A Cross Section of Psychological Research

Journal Articles for Discussion and Evaluation

Second Edition

Andrea K. Milinki

Editor

Pyrczak Publishing

P.O. Box 250430 ❖ Glendale, CA 91225

Pyrczak Publishing is an imprint of Fred Pyrczak, Publisher, A California Corporation.

Editorial assistance provided by Cheryl Alcorn, Randall R. Bruce, Karen M. Disner, Brenda Koplin, Erica Simmons, and Sharon Young.

Cover design by Robert Kibler and Larry Nichols.

Scanning services provided by Jack Petit.

Printed in the United States of America by Malloy, Inc.

ISBN 1-884585-69-8

Contents

Continued →

Quantitative Content Analysis

Meta-Analysis

Qualitative Research

Appendices

Notes:

Introduction to the Second Edition

This book is designed for students who are learning how to evaluate published psychological research. The 41 research articles in this collection provide the stimulus material for such a course.

Selection of the Articles

Several criteria were used in the selection of the articles. The first was that the articles be comprehensible to students taking their first research methods course. Thus, to be selected, an article needed to illustrate straightforward designs and the use of basic statistics.

Second, the articles needed to deal with topics of interest to psychology majors. To apply this criterion, psychology students were given the titles and abstracts (i.e., summaries) of a number of articles to rate for interest. Only those that received moderate to high average ratings survived the screening of the initial pool of potential articles.

Third, the articles needed to illustrate a wide variety of approaches to research. You will notice in the table of contents that the articles represent 12 types of research such as Survey Research, Content Analysis, Correlational Research, True Experimental Research, and so on.

Finally, the articles needed to be drawn from a large number of different journals. Since each journal has its own genre as well as criteria for the selection of submissions for publication, students can get a taste of the wide variations in psychological research only by reading articles from a wide variety of journals. Application of this criterion resulted in 41 articles drawn from 19 different journals.

How to Use This Book

In the field tests, one or two articles were assigned for homework at each class meeting. Students were required to read the article(s) and answer the questions at the end of each one. At the next class meeting, the article(s) were discussed with the instructor leading the discussion. Other arrangements are, of course, possible. For instance, each student might be respon-

sible for leading the discussion of one of the articles after all members of the class have read it.

About the Questions at the End of Each Article

There are three types of questions at the end of each article. First, there are *Factual Questions*. The answers for these are explicitly stated in the articles. In addition to writing down the answers, students should record the line numbers where they found the answers. The line numbers will facilitate discussions if there are disagreements on what constitutes a correct answer to a question.

Second, there are *Questions for Discussion*. Because these are designed to stimulate classroom discussions, most of them ask for students' opinions on various decisions made by the researchers in conducting and writing up their research. In the field tests, these questions led to lively classroom discussions. Since professional researchers often debate such issues with each other, students should not be surprised by such debates taking place in their own classrooms.

Third, students are asked to make *Quality Ratings* for each article. This is done by applying 13 fundamental criteria for evaluating research. These criteria may be supplemented by the more extensive list presented in Appendix A or with lists of criteria that are found in some research methods textbooks.

Reading the Statistics in This Book

Students who have taken a statistics class as a prerequisite to their research methods class should be able to comprehend the overwhelming majority of statistics found in this collection because articles that contained large numbers of obscure or highly advanced statistics were excluded from this book.

Students who are learning about statistics for the first time in the course for which they are using this book may need some additional help from their instructors. Keep in mind that it is not realistic to expect instructors of a one-semester research methods class to also teach a full-fledged course in statistical methods. Thus, there may be times when an instructor asks students to concentrate on the researcher's *interpretation* of statistics without getting bogged down in discussions of the theory underlying specific advanced statistics. It is possible to focus on the interpretation instead of specific statistics because almost all researchers describe their results in words as well as numbers.

The Classification of the Articles

If you examine a number of psychological research methods textbooks, you will probably find that they all differ to some extent in their system for classifying various types of research. While some labels such as "true experiment," "qualitative research," and "survey" are common to almost all textbooks, others that you find in your textbook may be more idiosyncratic. In addition, some categories of research overlap each other. For instance, when analyz- ing the results of a survey, a researcher may compute correlation coefficients, making it unclear whether it should be classified as a survey or as correlational research. An interesting classroom discussion topic is whether a given article can be classified as more than one type of research.

About the Second Edition

All of the research articles in this edition are new. In addition, this edition contains a larger number of articles than the previous one.

Acknowledgments

I am indebted to the publishers and researchers who hold the copyrights to the articles in this book. Without their cooperation, it would not be possible to amass a collection such as you find here.

Andrea K. Milinki

Article 1

Factors That Influence Fee Setting by Male and Female Psychologists

CAROL M. NEWLIN
University of Colorado at Boulder

JACQUELINE L. ADOLPH
University of Colorado at Boulder

LISA A. KREBER
University of Colorado at Boulder

ABSTRACT. What factors influence how psychologists in private practice set fees for self-pay clients? An anonymous survey in one county showed that male and female clinical psychologists did not differ in fees requested for services to self-pay clients, indicating that they equally value their time and work effort. They felt that their fees were strongly influenced by personal and local factors (i.e., education/qualifications, business experience, and local competition). Female psychologists indicated that local competition had a significantly greater influence on fee setting than did male psychologists. This perception among female psychologists might arise from competition with the larger number of nondoctoral therapists, who are predominately female, or from higher awareness through more active networking. The usefulness of this model for studies of self-employment is highlighted.

From *Professional Psychology: Research and Practice*, 35, 548–552. Copyright © 2004 by the American Psychological Association. Reprinted with permission.

Despite decades of activism and legal mandates, wage studies continue to report that women earn less than men. Surveys have documented this even for professionals; data published by the U.S. Census Bureau
5 (2000) show discrepancies between the 1998 incomes of men and women with professional degrees ($76,362 vs. $43,490 per annum) and doctoral degrees ($65,311 vs. $46,275). A nationwide "Fee, Practice, and Managed Care Survey" (2000) of private practice mental
10 health clinicians reported that female psychologists earned 78% of the income of male psychologists. They suggested that one reason for the gender gap in income across all mental health professionals is that men charge their self-pay clients more. In another study,
15 Sentell, Pingitore, Scheffler, Schwalm, and Haley (2001) analyzed the practices of members of the California Psychological Association and reported a difference in the median salary of full-time male and female psychologists ($80,000 vs. $62,000). They stated that
20 men's incomes were increased by having more self-pay clients. However, overall they found few differences between genders, and they thought there may have been differences in practices that were not revealed in their study.

25 Other studies have used different approaches to explore gender and fees in private practice. The "Fee, Practice, and Managed Care Survey" (2000) stated that men charge their self-pay clients more than women do. However, details were not described, and this may
30 have included nondoctoral clinicians. Parvin and Anderson (1999) also questioned whether male and female psychologists differ when making fee determinations. Because their efforts to interview psychologists about fees were met with strong resistance, their
35 study reported results from interviewing only 8 colleagues. Their 4 female participants charged standard fees, ranging from $95 to $120 ($M$ = $109), whereas their male participants charged $95 to $100 ($M$ = $98). A third study dealing with gender and fees was re-
40 ported by Lasky (1999). The data, which were derived from her 1984 survey of 60 clinicians scattered throughout the United States, contrasts with the localized survey of the present study. Lasky found that 75% of female *psychotherapists* (i.e., psychologists) charged
45 lower fees than men of the same level of experience in their geographic area. However, this study was conducted 17 years ago. Managed care fee structures may have influenced fee setting for self-pay clients, and the position of women in the work arena has changed.
50 Barnett and Hyde (2001) provided a thoughtful discussion about social changes and the need to revise research theories about gender relationships. They argued that researchers still rely on assumptions and research hypotheses that date to times, as recent as the 1950s,
55 when there was a high degree of gender segregation in relationships and in the workplace. They asserted that empirical data now fail to support predictions based on those old assumptions.

Different studies have investigated gender-related
60 financial aspects of practice from the standpoint of net income earned, rather than the financial value placed on a unit of work. Although such studies are not probing the same question, they are of interest in gaining overall perspective. Sentell et al. (2001) obtained data
65 on net income earned in a 1999 survey of 770 randomly selected members of the California Psychological Association. Net income from full-time work was derived from all positions as a psychologist, not only

from clinical services. Mean net income for men was $91,862, whereas mean net income for women was $71,831. Their findings suggested that men and women behave differently with regard to earning a living, as shown not only by differences in net income, but also in managed care contracting and proportion of self-pay clients. However, Sentell et al. concluded that gender differences in total income could not be fully explained by the factors they studied.

The study reported in this article was developed to identify the factors that influence men and women in setting fees for their self-pay clients by investigating the financial value that men and women place on their unit of time/work effort. The results can help private practice psychologists become aware of how they determine their own fees; the study methodology is easily repeatable in local areas to gain an understanding of local factors that influence fee setting.

Survey on Factors Affecting Fee Setting

This study used a distinctive approach for selecting participants. A two-page anonymous survey was mailed to all 75 individuals (36 male and 39 female) who advertised services as psychologists in the telephone business directory for one Colorado county. This provided a group of participants within a geographically localized, relatively homogeneous socioeconomic region.

This group of self-employed psychologists completed a survey about how they individually set fees for self-paying clients. The respondents were instructed to focus only on fees for self-pay clients seen in self-employed private practice. All respondents were licensed as clinical psychologists and saw at least some self-pay clients in private practice.

Clinical psychologists in private practice are a well-defined group for investigating factors that may influence fees of self-employed professionals in general. Advantages of this selection include (a) similar numbers of men and women advertised as psychologists, (b) equal qualifications implied by their doctoral degrees and licensing requirements for clinical psychologists, (c) well-defined unit of work effort according to standard codes for billing based on time and type of service, (d) freedom to choose their price for self-pay clients seen in private practice, (e) homogeneous socioeconomic factors that affect the profession, such as cost of doing business, wages, and cost of living, given that practitioners advertised and were located within one county.

The professional degrees (PhD, EdD, PsyD) and licensing requirements for clinical psychologists indicate essentially equal qualifications for all participants. The definition of services by current procedural terminology code (American Medical Association, 1999) standardizes time/work effort. The ability to ask any fee from self-paying clients and the customary prohibitions against organized group fee setting imply relative freedom for the individual to set the value of a unit of work.

The population of Larimer County in 2000, the year preceding this survey, was 252,494 (The Group, 2001). Caucasians comprised 91.4% of the population; 8.3% were Hispanic; and 3.4% were of another, unspecified background. Thirty percent of the population were under 20 years of age. Of those over 25 years of age, 32.2% had at least a bachelor's degree level of education. The 2000 median income for a family of four was $58,200; the median household income in the county was approximately $30,000 in 1990. This compares with a national median income in 2000 of $49,600 ($36,225 in 1990). The county includes both urban and rural populations. Psychological services were provided through public health and university counseling services, as well as through private practice. Thus, the population was also served by many psychologists who were not included in this study's survey.

Responses were analyzed using descriptive statistics as well as an unpaired t test whenever applicable. The number of respondents varies because some individuals did not answer every question. Seventy-five psychologists were surveyed; self-reported characteristics of respondents were as follows: The overall response rate was 55% ($n = 41$) after a second mailing, with 44% ($n = 16$) of men and 64% ($n = 25$) of women returning usable surveys. The average age of respondents was 50.61 years, and the ages of men ($M = 52.79$ years, range = 35–70) and women ($M = 49.1$ years, range = 32–70) did not differ significantly, $t(33) = 1.21, p = .24$.

Furthermore, the mean age at which men (35.08 years) and women (37.11 years) had entered self-employment did not differ significantly, $t(33) = -1.06, p = .30; M = 36.36$ years. Most respondents had been practicing for many years. There was no significant difference in years of experience between male (16.39 years, range = 4–26) and female (11.98 years, range = 1–25) respondents, $t(33) = 1.930, p = .06$.

Two questions were asked to ascertain whether the participants perceived gender bias related to fees. When asked whether they thought female therapists charged more, less, or the same as male therapists of the same qualifications, the majority reported that they felt that male and female therapists would charge the same. Very few men (1 of 15, or 7%) assumed that their female colleagues would charge less, whereas 8 of 22 (36%) women assumed that women would charge less. Of note, none of the 37 respondents felt that female psychologists would charge more. When asked whether they perceived a gender difference in clients' willingness to pay, most individuals perceived no difference between male and female clients. However, 3 of 22 female respondents (14%) believed that female clients would pay less, whereas no male participant held this belief.

Table 1 presents data on actual fees quoted for two time-specified procedure codes, 90801 (50- to 60-min evaluation) and 90806 (45- to 50-min psychotherapy)
185 when potential self-pay clients inquire. The data revealed that fees for initial evaluations had a normal distribution, and there were no significant gender differences in fees, $t(28) = 0.52$, $p = .61$. Although there was a trend toward male therapists asking a higher fee
190 for therapy (90806), their fees were not significantly different from those of female therapists, $t(33) = 1.09$, $p = .28$.

Table 1
Value of Work Effort: Prices Quoted for Self-Paying Clients

Participant	Price (in dollars)		
	M	SD	Mdn
Initial evaluation (CPT 90801)			
Men (n = 11)	97.27	16.34	97.5
Women (n = 19)	93.68	19.43	90.0
Psychotherapy (CPT 90806)			
Men (n = 14)	94.29	19.60	92.5
Women (n = 21)	88.10	14.10	90.0

Note. Initial evaluations were 50 to 60 min long; psychotherapy sessions were 45 to 50 min long. CPT = current procedural terminology.

It appeared that men and women differed in the practice of discounting fees. Whereas 56% of men re-
195 ported offering no discounts to self-paying clients, only 4% of females reported giving no discounts. When psychologists believed they had a gender bias in offering discounts, women clients were more likely to benefit, with 30% of females and 6% of males offering dis-
200 counts to women. No male or female psychologist was more likely to discount for men. Some participants volunteered discounting based on considerations other than gender, such as for students, friends, professionals, and single parents. It was beyond the scope of this
205 study to determine when discounts were offered (e.g., during the initial conversation or later in the relationship) or how much the fee was discounted.

The financial value of time/work effort was also assessed by willingness to give free brief initial meetings.
210 A substantial proportion of both women (41%) and men (53%) offered this to potential clients. Another question asked whether psychologists had changed their self-pay fees in the past 2 years. While many had kept fees the same over the 2-year period, 9% of
215 women decreased their self-pay fees. No men indicated a fee reduction, and a greater percentage of men (60%) increased fees compared with women (43%).

Fee setting may be influenced by other factors, such as office and personal expenses. Therefore, the survey
220 assessed whether men and women allocated practice income to any of the items shown in Table 2. A greater percentage of men indicated the use of part-time employees and word-processing services. A minority of both male and female practitioners were investing in
225 business real estate (7% and 14%, respectively). Only about 25% of psychologists reported providing medical insurance and retirement benefits for themselves from their practice income.

Table 2
Practice Expenditures

Expenditure	Participants who allocate funds (%)	
	Men	Women
Office overhead		
Solo office rental	47	36
Shared office rental	53	54
Malpractice insurance	100	100
Business phone/voice mail	100	95
Support services		
Full-time employee	7	9
Part-time employee	47	9
Billing service	47	50
Word-processing service	27	14
Real estate and benefits		
Purchasing business real estate	7	14
Paid-off business real estate	0	0
Medical insurance benefit	27	18
Retirement investment benefit	27	27

The survey also asked psychologists to rate the in-
230 fluence of 24 factors on how they set fees. Table 3 presents the items in the order that they were listed in the survey. Each item was categorized as having no influence, a little influence, or a lot of influence. As Table 3 illustrates, the majority of respondents endorsed at least
235 some influence from education/qualifications (87%), local competition (82%), business experience (76%), nonmonetary motivators (66%), clientele they wished to serve (63%), negotiating fees (63%), self-image (61%), money motivation (58%), and networking with
240 opposite sex colleagues (53%). Items that were scored as having a strong influence (*a lot of influence*) were education/qualifications (79%), business experience (47%), and local competition (47%).

Fewer than 5% of participants endorsed strong in-
245 fluence from these items: self-employed parent/family member, comparison with Medicare rates, guilt about charging for help, stage of practice—retiring or starting, professional newsletter/publications, financial consultants, and networking out of the local area.

250 To examine potential gender-related differences, numerically weighted scores were assigned to respondents' estimates of the importance of each item as follows: *no influence* = 0, *a little influence* = 1, and *a lot of influence* = 2. The numeric values were averaged for
255 each item. A weighted score of 2.00 indicated that all participants thought the factor was strongly influential, whereas a score of 0 indicated that no one regarded that factor as having any influence on fee setting. Intermediate scores reflect the combination of strong, weak,
260 and no influence.

Both men and women indicated that education/qualifications have the strongest influence on fees

3

Table 3
Factors That Influence Fees

Factor	All respondents (%)		Weighted score	
	Any influence	Strong influence	Men	Women
Business experience	76	47	1.30	1.17
Self-employed parent/family member/mentor	32	5	0.27	0.43
Education/qualifications	87	79	1.67	1.74
Network with same-sex colleagues	47	18	0.47	1.27
Network with opposite-sex colleagues	53	21	0.53	0.87
Local competition	82	47	0.93	1.50
Compare with Medicare rates	26	5	0.47	0.22
Compare with other insurance/managed care rates	37	8	0.40	0.48
Self-image	61	13	0.60	0.83
Money motivates me to work more	58	8	0.67	0.65
Nonmonetary motivators	66	18	0.73	0.91
Clientele you wish to serve	63	26	0.73	1.00
Guilt about charging for help	34	3	0.27	0.43
Other sources of family income	42	13	0.33	0.70
Stage of practice (starting)	11	3	0.07	0.17
Stage of practice (retiring)	24	5	0.20	0.35
Cost of your personal medical insurance	34	0	0.47	0.26
Index (e.g., consumer price or cost of living)	34	13	0.40	0.57
Professional newsletter/publications	26	3	0.33	0.26
Financial consultants	16	3	0.07	0.26
Networking out of local area	24	3	0.20	0.30
Major source of referrals	39	8	0.40	0.48
Setting a minimum fee	47	16	0.60	0.65
Negotiate fee with prospective client	63	13	0.67	0.83

Note. Scores of the importance of each item were numerically weighted (*no influence* = 0, *a little influence* = 1, *a lot of influence* = 2).

(1.67 and 1.74, respectively). Men then ranked business experience (1.30) as influential, followed by local competition (0.93). In comparison, women ranked local competition (1.50) as having a stronger influence than their other high-scoring factors of networking with same-sex colleagues (1.27), business experience (1.17), and clientele they wished to serve (1.00). Statistical analysis of these data indicates that the only significant gender-related difference is that women judged local competition as having more influence on fees asked of their self-pay clients than did men, $t(36) = -2.39$, $p = .02$.

Implications and Recommendations

The main focus of this study was on whether practitioners' gender influences fees for standard units of time/work effort defined by established current procedural terminology codes. Principal findings may be summarized as follows: (a) There was no statistically significant difference in fees asked by male and female psychologists; and (b) ratings of 24 factors that might influence fee setting revealed that personal and local factors, especially education/qualifications, business experience, and local competition, are the strongest influences. Of these factors, local competition was the only one that showed a statistically significant difference between genders, with women feeling the effect of this competition more strongly than men.

Several items suggest that many respondents, especially women, hold the common stereotype that female practitioners charge less than male practitioners, despite this study's finding that in this county, charges do not show a gender difference for equally qualified clinicians. In addition, some women thought that their female clients were willing to pay less than male clients.

To further investigate the perception of local competition, the authors examined additional listings in the telephone business directory. Not including psychiatrists (14 male and 2 female), there were 213 practitioners advertising as counselors, psychotherapists, or psychologists in the county. Of these, 130 (61%) were women, of whom 39 (30%) were psychologists. Of the 83 men (39% of total), 36 (43%) were psychologists. Therefore, the ratio of nondoctoral to doctoral female practitioners was approximately 2:1, whereas the ratio of nondoctoral to doctoral male practitioners was approximately 1:1. Limited data suggested that the male and female psychologists who responded to the survey did not differ markedly in types of expenditures for office overhead and benefits.

Some observations of this study suggest that psychologists in private practice may focus on the clientele they wish to serve and may incorrectly assess the potential market, as well as their position in the marketplace. That is, their perceptions may reflect common stereotypes about women's finances or may be influenced by comparisons of net income data for men and women in large populations. None of the respondents thought that men would charge less than women. However, a substantial number of participants, primarily women, believed that women psychologists would charge less than their male colleagues, which was not congruent with the fee data. Furthermore, there was a hint of gender bias in discounting fees for female clients.

There was a relatively small number of participants, and the proportion of women who responded was greater than the proportion of men who returned their surveys. It would be of interest to characterize nonresponders. Two individuals who did not complete the survey volunteered that they were not actually self-employed, but no further attempt was made to characterize nonresponders. It may also be of interest to try to find participants who do not advertise in the phone book (e.g., practitioners just getting started in private practice). The results of this study demonstrate that in this community, male and female psychologists charged similar fees for self-pay clients, contrary to common stereotypes.

Comparing responses from men and women, there was a clear difference in the perception of local competition. Women subjectively perceived more influence of local competition on setting fees, and this difference was statistically significant. The further investigation of potential competition from psychologists and others (primarily licensed clinical social workers and master's-level therapists) revealed that whereas psychologists include a nearly equal number of men (36) and women (39), nondoctoral therapists were predominately women (91 women and 47 men). Therefore, psychologists are outnumbered by therapists of other qualifications, and male and female psychologists appear to be competing in different arenas with regard to same-gender competition. Gender-based competition could arise from the preferences of self-pay clients. It could also relate to the impression that managed care panels favor nondoctoral therapists who charge less (Knapp, Bowers, & Metzler, 1992). The tendency for female psychologists to do more local networking may be a way of coping with the reality of greater competition from nondoctoral therapists, or the networking may simply heighten their awareness of competition.

The survey also suggests that men and women have similar types of business expenses. On the basis of the survey results (see Table 3), the greatest impact seems to come from personal and local factors, especially education/qualifications, business experience, and local competition. The strong effect of higher education levels on higher fees also has been documented by Knapp et al. (1992), who surveyed licensed psychologists with both doctoral and master's degrees. This study did not elicit information about family of origin, which Parvin and Anderson (1999) identified as a gender-related difference that could have influenced their findings (i.e., their female participants came from higher socioeconomic backgrounds and charged higher fees than their male participants). It was also noteworthy that in

this study, stage of practice did not have a stronger influence, since Sentell et al. (2001) reported that this affects net income. Furthermore, factors such as Medicare rates, managed care rates, price indexes, networking out of area, and publications did not rank highly.

We noted that stage of practice did not influence fees in the present survey. When Sentell et al. (2001) attempted to relate various factors to net income, they found that more years of experience correlated with higher net income. Thus, as noted above, net income probably does not parallel fees asked from self-pay clients. This would be of interest to study further, especially because expansion of self-pay practice has been encouraged as one means of countering the impact of managed care on use of time and income earned (Parvin & Anderson, 1999).

In conclusion, this study found that male and female psychologists (i.e. practitioners with equal education and qualifications) working in a socioeconomically homogeneous location price their time/work effort similarly if given the freedom to do so. Competition was more keenly felt by female respondents, which may have been related to the higher number of nonpsychologist practitioners who are female. The results of this study also suggest that the participants may be operating under common misconceptions about appropriate fees for their area and may be incorrectly assessing their position in the marketplace. This study found that fee setting is most strongly influenced by personal and local factors, suggesting that studies of income or fees at the national level would be less useful for self-employed practitioners than studies similar to this one, which used the local phone book to select relatively similar participants in a reasonably homogeneous socioeconomic setting.

References

American Medical Association (1999). *Current procedural terminology* (4th ed.). Chicago: Author.

Barnett, R. C., & Hyde, J. S. (2001). Women, men, work, and family: An expansionist theory. *American Psychologist, 56*, 781–796.

Fee, practice, and managed care survey. (2000, October). *Psychotherapy Finances, 26*, 1–12.

The Group, Inc. (2001). *Larimer County, Colorado, demographic profile, May 2001.* Fort Collins, CO: Author.

Knapp, S., Bowers, T. G., & Metzler, B. (1992). A survey of Pennsylvania psychologists. *Psychotherapy in Private Practice, 11*, 83–99.

Lasky, F. (1999). Psychotherapists' ambivalence about fees: Male-female differences. *Women and Therapy, 22*, 5–13.

Parvin, R., & Anderson, G. (1999). What are we worth? Fee decisions of psychologists in private practice. *Women and Therapy, 22*, 15–25.

Sentell, T., Pingitore, D., Scheffler, R., Schwalm, D., & Haley, M. (2001). Gender differences in practice patterns and income among psychologists in professional practice. *Professional Psychology: Research and Practice, 32*, 607–617.

U.S. Census Bureau (2000). Money income of persons—selected characteristics by income level: 1998. In *Statistical abstracts of the United States: 2000* (120th ed., Chart No. 750, p. 473). Washington, DC: Author.

About the authors: *Carol M. Newlin* received her PhD in pathology from the University of Pennsylvania in 1972. After receiving her MD from the Medical College of Pennsylvania in 1979, she completed her psychiatry residency at the Hospital, University of Pennsylvania. She is engaged in the private practice of psychiatry in Fort Collins, Colorado. *Jacqueline L. Adolph* completed her BA in preclinical psychology at the University of Northern Colorado in 1984. She works in private practice as a certified biofeedback/neurofeedback specialist in Fort Collins and Boulder, Colorado. *Lisa A. Kreber* received her MA in psychology in 2002 from the University of Colorado at Boulder, where she is pursuing a PhD in neuroscience.

Address correspondence to: Carol M. Newlin, 1305 Alford Street, Fort Collins, CO 80524. E-mail: cnewlin@holly.colostate.edu

Exercise for Article 1

Factual Questions

1. The survey was mailed to how many females?

2. The respondents were asked to focus only on fees for what type of clients?

3. Was the survey mailed a second time?

4. On the average, was the mean age of the men respondents significantly different from the mean age of the women respondents?

5. The researchers report that there was a trend toward male therapists asking a higher fee for therapy than female therapists. Was this difference statistically significant?

6. Only one of the differences between weighted scores for men and women in Table 3 was significant. Which one?

Questions for Discussion

7. Would you be willing to generalize the results of this study to psychologists who do not advertise in telephone business directories? Explain. (See lines 88–91 and 334–337.)

8. Is it important to know that the survey was anonymous? Do you think that the results might have been different if it were not anonymous? Explain. (See line 88.)

9. In your opinion, how important is the information about the county in which this study was conducted? (See lines 127–143.)

10. Are you surprised that the overall response rate is 55%? If you had conducted this study, would you have expected a higher response rate? A lower one? Explain. (See lines 149–152.)

11. The researchers indicate that it would be of interest to know more about nonresponders to this survey. Do you agree? Why? Why not? (See lines 327–334.)

12. If you were to conduct a study on the same topic, what changes in the research methodology, if any, would you make?

Quality Ratings

Directions: Indicate your level of agreement with each of the following statements by circling a number from 5 for strongly agree (SA) to 1 for strongly disagree (SD). If you believe an item is not applicable to this research article, leave it blank. Be prepared to explain your ratings. When responding to criteria A and B below, keep in mind that brief titles and abstracts are conventional in published research.

A. The title of the article is appropriate.
    SA   5   4   3   2   1   SD

B. The abstract provides an effective overview of the research article.
    SA   5   4   3   2   1   SD

C. The introduction establishes the importance of the study.
    SA   5   4   3   2   1   SD

D. The literature review establishes the context for the study.
    SA   5   4   3   2   1   SD

E. The research purpose, question, or hypothesis is clearly stated.
    SA   5   4   3   2   1   SD

F. The method of sampling is sound.
    SA   5   4   3   2   1   SD

G. Relevant demographics (for example, age, gender, and ethnicity) are described.
    SA   5   4   3   2   1   SD

H. Measurement procedures are adequate.
    SA   5   4   3   2   1   SD

I. All procedures have been described in sufficient detail to permit a replication of the study.
    SA   5   4   3   2   1   SD

J. The participants have been adequately protected from potential harm.
    SA   5   4   3   2   1   SD

K. The results are clearly described.
    SA   5   4   3   2   1   SD

L. The discussion/conclusion is appropriate.
    SA   5   4   3   2   1   SD

M. Despite any flaws, the report is worthy of publication.
    SA   5   4   3   2   1   SD

Article 2

Involvement of Fathers in Therapy:
A Survey of Clinicians

AMY M. DUHIG
University of South Florida

VICKY PHARES
University of South Florida

ROBYN W. BIRKELAND
University of South Florida

ABSTRACT. Clinicians providing treatment for children and families often question which family members to include in therapy. Historically, mothers were included in child-oriented therapy to a greater degree than were fathers. To determine actual rates of including fathers in therapy, 219 clinicians with specialization in clinical child psychology and family therapy were surveyed. In addition, personal and professional characteristics of clinicians were examined to establish the association between these characteristics and inclusion of fathers in treatment. Ways to help clinicians include fathers in child-oriented therapy are discussed in light of the findings.

From *Professional Psychology: Research and Practice, 33,* 389–395. Copyright © 2002 by the American Psychological Association. Reprinted with permission.

When referring children for treatment, parents or other family members frequently ask clinicians whom should be present at the first appointment. It is typically in the first contact with the clinician or the office staff that parents are educated as to how the treatment will involve them in their child's therapeutic services. Traditionally, parents' inclusion in treatment has been a theoretical matter—that is, depending on the type of treatment the therapist conducts.

Most cognitive-behavioral therapies focus solely on the child (Hibbs & Jensen, 1996; LeCroy, 1994), including parents in these sessions only in a psychoeducational manner to teach the parents what the children have been taught. Conversely, most family therapies focus on all family members and include parents in nearly all of the therapy sessions (Becvar & Becvar, 1993; Kaslow, Kaslow, & Farber, 1999). In fact, some family therapists do not include the children themselves in treatment depending on the focus of the problem. In a survey of family therapists, Johnson and Thomas (1999) found that family therapists were less likely to include children in therapy sessions when the children's problem was externalizing in nature, perhaps because children with these types of problems are considered challenging and disruptive in family sessions. Their findings also indicated that children were less likely to be included in sessions when the identified problem focused on one of the parent's issues. The

issue of involving parents in child-oriented therapy, other than behavioral parent training or family therapy, has largely been ignored (Kaslow & Thompson, 1998; Mash, 1998), often leaving the clinician with little guidance from an empirical viewpoint as to whom to include in treatment.

Parental issues, such as parental psychopathology, living circumstances, and marital and family functioning, are just a few of the factors that influence the nature and severity of the child's impairment, the degree of change in the therapeutic process, and the extent to which change is maintained at follow-up (e. g., Kazdin, 1995; Webster-Stratton, 1985a). Because of the complexities of treating children and adolescents, Kazdin and Weiss (1998) described child and adolescent therapy as "family-context" therapy, regardless of the conceptual view that underlies treatment.

Even when parents are included in therapy, often only mothers and not fathers are invited to be involved (Phares, 1997). Whether or not fathers are included in therapy may have important ramifications for the effectiveness of the therapy, and there has been speculation that engaging fathers (as well as mothers) in therapy and other services can enhance the therapeutic effectiveness of those services (Burns, Hoagwood, & Mrazek, 1999).

One question that arises when exploring fathers' involvement in therapy is the presence of fathers in children's lives. On the basis of U.S. Census data, Roberts (1993) documented that 61.1% of children under 18 years of age in the United States live with both biological parents, 10.8% of children live with one biological parent and step-parent, 24.2% live with their single mother, and 3.9% live with their single father. In a study examining referrals to an outpatient therapy clinic in a southeastern city, Phares and Lum (1997) found that slightly less than half (42.4%) of children and adolescents lived with their married biological parents. However, of the children who did not live with both biological parents, 40.0% still had at least monthly face-to-face contact with both biological parents. Given these findings, it appears incorrect for clinicians to assume that the majority of children referred for services do not have regular contact with their fathers (Phares & Lum, 1997). The inclusion of fathers in therapy remains an issue for many clinicians.

Including Fathers in Therapy

75   There are clear connections between psychopathology in fathers and their children (Phares, 1997, 1999; Phares & Compas, 1992). When compared with mothers, however, fathers have been ignored to a great extent by clinicians in the treatment of developmental
80 psychopathology (Barrows, 1999; Phares, 1992; Strean, 1997). A number of clinicians and theorists have argued that the inclusion of fathers in child-oriented therapy is important in order to provide comprehensive treatment for the child (Dienhart & Dolla-
85 hite, 1997; Hecker, 1991). Although the lack of attention to fathers is especially salient in cognitive-behavioral therapies, fathers have been ignored in family therapy as well (Carr, 1998; Hecker, 1991). Fathers were included in only 39% of studies on behavioral
90 parent training (Budd & O'Brien, 1982) and were included in 6–43% of family-oriented intake sessions (Churven, 1978; Szapocznik et al., 1988). In a survey of psychologists and social workers, Lazar, Sagi, and Fraser (1991) found that fathers were included in 6.3%
95 of therapy sessions with children, whereas mothers were included in 38.1% of such sessions. Thus, regardless of the orientation held by the therapist, fathers are rarely included in therapy for children's and adolescents' problems. This pattern is true for single-parent
100 (e.g., separated, divorced, or never-married parents) households as well as intact (e.g., married or remarried parents) families (Phares, 1996).

Therapeutic Benefits Related to Fathers' Inclusion in Treatment

    The next logical question relates to whether involving fathers in therapy increases the effectiveness of
105 therapy for children and adolescents. The ramifications of including fathers in therapy have primarily been studied with behavioral parent training. In general, studies have found that the inclusion of either mothers or fathers in behavioral parent training resulted in
110 comparable treatment outcomes (e.g., Nicol et al., 1988; Webster-Stratton, Hollinsworth, & Kolpacoff, 1989). However, other studies have found that the involvement of fathers enhanced maintenance and generalization of parent-training effects. Additionally, par-
115 ents can help reinforce and encourage each other in their efforts and remind each other of specific parent-training techniques (e.g., Webster-Stratton, 1985b). The inclusion of both mothers and fathers in such treatment can also be important in addressing marital
120 and coparenting issues (Coplin & Houts, 1991; Dienhart & Dollahite, 1997). Findings also suggest that child-parent interactions themselves are affected by including both fathers and mothers in treatment. In her study of conduct-problem children, Webster-Stratton
125 (1985a) found that when fathers and mothers were involved in parent training, mother-child interactions

were less negative than when fathers were absent from the therapeutic process. In another investigation, parenting similarities between mothers and fathers (i.e.,
130 fathers' reports of parenting alliance and discipline similarity) were found to be associated with lower parenting stress for mothers (Harvey, 2000). Another benefit of including fathers in child-oriented treatment is that this may help uncover underlying difficulties
135 that might have been missed when focusing solely on mothers and children (Prevatt, 1999).

    Thus, there is limited evidence of increased effectiveness when fathers are included in behavioral parent training; however, there are benefits for both the clini-
140 cian and the family when fathers are included in the process. Given the potential importance of including fathers in treatment for children's and adolescents' emotional/behavioral problems, it is essential to understand whether or not fathers are actually included in
145 treatment. In addition, it is important to know whether there are characteristics of clinicians that might be related to the inclusion of fathers in the therapeutic process.

Characteristics of Clinicians Who Include Fathers in Therapy

    Because fathers are rarely included in therapy for
150 children's and adolescents' emotional/behavioral problems, it appears worthwhile to investigate personal characteristics of clinicians associated with the inclusion of fathers in therapy. In a survey of social workers and psychologists working in child welfare agencies
155 and public schools, Lazar and colleagues (1991) found a number of personal and professional characteristics that were related to the inclusion of fathers in therapy. This inclusion was related to attending more family therapy courses in graduate school, being a male thera-
160 pist, having flexible hours for therapy appointments, and having fewer years of experience as a therapist. In addition, therapists who were maternally oriented and viewed fathers as secondary caretakers were less likely to include fathers in treatment. Unfortunately, it is not
165 clear whether these results are generalizable, given that the participants worked only within child protective agencies and public schools.

    The current study was designed to explore and extend these issues with a more generalizable sample—
170 specifically, with professionals who were actively engaged in therapy with children and adolescents. The current study attempted to include therapists working in a diverse array of therapy settings, with a range of experience, professions, and training in order to assess
175 their inclusion of fathers in therapy. In addition, personal and professional characteristics of therapists were explored to ascertain their connection to the inclusion of fathers in child-oriented therapy.

Exploratory Study on Fathers' Involvement in Child Therapy

    A total of 219 participants were included in this

180 study: 135 participants were members of the Society of
Clinical Child and Adolescent Psychology (Division
53) of the American Psychological Association (APA),
and 84 were members of the American Association for
Marriage and Family Therapy (AAMFT). By including
185 AAMFT members, we hoped to gain more variability
in theoretical orientation and in professional practice
experience and settings. It was also our intent to gain a
broad perspective from those clinicians practicing in
the field of child and adolescent treatment. We hoped
190 that by including a division outside of the APA, we
would gain a perspective not attainable by remaining in
the Association.

Surveys were mailed to a randomly selected group
of 500 members from each of the professional organi-
195 zations, along with postage-paid envelopes addressed
to the researchers. No one returned two surveys due to
membership in both organizations. A response rate of
27.0% for Division 53 and 16.8% for AAMFT was
obtained. This response rate is somewhat low com-
200 pared with that of other surveys of practitioners (e.g.,
Johnson & Thomas, 1999). Upon examining another
survey study that used the AAMFT population with a
higher response rate, we found that the demographics
in our study (i.e., gender, ethnicity, degree, and years
205 of experience) were well matched with their population
characteristics (Deacon, Kirkpatrick, Wetchler, &
Niedner, 1999).

Participants ranged in age from 23 to 74 years, with
an average age of 45.56 years (SD = 12.02). Women
210 constituted 63.8% of the sample, and men, 36.2%. Regarding ethnicity, participants were mainly Caucasian
(94.9%), and the others were Latino/Latina (2.3%),
African American (1.4%), Asian American (0.9%), or
labeled "other" (0.5%). A total of 67.0% of the sample
215 had earned a doctoral degree, 31.2% had earned a master's degree, and 1.8% had earned a bachelor's degree
and had some additional graduate training. Participants
had been involved in clinical practice with children
and/or adolescents for an average of 13.59 years (SD =
220 9.45). Clinicians were diverse in their therapeutic orientations, and most reported more than one orientation:
family systems (67.4%), cognitive-behavioral (63.3%),
behavioral (41.3%), eclectic/integrative (34.9%),
psychodynamic (28.4%), humanistic (15.1%), and
225 other (14.7%). Respondents also worked in a variety of
settings and sometimes in multiple settings: private
practice/independent practice (57.5%), academic/
university (26.0%), community mental health center
(20.1%), outpatient/hospital (19.2%), inpatient/hospital
230 (10.5%), medical school (8.7%), and other (16.4%).

Survey Completed by Clinicians

In an attempt to examine the association between
training issues, personal characteristics, structural issues of the clinics in which they worked, and the inclusion of mothers and fathers in treatment of children and
235 adolescents, we developed a questionnaire. As can be

seen in Table 1, training issues (such as coursework,
practicum experience, and continuing education), personal characteristics (such as years of experience and
egalitarian beliefs), and structural issues of the work
240 setting (such as the availability of evening and weekend appointments) were assessed.

Table 1
*Training Issues, Personal Characteristics, and Characteristics
of the Work Setting*

Variable	M	SD
Training issues		
No. of family therapy courses completed during graduate training	2.96	3.60
Months of clinical practicum training in family therapy in graduate training	12.60	12.26
No. of continuing education courses/seminars attended in past year	5.34	9.61
No. of family-related continuing education courses/seminars attended in past year	2.19	4.53
No. of family-related books read in past year	2.57	3.27
No. of family-related journal articles read in past year	12.55	17.68
Personal characteristics		
SRES total score	111.49	8.73
Years of clinical experience	14.50	9.63
Years of clinical practice with children/adolescents	13.59	9.45
Structural issues of work setting		
Weekend appointments available (per week)	0.27	0.51
Weekday evening appointments available (per week)	2.33	1.48

Note. SRES = Sex-Role Egalitarianism Scale.

Respondents were also asked to estimate the percentage of their treatment sessions that included different constellations of family members in treatment with
245 children (12 years of age and under) and adolescents
(13–18 years of age) for both intact (i.e., parents married or living in the same household) and single-parent
(where there is still contact with the noncustodial parent, usually the father) households, forming four cate-
250 gories in which to respond. Constellations for which
the clinicians could report (i.e., who they included in
therapy) were mother and child/adolescent; father and
child/adolescent; mother, father, and child/adolescent;
only father; only mother; only child; mother and father
255 only; and other family constellations. Participants were
asked that the sum of all their responses for each of the
four categories equal 100%. Respondents were also
asked to estimate what percentage of time fathers and
mothers agree to be involved in their child's or adoles-
260 cent's treatment sessions when asked to participate.

Measurement of Attitudes Toward Women and Men

In order to further explore Lazar and colleagues'
(1991) findings that maternally oriented therapists were
less likely to include fathers in treatment with their
children, the Sex-Role Egalitarianism Scale (SRES;
265 Beere, King, Beere, & King, 1984) was completed by

Table 2
Rates of Including Fathers and Mothers in Treatment with Children and Adolescents

Variable	Fathers involved (% of time)		Mothers involved (% of time)		
	M	*SD*	*M*	*SD*	*t*(200)
Intact families	39.46	26.85	62.00	26.07	−13.68[*]
Single-parent families[a]	21.22	23.13	55.64	24.53	−15.87[*]
Children (12 years and under)	29.79	23.36	65.45	25.13	−18.04[*]
Adolescents (13–18 years)	31.04	23.27	51.39	26.24	−11.27[*]

[a] Usually single-mother families.
[*] $p < .01$.

our population of clinicians. This scale was developed to reflect beliefs about the separate role behaviors of women and men, and it contains items that require judgments about the assumption of nontraditional roles
270 by both women and men (Beere et al., 1984). The short form KK, which contains 25 items, was used for the purposes of the present study. A 5-point rating format was used, ranging from 1 (*strongly agree*) to 5 (*strongly disagree*). Scores ranged from 25 to 125, with
275 higher scores indicating more egalitarian attitudes. Various estimates of reliability (e.g., internal consistency, test–retest, and alternate forms) and validity have been uniformly strong (King & King, 1993).

Findings

Reported Paternal and Maternal Involvement in Treatment

The percentage of involvement was computed sepa-
280 rately for mothers and fathers by adding up any inclusion of mothers or fathers in therapy (i.e., mother and child; father and child; mother, father, and child; mother only; father only; mother and father only) for each of the four categories (i.e., intact families with
285 children; intact families with adolescents; single-parent households with children where there is contact with noncustodial parent; single-parent households with adolescents where there is contact with noncustodial parent) and dividing by 4. This formula gave us general
290 participation rates in percentages for mothers and fathers separately.

Clinicians reported that, when asked to participate, mothers agreed to be involved in their child's or adolescent's treatment sessions ($M = 91.32$, $SD = 13.47$) a
295 greater percentage of time than fathers ($M = 62.63$, $SD = 28.94$), $t(200) = 15.67$, $p < .01$. Clinicians were also asked to report on their actual rates of including mothers and fathers in treatment. Overall, mothers ($M = 58.53$, $SD = 21.58$) were included significantly more
300 frequently than fathers ($M = 30.23$, $SD = 21.23$) in treatment of their children and adolescents, $t(142) = 15.57$, $p < .01$. Inclusion rates were also reported for younger children, adolescents, intact families, and single-parent (usually single-mother) households. The
305 percentage of time fathers were involved in treatment ranged from 21.2% for single-parent families with children and adolescents in treatment to 39.5% for in-

tact families with children and adolescents in treatment. The percentages of time mothers were included
310 in treatment ranged from 51.4% for adolescent treatment sessions to 65.5% for child treatment sessions. We conducted *t* tests to determine if rates of including parents differed across each of the four categories. Results suggest that overall, mothers are included more
315 frequently than fathers in treatment of both children and adolescents in both intact and single-mother households (see Table 2 for means, standard deviations, and *t* values). These findings are consistent with previous research (Lazar et al., 1991), suggesting that
320 fathers are included in therapy much less frequently than are mothers.

Training Issues

The training issues that were delineated in Table 1 (e.g., number of family therapy courses during graduate training, number of family-related journal articles
325 read in the past year) were correlated with the percentage of time that the clinicians included mothers and fathers in treatment sessions. Results suggested that the number of family therapy courses taken during graduate training, the months of clinical practicum training
330 in family therapy, and the number of continuing education seminars taken in the past year were not associated significantly with including mothers or fathers in treatment with their children and adolescents. However, the number of family-related continuing educa-
335 tion seminars attended by the clinician in the past year was significantly related to including both mothers ($r = .21$, $p < .01$) and fathers ($r = .36$, $p < .01$) in treatment with their children and adolescents.

Finally, both the number of family-related books
340 read in the past year and the number of family-related journal articles read in the past year were significantly related to including mothers ($r = .22$, $p < .01$ and $r = .24$, $p < .01$, respectively) and fathers ($r = .44$, $p < .01$, and $r = .24$, $p < .01$, respectively) in treatment with
345 their children and adolescents. These findings are consistent with research that has shown continuing education in family therapy to be associated with more professional involvement in family therapy (Guttman, Feldman, Engelsmann, Spector, & Buonvino, 1999).
350 The directionality of these associations is not clear, given that clinicians may seek out these educational

opportunities if they are already including parents in therapy. It may be, however, that these types of educational opportunities increase the likelihood that clinicians include parents in therapy sessions for children's and adolescents' emotional/behavioral problems (Allison, Powrie, Pearce, & Martin, 1995; Guttman et al., 1999).

Personal Characteristics of Clinicians

Using correlational procedures, we examined several personal characteristics of clinicians (i.e., therapeutic orientation, gender of clinician, egalitarian beliefs regarding gender roles, years of clinical practice, years of clinical practice with children and adolescents, and affiliation with AAMFT or APA Division 53) to determine their relation to clinicians' inclusion of parents in treatment with their children and adolescents. Results suggested that having a family systems orientation was significantly associated with including fathers ($r = .30$, $p < .01$), but not mothers ($r = .14$, $p > .05$), in treatment with their children and adolescents. All other correlations between therapeutic orientation and parental involvement were nonsignificant. The association between having a family systems orientation and including fathers in therapy is consistent with previous research (Guttman et al., 1999) that has shown connections between clinicians' orientations and their actual practices.

We also examined the gender of the clinician, and results suggested that men and women included mothers and fathers in treatment with their children and adolescents to a similar degree. Regarding egalitarian role beliefs as measured by the SRES, results suggested that there were no significant associations between these beliefs and involving either mothers or fathers in treatment. These findings are inconsistent with previous research (Lazar et al., 1991). One possible explanation for the lack of findings between egalitarian beliefs and parental participation is that the average score on the SRES was 111.49 ($SD = 8.73$). Because the upper limit on the scale is 125, it is possible that a ceiling effect occurred and that not enough variability was present to find such an effect.

There was a positive, significant association between number of years of clinical practice and involving fathers in treatment ($r = .32$, $p < .01$), but there was no significant association between variables for mothers ($r = .04$, $p > .05$). A similar pattern of results was found for number of years of clinical practice with children and adolescents; length of time was positively associated with including fathers ($r = .32$, $p < .01$) but not with including mothers ($r = .06$, $p > .05$). Given that the number of years of experience is associated with overall therapeutic effectiveness (Beutler, 1997) and given that there is some speculation that including fathers in therapy is more effective in treating family- and couple-related issues than not including them (Coplin & Houts, 1991; Prevatt, 1999), it is not surprising to find that more experienced clinicians are more likely to include fathers in therapy than are less experienced clinicians.

We conducted a series of independent t tests to determine if therapists' use of parental involvement differed by affiliation with AAMFT and APA Division 53. Results suggested that clinicians affiliated with AAMFT ($M = 63.66$, $SD = 21.99$) included mothers in treatment more often than did clinicians in APA Division 53 ($M = 55.22$, $SD = 20.78$), $t(141) = 2.32$, $p < .05$. A similar pattern of results was found for the inclusion of fathers, with AAMFT members involving fathers more frequently than did APA Division 53 members ($M = 37.94$, $SD = 24.05$ and $M = 25.28$, $SD = 17.64$, respectively), $t(141) = 3.63$, $p < .01$. The directionality of these findings is unclear, however, because clinicians' orientations and interests may lead to membership in these two divergent groups (Guttman et al., 1999).

Characteristics of the Work Environment

Correlations were also conducted to determine if working in certain settings (e.g., academia, community mental health center, private/independent practice), working weekend and evening hours, and level of commitment of the work setting toward family involvement in treatment were associated with including mothers and fathers in treatment with their children and adolescents. Results suggested that working in private practice was related to including fathers ($r = .25$, $p < .01$) but not mothers ($r = -.09$, $p > .05$) in treatment with their children and adolescents. All other correlations were nonsignificant. The finding that greater inclusion of fathers (but not mothers) was related to working in a private/independent practice setting may relate to these clinicians' greater control over the therapeutic process. Although clinicians who work in private or independent practice settings are influenced increasingly by health maintenance organizations and health insurance limitations (Crespi & Steir, 1996; Wolf, 1999), it appears that these clinicians may be freer to include fathers in therapy than are clinicians in other settings. Additionally, it is possible that the fathers themselves are contributing to these increased rates of participation in private/independent practice; that is, because they likely have a higher socioeconomic status, these fathers may have more personal freedom or resources that make them more physically available to attend these sessions.

We also examined the availability of weekend and weekday evening times for treatment. Results suggested that having weekday evening times available was not significantly related to including mothers or fathers in treatment with children or adolescents, nor was having weekend times available. Finally, clinicians were asked to report whether their work setting was committed, open, or not committed to family involvement in treatment. Correlations were conducted to de-

termine if level of commitment was associated with
including parents in treatment. Results suggested that
there was a nonsignificant association between level of
commitment of work setting and including mothers and
fathers in treatment. Although this finding is inconsistent with previous research in child welfare agencies
and school settings (Lazar et al., 1991), it may be that
the clinicians in the current sample had more control
over their own practices, and thus their own personal
characteristics were more influential in parental inclusion in treatment than were any work-setting variables.

Implications and Discussion

Overall, this study extends what was known previously about the involvement of fathers and mothers in
therapy related to children's and adolescents' emo-
tional/behavioral problems. The inclusion of parents
(either mothers or fathers) in therapy with children and
adolescents remains somewhat limited. Including parents in child-oriented therapy, however, has been
shown to be effective in addressing interparental conflict, coparenting issues, and marital issues that are
related to child functioning (Carr, 1998; Coplin &
Houts, 1991; Prevatt, 1999) and in allowing parents to
be supportive of the therapeutic gains that their children make in therapy (Burns et al., 1999). Because
there are connections between the psychological functioning of fathers, mothers, and children (Phares &
Compas, 1992), it makes sense that fathers and mothers
would be considered for inclusion in therapy when
children and adolescents show dysfunctional behavior.
Thus, it appears that there is some rationale for identifying and enhancing the characteristics associated with
including parents (especially fathers) in therapy for
children and adolescents.

Overall, fathers were included in therapy to a lesser
extent than were mothers. One potential reason for this
pattern of less paternal involvement in therapy may be
related to clinicians' reports that fathers were much
less likely to attend therapy sessions when compared
with mothers. Hecker (1991) noted that, consistent with
these findings, many clinicians assume that fathers are
more resistant to involvement in therapy. Hecker also
noted, however, that even if fathers do not initially
express interest in therapeutic involvement, it is incumbent upon clinicians to try to engage fathers in the
therapeutic process. Specifically, fathers can be provided with a rationale for their involvement in therapy
that emphasizes what they might gain from such involvement (Carr, 1998).

It appears that continuing education related to family therapy and reading books and journals on family
therapy may help clinicians realize the importance of
including fathers in therapy for children and adolescents (Guttman et al., 1999). Perhaps clinicians also
find additional techniques for engaging fathers in the
therapeutic process from these continuing education
activities on family therapy and in their family-related
readings. One of the most salient implications from this
study is that clinicians should increase their involvement in family-related continuing education and professional reading. These professional activities will
probably be associated with increased paternal and
maternal involvement in clinicians' therapy sessions.

Regarding the family systems orientation, it appears
that family therapists are becoming increasingly aware
of the importance of including fathers in family therapy. Although mother-blaming has been documented in
clinicians from a variety of theoretical orientations
(Phares, 1999), research with family therapists found
no evidence of mother-blaming in relation to a hypothetical vignette (McCollum & Russell, 1992). Interestingly, more parental culpability was assigned to which-
ever parent expressed more concern about the child's
emotional/behavioral problems (McCollum & Russell).
By attending to both mothers and fathers, family therapists are apparently following their training to explore
the family as a system rather than focusing on the
mother-child relationship exclusively (Becvar &
Becvar, 1993). One obvious implication of this work is
for clinicians to reflect on their own possible mother-
blaming tendencies and to explore whether these
thoughts have any relevance for their own clients. Even
if clinicians believe that a particular child client's problems are due to his or her mother, it is incumbent upon
the clinician to also explore the father's culpability for
that client's problems (or for the mother's problems).

Because the goal in treatment of children's and
adolescents' problems is to achieve generalization beyond the treatment setting (Stokes & Baer, 1977),
treatment must include key elements of other settings.
Parents represent the most obvious social elements in
the child's home environment, and therefore several
additional suggestions are offered to help clinicians
engage mothers and particularly fathers in the therapeutic process.

- Clinicians should be cognizant of the roles that parents play in the therapeutic process and should simply ask them to be involved. It would be helpful for
the clinician to talk to the father directly; this technique is typically and effectively used in engaging
reluctant family members (Anderson & Stewart,
1983).
- Prospective clients can be told that all family members, or both parents, are expected to attend the initial session (Hecker, 1991). Hecker also suggested
that the father should be reassured about his importance in the family and in relation to the therapeutic
change of the child, because fathers sometimes feel
marginalized in the therapeutic process.
- During the assessment process, parents can complete questionnaires about child symptomatology
and also about themselves and their family. Assessment information should be gathered by a variety of informants to include fathers, mothers, teach-

ers, and the children themselves because of the unique contributions of each informant (Achenbach, McConaughy, & Howell, 1987; Duhig, Renk, Epstein, & Phares, 2000) to help guide treatment conceptualization. If fathers participate in the assessment process, they may realize that their input is valuable, and they may be more willing to engage in the treatment process.

- Clinicians can point out to parents, especially fathers, that changes in the family situation depend on their participation (Hecker, 1991). In addition, it may be helpful to inform families of the current knowledge of how fathers can facilitate the child's therapeutic change and maintenance of change and to highlight the added benefits that studies have found for mothers involved in child-focused treatment with their partners.

- Within family therapy sessions, fathers appear to respond better to more structured and directive interactions, so these types of interactions appear to be appropriate when fathers are involved in therapy sessions (Carr, 1998).

- Fathers as well as mothers appear to respond well to being offered extra therapy sessions that can focus on parental concerns, such as job stress and personal concerns (Carr, 1998). Thus, clinicians may want to offer therapy sessions that would focus on parental concerns rather than on the concerns of the child.

- Clinicians can seek advice from more experienced therapists on ways they engage parents, especially fathers, in therapy. For additional suggestions about how to include fathers in therapy, see Carr (1998) and Hecker (1991). Interested clinicians are also encouraged to read more about fathers in contemporary society (Cabrera, Tamis-LeMonda, Bradley, Hofferth, & Lamb, 2000); the special needs of low-income, unmarried, and minority fathers (Coley, 2001), and the therapeutic issues that arise when working with gay fathers (Barret & Robinson, 2000; Bigner, 1996).

Overall, this study highlights the need to help clinicians learn about the benefits of including parents (and especially fathers) in child-oriented therapy and to learn ways in which parents (and especially fathers) can be engaged in therapy. This goal can be accomplished through training in family therapy in doctoral programs or through continuing education programs in family therapy.

References

Achenbach, T. M., McConaughy, S. H., & Howell, C. T. (1987). Child/adolescent behavioral and emotional problems: Implications for cross-informant correlations for situational specificity. *Psychological Bulletin, 101,* 213–232.

Allison, S., Powrie, R., Pearce, C., & Martin, G. (1995). Continuing medical education in marital and family therapy: A survey of South Australian psychiatrists. *Australian and New Zealand Journal of Psychiatry, 29,* 638–644.

Anderson, C. M., & Stewart, S. (1983). *Mastering resistance.* New York: Guilford Press.

Barret, R. L., & Robinson, B. E. (2000). *Gay fathers.* San Francisco: Jossey-Bass.

Barrows, P. (1999). Fathers in parent-infant psychotherapy. *Infant Mental Health Journal, 20,* 333–345.

Becvar, D. S., & Becvar, R. J. (1993). *Family therapy: A systemic integration* (2nd ed.). Boston: Allyn & Bacon.

Beere, C. A., King, D. W., Beere, D. B., & King, L. A. (1984). The Sex Role Egalitarianism Scale: A measure of attitudes toward the equality between the sexes. *Sex Roles, 10,* 563–576.

Beutler, L. E. (1997). The psychotherapist as a neglected variable in psychotherapy: An illustration by reference to the role of therapist experience and training. *Clinical Psychology: Science and Practice, 4,* 44–52.

Bigner, J. J. (1996). Working with gay fathers: Developmental, postdivorce parenting, and therapeutic issues. In J. Laird & R. J. Green (Eds.), *Lesbians and gays in couples and families: A handbook for therapists* (pp. 370–403). San Francisco: Jossey-Bass.

Budd, K. S., & O'Brien, T. P. (1982). Father involvement in behavioral parent training: An area in need of research. *Behavior Therapist, 5,* 85–89.

Burns, B. J., Hoagwood, K., & Mrazek, P. J. (1999). Effective treatment for mental disorders in children and adolescents. *Clinical Child and Family Psychology Review, 2,* 199–254.

Cabrera, N. J., Tamis-LeMonda, C. S., Bradley, R. H., Hofferth, S., & Lamb, M. E. (2000). Fatherhood in the twenty-first century. *Child Development, 71,* 127–136.

Carr, A. (1998). The inclusion of fathers in family therapy: A research based perspective. *Contemporary Family Therapy: An International Journal, 20,* 371–383.

Churven, P. G. (1978). Families: Parental attitudes to family assessment in a child psychiatry setting. *Journal of Child Psychology and Psychiatry, 19,* 33–41.

Coley, R. L. (2001). (In)visible men: Emerging research on low-income, unmarried, and minority fathers. *American Psychologist, 56,* 743–753.

Coplin, J. W., & Houts, A. C. (1991). Father involvement in parent training for oppositional child behavior: Progress or stagnation? *Child and Family Behavior Therapy, 13,* 29–51.

Crespi, T. D., & Steir, M. E. (1996). Managed care and mental health services: Facing the crisis in child and family treatment. *Psychotherapy in Private Practice, 15,* 15–25.

Deacon, S. A., Kirkpatrick, D. R., Wetchler, J. L., & Niedner, D. (1999). Marriage and family therapists' problems and utilization of personal therapy. *The American Journal of Family Therapy, 27,* 73–93.

Dienhart, A., & Dollahite, D. C. (1997). A generative narrative approach to clinical work with fathers. In A. J. Hawkins & D. C. Dollahite (Eds.), *Generative fathering: Beyond deficit perspectives* (pp. 183–199). Thousand Oaks, CA: Sage.

Duhig, A. M., Renk, K., Epstein, M. K., & Phares, V. (2000). Interparental agreement on internalizing, externalizing, and total behavior problems: A meta-analysis. *Clinical Psychology: Science and Practice, 7,* 435–453.

Guttman, H. A., Feldman, R. B., Engelsmann, F., Spector, L., & Buonvino, M. (1999). The relationship between psychiatrists' couple and family therapy training experience and their subsequent practice profile. *Journal of Marriage and Family Counseling, 25,* 31–41.

Harvey, E. A. (2000). Parenting similarity and children with attention-deficit/hyperactivity disorder. *Child and Family Behavior Therapy, 22,* 39–54.

Hecker, L. L. (1991). Where is Dad? 21 ways to involve fathers in family therapy. *Journal of Family Psychotherapy, 2,* 31–45.

Hibbs, E. D., & Jensen, P. S. (1996). *Psychosocial treatments for child and adolescent disorders: Empirically based strategies for clinical practice.* Washington, DC: American Psychological Association.

Johnson, L., & Thomas, V. (1999). Influences on the inclusion of children in family therapy. *Journal of Marital and Family Counseling, 25,* 117–123.

Kaslow, N. J., Kaslow, F. W., & Farber, E. W. (1999). Theories and techniques of marital and family therapy. In M. Sussman, S. K. Steinmetz, & G. W. Peterson (Eds.), *Handbook of marriage and the family* (pp. 767–792). New York: Plenum Press.

Kaslow, N. J., & Thompson, M. P. (1998). Applying the criteria for empirically supported treatments to studies of psychosocial interventions for child and adolescent depression. *Journal of Clinical Child Psychology, 27,* 146–155.

Kazdin, A. E. (1995). Child, parent, and family dysfunction as predictors of outcome in cognitive-behavioral treatment of antisocial children. *Behaviour Research and Therapy, 33,* 271–281.

Kazdin, A. E., & Weiss, J. R. (1998). Identifying and developing empirically supported child and adolescent treatments. *Journal of Consulting and Clinical Psychology, 66,* 19–36.

King, L. A., & King, D. W. (1993). *Manual for the Sex-Role Egalitarianism Scale: An instrument to measure attitudes toward gender-role equality.* Port Huron, MI: Sigma Assessment Systems.

Lazar, A., Sagi, A., & Fraser, M. W. (1991). Involving fathers in services. *Children and Youth Services Review, 13,* 287–300.

LeCroy, C. W. (1994). *Handbook of child and adolescent treatment manuals.* New York: Lexington Books.

Mash, E. J. (1998). Treatment of child and family disturbance: A behavioral systems perspective. In E. J. Mash & R. A. Barkley (Eds.), *Treatment of childhood disorders* (2nd ed., pp. 3–51). New York: Guilford Press.

McCollum, E. E., & Russell, C. S. (1992). Mother-blaming in family therapy: An empirical investigation. *American Journal of Family Therapy, 20,* 71–76.

Nicol, A. R., Smith, J., Kay, B., Hall, D., Barlow, J., & Williams, B. (1988). A focused casework approach to the treatment of child abuse: A controlled comparison. *Journal of Child Psychology and Psychiatry, 29,* 703–711.

Phares, V. (1992). Where's Poppa?: The relative lack of attention to the role of fathers in child and adolescent psychopathology. *American Psychologist, 47,* 656–664.

Phares, V. (1996). *Fathers and developmental psychopathology.* New York: Wiley.

Phares, V. (1997). Psychological adjustment, maladjustment, and father-child relationships. In M. E. Lamb (Ed.), *The role of the father in child development* (pp. 261–283). New York: Wiley.

Phares, V. (1999). *Poppa psychology: The role of fathers in children's mental well being.* Westport, CT: Greenwood.

Phares, V., & Compas, B. E. (1992). The role of fathers in child and adolescent psychopathology: Make room for daddy. *Psychological Bulletin, 111,* 387–412.

Phares, V., & Lum, J. (1997). Clinically referred children and adolescents: Fathers, family constellations, and other demographic factors. *Journal of Clinical Child Psychology, 26,* 219–223.

Prevatt, F. F. (1999). Milan systemic therapy. In D. M. Lawson & F. F. Prevatt (Eds.), *Casebook in family therapy* (pp. 188–209). Belmont, CA: Brooks/Cole.

Roberts, S. (1993). *Who we are: A portrait of America based on the latest U.S. census.* New York: Random House.

Stokes, T. F., & Baer, D. M. (1977). An implicit technology of generalization. *Journal of Applied Behavior Analysis, 10,* 349–367.

Strean, H. S. (1997). Who is father? Some facts, fantasies, and fallacies. *Journal of Analytic Social Work, 4,* 5–22.

Szapocznik, J., Perez-Vidal, A., Brickman, A. L., Foote, F. H., Santisteban, D., Hervis, O., & Kurtines, W. M. (1988). Engaging adolescent drug abusers and their families in treatment: A strategic structural systems approach. *Journal of Consulting and Clinical Psychology, 56,* 552–557.

Webster-Stratton, C. (1985a). The effects of father involvement in parent training for conduct problem children. *Journal of Child Psychology and Psychiatry, 26,* 801–810.

Webster-Stratton, C. (1985b). Predictors of treatment outcome in parent training for conduct disordered children. *Behavior Therapy, 16,* 223–243.

Webster-Stratton, C., Hollinsworth, T., & Kolpacoff, M. (1989). The long-term effectiveness and clinical significance of three cost-effective training programs for families with conduct-problem children. *Journal of Consulting and Clinical Psychology, 57,* 550–553.

Wolf, P. (1999). "Private" practice: An oxymoron in the age of managed care. In K. Weisgerber (Ed.), *The traumatic bond between the psychotherapist and managed care* (pp. 105–122). Northvale, NJ: Jason Aronson.

About the authors: *Amy M. Duhig* completed her PhD in clinical psychology at the University of South Florida. She completed her clinical internship at the Mailman Center for Child Development, University of Miami School of Medicine. She will complete her postdoctoral training at Yale University. *Vicky Phares* received her PhD in clinical psychology from the University of Vermont. She served on the faculty at the University of Connecticut and has been on the faculty at the University of South Florida since 1992. She is currently the director of clinical psychology training at the University of South Florida. *Robyn W. Birkeland* is currently completing her PhD in clinical psychology at the University of South Florida. She will be completing her clinical internship at the Children's Hospital Medical Center in Cincinnati, OH.

Address correspondence to: Vicky Phares, Department of Psychology, University of South Florida, 4202 East Fowler Avenue, PCD 4118G, Tampa, Florida 33620. E-mail: phares@luna.cas.usf.edu

Exercise for Article 2

Factual Questions

1. How many of the participants were members of Division 53 of the American Psychological Association?

2. What was the response rate for the members of Division 53?

3. For intact families, what is the mean percentage of time the therapists included mothers?

4. For intact families, what is the mean percentage of time the therapists included fathers?

5. Is the difference between your answers to Questions 3 and 4 statistically significant? If yes, at what probability level?

6. Was the length of time in clinical practice positively associated with including fathers? Explain.

Questions for Discussion

7. If you had conducted this survey, would you have included both APA and AAMFT members *or* would you have restricted it to members of only one association? Explain. (See lines 184–192.)

8. Is it important to know that the 500 individuals from each professional organization were selected at random? Explain. (See lines 193–195.)

9. The researchers characterize the response rates from the two professional organizations as "somewhat low." Do you agree with this characterization? Is this an important issue? Explain. (See lines 197–207.)

10. The researchers report that "the number of family-related continuing education seminars attended by the clinician in the past year was significantly related to including both mothers ($r = .21, p < .01$) and fathers ($r = .36, p < .01$) in treatment with their children and adolescents." Would you characterize these correlation coefficients (.21 and .36) as representing very strong relationships? Explain. (See lines 334–338.)

11. The researchers mention a possible "ceiling effect" in lines 390–391. Speculate on the meaning of this term.

12. The researchers report that the relationship between both the number of family-related books read in the last year and the number of journal articles read in the last year were significantly related to including mothers and fathers in treatment. In your opinion, is this evidence that reading such materials *cause* therapists to be more likely to include mothers and fathers? Explain. (See lines 339–345 and 512–525.)

Quality Ratings

Directions: Indicate your level of agreement with each of the following statements by circling a number from 5 for strongly agree (SA) to 1 for strongly disagree (SD). If you believe an item is not applicable to this research article, leave it blank. Be prepared to explain your ratings. When responding to criteria A and B below, keep in mind that brief titles and abstracts are conventional in published research.

A.   The title of the article is appropriate.

SA   5   4   3   2   1   SD

B.   The abstract provides an effective overview of the research article.

SA   5   4   3   2   1   SD

C.   The introduction establishes the importance of the study.

SA   5   4   3   2   1   SD

D.   The literature review establishes the context for the study.

SA   5   4   3   2   1   SD

E.   The research purpose, question, or hypothesis is clearly stated.

SA   5   4   3   2   1   SD

F.   The method of sampling is sound.

SA   5   4   3   2   1   SD

G.   Relevant demographics (for example, age, gender, and ethnicity) are described.

SA   5   4   3   2   1   SD

H.   Measurement procedures are adequate.

SA   5   4   3   2   1   SD

I.   All procedures have been described in sufficient detail to permit a replication of the study.

SA   5   4   3   2   1   SD

J.   The participants have been adequately protected from potential harm.

SA   5   4   3   2   1   SD

K.   The results are clearly described.

SA   5   4   3   2   1   SD

L.   The discussion/conclusion is appropriate.

SA   5   4   3   2   1   SD

M.   Despite any flaws, the report is worthy of publication.

SA   5   4   3   2   1   SD

Article 3

Screening for Domestic Violence: Recommendations Based on a Practice Survey

SARAH L. SAMUELSON
George Fox University

CLARK D. CAMPBELL
George Fox University

ABSTRACT. How do practicing psychologists identify female victims of domestic violence? When asking about harm to self and others, do they also ask if the client is in danger of being harmed by another in an intimate relationship? A national survey of practicing psychologists revealed that 95% agreed that it is their responsibility to assist victimized clients, but fewer than 19% routinely screen for domestic violence. Psychologists report several barriers to screening at intake, which coupled with low screening rates, suggest that psychologists are missing important opportunities to assist clients who are at risk for assault. Several recommendations designed to improve psychologists' screening rates for domestic violence are provided.

Professional Psychology: Research and Practice, 36, 276–282.

The need to identify and assist victims of domestic violence will remain an issue as long as society is not violence free. Insofar as clients who suffer domestic violence seek professional help for mental health is-
5 sues, clinical psychologists play an important role in the detection and treatment of this problem. It has become common practice for psychologists to routinely assess areas of client safety such as risk of harm to self or others. The questions are as follows: Do practicing
10 psychologists routinely screen clients for harm experienced at the hands of an intimate partner? What methods of screening do they use, and what factors may affect their screening practices? These questions are addressed in this exploratory survey, and practice and
15 research recommendations are provided based on survey results.

The Problem of Domestic Violence

The physical and psychological consequences of domestic violence are both acute and chronic. Physical injuries range from temporary bruises and broken
20 bones to scars, physical disability, or even death (Browne, 1993; Plichta, 1996). Many times domestic violence begins when a woman becomes pregnant. Pregnant women and their unborn children may sustain especially severe injuries as a result of physical abuse:
25 placental separation, fetal fractures, rupture of the

uterus, and premature labor (Goodman, Koss, & Russo, 1993). The effects of domestic violence can be either a contributing or an underlying factor in women's mental health problems as well. Psychological problems asso-
30 ciated with domestic violence include depression, post-traumatic stress disorder, anxiety, panic disorder, sexual dysfunction, suicidality, and substance abuse disorder (Garimella, Plichta, Houseman, & Garzon, 2000; Rodriguez, Bauer, McLoughlin, & Grumbach, 1999).
35 There is much discussion in the literature regarding mutuality of assault between intimate partners, and we know that both women and men are victims of domestic violence. The majority of studies suggests, however, that men are the primary perpetrators of domestic vio-
40 lence. Women are more likely to sustain physical injury as a result of abusive acts (e.g., Browne, 1993; O'Leary & Murphy, 1992) and are more likely to require medical attention (Stets & Straus, 1990). In fact, in women between the ages of 15 and 44, domestic
45 violence is found to be the leading cause of acute injury (Grisso et al., 1991). Studies also indicate that men act more aggressively and perpetrate more severe abusive acts than do women during episodes of domestic violence. Sometimes the injuries that men incur are the
50 result of their aggression against their partner. (For greater detail on mutuality of assault, see Browne, 1993.)
Prevalence estimates for physical abuse against women in the general population vary depending on
55 which study is examined (e.g., Browne, 1993; Glick, Johnson, & Pham, 1999; Koss et al., 1994; Plichta, 1996). Estimates range from 8% to 12%. This means that 1 out of 8–13 women in the United States reportedly experiences one or more acts of physical abuse
60 each year. Of every 4 abused women, 3 experience multiple acts of physical abuse, and more than 1 of every 4 experience more than 12 acts of physical abuse each year (Glick et al., 1999). Approximately 30% of all women are physically abused at least once by a
65 male intimate during their adulthood (Plichta, 1996).
Prevalence figures likely underestimate domestic violence according to Browne (1993). National surveys typically do not interview the very poor, non-English-speaking persons, military families living on a base, or

70 those who are incarcerated, homeless, hospitalized, or institutionalized. Surveys do not include those who are not at home when interviewers attempt contact, those who are unwilling to talk to interviewers, and those who respond but are, even anonymously, unwilling to
75 report their experiences of domestic violence.

Far less is known about frequency and severity of domestic violence in same-sex relationships or about the experiences of heterosexual male victims. A sense of stigma and the feeling that others will not under-
80 stand contribute to difficulties in obtaining information about violence in these relationships.

Screening for Domestic Violence

Several studies have examined domestic violence screening practices of physicians. In a survey of California physicians, Rodriguez et al. (1999) found that a
85 majority of the 400 respondents (79%) reported that they routinely screened women for domestic violence if they presented with some evidence of injury. Far fewer (10%) reported that they routinely screened their new patients. More female than male and more younger
90 than older physicians reported that they screened new patients. Physicians who worked in public health clinics reported the highest rate of new patient screening (37%), followed by private office (9%), HMOs (1%), and "other practice settings" (12%).
95 The psychological community has come late to the issue of domestic violence. Not until February 1999 did the American Psychological Association (APA) officially adopt the *Resolution on Male Violence Against Women*, making it clear that it is the duty of psycholo-
100 gists to assist victims of domestic violence. In 1993, Browne commented that the psychological community is "ideally suited to make a vital contribution ...[but] rarely involves itself in proactive interventions with women abused by male partners" (p. 1082). Since then,
105 steps have been taken to expand psychology's knowledge base. There is concern that psychologists may misunderstand and minimize the magnitude of the problem.

Pruitt and Kappius (1992) evaluated the abuse as-
110 sessment rate of psychologists in independent practice and found that 51% of psychologists reported that they asked all or at least most of their clients about sexual abuse at some time during the course of therapy. The focus of this study, however, was assessment of client
115 sexual abuse history rather than screening for current or recent domestic violence involvement. Furthermore, psychologists were asked whether they inquired about sexual abuse *at some time* during the course of therapy rather than at the time of initial client intake.
120 Glick et al. (1999) surveyed 365 public and community-based agencies regarding their screening practices for domestic violence. This sample included hospital emergency departments, public and community-based medical clinics, counseling services, social ser-
125 vices, criminal/legal services, services for special populations (seniors, women, children, ethnic groups, gay men/lesbians, and persons with disabilities), and domestic violence services. They found that 36% of the agencies in the sample had no protocol in place for
130 screening women for domestic violence. Furthermore, 49% of the agencies reported that they did not routinely ask women about involvement in domestic violence. Those agencies that did have a protocol used it most of the time compared with those agencies with no estab-
135 lished screening protocol (71% vs. 16%).

Glick et al. (1999) also interviewed 1,855 women in a stratified random sample that was representative of all women in the state of Oregon. Of this sample, 461 women reported that they had experienced physical
140 abuse: 251 within the past year and 210 within the past 10 years, but not during the past year. More than 90% of the abused women in this study reported that they had sought outside support and protection. Mental health providers were the third most sought out source
145 of help (34%) after friends or family (80%) and police (35%). Nearly all of the abused women (93%) felt that mental health providers were supportive and respectful of them, but only 55% reported that mental health providers offered information on domestic violence ser-
150 vices (Glick et al., 1999).

The Domestic Violence Screening Survey

Because so little is known about screening in the practice setting, we developed a questionnaire to assess how and when psychologists screen for domestic violence, as well as their attitudes about the screening
155 process. The questionnaire was based on published research by Browne (1993); Dill, Chu, Grob, and Eisen (1991); and Rodriguez, Quiroga, and Bauer (1999). Prevalence rates and severity of assault in domestic violence appear to be greatest for female victims, so
160 the screening questionnaire focused on this population. Respondents were asked to use the following definition of domestic violence as they formulated their responses:

Domestic violence is physically and sexually abusive acts
165 perpetrated against a woman by an intimate partner. These acts include, but are not limited to, threats of violence or acts of violence such as hitting, kicking, or other physical harm or forcing a woman to engage in sexual activity by use of physical coercion.

170 Safety assessment is fundamental to domestic violence screening, thus the term *threats of violence* was included in the definition. Although they may not be physical in nature, threats often escalate into direct acts of perpetration. Even if threats do not escalate into
175 physical violence, they are emotionally abusive and greatly affect a woman's perception of risk and safety. Threats can be both verbal and nonverbal, and examples of nonverbal threats include punching a wall, throwing objects across the room, or menacing body
180 postures. Other forms of emotional abuse, including

Table 1
Demographic Information for the Study Sample

Demographic	%	M (in years)	SD
Age			
Male		55.5	9.1
Female		50.0	8.7
Time in practice		21.9	9.0
Gender			
Male	51.0		
Female	49.0		
Ethnicity			
European American	90.6		
Hispanic American	3.1		
Asian American	2.4		
Other and not specified	2.3		
Native American	1.6		
Practice region			
Northeast	29.1		
Midwest	28.3		
Northwest, Southwest, Hawaii, Alaska	25.3		
Southeast, South	17.3		
Population served			
Adult females	45.4		
Adult males	32.5		
Adolescents	11.3		
Children	10.8		
Encounter DV victims in practice			
Almost always	0.8		
Quite often	22.8		
Sometimes	63.0		
Almost never	13.4		
Feel a responsibility to assist DV clients			
Strongly agree	71.7		
Mostly agree	18.9		
Agree a little	4.7		
Disagree a little	0.0		
Mostly disagree	1.6		
Strongly disagree	3.1		
Screen for DV on intake form	16.3		
Previous training in DV issues[a]			
Clinical presentations (e.g., grand rounds, practicum didactics)	71.8		
Continuing education course	67.8		
Clinical supervision	55.1		
Lecture on DV in graduate school	47.4		
Class on DV in graduate school	7.5		
Witnessed DV between caregivers as a child			
Male	8.0		
Female	6.0		
Physically hurt or feared for safety by current or previous intimate partner			
Male	6.0		
Female	9.0		

Note. $N = 128$. DV = domestic violence.
[a]Total does not equal 100% because participants endorsed more than one category.

intense criticisms, name calling, and put-downs, can escalate into physical violence as well.

Three hundred psychologists, randomly selected from a list of 47,000 licensed psychologists who were also members of the APA, were sent the questionnaire. These psychologists were residents of the United States, and indicated that they were in independent practice, provided mental health related services in an agency setting, or supervised those who provided such services.

Completed questionnaires were received from 128 respondents for a return rate of 43%. Given the low response rate, z-statistical tests were used to look for significant differences between the sample and the original population of psychologists. No significant differences were found for age, gender, and geographic region. However, a larger proportion of the respondents, 90.6%, identified themselves as European American than did those in the original population, 78.8% ($z = 3.10$, $p = .001$). Results should be interpreted with this in mind. Psychologist demographics are presented in Table 1.

To gauge psychologists' knowledge regarding domestic violence prevalence rates, they were asked to estimate the percentage of women in the general population who experience one or more acts of domestic violence each year. Estimates ranged from 2% to 80%. The majority of psychologists gave an estimate be-

Table 2
Psychologists' Preferred Method of Screening for Domestic Violence

Preferred method of screening	Combined male & female endorsement		Male endorsement		Female endorsement	
	%	n^a	%	n^b	%	n^c
Screen if client brings up the subject	10.2	13	16.9	11	3.2	2
Screen during the course of treatment if suspect that it could be an issue	26.6	34	23.1	15	30.1	19
Screen all adult female clients at some time during the course of treatment	19.5	25	23.1	15	15.9	10
Screen during the intake interview if suspect that it could be an issue	22.7	29	16.9	11	28.6	18
Screen all adult female clients during the intake interview	18.7	24	16.9	11	20.6	13
Domestic violence is not an issue that comes up in my practice	2.3	3	3.1	2	1.6	1

$^a n = 128.$ $^b n = 65.$ $^c n = 63.$

tween 20% and 30%, and the most frequent estimate was 20%. This figure was higher than the 8%–12% reported in previous research (e.g., Browne, 1993; Glick et al., 1999; Koss et al., 1994; Plichta, 1996; Straus & Gelles, 1990). Perhaps respondents had a clinical population in mind rather than the general population.

Perceived barriers to asking female clients about domestic violence during the intake interview process were identified by supplying psychologists with a list of 12 potential barriers. They were asked to rank order their top four concerns regarding screening at intake. These top concerns in rank order were

1. The client might be unwilling to disclose information.
2. The psychologist lacked training in domestic violence issues.
3. Screening might be overwhelming to the client.
4. There is too little time during the intake process to screen.

Ranking very closely to the fourth concern was a fifth concern; that is, that questioning about domestic violence felt intrusive or awkward to the psychologist.

Psychologists were also asked to identify one of six statements that most closely represented their current domestic violence screening practices. The most frequently endorsed statement (26.6%) was as follows: "Screen during the course of treatment if suspect it could be an issue." The six statements and percentages of endorsement for each response are summarized in Table 2.

To determine if there were differences in screening practices according to age, a median split was used to divide the respondents into two age groups: younger (<53) versus older (≥53). A Pearson chi-square test revealed no significant differences between the groups, $\chi^2(4, N = 125) = 4.81, p > .05$. To determine if there were differences in screening practices according to years since graduation, the respondents were divided into two groups: those in practice 20 years or less and those with more than 20 years of practice. A Pearson chi-square test revealed no significant differences between the groups, $\chi^2(4, N = 125) = 4.15, p > .05$.

A Pearson chi-square test was performed to determine if psychologists who reported a personal history of domestic violence might be more sensitive to domestic violence issues and would, therefore, screen at higher rates than psychologists who did not report such experiences. The number of respondents in various cells was too low, however, to accurately determine whether personal involvement in domestic violence had any effect on screening practices. A Pearson chi-square test was performed to determine if various training scenarios were associated with increased screening rates, but because of low response rates, that question remains unanswered as well.

To determine how often psychologists used specific interventions once they discovered that a female client was a victim of domestic violence, respondents were asked to rate 11 intervention strategies on a 4-point Likert scale, indicating whether they used the strategy 1 (*almost never*), 2 (*sometimes*), 3 (*quite often*), or 4 (*almost always*). Seven of the strategies were used almost always by 78% or more of the responders. Results are summarized in Table 3.

Implications and Recommendations for Practice

Results of this study suggest that psychologists recognize domestic violence to be an issue with serious implications for clients of mental health providers, but with such low levels of screening, psychologists are missing important opportunities to intervene on behalf of clients who are experiencing abuse.

One concern regarding screening was client nondisclosure. It can be the case that, given a victim's current situation and the paralyzing fear she is experiencing, an abused client may find it difficult to raise the subject of abuse on her own. Psychologists can assist by initiating the topic. To reduce awkward feelings, they might transition into asking about domestic violence by saying something like, "I am going to ask you

Table 3
Interventions Psychologists Use with Domestic Violence Victims

Intervention	Psychologist endorsement (%)			
	Almost never	Sometimes	Quite often	Almost always
Express to the client that acts of domestic violence are unacceptable	2	4	4	90
Ask the client about her current level of safety	1	1	9	89
Ask the client to describe the extent of the abuse (how often, specific behavior of the abuser, client's typical response to the abuse)	1	4	9	86
Record the client's disclosure in her chart notes	2	6	8	84
Express concern for the future safety of the client	1	6	10	83
Help the client formulate a plan of action given her most pressing need	1	5	13	81
Arrange for follow-up contact with the client	1	3	18	78
Ask the client about guns or other weapons in the home	3	17	21	59
Remind the client that her disclosure is confidential	10	13	19	58
Offer the client educational information about domestic violence	13	26	24	37
Offer the client written information about shelters and other domestic violence services	22	22	21	35

some questions that I ask everyone I see." Even though talking about her current level of safety may be anxiety producing, most women report that they are not overwhelmed if the topic is raised appropriately (Caralis & Musialowski, 1997; Friedman, Samet, Roberts, Hudlin, & Hans, 1992; Morrison, Allan, & Grunfeld, 2000). The opportunity to discuss her situation with a supportive and nonjudgmental professional in the safety of a private setting will often lessen her anxious feelings.

With regard to psychologists' concerns of intrusiveness, studies indicate that women prefer health care providers to ask them directly about their level of safety (Caralis & Musialowski, 1997; Friedman et al., 1992; Morrison et al., 2000). Furthermore, abused women negatively evaluate providers who skirted the issue or appear to avoid it altogether. They interpret this as an indication that the subject of their abuse is unimportant or somehow causes the health care provider to feel embarrassed (Rodriguez et al., 1996).

The methods and wording used to assess experiences of domestic violence in women directly affect the reported frequency of violence. Detection of domestic violence events increases when abused women are asked behaviorally specific questions (e.g., punch, kick) rather than questions that label events (e.g., abuse, rape; Weaver, 1998). Dill et al. (1991) found that a written self-report format was twice as likely to elicit reports of domestic violence as was a verbal questioning format.

Physical and psychological abuse against women can be reliably measured (O'Leary, 1999). The most widely used instruments are the Conflict Tactics Scale (CTS) developed by Straus (1979) and the Index of Spouse Abuse (ISA; Hudson & McIntosh, 1981); however, more recently, the Partner Violence Screen (PVS; Feldhaus et al., 1997) has proven useful as a screening

instrument. The length of the PVS directly addresses psychologists' concern that there is too little time during the intake process to screen for domestic violence. The PVS is quite short, taking an average of 20 s to administer. When tested in an emergency room setting, prevalence rates for detection of domestic abuse using the CTS and the ISA were 24.3% and 27.4%, respectively. The prevalence rate for the PVS was 29.5%. In fact, the first question alone detected nearly as many victims as did the entire PVS (Feldhaus et al., 1997). The first question addresses physical assault, and the remaining two address a woman's perception of her level of safety. Women are asked the following questions: "Have you been hit, kicked, punched, or otherwise hurt by someone within the past year? If so, by whom?" "Do you feel safe in your current relationship?" and "Is there a partner from a previous relationship who is making you feel unsafe now?" (Feldhaus et al., 1997, p. 1358). One limitation of the PVS is that it includes no direct question regarding sexual assault. Another short screening instrument to consider is the HITS (hits, insults, threatens, and screams) screening tool developed by Sherin, Sinacore, Li, Zitter, and Shakil (1998). The HITS correlates highly with the CTS and has demonstrated an ability to differentiate domestic violence victims from nonvictims in a family practice setting.

It is important for psychologists to have an understanding of the dynamics of abusive relationships and the variety of psychological and physical sequelae that ensue as a result of traumatic victimization. They should become familiar with diagnostic considerations and treatment goals. More training can increase the comfort level of psychologists who are concerned that they do not have the skills to effectively inquire and intervene in domestic violence cases. As important as

360 this knowledge is, however, it is unlikely sufficient to persuade psychologists to change their practice to include routine screening. We have seen that education alone does not have much impact on screening rates.
365 Studies in nonpsychological health care settings have shown that additional training had only a minimal effect on increased screening rates (Knight & Remington, 2000; Rodriguez et al., 1999).

Recommendations for Standard of Practice

Policies to formalize standard of practice expectations should be implemented by psychologists to en-
370 sure that clients victimized by violent partners are identified and assisted in gaining safety. The findings of this study clearly indicate that the psychological community, as a whole, could do more to support these victims. Browne (1993) contended that

> the same attitudes that produced decades of resistance to recognition of the prevalence and severity of violence by men against their female partners—and that lead medical doctors to simply itemize injuries and not inquire as to the context, perpetrator, or ongoing risk to the patient—are evident in the psychological community's failure to incorporate current knowledge on intimate violence into routinized psychological practice. (p. 1082)

375 Koss (1990) observed that "standard procedures of psychological history-taking, evaluation of suicide risk, assessment of psychopathology and personality, and measurements of life events all routinely fail to include questions about victimization by violence" (p. 376). It
380 has become common practice for psychologists to routinely assess other areas of client safety (e.g., risk of harm to self or others). Common screening protocols should be expanded to include questions regarding harm experienced at the hands of an intimate partner as
385 well. Unless the psychological community joins together in endorsing policies that call for routine screening, the current standard of practice will, more than likely, remain the same.

For practice standards to be effective, important in-
390 dividual attitudes must change. Psychologists agree that it is their responsibility to assist domestic violence victims, yet they seldom make it their practice to identify these victims early on. Although studies in a psychological setting regarding the benefits of screening at
395 intake as compared with other screening scenarios arc lacking, there appear to be few risks of harm in inquiring. Given high prevalence rates of domestic violence, is it ethical for psychologists to wait for research results on the benefits of universal screening to imple-
400 ment routine screening? Perhaps psychologists should ask if it is ethical to neglect screening at intake. It is possible that psychologists who are unaware of a client's current level of safety could suggest interventions that would, in fact, increase her risk for further abuse.
405 In circumstances in which an unidentified victim does not return for treatment following the initial visit, the opportunity to communicate concern for the client's

safety and to assist her in finding ways to gain that safety is lost. Knowing that a proactive stance could
410 make a difference in the level of the physical safety of their clients, psychologists must decide if they are willing to facilitate a safety intervention on behalf of victims of domestic violence.

Screening Recommendations

What are some steps that psychologists can take to
415 assist victims of domestic violence? Practice recommendations are offered next. Refer to Table 4 for a summary of these steps.

Table 4
Steps That Psychologists Can Take to Assist Victims of Domestic Violence

Decide to implement a screening protocol.
Obtain more training as needed. Previous training may be insufficient or outdated.
Establish links with community resources prior to screening implementation.
Obtain information regarding hotline numbers, local shelters, domestic violence therapy groups, law enforcement, legal aid, advocacy groups, educational and financial services, and food and housing assistance.
Maintain a supply of domestic violence literature to offer to clients.
Screen all adolescent and adult clients for domestic violence at the time of intake.
Also include questions regarding personal safety on client-completed intake forms.
Screen in privacy and maintain confidentiality.
Screen couples individually. Emphasize that this is a standard component of the intake process.
Validate identified victims' experiences.
Acknowledge that many women experience domestic violence, that domestic violence is illegal and inappropriate, that it results in physical and psychological damage, and that a variety of resources are available for victims.
Assess identified victims' level of safety.
What threats have been made to the client?
How accessible is the client to the abuser at this time?
Is the client requesting immediate protection by law enforcement or the safety of a shelter?
If the client is not in imminent danger, has she devised a plan to protect herself and any children if the danger escalates?
Does the client know how to access community resources if she feels unsafe?

Decide to Implement a Screening Protocol

Psychologists must make a conscious decision to implement a screening protocol, deciding to screen all
420 adolescent and adult clients for intimate partner abuse at the time of intake. We must not assume that only female clients are in danger. Several national medical organizations and public health organizations have endorsed the use of screening protocols. Routine
425 screening in nonpsychological clinical settings and hospital emergency rooms has been shown to be effective (American Academy of Family Physicians, 1994; American Public Health Association, 1993; Novello, Rosenberg, Saltzman, & Shosky, 1992). If more train-
430 ing is needed to recognize and treat victims of violence, psychologists should obtain this prior to screening implementation. It is important to note that research

in the area of domestic violence continues to evolve, and it may be the case that previous training is insufficient or outdated.

Establish Links with Community Resources

Links with community resources should be established prior to screening implementation. Networking with local domestic violence professionals has the potential to enhance prevention and treatment options. Information regarding hotline numbers, local shelters, domestic violence therapy groups, law enforcement, legal aid, advocacy groups, educational and financial services, and food and housing assistance should be located in order that it can be made available to clients who need it. It would also be helpful to maintain a supply of domestic violence literature to offer clients, including small pamphlets that can be hidden in one's shoe. Offering educational material and information about local resources can be empowering to a victim because it reduces feelings of isolation and expands her perception of the range of available options. It is important to recognize that an abusive partner may not want the victim to have this information about resources. Psychologists may need to help the client decide how it can be stored without compromising her safety.

Screen All Clients During the Intake Interview

Psychologists should routinely inquire about violence at the time of intake and also include questions regarding personal safety on client-completed intake forms. These could be added alongside other questions that address physical health. Inquiries can be as brief as asking the three PVS questions (Feldhaus et al., 1997). This would address both physical and emotional abuse. Psychologists should note that a victim may not feel safe enough to answer such questions in the presence of her abuser. Issues of privacy and confidentiality are of utmost importance during the screening process, and careless disclosure of reports of violence could compromise the safety of a victim. Asking someone about physical abuse in the presence or within the hearing of a potential abuser could increase a victim's risk for retaliation and coercion postinterview. If interviewed together, give partners some time to speak with you privately as well. Emphasize that this is a standard component of the intake process.

Validate Identified Victims' Experiences

Validating the abuse experience is another important factor in the screening process. Browne (1993) suggested, "for many victims, [validating] statements by a professional are a first step toward reframing abusive experiences and seeking intervention or counsel" (p. 1083). When addressing victims of violence, she suggested that clinicians acknowledge to their client that

many women experience physical and sexual assault from intimates, that such assaults may lead to a range of physical and psychological sequelae, that such assaults are illegal and inappropriate, and that a variety of resources exist for individuals who have experienced these assaults. (Browne, 1993, p. 1083)

This information will probably need to be shared a number of times. When a client feels powerless and overwhelmed, she is far less likely to retain important information related to her health.

Assess Identified Victims' Current Level of Safety

All screening for domestic violence should include an assessment of the victim's current level of safety. Even if the abuser is no longer physically present, the client may still be in danger of revictimization. Although prediction of violence is difficult, it may be useful to help the client think through some of the predisposing, protective, and precipitating factors in the threatening situation. This is analogous to assessing suicidality in clients and may be beneficial in helping victims of domestic violence take a more objective look at the potentially violent situation. Predisposing factors may include a history of threatening words and behaviors, while precipitating factors may include alcohol abuse. Although a victim of domestic violence has no control over these factors in the abuser's behavior, she can evaluate these factors in determining her level of safety.

The victim can, however, evaluate her own protective factors that are involved in safety planning. Safety planning should address both immediate and future protective factors. Potential safety questions include the following:

- What threats have been made to the client?
- How accessible is the client to the abuser at this time?
- Is the client requesting immediate protection by law enforcement or the safety of a shelter?
- If the client is not in imminent danger, has she devised a plan to protect herself and any children if the danger escalates?
- Does the client know how to access community resources if she feels unsafe?

Discussing options and formulating a safety plan with a client increase her current and anticipated feelings of safety, both of which are basic to the attainment of psychological and physical health.

Conclusion

Psychologists have a critical role to play in the early identification and assistance of victims who are experiencing domestic violence. The practice recommendations that we have proposed could be helpful to psychologists in the screening, assessment, and treatment of these clients.

References

American Academy of Family Physicians (1994). Family violence: An AAFP white paper. *American Family Physician, 50,* 1636–1640, 1644–1646.

American Psychological Association (1999, February). *Resolution on male violence against women.* Retrieved February 19, 2000, from http://www.apa.org/pi/wpo/maleviol.html

American Public Health Association (1993). Policy statement 9211 (PP): Domestic violence. *American Journal of Public Health, 83,* 458–463.

Browne, A. (1993). Violence against women by male partners. *American Psychologist, 48,* 1077–1087.

Caralis, P. V., & Musialowski, R. (1997). Women's experience with domestic violence and their attitudes and expectations regarding medical care of abuse victims. *Southern Medical Journal, 9,* 1075–1080.

Dill, D. L., Chu, J. A., Grob, M. C., & Eisen, S. V. (1991). The reliability of abuse history reports: A comparison of two inquiry formats. *Comprehensive Psychiatry, 32,* 166–169.

Feldhaus, K. M., Koziol-McLain, J., Amsbury, H. L., Norton, I. M., Lowenstein, S. R., & Abbott, J. T. (1997). Accuracy of 3 brief screening questions for detecting partner violence in the emergency department. *Journal of the American Medical Association, 277,* 1357–1361.

Friedman, L. S., Samet, J. H., Roberts, M. S., Hudlin, M., & Hans, P. (1992). Inquiry about victimization experiences: A survey of patient preferences and physician practices. *Archives of Internal Medicine, 152,* 1186–1190.

Garimella, R., Plichta, S. B., Houseman, C., & Garzon, L. (2000). Physician beliefs about victims of spouse abuse and about the physician role. *Journal of Women's Health & Gender-Based Medicine, 9,* 405–411.

Glick, B., Johnson, S., & Pham, C. (1999). *1998 Oregon domestic violence needs assessment: A report to the Oregon governor's council on domestic violence.* Salem, OR: Oregon Health Division and Multnomah County Health Department.

Goodman, L. A., Koss, M. P., & Russo, N. F. (1993). Violence against women: Physical and mental health effects. *Applied and Preventive Psychology, 2,* 79–89.

Grisso, J. A., Wishner, A. R., Schwarz, D. F., Weene, B. A., Holmes, J. H., & Sutton, R. L. (1991). A population-based study of injuries in inner city women. *American Journal of Epidemiology, 134,* 59–68.

Hudson, W. W., & McIntosh, S. (1981). The Index of Spouse Abuse. *Journal of Marriage and the Family, 43,* 873–888.

Knight, R. A., & Remington, P. L. (2000). Training internal medicine residents to screen for domestic violence. *Journal of Women's Health and Gender-Based Medicine, 9,* 167–174.

Koss, M. P. (1990). The women's mental health research agenda: Violence against women. *American Psychologist, 45,* 374–380.

Koss, M. P., Goodman, L. A., Browne, A., Fitzgerald, L. F., Keita, G. P., & Russo, N. F. (1994). *No safe haven: Violence against women at home, at work, and in the community* (Report of the Male Violence Against Women Task Force). Washington, DC: American Psychological Association.

Morrison, L. J., Allan, R., & Grunfeld, A. (2000). Improving the emergency department detection rate of domestic violence using direct questioning. *The Journal of Emergency Medicine, 19,* 117–124.

Novello, A. C., Rosenberg, M., Saltzman, L., & Shosky, J. (1992). From the Surgeon General, U.S. Public Health Service. *Journal of the American Medical Association, 267,* 3132.

O'Leary, K. D. (1999). Psychological abuse: A variable deserving critical attention in domestic violence. *Violence and Victims, 14,* 3–23.

O'Leary, K. D., & Murphy, C. (1992). Clinical issues in the assessment of spouse abuse. In R. T. Ammerman & M. Hersen (Eds.), *Assessment of family violence: A clinical and legal sourcebook* (pp. 26–46). New York: Wiley.

Plichta, S. B. (1996). Violence and abuse: Implications for women's health. In M. M. Falik & K. S. Collins (Eds.), *Women's health: The Commonwealth survey* (pp. 237–270). Baltimore, MD: Johns Hopkins University Press.

Pruitt, J. A., & Kappius, R. E. (1992). Routine inquiry into sexual victimization: A survey of psychologists' practices. *Professional Psychology: Research and Practice, 23,* 474–479.

Rodriguez, M. A., Bauer, H. M., McLoughlin, E., & Grumbach, K. (1999). Screening and intervention for intimate partner abuse: Practices and attitudes of primary care physicians. *Journal of the American Medical Association, 282,* 468–474.

Rodriguez, M. A., Quiroga, S. S., & Bauer, H. M. (1996). Breaking the silence: Battered women's perspectives on medical care. *Archives of Family Medicine, 5,* 153–158.

Sherin, K. M., Sinacore, J. M., Li, X. Q., Zitter, R. E., & Shakil, A. (1998). HITS: A short domestic violence screening tool for use in a family practice setting. *Family Medicine, 30,* 508–512.

Stets, J. E., & Straus, M. A. (1990). Gender differences in reporting marital violence and its medical and psychological consequences. In M. A. Straus & R. J. Gelles (Eds.), *Physical violence in American families* (pp. 151–165). New Brunswick, NJ: Transaction Press.

Straus, M. A. (1979). Measuring intrafamily conflict and violence: The Conflict Tactics (CT) scales. *Journal of Marriage and the Family, 41,* 75–78.

Straus, M. A., & Gelles, R. J. (1990). *Physical violence in American families: Risk factors and adaptations to violence in 8,145 families.* New Brunswick, NJ: Transaction.

Weaver, T. L. (1998). Method variance and sensitivity of screening for traumatic stressors. *Journal of Traumatic Stress, 11,* 181–185.

Acknowledgment: This article was supported by a Richter Scholars Research Grant and is based on a doctoral dissertation completed by Sarah L. Samuelson. Portions of this research were presented at the 112th Annual Convention of the American Psychological Association, Honolulu, Hawaii, July 2004.

About the authors: *Sarah L. Samuelson* received her PsyD in clinical psychology from the Graduate School of Clinical Psychology at George Fox University. She was a doctoral student at the time this article was written. She is now a psychologist resident in independent practice in Newberg, Oregon. *Clark D. Campbell* received his PhD in clinical psychology from the Graduate School of Clinical Psychology at Western Seminary, Portland, Oregon. He is a professor and director of clinical training in the Graduate Department of Clinical Psychology at George Fox University and an adjunct associate professor in the Departments of Psychiatry and Family Medicine at Oregon Health and Science University. He maintains a small independent practice in Newberg, Oregon, and conducts research on rural psychology.

Address correspondence to: Correspondence concerning this article should be addressed to Sarah L. Samuelson, Valley Psychological Associates, 470 Villa Road, Newberg, OR 97132. E-mail: s.l.samuelson@worldnet.att.net

Exercise for Article 3

Factual Questions

1. According to the literature review, prevalence estimates for physical abuse against women in the general population range from 8% to what higher percentage?

2. Does the definition of domestic violence the respondents were asked to use include *both* physically and sexually abusive acts?

3. How were the 300 psychologists selected from the list of 47,000?

4. The respondents were asked to estimate the percentage of women in the general population who experience one or more acts of domestic violence each year. What is the range of their responses?

5. Did a higher percentage of "males" *or* "females" endorse this statement: "Screen all adult female clients during the intake interview"?

6. Were the differences in screening practices between younger and older psychologists statistically significant? If yes, at what probability level?

Questions for Discussion

7. Do you agree with a suggestion in the literature review that prevalence figures might underestimate domestic violence? Explain. (See lines 66–75.)

8. In the literature review, the researchers use the term "stratified random sample." What is your understanding of the meaning of this term? (See line 137.)

9. The researchers characterize the return rate of 43% as a "low response rate." Do you agree with this characterization? If you had conducted this survey, would you have expected a higher rate of return? (See lines 191–193.)

10. The researchers compared those who returned the questionnaires with the original population of psychologists in terms of age, gender, and geographic region. In your opinion, was it important to do this? Why? Why not? (See lines 192–202.)

11. In line 241, the researchers use the term "median split." What is your understanding of the meaning of this term?

12. The Discussion section of this article (i.e., Implications and Recommendations for Practice) is longer and more detailed than those in most other articles in this book. In your opinion, is a long discussion desirable? Is it helpful? Are the implications and recommendations based closely on the data generated by the research reported in this article? Explain. (See lines 274–535.)

Quality Ratings

Directions: Indicate your level of agreement with each of the following statements by circling a number from 5 for strongly agree (SA) to 1 for strongly disagree (SD). If you believe an item is not applicable to this research article, leave it blank. Be prepared to explain your ratings. When responding to criteria A and B below, keep in mind that brief titles and abstracts are conventional in published research.

A. The title of the article is appropriate.

   SA   5   4   3   2   1   SD

B. The abstract provides an effective overview of the research article.

   SA   5   4   3   2   1   SD

C. The introduction establishes the importance of the study.

   SA   5   4   3   2   1   SD

D. The literature review establishes the context for the study.

   SA   5   4   3   2   1   SD

E. The research purpose, question, or hypothesis is clearly stated.

   SA   5   4   3   2   1   SD

F. The method of sampling is sound.

   SA   5   4   3   2   1   SD

G. Relevant demographics (for example, age, gender, and ethnicity) are described.

   SA   5   4   3   2   1   SD

H. Measurement procedures are adequate.

   SA   5   4   3   2   1   SD

I. All procedures have been described in sufficient detail to permit a replication of the study.

   SA   5   4   3   2   1   SD

J. The participants have been adequately protected from potential harm.

   SA   5   4   3   2   1   SD

K. The results are clearly described.

   SA   5   4   3   2   1   SD

L. The discussion/conclusion is appropriate.

   SA   5   4   3   2   1   SD

M. Despite any flaws, the report is worthy of publication.

   SA   5   4   3   2   1   SD

Article 4

Students' Ratings of Teaching Effectiveness: A Laughing Matter?

GARY ADAMSON
University of Ulster at Magee College

DAMIAN O'KANE
University of Ulster at Magee College

MARK SHEVLIN
University of Ulster at Magee College

ABSTRACT. Gump in 2004 identified a positive significant relationship between awareness of daily class objectives and ratings of the instructor's overall teaching effectiveness. The idea that rating of teaching effectiveness can be related to other nonteaching related attributes of the lecturer was further examined. Correlations based on ratings of teaching effectiveness from 453 undergraduate students (M = 21 yr., SD = 5.5; 73% women) showed that another nonteaching related variable, namely, how funny the instructor was perceived, was significantly related to indicators of teaching effectiveness.

From *Psychological Reports*, *96*, 225–226. Copyright © 2005 by Psychological Reports. Reprinted with permission.

The practice of having students evaluate teaching in universities is widespread in the UK and the USA, and the information from such surveys can be a useful guide for potential changes in course material and method of delivery (QAA, 1997). For students' evaluation of teaching questionnaires to be used, there should be clear evidence that such measures are producing valid scores, that is, that such questionnaires are actually measuring teaching effectiveness.

Research suggests that ratings of teaching effectiveness are positively related to teaching and student-related variables such as awareness of daily class objectives (Gump, 2004), expected grades (Feldman, 1976; Marsh, 1987), the students' prior interest in the topic (Marsh & Roche, 1997), and grading leniency (Greenwald & Gillmore, 1997). More alarmingly Shevlin, Banyard, Davies, and Griffiths (2000) tested a model that specified ratings of the lecturers' charisma, measured by a single item, as a predictor of teaching effectiveness, in particular "lecturer ability" and "module attributes." Using structural equation modeling, they found that the charisma ratings accounted for 69% of the variation of the lecturer ability factor and 37% of the module attributes factor.

The idea that ratings of teaching effectiveness can be related to other nonteaching related attributes of the lecturer was further examined. An additional item, "The lecturer was funny," was included in a larger questionnaire designed to measure teaching effectiveness. All items used a 5-point Likert response format with anchors of 1 (Strongly Disagree) and 5 (Strongly Agree). This questionnaire was administered at a UK university to a sample of 453 undergraduate students who were enrolled in full-time courses within a department of social sciences (M age = 21 yr., SD = 5.5; 73% women). In total, six lecturers were rated (four men and two women) in this study.

Analysis showed items designed to reflect aspects of effective teaching were positively correlated with rating how funny the lecturer was. Scores on the item "The lecturer was funny" were positively correlated with scores on the items "The lecturer helped me to develop an interest in the subject matter" (r = .60, p < .01), "I wanted to learn more about the topic" (r = .49, p < .01), "The lectures were well organised (r = .40, p < .01), and "The lecturer is successful in encouraging students to do supplementary reading on the subject matter of the module" (r = .38, p < .01).

The results suggest that students' perceptions of funniness were moderately and significantly associated with ratings of teaching-related activity.

Whereas previous research has focused mainly on the dimensionality of measures of teaching effectiveness (Abrami, d'Apollonia, & Rosenfield, 1997), it is suggested here that the validity of scores derived from any measure of teaching effectiveness ought to be ascertained prior to use of the measure.

References

Abrami, P. C., d'Apollonia, S., & Rosenfield, S. (1997). The dimensionality of student ratings of instruction: What we know and what we do not. In R. P. Perry & J. C. Smart (Eds.), *Effective teaching in higher education: Research and practice*. New York: Agathon Press. pp. 321–367.

Feldman, K. A. (1976). Grades and college students' evaluations of their courses and teachers. *Research in Higher Education, 18*, 3–124.

Greenwald, A. G., & Gillmore, G. M. (1997). Grading leniency is a removable contaminant of student ratings. *American Psychologist, 52*, 1209–1217.

Gump, S. E. (2004). Daily class objectives and instructor's effectiveness as perceived by students. *Psychological Reports, 94*, 1250–1252.

Marsh, H. W. (1987). Students' evaluations of university teaching: Research findings, methodological issues, and directions for future research. *International Journal of Educational Research, 11*, 253–388.

Marsh, H. W., & Roche, L. A. (1997). Making students' evaluations of teaching effectiveness effective. *American Psychologist, 52*, 1187–1197.

Quality Assurance Agency for Higher Education. (1997). *Subject review handbook: October 1998 to September 2000*. (QAA 1/97) London: Quality Assurance Agency for Higher Education.

Shevlin, M., Banyard, P., Davies, M. D., & Griffiths, M. (2000). The validity of student evaluation of teaching in higher education: Love me, love my lectures? *Assessment and Evaluation in Higher Education, 25*, 397–405.

Address correspondence to: Dr. Mark Shevlin, School of Psychology, University of Ulster at Magee Campus, Londonderry, BT48 7JL, UK.

Exercise for Article 4

Factual Questions

1. What were the anchors for the statement, "The lecturer was funny"?

2. How many students participated in this study?

3. What was the average age of the students in this study?

4. What is the value of the correlation coefficient for the relationship between "The lecturer was funny" and "I wanted to learn more about the topic"?

5. The strongest correlation was between the lecturer being funny and what other item?

6. Do all the correlation coefficients reported in this study indicate direct (positive) relationships?

Questions for Discussion

7. The researchers characterize being funny as a "nonteaching related" attribute. Do you agree with this characterization (i.e., that being funny is not a teaching attribute)? (See lines 25–30.)

8. Six lecturers were rated by the students. Would you recommend using a larger number of lecturers in a future study on this topic? Explain. (See lines 36–37.)

9. After each correlation coefficient, this information appears: $p < .01$. What does this tell you about the correlation coefficients? (See lines 43–48.)

10. Would you characterize any of the correlation coefficients in lines 43–48 as representing very strong relationships?

11. The relationships reported in this study are positive. If you had planned this study, would you have anticipated finding any inverse (negative) relationships among the variables studied? Explain.

12. Do you think that this study shows a *causal* relationship between being funny and perceptions of other teaching attributes (i.e., does it provide evidence that being funny causes higher ratings on other items)? Explain.

13. This research report is shorter than others in this book. In your opinion, is its brevity a defect of the report? A strength of the report? Explain.

Quality Ratings

Directions: Indicate your level of agreement with each of the following statements by circling a number from 5 for strongly agree (SA) to 1 for strongly disagree (SD). If you believe an item is not applicable to this research article, leave it blank. Be prepared to explain your ratings. When responding to criteria A and B below, keep in mind that brief titles and abstracts are conventional in published research.

A. The title of the article is appropriate.

    SA 5 4 3 2 1 SD

B. The abstract provides an effective overview of the research article.

    SA 5 4 3 2 1 SD

C. The introduction establishes the importance of the study.

    SA 5 4 3 2 1 SD

D. The literature review establishes the context for the study.

    SA 5 4 3 2 1 SD

E. The research purpose, question, or hypothesis is clearly stated.

    SA 5 4 3 2 1 SD

F. The method of sampling is sound.

    SA 5 4 3 2 1 SD

G. Relevant demographics (for example, age, gender, and ethnicity) are described.

    SA 5 4 3 2 1 SD

H. Measurement procedures are adequate.

    SA 5 4 3 2 1 SD

I. All procedures have been described in sufficient detail to permit a replication of the study.

    SA 5 4 3 2 1 SD

J. The participants have been adequately protected from potential harm.

    SA 5 4 3 2 1 SD

K. The results are clearly described.

    SA 5 4 3 2 1 SD

L.   The discussion/conclusion is appropriate.

        SA   5   4   3   2   1   SD

M.   Despite any flaws, the report is worthy of publication.

        SA   5   4   3   2   1   SD

Article 5

Psychological Correlates of Optimism in College Students

R. L. MONTGOMERY
University of Missouri–Rolla

F. M. HAEMMERLIE
University of Missouri–Rolla

D. M. RAY
University of Missouri–Rolla

ABSTRACT. This study assessed optimism held by 300 college students at a midwestern university using Scheier and Carver's Life Orientation Test. Optimism ratings were compared to measures of psychological functioning. Analysis showed that optimism was significantly associated with all of the adjustment measures (social, academic, personal, and goal commitment) assessed with Baker and Siryk's Student Adaptation to College Questionnaire, higher self-esteem measured with Rosenberg's Self-Esteem Scale, and with lower ratings of loneliness as assessed with the Revised UCLA Loneliness Scale.

From *Psychological Reports, 92,* 545–547. Copyright © 2003 by Psychological Reports. Reprinted with permission.

Seligman[13] asserted that an important goal for psychology in the new millennium is to create a more positive focus and to increase our understanding of strength and virtue, and not just focus on negative states such as anxiety, depression, prejudice, and poverty. One topic receiving such research attention has been optimism—the tendency to see one's abilities and situations in a positive light. Optimism has been associated with less emotional disturbance in response to a variety of stressful events, e.g., adjustment to law school[12] and coping with breast cancer.[4] Also, students who had previously been identified as optimistic reported less fatigue and fewer coughs, aches, and pains during the last month of a semester than those who rated optimism low.[11] The present study assessed the relations between optimism and several domains of college students' functioning, including adjustment to college, self-esteem, and loneliness. It was hypothesized that students who rated optimism high would also score more positively on adjustment, higher on self-esteem, and lower on loneliness.

Method

Three hundred undergraduates completed a series of questionnaires as part of the requirements for Introductory Psychology courses. Subjects took Scheier and Carver's measure of optimism, the Life Orientation Test.[10] This eight-item scale measures respondents' expectations regarding the favorability of future outcomes. Cronbach alpha was .78.[3] Students also completed the Student Adjustment to College Questionnaire,[2] which provides measures of Personal Adjustment, Social Adjustment, Academic Adjustment, and Commitment to the goal of completing one's degree, and a Total score. The reported coefficients alpha were in the .90s[1] for the overall score and evidence of criterion validity that included positive correlations between this measure and freshman grade-point average as well as with participation in social events.

Also, subjects completed the Rosenberg Self-Esteem Scale,[8] and the Revised UCLA Loneliness Scale.[9] The Rosenberg scale has 10 items and has shown good estimates of validity and reliability.[5,8] The Revised UCLA Loneliness Scale measures feelings of loneliness experienced in interpersonal relationships and has been shown to have high test–retest reliability [$r = .85$][6] and good validity in its correlation with measures of social support.[7]

Results

Means and standard deviations for each of these tests are shown in Table 1. Students' ratings on the Life Orientation Test correlated positively and significantly ($p < .0001$) with the Total adjustment score of the Student Adjustment to College Questionnaire ($r = .34$) and those of all four subscales: Personal Adjustment ($r = .33$), Social Adjustment ($r = .36$), Academic Adjustment ($r = .36$), and Goal Commitment ($r = .35$). Ratings on optimism correlated significantly and positively with the Rosenberg scale ($r = .51$) and negatively with the Revised UCLA Loneliness Scale ($r = -.40$).

Table 1
Means and Standard Deviations for Measures Used

Measure	M	SD
Life Orientation Test	20.5	6.4
Student Adaptation, Total Score	437.5	78.8
Personal Adjustment	87.4	19.1
Social Adjustment	123.5	22.9
Academic Adjustment	139.5	25.1
Goal Commitment	91.6	17.1
Rosenberg Self-Esteem Scale	22.6	5.7
Revised UCLA Loneliness Scale	36.5	10.2

Overall, these moderate correlations indicated that
60 rated optimism tended to be associated with more positive psychological functioning (i.e., better adjustment
to college, higher self-esteem, and less loneliness). The
more optimistic students were, the more positive were
their psychological tendencies. However, given use of
65 correlations, experimental designs with additional
samples of college students are required to assess directionality among various domains of psychological
functioning. Consistent with previous research,[4,11,12]
optimism appears to be a positive individual trait with
70 potential benefits worthy of further study.

References

1. Baker, R. W., & Siryk, B. (1986). Exploratory intervention with a scale measuring adjustment to college. *Journal of Counseling Psychology, 33,* 31–38.
2. Baker, R. W., & Siryk, B. (1989). *Student Adaptation to College Questionnaire manual.* Los Angeles, CA: Western Psychological Services.
3. Brissette, I., Scheier, M. F., & Carver, C. S. (2002). The role of optimism in social network development, coping, and psychological adjustment during a life transition, *Journal of Personality and Social Psychology, 82,* 102–111.
4. Carver, C. S., Pozo, C., Harris, S. D., Noriega, V., Scheier, M. F., Robinson, D. S., Ketcham, A. S., Moffat, F. L., Jr., & Clark, K. C. (1993). How coping mediates the effect of optimism on distress: a study of women with early stage breast cancer. *Journal of Personality and Social Psychology, 65,* 375–390.
5. Crandall, R. (1973). The measurement of self-esteem and related concepts. In J. P. Robinson & P. R. Shaver (Eds.), *Measures of social psychological attitudes,* Ann Arbor, MI: Univer. of Michigan Press. pp. 45–167.
6. Hartshorne, T. S. (1993). Psychometric properties and confirmatory analysis of the UCLA Loneliness Scale. *Journal of Personality Assessment, 61,* 182–195.
7. Pierce, G. R., Sarason, I. G., & Sarason, B. R. (1991). General and relationship-based perceptions of social support: Are two constructs better than one? *Journal of Personality and Social Psychology, 61,* 1028–1039.
8. Rosenberg, M. (1965). *Society and the adolescent self-image.* Princeton, NJ: Princeton Univer. Press.
9. Russell, D., Peplau, L., & Cutrona, C. (1980). The Revised UCLA Loneliness Scale: Concurrent and discriminant validity evidence. *Journal of Personality and Social Psychology, 39,* 472–480.
10. Scheier, M. F., & Carver, C. S. (1985). Optimism, coping, and health: Assessment and implications of generalized outcome expectancies. *Health Psychology, 4,* 219–247.
11. Scheier, M. F., & Carver, C. S. (1992). Effects of optimism on psychological and physical well-being: Theoretical overview and empirical update. *Cognitive Therapy and Research, 16,* 201–228.
12. Segerstrom, S. C., Taylor, S. E., Kemeny, M. E., & Fahey, J. L. (1998). Optimism is associated with mood, coping, and immune change in response to stress. *Journal of Personality and Social Psychology, 4,* 1646–1655.
13. Seligman, M. E. P. (2002). Positive psychology, positive prevention, and positive therapy. In C. R. Snyder & S. H. Lopez (Eds.), *Handbook of positive psychology.* London: Oxford Univer. Press. pp. 3–9.

Address correspondence to: Robert L. Montgomery, Department of Psychology, University of Missouri–Rolla, Rolla, MO 65401-0249. E-mail: bobm@umr.edu

Exercise for Article 5

Factual Questions

1. What is the hypothesis for this study?

2. Were the students required to participate in this study?

3. What is the name of the instrument used to measure optimism in this study?

4. Do the researchers provide information on the validity of the Student Adjustment to College Questionnaire?

5. Which one of the correlation coefficients in the results section of this report represents the strongest relationship?

6. How many of the correlation coefficients in this report indicate inverse relationships?

Questions for Discussion

7. In your opinion, have the researchers provided sufficient information on the Life Orientation test? Explain. (See lines 25–28.)

8. In line 28, the researchers state that "Cronbach alpha was .78." What do you think this means?

9. In your opinion, the correlation coefficient of –.40 in lines 57–58 indicates which of the following? Explain your choice.
   A. Those with higher optimism scores tend to have lower loneliness scores.
   B. Those with higher optimism tend to have higher loneliness scores.

10. In line 59, the researchers state that the correlations reported in this study are "moderate." Do you agree that they are moderate? Explain.

11. Do any of the results in this study surprise you? Explain.

Quality Ratings

Directions: Indicate your level of agreement with each of the following statements by circling a number from 5 for strongly agree (SA) to 1 for strongly disagree (SD). If you believe an item is not applicable to this research article, leave it blank. Be prepared to explain your ratings. When responding to criteria A and B below, keep in mind that brief titles and abstracts are conventional in published research.

A. The title of the article is appropriate.
   SA   5   4   3   2   1   SD

B. The abstract provides an effective overview of the research article.
   SA   5   4   3   2   1   SD

C. The introduction establishes the importance of the study.

  SA   5   4   3   2   1   SD

D. The literature review establishes the context for the study.

  SA   5   4   3   2   1   SD

E. The research purpose, question, or hypothesis is clearly stated.

  SA   5   4   3   2   1   SD

F. The method of sampling is sound.

  SA   5   4   3   2   1   SD

G. Relevant demographics (for example, age, gender, and ethnicity) are described.

  SA   5   4   3   2   1   SD

H. Measurement procedures are adequate.

  SA   5   4   3   2   1   SD

I. All procedures have been described in sufficient detail to permit a replication of the study.

  SA   5   4   3   2   1   SD

J. The participants have been adequately protected from potential harm.

  SA   5   4   3   2   1   SD

K. The results are clearly described.

  SA   5   4   3   2   1   SD

L. The discussion/conclusion is appropriate.

  SA   5   4   3   2   1   SD

M. Despite any flaws, the report is worthy of publication.

  SA   5   4   3   2   1   SD

Article 6

Relationships of Assertiveness, Depression, and Social Support Among Older Nursing Home Residents

DANIEL L. SEGAL
University of Colorado at Colorado Springs

ABSTRACT. This study assessed the relationships of assertiveness, depression, and social support among nursing home residents. The sample included 50 older nursing home residents (mean age = 75 years; 75% female; 92% Caucasian). There was a significant correlation between assertiveness and depression ($r = -.33$), but the correlations between social support and depression ($r = -.15$) and between social support and assertiveness ($r = -.03$) were small and nonsignificant. The correlation between overall physical health (a subjective self-rating) and depression was strong and negative ($r = -.50$), with lower levels of health associated with higher depression. An implication of this study is that an intervention for depression among nursing home residents that is targeted at increasing assertiveness and bolstering health status may be more effective than the one that solely targets social support.

From *Behavior Modification*, 29, 689–695. Copyright © 2005 by Sage Publications. Reprinted with permission.

Most older adults prefer and are successful at "aging in place"—that is, maintaining their independence in their own home. For the frailest and most debilitated older adults, however, nursing home placement is oftentimes necessary. About 5% of older adults live in a nursing home at any point in time, a figure that has remained stable since the early 1970s (National Center for Health Statistics, 2002). Depression is one of the most prevalent and serious psychological problems among nursing home residents: About 15% to 50% of residents suffer from diagnosable depression (see review by Streim & Katz, 1996).

Social support is also an important factor in mental health among nursing home residents, and psychosocial interventions often seek to bolster the resident's level of supportive relationships.

Assertiveness training plays an important role in traditional behavioral therapy with adults, and it has been recommended as a treatment component among older adults with diverse psychological problems as well (Gambrill, 1986). Assertiveness may be defined as the ability to express one's thoughts, feelings, beliefs, and rights in an open, honest, and appropriate way. A key component of assertiveness is that the communication does not violate the rights of others, as is the case in aggressive communications. It is logical that nursing home residents with good assertiveness skills would more often get what they want and need. Having basic needs met is a natural goal of all people, and failure to do so could lead to depression or other psychological problems. Personal control has long been noted to improve mental health among nursing home residents (see Langer & Rodin, 1976), and assertiveness training would likely help residents express more clearly their desires and needs.

Two studies have examined links between assertiveness, depression, and social support among older adult groups. Among 69 community-dwelling older adults, Kogan, Van Hasselt, Hersen, and Kabacoff (1995) found that those who are less assertive and have less social support are at increased risk for depression. Among 100 visually impaired older adults, Hersen et al. (1995) reported that higher levels of social support and assertiveness were associated with lower levels of depression. Assertiveness may rightly be an important skill among nursing home residents because workers at the institutional setting may not be as attuned to the emotional needs of a passive resident and the workers may respond poorly to the aggressive and acting-out resident. However, little is known about the nature and impact of assertiveness in long-term care settings. The purpose of this study, therefore, was to assess relationships of assertiveness, social support, and depression among nursing home residents, thus extending the literature to a unique population.

Method

Participants were recruited at several local nursing homes. Staff identified potential volunteers who were ostensibly free of cognitive impairment. Participants completed anonymously the following self-report measures: Wolpe-Lazarus Assertiveness Scale (WLAS) (Wolpe & Lazarus, 1966), Geriatric Depression Scale (GDS) (Yesavage et al., 1983), and the Social Support List of Interactions (SSL 12-I) (Kempen & van Eijk, 1995). The WLAS consists of 30 yes/no

65 items and measures levels of assertive behavior. Scores can range from 0 to 30, with higher scores reflecting higher levels of assertiveness. The GDS includes 30 yes/no items and evaluates depressive symptoms spe-
70 cifically among older adults. Scores can range from 0 to 30, with higher scores indicating higher levels of depression. The SSL12-I is a 12-item measure of received social support that has good psychometric properties among community-dwelling older adults. Re-
75 spondents indicate on a 4-point scale the extent to which they received a specific type of support from a member of their primary social network (1 = seldom or never, 2 = now and then, 3 = regularly, 4 = very often). Scores can range from 12 to 48 with higher scores corresponding to higher levels of support. The sample
80 included 50 older adult residents (mean age = 74.9 years, SD = 11.9, age range = 50–96 years; 75% female; 92% Caucasian).

Results and Discussion

The mean WLAS was 18.1 (SD = 4.1), the mean GDS was 9.0 (SD = 5.5), and the mean SSL12-I was
85 29.2 (SD = 7.3). The correlation between the WLAS and GDS was moderate and negative ($r = -.33$, $p <$ .05), with lower levels of assertiveness associated with higher depression. The correlation between the SSL12-I and GDS was small and nonsignificant ($r = -.15$, ns),
90 indicating a slight negative relationship between overall support and depression. Similarly, the correlation between the SSL12-I and WLAS was small and nonsignificant ($r = -.03$, ns), indicating almost no relationship between overall support and assertiveness. Next,
95 correlations between a subjective self-rating of overall physical health status (0–100 scale, higher scores indicating better health) and the WLAS, GDS, and SSL12-I were calculated. As expected, the correlation between physical health and GDS was strong and negative ($r =$
100 $-.50$, $p < .01$), with poorer health associated with higher depression. The correlation between health and WLAS was positive in direction but small and nonsignificant ($r = .17$, ns), indicating little relationship between health and assertiveness. Similarly, the correla-
105 tion between health and SSL12-I was also small and nonsignificant ($r = -.02$, ns), indicating no relationship between health and overall support. The slight relationship between health and assertiveness is an encouraging sign because it suggests that assertiveness (which is
110 primarily achieved through effective verbalizations) is not limited to only the least physically impaired nursing home residents. Finally, gender differences on all dependent measures were examined (independent t tests) and no significant differences were found (all ps
115 > .05).

Notably, the mean assertion and depression scores among nursing home residents are consistent with means on identical measures in community-dwelling older adults (assertion M = 19.1; depression M = 7.9;
120 Kogan et al., 1995) and visually impaired older adults

(assertion M = 18.3; depression M = 10.4; Hersen et al., 1995), suggesting that the higher functioning group of nursing home residents are no more depressed and no less assertive than other samples of older persons.
125 Regarding social support, our nursing home sample appeared to show somewhat higher levels of overall support than community older adults in the normative sample (N = 5,279, M = 25.5) in the SSL12-I validation study (Kempen & van Eijk, 1995). This may pos-
130 sibly be due to the nature of institutional living and the large numbers of support staff and health care personnel.

The correlational results regarding the moderate negative association between assertion and depression
135 are consistent with data from community-dwelling older adults ($r = -.36$; Kogan et al., 1995) and visually impaired older adults ($r = -.29$; Hersen et al., 1995), suggesting a pervasive relationship among the variables in diverse older adult samples and extending the
140 findings to nursing home residents. Contrary to the literature, the relationship between social support and depression among nursing home residents was weaker than the one reported in community-dwelling older adults ($r = -.50$; Kogan et al., 1995) and visually im-
145 paired older adults ($r = -.48$; Hersen et al., 1995). The relationship between assertiveness and overall support in this study was almost nonexistent, also contrary to earlier reports in which the relationship was moderate and positive in direction. Our results are consistent
150 with prior research showing no gender differences among older adults in assertiveness, depression, and social support using similar assessment tools (Hersen et al., 1995; Kogan et al., 1995). This study also suggests a strong negative relationship between health status and
155 depression among nursing home residents. An implication of this study is that an intervention for depression among nursing home residents that is targeted at increasing assertiveness and bolstering health status may be more effective than the one that solely targets social
160 support.

Several limitations are offered concerning this study. First, the sample size was modest and the sample was almost exclusively Caucasian. Future studies with more diverse nursing home residents would add to the
165 knowledge base in this area. All measures were self-report, and future studies with structured interviews and behavioral assessments would be stronger. We are also concerned somewhat about the extent to which the WLAS is content valid for older adults. Notably, a
170 measure of assertive behavior competence has been developed specifically for use with community-dwelling older adults (Northrop & Edelstein, 1998), and this measure appears to be a good choice for future research in the area. A final limitation was that partici-
175 pants were likely the highest functioning of residents because they were required to be able to complete the measures independently and were selected out if there was any overt cognitive impairment (although no for-

mal screening for cognitive impairment was done),
180 thus limiting generalizability to more frail nursing
home residents. Cognitive screening should be done in
future studies. Nonetheless, results of this study suggest a potentially important relationship between assertiveness and depression among nursing home residents.
185   Finally, it is imperative to highlight that there are
many types of interventions to combat depression
among nursing home residents: behavioral interventions to increase exercise, participation in social activities, and other pleasurable activities; cognitive inter-
190 ventions to reduce depressogenic thoughts; and pharmacotherapy, to name a few. (The interested reader is
referred to Molinari, 2000, for a comprehensive description of psychological issues and interventions
unique to long-term care settings.) The present data
195 suggest that training in assertiveness may be yet one
additional option for psychosocial intervention in nursing homes. A controlled outcome study is warranted in
which intensive assertiveness training is compared to a
control group of nursing home residents who do not
200 receive such training. Only with such a study can
cause-and-effect statements be made about the role that
assertiveness skills training may play in the reduction
of depressive symptoms among nursing home residents.

References

Gambrill, E. B. (1986). Social skills training with the elderly. In C. R. Hollin & P. Trower (Eds.), *Handbook of social skills training: Applications across the lifespan* (pp. 211–238). New York: Pergamon.

Hersen, M., Kabacoff, R. L, Van Hasselt, V B., Null, J. A., Ryan, C. F., Melton, M. A., et al. (1995). Assertiveness, depression, and social support in older visually impaired adults. *Journal of Visual Impairment and Blindness, 7*, 524–530.

Kempen, G. I. J. M., & van Eijk, L. M. (1995). The psychometric properties of the SSL12-I, a short scale for measuring social support in the elderly. *Social Indicators Research, 35,* 303–312.

Kogan, S. E., Van Hasselt, B. V., Hersen, M., & Kabacoff, I. R. (1995). Relationship of depression, assertiveness, and social support in community-dwelling older adults. *Journal of Clinical Geropsychology, 1*, 157–163.

Langer, E. J., & Rodin, J. (1976). The effects of choice and enhanced personal responsibility for the aged: A field experiment in an institutional setting. *Journal of Personality and Social Psychology, 34*, 191–198.

Molinari, V. (Ed.). (2000). *Professional psychology in long term care: A comprehensive guide.* New York: Hatherleigh.

National Center for Health Statistics. (2002). *Health, United States, 2002.* Hyattsville, MD: Author.

Northrop, L. M. E., & Edelstein, B. A. (1998). An assertive-behavior competence inventory for older adults. *Journal of Clinical Geropsychology, 4*, 315–331.

Streim, J. E., & Katz, I. R. (1996). Clinical psychiatry in the nursing home. In E. W. Busse & D. G. Blazer (Eds.), *Textbook of geriatric psychiatry* (2nd ed., pp. 413–432). Washington, DC: American Psychiatric Press.

Wolpe, J., & Lazarus, A. A. (1966). *Behavior therapy techniques.* New York: Pergamon.

Yesavage, J. A., Brink, T. L., Rose, T. L., Lum, O., Huang, V, Adey, M., et al. (1983). Development and validation of a geriatric depression screening scale: A preliminary report. *Journal of Psychiatric Research, 17*, 314–317.

Acknowledgment: The author thanks Jessica Corcoran, M.A., for assistance with data collection and data entry.

About the author: Daniel L. Segal received his Ph.D. in clinical psychology from the University of Miami in 1992. He is an associate professor in the Department of Psychology at the University of Colorado at Colorado Springs. His research interests include diagnostic and assessment issues in geropsychology, suicide prevention and aging, bereavement, and personality disorders across the lifespan.

Exercise for Article 6

Factual Questions

1. Were the participants cognitively impaired?

2. Was the mean score for the participants on the GDS near the highest possible score on this instrument? Explain.

3. What is the value of the correlation coefficient for the relationship between the WLAS and the GDS?

4. Was the relationship between SSL12-I and GDS strong?

5. Was the correlation coefficient for the relationship between SSL12-I and GDS statistically significant?

6. Was the relationship between physical health and GDS a direct relationship *or* an inverse relationship?

Questions for Discussion

7. The researcher obtained participants from "several" nursing homes. Is this better than obtaining them from a single nursing home? Explain. (See lines 56–57.)

8. The researcher characterizes the *r* of −.33 in line 86 as "moderate." Do you agree with this characterization? Explain.

9. In lines 85–107, the researcher reports the values of six correlation coefficients. Which one of these indicates the strongest relationship? Explain the basis for your choice.

10. In lines 85–107, the researcher reports the values of six correlation coefficients. Which one of these indicates the weakest relationship? Explain the basis for your choice.

11. For the *r* of −.50 in line 100, the researcher indicates that "*p* < .01." What is your understanding of the meaning of the symbol "*p*"? What is your understanding of ".01"?

12. Do you agree with the researcher that a different type of study is needed in order to determine the role of assertiveness skills training in the reduction of depressive symptoms? Explain. (See lines 197–204.)

Quality Ratings

Directions: Indicate your level of agreement with each of the following statements by circling a number from 5 for strongly agree (SA) to 1 for strongly disagree (SD). If you believe an item is not applicable to this research article, leave it blank. Be prepared to explain your ratings. When responding to criteria A and B below, keep in mind that brief titles and abstracts are conventional in published research.

A. The title of the article is appropriate.

SA   5   4   3   2   1   SD

B. The abstract provides an effective overview of the research article.

SA   5   4   3   2   1   SD

C. The introduction establishes the importance of the study.

SA   5   4   3   2   1   SD

D. The literature review establishes the context for the study.

SA   5   4   3   2   1   SD

E. The research purpose, question, or hypothesis is clearly stated.

SA   5   4   3   2   1   SD

F. The method of sampling is sound.

SA   5   4   3   2   1   SD

G. Relevant demographics (for example, age, gender, and ethnicity) are described.

SA   5   4   3   2   1   SD

H. Measurement procedures are adequate.

SA   5   4   3   2   1   SD

I. All procedures have been described in sufficient detail to permit a replication of the study.

SA   5   4   3   2   1   SD

J. The participants have been adequately protected from potential harm.

SA   5   4   3   2   1   SD

K. The results are clearly described.

SA   5   4   3   2   1   SD

L. The discussion/conclusion is appropriate.

SA   5   4   3   2   1   SD

M. Despite any flaws, the report is worthy of publication.

SA   5   4   3   2   1   SD

Article 7

Correlations Between Humor
Styles and Loneliness

WILLIAM P. HAMPES
Black Hawk College

ABSTRACT. In a previous study, a significant negative correlation between shyness with affiliative humor and a significant positive one with self-defeating humor were reported. Since shyness and loneliness share many of the same characteristics, poor social skills and negative affect, for example, significant negative correlations of loneliness with affiliative and self-enhancing humor and a significant positive one with self-defeating humor were hypothesized. 106 community college students (34 men, 72 women) ranging in age from 17 to 52 years ($M = 23.5$, $SD = 7.7$) were tested. The hypotheses were supported. Interrelationships among humor, shyness, and loneliness should be examined within one study.

From *Psychological Reports, 96*, 747–750. Copyright © 2005 by Psychological Reports. Reprinted with permission.

Various studies, using self-report and rating scales, have yielded correlations of .40 or more between shyness and loneliness (Cheek & Busch, 1981; Jones, Freeman, & Goswick, 1981; Moore & Schultz, 1983; Anderson & Arnoult, 1985). Research studies have shown that those high in both variables tend to have poor social skills (Zahaki & Duran, 1982; Moore & Schultz, 1983; Wittenberg & Reis, 1986; Miller, 1995; Carducci, 2000; Segrin & Flora, 2000), poor interpersonal relationships (Jones, 1981; Jones, Rose, & Russell, 1990; Carducci, 2000), and low self-esteem (Jones et al., 1981; Olmstead, Guy, O'Malley, & Bentler, 1991; Kamath & Kanekar, 1993; Schmidt & Fox, 1995).

Hampes (in press) reported shyness negatively correlated with affiliative humor and positively correlated with self-defeating humor. Affiliative humor is an interpersonal form of humor that involves use of humor (telling jokes, saying funny things, or witty banter, for example), to put others at ease, amuse others, and to improve relationships (Martin, Puhlik-Doris, Larsen, Gray, & Weir, 2003). Since those high on affiliative humor tend to score high on extraversion and intimacy (Martin et al., 2003), and lonely people, like shy people, have poor social skills and relationships, it was hypothesized that loneliness would be negatively correlated with affiliative humor.

Self-defeating humor "involves excessively self-disparaging humor, attempts to amuse others by doing or saying funny things at one's expense as a means of ingratiating oneself or gaining approval, allowing oneself to be the 'butt' of others' humor, and laughing along with others when being ridiculed or disparaged" (Martin et al., 2003, p. 54). Since both lonely and shy people tend to have low self-esteem, and those high in self-defeating humor tend to score low on self-esteem (Martin et al., 2003), it was hypothesized that loneliness and self-defeating humor would be positively correlated.

Hampes (in press) did not find a significant correlation for his total group of 174 subjects between scores on shyness and self-enhancing humor, an adaptive intrapersonal dimension of humor that "involves a generally humorous outlook on life, a tendency to be frequently amused by the incongruities of life, and to maintain a humorous perspective even in the face of stress or of adversity" (Martin et al., 2003, p. 53). However, Martin et al. reported self-enhancing humor scores were positively correlated with those on self-esteem, social intimacy, and social support, just the opposite of the relationships between loneliness and self-esteem, social intimacy, and social support. Therefore, it was hypothesized that loneliness and self-enhancing humor would be negatively correlated.

Hampes (in press) did not find a significant correlation for his total group between scores on shyness and aggressive humor (a maladaptive interpersonal type of humor, involving sarcasm, teasing, ridicule, derision, hostility, or disparagement humor) for the total group. Therefore, it was hypothesized that there would be a nonsignificant correlation between loneliness and aggressive humor.

Method

The subjects were 106 students (34 men, 72 women) at a community college in the midwestern United States. These students ranged in age from 17 to 52 years ($M = 23.5$, $SD = 7.7$). Students in four psychology classes were asked to participate, and those who volunteered were included in the sample.

The UCLA Loneliness Scale (Version 3) measures loneliness as a unidimensional emotional response to a

difference between desired and achieved social contact. It contains 20 items, each of which has four response options in a Likert-type format, anchored by 1 = Never and 4 = Always (e.g., "How often do you feel isolated
75 from others?"). Coefficients alpha for the scale ranged from .89 to .94 (Russell & Cutrona, 1988). Russell, Kao, and Cutrona (1987) reported a 1-yr. test–retest correlation of .73 and estimated discriminant validity through significant negative correlations between
80 scores on loneliness with those on social support and measures of positive mental health status.

In the Humor Styles Questionnaire, each of four scales has eight items. Each item has seven response options in a Likert-type format, anchored by 1 = To-
85 tally Disagree and 7 = Totally Agree. The Cronbach alpha for the four scales ranged from .77 to .81. The convergent validity for the Affiliative Humor Scale was indicated by significant correlations with scores on the Miller Social Intimacy Scale and Extraversion on
90 the NEO PI–R. Discriminant validity for the Self-enhancing Humor Scale was estimated by a significant negative correlation with scores on Neuroticism of the NEO PI–R, and convergent validity was estimated with significant positive correlations with the Coping Hu-
95 mor Scale and the Humor Coping subscale of the Coping Orientations to Problems Experienced Scale. Convergent validity for the Aggressive Scale was supported by a significant correlation with scores on the Cook-Medley Hostility Scale. Discriminant validity for
100 the Self-defeating Scale was based on significant negative correlations with ratings on the Rosenberg Self-esteem Scale and on the Index of Self-esteem (Martin et al., 2003).

Results and Discussion

Four Pearson product-moment correlations were
105 computed for the scores on the UCLA Loneliness Scale-Version 3 ($M = 41.1$, $SD = 10.7$) and those on each of four humor scales: Affiliative ($M = 45.5$, $SD = 7.3$), Self-enhancing ($M = 37.4$, $SD = 8.4$), Aggressive ($M = 25.8$, $SD = 7.4$), and Self-defeating ($M = 26.0$, SD
110 $= 8.9$). In each case, the hypotheses were supported, as correlations were significant for scores in Loneliness with Affiliative Humor ($r = -.47$, $p < .001$, $CI_{95} = -.28$ to $-.66$), Self-enhancing Humor ($r = -.39$, $p < .001$, $CI_{95} = -.20$ to $-.58$) and Self-defeating Humor ($r = .32$,
115 $p < .001$, $CI_{95} = .13$ to $.51$). The correlation between scores on Loneliness and Aggressive Humor was not significant ($r = -.04$, $p > .05$, $CI_{95} = -.23$ to $.15$).

Dill and Anderson (1999) posited that shyness precedes loneliness. Given their social anxiety, shy people
120 tend to be unsuccessful in social situations, and so they try to avoid these. Even if they do not avoid social relationships, they tend not to have satisfying personal relationships. As a result, they may report being lonely. The idea that shyness precedes loneliness is supported
125 by the developmental research of Kagan (1994), who stated that shyness has a strong genetic component and

is manifested early in infancy, and Cheek and Busch (1981), who found shyness influenced loneliness reported by students in an introductory psychology
130 course. If shyness does precede loneliness, it could be in part because shy individuals do not use affiliative humor and self-enhancing humor to help them be more successful in social situations and score high in self-defeating humor, which other people might not find
135 appealing. Further studies are needed to evaluate the causal relationships among shyness, loneliness, and styles of humor.

References

Anderson, C. A., & Arnoult, L. H. (1985). Attributional style and everyday problems in living: Depression, loneliness, and shyness. *Social Cognition, 3,* 16–35.

Carducci, B. (2000). *Shyness: a bold new approach.* New York: Perennial.

Cheek, J. M., & Busch, C. M. (1981). The influence of shyness on loneliness in a new situation. *Personality and Social Psychology Bulletin, 7,* 572–577.

Dill, J. C., & Anderson, C. A. (1999). Loneliness, shyness, and depression: the etiology and interrelationships of everyday problems in living. In T. Joiner & J. C. Coyne (Eds.), *The interactional nature of depression* (pp. 93–125) Washington, DC: American Psychological Association.

Hampes, W. P. (in press). The relation between humor styles and shyness. *Humor: The International Journal of Humor Research.*

Jones, W. H. (1981) Loneliness and social contact. *Journal of Social Psychology, 113,* 295–296.

Jones, W. H., Freeman, J. A., & Goswick, R. A. (1981). The persistence of loneliness: Self and other determinants. *Journal of Personality, 49,* 27–48.

Jones, W. H., Rose, J., & Russell, D. (1990). Loneliness and social anxiety. In H. Leitenberg (Ed.), *Handbook of social evaluation anxiety* (pp. 247–266) New York: Plenum.

Kagan, J. (1994). *Galen's prophecy: temperament in human nature.* New York: Basic Books.

Kamath, M., & Kanekar, S. (1993). Loneliness, shyness, self-esteem, and extraversion. *The Journal of Social Psychology, 133,* 855–857.

Martin, R. A., Puhlik-Doris, P., Larsen, G., Gray, J., & Weir, K. (2003). Individual differences in uses of humor and their relation to psychological well-being: Development of the Humor Styles Questionnaire. *Journal of Research in Personality, 37,* 48–75.

Miller, R. S. (1995). On the nature of embarassability, shyness, social evaluation, and social skill. *The Journal of Psychology, 63,* 315–339.

Moore, D., & Schultz, N. R. (1983). Loneliness at adolescence: correlates, attributions and coping. *Journal of Youth and Adolescence, 12,* 95–100.

Olmstead, R. E., Guy, S. M., O'Malley, P. M., & Bentler, P. M. (1991). Longitudinal assessment of the relationship between self-esteem, fatalism, loneliness, and substance abuse. *Journal of Social Behavior and Personality, 6,* 749–770.

Russell, D. W., & Cutrona, C. E. (1988). Development and evolution of the UCLA Loneliness Scale. (Unpublished manuscript, Center for Health Services Research, College of Medicine, University of Iowa)

Russell, D. W., Kao, C., & Cutrona, C. E. (1987). Loneliness and social support: Same or different constructs? Paper presented at the Iowa Conference on Personal Relationships, Iowa City.

Schmidt, L. A., & Fox, N. A. (1995). Individual differences in young adults' shyness and sociability: Personality and health correlates. *Personality and Individual Differences, 19,* 455–462.

Segrin, C., & Flora, J. (2000). Poor social skills are a vulnerability factor in the development of psychosocial problems. *Human Communication Research, 26,* 489–514.

Wittenberg, M. T., & Reis, H. T. (1986). Loneliness, social skills, and social perception. *Personality and Social Psychology Bulletin, 12,* 121–130.

Zahaki, W. R., & Duran, R. L. (1982). All the lonely people: The relationship among loneliness, communicative competence, and communication anxiety. *Communication Quarterly, 30,* 202–209.

Address correspondence to: William Hampes, Department of Social, Behavioral, and Educational Studies, Black Hawk College, 6600 34th Avenue, Moline, IL 61265. E-mail: hampesw@bhc.edu

Exercise for Article 7

Factual Questions

1. In the introduction to the research article, the researcher hypothesizes a positive correlation between which two variables?

2. What was the mean age of the students in this study?

3. The correlation coefficient for the relationship between Loneliness and Affiliative Humor was −.47. This indicates that those who had high loneliness scores tended to have

   A. low Affiliative Humor scores.
   B. high Affiliative Humor scores.

4. In lines 112–117, the researcher reports four correlation coefficients. Which correlation coefficient indicates the strongest relationship?

5. Is the correlation coefficient for the relationship between loneliness and Self-enhancing Humor statistically significant? If yes, at what probability level?

6. Is the correlation coefficient for the relationship between Loneliness and Aggressive Humor statistically significant? If yes, at what probability level?

Questions for Discussion

7. In your opinion, does the use of volunteers affect the quality of this study? (See lines 63–68.)

8. The correlation coefficient between Loneliness and Affiliative Humor equals −.47. The researcher also reports the 95% confidence interval (CI_{95}) for this correlation coefficient. What is your understanding of the meaning of the confidence interval? (See lines 112–113.)

9. Would you characterize any of the correlation coefficients reported in lines 112–117 as representing a "very strong" relationship? Explain.

10. Would you characterize any of the correlation coefficients reported in lines 112–117 as representing a "very weak" relationship? Explain.

11. The researcher mentions "causal relationships" in line 136. In your opinion, do the results of this study offer evidence regarding causal relationships? Explain.

Quality Ratings

Directions: Indicate your level of agreement with each of the following statements by circling a number from 5 for strongly agree (SA) to 1 for strongly disagree (SD). If you believe an item is not applicable to this research article, leave it blank. Be prepared to explain your ratings. When responding to criteria A and B below, keep in mind that brief titles and abstracts are conventional in published research.

A. The title of the article is appropriate.

   SA   5   4   3   2   1   SD

B. The abstract provides an effective overview of the research article.

   SA   5   4   3   2   1   SD

C. The introduction establishes the importance of the study.

   SA   5   4   3   2   1   SD

D. The literature review establishes the context for the study.

   SA   5   4   3   2   1   SD

E. The research purpose, question, or hypothesis is clearly stated.

   SA   5   4   3   2   1   SD

F. The method of sampling is sound.

   SA   5   4   3   2   1   SD

G. Relevant demographics (for example, age, gender, and ethnicity) are described.

   SA   5   4   3   2   1   SD

H. Measurement procedures are adequate.

   SA   5   4   3   2   1   SD

I. All procedures have been described in sufficient detail to permit a replication of the study.

   SA   5   4   3   2   1   SD

J. The participants have been adequately protected from potential harm.

   SA   5   4   3   2   1   SD

K. The results are clearly described.

   SA   5   4   3   2   1   SD

L. The discussion/conclusion is appropriate.

   SA   5   4   3   2   1   SD

M. Despite any flaws, the report is worthy of publication.

   SA   5   4   3   2   1   SD

Article 8

Effects of Laughing, Smiling, and Howling on Mood

CHARLES C. NEUHOFF
Fairleigh Dickinson University

CHARLES SCHAEFER
Fairleigh Dickinson University

ABSTRACT. This study examined the effects of forced laughter on mood and compared laughter with two other possible mood-improving activities, smiling and howling. While howling did not substantially improve mood, both smiling and laughing did. Moreover, laughter seemed to boost positive affect more than just smiling by 22 adults.

From *Psychological Reports*, *91*, 1079–1080. Copyright © 2002 by Psychological Reports. Reprinted with permission.

Studies of the physical health benefits of laughter have found both analgesic and stress-hormone-reduction properties of laughter (Provine, 2000). Martin (2001), however, noted methodological weaknesses in the investigations and concluded that more focal research is required. Short-term increases in mood after laughter, on the other hand, have clearly been supported to date (Keltner & Bonanno, 1997; Foley, Matheis, & Schaefer, 2002).

After reviewing the literature on laughter, Provine (2000) specified three areas which have not been addressed in current research. First, no study separates the effects of laughter from those of humor (e.g., forced laughter—without a humor component). Second, "no study controls for the possibility that the presumed effects of laughter may really derive from the playful social settings associated with these behaviors, not the acts themselves" (Provine, 2000). Third, no study evaluated the uniqueness of laughter's physiological profile by contrasting it with other energetic but arbitrary vocalizations (e.g., howling). While a recent study (Foley, et al., 2002) did indicate that forced laughter in a social setting improved mood, the second and third areas have not yet been studied.

The present study assessed the role of laughter in improving mood, while taking these three variables into consideration. To control for the first issue raised by Provine (2000), forced laughter was included. Moreover, laughter was to be done individually rather than in a social setting, to control for the second issue. Finally, participants were also asked to engage in howling and smiling to compare the effects of laughter relative to other physiological activities.

Method

Twenty-two adult subjects were instructed to engage individually in three different tasks on three separate occasions in any order desired. The tasks included 60 sec. of broad (Duchenne) smiling, 60 sec. of forced hearty laughter, and 60 sec. of howling. Researchers demonstrated the tasks to the participants and also provided a verbal description of each one. Participants were provided six sheets, on each of which were seven faces, showing a series from a broad smile (score of 7) to a broad frown (score of 1), and were asked to circle the face that most represented their current mood before and after engaging in each of the three tasks. Eighteen participants were enrolled in graduate courses; the remaining four were recruited from the community. Twenty were Caucasian, and two were African American. The ages of the 15 women and 7 men ranged from 21 to 43 years, with a median age of 27.

Results

Subjects rated their pretest mood as slightly positive across conditions (smiling $M = 4.5$; both laughing and howling $M = 4.7$). Although 1 min. of howling was not followed by a significant increase in posttest mood ($M = .3$, $SD = .8$; $t_{21} = 154, p > .10$), 1 min. of smiling was followed by an increase ($M = .7$, $SD = .7$; $t_{21} = 4.95$ $p < .01$). An even greater posttest mood increase was found for forced laughter ($M = 1.2$, $SD = 1.0$; $t_{21} = 5.92, p < .01$). The results indicated that both laughter and smiling improved mood, even when not done in social settings. Further, 1 min. of laughter showed a significantly greater improvement in mood than 1 min. of smiling ($M = .6$, $SD = 1.0$; $t_{21} = 2.53$, $p < .05$). These results suggest that adults who act happy (broad smile; hearty laugh) for a minute a day are likely to elevate their mood for at least a few seconds. Further studies of laughter/smiling should assess the robustness of these findings across different and larger populations and time periods as actual differences in ratings were small. Introduction of controls, measures other than self-reports and with fewer demand characteristics should be addressed in the design of further research.

References

Foley, E., Matheis, R., & Schaefer, C. E. (2002) Effects of forced laughter on mood. *Psychological Reports*, 90, 184.

Keltner, D., & Bonanno, G. A. (1997) A study of laughter and dissociation: distinct correlates of laughter and smiling during bereavement. *Journal of Personality and Social Psychology, 73*, 687–702.

Martin, R. A. (2001) Humor, laughter, and physical health: methodological issues and research findings. *Psychological Bulletin, 127*, 504–519.

Provine, R. R. (2000) *Laughter: a scientific investigation.* New York: Viking Penguin.

Address correspondence to: Charles Schaefer, Ph.D., Professor of Psychology, Fairleigh Dickinson University, 139 Temple Avenue, Hackensack, NJ 07601. E-mail: SchaeferCE@aol.com

Exercise for Article 8

Factual Questions

1. Why was forced laughter included in this study?

2. How many subjects participated in this study?

3. What did the participants circle to indicate their current mood?

4. What was the average age of the participants?

5. Did one minute of howling result in a statistically significant increase in mood? If yes, at what probability level?

6. Was the increase in mood after smiling statistically significant? If yes, at what probability level?

Questions for Discussion

7. At some points, the researchers use the term "subjects" (e.g., line 34) and at other points "participants" (e.g., line 39). In your opinion, are the two terms interchangeable? Explain.

8. The researchers suggest using "controls" in further studies on this topic. In your opinion, how desirable would this be? (See lines 71–73.)

9. The researchers suggest using measures other than self-reports in further studies. In your opinion, are there limitations associated with the use of self-reports? (See lines 71–73.)

10. The researchers use the term "demand characteristics" in line 72. Are you familiar with this term? If yes, what does it mean?

11. In your opinion, is it clear from this study that smiling *causes* an elevation in mood? Explain.

12. In the table of contents of this book, this article is classified as an example of "pre-experimental research." If you are familiar with the terminology for classifying experiments, what does this classification mean? Is it the best method of experimentation? Explain.

Quality Ratings

Directions: Indicate your level of agreement with each of the following statements by circling a number from 5 for strongly agree (SA) to 1 for strongly disagree (SD). If you believe an item is not applicable to this research article, leave it blank. Be prepared to explain your ratings. When responding to criteria A and B below, keep in mind that brief titles and abstracts are conventional in published research.

A. The title of the article is appropriate.

SA   5   4   3   2   1   SD

B. The abstract provides an effective overview of the research article.

SA   5   4   3   2   1   SD

C. The introduction establishes the importance of the study.

SA   5   4   3   2   1   SD

D. The literature review establishes the context for the study.

SA   5   4   3   2   1   SD

E. The research purpose, question, or hypothesis is clearly stated.

SA   5   4   3   2   1   SD

F. The method of sampling is sound.

SA   5   4   3   2   1   SD

G. Relevant demographics (for example, age, gender, and ethnicity) are described.

SA   5   4   3   2   1   SD

H. Measurement procedures are adequate.

SA   5   4   3   2   1   SD

I. All procedures have been described in sufficient detail to permit a replication of the study.

SA   5   4   3   2   1   SD

J. The participants have been adequately protected from potential harm.

SA   5   4   3   2   1   SD

K. The results are clearly described.

SA   5   4   3   2   1   SD

L. The discussion/conclusion is appropriate.

SA   5   4   3   2   1   SD

M. Despite any flaws, the report is worthy of publication.

    SA   5   4   3   2   1   SD

Article 9

Alcohol, Tobacco, and Other Drugs: College Student Satisfaction with an Interactive Educational Software Program

ROB J. ROTUNDA
University of West Florida

LAURA WEST
University of West Florida

JOEL EPSTEIN
Missouri Institute of Mental Health

ABSTRACT. Alcohol and drug use education and prevention continue to be core educational issues. In seeking to inform students at all levels about drug use, the present exploratory study highlights the potential educational use of interactive computer programs for this purpose. Seventy-three college students from two substance abuse classes interacted for at least 20 minutes with a CD-ROM program that was developed to explicitly teach and demonstrate concepts of addiction and recovery. Results indicated that most participants reported increased interest in course material and felt they had learned more about various drugs and their consequences after using the interactive program. Specifically, 81% of the participants indicated that the program increased their knowledge of drug use and addiction. Components of the interactive exercises were also evaluated separately. One implication of the study is that multimedia programs can be effective tools that complement current substance abuse education methods.

From *Journal of Teaching in the Addictions, 2*, 59–66. Copyright © 2003 by The Haworth Press, Inc. Reprinted with permission.

Programs for alcohol and drug use awareness and prevention are increasing in school systems due to the continual risk of children being exposed to and using alcohol, tobacco products, and other drugs. The pro-
5 grams disseminate information to children utilizing a variety of methods, including government-sponsored information campaigns and community-based programs like D.A.R.E (Drug Abuse Resistance Education). Now that most children and young adults have
10 access to computers and the Internet at home and in schools, and since many are also interested in multimedia activities (e.g., computer games), a trend is emerging for reinforcing classroom education at all levels with computer-based educational programs that stimu-
15 late student interest in drug education.

One such computer-based program is Alcohol, Tobacco and Other Drugs Television (ATOD-TV, 1996). This CD-ROM program was developed by the Missouri Institute of Mental Health, with the financial
20 support of the National Institute of Drug Abuse (NIDA), to teach the public about the causes, symp-
toms, and treatments for substance abuse. The software was initially contained in kiosks located in public areas in the St. Louis area. Using audio, video, photo-
25 graphs, and animation, the program employs a television motif to encourage users to explore various learning modules. A structured pre/post evaluation using 276 adults at a large, urban shopping mall indicated that users demonstrated greater knowledge about sub-
30 stance abuse and more positive attitudes toward substance abuse research and treatment after viewing the program (Epstein & McGaha, 1999a; Epstein & McGaha, 1999b). The program also serves as a resource for obtaining help for an alcohol or drug prob-
35 lem by providing an extensive list of treatment providers and support groups available nationwide. Additionally, a recent NIDA initiative resulted in the distribution of ATOD-TV to every public middle school in the United States (over 19,000 schools), and the pro-
40 gram was recently featured in the *Monitor,* a widely disseminated publication of the American Psychological Association (Chamberlin, 2001).

Since there is a limited amount of empirical literature that describes or evaluates the utilization of alco-
45 hol and drug educational software (see also Glover, 1995; LaGuardia, 1998), especially on the college level, the present exploratory study of ATOD-TV software was conducted and the feasibility of using it with young adults in a college setting was assessed.

Method

Participants

50 Participants were 73 undergraduate college students (57 women and 16 men) from two sections of an upper-level substance abuse course taught in consecutive semesters at the University of West Florida, a regional state university where the student population
55 median age is 25 years and students' ethnic background is primarily Caucasian (81%). Most enrolled in the courses were majoring in psychology.

Materials

Materials included a copy of the ATOD-TV software and an anonymous survey used to obtain Likert-

Table 1
Impact of ATOD-TV interactive program on students' perceptions of course-related interest and knowledge.

Statement	Strongly Disagree	Disagree	Neither Disagree or Agree	Agree	Strongly Agree
Increased my interest in the class	4%	7%	32%	51%	7%
Should positively affect my performance in the class	1%	7%	30%	47%	15%
Will prompt me to read more about particular topics	5%	5%	34%	41%	14%
Increased my interest in becoming a psychologist or human service professional*	4%	7%	51%	24%	14%
Revealed a personal strength	3%	11%	48%	29%	10%
Revealed a personal limitation*	4%	15%	57%	17%	7%
Increased my knowledge of drug use and addiction	1%	7%	11%	47%	34%

Note: N = 73 except where indicated by * in which case N = 72.

60 type ratings and open-ended comments about the software from each student. Satisfaction ratings on a 5-point scale (poor, fair, good, very good, excellent) for each of seven separate ATOD learning modules were obtained, as well as ratings of how the program influ-
65 enced student interest and addiction knowledge.

Program

Thematically designed as a television set, the software allows students to change "channels" by clicking on various prompts and interact with learning modules, some of which are named after popular television pro-
70 grams. This is evident by the names of the modules: St. Nowhere, The Torn and the Troubled, Wheels of Misfortune, NeuroNet, Mainline, Recovery, and Verdict (see Appendix at the end of this article for descriptions). For example, Wheels of Misfortune is a game
75 show that focuses on the epidemiology of substance abuse. In Verdict, a courtroom drama about the societal consequences of substance abuse, viewers have the opportunity to make a judgment regarding the guilt or innocence of various drugs and their relationship to
80 crime and violence, disease, and accidents.

As with most successful software programs, ATOD-TV includes readily accessible help features. There are two different types of help offered to the students. The first feature offers the student help with
85 utilizing the software program while the second assists the student in finding treatment for substance abuse problems. There is a comprehensive list of names and telephone numbers of agencies available to help. This is important for students who have come to understand
90 that they or someone they know need help with a drug or alcohol problem.

The program uses a variety of techniques for interaction including a mixture of real audio and video as well as colorful caricatures. Teachers will appreciate
95 the clear intuitive navigation that this package offers, allowing students to work without assistance. After each module, a brief quiz is given and the CD keeps track of scores, so students may review their own progress. The program is available for both Macintosh®
100 and Windows™ based computers, is 92 MB, and uses over 460 MB of supporting video.

Procedure

Students were asked to interact for at least 20–30 minutes with the program outside of class and com-
105 plete the evaluation form. Students reviewed the program using a computer in the university lab or library. Specific instructions were not given regarding particular learning modules (i.e., how long or whether to explore specific components of the program), although
110 participants indicated which modules they did or did not explore. The students were given course credit for completing and returning the evaluation form, but their performance and level of involvement with the program were not observed or graded.

Results and Discussion

Results are presented for the self-reported impact
115 the ATOD-TV interactive program had on the college student participants (see Table 1). After interaction with ATOD-TV, 58% of the respondents agreed (sum of *Agree* and *Strongly Agree* responses) that the program increased his or her interest in the class. Sixty-
120 two percent agreed that the program would positively affect their performance in the class, and 55% indicated that the program would prompt them to read more about a particular subject regarding alcohol or other drugs. Thirty-eight percent agreed the program in-
125 creased interest in becoming a human service professional, while 39% agreed that the program helped them realize or identify a personal strength. Perhaps most important, 81% of these students indicated that the program increased their knowledge of substance use
130 and addiction. It should be noted that some participants responded neutrally to these impact-related questions, perhaps because, while many thought the program contributed to their knowledge base in this area, they did not find or think it would influence them more broadly.

135 Additional results are presented for student satisfaction with the individual ATOD-TV program modules in Table 2. The individual modules students rated the highest were Recovery and Verdict, as reflected by combined *Very Good* and *Excellent* ratings from 67%
140 and 52% of the respondents, respectively. In general, participants were satisfied with the quality of the interactive exercises, and almost all rated each exercise to be at least *Fair*. However, the Wheels of Misfortune

Table 2
Student satisfaction with individual modules of ATOD-TV interactive program.

	Poor	Fair	Good	Very Good	Excellent	N/A
St. Nowhere	4%	15%	31%	21%	25%	4%
The Torn and the Troubled	11%	14%	25%	18%	18%	14%
Wheels of Misfortune	17%	26%	18%	19%	15%	4%
NeuroNet	7%	11%	28%	25%	15%	14%
Mainline	6%	14%	29%	26%	14%	11%
Recovery	1%	4%	24%	31%	36%	4%
Verdict	3%	11%	26%	24%	28%	8%

Note: N = 72; Not Applicable indicates that the student did not access or interact with the particular learning module.

module received the highest percentage of *Poor* ratings. This finding is interesting since this module was rated as *Very Good* or *Excellent* by 34% of the participants. Through written and verbal feedback, it was learned that some participants experienced minor trouble with operating the CD-ROM at the university library computer station. This is supported by the comment from one student who stated that "This one (Wheels of Misfortune) was my favorite, even though it didn't work properly the whole time. It was entertaining, while educating!" This occurrence, although quickly and easily corrected, may account for lower evaluation scores on some modules.

Other written comments about ATOD-TV included:

...CD-ROM was very informative and reinforced much of what has been said in class.

Very interesting, (the ATOD-TV CD) should be included with the textbook so one can use this more often and actually get to see all things on CD. Very real. Wish I could spend more time with it.

This particular CD-ROM was very informative. It provides information in a manner that is focused and easy to relate to.... I enjoyed going through the exercises and playing along.

I enjoyed the CD-ROM. It wasn't boring like a lot of assignments like this I've done in the past.

These exercises made me realize just how addicts appear to be normal citizens instead of the stereotypical, poor, dirty addicts.

In summary, the positive response to, and satisfaction with, the ATOD-TV educational CD program supports the contention that interactive computer methods can be used to enhance college student knowledge about, and interest in, addictive behaviors and recovery from addiction. ATOD-TV appears to be worthy of future controlled evaluations of student learning. Future investigations should sample middle and high school students as well as college-based users, randomly assign participants to experimental (i.e., incorporating use of ATOD-TV in addition to what is typically taught and how it is usually delivered) and control conditions (i.e., typical content and teaching methods), and use independent measures of knowledge acquisition and attitude change about substance misuse and recovery concepts. In addition, the specific modules of this program could be compared to gauge relative effectiveness in teaching students particular types of material (factual information versus critical thinking skills). Ideally, qualitative methods of exploring student learning and reactions to the program (e.g., focus groups) could be utilized to complement quantitative methods of evaluation. In this way, evaluations of ATOD-TV in various educational contexts (including the Internet) can result in updated versions of the program or others similar in scope to it, and improved interactive technologies that efficiently teach critical addiction-related content and concepts.

References

Alcohol, Tobacco and Other Drugs Television (ATOD-TV) (1996). [Computer Software] Curators of the University of Missouri, Columbia, MO.
Chamberlin, J. (2001, June). Targeting middle schools with prevention. *APA Monitor*, 74–75.
Epstein, J., & McGaha, A. (1999a). Evaluation of an interactive multimedia program to educate the general public about substance abuse. *Computers in Human Behavior*, *15*, 73–83.
Epstein, J., & McGaha, A. (1999b). ATOD-TV: A case study on developing interactive multimedia. *Technology in Human Services*, *16*, 17–31.
Glover, B. (1995). DINOS (Drinking Is Not Our Solution): Using computer programs in middle school drug education. *Elementary School Guidance and Counseling*, *30*, 55–62. [ERIC Document No: EJ513134].
LaGuardia, C. (1998). Understanding alcohol and other drugs: A multimedia resource. (CD-ROM). *Library Journal*, *123*, 179.

Appendix

Descriptions of Interactive CD Learning Modules

NeuroNet. A news program devoted to the biology of substance abuse. Meet Marcus and his father and listen as they talk about their family's history of addiction. See an inside view of the brain and what drugs do to it.

St. Nowhere. Dr. Ken Jones visits five families addicted to different drugs. Accompany him on his rounds as he listens to their stories. Learn how drugs have affected their lives and their health.

The Torn and the Troubled. While Chad and Beth argue about drinking, their daughter is arrested for marijuana possession. Meanwhile, James struggles with his addiction to cigarettes. Tune in to learn about the myths and facts of substance abuse.

Wheels of Misfortune. Each time you spin the Wheels of Misfortune, you will hear and see some facts about drug use in the United States.

Mainline. Vanessa Chance goes on a behind-the-scenes investigation to discover the causes of substance abuse. From family, friends, and society, she explores the many reasons why people become addicted.

Recovery. Meet four recovering addicts and ask them questions about how substance abuse has affected their lives.

Verdict. A courtroom drama about the societal consequences of substance abuse. The Honorable Alton Wiley puts alcohol, tobacco, and illegal drugs on trial. From AIDS and other diseases, to accidents and crime, you can help the judge make the verdict.

About the authors: *Rob J. Rotunda* and *Laura West* are affiliated with the Department of Psychology, University of West Florida. Joel Epstein is affiliated with the Missouri Institute of Mental Health.

Address correspondence to: Dr. Rob Rotunda, Psychology Department, University of West Florida, Pensacola, FL 32561. E-mail: rrotunda@uwf.edu, or Dr. Joel Epstein, Missouri Institute of Mental Health, 5247 Fyler Street, St. Louis, MO 63139. E-mail: epsteinj @mimh.edu

Exercise for Article 9

Factual Questions

1. How many of the participants were men?

2. Students were asked to interact with the program for at least how many minutes?

3. What did the students receive in exchange for completing and returning the evaluation form?

4. Was student performance using the program and their level of involvement observed?

5. In the discussion of the results in Table 1, the researchers summed two categories of response. What categories were summed?

6. In Table 1, which statement had the highest percentage of disagreement?

Questions for Discussion

7. In a future study, would you recommend that the researchers use a more diverse sample of participants? (See lines 50–57.)

8. In your opinion, could the outcomes of this study have been influenced by the fact that the participants in this study were enrolled in a substance abuse course? Explain. (See lines 50–52.)

9. In your opinion, are the program modules described in sufficient detail? Explain. (See lines 135–156 and the Appendix at the end of the article.)

10. The researchers suggest that in future studies on the effectiveness of the program, participants should be assigned to experimental and control conditions at random. In your opinion, how important is this suggestion? Explain. (See lines 179–185.)

11. The researchers suggest that in future studies on the effectiveness of the program, the acquisition of knowledge be examined. In your opinion, how important is this suggestion? Explain. (See lines 186–187.)

12. How desirable would it have been to examine attitude change (i.e., changes in attitudes from pretest to posttest) when evaluating the program? (See line 186.)

13. In the table of contents of this book, this article is classified as "pre-experimental research." Do you agree with this classification? Why? Why not?

Quality Ratings

Directions: Indicate your level of agreement with each of the following statements by circling a number from 5 for strongly agree (SA) to 1 for strongly disagree (SD). If you believe an item is not applicable to this research article, leave it blank. Be prepared to explain your ratings. When responding to criteria A and B below, keep in mind that brief titles and abstracts are conventional in published research.

A. The title of the article is appropriate.

SA   5   4   3   2   1   SD

B. The abstract provides an effective overview of the research article.

SA   5   4   3   2   1   SD

C. The introduction establishes the importance of the study.

SA   5   4   3   2   1   SD

D. The literature review establishes the context for the study.

SA   5   4   3   2   1   SD

E. The research purpose, question, or hypothesis is clearly stated.

SA   5   4   3   2   1   SD

F. The method of sampling is sound.

SA   5   4   3   2   1   SD

G. Relevant demographics (for example, age, gender, and ethnicity) are described.

SA   5   4   3   2   1   SD

H. Measurement procedures are adequate.

SA   5   4   3   2   1   SD

I. All procedures have been described in sufficient detail to permit a replication of the study.

SA   5   4   3   2   1   SD

J. The participants have been adequately protected from potential harm.

SA   5   4   3   2   1   SD

K. The results are clearly described.

SA   5   4   3   2   1   SD

L. The discussion/conclusion is appropriate.

SA   5   4   3   2   1   SD

M. Despite any flaws, the report is worthy of publication.

SA   5   4   3   2   1   SD

Article 10

Multimodal Behavioral Treatment of Nonrepetitive, Treatment-Resistant Nightmares: A Case Report

BARRY A. TANNER

Detroit Receiving Hospital and University Health Center

ABSTRACT. A 23-yr.-old woman presenting with a 17-yr. history of nightmares was treated with a variety of behavioral and self-regulatory techniques. The nightmares were unusual in that they did not have an obviously common theme as in most published reports, and, therefore, did not readily lend themselves to several frequently used techniques. Although previous treatment episodes had not affected the incidence of the nightmares, a combination of relaxation procedures, a mnemonic to increase lucid dreaming, and dream rehearsal upon waking from a nightmare resulted in a sharp decrease in the frequency of nightmares in four sessions. Further improvement was reported over the next nine months as additional techniques were introduced and other problems treated, and was maintained during a 9-mo. follow-up.

From *Perceptual and Motor Skills, 99,* 1139–1146. Copyright 2004 © by Perceptual and Motor Skills. Reprinted with permission.

Chronic nightmares are reported by roughly 5% of the general adult population (Bixler, Kales, Soldatos, Kales, & Healey, 1979; Coren, 1994), while as many as 29% of college students report monthly nightmares
5 (Feldman & Hersen, 1967). Nightmares are more common among women than men (Feldman & Hersen, 1967; Bixler, et al., 1979). This sex difference is consistent with treatment studies of nightmares for which three or four times as many women as men volunteer
10 for the studies (e.g., Krakow, Kellner, Pathak, & Lambert, 1995).

Nightmares are by definition frightening (Hartmann, 1994). Patients may be awakened by the nightmares and have trouble falling asleep once more. They
15 may also avoid sleep for fear of having yet another nightmare. This may involve avoiding the bed, sitting up watching television, or engaging in other late night activity, all of which are likely to disrupt sleep schedules.

20 Controlled studies have found that relaxation alone is as effective as relaxation with desensitization in treating nightmares (Miller & DiPlato, 1983), and that desensitization is more effective than placebo treatment (Cellucci & Lawrence, 1978) or remaining on a waiting
25 list for treatment (Miller & DiPlato, 1983). Instruction in desensitization and rehearsal of an altered dream in imagination (dream rehearsal) are equally effective in reducing the frequency of self-reported nightmares. However, only self-desensitization decreases emotional
30 arousal, while neither intervention decreases self-reported psychophysiological arousal (Kellner, Neidhardt, Krakow, & Pathak, 1992). Dream rehearsal is more effective than relaxation among participants following a manual for self-treatment at home for recur-
35 rent nightmares (Burgess, Gill, & Marks, 1998). Krakow and colleagues have provided support for the effectiveness of dream rehearsal in a series of additional studies (Neidhardt, Krakow, Kellner, & Pathak, 1992; Krakow, Kellner, Neidhardt, Pathak, & Lambert, 1993;
40 Krakow, Germain, Tandberg, Koss, Schrader, Hollifield, Cheng, & Edmond, 1996; Krakow, McBride, Hollifield, Schrader, Yau, & Tandberg, 1996; Krakow, Tandberg, Cutchen, McBride, Hollifield, Lauriello, Schrader, Yau, & Cheng, 1997; Krakow, Hollifield,
45 Schrader, Koss, Tandberg, Lauriello, McBride, Warner, Cheng, Edmond, & Kellner, 2000; Krakow, Hollifield, Johnston, Koss, Schrader, Warner, Tandberg, Lauriello, McBride, Cutchen, Cheng, Emmons, Germain, Melendrez, Sandoval, & Prince, 2001; Krakow,
50 Johnston, Melendrez, Hollifield, Warner, Chavez-Kennedy, & Herlan, 2001).

Case studies have reported the effectiveness of dream rehearsal, both with hypnosis (Erickson, 1959; Eichelman, 1985; Kingsbury, 1993) and with-
55 out it (Halliday, 1982; Bishay, 1985; Palace & Johnston, 1989; Kellner, Singh, & Irigoyen-Rascon, 1991; Forbes, Phelps, & McHugh, 2001; Forbes, Phelps, McHugh, Debenham, Hopwood, & Creamer, 2003). Additional case studies have re-
60 ported the effectiveness of imagining the nightmare without instructions to alter content (Marks, 1978; Cutting, 1979; Gorton, 1988; Burgess, Marks, & Gill, 1994). Both desensitization (Geer & Silverman, 1967; Cautela, 1968; Silverman & Geer,
65 1968; Cavior & Deutsch, 1975; Schindler, 1980; Ec-

cles, Wilde, & Marshall, 1988) and autogenic training (Sadigh, 1999) have been reported effective. Several authors also report case studies (Halliday, 1982; Brylowski, 1990; Abramovitch, 1995) or series
70 (Zadra & Pihl, 1997) treated with lucid dreaming in conjunction with other techniques, generally including imagining the dream and altering the dream's content.

All of these cases involved recurrent dreams that
75 facilitated the use of imagining the nightmare, altering the content of the imagined dream, or desensitization hierarchies because a common theme allows easier development of a script or a hierarchy. The case reported here differed in that the chronic nightmares did
80 not share a common content, making those procedures with the greatest experimental support more difficult to apply and suggested training in lucid dreaming (La-Berge, 1980; Tholey, 1983; Purcell, Mullington, Moffitt, Hoffman, & Pigeau, 1986). It was not until the
85 third session that I figured out how this woman could effectively alter the dream's content to her benefit.

Case Report

Mrs. X, a 23-yr.-old married woman, presented with a 17-yr. history of nightmares. She reported that the nightmares typically occurred three times per night
90 and four nights per week. The nightmares ranged from threatening figures to abstract shapes and colors and had no common content other than their bizarre and frightening nature. She practiced good sleep hygiene other than taking an over-the-counter sleep aid and
95 slept 7 to 8 hours per night so long as she took the sleep aid and an antidepressant. She averaged 40 min. to fall asleep, qualifying her for a diagnosis of insomnia (Hauri, 1994). She described three prior episodes of psychotherapy beginning at age 17, with the most re-
100 cent lasting 18 months while she was in graduate school. She had been placed on Wellbutrin, 150 mg daily, by a psychiatrist for depression while a graduate student and was still taking it when she came to see me shortly after graduating and moving from her home
105 state. She was a bright and pleasant young woman who described a fear of going to sleep as well as a more general nighttime anxiety. The fear increased when her husband was out of town on business, at which time she typically refused to sleep in her own bed. She de-
110 scribed her mood as generally "below average" and only "average on a good day."

The initial session was spent taking a history and developing a treatment plan. She agreed at that session to keep a sleep log, which she would bring to subse-
115 quent sessions.

Diaphragmatic breathing (Schwartz, 1995) was introduced for relaxation at the second session. She was instructed to practice it while driving and at bedtime. She was also instructed to use a mne-
120 monic at bedtime designed to increase lucid dreaming (LaBerge, 1980). While lying in bed with her

eyes closed, she silently repeated 10 times, "I must remember when I'm dreaming to remind myself that I'm dreaming." She reported one nightmare on each
125 of three nights during the previous week.

She reported at the next session that she had discontinued the sleep medication, with a resulting increase in time to fall asleep but no further change in the frequency of nightmares. She reported a good experience
130 with diaphragmatic breathing and was instructed to modify it, with slower breathing using pursed lip expiration (Schwartz, 1995). She said she did not experience lucidity while dreaming, but stated that the mnemonic helped her more quickly to attain lucidity upon
135 waking from a nightmare, thereby decreasing her distress. She was asked to repeat the mnemonic upon waking from a nightmare. She was then to change the nightmare so as to make it more acceptable to her and to imagine the altered nightmare before returning to
140 sleep.

The patient reported at the fourth session that she had fallen asleep more quickly and experienced less anxiety at night, although she again had a single nightmare on each of three nights. She reported diffi-
145 culty in imagining a modified dream upon waking from a nightmare, because it was difficult to focus and anxiety was associated with the dream. She was encouraged to leave the bed and read for 15 min. before returning to bed and imagining a modified version of the dream.
150 An attempt to teach her an abbreviated progressive relaxation procedure (Tanner & Parrino, 1975) was discontinued when the patient reported relaxation induced anxiety and fear of closing her eyes (Schwartz & Schwartz, 1995). Autogenic training (Schultz & Luthe,
155 1969) was then introduced, emphasizing the cognitive as opposed to the muscle-relaxing aspects of it. However, she found the autogenic statements distressing, as they reminded her of prior unpleasant experiences, and she was unable to make good use of them.
160 She reported no nightmares at the fifth session. She continued to repeat her lucidity mnemonic at bedtime but could not imagine a changed nightmare in the absence of any disturbing dreams. She was taught thought stopping (Tanner & Parrino, 1975) because she com-
165 plained of chronic intrusive and disturbing thoughts that increased her anxiety and interfered with sleep. Thought stopping was not helpful, so she was instructed in disrupting irrational thoughts (Ellis & Greiger, 1977) and in covert reinforcement of incom-
170 patible thoughts such as "I am safe" (Homme, 1965). At the ninth session, she reported two nightmares. She reported imagining a modified dream once she was fully alert and then sleeping well for the remainder of the night after each of these nightmares. She said that
175 she was satisfied with the continuing decrease in her nightmares, nighttime anxiety, and in her time to fall asleep and asked that we focus instead on a sexual dysfunction.

180 She continued to monitor her nighttime anxiety, sleep, and nightmares while we focused on other areas. She began to work part-time in her chosen profession after the 17th session. Her anxiety was now specific to current concerns such as not having prepared ade-quately for the next day's work, as opposed to the pre-
185 vious free-floating anxiety. The dreams were less bi-zarre and less upsetting than previously experienced. She reported that they generally did not wake her, had less negative effect on her mood the following day, and were "more like strange dreams than nightmares." She
190 informed me later that she had also discontinued the Wellbutrin between the 17th and 18th sessions. She reported nine disturbing dreams during the remaining 19 treatment sessions.

We jointly agreed to terminate after the 37th ses-
195 sion and 10 months of treatment as all of her objectives had been reached or surpassed. She agreed to my con-tacting her for follow-up.

Ten months after beginning treatment, she reported less than one nightmare per month, experiencing no
200 anxiety at night, and feeling rested during the day. She was now falling asleep within 10 to 15 minutes without medication, and no longer met the usual criteria for insomnia (Hauri, 1994). This compared with more than 50 nightmares per month at the start of treatment, 40
205 minutes to fall asleep with medication, a bedtime anxi-ety score of 40 on a scale of 0 to 100, and feeling tired much of the time.

Nine months after termination, Mrs. X reported that she averaged about two nightmares per month and that
210 nighttime anxiety averaged 15 on the scale of 0 to 100, since termination of treatment. She also averaged 15 min. to fall asleep, putting her at or below the custom-ary cutoff for diagnosing insomnia (Hauri, 1994). Fig-ure 1 summarizes the changes in nightmare frequency
215 and time to fall asleep from pretreatment through the 9-mo. follow-up. While both the number of nightmares and the number of nights on which nightmares occur are common measures of nightmare behavior (e.g., Krakow, Hollifield, Johnston, Koss, Schrader, Warner,

220 Tandberg, Lauriello, McBride, Cutchen, Cheng, Emmons, Germain, Melendrez, Sandoval, & Prince, 2001), those two measures were identical for this pa-tient once treatment began. Therefore, number of nights with nightmares was not included in Figure 1.
225 Although the merely unpleasant dreams without awak-ening which occurred after the ninth session do not strictly qualify as nightmares (Hartmann, 1994), those dreams are nonetheless counted as nightmares in Fig-ure 1. Data are missing for minutes to fall asleep for
230 one month during which she did not record this infor-mation.

Mrs. X also reported at follow-up that she had been working full-time for over seven months. This was quite an accomplishment, as she had never previously
235 worked full-time. Unfortunately, the job appeared to be the source of her increased anxiety and time to fall asleep. She said that her boss was unpleasant, that she found her job stressful, and that her depressed mood had returned. I offered to treat her for this or refer her
240 elsewhere, but she declined.

While others have documented effective inter-ventions for repetitive nightmares, this paper represents the first known published report of suc-cessful treatment of nonrepetitive, chronic nightmares
245 with combined direct treatment. Although Mrs. X denied attaining lucidity while dreaming, she be-lieved that the lucidity mnemonic helped her more quickly achieve lucidity upon waking from a nightmare and reduced her distress. The patient
250 responded quickly to instruction in diaphragmatic breathing, lucid dreaming, and imaginary dream rehearsal and maintained much of her gain over the ensuing 18 months of treatment and follow-up. Although the use of multiple techniques provides less
255 information about the specific active ingredients of treatment, it is probably closer to what clinicians face in daily practice, and may, therefore, be of help to those treating patients with similar presen-tations.

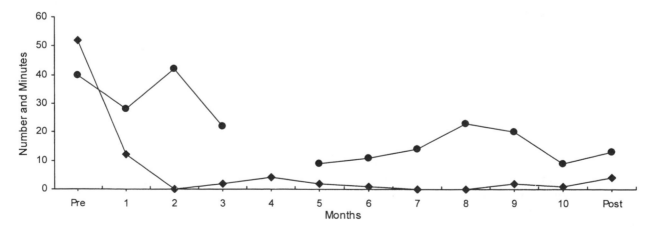

Figure 1. Nightmare frequency (♦) and time to fall asleep in minutes (●); Pre = pretherapy, Post = posttherapy.

References

Abramovitch, H. (1995). The nightmare of returning home: a case of acute onset nightmare disorder treated by lucid dreaming. *Israeli Journal of Psychiatry and Related Sciences, 32,* 140–145.

Bishay, N. (1985). Therapeutic manipulation of nightmares and the management of neuroses. *British Journal of Psychiatry, 14,* 67–70.

Bixler, E., Kales, A., Soldatos, C. R., Kales, J., & Healey, S. (1979). Prevalence of sleep disorders in the Los Angeles metropolitan area. *American Journal of Psychiatry, 79,* 2157–2162.

Brylowski, A. (1990). Nightmares in crisis: clinical applications of lucid dreaming techniques. *Psychiatric Journal of the University of Ottawa, 15,* 79–84.

Burgess, M., Gill, M., & Marks, I. (1998). Postal self-exposure treatment of recurrent nightmares. *British Journal of Psychiatry, 172,* 257–262.

Burgess, M., Marks, I., & Gill, M. (1994). Postal self-exposure treatment of recurrent nightmares. *British Journal of Psychiatry, 165,* 388–391.

Cautela, J. (1968). Behavior therapy and the need for behavioral assessment. *Psychotherapy: Therapy, Research and Practice, 5,* 175–179.

Cavior, N., & Deutsche, A-M. (1975). Systematic desensitization to reduce dream-induced anxiety. *Journal of Nervous and Mental Disease, 161,* 433–435.

Cellucci, A., & Lawrence, P. (1978). The efficacy of systematic desensitization in reducing nightmares. *Journal of Behavior Therapy and Experimental Psychiatry, 9,* 109–114.

Coren, S. (1994). The prevalence of self-reported sleep disturbances in young adults. *International Journal of Neuroscience, 79,* 67–73.

Cutting, D. (1979). Relief of nightmares. *British Journal of Psychiatry, 134,* 647.

Eccles, A., Wilde, A., & Marshall, W. (1988). In vivo desensitization in the treatment of recurrent nightmares. *Journal of Behavior Therapy and Experimental Psychiatry, 19,* 285–288.

Eichelman, B. (1985). Hypnotic change in combat dreams of two veterans with posttraumatic stress disorder. *American Journal of Psychiatry, 142,* 17–20.

Ellis, A., & Greiger, R. (1977). *Handbook of Rational-Emotive Therapy.* New York: Springer.

Erickson, M. (1959). Further clinical techniques of hypnosis: utilization techniques. *American Journal of Clinical Hypnosis, 2,* 3–21.

Feldman, M., & Hersen, M. (1967). Attitudes toward death in nightmare subjects. *Journal of Abnormal Psychology, 72,* 421–425.

Forbes, D., Phelps, A., & McHugh, A. (2001). Imagery rehearsal in the treatment of posttraumatic nightmares in combat-related PTSD. *Journal of Traumatic Stress, 14,* 433–442.

Forbes, D., Phelps, A., McHugh, A., Debenham, P., Hopwood, M., & Creamer, M. (2003). Imagery rehearsal in the treatment of posttraumatic nightmares in Australian veterans with chronic combat-related PTSD: 12-month follow-up data. *Journal of Traumatic Stress, 16,* 509–513.

Geer, J., & Silverman, I. (1967). Treatment of a recurrent nightmare by behavior-modification procedures: a case study. *Journal of Abnormal Psychology, 72,* 188–190.

Gorton, G. (1988). Life-long nightmares: an eclectic treatment approach. *American Journal of Psychotherapy, 42,* 610–618.

Halliday, G. (1982). Direct alteration of a traumatic nightmare. *Perceptual and Motor Skills, 54,* 413–414.

Hartmann, E. (1994). Nightmares and other dreams. In M. Kryger, T. Roth, & W. Dement (Eds.), *Principles and practice of sleep medicine.* (2nd ed.) Philadelphia, PA: Saunders. pp. 407–410.

Hauri, P. (1994). Primary insomnia. In M. Kryger, T. Roth, & W. Dement (Eds.), *Principles and practice of sleep medicine.* (2nd ed.) Philadelphia, PA: Saunders pp. 494–499.

Homme, L. (1965). Control of coverants, the operants of the mind. *Psychological Record, 15,* 501–511.

Kellner, R., Neidhardt, J., Krakow, B., & Pathak, D. (1992). Changes in chronic nightmares after one session of desensitization or rehearsal instructions. *American Journal of Psychiatry, 149,* 659–663.

Kellner, R., Singh, G., & Irigoyen-Rascon, F. (1991). Rehearsal in the treatment of recurring nightmares in post-traumatic stress disorders and panic disorder: case histories. *Annals of Clinical Psychiatry, 3,* 67–71.

Kingsbury, S. (1993). Brief hypnotic treatment of repetitive nightmares. *American Journal of Clinical Hypnosis, 35,* 161–169.

Krakow, B., Germain, A., Tandberg, D., Koss, M., Schrader, R., Hollifield, M., Cheng, D., & Edmond, T. (1996). Long term reduction in nightmares with imagery rehearsal treatment. *Behavioural and Cognitive Psychotherapy, 24,* 135–148.

Krakow, B., Hollifield, M., Johnston, L., Koss, M., Schrader, R., Warner, T., Tandberg, D., Lauriello, J., McBride, L., Cutchen, L., Cheng, L., Emmons, S., Germain, A., Melendrez, D., Sandoval, D., & Prince, H. (2001). Imagery rehearsal for chronic nightmares in sexual assault survivors with posttraumatic stress disorder: a randomized controlled trial. *Journal of the American Medical Association, 286,* 537–545.

Krakow, B., Hollifield, M., Schrader, R., Koss, M., Tandberg, D., Lauriello, J., McBride, L., Warner, T., Cheng, D., Edmond, T., & Kellner, R. (2000). A controlled study of imagery rehearsal for chronic nightmares in sexual assault survivors with PTSD: a preliminary report. *Journal of Traumatic Stress, 13,* 589–609.

Krakow, B., Johnston, L., Melendrez, D., Hollifield, M., Warner, T., Chavez-Kennedy, D., & Herlan, M. (2001). An open-label trial of evidence-based cognitive behavior therapy for nightmares and insomnia for crime victims with PTSD. *American Journal of Psychiatry, 158,* 2043–2047.

Krakow, B., Kellner, R., Neidhardt, J., Pathak, D., & Lambert, L. (1993). Imagery rehearsal treatment of chronic nightmares: with a thirty month follow-up. *Journal of Behavior Therapy and Experimental Psychiatry, 24,* 325–330.

Krakow, B., Kellner, Pathak, P., & Lambert, L. (1995). Imagery rehearsal treatment for chronic nightmares. *Behaviour Research and Therapy, 33,* 837–843.

Krakow, B., McBride, L., Hollifield, M., Schrader, R., Yau, C. L., & Tandberg, D. (1996). Treatment of chronic nightmares in sexual assault survivors. *Sleep Research, 25,* 137.

Krakow, B., Tandberg, D., Cutchen, L., McBride, L., Hollifield, M., Lauriello, J., Schrader, R., Yau, C. L., & Cheng, D. (1997). Imagery rehearsal treatment of chronic nightmares in PTSD: a controlled study. *Sleep Research, 26,* 245.

LaBerge, S. (1980). Lucid dreaming as a learnable skill: a case study. *Perceptual and Motor Skills, 51,* 1039–1042.

Marks, I. (1978). Rehearsal relief of a nightmare. *British Journal of Psychiatry, 133,* 461–465.

Miller, W., & DiPlato, M. (1983). Treatment of nightmares via relaxation and desensitization: a controlled evaluation. *Journal of Consulting and Clinical Psychology, 51,* 870–877.

Neidhardt, E., Krakow, B., Kellner, R., & Pathak, D. (1992). The beneficial effects of one treatment session and recording of nightmares on chronic nightmare sufferers. *Sleep, 15,* 470–473.

Palace, E., & Johnston, C. (1989). Treatment of recurrent nightmares by the dream reorganization approach. *Journal of Behavior Therapy and Experimental Psychiatry, 20,* 219–226.

Purcell, S., Mullington, J., Moffitt, A., Hoffman, R., & Pigeau, R. (1986). Dream self-reflectiveness as a learned cognitive skill. *Sleep, 9,* 423–437.

Sadigh, M. (1999). The treatment of recalcitrant post-traumatic nightmares with autogenic training and autogenic abreaction: a case study. *Applied Psychophysiology and Biofeedback, 24,* 203–210.

Schindler, F. (1980). Treatment by systematic desensitization of a recurring nightmare of a real life trauma. *Journal of Behavior Therapy and Experimental Psychiatry, 11,* 53–54.

Schultz, J., & Luthe, W. (1969). *Autogenic therapy.* Vol. 1. *Autogenic methods.* New York: Grune & Stratton.

Schwartz, M. (1995). Breathing therapies. In M. Schwartz & Associates (Eds.), *Biofeedback: a practitioner's guide.* (2nd ed.) New York: Guilford. pp. 248–287.

Schwartz, M., & Schwartz, N. (1995). Problems with relaxation and biofeedback-assisted relaxation and guidelines for management. In M. Schwartz & Associates (Eds.), *Biofeedback: a practitioner's guide.* (2nd ed.) New York: Guilford. pp. 288–300.

Silverman, I., & Geer, J. (1968). The elimination of a recurrent nightmare by desensitization of a related phobia. *Behaviour Research and Therapy, 6,* 109–111.

Tanner, B., & Parrino, J. (1975). *Helping others: behavioral procedures for mental health workers.* Eugene, OR: E-B Press.

Tholey, P. (1983). Techniques for inducing and manipulating lucid dreams. *Perceptual and Motor Skills, 57,* 79–90.

Zadra, A., & Pihl, R. (1997). Lucid dreaming as a treatment for recurrent nightmares. *Psychotherapy and Psychosomatics, 66,* 50–55.

Address correspondence to: Barry A. Tanner, Ph.D., Life Stress Center 3S-14, Detroit Receiving Hospital and University Health Center, 4201 St. Antoine, Detroit, MI 48201.

Exercise for Article 10

Factual Questions

1. How did the case reported in this article differ from previous cases in terms of the type(s) of chronic nightmares?

2. What words was the client asked to repeat 10 times?

3. Did the client take an antidepressant?

4. After 10 months of treatment, did the client still meet the criteria for insomnia?

5. Does Figure 1 include data on "unpleasant dreams" that do not strictly qualify as nightmares?

6. According to the researcher, this article represents the first published report of what?

Questions for Discussion

7. In lines 38–51 in the literature review, the researcher provides a number of references regarding a finding reported in the literature. Does the large number of references give you confidence in the finding? Would a smaller number be just as effective? Explain.

8. In your opinion, are the client's nightmares described in sufficient detail? Explain. (See lines 90–93.)

9. How helpful is Figure 1 in helping you understand the results of this case study? Would the research report be as effective without the figure? Explain.

10. When working with a single case, researchers sometimes alternate treatments (e.g., first, give the treatment for a while, then stop the treatment for a while, and then give the treatment again). In your opinion, would it have been desirable to do something along these lines in this study? Would it have been ethical? Explain.

11. Has the researcher convinced you that the treatment used with this client was effective? Explain.

12. In light of your reading of this study, do you think that case studies employing only a single case are helpful in advancing scientific knowledge? Why? Why not?

Quality Ratings

Directions: Indicate your level of agreement with each of the following statements by circling a number from 5 for strongly agree (SA) to 1 for strongly disagree (SD). If you believe an item is not applicable to this research article, leave it blank. Be prepared to explain your ratings. When responding to criteria A and B below, keep in mind that brief titles and abstracts are conventional in published research.

A. The title of the article is appropriate.

SA   5   4   3   2   1   SD

B. The abstract provides an effective overview of the research article.

SA   5   4   3   2   1   SD

C. The introduction establishes the importance of the study.

SA   5   4   3   2   1   SD

D. The literature review establishes the context for the study.

SA   5   4   3   2   1   SD

E. The research purpose, question, or hypothesis is clearly stated.

SA   5   4   3   2   1   SD

F. The method of sampling is sound.

SA   5   4   3   2   1   SD

G. Relevant demographics (for example, age, gender, and ethnicity) are described.

SA   5   4   3   2   1   SD

H. Measurement procedures are adequate.

SA   5   4   3   2   1   SD

I. All procedures have been described in sufficient detail to permit a replication of the study.

SA   5   4   3   2   1   SD

J. The participants have been adequately protected from potential harm.

SA   5   4   3   2   1   SD

K. The results are clearly described.

SA   5   4   3   2   1   SD

L. The discussion/conclusion is appropriate.

SA   5   4   3   2   1   SD

M. Despite any flaws, the report is worthy of publication.

SA   5   4   3   2   1   SD

Article 11

Continuous White Noise to Reduce Resistance Going to Sleep and Night Wakings in Toddlers

LEANNE M. FORQUER
Central Michigan University

C. MERLE JOHNSON
Central Michigan University

ABSTRACT. White noise generators were turned on at 75 dB at bedtime and kept on all night to treat resistance going to sleep and night wakings in one-year-old toddlers. In a multiple baseline design, four sets of parents recorded duration of resistance going to sleep, number of night wakings, completed surveys of their child's feeding and sleeping patterns, and the Parenting Stress Index (PSI). Three of four toddlers were sleeping better at the end of treatment; however, one child's night wakings returned at follow-up when white noise was discontinued. All parents were comfortable with the white noise and most would recommend it to others. White noise may be effective for childhood night wakings and resistance going to sleep without being combined with other validated treatments.

From *Child & Family Behavior Therapy*, 27, 1–10. Copyright © 2005 by The Haworth Press, Inc. Reprinted with permission.

The most common sleep problems for infants and preschoolers are bedtime struggles and night wakings (Ferber, 1985; Kuhn & Weidinger, 2000; Mindell, 1999). In a telephone survey of parents in one U.S. community, of all 12- to 35-month-old children listed in a directory, 42% resisted going to bed and 35% awoke and cried during the night (Johnson, 1991). Sleep problems are stressful for parents and are associated with maternal depression, marital dissatisfaction, and child abuse (France & Hudson, 1990).

The first step in managing infant or childhood sleep problems is consultation with a family physician or pediatrician to eliminate potential physiological causes. Once these are ruled out, there are methods for decreasing sleep disturbances including medication and behavioral procedures (Ferber, 1985; Mindell, 1999; Sadeh, 2001). Overall, medication does not appear effective (Mindell, 1999; Ramchandani, Wiggs, Webb, & Stores, 2000). While drugs may reduce night wakings, these often return once medication is discontinued (Richman, 1985). Alternatively, behavior therapy techniques such as extinction, graduated extinction, scheduled awakenings, and positive bedtime routines are effective. However, parents often use these inappropriately or inconsistently, or end them prematurely (Ed-

wards & Christophersen, 1994; Kuhn & Weidinger, 2000; Lawton, France, & Blampied, 1991; Mindell, 1999). Therefore, at least some parents need easier techniques.

One alternative is white noise, that is, sound that covers the entire range of human hearing (20–20,000 Hertz). White noise promotes recovery from heart bypass surgery in adults in hospitals (Williamson, 1992). Another study examined the effects of white noise on the fetus. Zimmer, Jakobi, Talmon, Shenhav, and Weissman (1993) administered white noise at 100 decibels (dB) to the mother's abdomen for five minutes while fetal heart rate and activity were measured. No change was observed; however, the noise may have been insufficient in duration or intensity considering the sound level in the womb is 85 dB (Grimwade, Walker, & Wood, 1993).

Brackbill, Adams, Crowell, and Gray (1966) studied continuous auditory stimulation on arousal in neonates and preschool children. They compared four conditions: no sound, heartbeat, beating of a metronome, and lullabies. Children in sound conditions were awake less than those in no sound; however, no difference was found between any of the sound conditions. Brackbill (1970) extended these findings when she compared continuous, intermittent, and no sound on arousal of 30-day-old infants. Arousal was lowest for continuous and highest for intermittent sound. Brackbill (1971) later examined continuous stimulation on arousal of 27-day-old infants. In her laboratory study, 24 infants were presented either no extra stimulation (control condition) or continuous stimulation of one, two, three, or four modalities (85 dB sound, temperature, movement, and vision). Results indicate an inverse relationship between the number of modalities stimulated and arousal. Spencer, Moran, Lee, and Talbert (1990) examined five minutes of continuous heartbeat, ranging from 67 to 72.5 dB, with 40 two- to seven-day-old infants. Neonates exposed to heartbeats fell asleep sooner. Brackbill (1973) extended her 1971 findings by simultaneously stimulating the four modalities for two hours. This produced decreases in heart

rate, respiration, motor activity, and improved sleep within 40 minutes that endured over the two hours.
70 These studies indicate that continuous white noise, as well as heartbeat sounds, can reduce arousal and induce sleep, at least in laboratory settings.

Johnson's (1991) survey found acceptability of white noise to assist sleep; however, this does not tell
75 us if parents actually use it. Some used approximations of white noise, such as fans, air conditioners, or humidifiers. Although these studies offer information about the efficacy and acceptability of white noise, they fail to research into natural environments over
80 lengthy periods.

Borkowski, Hunter, and Johnson (2001) examined white noise at 75 dB for four-month-olds in their homes for the entire night in a multiple baseline design. White noise decreased wakings in two of five infants.
85 Most parents believed it helped even when data did not reflect a change. The infants were at ages when sleeping through the night is possible (Ferber, 1985; Sadeh, 2001), but perhaps all five were not sufficiently mature to consolidate uninterrupted sleep. In a second study,
90 they found that continuous noise, in conjunction with positive bedtime routines, reduced bedtime struggles and night wakings in 14- to 48-month-olds. Results indicate sleep problems decreased in three of four children that were maintained for six weeks. Parents re-
95 ported satisfaction with both white noise and bedtime routines and said they would recommend these.

We examined the efficacy of white noise on resistance going to sleep and night wakings in one-year-old children whose parents indicated they had sleep prob-
100 lems. Except for Borkowski et al. (2001), previous studies were carried out in laboratory settings and for no more than two hours, which is considerably shorter than a full night of sleep. This experiment differed from the Borkowski et al. study because these infants
105 were older than the four-month-olds in their first experiment; thus they were more likely to be able to sleep for longer periods of time. In addition, these toddlers were all less than two years old so the age range was not as wide as the range in their second experiment.
110 Moreover, white noise was presented alone, without potential confounds of positive bedtime routines in their treatment package for experiment two for young children who exhibited common sleep difficulties.

Method

Participants

Four families with 13- to 23-month-old children
115 participated. The criteria to participate were: (1) waking an average of once per night or resisting sleep for at least a half hour each night after being placed in the crib, (2) not already using a form of white noise (e.g., fan or humidifier) or sound was less than 75 dB, (3) no
120 medical condition that might be responsible for their sleep problem, and (4) not sleeping with parents. Families were recruited from a database of 12-month-old infants whose parents had participated in a telephone survey concerning sleep and attachment. Seven parents
125 who indicated sleep problems in the survey were contacted to see if their infants met criteria and were willing to participate in this project. Four met criteria and all agreed to participate. Parents were informed of the purpose of this study, gave written consent, and were
130 advised to obtain a physician's approval before participation as required by the Institutional Review Board (IRB).

Apparatus

The apparatus was a Tranquil Moments Plus white noise generator (Brookstone model #348516 for ap-
135 proximately $50) set at 75 dB sound pressure level (SPL) measured at the child's ear (calibrated by a technician). This volume level was determined not to be harmful to the child's hearing in the Borkowski et al. (2001) study of younger infants and was approved by
140 the IRB.

Procedure

A home visit was scheduled for families who agreed to participate. During this visit parents were given an explanation of the study, the child's crib and bedroom were examined, and written consent was ob-
145 tained. Sleep diaries were distributed and these included questions regarding location, time and length of naps, planned and actual bedtimes, time between placing their child in the crib and falling asleep (indicated by silence), number and length of night wakings, time
150 awake in the morning, and any unusual circumstances (e.g., vacations or illness). Sleep diaries completed by parents were commonly employed and validated by videotapes (Burke, Kuhn, & Peterson, 2004; Mindell & Durand, 1993). Parents completed a modified version
155 of Morrell's (1999) infant sleep questionnaire (ISQ). This survey determined the existence and severity of sleep problems and it included questions regarding feeding patterns. Parents also completed the Parenting Stress Inventory (PSI) Short Form (Abidin, 1995)
160 which consists of 36 items derived from the full PSI. The PSI was employed to measure the self-reported levels of parental stress.

A non-concurrent multiple baseline across families design was used (Kazdin, 1982). During baseline par-
165 ents kept diaries and responded to bedtime struggles and night waking as in the past. Baseline continued until sleep patterns stabilized. Another home visit occurred after baseline to set up the white noise generator and instruct parents in its use. Machines were placed
170 where they were set at 75 dB and inaccessible to the child.

Intervention lasted at least one month. White noise was used during all sleep periods, including naps if the child napped at home. Parents continued typical bed-
175 time activities but turned on the white noise before placing their child in the crib. Machines ran all night and were turned off before taking their toddler out of

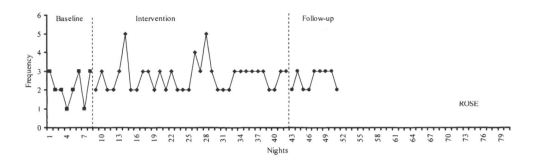

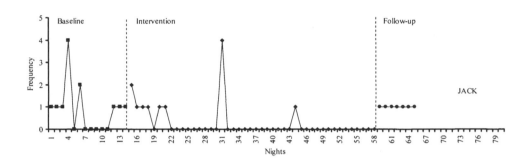

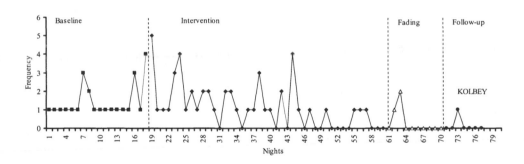

Figure 1. Number of night wakings for three of the toddlers (Rose, Jack, and Kolbey) during each phase of the experiment.

the crib the next morning. White noise was to serve as stimulus control, signaling time to sleep when on but
180 not when off. Parents were called twice each week to collect data and promote compliance. Sleep diaries were mailed weekly.

Following intervention, parents faded out the white noise. Fading involved turning the sound down ap-
185 proximately 5 to 10 dB every night until the machine was off. After one to two weeks of fading, a third home visit was made to complete the survey, PSI, and re- trieve the machine.

One month after fading there was a one-week fol-
190 low-up. A final home visit included the parent survey, PSI, white noise evaluation, and answering questions. The evaluation included questions regarding parent satisfaction with treatment. If sleep problems continued after follow-up, parents were provided information on
195 how to purchase a white noise generator or given in-

formation on other validated sleep techniques (Kuhn & Weidinger, 2000; Mindell, 1999; Ramchandani et al., 2000).

Results

The number of night wakings and length of bedtime
200 struggles were recorded across successive nights and these data are displayed in Figures 1 and 2. All families took at least one vacation during which white noise was not used and these nights were excluded. PSI scores were calculated for each mother during each
205 phase and parents' opinions were obtained at follow- up.

Rose was a 15-month-old who was breastfed to sleep. Rose's sleep disturbance was night wakings dur- ing which she cried until held and rocked back to sleep
210 or taken to her parent's bed. Rose consistently woke up at least twice a night and these rates changed little dur-

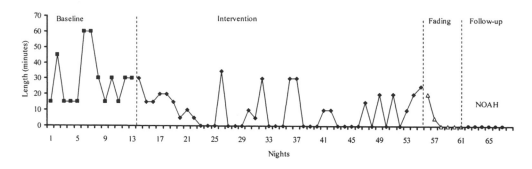

Figure 2. Minutes of bedtime struggles for Noah during each phase of the experiment.

ing the study (mean of 2.1 during baseline, 2.7 during intervention, and 2.5 during follow-up). Interestingly, her mother's level of stress decreased slightly across phases (10th percentile during baseline, 5th during intervention, 1st during follow-up) even though white noise did not appear to decrease Rose's night wakings.

Jack was a 21-month-old who was bottle-fed. Jack's sleep problem involved night wakings during which he was either comforted back to sleep or he was taken to his parents' bed. He exhibited an average of 0.9 night wakings during baseline; which decreased to 0.3 during intervention, then returned to 1.0 at follow-up. Jack's mother reported increased levels of stress from baseline to intervention (5th percentile during baseline to 20th during white noise), followed by a decrease to the 1st percentile at follow-up.

Kolbey was a 15-month-old who was in the process of being weaned from breastfeeding. Kolbey's sleep problem involved waking once per night during which she was either comforted back to sleep or taken to her parents' bed. Kolbey's night wakings decreased from a mean of 1.4 during baseline to 1.0 during intervention and 0.1 at follow-up. Parent stress reported by Kolbey's mother varied greatly from the 60th percentile at baseline to the 1st percentile during intervention and back up to the 50th percentile at follow-up.

Noah was a 13-month-old, recently weaned, whose sleep disturbance was resistance going to sleep for approximately a half hour after being placed in his crib awake. His bedtime struggles decreased from a mean of 28.9 minutes during baseline to 9.2 during intervention and to 0 during follow-up. His mother's stress changed little (25th percentile at baseline and intervention to 30th percentile at follow-up).

Parents' usage of white noise, based on nightly sleep diaries over the month of intervention, were 100% for Jack, 98% for Kolbey, 91% for Noah, and 87% for Rose. Rose's mother, however, had the volume set at less than 75 dB initially because it bothered her and gradually she increased it. Therefore, treatment fidelity of 87% may be a high estimate. The other mothers reported following the treatment protocol. Overall, all mothers except Rose's were satisfied with the white noise. On a 5-point, Likert-type scale of strongly agree (1) to neutral or no opinion (3) to strongly disagree (5), Rose's mother indicated a 3, Noah's a 2, Jack's a 1, and Kolbey's a 2. Moreover, Noah's mother purchased a white noise generator after the study, Jack's mother was considering a purchase, Kolbey's mother did not because she began sleeping unaided, and Rose's mother did not want a sound machine.

Discussion

The results demonstrate the efficacy of white noise for both bedtime struggles and night wakings in toddlers; three of four children improved. Two of three with frequent night wakings showed reductions during intervention; however, Jack's rate returned at follow-up. Noah, who resisted going to sleep, showed improvements that maintained at follow-up. All except Rose's mother were pleased with white noise; during follow-up Noah's mother recommended it to a friend.

One explanation for the effectiveness is due to decreased arousal and this is not limited to auditory stimulation (Brackbill, 1971). Second, white noise may help induce and maintain sleep by masking household noises that might awaken sleeping infants. Third, white noise may function as stimulus control, that is, after applied for a few weeks infants sleep when it is present and awaken when absent. Another possibility is management of circadian rhythms (Czeisler et al., 1981). This involves resetting the person's biological clock to establish a 24-hour cycle. Failure to maintain a consistent sleep schedule disrupts circadian rhythms. White noise may be resetting this biological clock when turned on at the same time every night and again when turned off in the morning (i.e., a zeitgeber).

This study, as well as Borkowski, Hunter, and Johnson (2001), used an approximation to white noise. Although several sounds have been utilized (Brackbill, 1966; Williamson, 1992), true white noise may be more effective. Therefore, comparing various sounds to true white noise should be examined in the future. In addition, different intensity levels need to be researched. A replication with a group design that employs a parametric analysis of different decibel levels would be useful.

Ferber (1985) does not support using white noise because children become dependent on it and therefore
300 cannot sleep when it is not present. Jack's return to night wakings during follow-up supports this caveat. This may be similar to medication, once discontinued sleep problems return (Mindell, 1999; Ramchandani et al., 2000). However, if white noise helps and parents
305 are comfortable, there is little need to eliminate it. Moreover, if parents desire, it can be gradually faded out easier than medication. Further, Ferber's recommendation to let children self-soothe was supported by Rose who was breastfed to sleep and who did not im-
310 prove.

In conclusion, white noise appears promising in reducing bedtime struggles and night wakings in toddlers; however, disturbances may return when discontinued. Inconsistent results on parent stress suggest
315 other stressors in the family may be more salient than sleep disturbances. Finally, most of the parents seem comfortable with white noise and would recommend it.

References

Abidin, R. R. (1995). *Parenting stress index* (3rd ed.). Odessa, FL: PAR.

Borkowski, M. M., Hunter, K. E., & Johnson, C. M. (2001). White noise and scheduled bedtime routines to reduce infant and childhood sleep disturbances. *The Behavior Therapist, 24,* 29–47.

Brackbill, Y., Adams, G., Crowell, D. H., & Gray, M. L. (1966). Arousal level in neonates and preschool children under continuous auditory stimulation. *Journal of Experimental Child Psychology, 4,* 178–188.

Brackbill, Y. (1970). Acoustic variation and arousal level in infants. *Psychophysiology, 6,* 517–526.

Brackbill, Y. (1971). Cumulative effect of continuous stimulation on arousal level in infants. *Child Development, 42,* 17–26.

Brackbill, Y. (1973). Continuous stimulation reduces arousal level: Stability of the effect over time. *Child Development, 44,* 43–46.

Burke, R. V., Kuhn, B. R., & Peterson, J. L. (2004). A "storybook" ending to children's bedtime problems—The use of a rewarding social story to reduce bedtime resistance and frequent night wakings. *Journal of Pediatric Psychology, 29,* 389–396.

Czeisler, C. A., Richardson, G. S., Coleman. R. M., Zimmerman, J. C., Moore-Ede, M. C., Dement, W. C., & Weitzman, E. D. (1981). Chronotherapy: Resetting the circadian clocks of patients with delayed sleep phase insomnia. *Sleep, 4,* 1–21.

Edwards, K. J., & Christophersen, E. R. (1994). Treating common sleep problems of young children. *Journal of Developmental and Behavioral Pediatrics, 15,* 207–213.

Ferber, R. (1985). *Solve your child's sleep problems.* New York: Simon and Schuster.

France, K. G., & Hudson, S. M. (1993). Management of infant sleep disturbance: A review. *Clinical Psychology Review, 13,* 635–647.

Grimwade, J. C., Walker, D. W., & Wood, C. (1993). Sensory stimulation of the human fetus. *Australian Journal of Mental Retardation, 2,* 63–64.

Johnson, C. M. (1991). Infant and toddler sleep: A telephone survey of parents in one community. *Journal of Developmental and Behavioral Pediatrics, 12,* 108–114.

Kazdin, A. E. (1982). *Single-case research designs: Methods for clinical and applied settings.* New York: Oxford University Press.

Kuhn, B. R., & Weidinger, D. (2000). Intervention for infant and toddler sleep: A review. *Child & Family Behavior Therapy, 22,* 33–50.

Lawton, C.. France, K. G., Blampied, N. M. (1991). Treatment of infant sleep disturbance by graduated extinction. *Child & Family Behavior Therapy, 13,* 39–56.

Mindell, J. A. (1999). Empirically supported treatments in pediatric psychology: Bedtime refusal and night wakings in young children. *Journal of Pediatric Psychology, 24,* 465–481.

Mindell. J. A., & Durand, V. M. (1993). Treatment of childhood sleep disorders: Generalization across disorders and effects on family members. *Journal of Pediatric Psychology, 18,* 731–750.

Morrell, J. M. B. (1999). The infant sleep questionnaire: A new tool to assess infant sleep problems for clinical and research purposes. *Child Psychology & Psychiatry Review, 4,* 20–26.

Ramchandani, P., Wiggs, L., Webb, V., & Stores, G. (2000). A systematic review of treatments for settling problems and night waking in young children. *British Medical Journal, 320,* 209–213.

Richman, N. (1985). A double-blind drug trial in young children with waking problems. *Journal of Child Psychology and Psychiatry, 26,* 591–598.

Sadeh, A. (2001). *Sleeping like a baby.* New Haven, CT: Yale University Press.

Spencer, J. A. D., Moran, D. J., Lee, A., & Talbert, D. (1990). White noise and sleep induction. *Archives of Disease in Childhood, 65,* 135–137.

Williamson. J. W. (1992). The effects of ocean sound on sleep after coronary artery bypass graft surgery. *American Journal of Critical Care, 1,* 91–97.

Zimmer, E. Z., Jakobi, P., Talmon, R., Shenhav, R., & Weissman, A. (1993). White noise does not induce fetal sleep. *Fetal Diagnosis and Therapy, 8,* 209–210.

About the authors: *LeAnne M. Forquer*, MS, is a doctoral student in applied experimental psychology at Central Michigan University. *C. Merle Johnson*, PhD, is Professor of Psychology, Central Michigan University.

Address correspondence to: LeAnne M. Forquer, Department of Psychology, Central Michigan University, Mount Pleasant, MI 48859. E-mail: forqu1l@cmich.edu

Exercise for Article 11

Factual Questions

1. White noise is sound that covers what range?

2. Did the children in this study sleep with their parents?

3. Why were the parents called twice each week?

4. What did "fading" involve?

5. Jack had an average of 0.9 night wakings during baseline. This decreased to what average during intervention?

6. The parent of which child had the lowest fidelity of treatment?

Questions for Discussion

7. In lines 129 and 144–145, the researchers mention that written consent was obtained. In your opinion, is it important for researchers to report whether such consent was obtained? Explain.

8. In your opinion, is the Parenting Stress Inventory described in sufficient detail? Explain. (See lines 158–162.)

9. The term "baseline" is used throughout this report (e.g., lines 163–166 and the figures). How would you define this term?

10. In lines 232–234, the results for Kolbey are presented using averages: "Kolbey's night wakings decreased from a mean of 1.4 during baseline to 1.0 during intervention and 0.1 at follow-up." The results for her are also presented in the bottom part of Figure 1. In your opinion, are both types of reports of results of equal value? Are they both informative? Explain.

11. In your opinion, how important is the follow-up data? Would this research report be as informative without follow-up data? Explain.

12. To what extent do you agree with the conclusion the researchers state in lines 311–317? Explain.

Quality Ratings

Directions: Indicate your level of agreement with each of the following statements by circling a number from 5 for strongly agree (SA) to 1 for strongly disagree (SD). If you believe an item is not applicable to this research article, leave it blank. Be prepared to explain your ratings. When responding to criteria A and B below, keep in mind that brief titles and abstracts are conventional in published research.

A. The title of the article is appropriate.

SA   5   4   3   2   1   SD

B. The abstract provides an effective overview of the research article.

SA   5   4   3   2   1   SD

C. The introduction establishes the importance of the study.

SA   5   4   3   2   1   SD

D. The literature review establishes the context for the study.

SA   5   4   3   2   1   SD

E. The research purpose, question, or hypothesis is clearly stated.

SA   5   4   3   2   1   SD

F. The method of sampling is sound.

SA   5   4   3   2   1   SD

G. Relevant demographics (for example, age, gender, and ethnicity) are described.

SA   5   4   3   2   1   SD

H. Measurement procedures are adequate.

SA   5   4   3   2   1   SD

I. All procedures have been described in sufficient detail to permit a replication of the study.

SA   5   4   3   2   1   SD

J. The participants have been adequately protected from potential harm.

SA   5   4   3   2   1   SD

K. The results are clearly described.

SA   5   4   3   2   1   SD

L. The discussion/conclusion is appropriate.

SA   5   4   3   2   1   SD

M. Despite any flaws, the report is worthy of publication.

SA   5   4   3   2   1   SD

Article 12

Multiple Uses of a Word Study Technique

LAURICE M. JOSEPH
The Ohio State University

ANDREW ORLINS
The Ohio State University

ABSTRACT. This paper presents two case studies that illustrate the multiple uses of word sorts, a word study phonics technique. Case study children were Sara, a second grader, who had difficulty with reading basic words, and John, a third grader, who had difficulty with spelling basic words. Multiple baseline designs were employed to study the effects of word sorts across sets of words for helping Sara improve and maintain her word recognition performance and helping John improve and maintain his spelling performance. Findings revealed that word sorts helped Sara and John improve on their basic literacy performance in contrast to their performance during baseline conditions before word sorts were implemented. These case studies illustrate that the use of word sorts serves multiple purposes as it may be implemented to teach reading as well as spelling skills.

From *Reading Improvement*, 42, 73–79. Copyright © 2005 by Project Innovation, Inc.. Reprinted with permission.

Word study techniques have gained much attention by reading educators, and many educators are incorporating them in their literacy programs. Word study techniques have also been coined a contemporary way
5 to teach phonics and considered to be spelling-based phonic techniques (Stahl, Duffy-Hester, & Stahl, 1998). There are various word study techniques, but one that has been described and researched is word sorts (Bear, Invernizzi, Templeton, & Johnston, 1996;
10 Cunningham, 1995). Word sorts are designed to help children examine, discriminate, and categorize words according to spelling and sound patterns (Barnes, 1989). Word sorts have multiple uses. Word sorts can be useful for helping children spell words, helping
15 children recognize words, make word analogies, become aware of the phonemic structure of words, learn about morphemic structures of words, and gain meaning of words (vocabulary) (Bear, Invernizzi, Templeton, & Johnston, 1996).
20 There have been few investigations studying the effectiveness of word sorts. Some of the investigations involved examining the effectiveness of programs that have incorporated word sorts as part of a comprehensive literacy program. For instance, Santa and Hoien
25 (1999) included word sorts within their Early Steps program, and Morris, Shaw and Perney (1990) included word sort activities within their Howard Street

Tutoring program. The findings of these studies supported the usefulness of these programs, but it was dif-
30 ficult to decipher whether word sorts contributed to the effectiveness of these programs in these investigations.

Word sorts have also been investigated in isolation (not embedded within a program). For instance, Dangle (1989) found that word sorts were more effective than
35 traditional spelling instruction for improving spelling performance on spelling tests. Joseph (2000) found that word sorts compared to two other phonic techniques (word boxes and traditional phonics instruction) were especially effective for helping first grade children im-
40 prove their spelling performance. In another study, variation in spelling performance using word sort was evident in a group of children with mental retardation and a group of children without disabilities (Joseph & McCachran, 2003). In most of these studies, word sorts
45 have been used to help children improve on their spelling performance. However, word sorts may also be used to help children read words, although more research is needed to verify this claim.

The purpose of the following two case studies is to
50 illustrate the multiple purposes of a word sorting technique. The first case describes the usefulness of word sorts for helping a student improve her word recognition performance, and the other case study illustrates the use of word sorts to help a student improve his
55 spelling performance.

Word Sorts Help Sara Improve
Word Recognition Performance

Sara, a second grade student, was diagnosed with Attention Deficit Hyperactive Disorder, and was receiving special education services in an urban school district in Central Ohio. She was referred to the school
60 psychologist for demonstrating severe delays in reading. She was assessed with the Wechsler Individual Achievement Test-Second Edition (WIAT-II) and obtained a standard score of 68, which reflected well below average basic reading performance compared to
65 other children her age. According to her second grade teacher, she was able to identify some two and three letter words but had difficulty reading words that contained more than three letters. Sara was clearly in need of intervention to help her recognize words. Therefore,
70 she was administered a 120 word screening measure that contained several four letter words such as conso-

nant-vowel-consonant-vowel, double consonant-vowel-consonant, consonant-double vowel-consonant, and consonant-vowel-double consonant patterned words.
75 The words she read incorrectly or words that were unknown to her were placed on three sets of word lists.

Procedures

A multiple baseline design was employed to determine the effectiveness of a word sort technique across Sara's reading performance on three different sets of
80 words. Each set of words contained a list of 10 words. Probes were administered during baseline sessions. They contained the sets of words printed on index cards. During baseline conditions, probes containing set 1, 2, and 3 words were given to Sara. Set #1 con-
85 sisted of the following words: Mold, bold, told, bank, rank, tank, rent, vent, and dent. Set #2 consisted of the following words: Wave, save, gave, cave, tore, pore, sore, mate, date, and hate. Set #3 consisted of the following words: Wade, made, fade, back, lack, rack,
90 tack, spin, shin, and skin. The words were shuffled and mixed up each time they were presented. On each probe, a word printed on an index card was presented, and Sara was asked to read it orally. Word sort intervention was implemented on the first set of words after
95 two sessions of baseline, leaving the other two sets of words in baseline. In other words, Sara was taught the first set of words using the word sort technique, and sets 2 and 3 were tested through administration of probes during baseline conditions but were not yet
100 taught using the word sorts. Word sort instruction consisted of having Sara sort a set of 10 words printed on index cards into three categories. The categories were determined by the instructor. After the sort was completed, Sara was asked to read the sorted words. She
105 was encouraged to self-correct if she read a word incorrectly or sorted the word in the wrong category. She was also provided with corrective feedback by the instructor if she was unable to make self-corrections.

At the end of each word sort session, Sara was ad-
110 ministered a probe containing the list of words that were sorted. Criterion levels of performance were 90% of the words read correctly on the probes during two consecutive instructional probes. Once Sara reached mastery criterion levels on a set of words, instruction
115 using the word sorts ended for that specific set of words and began on the second set of words and so forth. Thus, word sort instruction was implemented in a staggered-like fashion across the sets of words so that experimental control could be demonstrated. Experi-
120 mental control is demonstrated when performance remains relatively stable and low across baseline conditions and changes across instructional conditions. Probes containing the words mastered were assessed over time once instruction on those words ended to
125 assess maintenance performance on reading words mastered during instructional conditions.

Findings

Figure 1 presents Sara's performance across sets of words during three experimental conditions. Sara reached mastery criterion levels on all sets of words
130 during instructional conditions in contrast to baseline conditions where she demonstrated relatively consistently low performance levels. It was only when the word sorts were implemented that Sara demonstrated mastery levels on word recognition performance on the
135 probes. In fact, she demonstrated an immediate increase from baseline performance to performance during word sort instructional conditions. She was able to maintain recognition on three sets of words once instruction using the word sorts ended. Her maintenance
140 probe performance ranged from 90–100% accuracy.

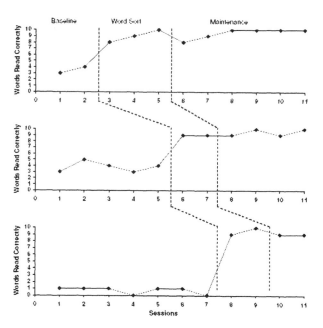

Figure 1. Sara's word recognition performance across experimental conditions.

Word Sorts Help John Improve Spelling Performance

John, a third grader, was referred by his teacher due to exhibiting difficulty with spelling. He was adminis-
145 tered the Diagnostic Achievement Battery-Third Edition. He performed one standard deviation below the mean on a spelling measure indicating well below average spelling performance. To more specifically determine his spelling performance level, a 40 word
150 screener was administered and words spelled incorrectly were recorded and included on three sets of words each containing 10 words.

Procedures

A multiple baseline design across sets of words was employed to examine the effectiveness of a word sort-
155 ing technique to improve John's spelling performance. Baseline conditions across three sets of words con-

sisted of administering 10-item spelling probes. Set #1 consisted of the following words: Carry, marry, pretty, silly, happy, scary, lazy, angry, fancy, and weary. Set #2 consisted of the following words: Coil, foil, boil, soil, broil, foul, loud, shout, route, and cloud. Set #3 consisted of the following words: Burn, turn, blur, fur, church, torn, storm, born, core, and dorm. Each word was orally presented to John, used in a sentence, and then presented orally again. John was given a numbered sheet of paper to write his responses. After baseline levels of performance was established on the first set of words, instruction using the word sorting technique began on the first set of words. The words were printed on index cards. The category words were created by the instructor. John was instructed to sort a set of words that shared similar spelling patterns into two categories. He was encouraged to make self-corrections if he sorted a word in the wrong category. He was provided with corrective feedback by the instructor if he was unable to self correct an error. At the end of each instructional session, John was administered a spelling probe (same as those administered during baseline conditions). Criterion levels of performance on probes were 90% correct on two consecutive probes. Once this level was attained, instruction using the word sorts ended. Maintenance probes containing the spelling words were administered over time to determine if he maintained the words that were taught.

Findings

Figure 2 presents John's performance on spelling probes across baseline, word sort instruction, and maintenance conditions for three sets of words. John made a gradual increase in number of words spelled correctly for set #1 during word sort condition in comparison to his performance during baseline for set #1. It took him six trials to reach criterion levels of performance on spelling set #1 words. In contrast to baseline conditions, he made an immediate increase in words spelled correctly on sets #2 and 3, and he reached criterion levels of performance after approximately three trials during the word sort condition. These findings indicate that it was only when the word sorts were implemented that John's spelling improved and criterion levels were reached across all sets of words. He was able to maintain criterion levels of performance on spelling all three sets of words taught during word sort instruction. He maintained scores ranging from 90% to 100% on spelling probes.

Implications

John and Sara improved their performance on probes across various sets of words using word sorts in contrast to their performance on probes during baseline conditions (before word sorts were implemented). These case studies illustrate that word sorts may be used to teach spelling and word recognition to children who have word recognition and spelling difficulties. Teachers can integrate teaching reading with spelling using word sorts. This may help children make connections between reading and spelling skills more easily. Word sorts, although not illustrated here, may also be used to teach vocabulary skills and morphemic units of words such as prefixes and suffixes. Additionally, word sorts are an inexpensive way to teach multiple literacy skills.

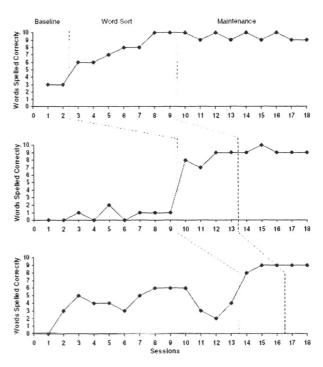

Figure 2. John's spelling performance across experimental conditions.

References

Barnes, G. W. (1989). Word sorting: The cultivation of rules for spelling in English. *Reading Psychology, 10,* 293–307.

Bear, D. R., Invernizzi, M. A., Templeton, S., & Johnston, F. (1996). *Words their way: Word study for phonics, vocabulary, and spelling.* Englewood Cliffs, NJ: Prentice Hall.

Cunningham, P. (1995). *Phonics they use: Words for reading and writing.* New York: Harper Collins.

Dangel, H. L. (1989). The use of student directed spelling strategies. *Academic Therapy, 25,* 43–51.

Joseph, L. M. (2000). Developing first grader's phonemic awareness, word identification, and spelling performance: A comparison of two contemporary phonic approaches. *Reading Research and Instruction 39,* 160–169.

Joseph, L. M., & McCachran, M. (2003). Comparison of a word study phonics technique between students with moderate to mild mental retardation and struggling readers without disabilities. *Education and Training in Mental Retardation and Developmental Disabilities, 38,* 192–199.

Morris, D., Shaw, B., & Perney, J. (1990). Helping low readers in grades 2 and 3: An after-school volunteer tutoring program. *The Elementary School Journal, 91,* 133–150.

Santa, C. M., & Hoien, T. (1999). An assessment of Early Steps: A program for early intervention of reading problems. *Reading Research Quarterly, 34,* 54–79.

Shahl, S. A., Duffy-Hester, A., & Stahl, K. A. (1998). Theory and research into practice: Everything you wanted to know about phonics (but were afraid to ask). *Reading Research Quarterly, 33,* 338–355.

Address correspondence to: Dr. Laurice M. Joseph, Assistant Professor of School Psychology, 356 Arps Hall, 1945 North High Street, Columbus, OH 43210. E-mail: joseph.21@osu.edu

Exercise for Article 12

Factual Questions

1. The word sort intervention for the first set of words for Sara was implemented after how many sessions of baseline?

2. During the word sort intervention, did the instructor provide corrective feedback?

3. For Sara, what was the mastery criterion level for a set of words?

4. When each word was presented to John, was it presented to him in a sentence?

5. For set #1, did John make "dramatic" *or* "gradual" improvement while the word sort technique was being used?

6. Do the researchers indicate that the word sorts are expensive?

Questions for Discussion

7. The word sort instruction consisted of putting the words into three categories determined by an instructor. Would you be interested in knowing what categories were used? Explain. (See lines 100–103.)

8. What is your understanding of the meaning of "baseline" as it is used in this research article? For instance, the word baseline is used in Figures 1 and 2.

9. In your opinion, is having each of the three baselines end at a different point in time a strength of this study? Explain. (Note that Figures 1 and 2 show the lengths of each baseline.)

10. To what extent do Figures 1 and 2 help you understand the design and results of this study? Explain.

11. Overall, are you convinced that the word sort technique was effective for Sara and John? Explain.

12. In your opinion, is the study of value even though only two participants were used? Explain.

Quality Ratings

Directions: Indicate your level of agreement with each of the following statements by circling a number from 5 for strongly agree (SA) to 1 for strongly disagree (SD). If you believe an item is not applicable to this research article, leave it blank. Be prepared to explain your ratings. When responding to criteria A and B below, keep in mind that brief titles and abstracts are conventional in published research.

A. The title of the article is appropriate.
SA   5   4   3   2   1   SD

B. The abstract provides an effective overview of the research article.
SA   5   4   3   2   1   SD

C. The introduction establishes the importance of the study.
SA   5   4   3   2   1   SD

D. The literature review establishes the context for the study.
SA   5   4   3   2   1   SD

E. The research purpose, question, or hypothesis is clearly stated.
SA   5   4   3   2   1   SD

F. The method of sampling is sound.
SA   5   4   3   2   1   SD

G. Relevant demographics (for example, age, gender, and ethnicity) are described.
SA   5   4   3   2   1   SD

H. Measurement procedures are adequate.
SA   5   4   3   2   1   SD

I. All procedures have been described in sufficient detail to permit a replication of the study.
SA   5   4   3   2   1   SD

J. The participants have been adequately protected from potential harm.
SA   5   4   3   2   1   SD

K. The results are clearly described.
SA   5   4   3   2   1   SD

L. The discussion/conclusion is appropriate.
SA   5   4   3   2   1   SD

M. Despite any flaws, the report is worthy of publication.
SA   5   4   3   2   1   SD

Article 13

Use of an Antecedent Procedure to Decrease Night Awakening in an Infant: A Replication

JOSEPH CAUTILLI
St. Joseph's University

SUMMARY. Borkowski, Hunter, and Johnson (2001) found that an antecedent strategy such as white noise could decrease sleep awakenings for infants in the natural home environment. This study attempts to replicate the findings using an ABAB reversal design. A five month and one week old child, who had difficulty with waking an average of four times per night, was placed on a white noise program. This program consisted of the parents placing a FamilyCare air purifier and ionizer next to the infant's crib and turning the machine on just before the infant's parents began to rock the infant and then place the infant in the crib for sleep. This antecedent procedure was successful in reducing the number of infant wakenings to 1.3 episodes/night.

From *Journal of Early and Intensive Behavior Intervention*, 2, 9–13. Copyright © 2005 by Joseph Cautilli. Reprinted with permission.

Introduction

As a greater reliance on functional assessment is occurring in behavior therapy (Sturmey, 1996), behavioral interventionists are placing growing weight on neutralizing routines and antecedent control strategies
5 as alternatives to contingency management strategies. As part of this trend, a greater emphasis is being placed on establishing positive routines (Adams & Rickert, 1989; Milan, Mitchell, Berger, & Pierson, 1981), neutralizing routines at the onset of problems (Cautilli &
10 Dziewolska, 2004), and antecedent control strategies (Rolider & Axelrod, 1999; Cautilli & Tillman, 2004). This research stretches across many areas but one area of particular importance for new parents is that of sleep.
15 Establishing a sleep wake cycle in infants is an important part of parenting (Novak & Pelaez, 2004) and typically one of parents' earliest challenges. Sleep problems for typical children are common (Kuhn & Weidinger, 2000). One of the earliest interventions
20 tried was the use of white noise (Borkowski, Hunter, & Merele, 2001; Schmidt, 1975). The white noise procedure is the simple use of continuous sounds to block out the occurrence of other sounds and to create an "airy" sound effect. (For a complete theoretical analy-
25 sis of white noise, see Borkowski and colleagues, 2001. The procedure builds on a combination of stimulus control in which sleep is seen as a reinforcer and respondent conditioning. Continued sleep is seen as a factor of behavioral momentum).
30 Borkowski and colleagues (2001) explored the use of white noise as an antecedent for sleep time combined with scheduled bedtime routines for five infants, who were four months old. They found the intervention helpful in three infants who were bottle-fed but not
35 helpful for the two infants who were breastfed. This study attempted to replicate their findings in clinical practice with a five month, one week old child.

Method

Participant

The participant was an only child in his family and typically developing. The child was mostly breastfed;
40 however, due to hectic life schedules the parents fed formula at least three times/week. The child was fed between four and six ounces of milk during the last feeding before sleep. The participant was a five month and one week old child with a history of difficulty with
45 waking during the night after his parents placed him in his crib for sleep. The participant was roughly averaging four instances of waking each night. The instances of problems sleeping reached the point of being so severe that the parents brought the participant to the hos-
50 pital emergency room in order to determine if a physical problem was present. After the physician told the parents that waking during the night was common, the physician sent the parents and the participant home. Two days later, the infant's parents sought out the aid
55 of the author by email on the Internet.

Setting

The participant slept in parents' room. The setting was a standard 12x14 room. The room housed one standard crib for the infant and a queen-sized bed.

Apparatus

Initially, the author wanted to use the white noise
60 generator (model #190405, Brookstone); however,

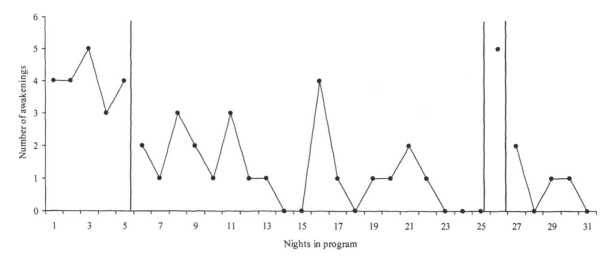

Figure 1. The number of awakenings each night over the course of the study.

parents had difficulty locating the machine. A switch was made to a common air purifier that emitted a similar sound. It was the FamilyCare Air Purifier/Ionizer (model HAP221) turned to the high setting.

Procedure

65   The experimenter employed an ABAB reversal design. The parents kept individual diaries recording the infant's sleep patterns and night awakenings. Baseline data consisted of the sleep diary report from the mother. During the intervention phases, before the par-
70   ent began to rock the participant to sleep, the parents would turn on the air purifier. Once the child was asleep, he was placed in the crib. Usually, this process was completed by 8:30 p.m. The air purifier ran through the night and the parent turned off the ma-
75   chines the next morning. Initially, the experimenter planned the reversal for three nights. The experimenter instructed the parents that the removal was important because it would allow them to see if the intervention was still needed. The parents decided to lessen the re-
80   versal phase to one night after the first night without intervention, which proved difficult. Normal wakeup time for the infant was 6:45 a.m. Waking up between 6:20 a.m. to 6:45 a.m. was not scored as night waking for this study.

Interobserver Agreement

85   Hawkins and Fabry (1979) stressed the importance of ensuring interobserver agreement in data collection. Each parent kept a separate book with the number of times that the infant woke up during the course of the evening. The experimenter calculated the interobserver
90   agreement between the parents' books of infant wakening. The experimenter randomly chose four sessions and compared two baseline phases and two treatment phases. The experimenter scored agreement if both parents stated the same number of wakenings for that
95   night. The experimenter scored disagreement if the two

scored differently. Of the 31 days of the study, the numbers matched on 28 compared, using the equation of agreements/agreements + non-agreements multiplied by 100, to calculate the percent of agreement. Thus,
100   90% coding agreement occurred between the parents.

Results/Discussion

Figure 1 displays the data for nighttime waking. During the baseline phase, the average instance of wakening for the participant was four episodes/night. In the first intervention phase, the average decreased to
105   1.3 episodes/night. The return to baseline phase was one data point. It was initially supposed to be three nights for the parents to decide if the participant still needed the program, but after the first night in which five instances of wakening occurred, the parents de-
110   cided on reinstitution of the program. In the reinstitution of the program, the average for awakening each evening was .8.

This study represents a replication of the work by Borkowski and colleagues (2001). The results suggest
115   that antecedent interventions could have a powerful effect in helping to establish sleep and wake routines in infants. Since DeCasper found that infants prefer mother's voice, mother's voice sounds might represent a good stimulus on a tape recorder to aid in stimulus
120   control. Also, the basis for the preference for maternal and paternal voice appears to be in-utero exposure (DeCasper, Lecanuet, Maugais, Granier-Deferre, & Busnel, 1994; DeCasper & Prescott, 1984; DeCasper, & Spence, 1986). Even more common in-utero is expo-
125   sure to maternal heart sounds. An interesting question that would seem relevant would be whether white noise is more efficient than say the mother's heart sounds. This question might have potential for even earlier levels of sleep scheduling.

References

Adams, L. A., & Rickert, V. I. (1989). Reducing bedtime tantrums: Comparison between positive bedtime routines and graduated extinction. *Pediatrics, 84,* 756–761.

Borkowski, M. M., Hunter, K. E. & Johnson, C. M. (2001). White noise and scheduled bedtime routines to reduce infant and childhood sleep disturbances. *The Behavior Therapist, 24,* 29–31.

Cautilli, J. D. & Dziewolska, H. (2004). The neutralizing effects of stimulus control intervention for sleep on escape behavior and token performance of a nine-year-old child with Oppositional Defiant Disorder. *Journal of Early and Intensive Behavioral Intervention, 1* (2).

Cautilli, J., & Tillman, T. C. (2004). Evidence based practice in the home and school to help educate the socially maladjusted child. *Journal of Early and Intensive Behavioral Intervention 1,* 28–34.

Dahl, R. E., Pelham, W. E., & Wierson, M. (1991). The role of sleep disturbances in attention deficit disorder symptoms: a case study. *Journal of Pediatric Psychology, 16,* 229–239.

DeCasper, A. J., Lecanuet, J. P., Maugais, R., Granier-Deferre, C., & Busnel, M. C. (1994). Fetal reactions to recurrent maternal speech. *Infant Behavior and Development, 17,* 159–164.

DeCasper, A. J., & Prescott, P. (1984). Human newborns' perception of male voices: Preference, discrimination, and reinforcing value. *Developmental Psychobiology, 17,* 481–491.

DeCasper, A. J., & Spence, M. J. (1986). Prenatal maternal speech influences newborns' perception of speech sounds. *Infant Behavior and Development, 9,* 133–150.

Hawkins, R. P., & Fabry, B. D. (1979). Applied behavior analysis and interobserver reliability: A commentary on two articles by Birkimer and Brown. *Journal of Applied Behavior Analysis, 12,* 545–552.

Kuhn, B. R., & Weidinger, D. (2000). Interventions for infant and toddler sleep disturbance: A review. *Child and Family Behavior Therapy, 22,* 33–50.

Milan, M. A., Mitchell, Z. P., Berger, M.I., & Pierson, D.F. (1981). Positive routines: A rapid alternative to extinction for elimination of bedtime tantrum behavior. *Child Behavior Therapy, 3,* 13–25.

Novak, G., & Pelaez, M. (2004). *Child and adolescent development: A behavioral systems approach.* Sage Publications: Thousand Oaks.

Rolider, A., & Axelrod, S. (2001). *How to teach self-control through trigger analysis.* Austin, Texas: Pro-Ed.

Schmidt, K. (1975). The effects of continuous stimulation on the behavioral sleep of infants. *Merrill-Palmer Quarterly, 21,* 77–88.

Sturmey, P. (1996). *Functional analysis in clinical psychology.* New York: Wiley.

Address correspondence to: Joe Cautilli, Children Crisis Treatment Center, 1823 Callowhill, Philadelphia, PA 19130. E-mail: jcautilli@cctckids.com.

Exercise for Article 13

Factual Questions

1. Did the child sleep in the parents' room?

2. Expressed as a percentage, what was the rate of agreement between the two parents?

3. During the baseline, what was the average number of wakening episodes per night?

4. In the first intervention phase, what was the average number of wakening episodes per night?

5. The researcher planned a reversal for three nights. Who decided to make it only one night?

Questions for Discussion

6. In lines 59–64, the researcher gives the brand names and model numbers of the equipment to produce white noise. In your opinion, how important is it to be this specific in the description of the equipment for a study of this type? Explain.

7. In lines 65–66, the researcher states that he employed an "ABAB reversal design." What do you think this term means?

8. The researcher uses the term "baseline" in lines 67, 92, 102, and 105. What do you think the term "baseline" means?

9. In your opinion, is the information on interobserver agreement an important part of this research report? (See lines 85–100.)

10. In lines 101–112, the results are reported in terms of averages. The results are also illustrated in Figure 1. Are both types of reports of the results important? Is one more informative than the other? Explain.

11. In lines 114–117, the researcher suggests that interventions such as the one in this study "could have a powerful effect." Do the data in this study convince you that this is true? Explain.

12. How much credence are you willing to give this study in light of the fact that the sleep behavior of only one child was studied? Would you recommend additional studies on this topic with additional children? Explain.

Quality Ratings

Directions: Indicate your level of agreement with each of the following statements by circling a number from 5 for strongly agree (SA) to 1 for strongly disagree (SD). If you believe an item is not applicable to this research article, leave it blank. Be prepared to explain your ratings. When responding to criteria A and B below, keep in mind that brief titles and abstracts are conventional in published research.

A. The title of the article is appropriate.

   SA   5   4   3   2   1   SD

B. The abstract provides an effective overview of the research article.

   SA   5   4   3   2   1   SD

C. The introduction establishes the importance of the study.

SA   5   4   3   2   1   SD

D. The literature review establishes the context for the study.

SA   5   4   3   2   1   SD

E. The research purpose, question, or hypothesis is clearly stated.

SA   5   4   3   2   1   SD

F. The method of sampling is sound.

SA   5   4   3   2   1   SD

G. Relevant demographics (for example, age, gender, and ethnicity) are described.

SA   5   4   3   2   1   SD

H. Measurement procedures are adequate.

SA   5   4   3   2   1   SD

I. All procedures have been described in sufficient detail to permit a replication of the study.

SA   5   4   3   2   1   SD

J. The participants have been adequately protected from potential harm.

SA   5   4   3   2   1   SD

K. The results are clearly described.

SA   5   4   3   2   1   SD

L. The discussion/conclusion is appropriate.

SA   5   4   3   2   1   SD

M. Despite any flaws, the report is worthy of publication.

SA   5   4   3   2   1   SD

Article 14

Brief Functional Analysis and Intervention Evaluation for Treatment of Saliva-Play

JAMES K. LUISELLI
The May Institute

SARAH SCHMIDT
Health South

JOSEPH N. RICCIARDI
Hampstead Hospital

MELISSA TARR
Woburn Public Schools

ABSTRACT. We conducted a brief (8 days) functional analysis to identify sources of control over persistent saliva-play displayed by a 6-year-old child with autism in a school setting. The functional analysis suggested that saliva-play was maintained by automatic reinforcement, leading to an intervention evaluation (3 days) that compared two methods of providing alternative sensory consequences. Saliva-play was eliminated when the child had access to an acceptable form of oral stimulation, mouthing a chew object, but was unaffected when he chewed gum. We discussed the merits of brief functional analysis and intervention evaluation in applied settings, and clinical issues influencing the treatment of stereotypic behaviors that are automatically reinforced.

From *Child & Family Behavior Therapy*, 26, 53–61. Copyright © 2004 by The Haworth Press, Inc. Reprinted with permission.

Some children who have a developmental disability exhibit maladaptive oral behaviors such as spitting (Luiselli, 1988; St. Lawrence & Drabman, 1984) or drooling (Drabman, Cordua, Ross, & Lynd, 1979; 5 Reddihough & Johnson, 1999). The presence of saliva on the body, clothing, and physical surroundings is unappealing, may have a foul odor, and interferes with instruction. Furthermore, there could be a potential health risk because certain viruses and bacterial dis-10 eases can be transmitted through saliva (Blackman, 1983; Boniuk, 1972).

Putting hands in mouth is a behavior that also produces contact with saliva. Miltenberger and associates (Ellingson, Miltenberger, Strickler et al., 2000; Rapp, 15 Miltenberger, Galensky, Roberts, & Ellingson, 1999) demonstrated the benefit of brief functional analysis in formulating interventions for oral-digital behaviors (finger and thumb sucking) in children with or without disabilities. The functional analyses confirmed that the 20 behaviors were maintained by automatic reinforcement, and the resulting interventions had the objective of interfering with or attenuating the response produced, pleasurable sensory consequences. Our concern in this single-case study was to test the utility of a brief 25 functional analysis in identifying the maintaining con-

sequences for persistent saliva-play by a child with autism. A second objective was to perform a rapid evaluation of intervention methods suggested by the functional analysis.

Method

Participant

30 Matt was a 6-year-old boy diagnosed with autistic disorder. His expressive language consisted of 4–6 word phrases and sentences, while receptively able to carry out simple (1–2-step) instructions. Matt enjoyed playing with a variety of toys and materials such as 35 clay, building blocks, beads, and interlocking objects. With partial physical assistance from an adult, he could complete basic self-care routines, but he was not fully toilet-trained. The focus of his classroom instruction was teaching him preacademic, communication, and 40 daily living skills.

Setting

Matt attended a private school for children with developmental disabilities. His classroom included 6 other students, a primary teacher, and 2 assistants. Classroom activities were scheduled 6 hours each 45 weekday. Both the functional analysis (Phase I) and intervention evaluation (Phase II) were conducted in a designated location in the classroom. During sessions, Matt sat at a table beside a therapist who implemented procedures. Other students were present in the class-50 room but they were not in proximity to Matt and did not interact with him.

Measurement

Matt engaged in saliva-play by placing hands in his mouth, and manipulating the saliva with his fingers, sometimes accompanied by drooling saliva on his chin, 55 which he immediately re-ingested. For the purpose of data collection, saliva-play was defined as anytime Matt's hand crossed the plane of his lips, or if he expectorated saliva onto his chin and "sucked" it back into his mouth. Using a frequency count measure, an 60 observer recorded each occurrence of saliva-play during a 10-minute session.

Interobserver Agreement

To assess interobserver agreement (IOA), a second individual recorded data simultaneously with the primary observer during 100% of sessions in Phase I and Phase II. IOA was calculated by dividing the smaller recorded frequency by the larger recorded frequency and multiplying by 100. Average IOA was 95%.

Phase I

This was a brief functional analysis following the experimental analog methodology reported by Iwata et al. (1982). During each 10-minute session, the therapist interacted with Matt according to the conditions described below. Four sessions were scheduled per condition over an 8-day period.

Attention. The therapist sat beside Matt at the table but did not interact with him. When saliva-play occurred, the therapist responded with the verbal directive, "No, don't put hands in your mouth/spit."

Demand. Using learning tasks selected from Matt's individualized educational program, the therapist provided instruction during the session. Prompts by the therapist were delivered according to a verbal-partial physical assistance-full physical assistance hierarchy. If Matt engaged in saliva-play, the therapist removed materials and ceased instruction for 30-s.

Play. Matt sat at the table beside the therapist and had access to several toys. The therapist presented noncontingent attention to him (e.g., "I like your shirt.") for approximately 1–2 s. on a fixed-interval 30-s. schedule. There was no consequence for saliva-play.

Ignore. This condition was identical to the attention condition but when saliva-play occurred, the therapist did not respond to Matt.

Results

Figure 1 shows the frequency of saliva-play during the 4 functional analysis conditions. These data indicate undifferentiated responding, with saliva-play displayed at high frequency in all sessions. Of note was the accelerating response trend within the demand condition. Otherwise, frequencies were stable during the attention ($M = 24.5$), ignore ($M = 42.7$), and play ($M = 43.2$) conditions.

Discussion

The results of Phase I suggest that Matt's saliva-play was automatically reinforced. However, the response trend within the demand condition also implicated an escape-motivated function, indicating that saliva-play possibly had multiple sources of control (Kodak, Miltenberger, & Romaniuk, 2003). In this situation, saliva-play may have been negatively reinforced by the behavior contingent withdrawal of instructional demands. Given the preceding formulation, the objective of intervention was to provide Matt with alternative oral stimulation that conceivably would compete with the pleasurable sensation of saliva-play and additionally attenuate escape-motivated responding.

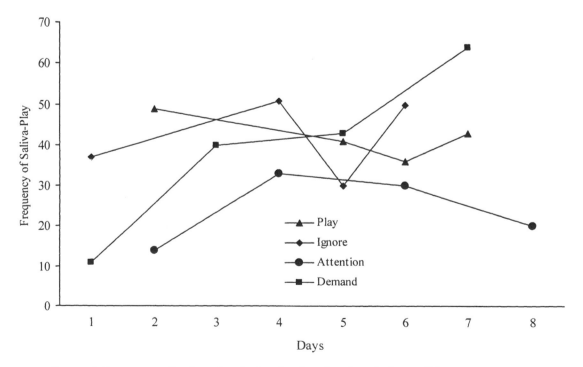

Figure 1. Frequency of saliva-play during the functional analysis conditions.

Phase II

115   In an alternating treatments design (Barlow & Hayes, 1979), Matt participated in 3, 10-minute sessions each day over a 3-day period. The 3 daily sessions included 2 intervention procedures and a control condition. Sessions were scheduled in random order

120   each day, with an intersession interval of approximately 30 minutes.

During all sessions, the ignore condition described in Phase I was in effect: Matt sat at the table, was not required to participate in an activity, and did not inter-

125   act with the therapist. There was no consequence for saliva-play.

Control. Matt was observed during the session without intervention.

Gum. Immediately preceding the session, the thera-

130   pist presented Matt with one stick of chewing gum. Gum was considered a preferred stimulus for Matt, and he always accepted it when presented. When the session concluded, the therapist had him remove the gum from his mouth and discard it.

135   *Chew Object.* Immediately preceding the session, the therapist gave Matt a chew object, which he could put in his mouth, and have access to for the duration of the session. The chew object was a commercially available therapeutic device (*Pocket Full of Ther-*

140   *apy®*), used frequently by occupational therapists with children and adults to induce additional proprioceptive stimulation to the jaw and associated oral musculature. The "T shaped" object had a non-flavored and non-toxic surface, with a 3-inch stem that could be mouthed

145   or chewed safely. There was an accompanying neck-

lace that enabled Matt to remove the chew object from his mouth without dropping or losing it during sessions.

Results

Figure 2 shows the frequency of saliva-play per session recorded during the 3 intervention evaluation

150   conditions. Saliva-play occurred most frequently when Matt chewed gum *(M* = 45.3). During the control condition, average frequency was 31.7 per session. Matt did not exhibit saliva-play in any of the sessions where the chew object was available.

Discussion

155   Giving Matt noncontingent access to an alternative form of oral stimulation eliminated his saliva-play. However, the positive intervention effect occurred only with the chew object and not when he chewed gum. One explanation for these findings is that when Matt

160   contacted the chew object, it prevented putting fingers into mouth, or possibly it made expectorating saliva more difficult. We observed that he often maintained the chew object in his mouth (30–60-s. at a time), but also removed it frequently during sessions. Chewing

165   gum appeared to be less incompatible with putting fingers into mouth, and also may have had a provocative effect because Matt took it out and returned it to his mouth during many incidents of saliva-play. Unfortunately, we did not record how long (percent of session

170   duration) Matt kept gum and the chew object in his mouth. Therefore, although Phase II of the study documented an intervention that eliminated saliva-play, it is unclear what caused this effect.

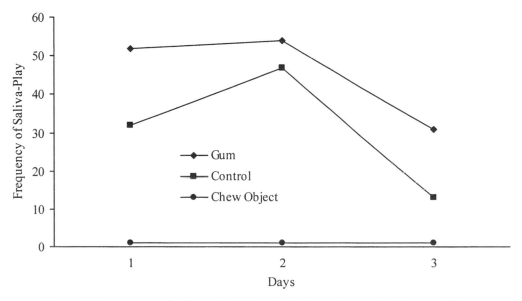

Figure 2. Frequency of saliva-play during the intervention evaluation conditions.

General Discussion

175   This study illustrates use of brief functional analysis to guide intervention formulation and implementation with a child displaying high frequency oral-digital stereotype in the form of saliva-play. The evaluation methodology was selected largely because Matt was enrolled in a school setting, necessitating procedures 180 that could be adopted easily by direct-care practitioners. Both Phase I (8 days) and Phase II (3 days) components of the study were accomplished with brevity, integrated within Matt's typical school day, and were well received by staff responsible for his education. An 185 important result was the ability to identify a functionally determined intervention that was effective with a chronic and previously treatment-resistant challenging behavior.

    One criticism of the study is that the intervention 190 evaluation phase lasted only 3 days. Additional sessions may have been warranted, particularly given the decreasing trend in saliva-play recorded on the final day of the gum and control conditions. However, because the purpose of an alternating treatments design is 195 to compare the differential effectiveness of two or more interventions, the issue of trend variability may be less of a concern when interpreting clinical significance (Barlow & Hersen, 1994). Another limitation is that the study did not assess whether the chew object 200 intervention reduced saliva-play outside of the controlled evaluation sessions. After the study, Matt's teacher and ancillary staff were advised to use the procedure during instructional activities and they reported good success when implemented accordingly. Note 205 also that we did not record data to judge if the elimination of saliva-play was dependent on continuous availability of the chew object, or whether positive effects could have been supported while gradually reducing (fading) the time Matt had access to it. Ellingson et al. 210 (2000), for example, found that having a typically developing child wear an athletic glove eliminated automatically reinforced finger sucking and that with systematic fading (removing small portions from the fingertips of the glove), he did not suck his fingers once 215 the glove had been removed. Consideration of fading and possibly withdrawing stimuli such as gloves, protective equipment, and the object evaluated in this study is important because they have a conspicuous appearance, and some people may view them as stig-220 matizing.

    Future studies should continue to explore the utility of functional analysis methodology for stereotypic behaviors. Where stereotypy is automatically reinforced (Kennedy, 1994), intervention research likely will ad-225 dress manipulation of behavior elicited sensory consequences through procedures such as sensory extinction, response competition, or reinforcer substitutability. As demonstrated in this study, brief functional analysis can identify interventions that can be evaluated rapidly 230 and produce desirable behavior change.

References

Barlow, D. H., & Hayes, S. C. (1979). Alternating treatments design: One strategy for comparing the effects of two treatments in a single subject. *Journal of Applied Behavior Analysis, 12,* 199–210.

Barlow, D. H., & Hersen, M. (1984). Single case experimental designs: Strategies for studying behavior change. Elmsford, NY: Pergamon Press.

Blackman, J. A. (1983). *Medical aspects of developmental disabilities in children birth to three.* Iowa City, IA: University of Iowa.

Boniuk, M. (1972). *Rubella and other intraocular viral diseases in infancy.* Boston, MA: Little, Brown, and Company.

Drabman, R. S., Cordua, G., Ross, J., & Lynd, S. (1979). Suppression of chronic drooling in mentally retarded children and adolescents: Effectiveness of a behavioral treatment package. *Behavior Therapy, 10,* 46–56.

Ellingson, S. A., Miltenberger, R. G., Stricker, J. M., Garlinghouse. M. A., Roberts, J., & Galensky, T. L. (2000). Analysis and treatment of finger sucking. *Journal of Applied Behavior Analysis, 33,* 41–52.

Iwata, B. A., Dorsey, M. F., Slifer, K. J., Bauman, K. E., & Richman, G. S. (1982). Toward a functional analysis of self-injury. *Analysis and Intervention in Developmental Disabilities, 2,* 3–20.

Kennedy, C. H. (1994). Automatic reinforcement: Oxymoron or hypothetical construct? *Journal of Behavioral Education, 4,* 387–396.

Kodak, T., Miltenberger, R. G., & Romaniuk, C. (2003). A comparison of differential reinforcement and noncontingent reinforcement for the treatment of a child's multiply controlled problem behavior. *Behavioral Interventions, 18,* 267–278.

Luiselli, J. K. (1988). Multicomponent behavioral treatment of high-rate spitting and object-mouthing in a child with cytomegalovirus. *Journal of the Multihandicapped Person, 1,* 175–182.

Rapp, J. T., Miltenberger, R. G., Galensky, T., Roberts, J., & Ellingson, S. A. (1999). Brief functional analysis and simplified habit reversal treatment of thumb sucking in fraternal twin brothers. *Child & Family Behavior Therapy, 21,* 1–17.

Reddihough, D. S., & Johnson, H. (1999). Assessment and management of saliva control problems in children and adults with neurological impairment. *Journal of Physical and Developmental Disabilities, 11,* 17–24.

St. Lawrence, J. S., & Drabman, R. S. (1984). Suppression of chronic high frequency spitting in a multiply handicapped and mentally retarded adolescent. *Child & Family Behavior Therapy, 6,* 45–55.

About the authors: *James K. Luiselli*, EdD, ABPP, BCBA, is Senior Vice President-Applied Research, Clinical Training, and Peer Review affiliated with The May Institute, One Commerce Way, Norwood, MA 02062. *Joseph N. Ricciardi*, PsyD, ABPP, is affiliated with Developmental Disabilities Unit, Hampstead Hospital, 218 East Road, Hampstead, NH 03841-2305. *Sarah Schmidt*, PsyD, ABPP, is affiliated with Health South. *Melissa Tarr*, PsyD, ABPP, is affiliated with the Woburn Public Schools.

Address correspondence to: James K. Luiselli, May Center for Early Childhood Education, 10 Action Street, Arlington, MA 02476-6013. E-mail: jluiselli@mayinstitute.org

Exercise for Article 14

Factual Questions

1. Where were Phase I and Phase II of this study conducted?

2. How was "saliva-play" defined?

3. Each session lasted how many minutes?

4. In Phase I, which condition resulted in increased frequency of saliva-play across time?

5. In Phase II, what was the mean frequency of saliva-play under the chewing gum condition?

6. In Phase II, did Matt exhibit any saliva-play in the sessions where the chew object was available?

Questions for Discussion

7. How important is the information on interobserver agreement? By how much does it increase your confidence in the results of this study? (See lines 62–67.)

8. The researchers state that in Phase II an "alternating treatments design" was used. How would you define this type of design? (See lines 115–121.)

9. Phase II lasted only three days. In your opinion, was this long enough? Explain. (See lines 189–198.)

10. Would it have been desirable for the researchers to study formally the effects of the chew object outside the controlled experimental setting (e.g., in the normal classroom setting)? Explain. (See lines 198–204.)

11. Would you recommend a future study in which "fading" was studied? Why? Why not? (See lines 204–220.)

12. In your opinion, does this study make a valuable contribution to understanding the variables that were studied even though only one research participant was used? Explain.

Quality Ratings

Directions: Indicate your level of agreement with each of the following statements by circling a number from 5 for strongly agree (SA) to 1 for strongly disagree (SD). If you believe an item is not applicable to this research article, leave it blank. Be prepared to explain your ratings. When responding to criteria A and B below, keep in mind that brief titles and abstracts are conventional in published research.

A. The title of the article is appropriate.

    SA   5   4   3   2   1   SD

B. The abstract provides an effective overview of the research article.

    SA   5   4   3   2   1   SD

C. The introduction establishes the importance of the study.

    SA   5   4   3   2   1   SD

D. The literature review establishes the context for the study.

    SA   5   4   3   2   1   SD

E. The research purpose, question, or hypothesis is clearly stated.

    SA   5   4   3   2   1   SD

F. The method of sampling is sound.

    SA   5   4   3   2   1   SD

G. Relevant demographics (for example, age, gender, and ethnicity) are described.

    SA   5   4   3   2   1   SD

H. Measurement procedures are adequate.

    SA   5   4   3   2   1   SD

I. All procedures have been described in sufficient detail to permit a replication of the study.

    SA   5   4   3   2   1   SD

J. The participants have been adequately protected from potential harm.

    SA   5   4   3   2   1   SD

K. The results are clearly described.

    SA   5   4   3   2   1   SD

L. The discussion/conclusion is appropriate.

    SA   5   4   3   2   1   SD

M. Despite any flaws, the report is worthy of publication.

    SA   5   4   3   2   1   SD

Article 15

Sex Differences on a Measure of Conformity in Automated Teller Machine Lines

STEPHEN REYSEN
California State University Fresno

MATTHEW B. REYSEN
Purdue University

ABSTRACT. Sex differences in conformity were examined as participants approached two ATMs, one of which was occupied by three confederates and the other immediately available. The number of men and women in the line in front of one of the ATMs was manipulated (3 men or 3 women), and an unobtrusive observer recorded the sex of each participant. The results indicated that women were more likely than men to wait in line to use the ATM regardless of the makeup of the line. Thus, the present study provides evidence in favor of the idea that sex differences in conformity are evident on a common task performed in a natural setting.

From *Psychological Reports, 95,* 443–446. Copyright © 2004 by Psychological Reports. Reprinted with permission.

In a highly influential series of experiments conducted in the 1950s, Solomon Asch (1952, 1955, 1956) examined conformity pressure in a group situation. Asch's classic conformity studies involved individuals
5 making line-length judgments in the presence of others also making judgments about the same stimuli. Asch found that participants often agreed with incorrect confederate responses even though, presumably, they could easily discern which of three presented lines
10 matched a target line. Based on Asch's results, it is clear that the behavior of others can influence an individual's own behavior.

Since Asch's experiments (1952, 1955, 1956), a great many studies have examined conformity in be-
15 havior (see McIlveen & Gross, 1999; Wren, 1999, for reviews). One important area of this research concerns whether women are more likely to conform than men. Sistrunk and McDavid (1971) reported that women conform more often than men on judgment tasks com-
20 pleted in the laboratory. They determined that the nature of the task plays a large role in contributing to sex differences in conformity and that a cultural role explanation is inadequate to explain the effect. A number of other studies have also demonstrated that women
25 tend to conform more than men in laboratory situations (e.g., Krech, Crutchfield, & Ballachey, 1962; Aronson, 1972; Worchel & Cooper, 1976).

Based on the results of a meta-analysis, Eagly (1978) concluded that women may be conditioned to
30 yield to men under certain circumstances. Eagly suggested that this tendency was the primary explanation for why women tend to conform more often than men. The current study was designed to analyze sex differences in conformity on a common task in a real world
35 setting. Examining a situation in which participants complete a common task in their natural environment provides a much-needed test of the external validity of more artificial laboratory paradigms. A sex-neutral task was chosen in which men and women are likely to be
40 equally competent.

In the present experiment, a line of two confederates was created behind another confederate using one of two adjacent ATMs. The three confederates were either all men or all women. The primary purpose of
45 the study was to assess whether women would conform to the group more often than men. Conformity was operationally defined by number of times a participant stood in line behind the confederates for at least 5 sec. instead of using the vacant ATM. A participant who
50 waited in line was assumed to accept implicitly the confederates' judgment that the available ATM was nonfunctional.

Method

Participants

Two hundred ATM users were observed at an outdoor shopping area in a small coastal town in Califor-
55 nia. This sample included 106 men and 94 women.

Design and Procedure

The purpose of the present experiment was to observe individuals' behavior while they used a public automated teller machine. To accomplish this, we located two ATMs at a local shopping area that met sev-
60 eral specifications. The ATMs were less than 1 ft. apart and were not separated by a divider. There were no overt signs that either of the machines was nonfunctional. In fact, both of the machines were in perfect working order. The procedure used was straightfor-
65 ward. Two confederates stood behind another confederate using one of the two ATMs. On half of the trials, the left ATM was used and on the other half of the trials the right ATM was used. Thus, on every trial, the participant approached two ATMs, one vacant and the

70 other in use with two people waiting in line. In half of the trials, two men stood in line behind a man, while in the other half of the trials two women stood in line behind a woman.

A trial began when an individual approached the
75 two ATMs. To constitute a usable trial, the person had to be alone and easily identifiable as being in line. An observer, sitting unobtrusively at a nearby table, recorded the sex of the participant and whether the participant stood in line or used the vacant ATM. "Wait-
80 ing in line" was operationally defined as standing in line behind the confederates for a period of at least 5 sec. Two hundred trials were recorded on weekday afternoons over the course of two weeks. Approximately 25 trials were recorded each day that observa-
85 tions were made.

Results and Discussion

The primary purpose of the present experiment was to examine whether men and women showed differential conformity on this common task. Our hypothesis, based on previous laboratory observations, was that
90 women would tend to conform more often than men. The data appear to support our hypothesis. The 89 women did, in fact, tend to wait in line more often than the 78 men (74%) for a period of at least 5 sec. This difference in distribution gave a statistically significant
95 chi-square (χ_1^2 ($N = 200$) = 16.09, $p < .001$).

Interestingly, the sex makeup of the line seemed to play little role in influencing the participants' behavior. Women tended to wait in line more often than men regardless of the sex of the confederates. With two
100 male confederates in line, 43 (91%) of the women waited in line, while only 35 (66%) of the men did so. This difference was statistically significant (χ_1^2 ($N = 100$) = 9.40, $p < .01$). In addition, when female confederates were in line, 46 (98%) of the women stood in
105 line, while only 43 (81%) of the men waited in line. This difference was also statistically significant (χ_1^2 ($N = 100$) = 7.13, $p < .01$). Thus, even when the sex composition of the line was manipulated, women were still more likely than men to wait in line.

110 The sex-role socialization explanation has been proposed to account for sex differences in conformity (Crutchfield, 1955; Tuddenham, 1958; Eagly, 1978). This account suggests that sex differences in conformity are a result of socialization. According to this
115 idea, women adopt a sex role that includes traits such as submissiveness and a tendency to rely on others. This idea could potentially explain why the women in our study may have been reluctant to challenge the judgment of others and instead chose to wait in line
120 rather than trying the vacant ATM. Whereas the present results seem to support the sex-role socialization theory, they are not consistent with several other prominent explanations for sex differences in conformity, namely, the information-deficit explanation (see
125 Allen, 1965; Endler, Wiesenthal, Coward, Edwards, & Geller, 1975), the verbal processing account (Eagly & Warren, 1976), and status allocation differences (Eagly, Wood, & Fishbaugh, 1981; Santee & Maslach, 1982; Eagly, 1987).

130 One limitation that must be considered with respect to the present results is the location in which the trials took place. The experiment was conducted in a small coastal town in California. It is unclear whether the results would remain consistent in a different setting. In
135 fact, this realization suggests other possible questions. For example, it would be interesting to evaluate whether manipulating the race, age, or status of the confederates would affect the outcome. It would also be informative to include a condition in which a line of
140 persons of mixed sex was used. In sum, the present data suggest that women conform more often than men when conducting a common task in a real world setting. This observation suggests that results obtained in laboratory paradigms using similar methods may not be
145 limited with respect to external validity.

References

Allen, V L. (1965). Situational factors in conformity. In L. Berkowitz (Ed.), *Advances in experimental social psychology*. Vol. 2. (pp. 133–176). New York: Academic Press.

Aronson, E. (1972). *The social animal*. (2nd ed.) Oxford, UK: Freeman.

Asch, S. E. (1952). *Social psychology*. Englewood Cliffs, NJ: Prentice-Hall.

Asch, S. E. (1955). Opinions and social pressure. *Scientific American, 193*, 31–35.

Asch, S. E. (1956). Studies of independence and conformity: a minority of one against a unanimous majority. *Psychological Monographs, 70*, Whole No. 416.

Crutchfield, R. S. (1955). Conformity and character. *American Psychologist, 10*, 191–198.

Eagly, A. H. (1978). Sex differences in influenceability. *Psychological Bulletin, 85*, 86–116.

Eagly, A. H. (1987). *Sex differences in social behavior: a social-role interpretation*. Hillsdale, NJ: Erlbaum.

Eagly, A. H., & Warren, R. (1976). Intelligence, comprehension, and opinion change. *Journal of Personality, 44*, 226–242.

Eagly, A. H., Wood, W, & Fishbaugh, L. (1981). Sex differences in conformity: surveillance by the group as a determinant of male nonconformity. *Journal of Personality and Social Psychology, 40*, 384–394.

Endler, N. S., Wiesenthal, D. L., Coward, T., Edwards, J., & Geller, S. H. (1975). Generalization of relative competence mediating conformity across differing tasks. *European Journal of Social Psychology, 5*, 281–287.

Krech, D., Crutchfield, R. S., & Ballachey, E. L. (1962). Individual in society: a textbook of social psychology. New York: McGraw-Hill.

McIlveen, R., & Gross, R. (1999). *Social influence*. London: Hodder & Stoughton.

Santee, R. T., & Maslach, C. (1982). To agree or not to agree: personal dissent amid social pressure to conform. *Journal of Personality and Social Psychology, 42*, 690–700.

Sistrunk, F., & McDavid, J. (1971). Sex variable in conforming behavior. *Journal of Personality and Social Psychology, 17*, 200–207.

Tuddenham, R. D. (1958). The influences of a distorted group norm upon individual judgment. *Journal of Psychology, 46*, 227–241.

Worschel, S., & Cooper, J. (1976). *Understanding social psychology*. Oxford, UK: Dorsey.

Wren, K. (1999). *Social influences*. Florence, KY: Taylor & Francis/Routledge.

Acknowledgments: Thanks to Faye Crosby, Robert Levine, and Ellen Ganz for their helpful comments on previous versions of this article.

Address correspondence to: Stephen Reysen, Department of Psychology, California State University Fresno, Fresno, CA 93740-8019. E-mail: sreysen@jasnh.com

Matthew Reysen is now at University of Mississippi.

Exercise for Article 15

Factual Questions

1. How did the researchers operationally define "conformity"?

2. In half the trials, two men stood behind another man. Who stood in line in the other half?

3. With two male confederates in line, what percentage of the women waited in line? What percentage of the men did so?

4. Was the difference between the men and women in Question 3 above statistically significant? If yes, at what probability level?

5. When two female confederates were in line, what percentage of the men waited in line?

6. What is the limitation of the study that the researchers briefly discuss?

Questions for Discussion

7. This research report begins with a literature review with references to studies conducted in the 1950s. In your opinion, is it appropriate to cite older literature? Explain.

8. The researchers suggest that studying the variables of interest in their "natural environment" is needed. In your opinion, is this important? Explain. (See lines 35–38.)

9. Because the study was conducted in a natural environment, the researchers could not assign the individuals who approached the ATMs at random to the experimental conditions. In your opinion, is this an important issue? Explain.

10. In your opinion, is it important that the observer was unobtrusive? Explain. (See lines 76–79.)

11. Has this study convinced you that there are gender differences in conformity? Explain.

12. Do you agree with the researchers that it would be interesting to evaluate whether manipulating the race, age, or status of the confederates would affect the outcome? Explain. (See lines 136–138.)

Quality Ratings

Directions: Indicate your level of agreement with each of the following statements by circling a number from 5 for strongly agree (SA) to 1 for strongly disagree (SD). If you believe an item is not applicable to this research article, leave it blank. Be prepared to explain your ratings. When responding to criteria A and B below, keep in mind that brief titles and abstracts are conventional in published research.

A. The title of the article is appropriate.

SA   5   4   3   2   1   SD

B. The abstract provides an effective overview of the research article.

SA   5   4   3   2   1   SD

C. The introduction establishes the importance of the study.

SA   5   4   3   2   1   SD

D. The literature review establishes the context for the study.

SA   5   4   3   2   1   SD

E. The research purpose, question, or hypothesis is clearly stated.

SA   5   4   3   2   1   SD

F. The method of sampling is sound.

SA   5   4   3   2   1   SD

G. Relevant demographics (for example, age, gender, and ethnicity) are described.

SA   5   4   3   2   1   SD

H. Measurement procedures are adequate.

SA   5   4   3   2   1   SD

I. All procedures have been described in sufficient detail to permit a replication of the study.

SA   5   4   3   2   1   SD

J. The participants have been adequately protected from potential harm.

SA   5   4   3   2   1   SD

K. The results are clearly described.

SA   5   4   3   2   1   SD

L. The discussion/conclusion is appropriate.

SA   5   4   3   2   1   SD

M. Despite any flaws, the report is worthy of publication.

SA   5   4   3   2   1   SD

Article 16

Effects of Participants' Sex and Targets' Perceived Need on Supermarket Helping Behavior

PAMELA C. REGAN
California State University Los Angeles

DELIA M. GUTIERREZ
California State University Los Angeles

ABSTRACT. A field experiment was focused on whether participants' sex and targets' perceived need influenced helping behavior. Confederates approached 332 (166 women, 166 men) same-sex participants in a supermarket and asked for 25 cents to help purchase one of three randomly assigned food items: milk, which was defined as a high-need item; frozen cookie dough, which served as a low-need item; or alcohol, which was a low-need item with negative social connotations. The dependent variable was whether a participant provided help. Participants' sex was not associated with helping behavior as equal proportions of men and women provided assistance to the confederate; however, perceived need strongly influenced whether the confederate received help. Specifically, the high-need item produced more helping behavior than did either of the low-need items, and the socially acceptable low-need item of cookie dough produced more helping behavior than the socially unacceptable low-need item of alcohol. This may be interpreted as showing that what one buys and how deserving of help one appears to be influence whether one is helped by others.

From *Perceptual and Motor Skills*, *101*, 617–620. Copyright © 2005 by Perceptual and Motor Skills. Reprinted with permission.

Social psychologists have extensively documented the variables associated with prosocial or helping behavior (Batson, 1998). Much of this research has focused upon characteristics of the person in need. Physi-
5 cally attractive individuals, for example, are more likely to receive help than are their less attractive peers (Wilson, 1978; Regan & Llamas, 2002). Another perhaps equally important variable in helping behavior is the target's perceived need; that is, how deserving of
10 assistance the person appears to be. In general, targets in greater need of assistance tend to elicit more helping behavior from others (Enzle & Harvey, 1978; Sinha & Jain, 1986). For example, an early classic field experiment conducted by Bickman and Kamzan (1973) indi-
15 cated women shoppers were more likely to help a female confederate who asked for 10 cents when she was attempting to buy a high-need food item like milk, and thereby presumably appeared more deserving of help, than when she was purchasing a low-need food item

20 such as frozen cookie dough. The present field experiment was designed to replicate and extend this earlier work by investigating the extent to which two variables, participants' sex and target's perceived need, would influence helping behavior. Perceived need was
25 manipulated by using three different food items: milk (a high-need item), frozen cookie dough (a low-need item), and alcohol (a low-need item with negative social connotations). Based upon earlier research, the high-need item was predicted to elicit greater helping
30 behavior than either of the low-need items. Because previous research exploring the association between participants' sex and helping behavior has yielded inconsistent results (Eagly & Crowley, 1986), there were no *a priori* predictions concerning this variable.

Methods

Participants

35 Participants were 332 adult (166 women, 166 men; estimated *M* age = 26 yr., *SD* = 4 yr.) shoppers at three large supermarkets located in Southern California. Participants were selected for inclusion in the experiment if they were the same sex as the confederate, appeared
40 to be over 21 years of age, were shopping alone as defined by being unaccompanied by friends or family members, and appeared to be somewhat relaxed and not in a hurry to find a particular item or finish their shopping.
45 Confederates were four university students, two men and two women, whose ages ranged from 24 to 31 years (*M* age = 27 yr., *SD* – 2.5 yr.). Each dressed in clean, informal attire (pants with a shirt or blouse). Two confederates were present for each experimental
50 session; one acted as an observer while the other approached the participant. Prior to entering the supermarket, each confederate team randomly selected the item they would use when soliciting help: a quart of milk, which served as a high-need item; a roll of frozen
55 cookie dough, which was defined as low need; or a large bottle of beer, which represented a low-need item with negative social connotations.

Procedure

Upon entering the store, Confederate 1 picked up the assigned food item and proceeded down the next
60 adjacent aisle. Confederate 2, masquerading as a shopper with a cart, followed at a discreet distance to observe the interaction, record the participant's response, and estimate the participant's age. The first shopper in the aisle who fulfilled the selection criteria was ap-
65 proached. Specifically, Confederate 1 approached the participant with two dollar bills and some change crumpled in one hand and with the selected food item held in the other. The confederate's statement was "Hi. I'm a little embarrassed, but I'm short 25 cents for this
70 [carton of milk/package of cookie dough/bottle of beer]. Can you spare a quarter?" If the participant questioned the confederate, he or she replied, "I thought I had enough money with me."

The participant's response of help or no help served
75 as the dependent variable. If the participant responded negatively to the confederate's request, the confederate said, "No problem, I understand" and proceeded to exit the aisle. If the participant responded affirmatively to the request and gave the confederate a quarter, the con-
80 federate accepted the quarter, thanked the participant, began to walk away, and then suddenly "found" a quarter in his or her own pocket. He or she immediately returned the participant's quarter, thanked the participant, and exited the aisle. Note that 23 participants
85 insisted that the confederate keep the quarter.

Results and Discussion

In Table 1 are the number and percentage of participants who provided help in each of the three conditions. There was no sex difference in rates of helping behavior; across conditions, roughly equal percentages
90 of men (51.2%) and women (56.6%) gave a quarter to the confederate when asked ($z = 0.99$, ns); however, perceived need clearly influenced helping behavior. As hypothesized, the high-need item produced greater helping behavior than both of the low-need items. Spe-
95 cifically, a series of z tests for proportions indicated that significantly more participants gave assistance to the confederate when he or she was trying to purchase milk than when he or she was trying to purchase frozen cookie dough (70.1 % vs 52.6%; $z = 2.85$, $p < .005$) or
100 alcohol (70.1% vs 29.3%; $z = 5.86$, $p < .0001$). Similarly, cookie dough, a low-need but nonetheless socially acceptable item, produced greater helping behavior than did alcohol, a low-need item with questionable social desirability (52.6% vs 29.3%; $z = 3.27$, $p <$
105 .001). In addition and in keeping with the lack of an overall sex difference in helping rates, the same result pattern was obtained when the responses of the men and women were examined separately.

These findings indicate that people in general are
110 fairly helpful. Over half of the participants and equal numbers of men and women gave assistance to the confederate when asked. They did not help indiscrimi-

nately, however, but based their decision to provide assistance, at least in part, on how deserving of help the
115 confederate appeared to be. Although other researchers also have found high rates of helping behavior (North, Tarrant, & Hargreaves, 2003), it is important to recognize that the scenario created here to elicit helping behavior from participants involved little risk of personal
120 endangerment and low involvement with the target. It is possible that rates of helping behavior would be significantly lower in situations requiring greater personal involvement or risk.

Table 1
Helping Behavior As a Function of Targets' Perceived Need

Group		Milk	Cookie dough	Alcohol
Women	Total *N*	68	58	40
	Participants who helped			
	n	49	32	13
	%	72.0	55.2	32.5
Men	Total *N*	66	58	42
	Participants who helped			
	n	45	29	11
	%	68.2	50.0	26.2
Total	Total *N*	134	116	82
	Participants who helped			
	n	94	61	24
	%	70.1[ab]	52.6[ac]	29.3[bc]

Note. Percentages that share a superscript are significantly different. *Z* and *p* values are given in the text. Response patterns for men and women separately are identical with that of the total sample.

References

Batson, C. D. (1998). Altruism and prosocial behavior. In D. T. Gilbert, S. T. Fiske, & G. Lindzey (Eds.), *The handbook of social psychology.* (4th ed.) Vol. 2. Boston, MA: McGraw-Hill. Pp. 282–316.

Bickman, L., & Kamzan, M. (1973). The effect of race and need on helping behavior. *Journal of Social Psychology, 89,* 73–77.

Eagly, A. H., & Crowley, M. (1986). Gender and helping behavior: A meta-analytic review of the social psychological literature. *Psychological Bulletin, 100,* 283–308.

Enzle, M. E., & Harvey, M. D. (1978). Recipient vs. third-party requests, recipient need, and helping behavior. *Personality and Social Psychology Bulletin, 4,* 620–623.

North, A. C., Tarrant, M., & Hargreaves, D. J. (2003). The effects of music on helping behavior: A field study. *Environment and Behavior, 36,* 266–275.

Regan, P. C., & Llamas, V. (2002). Customer service as a function of shopper's attire. *Psychological Reports, 90,* 203–204.

Sinha, A. K., & Jain, A. (1986). The effects of benefactor and beneficiary characteristics on helping behavior. *Journal of Social Psychology, 126,* 361–368.

Wilson, D. W. (1978). Helping behavior and physical attractiveness. *Journal of Social Psychology, 104,* 313–314.

Acknowledgment: This research was supported in part by NIH MBRS-RISE Grant R25 GM61331.

Address correspondence to: Pamela Regan, Ph.D., Department of Psychology, California State University, 5151 State University Drive, Los Angeles, CA 90032-8227. E-mail: pregan@calstatela.edu

Exercise for Article 16

Factual Questions

1. According to the literature review, have high-need and low-need items been examined in an earlier experiment?

2. Confederate 2 masqueraded as what?

3. According to the researchers, what is the "dependent variable" in this experiment?

4. Was there a statistically significant sex difference in rates of helping behavior?

5. For the total sample, did cookie dough produce significantly greater helping behavior than alcohol?

6. Of the 66 men who were asked to help purchase milk, how many helped?

Questions for Discussion

7. This article is classified as an example of an experiment in the table of contents of this book. In your opinion, is this classification correct? If yes, what feature of this study makes it an experiment?

8. In your opinion, are the criteria for inclusion of participants in this study reasonable? Explain. (See lines 37–44.)

9. Is the procedure in lines 58–85 sufficiently detailed so that you could conduct a replication of this study? Explain.

10. Do you agree with the researchers' concluding comment in lines 115–123? Explain.

11. This research article is shorter than most others in this book. In your opinion, is the article informative despite its brevity? Does it provide important results? Explain.

12. If you were on a funding board (e.g., on the board of a foundation that sponsors research), would you recommend funding for additional studies on this topic? Explain.

Quality Ratings

Directions: Indicate your level of agreement with each of the following statements by circling a number from 5 for strongly agree (SA) to 1 for strongly disagree (SD). If you believe an item is not applicable to this research article, leave it blank. Be prepared to explain your ratings. When responding to criteria A and B below, keep in mind that brief titles and abstracts are conventional in published research.

A. The title of the article is appropriate.

SA   5   4   3   2   1   SD

B. The abstract provides an effective overview of the research article.

SA   5   4   3   2   1   SD

C. The introduction establishes the importance of the study.

SA   5   4   3   2   1   SD

D. The literature review establishes the context for the study.

SA   5   4   3   2   1   SD

E. The research purpose, question, or hypothesis is clearly stated.

SA   5   4   3   2   1   SD

F. The method of sampling is sound.

SA   5   4   3   2   1   SD

G. Relevant demographics (for example, age, gender, and ethnicity) are described.

SA   5   4   3   2   1   SD

H. Measurement procedures are adequate.

SA   5   4   3   2   1   SD

I. All procedures have been described in sufficient detail to permit a replication of the study.

SA   5   4   3   2   1   SD

J. The participants have been adequately protected from potential harm.

SA   5   4   3   2   1   SD

K. The results are clearly described.

SA   5   4   3   2   1   SD

L. The discussion/conclusion is appropriate.

SA   5   4   3   2   1   SD

M. Despite any flaws, the report is worthy of publication.

SA   5   4   3   2   1   SD

Article 17

Failure of a Traffic Control "Fatality" Sign to Affect Pedestrians' and Motorists' Behavior

W. ANDREW HARRELL
University of Alberta

MARIA DAVID-EVANS
University of Alberta

JOHN GARTRELL
University of Alberta

ABSTRACT. The behavior of 643 pedestrians and 1,749 motorists at two signal-controlled intersections was observed over a 2-mo. period of observation in March and November. One intersection had a coffin-shaped traffic sign with the wording "Fatality" erected during the first month of observation (March). The second intersection was identical in traffic and pedestrian volume but lacked a "Fatality" sign in either March or November. "Fatality" signs are erected and maintained by the City of Edmonton for 6 mo. whenever a pedestrian death has occurred, and they are intended to raise the awareness of both pedestrians and motorists concerning the risks at dangerous intersections. This sign had been removed for nearly 3 mo. when a follow-up observation was made in November. While female pedestrians and pedestrians over the age of 50 years showed greater caution at both intersections, the presence or absence of the "Fatality" sign had no statistically significant influence on safety. Similarly, the presence or absence of a sign did not significantly influence motorists' behavior. Of motorists, 7.6% ran either amber or red traffic control lights at the two intersections. The "Fatality" sign did not affect the rates of these violations.

From *Psychological Reports*, *95*, 757–760. Copyright © 2004 by Psychological Reports. Reprinted with permission.

About 14% of all traffic deaths in North America involve pedestrians (Brainard, Slauterbeck, Benjamin, Hagaman, & Higie, 1989; Vestrup & Reid, 1989). A field experiment in Canada reported that posting a
5 "Stop Here for Pedestrians" sign reduced the percentage of motor vehicle-pedestrian conflicts in which a motorist did not stop to allow a pedestrian to cross (Van Houten & Malenfant, 1992). Another study, however, reported that accidents between pedestrians and
10 vehicles actually increased during the daytime when a yield sign was replaced with a stop sign (Polus, 1985). For the most part, the literature suggests that road signs have small effects on accident rates and that motorists tend to pay little attention to many kinds of signs that
15 involve pedestrians (Harrell, 1991, 1992; Johannson & Rumar, 1966; McKelvey, 1984).

The present study examined the impact of a prominently posted "Fatality" sign at a busy urban intersection on cautionary behaviors by both pedestrians and
20 motorists.

Method

Sample

Subjects were 643 pedestrians observed crossing at two signal-controlled urban intersections during 80 hr. of observation during the months of March and November. In addition, the behavior of 1,749 motorists
25 passing through these intersections was also observed.

Locations

Observations were conducted at two busy urban intersections one block apart. Pretest observations verified that the volume of traffic through these intersections was approximately the same. Phasing of traffic
30 signals and the length of walk–don't walk signs for pedestrians were also equal. One intersection (with only southbound traffic) had a large 80-cm high by 67-cm wide coffin-shaped sign with the word "Fatality" written in black lettering on a white background. The
35 sign was mounted on a light standard 3.7 m above the ground on the southeastern corner and facing southbound traffic and pedestrians. The sign was erected in February and remained in place until the end of July. It is the policy of the City of Edmonton to erect
40 such signs on roadways for a period of 6 mo. following a fatal accident involving a pedestrian. In the present case, the sign was posted after a pedestrian had been hit and killed by a city bus. Other than the standard street signs on each corner of the intersections there were no
45 other prominent signs that interfered with the view of the "Fatality" sign. Four lanes of traffic in the southbound street featuring the "Fatality" sign passed through a four-lane arterial with east–west traffic. One block to the east was the control intersection. Four
50 lanes of northbound traffic passed through the four-lane arterial with east-west traffic.

Measures

An index of pedestrian safety was constructed by recording whether a pedestrian moved the head to look one way or two ways before crossing, whether a pedes-
55 trian walked only when the "walk" sign was indicated, and the distance stood from the curb. Failure to look in either direction was scored 0. A one-way look was scored 1, and looking both ways was scored 2. A pedestrian who walked before the "walk" light was illu-

60 minated received a score of 0, while a score of 1 was given for waiting for the signal. Tape was placed on the pavement at premeasured distances from the curb. A score of 1 was given if the pedestrian stood closer than one foot from the curb; a 2 was given if the distance

65 was between two and three feet, and a 3 was assigned if the pedestrian stood three or more feet from the curb. The composite safety index was ordinal in nature and ranged from 1 to a maximum of 6. The sex of each subject, as well as an estimate of subject's age, was

70 recorded. For purposes of analysis, four age categories were created, representing subjects less than 20 years, 21–35 years, 36–50 years, and subjects over age 50 years. No effort was made to interview subjects to obtain their actual ages or other demographic data. Sam-

75 ples of motor vehicle traffic were taken during this time frame and simultaneously with observations of pedestrians. A tally was made of motorists who ran an amber light (i.e., passing through the intersection if the signal light changed to yellow before the motorist en-

80 tered the intersection) and runners of a red light.

Procedure

A single, trained observer sampled both pedestrians' and motorists' behaviors for a total of 80 hr. during March. Observations were made from 10:00 a.m. to 4:00 p.m. during weekdays. These observations oc-

85 curred during the period of time the "Fatality" sign was displayed. An additional 80 hr. of observation was made in November after the sign had been removed. During these months the observed streets were comparable in terms of the quality of the roadway and

90 weather conditions.

Results

Fifty-one percent of the subjects were men ($n = 327$) and 49% women ($n = 316$). Two hundred and fifteen subjects were observed at the intersection with the "Fatality" sign, 214 at this same intersection with-

95 out the sign, and 214 at the control intersection. Those under 20 years were the largest age group at 42% of the sample ($n = 270$). Thirty-three percent were 20–35 years ($n = 213$). Fifteen percent were 36–50 years ($n = 97$), and 10% were over 50 years ($n = 63$). A total of

100 1,749 motorists were observed passing through the intersections. Six hundred and forty were observed at the intersection with the "Fatality" sign (36.6%). Thirty-four percent were observed at this same intersection without the sign ($n = 594$), and 29.5% ($n = 515$)

105 were observed at the control intersection.

The influence of the "Fatality" sign on pedestrians' behavior was not significant ($F_{2,499} = 2.3, p < .11$). The mean safety score for pedestrians at the intersection with the "Fatality" sign in place was slightly higher

110 than when the "Fatality" sign was absent from this intersection, but not significant. (See Table 1.) The mean safety score of 4.5 recorded at the control intersection was slightly lower than the safety score for the intersection with the "Fatality" sign, but the difference also

115 was not statistically significant. Safety scores were significantly higher for women than for men ($F_{1,499} = 19.4, p < .001$). In addition, scores were progressively higher with greater age ($F_{3,499} = 16.7, p < .001$).

Table 1
Means and Standard Deviations for Safety Scores

Variable	M	SD
Fatality Sign		
Present	4.6	0.8
Absent	4.8	1.1
Control Intersection	4.5	0.9
Pedestrian's Sex		
Men	4.6	1.0
Women	4.8	0.8
Pedestrian's Age		
<20	3.1	1.0
20–35	4.4	0.9
36–50	4.6	1.0
>50	5.0	0.6

In all of the intersections, a total of 7.6% of the mo-

120 torists observed ran either amber or red lights. For the intersection with the "Fatality" sign, 8.5% of the motorists ran amber or red lights. When the "Fatality" sign was removed, 6.7% of the motorists ran the light. In the control intersection, 7.1% of the motorists ran amber or

125 red lights. A chi-square analysis yielded no significant difference in distributions for the two intersections.

Discussion

It was the intent of the City that these "Fatality" signs would raise awareness of traffic risks, thereby increasing safe street crossing behaviors by pedestri-

130 ans. It was also felt that the signs would evoke safer driving by motorists. Evidence from this study suggests that this is not the case. Pedestrians did not act more safely when "Fatality" signs were present than when they were absent. Motorists were just as likely to run

135 amber or red lights when the signs were present as when they were absent.

References

Brainard, B. J., Slauterbeck, J., Benjamin, S. B., Hagaman, R. M., & Higie, S. (1989). Injury profiles in motor vehicle trauma. *Annals of Emergency Medicine, 18,* 881–883.

Harrell, W A. (1991). Factors influencing pedestrian cautiousness in crossing streets. *Journal of Social Psychology, 131,* 367–372.

Harrell, W. A. (1992). Driver response to a disabled pedestrian using a dangerous crosswalk. *Journal of Environmental Psychology, 12,* 345–352.

Johannson, G., & Rumar, K. (1966). Drivers and road signs: A preliminary investigation of the capacity of car drivers to get information from road signs. *Ergonomics, 9,* 57–62.

McKelvey, R. K. (1994). Can children learn to discriminate safe road-crossing intervals? *Journal of Safety Research, 15,* 57–67.

Polus, A. (1985). Driver behavior and accident records at unsignalled urban intersections. *Accident Analysis & Prevention, 22,* 549–559.

Van Houten, R., & Malenfant, L. (1992). The influence of signs prompting motorists to yield before marked crosswalks on motor vehicle-pedestrian conflicts at crosswalks with flashing amber lights. *Accident Analysis & Prevention, 24,* 217–225.

Vestrup, J. A., & Reid, J. D. (1989). A profile of urban pedestrian trauma. *Journal of Trauma, 29,* 741–745.

Address correspondence to: W. Andrew Harrell, University of Alberta, Tory Bldg., Rm. 5–21, Edmonton, AB, Canada. E-mail: aharrell@gpu.srv.ualberta.ca

Exercise for Article 17

Factual Questions

1. The observation period in March lasted how many hours?

2. For looking before crossing, what does a score of 2 indicate?

3. What was the total possible score for the composite safety index?

4. What percentage of the 1,749 motorists who were observed went through the control intersection?

5. What was the mean safety score when the "Fatality" sign was present? What was the mean safety score at the control intersection?

6. Were the differences in the percentage of cars that ran amber/red lights statistically significant?

Questions for Discussion

7. Is it important to know that the volume of traffic through the two intersections was approximately the same? Explain. (See lines 26–29.)

8. What is your opinion on the ability of observers to estimate age through observation? (See lines 68–74.)

9. This study did not include a second observer in order to estimate interobserver reliability (i.e., the extent to which two observers would obtain the same data when observing the same phenomena). In your opinion, is this a serious omission? Explain. (See lines 81–82.)

10. At the first intersection, observations with the sign present were made in March, while the observations at the same intersection with the sign removed were made in November. Could the difference in months affect the difference between the mean safety scores for these two conditions? Would alternating daily or weekly (e.g., one week with the sign, the next week without the sign) have improved this study? Explain. (See lines 81–90.)

11. In line 107, the researchers report "$p < .11$." What does this tell you?

12. In the table of contents of this book, this research article is classified as an example of "quasi-experimental research." If you are familiar with the terminology for classifying experiments, explain why this experiment is not classified as "true experimental research."

13. Despite the fact that the main differences were statistically insignificant, would you recommend additional studies on the effects of fatality signs on pedestrians' and motorists' behavior? Explain.

Quality Ratings

Directions: Indicate your level of agreement with each of the following statements by circling a number from 5 for strongly agree (SA) to 1 for strongly disagree (SD). If you believe an item is not applicable to this research article, leave it blank. Be prepared to explain your ratings. When responding to criteria A and B below, keep in mind that brief titles and abstracts are conventional in published research.

A. The title of the article is appropriate.

SA   5   4   3   2   1   SD

B. The abstract provides an effective overview of the research article.

SA   5   4   3   2   1   SD

C. The introduction establishes the importance of the study.

SA   5   4   3   2   1   SD

D. The literature review establishes the context for the study.

SA   5   4   3   2   1   SD

E. The research purpose, question, or hypothesis is clearly stated.

SA   5   4   3   2   1   SD

F. The method of sampling is sound.

SA   5   4   3   2   1   SD

G. Relevant demographics (for example, age, gender, and ethnicity) are described.

SA   5   4   3   2   1   SD

H. Measurement procedures are adequate.

SA   5   4   3   2   1   SD

I. All procedures have been described in sufficient detail to permit a replication of the study.

SA   5   4   3   2   1   SD

J. The participants have been adequately protected from potential harm.

SA   5   4   3   2   1   SD

K. The results are clearly described.

SA   5   4   3   2   1   SD

L. The discussion/conclusion is appropriate.

SA   5   4   3   2   1   SD

M. Despite any flaws, the report is worthy of publication.

SA   5   4   3   2   1   SD

Article 18

Project Trust: Breaking Down Barriers Between Middle School Children

MARY ELLEN BATIUK
Wilmington College

JAMES A. BOLAND
Wilmington College

NORMA WILCOX
Wright State University

ABSTRACT. This paper analyzes the success of a camp retreat weekend called Project Trust involving middle school students and teachers. The goal of the camp is to break down barriers between cliques identified as active in the school. The camp focuses on building team relationships across clique membership and incorporates elements of peace education and conflict resolution. A treatment group (campers) and comparison group (noncampers) were administered an adaptation of the Bogardus Social Distance Test and the Piers-Harris Children's Self-Concept Scale before and after the camp. Attendance was found to lower social distance scores for nine of the ten groups/cliques. Campers also had higher self-concept scores after the retreat.

From *Adolescence, 39,* 531–538. Copyright © 2004 by Libra Publishers, Inc. Reprinted with permission.

The *Final Report and Findings of the Safe School Initiative* indicates that from 1993 to 1997, the "odds that a child in grades 9–12 would be threatened or injured with a weapon in school were 8 percent, or 1 in
5 13 or 14; the odds of getting into a physical fight at school were 15 percent, or 1 in 7" (Vossekuil, Fein, Reddy, Borum, & Modzeleski, 2002, p. 12). Such widespread experiences of school violence have led to what McLaren, Leonardo, and Allen (2000) call a
10 "bunker mentality" on many school campuses. As Tompkins (2000) points out, "increased levels of security suggest to students and teachers that they learn and teach in a violent environment where students cannot be trusted and are under suspicion" (p. 65). This is
15 doubly unfortunate, not only because positive school climates promote learning, but that they have been found to be strong predictors of the absence of school violence (Welsh, 2000).

Further, one of the ten key findings of the analysis
20 of the Safe School Initiative is that "many attackers felt bullied, persecuted or injured by others prior to the attack" (Vossekuil et al., 2002, p. 18). In a word, attackers felt excluded. Kramer (2000) has established that patterns of individual exclusion in school settings
25 contribute to violence among students because exclusion separates them from the informal social control networks provided by parents, schools, and communi-

ties. This lack of informal social control has been linked to diminishing social and cultural capital
30 (Hagen, 1985) and ultimately delinquency (Cullen, 1994, Currie, 1998; Sampson & Laub, 1993). Exclusion also preempts the kind of dialogue that can resolve conflicts (Aronowitz, 2003).

As a result, many educators have called for curricu-
35 lar changes incorporating programs in peace education (Caulfield, 2000; Harris, 1996; Pepinsky, 2000) and conflict resolution (Bretherton, 1996; Children's Defense Fund, 1998). For example, 10 years ago, Wilmington College collaborated with a local middle
40 school to provide programming aimed at eliminating patterns of mistrust and exclusion fostered by student cliques. The collaboration was a natural one since Wilmington College offers extensive teacher education programs and maintains a strong tradition of conflict
45 resolution and peacemaking tied to its Quaker heritage.

The training emphasized a mutual and reflexive process of problem solving and conflict resolution in which involved parties actively frame the understanding of both the problem and its solution. Teachers and
50 students at the middle school overwhelmingly pointed to the ongoing problem of conflicts arising from student cliques. As a response, teachers and students designed activities that would help break down barriers among the cliques. From this collaboration emerged
55 Project Trust—a weekend camp retreat in which student opinion/clique leaders engaged in discussions, role-playing, and noncompetitive risk-taking tasks.

The present paper focuses on a program for middle school children that incorporates principles of peace
60 education and conflict resolution techniques to address the pervasive sources of these conflicts within networks of student cliques. It was hypothesized that by engaging student leaders in activities focused on cooperation and breaking down barriers, these same stu-
65 dents would become more receptive to interacting with members of other cliques. It was also hypothesized that participation in the retreat weekend would lead to increased self-esteem in the participants.

Method

Project Trust

In the fall of 1990, middle school teachers and stu-

70 dents were asked to brainstorm about the kinds of cliques that were active in the school. A list of 24 groups, active within the school, emerged from these initial brainstorming sessions. Discussions with both students and teachers allowed project managers to hone
75 the list to eight, and these groups became the focal point for Project Trust. The groups included: (1) preps—smart and well dressed, well to do or at least giving the perception that they are, doing what they are told to do; (2) alternatives—baggy clothes, various
80 colors of hair, might be skaters, long hair; (3) jocks—athletes or individuals whose lives are dominated by sports interests, wearing NBA and NFL jerseys; (4) hoods/gangsters/thugs—rule-breakers, tough, like to fight, might be in a gang, wearing black; (5) dorks—
85 geeks, socially awkward, nonathletic; (6) cheerleaders—attractive and active girls; (7) hicks/hillbillies—rural kids, possibly live in trailer parks, like country music; and (8) dirties—poor kids, dirty and cannot help it, poor hygiene.
90 The names of the cliques came directly from the students and teachers. Ethnic groups were not mentioned by the students but were added by the project managers after discussions with the teachers (i.e., whites and African Americans).

Treatment and Comparison Groups

95 Project Trust camp retreats include student opinion/clique leaders who are identified by teachers and invited to spend the weekend at a local camp that regularly provides team-building exercises to local civic groups and businesses. Middle school teachers receive
100 training from Wilmington College project managers in group process and team building. Both teachers and Wilmington College professors lead the retreats. Once at the camp, students and teachers are placed into Family Groups of 8–10 members designed to cut across
105 clique memberships. Students are encouraged to take ownership of the weekend agenda by developing contracts with retreat leaders. Contracting processes involve eliciting from students what they hope to "get" from the weekend (everything from food to fun activi-
110 ties) and what they are willing to "give" to get those things. During the course of the weekend (Friday evening through Sunday afternoon), student family groups take part in discussions, cooperative tasks, and team building and survival exercises.
115 One team-building activity, titled Toxic Waste, involves blindfolded team members "dumping" a cupful of sludge into another cup inside of a 4 × 4 square. Unsighted family team members cannot cross into the square, have access only to 4 bungee cords, the cup of
120 sludge and a rubber band, and are given directions by their sighted team members. Another activity, called Plane Crash, involves the completion of various tasks by team members who have received several handicaps (broken bones, loss of sight) and limited supplies
125 (food, water, blankets). Also included in the retreat are an extended outdoor trust walk and a structured discussion about the harmful effects of put-downs and techniques for resolving conflicts around them. Students and teachers discuss the case study of a young girl who
130 committed suicide, leaving a note explaining the exclusion she felt because of being called a "fat hog" by her classmates.

Family groups are brought together regularly to assess how the retreat is progressing. Plenty of snacks,
135 pizza, and pop are provided to foster an environment of fun and relaxation during the time that students and teachers spend together.

In addition to this treatment group, fellow students who did not attend the camp were selected on the basis
140 of availability and assessed using the same instrument, for the purposes of comparison. Treatment group students were identified by teachers on the basis of being "opinion leaders."

Assessments

Assessment of Project Trust weekends relies pri-
145 marily on an adaptation of the Bogardus (1933) Social Distance Scale to measure the social distances between the students and identified groups before and after the camp experience. The scale was chosen because of its ease of scoring and high reliability (Miller, 1991;
150 Owen et al., 1981). In addition, the scale has also been successfully and widely adapted for use with school-age children (Cover, 2001; Lee, Sapp, & Ray, 1996; Mielenz, 1979; Payne, 1976; Williams, 1992). On this modified scale, students were asked to rate all ten
155 groups on a scale of 0–7, with 7 representing the greatest degree of social distance: 0–be best friends with; 1–invite over to my house; 3–choose to eat lunch with; 4–say "hi" to only; 5–as a member of my homeroom only; 6–as a member of my school only; 7–exclude
160 them from my school. Both treatment and comparison groups completed this scale immediately before the retreat weekend and within one month after the camp.

In addition, treatment and nontreatment groups completed the Piers-Harris Children's Self-Concept
165 Scale (Piers, 1984). This self-report scale measures self-concept using 80 yes/no questions and is intended for use with youths aged 8–18. The scale was administered to the treatment group before and after the camp experience, and to the comparison group before the
170 camp experience.

Results

Camps have been held from 1998 through 2002 in both the fall and spring. An independent-samples *t* test (equal variances not assumed) comparing the pretest mean scores of the treatment group (*n* = 298) and com-
175 parison group (*n* = 215) found significant differences between only two groups: preps (*t* = 5.058, *df* = 405, *p* < .01) and jocks (*t* = 2.654, *df* = 378, *p* < .01). In both cases, the means of the treatment group social distance scores were lower than for the comparison group: preps
180 (*M* = 2.28, *SD* = 2.06, for campers, vs. *M* = 3.34, *SD* =

2.24, for noncampers), jocks ($M = 2.07$, $SD = 2.14$, for campers, vs. $M = 2.66$, $SD = 2.43$, for noncampers). Thus, treatment and comparison students were roughly equivalent in their perceptions of social distance from
185 their classmates with the exception of the preps and the jocks. In these two instances, the campers reported statistically significant lower social distance scores when compared to noncampers.

A paired-samples t test was calculated for both the
190 treatment group ($n = 216$) and comparison group ($n = 80$). Table 1 reports the results for the treatment group. For all eight cliques, attendance at the camp significantly reduced perceptions of social distance. In addition, perceptions of social distance were significantly
195 reduced for African Americans but not whites. Mean scores for whites were already low (pretest $M = .54$, $SD = 1.00$) and did fall (posttest $M = .47$, $SD = .86$), though not to a statistically significant degree. The greatest change for campers was in their perceptions of
200 dirties, moving an average of 1.55 points on the 7-point scale (pretest $M = 5.55$, $SD = 1.40$; posttest $M = 4.00$, $SD = 1.71$); dorks, moving an average of 1.37 points (pretest $M = 4.60$, $SD = 2.10$; posttest $M = 3.23$, $SD = 1.65$); and hicks, moving an average of 1.23 points
205 (pretest $M = 4.38$, $SD = 2.07$; posttest $M = 3.15$, $SD = 1.96$).

Table 1

Paired-Samples Two-Tailed t Test for the Treatment Group (n = 216)

Campers	t	df	p
Preps	6.816	212	.000
Alternatives	5.254	196	.000
Jocks	6.532	207	.000
Hoods	6.709	205	.000
Dorks	10.810	206	.000
Cheerleaders	3.282	213	.001
Hicks	8.608	203	.000
Dirties	11.751	204	.000
African Americans	2.500	208	.013
Whites	1.141	206	.255

Table 2 reports the results for the comparison group (noncampers). The only statistically significant shift was for preps (pretest $M = 3.18$, $SD = 2.23$; posttest M
210 $= 2.74$, $SD = 2.37$). In all other instances, there were no statistically significant changes. However, there were two instances, for dorks and African Americans, in which social distance scores actually regressed.

On the Piers-Harris Children's Self-Concept Scale,
215 self-concept scores also shifted for the treatment (camper) group. The mean score on the pretest was 61.37 ($SD = 12.6$) and the mean on the posttest was 66.13 ($SD = 11.32$). The difference was statistically significant ($p < .01$).

Conclusions

220 The results suggest that educational programs for middle school children that incorporate peace education and conflict resolution hold potential for reducing divisive student cliques built around difference, mistrust, and exclusion, that often result in the violence
225 found in schools today. While this is only one study in a rural area of a mid-Atlantic state with a unique subculture, it does offer hope of greater validity and reliability with its longitudinal character. Obviously, the study needs to be replicated in a variety of cultural and
230 institutional contexts and across different age groups. However, there is much to be gained by such replication in a society struggling to understand the attitudes of the "other."

Table 2

Paired-Samples Two-Tailed t Test for the Comparison Group (n = 80)

Noncampers	t	df	p
Preps	2.035	72	.046
Alternatives	0.967	63	.337
Jocks	0.150	65	.881
Hoods	0.567	61	.573
Dorks	−0.068	68	.946
Cheerleaders	0.935	72	.353
Hicks	2.264	72	.353
Dirties	1.589	67	.117
African Americans	−0.271	74	.787
Whites	0.090	206	.928

References

Aronowitz, S. (2003). Essay on violence. In *Smoke and mirrors: The hidden context of violence in schools and society* (pp. 211–227). New York: Rowman and Littlefield.

Bogardus, E. S. (1933). A social distance scale. *Sociology and Social Research, 17*, 265–271.

Bretherton, D. (1996). Nonviolent conflict resolution in children. *Peabody Journal of Education, 71*, 111–127.

Caulfield, S. L. (2000). Creating peaceable schools. *ANNALS: The American Academy of Political and Social Science, 567*, 170–185.

Children's Defense Fund. (1998). *Keeping children safe in schools: A resource for states.* Available: http://www.childrensdefense.org.

Cover, J. D. (1995). The effects of social contact on prejudice. *The Journal of Social Psychology, 135*, 403–405.

Cullen, F. T. (1994). Social support as an organizing concept for criminology: Presidential address to the Academy of Criminal Justice Sciences. *Justice Quarterly, 11*, 527–559.

Currie, E. (1998). *Crime and punishment in America.* New York: Metropolitan Books.

Hagen, J. (1985). *Modern criminology: Crime, criminal behavior and its control.* New York: McGraw-Hill.

Harris, I. M. (1996). Peace education in an urban school district in the United States. *Peabody Journal of Education, 71*, 63–83.

Kramer, R. (2000). Poverty, inequality, and youth violence. *ANNALS: The American Academy of Political and Social Science, 567*, 123–139.

Lee, M. Y., Sapp, S. G., & Ray, M. C. (1996). The Reverse Social Distance Scale. *The Journal of Social Psychology, 136*, 17–24.

McLaren, P., Leonardo, Z., & Allen, R. L. (2000). Rated "cv" for cool violence. In S. U. Spina (Ed.), *Smoke and mirrors: The hidden context of violence in schools and society* (pp. 67–92). New York: Rowman and Littlefield.

Mielenz, C. C. (1979). Non-prejudiced Caucasian parents and attitudes of their children toward Negroes. *The Journal of Negro Education, 1979*, 12–21.

Miller, D. (1991). *Handbook of research design and social measurement.* Newbury Park, CA: Sage Publications.

Owen, C. A., Eisner, H. C., & McFaul, T. R. (1981). A half century of social distance research: National replication of the Bogardus studies. *Sociology and Social Research, 66*, 80–98.

Payne, W. J. (1976). Social class and social differentiation: A case for multidimensionality of social distance. *Sociology and Social Research, 61*, 54–67.

Pepinsky, H. (2000). Educating for peace. *ANNALS: The American Academy of Political and Social Science, 567,* 157–169.

Piers, E. V. (1984). *Piers-Harris Children's Self-Concept Scale revised manual 1984.* Los Angeles: Western Psychological Services.

Sampson, R. J., & Laub, J. H. (1993). *Crime in the making: Pathways and turning points through life.* Cambridge, MA: Harvard University Press.

Tompkins, D. E. (2000). School violence: Gangs and a culture of fear. *AN-NALS: The American Academy of Political and Social Science, 567,* 54–71.

Vossekuil, B., Fein, R A., Reddy, M., Borum, R., & Modzeleski, W. (2002). *The final report and findings of the Safe School Initiative: Implications for the prevention of school attacks in the United States.* Washington, DC: U.S. Secret Service and U.S. Department of Education.

Welsh, W. N. (2000). The effects of school climate on school disorder. *AN-NALS: The American Academy of Political and Social Science, 567,* 88–107.

Williams, C. (1992). The relationship between the affective and cognitive dimensions of prejudice. *College Student Journal, 26,* 50–54.

About the authors: *Mary Ellen Batiuk*, Department of Social and Political Studies, Wilmington College. *James A. Boland*, Department of Education, Wilmington College. *Norma Wilcox*, Department of Sociology, Wright State University.

Address correspondence to: Mary Ellen Batiuk, Department of Social and Political Studies, Wilmington College, Wilmington, OH 45177. E-mail: mebatiuk@wilmington.edu

Exercise for Article 18

Factual Questions

1. What resulted from the brainstorming sessions?

2. On the Social Distance Scale, what does a rating of "3" represent?

3. On the Social Distance Scale, does a high rating (e.g., "7") represent the greatest degree of social distance *or* does it represent the least degree of social distance?

4. In terms of social distance, the greatest change for campers from pretest to posttest was in their perceptions of what group?

5. In Table 1, all differences are statistically significant except for one group. Which group?

6. Was the treatment group's pretest to posttest difference on self-concept statistically significant? If yes, at what probability level?

Questions for Discussion

7. Keeping in mind that this is a research report and not an instructional guide, is the description of the treatment in lines 95–137 sufficiently detailed so that you have a clear picture of it? Explain.

8. For the comparison group, fellow students who did not attend the camp were selected on the basis of availability. How much stronger would this experiment have been if students had been ran-domly assigned to the treatment and comparison groups? Explain. (See lines 138–143.)

9. In your opinion, is the Piers-Harris Children's Self-Concept Scale described in sufficient detail? Explain. (See lines 163–170.)

10. The researchers state that "the study needs to be replicated in a variety of cultural and institutional contexts and across different age groups." (See lines 228–230.) In your opinion, are the results of this study sufficiently promising to warrant such replications? Explain.

11. What changes, if any, would you suggest making in the research methodology used in this study?

Quality Ratings

Directions: Indicate your level of agreement with each of the following statements by circling a number from 5 for strongly agree (SA) to 1 for strongly disagree (SD). If you believe an item is not applicable to this research article, leave it blank. Be prepared to explain your ratings. When responding to criteria A and B below, keep in mind that brief titles and abstracts are conventional in published research.

A. The title of the article is appropriate.

   SA   5   4   3   2   1   SD

B. The abstract provides an effective overview of the research article.

   SA   5   4   3   2   1   SD

C. The introduction establishes the importance of the study.

   SA   5   4   3   2   1   SD

D. The literature review establishes the context for the study.

   SA   5   4   3   2   1   SD

E. The research purpose, question, or hypothesis is clearly stated.

   SA   5   4   3   2   1   SD

F. The method of sampling is sound.

   SA   5   4   3   2   1   SD

G. Relevant demographics (for example, age, gender, and ethnicity) are described.

   SA   5   4   3   2   1   SD

H. Measurement procedures are adequate.

   SA   5   4   3   2   1   SD

I. All procedures have been described in sufficient detail to permit a replication of the study.

   SA   5   4   3   2   1   SD

J. The participants have been adequately protected from potential harm.

    SA   5   4   3   2   1   SD

K. The results are clearly described.

    SA   5   4   3   2   1   SD

L. The discussion/conclusion is appropriate.

    SA   5   4   3   2   1   SD

M. Despite any flaws, the report is worthy of publication.

    SA   5   4   3   2   1   SD

Article 19

Psychotherapy Using Distance Technology: A Comparison of Face-to-Face, Video, and Audio Treatment

SUSAN X DAY
University of Illinois at Urbana—Champaign,
Iowa State University, and University of Houston

PAUL L. SCHNEIDER
University of Illinois at Urbana—Champaign
and GeoLearning, Inc.

ABSTRACT. This study compared selected process and outcome variables across 3 modes of psychotherapy: face-to-face, real-time video conference, and 2-way audio (analogous to telephone). Results from 80 randomly assigned clients suggested that differences in process and outcome among the 3 treatments were small and clinically promising in comparison with the untreated control group.

From *Journal of Counseling Psychology*, 49, 499–503. Copyright © 2002 by the American Psychological Association. Reprinted with permission.

Experimental comparisons of process and outcome in distant versus face-to-face conditions may influence the future practice of psychology. Conventional wisdom insists that, for most purposes, the therapist and
5 client must be in the same room. Overall, our training as psychologists has emphasized face-to-face contact as the ideal. It will be interesting to discover whether this is true. Moreover, what conditions are required to establish psychological contact with another person
10 and, in fact, what constitutes psychological contact at all, are salient questions in the age of Internet discourse (e.g., Kraut et al., 1998). These research questions are significant for therapist training, choice of treatment, and application of previous research findings.
15 Our effort to compare face-to-face, video, and audio individual therapy addressed two aspects of substitutability. On the process side, the working alliance was examined in all three conditions. Bordin (1979) conceptualized this alliance as the emotional bond be-
20 tween client and therapist, the quality of client and therapist involvement in the tasks of therapy, and the amount of concordance on goals between therapist and client. Reviewing studies of the predictive validity of the alliance variable, Henry, Strupp, Schacht, and Gas-
25 ton (1994) found empirical support for alliance-outcome associations no matter how outcome was measured, who measured it, or what psychotherapeutic school of thought was represented. These reviewers entertained the "hypothesis that the alliance is a causal
30 ingredient of change" (p. 485).

On the outcome side, several assessments were combined, following the advice of Strupp and Hadley (1977) that evaluation of outcome should include multiple sources of information (therapist and client) and
35 multiple targets for change (symptom change, satisfaction level, problem resolution).

As implied above, our research questions were straightforward:

Does level of working alliance differ according to
40 mode of delivery (face-to-face, audio, or video)?

Does outcome differ according to mode of delivery and in comparison to a no-treatment wait-list control group?

Method

Participants

Clients were recruited from a wide variety of
45 sources so that the sample mirrored a community counseling center clientele. These sources included self-referrals from radio and print ads and referrals from local businesses, community colleges, and clinicians. We estimate that 75% were gathered from newspaper
50 ads, letters to the editor, and radio ads. Clients presented a wide range of problems, from weight concerns to personality disorders. As expected, given our community sample and random assignment, the variety of problems was wide and their frequency among modes
55 comparable. A tally revealed that the problems most frequently reported concerned body image/weight (audio = 3, video = 4, face-face = 4), family relationships (audio = 4, video = 3, face-face = 2), other relationships (audio = 9, video = 7, face-face = 10), self-
60 esteem (audio = 3, video = 3, face-face = 4), and work/school (audio = 3, video = 5, face-face = 4). Random assignment also fostered similar pretreatment status across groups, with global assessment of functioning (GAF; 1 to 100, 100 being the highest function-
65 ing) means at 69.2 for face-to-face, 70.6 for video, and 69.3 for audio, and symptom checklist means (range = 0–212, 212 being the highest number of symptoms) at 43 for face-to-face, 45 for video, and 46 for audio. These averages reflect mild symptoms or some diffi-

70 culty in social, occupational, or school functioning. The clients who completed treatment ($n = 80$) ranged in age from 19 to 75 years ($M = 39.35$, $SD = 15.88$), included 52 women and 28 men, and reported ethnic

75 identities of White (66), African American (8), Asian (3), and other (3). We were successful in our efforts to avoid a sample dominated by university students.

In the face-to-face condition, 27 clients completed the five sessions; in video, 26 clients completed them; and in audio, 27 completed them. There were 11 drop-

80 outs, reporting a variety of reasons for noncompletion. Five audio clients, 4 video clients, and 2 face-to-face clients did not complete the sessions, $\chi^2(2, N = 80) = 1.13$, $p > .05$. No systematic effects of sex or reported ethnicity were perceptible among the dropouts. When

85 interviewed, clinicians did not believe that treatment mode contributed to their clients' early termination.

Participants were told during the informed-consent process that the study sought to compare psychotherapy delivered face-to-face, over video, and over audio

90 and that they would be randomly assigned to one of these modes. In debriefing, they were provided more detail about what factors we were investigating.

Instruments

Process measurement. Observer ratings on three subscales of the Vanderbilt Psychotherapy Process

95 Scale (VPPS; Strupp, Hartley, & Blackwood, 1974) represented the working alliance. The subscales were Client Participation, Client Hostility (reverse scored), and Therapist Exploration as demonstrated on videotapes of Session 4, by which time the alliance is stably

100 established (Sexton, Hembre, & Kvarme, 1996). The three Vanderbilt subscales have reported reliabilities (Cronbach's alphas) of .93 for Client Participation, .83 for Client Hostility, and .96 for Therapist Exploration (O'Malley, Suh, & Strupp, 1983). The scales have

105 demonstrated concurrent validity ($p < .001$) with scales from the Penn Helping Alliance Method and the Therapeutic Alliance Rating System (Bachelor, 1991). The scales were chosen for this type of conceptual reflection of accepted positive and negative elements of

110 the working alliance. Five other subscales of the VPPS were not used in order to avoid redundant or irrelevant variables.

Raters were three professional psychotherapists not associated with clinic operations. They were master's-

115 level clinicians who had worked full-time as psychotherapists at community mental health agencies for at least 7 years. They were provided with item-level guidelines developed by the scale creators and designed to lower the amount of inference needed to in-

120 terpret each item (Strupp et al., 1974). In a 1-day training session, raters watched sample segments of videotape, rated them, discussed their ratings and revised them if necessary, and continued this process until they reached an acceptable level of agreement consistently

125 on the first rating attempt (as a guideline, a range of 2

or less, 90% of the time). The raters met every 2–3 weeks to rate sample segments together and recalibrate in an effort to prevent rater drift. Raters were paid by the hour for their work.

130 Raters watched three 5-min segments of each videotape (samples from beginning, middle, and end). The visual element made it impossible for them to be blind to the condition they were rating; however, the raters reported that they usually forgot what mode they

135 were watching as they rated.

Outcome measurement. Several outcome measures assessed results from both clients' and clinicians' points of view and from various definitions of outcome. The Brief Symptom Inventory (BSI; Derogatis,

140 1993) provided a standardized symptom checklist from the client. The BSI contains 53 items scored on a scale of 0 (*not at all*) to 4 (*extremely*) for how much each symptom has bothered the client in the past week. Test–retest reliability among 60 outpatients over 2-

145 week intervals was .90 (Derogatis & Melisaratos, 1983).

The GAF (American Psychiatric Association, 1994) assessed overall functioning from the therapist's perspective. The GAF is a slightly modified version of the

150 Global Assessment Scale (GAS; Endicott, Spitzer, Fleiss, & Cohen, 1976), which has shown relatively high and consistent interrater reliability. The scale also demonstrated good reliability for use over a wide range of severity levels, with an intraclass correlation coeffi-

155 cient of .69 to .91 over five studies, and acceptable concurrent, predictive, and discriminant validity. The scale yielded the greatest sensitivity to change when compared with other measures of overall change. Sensitivity to change was of particular importance, given

160 the brevity of our intervention.

The Target Complaints method (TC; Battle et al., 1966; Mintz & Kiesler, 1982) is an individualized self-report of one to three presenting problems and their severity level. The measure asks the clients to list three

165 problems for which they are seeking help and rate the severity of the problem on a scale from 10 (*couldn't be worse*) to 1 (*not at all*). The therapist also filled out TCs for each client. The TC is highly correlated with other treatment outcome measures (Mintz & Kiesler,

170 1982).

Both client and therapist completed measures of satisfaction, modified from Tracey and Dundon's 7-item Client and Therapist Satisfaction Scales (CSS and TSS, respectively; Tracey & Dundon, 1988), which

175 reflected each party's opinion of the worth of the therapeutic experience. The measure has produced an internal consistency of .94 (Tracey & Dundon, 1988). In the current study, the modified CSS produced an internal consistency of .88. The TSS, filled out by the

180 therapist, is a similar measure adapted for the clinician's point of view. In this study, it was found to have an internal consistency of .84.

The BSI, the GAF, and the TCs were completed at the beginning and end of the five-session sequence. Each client's therapist gave the GAF ratings. These clinicians were trained in diagnoses of the *Diagnostic and Statistical Manual of Mental Disorders* (*DSM-IV*; American Psychiatric Association, 1994), including GAF rating, in their doctoral programs. The CSS and TSS were completed at the end of treatment. Predicting 30 clients in each group, an a priori estimate gave the multivariate analysis of variance (MANOVA) a .70 power to detect a moderate effect size of .375 (Lauter, 1978).

Procedure

Clients received five free sessions of cognitive-behavioral therapy (CBT) delivered by experienced doctoral students at a large midwestern university.[1] These therapists attended a 1-day training program in which they were provided a session-by-session treatment plan. This plan relied on standard CBT psychoeducational dialogues and use of traditional materials such as daily graphs, ABCD charts for negative events (Activation, Belief, Consequence, and Disputation), and goaling ladders. However, this was not the only CBT training they had received because all of them attended doctoral programs that valued and taught this approach, and several worked in clinics with this orientation. All therapists worked in all three modes (face-to-face, video, and audio), were aware that the study involved comparing these modes, and knew that they were expected to provide equivalent treatment in each mode. Clinicians ranged in age from 22 to 45. Self-reported ethnic backgrounds included White (11), Asian American (1), African American (2), and Latina (2). Our clinicians also represented lesbian and physically handicapped groups.

On calling the clinic for appointments, clients were assigned to one of the three conditions according to a randomized list; one quarter were also assigned to a 4- or 5-week wait-list to serve as outcome control participants, after which they joined their appointed group for therapy. All sessions were videotaped, even when the dyad members never saw each other (in the audio condition), for purposes of rating the alliance. In the face-to-face condition, the pair occupied the same room in

the ordinary manner. In the video condition, each member of the pair sat in a separate room and viewed the other person over a closed-circuit 20-inch television monitor. In the audio condition, each client used a hands-free audio-only system to connect and speak with the therapist, again from a separate room. In both experimental conditions, the client never saw the therapist in person and was not aware that the therapist's room was nearby. Thus, although the centralization of locale did not replicate the conditions of real-world distance technology, it did provide similarity while maintaining control of the physical setting, which might have otherwise introduced unmeasured variability among clients (e.g., faulty technology, lack of privacy, and problems of access).

A site coordinator managed the clinic operations and received the clients at each session. At Session 1, clients were excluded from the study (a) if their scores on the General Severity Index of the BSI (Derogatis, 1993) were above the 50th percentile of adult nonpatient norms and they could not name a specific problem to work on ($n = 2$); (b) if they indicated that they would be unable to complete five sessions; or (c) if they were assessed to be a danger to self or others or actively psychotic, for which contingency we planned a referral system. It was never necessary to invoke the last two exclusion criteria.

Results

Process

Raters demonstrated excellent interrater agreement on the Vanderbilt subscales, with intraclass correlations of .75 for Participation, .72 for Hostility, and .82 for Exploration (all $ps < .0001$). Scale reliabilities (Cronbach's alphas) were .87 for Participation, .72 for Hostility, and .89 for Exploration.

Table 1
Descriptive Statistics for Working Alliance Variables (Vanderbilt Psychotherapy Process Scale)

Variable	n	M	SD	Item score range
Client participation				1.5–5
Face-to-face	27	3.99	0.31	
Video	26	4.19	0.34	
Audio	27	4.15	0.23	
Client hostility				1–4
Face-to-face	27	1.09	0.12	
Video	26	1.12	0.11	
Audio	27	1.17	0.24	
Therapist exploration				1–5
Face-to-face	27	3.33	0.41	
Video	26	3.10	0.43	
Audio	27	3.29	0.41	

Table 1 profiles the sample sizes, means, standard deviations, and ranges of item scores for all participants. A MANOVA on the sample ($N = 80$) revealed a statistically significant, $F(6, 150) = 2.51$, $p < .05$, difference among the groups on the set of alliance vari-

---

[1] Therapists were given training in CBT as well as having studied it in coursework. However, they were allowed flexibility in treatment in order to reproduce the conditions of real-world therapy. Therapists gave self-reports of adherence to the CBT model after each treatment. Mean therapy adherence scores, on a scale of 1 to 10 for each of the three treatment groups ($1 = I\ did\ not\ use\ CBT$, $10 = I\ used\ CBT\ completely$), were 7.04 for face-to-face ($SD = 2.08$), 7.12 for video ($SD = 2.05$), and 6.56 for audio ($SD = 2.06$). Analysis of variance revealed no significant differences in therapy adherence across groups. The secondary approach most used was emotional support. Self-rating was considered the best available measure because tape observers saw only parts of the therapy sequence.

ables. Follow-up analyses (pairwise comparisons with Bonferroni adjustment) showed that the meaningful difference lay in the Client Participation dimension—but not in the expected direction. Clients participated *less* in the face-to-face mode than in either of the technologically mediated treatments, with effect sizes of .62 for face-to-face versus video and .57 for face-to-face versus audio.

Outcome

Table 2 profiles the sample sizes, means, and standard deviations for all participants on outcome measures. A MANOVA comparing treatment groups with the control group on outcome measures discovered a significant superiority of treatment to no treatment, as expected, $F(12, 265) = 1.82$, $p = .01$. This superiority was particularly reflected in Target Complaints severity levels, which makes sense given that the brief cognitive-behavioral model focuses on specific problem areas. From clients' TC ratings, effect sizes were 1.04 for face-to-face over control, 1.16 for video over control, and .73 for audio over control. (Among treatment groups, these effect sizes were .18 for audio over face-to-face, .07 for face-to-face over video, and .06 for audio over video.) From therapists' TC ratings, effect sizes were 1.05 for face-to-face over control, 1.26 for video over control, and 1.43 for audio over control. (Among treatment groups, these effect sizes were .19 for face-to-face over audio, .13 for face-to-face over video, and .09 for video over audio.) In the Global Assessment of Functioning, effect sizes were .69, .72, and .56 for face-to-face, video, and audio treatments, respectively, over control group levels. As Table 2 makes plain, effect sizes for symptom inventory (BSI) means were negligible, perhaps because of raised awareness or arousal of symptoms after five sessions of treatment. We speculate that this might arise from intensified introspection among already troubled people.

To examine possible differences among face-to-face, video, and audio groups in therapy outcome, the three groups were compared by MANOVA on the set of outcome variables. Although the researcher set the significance level at .15 to enhance the procedure's power to perceive differences when they existed (Stevens, 1996), no significant differences among the groups were found, $F(12, 144) = .67$, $p > .15$. This means that the closing symptom checklists, assessments of functioning, levels of target complaints, and satisfaction measures, taken as a composite variable that maximized the differences among groups, did not distinguish in which mode the client was treated. Raw outcome scores were used because randomization equalized pretreatment conditions across groups, making unnecessary any further operations to adjust for pretest scores.

As research and theory predicted, the working alliance was significantly and positively correlated with overall outcome in this study ($r = .22$, $p = .05$), using the mean of standardized scores for all outcome measures. In each separate condition, the alliance-outcome correlation did not reach significance because of the number of participants.

Table 2
Descriptive Statistics for Outcome Measures

Measure	n	M	SD
BSI (GSI)			
Face-to-face	27	35.73	30.56
Video	26	32.84	21.44
Audio	27	32.36	24.83
Control	27	35.37	25.64
GAF			
Face-to-face	27	77.60	10.60
Video	26	77.85	10.03
Audio	27	76.30	12.39
Control	27	71.00	9.51
TC—Client			
Face-to-face	27	5.99	3.17
Video	26	5.78	2.88
Audio	27	6.56	3.04
Control	27	7.90	1.83
TC—Therapist			
Face-to-face	27	5.81	3.14
Video	26	5.47	2.11
Audio	27	5.22	3.16
Control	27	7.46	1.57
CSS			
Face-to-face	27	6.19	1.17
Video	26	5.97	0.92
Audio	27	5.77	1.07
TSS			
Face-to-face	27	5.90	0.90
Video	26	5.73	0.89
Audio	27	5.38	1.32

Note. BSI (GSI) = Brief Symptom Inventory (Global Severity Index); GAF = Global Assessment of Functioning; TC = Target Complaints; CSS = Client Satisfaction Scale; TSS = Therapist Satisfaction Scale.

Discussion

Our overall conclusions support the continued exploration of distance psychotherapy for individuals. The similarities among the three treatment groups—face-to-face, video teleconference, and audio conference—came through more strongly than any differences. The major difference we found could be construed as favorable to the distance modes: Statistics indicate that Client Participation scores were higher when clients were not face to face with their therapists. This dimension included ratings on such features as clients' activity level, initiative, trust, spontaneity, and disinhibition—aspects that we would expect to be dampened by the introduction of a strange therapeutic situation. Evidently, they were not. Two speculations about the cause of this unusual result are that clients in the distance modes made more of an effort to communicate, taking more responsibility for the interaction than they did in face-to-face traditional therapy, or that distance made openness seem safer. The pattern of the clients becoming more active in the distance modes is certainly an intriguing one. It may be that clients tried

345 harder to get their voices heard when technology came between them and their therapists.

The results of the outcome analysis found no significant differences among treatment groups, thus failing to reject the null hypothesis of no treatment differ-
350 ences. It would appear that in a brief therapy situation, the outcome of delivery over two-way audio or video is comparable to face-to-face treatment. The observed power in the outcome analysis (.60) would have allowed us to detect large differences in results between
355 the modes, but medium effects could be missed and small ones certainly would be. In sum, initial evaluations indicate that two-way audio, video, and face-to-face treatment delivery modes can be used to provide similarly effective treatment; however, several features
360 must still be examined before we can declare equivalent effectiveness across the board.

Limitations of the Study

Despite attempts to achieve generalizable results, this project remains an analogue study. Clients were deprived of the obvious benefits of telemedicine—that
365 is, they were not able to receive their therapy from a location more convenient than their local clinic because they were required to come to our clinic for videotaping and control purposes. All treatment was limited to five sessions, with clients referred elsewhere for con-
370 tinuing therapy. The fact that we drew from the nearby and mobile population meant that the sample did not include rural residents or the homebound, who are main beneficiaries of telemedicine. From one point of view, these facts only strengthen the indicators of our
375 study because one might expect even better results from clients relieved from travel, inconvenience, or plain absence of services.

As usual, generalization to a larger population may be limited by our research design. First, standard devia-
380 tions on process variables (Table 1) are less than half a point on a 5-point scale. The small variability in Therapist Exploration scores is understandable because the therapists and techniques were so homogenous. The small standard deviations for client process variables
385 were surprising, considering a varied group of ages, problem types, and severity among clients. Raters did not appear to be avoiding extremes on the scale (see Table 1). We must conclude that there was a good deal of similarity among therapy sessions overall in this
390 study. Second, our master's-level therapists may have performed differently from PhD-level therapists; however, it must be acknowledged that most front-line therapists *are* at the master's level. Third, findings from cognitive-behavioral techniques may not repre-
395 sent what would happen if other approaches were emphasized. Fourth, our decision to include a wide variety of presenting problems improved generalizability in one way while precluding insight into the preferred treatment for a specific problem, and the average mild
400 level of distress among our participants precludes judgments about treatment of more severe disorders. Finally, because we did not do a follow-up study, we do not know whether one mode of treatment had longer-lasting effects than any other.

Future Directions

405 The next step on a larger scale is to collect data and analyze it in naturalistic settings in which communications technology is used to achieve access to clients in remote sites. Extensions of teletherapy to people in restricted conditions such as prisons, hospices, and
410 nursing homes need to be studied.

Because it appears that the alliance can be built regardless of treatment mode (face-to-face, video, or audio), investigations into using features of distance communication to treat specific problems will be inter-
415 esting clinically. Mode-by-problem matching is an area ripe for study. For example, like the alcohol abusers in Kobak et al.'s (1997) study, anorexic women reported admitting to more pathological behavior in a voice-only communication than they ever had in face-to-face
420 counseling.

Along the same lines, several psychological disorders result in extreme discomfort with human contact. Agoraphobics, socially anxious, and avoidant personalities often find close proximity with unfamiliar others
425 intolerable. One possible tactic involves using telephone, video, and face-to-face communication with the psychotherapist as such a client gains trust and comfort. Because keeping these clients in continuous treatment is a challenge, this flexibility could prove
430 extremely valuable in their course of therapy by maintaining the relationship under adverse conditions.

An extension of this study to another widely used but unstudied phenomenon—the use of on-line systems to conduct psychotherapy—is a tempting line of future
435 endeavors. Because the nature of relationships formed over the Internet has recently been found lacking (e.g., in failing to ameliorate loneliness; Kraut et al., 1998), it would be interesting to discover whether the therapeutic alliance established by electronic keyboard shares
440 the healing qualities of the relationship established in other technologically mediated ways.

References

American Psychiatric Association (1994). *Diagnostic and statistical manual of mental disorders* (4th ed.). Washington, DC: Author.

Bachelor, A. (1991). Comparison and relationship to outcome of diverse dimensions of the helping alliance as seen by client and therapist. *Psychotherapy, 28*, 534–549.

Battle, C. C., Imber, S. D., Hoehn-Saric, R., Stone, A. R., Nash, E. R., & Frank, J. D. (1966). Target complaints as criteria for improvement. *American Journal of Psychotherapy, 20*, 184–192.

Bordin, E. S. (1979). The generalizability of the psychoanalytic concept of working alliance. *Psychotherapy: Theory, Research and Practice, 16*, 252–260.

Derogatis, L. R. (1993). *Brief Symptom Inventory: Administration, scoring, and procedures manual.* Minneapolis, MN: National Computer Systems.

Derogatis, L. R., & Melisaratos, N. (1983). The Brief Symptom Inventory: An introductory report. *Psychological Medicine, 13*, 595–605.

Endicott, J., Spitzer, R. L., Fleiss, J. L., & Cohen, J. (1976). The Global Assessment Scale. *Archives of General Psychiatry, 33*, 766–771.

Henry, W. P., Strupp, H. H., Schacht, T. E., & Gaston, L. (1994). Psychodynamic approaches. In A. E. Bergin & S. L. Garfield (Eds.), *Handbook of psychotherapy and behavior change* (4th ed., pp. 467–508). New York: Wiley.

Kobak, K. A., Taylor, L. vH., Dottl, S. L., Greist, J. H., Jefferson, J. W., & Burroughs, D. (1997). A computer-administered telephone interview to identify mental disorders. *Journal of the American Medical Association, 278,* 905–910.

Kraut, R., Patterson, M., Lundmark, V., Kiesler, S., Mukopadhyay, T., & Scherlis, W. (1998). Internet paradox: A social technology that reduces social involvement and psychological well-being? *American Psychologist, 53,* 1017–1031.

Lauter, J. (1978). Sample size requirements for the T^2 test of MANOVA. *Biometrical Journal, 20,* 389–406.

Mintz, J., & Kiesler, D. J. (1982). Individualized measures of psychotherapy outcome. In P. C. Kendall & J. N. Butcher (Eds.), *Handbook of research methods in clinical psychology* (pp. 429–460). New York: Wiley.

O'Malley, S. S., Suh, C. S., & Strupp, H. H. (1983). The Vanderbilt Psychotherapy Process Scale: A report on the scale development and a process-outcome study. *Journal of Consulting and Clinical Psychology, 51,* 581–586.

Sexton, H. C., Hembre, K., & Kvarme, G. (1996). The interaction of the alliance and therapy microprocess: A sequential analysis. *Journal of Consulting and Clinical Psychology, 64,* 471–480.

Stevens, J. (1996). *Applied multivariate statistics for the social sciences* (3rd ed.). Mahwah, NJ: Erlbaum.

Strupp, H. H., & Hadley, S. W. (1977). A tripartite model of mental health and therapeutic outcomes. *Archives of General Psychiatry, 36,* 1125–1136.

Strupp, H. H., Hartley, D., & Blackwood, G. L., Jr. (1974). *Vanderbilt Psychotherapy Process Scale and rater's manual.* Unpublished manuscript, Vanderbilt University, Nashville, TN.

Tracey, T. J., & Dundon, M. (1988). Role anticipations and preferences over the course of counseling: An interactional examination. *Journal of Counseling Psychology, 31,* 13–27.

Acknowledgments: This study was partially funded by a University of Illinois Graduate College Dissertation Grant (1998) and a University of Illinois Research Board Grant (1998). We warmly thank our dissertation committee: James Rounds, Terence J. G. Tracey, Lizanne Destefano, Thomas Moore, and Rob Glueckauf. Our project depended on the efforts of many others to whom we owe our gratitude: therapists, supervisors, site coordinators, Psychological Services Center staff at UIUC, donators of equipment and labor, and cognitive-behavioral therapy trainers.

Address correspondence to: Susan X Day, Department of Educational Psychology, University of Houston, 491 Farish Hall, Houston, TX 77204-5029. E-mail: sxday@iastate.edu

Exercise for Article 19

Factual Questions

1. Some of the clients for this study were obtained from self-referrals from what two sources?

2. What was the age range of clients who completed treatment?

3. Were the psychotherapists who rated the working alliance trained for this study?

4. Did clients participate "more" or did they participate "less" in the face-to-face mode than in the other two modes?

5. According to the researchers, why did they report only posttest scores (and not pretest scores) in Table 2?

6. To test for significant differences on the outcome measures, the researchers used what probability level?

Questions for Discussion

7. In the table of contents of this book, this research article is classified as true experimental research. What is your understanding of the meaning of this term?

8. The researchers selected a sample with a wide range of problems. If you were conducting a study on the same topic, would you use such a sample or would you use a sample with a limited range of problems? Explain. (See lines 50–61 and 383–386.)

9. The researchers used only cognitive-behavioral therapy. If you were conducting a study on the same topic, would you use only one type of therapy? Explain. (See lines 195–197.)

10. In your opinion, how important is the information given in the footnote on the third page of this article? Explain.

11. "Effect sizes" are given for a number of the comparisons. What is your understanding of the meaning of this statistic? (See lines 281–299.)

12. The researchers point out a number of limitations in lines 362–404. In your opinion, are they all equally important? Explain.

13. The researchers make a number of recommendations for future directions in research on their research topic in lines 405–441. If you were planning a follow-up study on the same topic, which of the recommendations, if any, would you incorporate in your plans?

Quality Ratings

Directions: Indicate your level of agreement with each of the following statements by circling a number from 5 for strongly agree (SA) to 1 for strongly disagree (SD). If you believe an item is not applicable to this research article, leave it blank. Be prepared to explain your ratings. When responding to criteria A and B below, keep in mind that brief titles and abstracts are conventional in published research.

A. The title of the article is appropriate.

SA   5   4   3   2   1   SD

B.   The abstract provides an effective overview of the research article.

SA   5   4   3   2   1   SD

C.   The introduction establishes the importance of the study.

SA   5   4   3   2   1   SD

D.   The literature review establishes the context for the study.

SA   5   4   3   2   1   SD

E.   The research purpose, question, or hypothesis is clearly stated.

SA   5   4   3   2   1   SD

F.   The method of sampling is sound.

SA   5   4   3   2   1   SD

G.   Relevant demographics (for example, age, gender, and ethnicity) are described.

SA   5   4   3   2   1   SD

H.   Measurement procedures are adequate.

SA   5   4   3   2   1   SD

I.   All procedures have been described in sufficient detail to permit a replication of the study.

SA   5   4   3   2   1   SD

J.   The participants have been adequately protected from potential harm.

SA   5   4   3   2   1   SD

K.   The results are clearly described.

SA   5   4   3   2   1   SD

L.   The discussion/conclusion is appropriate.

SA   5   4   3   2   1   SD

M.   Despite any flaws, the report is worthy of publication.

SA   5   4   3   2   1   SD

Article 20

Differences in Readers' Response Toward Advertising versus Publicity

SANJAY PUTREVU
Bryant University

ABSTRACT. Publicity is assumed to have higher credibility than advertising, prompting communication specialists to call for its use alongside traditional advertising to achieve overall communication goals. To test the differences in readers' response toward advertisements and publicity, a sample of students (*N*=104; 52 men and 52 women) were shown printed messages identified as advertising or publicity. The publicity format appeared to be associated with deeper processing because participants had higher recall, more message-relevant thoughts, and better discrimination for the publicity message. In addition, participants rated the publicity message higher on Source Credibility, Brand Attitude, and Purchase Intent than a comparable advertisement.

From *Psychological Reports*, 96, 207–212. Copyright © 2005 by Psychological Reports. Reprinted with permission.

There is growing concern and unease among advertisers with the sole or excessive reliance on advertising to accomplish their communication objectives (Blacker, 1994; Perry, 1994). Advertising proliferation, shorter messages, technological advances, higher costs, and viewer distrust have made advertisers reassess their communication strategy. One potential solution is integrated marketing communications, an approach that recommends the simultaneous use of multiple communication methods such as advertising and publicity (Lord & Putrevu, 1998; Buer, 2002; Jin, 2003).

Advertising is generally defined as any paid form of nonpersonal presentation of ideas, goods, or services by an identified sponsor, whereas publicity is depicted as the task of securing editorial space, as opposed to paid space, in print and broadcast media to promote a product, place, or person (Kotler, 2003). It is widely assumed that publicity is more credible and has a stronger influence on affect and brand sales than advertising (Ellenis, 1989; Levy, 1989; Ries & Ries, 2002; Hausman, 2003). While the empirical evidence comparing the two formats is very sparse, some past research has found larger readership (Lord & Putrevu, 1998), less miscomprehension (Preston & Scharbach, 1971), and higher credibility (Hausknecht, Wilkinson, & Brough, 1989; D'Astous & Hebert, 1991) for publicity over advertising.

It is reasonable to expect consumers to place more value on information obtained from a highly credible source. Hence, based on the assumption of publicity's higher credibility, Lord and Putrevu (1993) proposed an information-processing model wherein publicity was associated with higher processing motivation and hence deeper processing than advertising. Such deeper processing should, in turn, lead to higher recall, more message-relevant thoughts, and better discrimination (recognition accuracy) for publicity (Petty, Ostrom, & Brock, 1981; Burnkrant & Howard, 1984; Lynch, Marmorstein, & Weigold, 1988). Also, the higher credibility associated with publicity should result in more positive Brand Attitude and Purchase Intent for publicity messages than advertisements. These assumptions and predictions of the Lord and Putrevu model (1993) were tested in the context of printed advertising and publicity messages. There were four hypotheses. (H1A) A higher proportion of the readers will recall the publicity message than a comparable advertisement. (H1B) Readers will generate more message-relevant cognitive responses for the publicity message than for a comparable advertisement. (H1C) The contents of the publicity message will be more accurately recognized than those of a comparable advertisement. (H2) Readers will rate the publicity message higher on Source Credibility, Brand Attitude, and Purchase Intent than a comparable advertisement.

Method

Data were collected from 104 (52 men and 52 women) undergraduate students from a university in the northeastern USA. Two distinct 12-page excerpts were created and presented as newly developed university magazines. The excerpts contained a cover page, instruction page, three buffer items, stimulus advertisement, three buffer items, stimulus news story (publicity), and two buffer items. The stimulus advertising and publicity messages were for fictitious brands of shampoo and pizza. The buffer items were university announcements, news stories, and advertisements for products and services available on campus. In the first excerpt the shampoo message was depicted as the advertisement, and the pizza message was depicted as the news story (publicity). In the second excerpt the shampoo message was depicted as the news story (publicity), and the pizza message was depicted as the advertisement.

The primary focus of the experiment was to test whether readers would respond differently toward the messages based on the format alone. Hence, to avoid potential confounds, the information content and presentation style were identical in the advertising and publicity conditions except for the title at the top of the page. In the advertising condition, the stimulus message was clearly identified as an advertisement by the title "ADVERTISEMENT" in boldface, 18-point font at the top of the page. Similarly, in the publicity condition, the stimulus message was clearly identified as a news story by the title "NEWS STORY" in boldface, 18-point font at the top of the page.

Participants were told that the purpose of the study was to obtain their opinions about the usefulness and relevance of the news magazine. They were instructed to read the magazine as they normally would and to skip over any items that were of little or no interest. Participants were randomly assigned to one of the two excerpts and were given a maximum of 10 min. to read the contents. After all participants had returned their copies, they completed the dependent measures and were debriefed and dismissed.

First, unaided recall was measured by asking participants to list all the advertisements, news stories, and announcements they recalled seeing in the magazine. They could potentially recall up to ten items—any of the eight buffer items and the two stimulus items (one advertisement and one publicity article). If the stimulus advertisement or publicity article was listed, it was coded 1, and if it was not listed, the code was 0. Second, participants were presented the brand name of the stimulus advertisement or publicity article in writing, and they were asked to write down their thoughts about the brand. These responses were coded as message-relevant thoughts and message-irrelevant thoughts by two independent judges (agreement rate = .96). There were very few message-irrelevant thoughts, and their inclusion or exclusion did not alter the results. Hence, only message-relevant thoughts were included in the analysis.

Next, participants were asked to identify features included in the stimulus message from a list of ten (five true and five foil) statements. Recognition accuracy (i.e., ability to identify correctly the details included in the message) was assessed using signal-detection scores (Grier, 1971). The scores were calculated as: $A' = 05 + [(y - x)(1 + y - x)]/[4y (1 - x)]$, where x is the probability of false alarm (wrong acceptance of a foil statement), and y is the probability of a hit (correct acceptance of a true statement). Signal-detection scores are useful measures of recognition since they provide a measure of discrimination uncontaminated by the response tendencies of subjects (Singh & Churchill,

1986; Putrevu, 2004). Source Credibility was assessed using six sets of 5-point bipolar adjectives: 1 = untrustworthy, 5 = trustworthy; 1= unfair, 5 = fair; 1 = not justified, 5 = justified; 1 = novice, 5 = expert; 1 = not credible, 5 = credible; and 1 = unreliable, 5 = reliable (alphas of .90 and .88 for advertising and publicity, respectively). Brand Attitude was measured using four sets of 5-point bipolar adjectives: 1 = dislike, 5 = like; 1 = bad, 5 = good; 1 = unfavorable, 5 = favorable; and 1 = useless, 5 = useful (alphas of .86 and .84 for advertising and publicity, respectively). Purchase Intent was measured using three sets of 5-point bipolar adjectives: 1 = unlikely, 5 = likely; 1 = improbable, 5 = probable; and 1 = impossible, 5 = possible (alphas of .91 and .83 for advertising and publicity, respectively).

Results

The results are summarized in Table 1. Compared to advertising, the publicity message was recalled by a higher proportion of respondents for both products (Shampoo: .77 versus .50; Pizza: .75 versus .60). Respondents generated more message-relevant thoughts in the publicity condition than in the advertising condition for both products (Shampoo: 2.87 versus 2.00; Pizza: 2.92 versus 1.94). The signal-detection scores showed that respondents had more accurate recognition in the publicity condition than in the advertising condition for both products (Shampoo: .78 versus .72; Pizza: .79 versus .72). Hence, Hypotheses H1A, B, and C are supported. The publicity message was rated higher on Source Credibility than the advertisement for both products (Shampoo: 3.8 versus 3.1; Pizza: 3.7 versus 3.1). The publicity condition had a more positive rating for Brand Attitude than the advertising condition for both products (Shampoo: 3.8 versus 3.3; Pizza: 3.8 versus 3.3). Also, participants rated the publicity message as higher in Purchase Intent compared to the advertising message for both products (Shampoo: 3.8 versus 3.1; Pizza: 3.8 versus 3.2). Therefore, the results support Hypothesis H2.

Discussion

The findings of this study support the assumptions and predictions of the Lord and Putrevu model (1993). Specifically, a higher proportion of participants recalled the message labeled publicity than that labeled an advertisement. In addition, the message labeled publicity was associated with more message-relevant thoughts and higher recognition accuracy. The better memory and more cognitive responses in the publicity condition suggest that the participants probably processed the publicity message more deeply than the comparable advertisement. The participants also rated the publicity message higher on Source Credibility, Brand Attitude, and Purchase Intent than the advertisement.

In conclusion, this research suggests that information identified as publicity elicits different responses than identical content identified as an advertisement. These effects were significant even though the manipu-

Table 1
Means and Standard Deviations for Dependent Variables

	Advertisement		Publicity			
	M	*SD*	*M*	*SD*	*t*	*p*
Unaided Recall						
Shampoo	0.50	0.51	0.77	0.43	−3.44	.01
Pizza	0.60	0.50	0.75	0.44	−2.22	.05
Number of Cognitive Responses						
Shampoo	2.00	0.93	2.87	0.97	−8.13	.01
Pizza	1.94	0.85	2.92	0.93	−10.11	.01
Signal-detection Scores						
Shampoo	0.72	0.10	0.78	0.10	−9.64	.01
Pizza	0.72	0.10	0.79	0.10	−9.56	.01
Source Credibility						
Shampoo	3.14	0.65	3.77	0.70	−11.99	.01
Pizza	3.12	0.65	3.74	0.70	−12.34	.01
Brand Attitude						
Shampoo	3.28	0.69	3.80	0.69	−8.41	.01
Pizza	3.26	0.66	3.77	0.72	−8.25	.01
Purchase Intent						
Shampoo	3.13	0.70	3.79	0.70	−16.39	.01
Pizza	3.15	0.69	3.83	0.68	−22.42	.01

185 lation was somewhat weak (i.e., the information content and presentation style were identical in the two formats). Hence, publicity could be used to enhance the credibility and effectiveness of marketing communications. Researchers should explore whether these results would generalize to the larger consumer population and 190 whether individual-difference variables such as need for cognition and involvement moderate these effects.

References

Blacker, S. M. (1994). Magazines' role in promotion: They're well suited to assist in relationship marketing. *Advertising Age (June 20)*, 32.

Buer, L. (2002). What have public affairs and advertising got in common? *Journal of Public Affairs, 2*, 293–295.

Burnkrant, R. E., & Howard, D. J. (1984). Effects of the use of introductory rhetorical questions versus statements on information processing. *Journal of Personality and Social Psychology, 47*, 1218–1230.

D'Astous, A., & Hebert, C. (1991). Une etude comparative des effets de la publicite ecrite conventionnelle et du publi-reportage. In T. Schellinck (Ed.), *ASAC marketing proceedings.* Niagara Falls, ON: Administrative Sciences Association of Canada. Pp. 102–112.

Ellenis, M. (1989). Generating maximum exposure with a limited marketing budget. *Economic Development Review, 7*, 45–46.

Grier, J. B. (1971). Nonparametric indexes for sensitivity and bias: computing formulas. *Psychological Bulletin, 75*, 424–429.

Hausknecht, D. R., Wilkinson, J. B., & Brough, G. E. (1989). Advertorials: Do consumers see the wolf in sheep's clothing? In P. Bloom, R. Winer, H. H. Kassarjian, D. L. Scammon, B. Weitz, R. Speckman, V. Mahajan, & M. Levy (Eds.), *AMA Educators' proceedings: Enhancing knowledge development in marketing.* Chicago, IL: American Marketing Association. Pp. 308–312.

Hausman, M. (2003). PR vs. ads: Are you getting what you paid for? *Brandweek, 44*, 24.

Jin, H. S. (2003). Compounding consumer interest: Effects of advertising campaign publicity on the ability to recall subsequent advertisements. *Journal of Advertising, 32*, 29–41.

Kotler, P. (2003). *Marketing management.* (11th ed.) Englewood Cliffs, NJ: Prentice Hall.

Levy, D. (1989). What public relations can do better than advertising. *Public Relations Quarterly, 34*, 7–9.

Lord, K. R., & Putrevu, S. (1993). Advertising and publicity: An information processing perspective. *Journal of Economic Psychology, 14*, 57–84.

Lord, K. R., & Putrevu, S. (1998). Communicating in print: A comparison of consumer responses to different promotional formats. *Journal of Current Issues and Research in Advertising, 20*, 1–18.

Lynch, L. G., Jr., Marmorstein, H., & Weigold, M. F. (1988). Choices from sets including remembered brands: Use of recalled attributes and prior evaluations. *Journal of Consumer Research, 15*, 169–184.

Perry, C. N. (1994). From trying harder to 'nothing but net,' ads lost their focus. *Advertising Age (May 16)*, 32.

Perry, R. E., Ostrom, T. M., & Brock, T. C. (1981). *Cognitive responses in persuasion.* Hillsdale, NJ: Erlbaum.

Preston, I. L., & Scharbach, S. E. (1971). Advertising: More than meets the eye? *Journal of Advertising Research, 3*, 19–24.

Putrevu, S. (2004). Sex differences in processing printed advertisements. *Psychological Reports, 94*, 814–818.

Ries, A., & Ries, L. (2002). *The fall of advertising and the rise of PR.* New York: HarperCollins.

Singh, S. N., & Churchill, G. A. (1986). Using the theory of signal detection to improve ad recognition testing. *Journal of Marketing Research, 23*, 327–336.

Address correspondence to: Sanjay Putrevu, Marketing Department, Bryant University, 1150 Douglas Pike, Smithfield, RI 02917-1284. E-mail: sputrevu@bryant.edu

Exercise for Article 20

Factual Questions

1. The researcher states four hypotheses. What is the first one?

2. What was the basis for assigning the participants to one of the two types of excerpts (publicity versus advertisement)?

3. In line 146, the researcher reports "proportions." In order to convert a proportion to a percentage, multiply the proportion by 100%. What percentage of those in the publicity-message group recalled the shampoo advertisement?

4. Did the "publicity group" *or* "advertisement group" give a higher rating on Purchase Intent for pizza?

5. How many of the twelve comparisons of means in Table 1 are statistically significant?

6. What is the name of the statistical test used in this study?

Questions for Discussion

7. This article is classified as an example of "true experimental research" in the table of contents of this book. Do you agree with this classification? Why? Why not?

8. The participants were 104 undergraduates. Would it be interesting to know how they were recruited? (See lines 56–58.)

9. The researcher uses the term "potential confounds" in line 77. Speculate on the meaning of this term.

10. The researcher uses the term "debriefed" in line 96. Speculate on the meaning of this term.

11. The researcher used two independent judges. Is this important? Is it a strength of the study? Explain. (See lines 108–110.)

12. If you were to conduct a study on the same topic, what changes, if any, would you make in the research methodology?

Quality Ratings

Directions: Indicate your level of agreement with each of the following statements by circling a number from 5 for strongly agree (SA) to 1 for strongly disagree (SD). If you believe an item is not applicable to this research article, leave it blank. Be prepared to explain your ratings. When responding to criteria A and B below, keep in mind that brief titles and abstracts are conventional in published research.

A. The title of the article is appropriate.

SA 5 4 3 2 1 SD

B. The abstract provides an effective overview of the research article.

SA 5 4 3 2 1 SD

C. The introduction establishes the importance of the study.

SA 5 4 3 2 1 SD

D. The literature review establishes the context for the study.

SA 5 4 3 2 1 SD

E. The research purpose, question, or hypothesis is clearly stated.

SA 5 4 3 2 1 SD

F. The method of sampling is sound.

SA 5 4 3 2 1 SD

G. Relevant demographics (for example, age, gender, and ethnicity) are described.

SA 5 4 3 2 1 SD

H. Measurement procedures are adequate.

SA 5 4 3 2 1 SD

I. All procedures have been described in sufficient detail to permit a replication of the study.

SA 5 4 3 2 1 SD

J. The participants have been adequately protected from potential harm.

SA 5 4 3 2 1 SD

K. The results are clearly described.

SA 5 4 3 2 1 SD

L. The discussion/conclusion is appropriate.

SA 5 4 3 2 1 SD

M. Despite any flaws, the report is worthy of publication.

SA 5 4 3 2 1 SD

Article 21

Online Instruction:
Are the Outcomes the Same?

LOUIS L. WARREN
East Carolina University

HAROLD L. HOLLOMAN, JR.
East Carolina University

ABSTRACT. Institutions of higher education are offering more and more online courses to students. Do students receive the same quality of instruction with an online class as an on-campus class? Specifically, is there a difference in students' outcomes between a face-to-face class and online class? This study addresses that question by collecting and assessing data between students enrolled in the same course as it is delivered to one section face-to-face and another section online. The results of this study reveal that there are no significant differences in the students' outcomes between the two sections. These results support that the quality of online instruction is equal to face-to-face instruction. However, more research is needed to address issues related to online instruction.

From *Journal of Instructional Psychology, 32*, 148–151. Copyright © 2005 by Project Innovation, Inc. Reprinted with permission.

Technology has made a significant impact on how instruction is delivered in higher education (Teh, 1999). The majority of colleges and universities offer some form of Web-based education (Palloff & Pratt,
5 2001). Each year, the number of courses being delivered over the Internet is increasing. The teaching methodology of higher education faculty has changed as the result of teaching online (Greenwood, 2000). The important question to address in this movement of online
10 course delivery is students' outcomes. Is the achievement level of students who take classes online equal to classes that are taught face-to-face? That is the question addressed in this study.

Online instruction is housed under the auspice of
15 distance education. Distance education began in the 19th century to provide students who could not attend traditional classes the chance to learn. The evolution of various instructional delivery methods of distance education has included such media as correspondence
20 courses, radio, television, and videotapes (Fender, 1999). Then in the 1990s, many higher education distance education programs adopted Internet-based delivery as the new mode to deliver courses (Khan, 1997; Moore & Kearsley, 1996; Porter, 1997).
25 Today, the Internet and its prevalence allow almost anyone to become a distance learner through online course offerings. This ease of use has been supplemented by the development of course management software with the purpose of making online courses
30 easy to develop and manage from the instructors' perspective and easy to undertake from the students' perspective.

There are several Computer Management System (CMS) programs being used for online classes with
35 Blackboard being the most popular (Olsen, 2001; Young, 2002). CMSs such as Blackboard have a structured format that allows instructors to post announcements, assignments, course documents, faculty credentials, and lecture notes that can be easily accessed by
40 students. Blackboard also is structured so small groups can be formed, and group work can be an integral part of how the course is taught. It allows the opportunity for direct communication between instructor and students and among students through e-mail, discussion
45 boards, and the virtual chat room.

So all the variables were in place (availability, convenience, ease of implementing, etc.) to take distance learning to levels it has never experienced in its path. There has been an accelerated rate of course offerings
50 through online delivery, and it appears to be growing exponentially (Bennett, 2001; Boettcher, 1996; Hiltz, 1997; Lewis, Snow, Farris, Levin, & Greene, 1999; National Center for Education Statistics, 2002).

Interestingly, with the increasing acceptance of
55 online classes (Owston, 1997; Rossman, 1992) few studies have examined the effectiveness of online courses and whether the achievement levels of meeting the courses' competencies and objectives were met (Navarro & Shoemaker, 1999; Schulman & Sims,
60 1999; Sener & Stover, 2000; Smeaton & Keogh, 1999; Russell, 1999; Spooner, Jordan, Algozzine, & Spooner, 1999). In addition, little research exists examining issues related to student satisfaction (Kirtley, 2002). This study was conducted by comparing the outcomes of
65 students when one section of a course was taught face-to-face and one section of the same course was taught online.

Method

Subjects

The participants were a total of 52 students who

were evenly divided into two sections of the same graduate course that dealt with the topics of teacher leadership and communication. The students were randomly assigned to each of the two sections. One section was delivered face-to-face and the other section was delivered totally online. The demographics of the students in both sections were very close with the face-to-face section being 80% female with an average age of 34 and an average of nine years of teaching experience. The online section was 75% female with an average age of 33 and average of eight years of teaching experience.

Design and Procedure

Students were assigned various course requirements that included: designing and publishing a personal professional Web page, writing a professional mission statement that included clearly defined goals, conducting interviews, producing a PowerPoint presentation, writing a research paper, article critiques, midterm, and final examinations. These requirements and products were organized in a portfolio and collected by the instructor. Three outside evaluators assessed these portfolios for their overall quality by rating them on a scale of one to seven with a one being the low and a seven being the high.

Students were pre-assessed at the beginning of the course and post-assessed at the end of the course in a self evaluation that examined their level of expertise in the course's competencies and objectives. This self-evaluation was conducted on a Likert scale (1 = no mastery, 7 = total mastery). These evaluations were conducted on the first class meeting and the last class meeting after the students had completed their final examination.

Data for course evaluations were collected and shared with the instructor. Course evaluations are conducted on all course offerings at the university where this study was conducted. Students responded to questions that addressed their satisfaction with the different aspects of the course delivery. A Likert scale of 1–7 was used (1 = strongly disagree, 7 = strongly agree). Questions included instructor's preparation, availability, amount of work, etc., with the final question being the instructor's overall effectiveness.

Results

The data generated from this study indicated that there was no significant difference between the face-to-face section and the online section. The outside evaluators' overall assessment of the face-to-face portfolios was an average of 6.00 (with a low of a three and a high of a seven) and for the online section the overall assessment was an average of 6.25 (with a low of a three and a high of a seven).

The self-assessment data for the pre-assessment were an overall of 2.9 for the face-to-face section and 3.0 for the online section. For the post assessment, the face-to-face section overall score was 6.6 and for the

online an overall score of 6.7 was calculated. These results once again reveal no significant difference between the two sections.

The distribution of final grades for the face-to-face section was as follows: 19 students earned an A; 6 students earned a B; and 1 student earned a C. For the online section, 20 students earned an A and 6 students earned a B. Once again, there is no significant difference in the grade distribution between the two sections.

Results of the course evaluations administered by the university reveal no significant difference in students' satisfaction between the two sections. The mean score for the instructors' overall effectiveness for the face-to-face section was 6.7 and for the online section the score was 6.8. The other areas of students' satisfaction addressed by the instrument revealed very similar results with none being at the significant level.

Discussion

The current trend in higher education is to provide more online course offerings. Institutions of higher learning are responding to student demand and are offering more and more courses online and are even increasing the number of complete degree programs being offered online. However, as online course offerings continue to increase, there needs to be research that examines the quality of the course offerings and the student outcomes. This research study addresses those questions and the results support that students' outcomes are equal between face-to-face sections and online sections of the same course. The results of this study are encouraging in supporting distance education as providing educational opportunities for an ever-increasing diverse and mobile society. However, more research is needed to address the issues related to online course delivery and its impact on students and society.

References

Bennett, G. (2001). Student learning in the online environment: No significant difference? *Quest, 53*, 13.

Fender, D. L. (1999). Professional Safety. *Distance Education, 44*. Retrieved September 3, 2003, from EBSCOHost Academic Search Elite database.

Greenwood. T. M. (2000). E-Class: Creating a guide to online course development for distance education: An examination and analysis of change. *Dissertations Abstract International, 61*, 2576.

Hiltz, S. (1997). Impacts of college-level courses via Asynchronous Learning Networks: Some preliminary results. *Journal of Asynchronous Learning Networks* [Online]. Available from http://eies.njit.edu/`hiltz/workingpapers/philly/philly.htm

Khan, B. H. (1997). *Web-based instruction*. Englewood Cliffs, NJ: Educational Technology Publications.

Kirtley, K. E. (2002). A Study of Student Characteristics and Their Effects on Student Satisfaction with Online Courses Dissertation, West Virginia University. [Online Abstract]. Available: http://etd.wvu.edu/templates/show ETD.cfm?recnum=2538

Lewis, L., Snow, K., Farris, F., Levin, D., & Greene, B. (1999). Distance education at postsecondary education institutions 1997–98. National Center for Education Statistics [Online]. Available:http://nces.ed.gov/pubs2000/2000013.pdf

Moore, M. G., & Kearsley. G. (1996). *Distance education: A systems view*. Belmont, CA: Wadsworth.

National Center for Education Statistics (2002). *A Profile of Participation in Distance Education: Postsecondary Education Descriptive Analysis Reports* (NCES 2003-154). Washington. D.C.: U.S. Department of Education.

Navarro, P., & Shoemaker, J. (1999). The power of cyber learning: An empirical test. *Journal of Computing in Higher Education, 11*, 33.

Olsen, F. (2001). Getting ready for a new generation of course-management systems. *Chronicle of Higher Education, 48*, A25.

Owston, R. (1997). The World Wide Web: A technology to enhance teaching and learning. *Educational Researcher, 26*, 2733.

Palloff, R. M., & Pratt, K. (2001). Lessons from cyberspace classroom: The realities of online teaching. San Francisco: Jossey-Bass.

Porter, L. R. (1997). *Creating virtual classroom: Distance learning with the Internet*. New York: Wiley.

Rossman, P. (1992). *The emerging worldwide electronic university: Information age global higher education*. Westport, CT: Greenwood Press.

Schulman, A. H., & Sims, R. L. (1999). Learning in an online format versus an in-class format: An experimental study. *T H E Journal, 26*, 54–56.

Sener. J., & Stover, M. (2000). Integrating ALN into an independent study distance education program: NVCC case studies. *Journal of Asynchronous Learning Network, 4*.

Smeaton, A., & Keogh, G. (1999). An analysis of the use of virtual delivery of undergraduate lectures. *Computers and Education, 32*, 83–94.

Spooner, F., Jordan, L., Algozzine, B., & Spooner, M. (1999). Student ratings of instruction in distance learning and on-campus classes. *Journal of Educational Research, 92*, 132–140. Retrieved July 15, 2003 from EBSCOHost Academic Search Elite database.

Teh, G. (1999). Assessing student perceptions of Internet-based online learning environments. *International Journal of Instructional Media, 26*, 397–406.

Young, J. R. (2002). Pricing shifts by Blackboard and WebCT cost some colleges much more. *Chronicle of Higher Education, 48*, A35.

About the authors: *Louis L. Warren*, Associate Professor, Department of Curriculum & Instruction, College of Education, East Carolina University. *Harold L. Holloman, Jr.*, Assistant Professor, Department of Educational Leadership, East Carolina University.

Address correspondence to: Louis L. Warren, Associate Professor, East Carolina University, Department of Curriculum & Instruction,. College of Education, East Carolina University.

Exercise for Article 21

Factual Questions

1. What was the total number of participants in this experiment?

2. On what basis were the participants assigned to each of the two sections?

3. What issue did the last question on the course evaluations address?

4. Was there a significant difference in the outside evaluators' overall assessments of the two groups of portfolios?

5. Was the average score for the portfolios of the two sections near the top of the scale? Explain.

6. Were the average ratings of overall effectiveness for the two sections similar? Explain.

Questions for Discussion

7. The participants in this study were graduate students in a professional preparation course. Would you be willing to generalize the results of this experiment to undergraduates? To students in other types of courses? Explain. (See lines 68–71.)

8. This study is classified as "true experimental research" in the table of contents of this book. If you are familiar with the classification of types of experiments, explain what makes this a true experiment.

9. To what extent is it important to know that the demographics of the students in both sections were very close? (See lines 74–80.)

10. The portfolios were evaluated by outside evaluators. Would you be interested in knowing more about how they evaluated the portfolios? Explain. (See lines 87–92.)

11. Three outcome measures were used in this experiment (portfolio ratings, students' self-ratings of their level of expertise, and course evaluations). In your opinion, are all equally important? Explain. (See lines 81–111.)

12. Do you agree that more research is needed? Explain. (See lines 155–158.)

Quality Ratings

Directions: Indicate your level of agreement with each of the following statements by circling a number from 5 for strongly agree (SA) to 1 for strongly disagree (SD). If you believe an item is not applicable to this research article, leave it blank. Be prepared to explain your ratings. When responding to criteria A and B below, keep in mind that brief titles and abstracts are conventional in published research.

A. The title of the article is appropriate.
    SA   5   4   3   2   1   SD

B. The abstract provides an effective overview of the research article.
    SA   5   4   3   2   1   SD

C. The introduction establishes the importance of the study.
    SA   5   4   3   2   1   SD

D. The literature review establishes the context for the study.
    SA   5   4   3   2   1   SD

E. The research purpose, question, or hypothesis is clearly stated.
    SA   5   4   3   2   1   SD

F. The method of sampling is sound.
    SA   5   4   3   2   1   SD

G.   Relevant demographics (for example, age, gender, and ethnicity) are described.

SA   5   4   3   2   1   SD

H.   Measurement procedures are adequate.

SA   5   4   3   2   1   SD

I.   All procedures have been described in sufficient detail to permit a replication of the study.

SA   5   4   3   2   1   SD

J.   The participants have been adequately protected from potential harm.

SA   5   4   3   2   1   SD

K.   The results are clearly described.

SA   5   4   3   2   1   SD

L.   The discussion/conclusion is appropriate.

SA   5   4   3   2   1   SD

M.   Despite any flaws, the report is worthy of publication.

SA   5   4   3   2   1   SD

Article 22

Effect of Petting a Dog
on Immune System Function

CARL J. CHARNETSKI
Wilkes University

SANDRA RIGGERS
Marywood University

FRANCIS X. BRENNAN
VA Medical Center, Philadelphia

ABSTRACT. The present study assessed the effect of petting a dog on secretory immunoglobulin A (IgA) levels. 55 college students were randomly assigned to either an experimental group or one of two control groups. Group 1 (*n* = 19) petted a live dog; Group 2 (*n* = 17) petted a stuffed dog, while Group 3 (*n* = 19) simply sat comfortably on a couch. Each participant was exposed to one of the three conditions for 18 min. Pre- and posttreatment saliva samples yielded a significant increase in IgA for Group 1 only. Participants were also asked to complete the Pet Attitude Scale of Templer, Salter, Dickey, Baldwin and Veleber (1981). Scores on this scale correlated with IgA increases only for participants in Group 2 (petting a stuffed animal). Results are discussed in terms of the beneficial effects of pets on health in general, and immunity in particular.

From *Psychological Reports*, 95, 1087–1091. Copyright © 2004 by Psychological Reports. Reprinted with permission.

A number of influences on immune system function have been documented during the past several decades (see Cohen & Herbert, 1996, for a review). The effects of stress and negative psychological states have been extensively studied (e.g., McLelland, Ross, & Patel, 1985). Far fewer studies have documented immuno-enhancing effects. We have published several studies in which increases in Immunoglobulin A (IgA) were noted (see Charnetski & Brennan, 2001, for a review). This protein is by far the most prevalent of the immunoglobulins in the body and is present in virtually all mucosal linings of the body as well as the bloodstream (Ogra, 1985). This underscores its importance as a first line of defense in the prevention of a wide variety of pathologies. IgA may increase after listening to music (e.g., Charnetski, Brennan, & Harrison, 1998), relaxing for 20 min. (Green & Green, 1987), or watching a humorous videotape (Dillon, Minchoff, & Baker, 1986).

In a separate literature, a number of studies have indicated the positive influence of pets on physical health in general (see Serpell, 1991). Prior research has shown that pets can positively influence physiological variables such as heart rate (e.g., Lynch, Thomas, Pastwity, Katcher, & Weir, 1977), blood pressure (e.g., Vormbrock & Grossberg, 1988), and even cholesterol and triglycerides (Anderson, Reid, & Jennings, 1992). The use of pets as therapeutic agents has become a common activity in many hospitals and long-term care facilities (Thomas, 1996). Studies of the effect of tactile contact on the heart and respiratory rates of dogs and horses have suggested that petting, as a form of touch, may be associated with physiological changes in humans (Baun, Bergstrom, Langston, & Thomas, 1984). Jenkins (1986) examined the physiological effects (i.e., heart rate and blood pressure) of pet owners petting their own dogs. Even the mere presence of a companion animal was beneficial as autonomic reactivity of women as defined by pulse rate, blood pressure, and skin conductance changed during a standard experimental stress task as compared to the presence of a human friend or no companion (Allen, Blascovich, Tomaka, & Kelsey, 1991).

Of all the studies of animals on human health-related issues, by far the most common animal studied is the dog. Consequently, we chose a Shelti for our study and hypothesized that petting the dog would have a positive effect on IgA. While no other such studies with animals could be located, we know from manipulation of other variables (e.g., music) that influence of IgA can occur in a relatively brief period of time.

Method

Participants

We recruited 59 college students for the current study and randomly assigned them to one of three conditions. The first group (*n* = 19) sat individually on a couch with the Shelti right next to them. They were instructed to pet the dog for 18 min. We specifically instructed the participants to control individual variation of interaction with the dog. A second group (*n* = 19) sat comfortably on the couch for 18 min. Finally, to control for the effect of tactile stimulation, we utilized a stuffed replica similar in size, shape, and texture to the dog to which our third group was exposed (*n* = 17). This group sat on the couch and spent 18 min. stroking the stuffed dog.

Materials

All participants were given the Pet Attitude Scale (Templer, Salter, Dickey, Baldwin, & Veleber, 1981)

prior to participation. In addition, unstimulated saliva samples were collected from each participant immediately before and after exposure to the conditions. The saliva samples were immediately frozen for later analy-
70 sis. IgA levels were determined via a single radial immunodiffusion technique (Mancini, Carbonara, & Heremens, 1965) that yielded IgA concentration data for pre- vs. postexposure comparisons.

A small, 10-yr.-old, 20-lb. female Shelti/mixed
75 breed dog, documented to be in good health by a veterinarian, was utilized in Group 1. A replica of the same size, colors, and proportions was utilized in Group 3.

Procedure

All participants were individually exposed to the
80 experimental conditions in a room with two chairs, a table, a desk, and a couch. After completing the Pet Attitude Scale in an adjacent room, participants were seated on the couch and were given a small cup and lid. They were then instructed to deposit a saliva sample.
85 All participants were then instructed to sit quietly until the experimenter indicated that time was up. To ensure that the dog remained on the couch with the participants, the experimenter remained in the room seated at one end of the couch for all three groups while the par-
90 ticipants sat at the other end. For Group 1, the experimenter (S.R.) brought the dog in from an adjacent room and placed the dog next to the participant on the couch. As mentioned earlier, Group 2 simply sat comfortably on the couch for 18 min. For Group 3, the ex-
95 perimenter brought in the stuffed replica of the dog. After the completion of the experimental manipulation, participants produced another saliva sample and were debriefed.

IgA Analysis

IgA analysis was performed after samples were
100 thawed at room temperature for 60 min. Twenty microliter aliquots of whole saliva were diluted 1:2 with albumin for each sample. Ten microliters of the diluted saliva were then pipetted into wells on agarose gel plates. The gel on the plates contained antihuman
105 monospecific IgA antibodies. After a 96-hr. incubation period, diffusion ring diameters were measured in millimeters and converted from a calibration curve into milligrams per liter. Technicians performing the assay were blind to experimental conditions.

Results

Analyses

110 The IgA of most of the subjects appeared to increase from pre- to the postexposure. The raw data are presented in Table 1. The two-factor (group × time), repeated-measures analysis of variance on IgA levels yielded a significant main effect of time ($F_{1,52} = 8.58$, p
115 $< .005$). Neither the main effect of group ($F_{2,52}$. 1.78, p $> .05$) nor the interaction ($F_{2,52} = 1.53$, $p > .05$) were significant. Post hoc tests yielded no significant change

in either the stuffed dog-petting group ($t = 2.43$, $p > .05$) or the control group ($t = 1.95$, $p > .05$). However,
120 significant pre- vs. postexposure differences were noted in IgA levels of the dog-petting group ($t = 3.28$, $p < .02$; Table 2). Further analyses included Pearson product-moment correlations between IgA changes, as ascertained by pre- vs. postexposure difference scores,
125 and scores on the Pet Attitude Scale. There was no significant overall correlation ($r = .23$, $p > .05$). Correlations for each group were not significant for the dog-petting group ($r = -.10$, $p > .05$) or the control group ($r = .13$, $p > .05$), but were for the stuffed dog group ($r = $
130 $.62$, $p < .001$).

Table 1
IgA Means and Standard Errors of Mean for Three Groups Pre- and Post-manipulation

Group	n	Pre-manipulation		Post-manipulation	
		M	SE	M	SE
Dog Group	19	712.6	60.5	947.4	92.3
Stuffed Dog Group	17	957.2	92.5	980.0	64.3
Control Group	19	705.8	60.2	910.3	91.5

Table 2
Difference Scores for Three Groups

Group	n	M	SD
Dog Group	19	235.2*	71.6
Stuffed Dog Group	17	34.6	97.1
Control Group	19	204.5	104.8

*$p < .05$

Comment

A significant increase in IgA levels occurred after petting a dog. The lack of significant correlation between IgA change and the Pet Attitude Scale scores in the dog-petting group indicates that one's attitude to-
135 ward pets is not relevant to benefit from this interaction. These results complement some of the general health benefits of animals that have been documented elsewhere in the literature. Examples on higher levels of IgA show relation to less frequent illness (e.g., Yod-
140 fat & Silvian, 1977) and less susceptibility to upper respiratory infection (Martin, Guthrie, & Pitts, 1993). Apparently, interactions with animals have many beneficial effects on humans, as other physiological measures have been positively influenced by the presence of
145 or interaction with animals. These results may have been associated with relaxation (Green, Green, & Santoro, 1988), which has been shown to have an enhancing effect on the immune system. However, the control group who sat comfortably should also have
150 experienced significant effects were relaxation the primary factor. However, we did not record an independent measure of relaxation.

The correlation between Pet Attitude Scale scores and IgA level change for the stuffed animal group may
155 indicate that those who have a more positive attitude toward pets may benefit, perhaps by way of Pavlovian conditioning, from interaction with even a stuffed animal. Alternative explanations also clearly exist. It seems entirely possible that subjects found the situation
160 humorous, and the correlation simply reflects that. Further research should be designed to ascertain whether the high correlation observed in this group was spurious.

Ader and Cohen (1975) found evidence for Pav-
165 lovian conditioning of immunosuppression; perhaps the opposite effect may be found as well. Perhaps persons with a more positive attitude toward pets have had more life experiences with pets. The act of petting an animal may then have more positive effects on them
170 than on someone with less of an affinity toward animals. Perhaps further investigation into each participant's experience with animals (i.e., do they have a pet, how long, etc.) as well as their attitudes toward animals, would be helpful to clarify this.

References

Ader, R., & Cohen, N. (1975). Behaviorally conditioned immunosuppression. *Psychosomatic Medicine, 37,* 333–340.

Allen, K. M., Blascovich, J., Tomaka, J., & Kelsey, R. M. (1991). Presence of human friends and pet dogs as moderators of autonomic responses to stress in women. *Journal of Personality and Social Psychology, 61,* 582–589.

Anderson, W. P., Reid, C. M., & Jennings, G. L. (1992). Pet ownership and risk factors for cardiovascular disease. *Medical Journal of Australia, 157,* 298–301.

Baun, M. M., Bergstrom, N., Langston, N. F., & Thomas, L. (1984). Physiological effects of human/companion animal bonding. *Nursing Research, 33,* 126–129.

Charnetski, C. J., & Brennan, F. X. (2001). *Feeling good is good for you: How pleasure can boost your immune system and lengthen your life.* Emmaus, PA: Rodale Press.

Charnetski, C. J., Brennan, F. X., & Harrison, J. F. (1998). Effect of music and auditory stimuli on secretory immunoglobulin A (IgA). *Perceptual and Motor Skills, 87,* 1169–1170.

Cohen, S., & Herbert, T. B. (1996). Health psychology: Psychological factors and physical disease from the perspective of human psychoneuroimmunology. *Annual Review of Psychology, 47,* 113–142.

Dillon, K. M., Minchoff, B., & Baker, K. H. (1986). Positive emotional states and enhancement of the immune system. *International Journal of Psychiatry in Medicine, 15,* 13–18.

Green, M. L., Green, R. G., & Santoro, W. (1988). Daily relaxation modifies serum and salivary immunoglobulins and psychophysiologic symptom severity. *Biofeedback and Self-Regulation, 13,* 187–199.

Green, R. G., & Green, M. L. (1987). Relaxation increases salivary immunoglobulin A. *Psychological Reports, 61,* 623–629.

Jenkins, J. L. (1986). Physiological effects of petting a companion animal. *Psychological Reports, 51,* 21–22.

Lynch, J. J., Thomas, S. A., Pastwity, D. A., Katcher, A. H., & Weir, L. O. (1977). Human contact and cardiac arrhythmia in a coronary care unit. *Psychosomatic Medicine, 39,* 188–192.

Mancini, G., Carbonara, A. O., & Heremens, J. F. (1965). Immunochemical quantification of antigens by single radial immunodiffusion. *Immunochemistry, 2,* 235–254.

Martin, R. B., Guthrie, C. A., & Pitts, C. G. (1993). Emotional crying, depressed mood and secretory immunoglobulin A. *Behavioral Medicine, 9,* 111–114.

McLelland, D. C., Ross, G., & Patel, V. (1985). The effect of an examination on salivary norepinephrine and immunoglobulin levels. *Journal of Human Stress, 11,* 52–59.

Ogra, P. L. (1985). Local immune responses. *British Medical Bulletin, 41,* 28.

Serpell, J. A. (1991). Beneficial effects of pet ownership on some aspects of human health and behavior. *Journal of the Royal Society of Medicine, 84,* 717–720.

Templer, D., Salter, C. A., Dickey, S., Baldwin, R., & Veleber, D. M. (1981). The construction of a pet attitude scale. *The Psychological Record, 31,* 343–348.

Thomas, W. H. (1996). *Life worth living.* Acton, MA: VanderWyk & Burnham.

Vormbrock, J. K., & Grossberg, J. M. (1988). Cardiovascular effects of human-pet dog interactions. *Journal of Behavioral Medicine, 11,* 509–517.

Yodfat, Y., & Silvian, H. (1977). A prospective study of acute respiratory infections among children in kibbutz. *Journal of Infectious Disease, 135,* 26–30.

Address correspondence to: Carl J. Charnetski, Ph.D., Department of Psychology, Wilkes University, Wilkes-Barre, PA 18766. E-mail: charnets@wilkes.edu

Exercise for Article 22

Factual Questions

1. What is the researchers' stated hypothesis?

2. What was the basis for assigning the students to the three conditions?

3. The researchers used a stuffed replica of a dog in order to control for the effect of what?

4. For the dog-petting group, the researchers found a significant difference from pre- to posttest. What significance test was used to test for the significance of this difference?

5. What is the value of the correlation coefficient for the relationship between the difference scores and the scores on the Pet Attitude Scale for the stuffed dog group?

6. What was the mean IgA score for the control group on the pretest? What was it on the posttest?

Questions for Discussion

7. This study is classified as an example of true experimental research in the table of contents of this book. If you are familiar with how to classify experiments, explain why this study is a true experiment.

8. The researchers indicate that after the experiment they "debriefed" the participants. What is your understanding of the meaning of this term? (See lines 96–98.)

9. The researchers state that the analysis of variance revealed a "significant main effect of time." What is your understanding of the meaning of this statement? (See lines 110–115.)

10. The researchers speculate that the stuffed animal group might have found the situation humorous and the humor could have affected the results. In a

future study, do you think that it would be advisable to question such a group on how humorous they found the task? Explain. (See lines 158–163.)

11. Has this study convinced you that petting a dog increases immune system function? Explain.

12. Do you think that this topic deserves further investigation? Explain. (See lines 171–174.)

Quality Ratings

Directions: Indicate your level of agreement with each of the following statements by circling a number from 5 for strongly agree (SA) to 1 for strongly disagree (SD). If you believe an item is not applicable to this research article, leave it blank. Be prepared to explain your ratings. When responding to criteria A and B below, keep in mind that brief titles and abstracts are conventional in published research.

A. The title of the article is appropriate.

SA   5   4   3   2   1   SD

B. The abstract provides an effective overview of the research article.

SA   5   4   3   2   1   SD

C. The introduction establishes the importance of the study.

SA   5   4   3   2   1   SD

D. The literature review establishes the context for the study.

SA   5   4   3   2   1   SD

E. The research purpose, question, or hypothesis is clearly stated.

SA   5   4   3   2   1   SD

F. The method of sampling is sound.

SA   5   4   3   2   1   SD

G. Relevant demographics (for example, age, gender, and ethnicity) are described.

SA   5   4   3   2   1   SD

H. Measurement procedures are adequate.

SA   5   4   3   2   1   SD

I. All procedures have been described in sufficient detail to permit a replication of the study.

SA   5   4   3   2   1   SD

J. The participants have been adequately protected from potential harm.

SA   5   4   3   2   1   SD

K. The results are clearly described.

SA   5   4   3   2   1   SD

L. The discussion/conclusion is appropriate.

SA   5   4   3   2   1   SD

M. Despite any flaws, the report is worthy of publication.

SA   5   4   3   2   1   SD

Article 23

The Profession of Psychology Scale: Sophisticated and Naïve Students' Responses

GARY T. ROSENTHAL
Nicholls State University

BARLOW SOPER
Louisiana Tech University

CHRIS RACHAL
Nicholls State University

RICHARD R. McKNIGHT
Nicholls State University

A. W. PRICE
Nicholls State University

ABSTRACT. The Profession of Psychology Scale (Rosenthal, McKnight & Price, 2001) was used to investigate whether taking more psychology courses results in a more accurate understanding of what is required to become a psychologist. Data indicate that though misconceptions exist in both Naïve students (those who had not completed any psychology courses) and Sophisticated students (those who had completed five to fourteen psychology courses), the concepts that most define who psychologists are and what they do (e.g. minimal qualifications, lack of prescription privileges) were mastered better by Sophisticated than Naïve students.

From *Journal of Instructional Psychology*, *31*, 202–205. Copyright © 2004 by Project Innovation, Inc. Reprinted with permission.

The public harbors misconceptions about who psychologists are and what they do. Accurate information concerning the profession is fairly obscure. Even psychology majors are prone to erroneous beliefs (Nauta, 2000), which can result in inappropriate career choices (Nauta, 2000).

Rosenthal, McKnight, and Price (2001) assessed perceptions of the profession of psychology with the Profession of Psychology Scale (PPS). Responses of introductory psychology students on the PPS indicated that most did not recognize the doctorate as the standard level of training for psychologists. Further, respondents significantly overestimated the number of psychologists who were health care providers (clinicians, counseling, and school specialists), as well as the number who are members of a minority group.

The current study examined the effect that the number of undergraduate psychology courses completed had on students' perceptions of the profession of psychology. The study specifically focused on whether or not taking more psychology courses relates to more accurate understandings of the profession, such as: training requirements, demographics, and job roles and functions. It was hypothesized that the more psychology courses students completed, the more knowledgeable they would be of the profession.

Method

Participants

One hundred fifty-four undergraduate students at a small rural southern university completed the Profession of Psychology Scale. All participants were volunteers and registered for one of six undergraduate psychology classes (introductory psychology, psychological measurement, abnormal psychology, research designs and methods, psychology of personality, or senior research seminar). From this sample, "Naïve" and "Sophisticated" comparison groups were created based on self-reports of the number of psychology courses completed. The 36 students (14 males and 22 females) in the Naïve group reported that they had not completed any psychology courses (high school or college); their mean age was 20.1 ($SD = 5.5$). All Naïve participants were enrolled in an introductory psychology class. The 38 students (4 males and 34 females) in the Sophisticated group reported they had completed from five to greater than fourteen courses (Mode = 5, Median = 7); their mean age was 23.2 ($SD = 4.6$).

Materials

The Profession of Psychology Scale (PPS)

The Profession of Psychology Scale is a self-report measure of perceptions of the profession of psychology and psychologists (e.g. qualifications, characteristics, and workplaces). The scale begins with a demographic section. The majority of items that follow require estimating a percentage, the remainder consist of Likert-type, one-choice, choose all that apply, and yes/no items.

Procedure

All participants completed the PPS scale on the first day of class before listening to any lecture material or reading the text (presumably). Students were encouraged to take as much time as necessary and to be truthful. They were assured that their responses would be anonymous and not affect their grades. Some participants received extra credit for completing the survey.

Analyses

Where appropriate, responses were compared to available factual data; then responses of Naïve and Sophisticated groups were compared using a variety of parametric and nonparametric tests for the significance
65 of a difference. An alpha level of .05 was used for all tests.

Results and Discussion

Results are presented in sections grouped by item. A section begins with a summary of what the scale indicates about undergraduates' views of a "typical"
70 psychologist and where appropriate is followed by statistical analyses.

Who are Psychologists?

Respondents were asked to provide their estimates of the percentage of psychologists who had certain demographic characteristics. The American Psycho-
75 logical Association (APA) reports that as of 1999, among Ph.D. psychologists, 46% were female and 54% were male (APA, 2003a). The Naïve group mean estimate of the percentage of female psychologists was 49.13% (SD = 19.3%), while the Sophisticated group
80 mean estimate was 52.37% (SD = 20.0%). A One-way ANOVA indicated that Naïve and Sophisticated mean estimates did not differ significantly $F(1, 72)$ = .53, p > .05. Both groups overestimated the representation of women within the profession, but a subsequent Test for
85 Significance of a Proportion (TSP) of the Sophisticated group estimate indicated that the overestimates were not significantly different from reality (z = .79, p > .05).

APA reports that as of 1999, 91% of all psycholo-
90 gists are white, while 9% are people of color (APA, 2003a). One-way ANOVA results indicated no significant difference between Naïve (M = 26.0%, SD = 14.8%) and Sophisticated (M = 24.7%, SD = 12.6%) mean estimates $F(1,72)$ = .16, p > .05. Both groups
95 again overestimated, but this time their estimates of minority psychologists significantly differed from reality (TSP for the Sophisticated group mean is z = 3.56, p < .001).

What Do Psychologists Do?

The APA Research Office lists the percentage of
100 Ph.D. health service providers (Clinical, Counseling and School Psychologists) as 50% (American Psychological Association, 2003b). To examine perceptions concerning health service providers, respondents answered the following item: "What percentage of psy-
105 chologists work mainly counseling or guiding adults or children with problems?" One-way ANOVA results indicated no significant difference between Naïve (M = 44.3%, SD = 24.3%) and Sophisticated (M = 41.7%, SD = 17.6%) mean estimates $F(1,72)$ = .28, p > .05.
110 Both groups underestimated the percentage of psychologist caregivers, but a subsequent (TSP) indicated

not significantly so (Sophisticated group mean was tested and z = 1.02, p > .05).

Another job-related item, "What percentage of psy-
115 chologists can write prescriptions?" proved very interesting. The exact percentage of psychologists who can prescribe is unknown. However, owing to the small number of states that allow this practice, and the recency of such privileges, it is reasonable to assume that
120 no more than five percent of psychologists can prescribe. The ANOVA indicated that the Naïve group mean estimate (M = 43.6%, SD = 33.9%) was significantly different from the Sophisticated group mean estimate (M = 6.2%, SD = 11.8%), $F(1,72)$ = 41.2, p <
125 .001. While both groups overestimated, the Naïve group's estimate was over six times as large as that of students in the Sophisticated group who had taken more psychology courses.

How Do You Become a Psychologist?

A choose-one item on the scale asked "What are the
130 minimal qualifications necessary to be a psychologist?" Choices ranged from "some undergraduate courses in psychology" to a "Doctorate in psychology." The correct answer is that to become an academic psychologist, you must complete a doctorate in psychology.
135 Since the data on this item are categorical, a nonparametric Test for Significance of a Difference Between Two Proportions (TSDBTP) was performed. The proportion of Naïve group subjects who answered correctly, converted to a percentage for clarity (16.7%),
140 was compared to the proportion of the Sophisticated group subjects who were correct (42.1%). The TSDBTP test statistic was significant (z = 3.26, p < .01), a significantly larger proportion of the Sophisticated group (those with more psychology courses) an-
145 swered this item correctly.

Three other "yes/no" items relevant to how to become a psychologist were analyzed. These items concerned training that is required for psychological practitioners.
150 The first item was "In addition to their coursework, in order to practice independently a psychologist must have a license from the government." The number of Naïve group subjects endorsing this item was 34 of 36 and the number of Sophisticated group subjects was 36
155 of 38. A chi-square analysis was not possible due to cell size restrictions. However, the data indicate that both Naïve and Sophisticated students are aware of this requirement.

The second item was "In addition to their course-
160 work, in order to practice independently a psychologist must complete a minimum number of hours under the supervision of a qualified psychologist." The number of Naïve group subjects endorsing this item was 34 of 36 and the number of Sophisticated group subjects was
165 36 of 38. Once again, a chi-square analysis was not possible due to cell size restrictions. But the "supervi-

sion" data again indicate that both Naïve and Sophisticated students are aware of this requirement.

170   The final item was "In addition to their coursework, in order to practice independently a psychologist must undergo personal psychotherapy." This is a common misperception about clinicians and counselors. The number of Naïve group subjects endorsing this item was 21 of 36 and the number of Sophisticated group

175   subjects was markedly less 10 of 38. A chi-square analysis was conducted (2 ($df = 1$) = 7.78, $p < .01$), and indicated that there was a significant difference between Naïve and Sophisticated students, with more Sophisticated students aware of the fact that this re-

180   quirement is a myth.

Conclusions

Regardless of the number of psychology classes completed, students continue to harbor several common misconceptions about psychologists. For example, the current study showed that students significantly

185   overestimated the number of minority psychologists. And, while they did not significantly misestimate the number of health care providers who are psychologists in this study, in a previous study (Rosenthal, McKnight, & Price, 2001) they did. Regardless of the

190   number of psychology classes completed, students accurately perceived the need for both a license and supervision to practice independently.

Although misconceptions in both Naïve and Sophisticated psychology students exist, those central

195   concepts that most define who psychologists are and what they do were mastered better by Sophisticated students than students who had taken no psychology courses. For example, students who had completed more psychology courses were more accurate in assess-

200   ing minimal qualifications for the profession. In addition, the Sophisticated were also more accurate in their estimates of the number of psychologists who prescribe medications, which suggests they are more knowledgeable about differences between psychologists and psy-

205   chiatrists. Finally, while not as important as training and prescription issues, students with no psychology courses were more likely to believe that practicing psychologists must undergo psychotherapy.

While Nauta (2000) has suggested that misconcep-

210   tions may adversely affect psychology student career choices, some misconceptions are probably not as potentially damaging as others. For example, it could be argued that perceptions of minority representation in psychology might affect student career choice, but not

215   as much as misunderstanding the training requirements to enter the field. According to the current study, taking more psychology courses seems to partially correct potentially damaging misconceptions. Further research might explore whether non-psychology majors con-

220   tinue to harbor misconceptions throughout their lifetime and explore possible gender differences.

References

American Psychological Association. (2003a). *APA Research Office—General Demographic Shifts in Psychology* [Online]. Available: http://research.apa.org/gen1.html

American Psychological Association. (2003b). APA Research Office—PhD Psychologists by Subfield: 1975, 1985, 1995 [Online]. Available: http://research.apa.org/docl5.html

Nauta, M. M. (2000). Assessing the accuracy of psychology undergraduates' perceptions of graduate admissions criteria. *Teaching of Psychology, 27*, 277–280.

Rosenthal, G. T., McKnight, R. R., & Price, A. W. (2001). Who, what, how and where the typical psychologist is…The Profession of Psychology Scale. *Journal of Instructional Psychology, 28*, 220–224.

Note: A summary of the results of this study was presented at the 49th Annual Southeastern Psychological Association Conference, New Orleans, LA, March 2003.

About the authors: *Gary T. Rosenthal*, Professor, Department of Psychology and Counselor Education, Nicholls State University. *Barlow Soper*, Professor, Department of Behavioral Sciences, Louisiana Tech University. *Chris Rachal*, Assistant Professor, Department of Psychology and Counselor Education, Nicholls State University. *Richard R. McKnight*, Professor, Department of Psychology and Counselor Education, Nicholls State University. *A. W. Price*, Professor, Department of Psychology and Counselor Education, Nicholls State University.

Address correspondence: If you would like to help gather a nationwide sample with the Revised Profession of Psychology Scale (a shorter instrument), please contact Gary T. Rosenthal, Department of Psychology and Counselor Education, Nicholls State University, P.O. Box 2075, Thibodaux, LA 70310. E-mail: psyc-gtr@nicholls.edu

Exercise for Article 23

Factual Questions

1. Was the Profession of Psychology Scale (PPS) used in a study prior to this one?

2. What is the hypothesis for this study?

3. What was the mean age of the Naïve group? What was the mean age of the Sophisticated group?

4. Did any of the participants receive extra credit for participating in this study?

5. Were the estimates of the percentage of female psychologists by Naïve and Sophisticated students statistically significant? If yes, at what probability level?

6. According to the researchers, what job-related item "proved very interesting"?

Questions for Discussion

7. In line 44, the researchers report the modal number of courses taken (5) and the median number taken (7). Both the mode and median are averages. If you know how they are defined, write their definitions.

8. In a future study, would it be interesting to compare responses to the PPS both before and after taking psychology courses? Would this provide more information than the current study? Explain.

9. In addition to the aspects of psychology as a profession mentioned in this article, are there others that might be interesting to explore in future research on this topic (e.g., compensation levels, percentage in private practice)? If yes, name some additional ones.

10. In the table of contents of this book, this article is classified as an example of "causal-comparative research" (i.e., research in which existing groups are compared for possible causes of differences among them). Based on your reading of experimental articles in this book, explain how causal-comparative research differs from experimental research.

11. Has this study convinced you that taking psychology courses *causes* an increase in knowledge of psychology as a profession? Explain.

12. Do the results of this study surprise you? Are any of the findings of special interest to you? Explain.

Quality Ratings

Directions: Indicate your level of agreement with each of the following statements by circling a number from 5 for strongly agree (SA) to 1 for strongly disagree (SD). If you believe an item is not applicable to this research article, leave it blank. Be prepared to explain your ratings. When responding to criteria A and B below, keep in mind that brief titles and abstracts are conventional in published research.

A. The title of the article is appropriate.

SA   5   4   3   2   1   SD

B. The abstract provides an effective overview of the research article.

SA   5   4   3   2   1   SD

C. The introduction establishes the importance of the study.

SA   5   4   3   2   1   SD

D. The literature review establishes the context for the study.

SA   5   4   3   2   1   SD

E. The research purpose, question, or hypothesis is clearly stated.

SA   5   4   3   2   1   SD

F. The method of sampling is sound.

SA   5   4   3   2   1   SD

G. Relevant demographics (for example, age, gender, and ethnicity) are described.

SA   5   4   3   2   1   SD

H. Measurement procedures are adequate.

SA   5   4   3   2   1   SD

I. All procedures have been described in sufficient detail to permit a replication of the study.

SA   5   4   3   2   1   SD

J. The participants have been adequately protected from potential harm.

SA   5   4   3   2   1   SD

K. The results are clearly described.

SA   5   4   3   2   1   SD

L. The discussion/conclusion is appropriate.

SA   5   4   3   2   1   SD

M. Despite any flaws, the report is worthy of publication.

SA   5   4   3   2   1   SD

Article 24

Untreated Recovery from Eating Disorders

SUSAN L. WOODS
Eastern Illinois University

ABSTRACT. This retrospective study explored the experience of recovery from anorexia nervosa and bulimia nervosa without professional treatment. An eight-question open-ended electronic survey was posted for a period of three months at a midwestern university. Sixteen female and two male respondents reported recovery from adolescent-onset full syndrome anorexia nervosa or bulimia nervosa. All respondents reported onset factors supporting a sociocultural etiology. Recovery was initiated through the empathic, participatory efforts of parents and friends, or was self-initiated. Respondents with the shortest disorder duration and most complete recovery reported early parental intervention. Onset factors similar to those in research with a clinically treated population were found. Implications of the findings are discussed.

From *Adolescence*, 39, 361–371. Copyright © 2004 by Libra Publishers, Inc. Reprinted with permission.

Eating disorders are the third most common chronic condition among adolescent females in the United States (Fisher et al., 1995). It is estimated that 1% to 3% of adolescent females suffer full syndrome ano-
5 rexia or bulimia nervosa, and up to 20% of high school- and college-age females have partial syndrome eating disorders (Sands et al., 1997). Eating disorders are associated with devastating physical, psychosocial, and financial consequences and have the highest mor-
10 tality rate of any mental health disorder (Fisher, 2003; Rome et al., 2003).

After two decades of research, there remains limited understanding of the eating disorder recovery process. Approximately 50% of patients do well after
15 inpatient treatment; 20% do poorly; and 30% do reasonably well but continue to have symptoms (Fisher, 2003). These recovery outcome results, however, have been based on studies of patients in specialized treatment centers. Schoemaker (1998) notes, "We don't
20 know in how many cases eating-disordered patients may improve or even recover without professional treatment" (p. 204). The present exploratory study was designed to examine the experience of recovery from an eating disorder without clinical treatment.

Method

Instruments

25 Based upon a review of literature and input from four undergraduate student research assistants, a quali-
tative, open-ended, electronic mail survey was developed for this study. This format allows respondents to describe events, perceptions, and experiences in their
30 own words. The survey questions were reviewed by a panel of four experts in eating disorder treatment and research, and was revised based upon panel suggestions. Following human subject research approval, eight survey questions were made available on the
35 study e-mail address: (1) When did your eating disorder symptoms begin/emerge? (2) How did they start? (3) What factor(s) led to the development of your behavior? (4) What behaviors did you engage in? (Please list or describe all behaviors.) (5) Was there a key turn-
40 ing point in the initiation of your recovery? (6) Did you see/consult with any of the following: physician(s), therapist(s), or dieticians(s)? If yes, please describe: Who was consulted? How often? Length of treatment? (7) Do any physical and/or psychological aspects of
45 your eating disorder persist? Please describe. (8) What and/or who do you find most helpful in keeping you from your former behaviors?

The survey cover page contained the study purpose, an explanation of confidentiality, a short demographic
50 section, instructions on paper mail-in for anonymity assurance, and a statement thanking the participant for his or her time and generosity. Respondents were given information on obtaining study results and were encouraged to contact the researcher by e-mail or faculty
55 telephone with any questions, suggestions, or thoughts.

Procedure

Several hundred survey flyers were placed on bulletin boards throughout the campus. The bold headline "Recovery from Eating Disorder Study" was followed by "If you have recovered from an eating disorder
60 without extensive outpatient or inpatient clinical treatment and would assist with a study on your experience of recovery, please contact (e-mail address). This eight-question e-mail study is confidential and can be answered anonymously. Your input is important and
65 greatly appreciated." At the bottom of the survey were tear-off e-mail address tab strips. Throughout the semester student assistants monitored and replaced the flyers. Surveys were collected for three months.

Design

Ground theory (Glaser & Strauss, 1967) was em-

70 ployed to sort through themes and connections in the data. This qualitative process attempts to discern the mechanisms and pathways of experience and the understanding of phenomena in the generation of theory.

Results

Demographics

Twenty-two respondents completed the e-mail sur-
75 vey. Four respondents had been in hospital and inpatient treatment programs prior to recovery. The recovery following inpatient treatment surveys were reviewed as a comparison group but are not included in the main analysis. Of the 18 respondents who reported
80 recovery without treatment, 16 were female (89%) and 2 (11%) were male. Seventeen of the respondents were white, and one female respondent was black. All respondents were 18–21 years of age and full-time students at one midsize, midwestern university. All re-
85 spondents met the DSM-IV (American Psychiatric Association, 2000) diagnostic criteria for full syndrome anorexia nervosa or purging type bulimia nervosa prior to recovery. Eight females and one male (50%) reported suffering from purging type bulimia, six females
90 and one male (39%) reported restricting type anorexia, and two females (11%) reported binge-eating/purging type anorexia nervosa. All respondents reported regular or intermittent excessive exercise throughout the duration of their disorder.
95 The respondents began their disordered behavior between the ages of 12 and 17 (modal age = 15). All respondents were competitive high school athletes in the following sports: gymnastics/cheerleading (10 females), elite junior-level figure skating (1 female),
100 cross-country/track (4 females, 1 male), softball (1 female), and football (1 male).

Onset and Duration

The period from onset of symptoms to the first steps toward recovery ranged from 6 months to 4 years, with a mean duration of 1.94 years.

Onset and Behavior Reinforcement Factors

105 A web of factors leading to onset was reported. The need to lose weight for sport performance/appearance; critical "fat for your sport" comments from family members, coaches and peers; and self-comparison to the "ideal" were common themes in all respondent nar-
110 ratives. No respondent in the recovery without treatment group reported abuse or sexual assault as a factor. Only two respondents (one female softball player and one football player) reported being "a little" overweight prior to disorder onset. All other respondents
115 noted they were within, or slightly below, the ideal recommended weight range for their height prior to initial weight loss.

All respondents reported that their behaviors were reinforced and maintained through successful weight
120 loss/control and the initial compliments of parents,

coaches, boyfriends, and peers on their appearance and/or weight loss achievements.

Recovery Turning Point

Four female respondents reported that an early empathic and supportive intervention by their mothers was
125 the key turning point toward recovery. These respondents met the criteria for restricting anorexia prior to intervention and reported the shortest duration from symptom onset to the beginning of recovery, with a mean of 9 months. Two females reported that after a
130 long period of confrontive anger, a heartfelt, emotional plea from their fathers was the turning point in their disorder. Both respondents met the criteria for restricting anorexia. The father intervention group had a disorder onset to turning point duration of 1.4 years. Five
135 female respondents, all meeting the criteria for bulimia nervosa, reported that their boyfriends provided the key turning point in their recovery. The mean duration of their disorder onset to turning point was 2.1 years. Two females and one male listed a "best college friend" as
140 the key to their recovery initiation. These three respondents were bulimic and reported the duration of their disorder to initial recovery turning point as approximately 3.0 years. Three female respondents reported that a combination of dental and gastrointestinal prob-
145 lems, along with the realization that they wanted to have an authentic life, not just the disorder, led to their recovery. Two respondents met the criteria for binge-eating/purging anorexia nervosa, and one respondent was bulimic. One male restricting anorexic reported
150 that his key turning point followed several months of constant fatigue and the subsequent inability to perform academically and physically. The four self-initiated recovery respondents reported the longest duration of their disorders, with a mean duration from onset to
155 turning point of approximately 3.9 years.

Professional Consultation

Two former restricting anorexic females reported that due to parental insistence, they had a physical exam with their primary care physician at the beginning of their recovery. One of these respondents also
160 reported that her primary care physician arranged a two-session family consultation with a dietician. No other respondent reported clinical treatment during their recovery process.

Physical Outcome

The nine respondents reporting recovery from bu-
165 limia noted that they experienced some intermittent gastrointestinal symptoms, including constipation, pancreatitis, acid reflux, and heartburn. Dental damage, requiring root canals, and/or major tooth restoration, were common to all recovering bulimics. Of the two
170 recovering binge-eating/purging anorexics, one reported all of the above symptoms, and one reported that despite a year of restricting and intermittent purg-

ing, she seems to have no signs of physical damage at this time with the exception of occasional heartburn.

175 One former restricting anorexic and one recovering binge-eating purging anorexic noted that recent bone scan testing has revealed that they are at high risk for osteoporosis. The six female and one former male restricting anorexics reported that, to their knowledge,
180 they evidence no residual physical damage from their disorder. The male respondent attributed his lack of symptoms to the use of daily vitamin, mineral, and protein supplements throughout his disorder and the careful nutritional balancing of his exact 1,200 calo-
185 rie/day food intake before beginning his recovery.

Psychological Outcome

Most respondents noted that some cognitive aspects of their disorder persist. Feeling "too full" after a large meal sometimes reactivates the two former binge-eating/purging anorexics' and nine bulimics' urges to
190 purge and stimulates anxiety for one former male and three former female restricting anorexics. These fifteen respondents report that by increasing their aerobic exercise the day after overeating and by engaging in positive self-dialogue, they are able to avoid the reactiva-
195 tion of further disordered thinking or behavior. (All study respondents exercise daily but noted that their levels of exercise are now within recommended levels.)

All but three females noted that accepting a higher weight or larger clothing size remains difficult and
200 troubling even after recovery. Both the male and thirteen female respondents describe that recovering, or discovering, a sense of authentic identity remains an ongoing process. The three females reporting no residual "disordered thinking" were all former restricting
205 anorexics whose turning point for recovery was early empathic intervention by their mothers prior to age 15.

Recovery Sustaining Factors

Fourteen respondents reported that the sustained and supportive reinforcement from a parent, boyfriend, or friend is most helpful in sustaining their recovery.
210 The four respondents whose recovery was self-initiated reported that the need to experience and enjoy an authentic life is the most helpful factor in sustaining their recovery. Both female former binge-eating/purging anorexics reported that their current primary care phy-
215 sician had recently prescribed a serotonin reuptake inhibitor after they described their history and current anxiety symptoms. These two respondents reported that the medications seem to have a positive impact on their continuing recovery.

Discussion

220 The results of this exploratory study support the feminist/sociocultural theory that eating disorders are culturally produced and culture-bound syndromes (Gordon, 2000; Bordo, 1997). A common theme in all female respondent narratives was the importance of

225 being exceptionally slender and fit in order to compete, gain positive attention, and win love and admiration.

Respondent 2: I feared gaining weight because I didn't want to be one of those girls that looked fat in their leotard.

230 Respondent 11: Being small and skinny in gymnastics and dance, to look good in general.

Respondent 9: I was the only black cheerleader at my mostly white high school. I heard remarks from the crowd about my big butt and size compared to the
235 white girls. That's when my disorder started.

Respondent 3: My parents were critical no matter how well I did. I thought I could please them by becoming the thinner daughter they wanted, but nothing changed.

240 As Bordo (1997) notes, "Families exist in cultural time and space. So does 'peer pressure,' 'perfectionism,' 'body-image distortion,' and all those other elements of individual and social behavior that clinical models have tended to abstract and pathologize" (pp.
245 119–120). Western adolescents find themselves in a space and time where the demands to perform, measure up, and excel seem relentless. The attitudes evidenced in these narratives are far from exceptional. They mirror the normative attitudes expressed by female stu-
250 dents at a regional midwestern university. The need to be exceptionally slender and fit seems a given—a vital component for success. (While male students have a differing standard for ideal—low fat but "buff," well-sculpted muscles—the necessity of meeting "ideal
255 standards" seems unquestioned.)

All former bulimics' and purging anorexics' narratives emphasized the normative nature of their disorder.

Respondent 7: Most of my friends and teammates
260 were throwing up and using laxatives. Along with my boyfriend, a turning point for me was when we taught a younger girl how to throw up at cheerleading camp. It made me kind of realize what we were doing.

Although a meta-analysis of 34 studies found no
265 significant eating disorder risk effects for gymnasts, dancers and elite athletes in sports emphasizing thinness were at increased risk (Smolak, Muren, & Ruble, 2000). Most of the athletes in this study felt that their coaches either overlooked or seemed pleased with their
270 weight loss. Half of the female respondents and both male respondents reported praise from coaches.

Respondent 16: My football coaches complimented me on my rapid 15-pound off-season weight loss, so did my teammates. My speed and mobility definitely
275 increased at first.

Respondent 10: When I'd lost around 10 pounds, my gymnastic coach said I looked great. The other girls on the team started to lose more weight then.

These respondents were describing events that oc-
280 curred in the mid-1990s, when eating disorders were

well recognized and widely publicized in the general press. The coaching attitudes described by the respondents in this study should be rare exceptions. In classroom discussions, students report that the coaching attitudes reflected in the respondent narratives are not uncommon in their experience. The most disturbing respondent narrative came from a female runner.

> Respondent 15: A teammate told my parents and track coach I was in trouble. I was upset, but relieved in a way. But the coach told my parents that she had seen anorexic girls before and I wasn't skinny enough to worry about it. So none of them did anything. I'd lost 30 pounds at that point, and I'd only been 120 pounds before the disorder began. My disorder went on for nearly three more years.

Two female respondents, however, reported the critical role their coaches played in initiating recovery.

> Respondent 5: My 9th-grade P.E. [physical education] teacher and coach called a conference with my parents. She told them I needed help and that she wouldn't let me participate in P.E. or cross-country until I was in much better condition.

> Respondent 6: My parents explained away my weight loss to other family members. They just didn't want to deal with it. It took my track coach's refusal to let me participate that season to get my parents involved. I give her a lot of credit, and will never forget her.

The results of this study were striking and consistent. The key turning point for most respondents was the empathic, nurturing support of a patient parent, boyfriend, or friend. The shortest disorder duration and greatest degree of recovery were reported by respondents whose mothers intervened with a firm but loving response early in the course of their disorder.

> Respondent 1: I came home from school and found my mom reading on my bed that was covered with books and videotapes. She said she was starting to understand and that we would work through this thing together. We did, and are much closer because of the experience.

> Respondent 2: My mom said, "We'll do anything it takes to help you. You should go ahead and quit gymnastics and work on getting well."

The key turning point for two respondents was an unexpected heartfelt expression of love from their fathers. Both described that their eating disorder symptoms had been a source of anger and confrontation, a battle of wills, with their fathers for over a year.

> Respondent 5: My dad came into my room and started crying. He told me he couldn't live if he lost me. It was like, this is it. It's over *now*.

> Respondent 6: I had never seen my father cry before. He told me he loved me and didn't know what to do, how to help me. I realized he really cared about me. That was the first day of my recovery.

The realization that they were loved for themselves—not solely their achievements—and the empathic parental expression of a determination to work *with* the child on overcoming the disorder were the key recovery initiators for six respondents. Sadly, twelve respondents described that their parents "explained away," overlooked, or seemed to ignore the symptoms of their eating disorder. Eight respondents found that the expression of love and support they needed to begin their recovery came from boyfriends or close friends. These nurturing friends were not only supportive but active intervention participants.

> Respondent 13: My friend acted more like a mother. She encouraged me to talk about feelings, monitored me at our sorority house, and accompanied me to the Ladies Room for over a year.

One boyfriend took a somewhat novel approach.

> Respondent 8: At his house, my boyfriend had his mother or sister hide in the bathtub and "surprise" me whenever I used their bathroom after eating. In public, he loiters outside the women's restroom door without embarrassment. I guess that's love. He never looks at skinny girls, and when I compare myself to them, he always tells me how beautiful I am.

Friends and boyfriends in this study appear to function as parental surrogates, providing a safe harbor for recovery. The pattern found in this study was consistent. The shortest disorder durations, with the most complete recoveries, were reported by respondents whose parents provided loving and supportive early interventions, followed by the respondents whose recovery was initiated and sustained by a significant other. The longest disorder duration occurred among the respondents whose recovery was self-initiated.

In a study of 1,171 patients, Kordy et al. (2002) reported that the mean duration of the illness for patients seeking clinical treatment at 43 German clinics was 8.2 years for bulimic and 5.7 years for anorexic patients. The four respondents in the present study (2 restricting anorexics, 2 binge-eating/purging anorexics) who had received inpatient treatment reported multiple hospitalizations, extensive and ongoing psychotherapy, and chronic physical outcomes, including osteoporosis, heart abnormalities, gastrointestinal disorders, and diminished memory and ability to concentrate. They reported the longest period from onset to initial recovery turning point, ranging from 4 to 7 years (mean 6.1 years) and considered themselves to be in the process of recovery, not recovered. These respondents reported that "disordered thinking" remains a constant and challenging aspect of their daily lives. Sadly, three of these four inpatient treatment respondents expressed the belief that they will always battle their disorder.

The findings of this exploratory study would suggest that recovery from eating disorders, with minimal clinical treatment, can occur when early symptoms are recognized by an empathic parent or significant other committed to a collaborative, participatory approach to recovery. The need for further research with a popula-

395 tion reporting recovery without clinical treatment is critical in advancing the working knowledge of eating disorder prevention and treatment.

Implications

Pressures for achievement can create and reinforce devastating self-destructive behavior. It is critical for
400 parents to consider Reindl's (2001) proposal that "the opposite of an eating disorder is accepting and respecting oneself as one is, and yet striving to develop one's potential as an increasingly whole, complex person" (p. 290).
405 The results of this study support Rome et al.'s (2003) conclusions that early detection and treatment help decrease eating disorder morbidity in the adolescent population. School systems, administrators, athletic directors, coaches, and teachers must make every
410 effort to ensure that their policies, programs, and personnel support a healthy environment for their students. Through primary prevention dialogue with parents, students, health professionals and community members, the prevention and early detection of eating
415 disorders could be better realized. Within the limits of what is possible, every effort must be made to create an environment that counteracts a toxic culture.

References

American Psychiatric Association (2000). *Diagnostic and statistical manual of mental disorders* (4th ed., text revision). Washington, DC: Author.

Bordo, S. (1997). Never just pictures. In S. Bordo (Ed.), *Twilight zones: The hidden life of cultural images from Plato to O.J.* (pp. 107–138). Berkeley, CA: University of California Press.

Fisher, M. (2003). The course and outcome of eating disorders in adults and adolescents: A review. *Adolescent Medicine, 14*, 149–158.

Fisher, M., Golden, N. H., Katzman, K. K., Kriepe, R. E., Rees, J., Schebendach, J., Sigman, G., Ammerman, S., & Hoberman, H. M. (1995). Eating disorders in adolescents: A background paper. *Journal of Adolescent Health, 16*, 20–37.

Glaser, B. G., & Strauss, A. L. (1967). *The discovery of ground theory.* Chicago, IL: Aldine.

Gordon, R. A. (2000). *Eating disorders: Anatomy of a social epidemic* (2nd ed.). Oxford, UK: Blackwell.

Kordy, H., Kramer, B., Palmer, R. L., Papezova, H., Pellet, J., Richard, M., & Treasure, J. (2002). Remission, recovery, relapse, and recurrence in eating disorders: Conceptualization and illustration of a validation strategy. *Journal of Clinical Psychology, 58*, 833–846.

Reindl, S. M. (2001). *Sensing the self: Women's recovery from bulimia.* Cambridge, MA: Harvard University Press.

Rome, E. S., Ammerman, S., Rosen, D. S., Keller, R. J., Lock, J., Mammel, K. A., O'Toole, J., Rees, J. M., Sanders, M. J., Sawyer, S. M., Schneider, M., Sigel, E., & Silber, T. J. (2003). Children and adolescents with eating disorders: The state of the art. *Pediatrics, 111*, 98–108.

Sands, R., Tricker, J., Sherman, C., Armatas, C., & Maschette, W. (1997). Disordered eating patterns, body image, self-esteem, and physical activity in preadolescent children. *International Journal of Eating Disorders, 21*, 159–166.

Schoemaker, C. (1998). The principles of screening for eating disorders. In W. Vandereycken & G. Noordenbos (Eds.), *The prevention of eating disorders* (pp. 187–213). New York: New York University Press.

Smolak, L., Muren, S. K., & Ruble, A. E. (2000). Female athletes and eating problems: A meta-analysis. *International Journal of Eating Disorders, 27*, 371–380.

Acknowledgments: In memory of Randy Woods. The author gratefully acknowledges the assistance of Jeanette Wilson; and students, Stefanie Bolling, Erin Hardiek, Erinn Kuebler, and Allison Flores, Eastern Illinois University.

Address correspondence to: Susan L. Woods, M.A., Department of Health Studies, Eastern Illinois University, 600 Lincoln Avenue, Charleston, Illinois 61920. E-mail: cfslw@eiu.edu

Exercise for Article 24

Factual Questions

1. Did the researcher receive human subject research approval?

2. Were participants informed of the purpose of the study?

3. Where were the flyers that announced the study placed?

4. How many respondents reported recovery without treatment?

5. What was the mean duration of symptoms during the period from their onset to the first steps toward recovery?

Questions for Discussion

6. The researcher collected responses for three months. (See line 68.) If you had planned this study, would you have planned to wait for this length of time? Explain.

7. The researcher used open-ended questions (i.e., questions without response choices). If you had conducted this study, would you have used open-ended questions? Explain.

8. In your opinion, is the description of the "design" in lines 69–73 sufficiently detailed? Explain.

9. In the discussion section of this research report, the researcher provides a number of quotations from participants. How effective are these in helping you understand the results of this study?

10. In your opinion, are the implications in lines 398–417 justified by the data presented? Explain.

Quality Ratings

Directions: Indicate your level of agreement with each of the following statements by circling a number from 5 for strongly agree (SA) to 1 for strongly disagree (SD). If you believe an item is not applicable to this research article, leave it blank. Be prepared to explain your ratings. When responding to criteria A and B below, keep in mind that brief titles and abstracts are conventional in published research.

A. The title of the article is appropriate.

    SA   5   4   3   2   1   SD

B. The abstract provides an effective overview of the research article.

    SA   5   4   3   2   1   SD

C. The introduction establishes the importance of the study.

    SA   5   4   3   2   1   SD

D. The literature review establishes the context for the study.

    SA   5   4   3   2   1   SD

E. The research purpose, question, or hypothesis is clearly stated.

    SA   5   4   3   2   1   SD

F. The method of sampling is sound.

    SA   5   4   3   2   1   SD

G. Relevant demographics (for example, age, gender, and ethnicity) are described.

    SA   5   4   3   2   1   SD

H. Measurement procedures are adequate.

    SA   5   4   3   2   1   SD

I. All procedures have been described in sufficient detail to permit a replication of the study.

    SA   5   4   3   2   1   SD

J. The participants have been adequately protected from potential harm.

    SA   5   4   3   2   1   SD

K. The results are clearly described.

    SA   5   4   3   2   1   SD

L. The discussion/conclusion is appropriate.

    SA   5   4   3   2   1   SD

M. Despite any flaws, the report is worthy of publication.

    SA   5   4   3   2   1   SD

Article 25

Does Therapist Experience Influence Interruptions of Women Clients?

RONALD JAY WERNER-WILSON
Iowa State University

MEGAN J. MURPHY
Iowa State University

JENNIFER LYNN FITZHARRIS
Iowa State University

ABSTRACT. The feminist critique of marriage and family therapy and studies of interruptions in conversation influenced the topic of the present study. We replicated methodology from a study (Werner-Wilson, Price, Zimmerman, & Murphy, 1997) in which the researchers reported that student therapists interrupted women clients more frequently than male clients. Those results may have been related to therapist inexperience—since the therapists were students. In the present study, we compared interruptions from student therapists to those identified as "master" therapists who had extensive clinical experience. Analysis of Variance was used to compare videotaped sessions of therapists in marriage and family therapy training sessions to therapists from the American Association for Marriage and Family Therapy (AAMFT) Masters series. Results suggest that there is no statistically significant difference between the rate of interruptions used by students versus experienced therapists. Both groups interrupted women clients more often than men clients, a finding that replicates the earlier study by Werner-Wilson and colleagues (1997), which increases the generalizability about this pattern in marriage and family therapy

From *Journal of Feminist Family Therapy*, *16*, 39–49. Copyright © 2004 by The Haworth Press, Inc. Reprinted with permission.

One of the first empirical quantitative analyses of power in marriage and family therapy investigated interruptions, which were viewed as a sign of conversational power. That study reported that women clients
5 were interrupted three times more often than men clients regardless of therapist gender (Werner-Wilson et al., 1997). The study published in 1997 included only student therapists so the findings could have been the result of limited professional training because therapist
10 inexperience seems to be associated with a more directive interviewing style (Auerbach & Johnson, 1978). The present study represents a replication of the 1997 study with a sample of therapists that includes some who have significantly more experience so interrup-
15 tions could be compared between student therapists and those identified by the American Association for Marriage and Family Therapy as "master" therapists. This present study was influenced by two themes: language and therapeutic discourse as well as the feminist cri-
20 tique of marriage and family therapy.

Relevant Literature

The Feminist Critique

Feminists have brought to the forefront the importance of attending to social and political issues within the therapeutic context, such as examining the effects of race/ethnicity on client problems, openly discussing
25 power and privilege one may or may not have within the context of a relationship, and making gender a central component of case conceptualization and intervention (Silverstein, 2003). Embedded within these suggestions is a central issue of power: How does power
30 play out in relationships? Do therapists recognize power differences in the couples and families they treat? How do therapists attend to these power differences in the therapeutic context, that is, both between members of a couple and between themselves and their
35 clients? Although feminists have long called for therapists to examine power in relationships, only recently have concrete suggestions been given regarding how therapists can address abstract concepts like power in therapy (Blanton & Vandergriff-Avery, 2001; Had-
40 dock, Zimmerman, & MacPhee, 2000).

In addition to offering ways of conceptualizing and intervening in family therapy, feminists have highlighted the differential treatment of men and women in therapy by their therapists. One of the themes of the
45 feminist critique is associated with therapeutic process: women's voices are to be encouraged, heard, and validated in therapy. Feminist therapists actively encourage equal participation from women and men in therapy and in relationships (Cantor, 1990). From a feminist
50 perspective, therapists should attend to gender issues rather than ignore gender hierarchies in relationships. If "therapeutic talk is, of course, all about the politics of influence" (Goldner, 1989, p. 58), then how well do therapists negotiate power in therapy? Are therapists
55 replicating or challenging existing power inequalities in therapy? Furthermore, are therapists aware of their own stereotypes regarding gender and communication? One frequently heard stereotype is that women talk more than men (O'Donohue, 1996). Do therapists con-
60 sciously mitigate their own gender-related biases? These questions seem relevant in light of recent studies that show a negative relationship between marital satis-

faction and power inequality (Gray-Little, Baucom, & Hamby, 1996; Whisman & Jacobson, 1990).

65   Recent research seems to provide empirical support for this feminist critique of therapy. For example, Haddock and Lyness (2002) reported that male therapists frequently and negatively challenged female clients. The same pattern was not found for male clients. Other

70 research suggests that therapists scored low on taking a stance against client behaviors intended to control another (Haddock, MacPhee, & Zimmerman, 2001). Even though therapists may be aware of the importance of attention to power and gender issues in therapy, it

75 appears that they may not follow through in terms of how they communicate and/or intervene regarding conversational power. It could be argued that therapists have an ethical responsibility to challenge the hierarchies inherent in couples' relationships. Failure to do

80 so would be maintaining the status quo. Therefore, therapists' use of self seems particularly important given the power they have in relation to their clients to shape, end, or shift conversation (Avis, 1991).

Language and Therapeutic Discourse

    Given that therapists are responsible for monitoring

85 and perhaps intervening in the relational and communicational therapeutic context, it seems important to pay attention to interruptions—especially those employed by therapists—in therapeutic conversation. The language and communication literature is helpful in this

90 regard. In their pioneering investigation of interruptions as a power tactic in conversation, Zimmerman and West (1975) reported that males more frequently interrupt females in cross-sex pairs, whereas interruptions occur in equal numbers between same-sex con-

95 versational partners. Some studies have not found support for males interrupting more, regardless of partner sex (Hannah & Murachver, 1999; Turner, Dindia, & Pearson, 1995). Explanations of mixed results in studies of interruptions may result from different defini-

100 tions of "interruption," situational context, and whether activities are structured (Anderson & Leaper, 1998). In their meta-analysis of studies of interruption, Anderson and Leaper (1998) suggested that definitions of interruption may moderate gender differences, gender dif-

105 ferences are larger in unstructured activities, and situational factors may influence interruptions more than gender.

    In the language theory literature, two theories have been used to explain gender miscommunication: *two-*

110 *cultures theory* and *dominance theory*. The *two-cultures theory* of gender-linked language differences suggest that boys and girls grow up in different gender cultures, in which they learn different ways of communicating (Mulac, Erlandson, Farrar, Hallett, Molloy, &

115 Prescott, 1998). Boys use questions, for example, to control conversation, whereas girls use questions to sustain conversation. These cultural differences produce miscommunication when children grow up to be

120 adults, when they are interacting more with others from "different cultures." From this position, men do not view interruptions as a display of power; rather, men and women use language differently based on their previous experiences in their cultural sub-groups.

    The *dominance theory* of gender-linked language

125 differences suggests that men's domination of conversations via interruption and topic introduction is reflective of the power they hold in larger society. From this perspective, men use questions, interruptions, and other means of communication as a way to dominate conver-

130 sation and to keep women in a subordinate position. The result is that women speak less and men talk more, again isomorphic to patterns at a larger, societal level in which men have more power than women.

    Proponents of both theories seem to suggest that

135 there are communication differences between men and women, yet the theories posit different explanations for why these differences exist. Given that there have been few empirical investigations of interruptions in therapy, the first step should be to first examine whether there

140 are differences between rates of interruption in the therapeutic context. If gender differences related to interruption are discovered, then therapists may be compelled to address these differences, particularly if these differences impact power within the couple rela-

145 tionship.

    In recent years, researchers have begun to explore interruptions within the context of therapy. Although there are differences in results about the influence of therapist gender on use of interruptions, two different

150 studies (Stratford, 1988; Werner-Wilson et al., 1997) reported that women clients were much more likely than men clients to be interrupted by therapists. Stratford (1998) found that male therapists were more likely than female therapists to interrupt clients; Stratford also

155 reported that female clients were more likely than male clients to be interrupted. Werner-Wilson and his colleagues (1997) also reported that women clients were more likely than men clients to be interrupted in therapy but did not find a difference between women and

160 men therapists. Stratford (1988)—noting that therapist inexperience is associated with a more directive interviewing style (Auerbach & Johnson, 1978)—suggested that the difference in findings about therapist gender and interruptions might be due to differences in thera-

165 pist experience: her study included experienced therapists while the Werner-Wilson et al. (1997) study included student therapists who have less experience. If Stratford's (1998) speculation is true, we might expect differences in interruption rates based on therapist ex-

170 perience level. The purpose of the present study is to investigate two related research questions:

1. Are women clients interrupted more than men clients?

2. Do student therapists interrupt women clients more

175   than experienced therapists?

Method

Participants

The sample for the present study included clients and therapists from two sources: (a) doctoral student therapists and clients at a nonprofit marriage and family therapy clinic at a major southern university that was accredited by the American Association for Marriage and Family Therapy, and (b) "master" therapists from the Master Series video collection distributed by the American Association for Marriage and Family Therapy. "The Master Series presents the world's most respected marriage and family therapists conducting live, unedited therapy sessions at AAMFT annual conferences" (AAMFT Catalog, 1993, p. 4). Including these master therapists provides an opportunity to compare therapy process between two levels of clinical experience: doctoral students versus master therapists. In each case, the session was the initial consultation with either the student therapist or the master therapist and it featured both an adult woman client and an adult man client who were romantic partners. Table 1 provides descriptive information about cases included in the study.

Procedures

We replicated the approach used by Werner-Wilson and colleagues (1997) to investigate interruptions in therapy process. We examined the first therapy session to control for treatment duration. Therapy sessions have predictable stages (e.g., social, engagement, information collection, intervention, closure), so we examined multiple time points in the session. Three five-minute segments were coded for every client from early, middle, and later stages in the session: (a) 10:00 to 15:00 minute segment; (b) 25:00 to 30:00 minute segment; and (c) 40:00 to 45:00 minute segment. Two senior-level undergraduate students, who were unaware of the purpose of this research, coded videotapes from the first therapy session.

Table 1
Descriptive Information about Videotapes

	Student Therapists	Master Therapists	Total
Therapist gender			
Men	52	14	66
Women	22	14	36
Total	74	28	102
Modality			
Marital	60	16	76
Family	14	12	26
Total	74	28	102

Coder training. Coders learned the coding scheme by practicing on tapes not featured in the sample until they achieved 80 percent agreement. A graduate student, who was also unaware of the purpose of the present study, coded every sixth session; these tapes were used to calculate interrater reliability. The coders maintained an acceptable level of interrater reliability throughout the coding process: intraclass correlations were .68.

Coding scheme. The transcripts were arranged with codes adjacent to each spoken turn to promote reliability by eliminating the need for coders to memorize codes: The coders viewed the video with the transcript and circled the appropriate code as they occurred during each speaking turn. A distinct set of codes was printed next to each speaker (e.g., therapist, woman client, man client) but each set of codes featured the same possible codes. For example, the therapist could interrupt either the woman or man client. Similarly, each client could interrupt either her/his partner or the therapist. In addition to enhancing reliability, this coding arrangement disguised the nature of the research project because coders identified conversational strategies used by each speaker, not just the therapist.

Dependent Measures

Interruptions. Interruptions—defined as a violation of a speaking turn, and operationalized as an overlap of speech that is disruptive or intrusive (West & Zimmerman, 1983; West & Zimmerman, 1977; Zimmerman & West, 1975)—were distinguished from other forms of overlap such as supportive statements that represent active listening skills. Statements that tailed off in tone or volume were not coded as interruptions because they represented invitations for reply. It is possible that people who talk more are interrupted more, so, following the procedure used by Werner-Wilson and colleagues (1997), we controlled for amount of client participation: A variable was constructed from the ratio of interruptions made by the therapist to number of speaking turns taken by the client. These ratios provided standardized measures to examine therapist interruptions.

Results

Based on our review of the literature, it seemed important to consider the influence of client gender, therapist gender, modality, and client experience since each variable has been found to have an influence on some dimension of therapy process. Analysis of Variance (ANOVA) was conducted to examine the following main effects on the dependent variable (ratio of therapist interruptions to number of client speaking turns): client gender (man, woman), therapist gender (man, woman), modality (couple, family), and therapist experience (student, AAMFT master therapist). Based on our review of the literature, it also seemed important to investigate the following interaction effects:

- Client gender × Therapist gender (Stratford, 1998; Werner-Wilson, Zimmerman, & Price, 1999);
- Client gender × Modality (Werner-Wilson, 1997; Werner-Wilson et al., 1999);

- Therapist gender × Modality (Werner-Wilson et al., 1999); Therapist gender × Therapist experience (Stratford, 1998); Client gender × Therapist gender × Modality (Werner-Wilson et al., 1999);
- Client gender × Therapist gender × Modality × Therapist experience (Stratford, 1998).

There was a statistically significant difference for gender of client on the dependent variable (see Table 2). Neither therapist gender, modality, therapist experience, nor the interaction of any variables was significant (see Table 2). On average, therapists in the present study interrupted women clients ($M = 0.064$) almost two times more often than men clients ($M = 0.037$).

Table 2
Analysis of Variance for Therapist Behaviors: Interruption

Source	MS	F
Client Gender	0.014	4.780*
Therapist Gender	0.007	2.497
Modality	0.001	0.259
Therapist Experience	0.009	3.312
Client Gender × Therapist Gender	0.004	1.370
Client Gender × Modality	0.000	0.046
Therapist Gender × Modality	0.006	2.189
Therapist Gender × Therapist Experience	0.003	0.923
Client Gender × Therapist Gender × Modality	0.005	0.189
Client Gender × Therapist Gender × Modality × Therapist Experience	0.002	0.869

$*p < .05, n = 102$

Discussion

Gender as a Process Issue

Results from the present study continue to suggest that women clients are interrupted more often than men clients in conjoint couple and family therapy, although the rate was slightly lower in the present study than in the original study published in 1997. For some aspects of therapy process (e.g., therapy alliance, goal setting), there seems to be an interaction effect between client gender and therapy modality (Werner-Wilson et al., 1997; Werner-Wilson, Zimmerman, & Price, 1999) but this effect was not demonstrated in the present study. Results from the present study also suggest that therapist experience—which was not measured in the 1997 study—does not significantly influence the number of interruptions directed toward women clients. In fact, master therapists interrupted women clients at a higher rate than student therapists, although it was not statistically significant.

Our findings contribute to the literature in providing evidence that women clients are interrupted more frequently than men clients, regardless of therapist gender or experience. Although the design of the current study could not directly test the validity of the two-cultures theory or the dominance theory (explain-

ing differences for men and women in language use), we tentatively suggest that these theories are too simplistic to adequately capture the complexity of interactions and power dynamics at play in relationships. Both theories, for example, posit that women may be more likely to be interrupted than men, *and* suggest that men use language in a way that is different from how women use language. One might hypothesize, from either theory of language use, that men therapists would be somehow different from women therapists in how often they interrupt clients, yet results from the current study do not support this view. Simply put, a more comprehensive theory that incorporates therapist and client markers of social standing may be more helpful for future researchers seeking to expand on the repeated finding in the therapy literature that women clients are more frequently interrupted than men clients.

Findings from the present study suggest an ongoing need to consider the influence of gender as a process variable in marriage and family therapy. Most therapists would agree to the notion that men and women should have relatively equal participation in therapy; it is likely that therapists are unaware that they tend to interrupt women far more frequently than men in therapy. The first step is for therapists to be aware of these patterns in therapy; the second step is for therapists to use their positional power to assist men and women to equitably share the therapeutic floor.

References

Anderson, K. J., & Leaper, C. (1998). Meta-analyses of gender effects on conversational interruption: Who, what, when, where, and how. *Sex Roles, 39*, 225–252.

Auerbach, A., & Johnson, M. (1978). Research on therapists' level of experience. In A. Gorman & A. Razin (Eds.), *The therapists' contribution to effective psychotherapy: An empirical assessment.* New York: Pergamon Press.

Avis, J, M. (1991). Power politics in therapy with women. In T. J. Goodrich (Ed.), *Women and power: Perspectives for family therapy* (pp. 183–200). New York: Norton.

Blanton, P. W., & Vandergriff-Avery, M. (2001). Marital therapy and marital power: Constructing narratives of sharing relational and positional power. *Contemporary Family Therapy, 23*, 295–308.

Cantor, D. W. (1990). Women as therapists: What we already know. In D. W. Cantor (Ed.), *Women as therapists: A multitheoretical casebook* (pp. 3–19). Northvale, NJ: Aronson.

Goldner, V. (1989). Generation and gender: Normative and covert hierarchies. In M. McGoldrick, C. M. Anderson, & F. Walsh (Eds.), *Women in families: A framework for family therapy* (pp. 42–60). New York: Norton.

Gray-Little., B., Baucom, D. H., & Hamby, S. L. (1996). Marital power, marital adjustment, and therapy outcome. *Journal of Family Psychology, 10*, 292–303.

Haddock, S., A., & Lyness, K. P. (2002). Three aspects of the therapeutic conversation in couples therapy: Does gender make a difference? *Journal of Couple & Relationship Therapy, 1*, 5–23.

Haddock, S. A., MacPhee, D., & Zimmerman, T. S. (2001). AAMFT Master Series Tapes: An analysis of the inclusion of feminist principles into family therapy practice. *Journal of Marital and Family Therapy, 27*, 487–500.

Haddock, S. A., Zimmerman, T. S., & MacPhee, D. (2000). The Power Equity Guide: Attending to gender in family therapy. *Journal of Marital and Family Therapy, 26*, 153–170.

Hannah, A., & Murachver, T. (1999). Gender and conversational style as predictors of conversational behavior. *Journal of Language and Social Psychology, 18*, 153–174.

Mulac, A., Erlandson, K. T., Farrar, W. J., Hallett, .T. S., Molloy, J. L., & Prescott, M. E. (1998). "Uh-huh. What's that all about?" Differing interpretations of conversational backchannels and questions as sources of miscommunication across gender boundaries. *Communication Research, 25*, 642–668.

O'Donohue, W. (1996). Marital therapy and gender-linked factors in communication. *Journal of Marital and Family Therapy, 22,* 87–101.

Silverstein, L. B. (2003). Classic texts and early critiques. In L. B. Silverstein & T. J. Goodrich (Eds.), *Feminist family therapy: Empowerment in social context* (pp. 17–35). Washington, DC: APA.

Stratford, J. (1998). Women and men in conversation: A consideration of therapists' interruptions in therapeutic discourse. *Journal of Family Therapy, 20,* 393–394.

Turner, L. H., Dindia, K., & Pearson, J. C. (1995). An investigation of female/male verbal behaviors in same-sex and mixed-sex conversations. *Communication Reports, 8,* 86–96.

Werner-Wilson, R. J. (1997). Is therapeutic alliance influenced by gender in marriage and family therapy? *Journal of Feminist Family Therapy, 9,* 3–16.

Werner-Wilson, R. J., Price, S. J., Zimmerman, T. S., & Murphy, M. J. (1997). Client gender as a process variable in marriage and family therapy: Are women clients interrupted more than men clients? *Journal of Family Psychology, 11,* 373–377.

Werner-Wilson, R. J., Zimmerman, T. S., & Price, S. J. (1999). Are goals and topics influenced by gender and modality in the initial marriage and family therapy session? *Journal of Marital and Family Therapy, 25,* 253–262.

West, C., & Zimmerman, D. H. (1977). Women's place in everyday talk: Reflections on parent-child interaction. *Social Problems, 24,* 521–529.

West, C. & Zimmerman, D. H. (1983). Small insults: A study of interruptions in cross-sex conversations between unacquainted persons. In B. Thorne, C. Kramarae, & N. Henley (Eds.), *Language, gender and society* (pp. 103–117). Rowley, MA: Newbury House.

Whisman, M. A., & Jacobson, N. S. (1990). Power, marital satisfaction, and response to marital therapy. *Journal of Family Psychology, 4,* 202–212.

Zimmerman, D. H., & West, C. (1975). Sex roles, interruptions, and silences in conversation. In B. Thorne & N. Henley (Eds.), *Language & sex: Difference & dominance* (pp. 105–129). Rowley, MA: Newbury House.

About the authors: *Ronald Jay Werner-Wilson*, PhD, Associate Professor and Marriage and Family Therapy Program and Clinic Director; *Megan J. Murphy*, PhD, Assistant Professor, and *Jennifer Lynn Fitzharris*, MS, are all affiliated with the Department of Human Development and Family Studies, Iowa State University, Ames, IA.

Address correspondence to: Ronald Jay Werner-Wilson, PhD, Department of Human Development and Family Studies, 4380 Palmer Building, Suite 1321, Iowa State University, Ames, IA 50011-4380. E-mail: rwwilson@iastate.edu

Exercise for Article 25

Factual Questions

1. The researchers state that recent studies show what type of relationship between marital satisfaction and power inequality?

2. Dominance theory suggests that men use questions, interruptions, and other means of communication as a way to do what?

3. Coding for interruptions in each therapy session was done for three segments. How long was each segment?

4. The researchers defined "interruptions" as a violation of a speaking turn. How was "interruptions" operationalized?

5. Was the difference between women clients and men clients being interrupted statistically significant? If yes, at what probability level?

6. Was the difference between men therapists and women therapists statistically significant? If yes, at what probability level?

Questions for Discussion

7. The researchers discuss theories relating to their research in lines 108–145 and lines 302–325. In your opinion, is this discussion an important strength of this research report? Explain.

8. This study examined interruptions in only the initial consultation with a therapist. Would you be willing to generalize the results to subsequent sessions? Explain. (See lines 191–192.)

9. The researchers state that the undergraduate students who coded the videotapes were unaware of the purpose of this research. Speculate on why the researchers did not make them aware of the purpose. (See lines 207–210.)

10. In your opinion, is the "coder training" described in lines 211–219 an important part of this study? Explain.

11. The current study does not support the view that men therapists are different from women therapists in how often they interrupt clients. Does this result surprise you? Explain. (See lines 315–319.)

12. In your opinion, does this study make an important contribution to understanding how clients' gender *influences* therapists' behavior? Explain.

Quality Ratings

Directions: Indicate your level of agreement with each of the following statements by circling a number from 5 for strongly agree (SA) to 1 for strongly disagree (SD). If you believe an item is not applicable to this research article, leave it blank. Be prepared to explain your ratings. When responding to criteria A and B below, keep in mind that brief titles and abstracts are conventional in published research.

A. The title of the article is appropriate.

SA 5 4 3 2 1 SD

B. The abstract provides an effective overview of the research article.

SA 5 4 3 2 1 SD

C. The introduction establishes the importance of the study.

SA 5 4 3 2 1 SD

D. The literature review establishes the context for the study.

SA   5   4   3   2   1   SD

E. The research purpose, question, or hypothesis is clearly stated.

SA   5   4   3   2   1   SD

F. The method of sampling is sound.

SA   5   4   3   2   1   SD

G. Relevant demographics (for example, age, gender, and ethnicity) are described.

SA   5   4   3   2   1   SD

H. Measurement procedures are adequate.

SA   5   4   3   2   1   SD

I. All procedures have been described in sufficient detail to permit a replication of the study.

SA   5   4   3   2   1   SD

J. The participants have been adequately protected from potential harm.

SA   5   4   3   2   1   SD

K. The results are clearly described.

SA   5   4   3   2   1   SD

L. The discussion/conclusion is appropriate.

SA   5   4   3   2   1   SD

M. Despite any flaws, the report is worthy of publication.

SA   5   4   3   2   1   SD

Article 26

Integrating Behavioral Health into Primary Care Settings: A Pilot Project

ANDREW KOLBASOVSKY
Health Insurance Plan of New York

ISRAEL ROMANO
Health Insurance Plan of New York

LEONARD REICH
Health Insurance Plan of New York

BEATRIZ JARAMILLO
Health Insurance Plan of New York

ABSTRACT. The integration of behavioral health into the primary care setting provides an opportunity for psychologists to improve care for the treatment of depression. In this study, a pilot program was created integrating psychologists into four medical centers. Results indicated a significant improvement in depressive symptoms and health status, and an improvement in overall antidepressant medication adherence. Physicians were highly satisfied with the integrated program. To guide behavioral health specialists considering work in the primary care setting, a description of the program and a discussion of the lessons learned from the project are provided.

From *Professional Psychology: Research and Practice*, *36*, 130–135. Copyright © 2005 by the American Psychological Association. Reprinted with permission.

Depression is a highly prevalent condition in primary care (Beck, 2001; Coyne, Thompson, Klinkman, & Nease, 2002), yet few psychologists currently work in this setting. Studies show that most treatment for
5 depression occurs in primary care, with as many as 66% to 75% of all depression cases treated by primary care physicians (PCPs) rather than by mental health specialists (Coyne et al., 2002; U.S. Department of Health and Human Services, 1993). Yet, despite its
10 prevalence and the importance of proper treatment, depression is frequently unrecognized and undertreated by PCPs (Finley, Rens, & Pont, 2003; U.S. Department of Health and Human Services, 1993), suggesting a strong need for behavioral health specialists to work
15 collaboratively with physicians for the treatment of depression.

In an effort to address this need, models integrating psychologists into the primary care setting for the treatment of depression have been developed (Beck,
20 2001; Coyne et al., 2002; Kaintz, 2002; McDaniel, Belar, Schroeder, Hargrove, & Freeman, 2002; Pruitt, Klapow, Epping-Jordan, & Dresselhaus, 1998). Integrated care models typically involve the co-locating of behavioral health specialists and PCPs to work collabo-
25 ratively in the medical center setting to provide depression care. Several integrated programs have demon-

strated promising results such as improving the quality of depression care provided, increasing adherence to antidepressant medication, and increasing satisfaction
30 with care (Beck, 2001; Coyne et al., 2002; Finley et al., 2003; Gill & Dansky, 2003; Kanapaux, 2004; Katon, Russo, & Von Korff, 2002; Katon, Von Korff, & Lin, 1995, 1997).

In response to the importance of providing high-
35 quality depression care in the primary care setting, a large northeastern HMO, with a grant from the New York State Department of Health, created a pilot program, co-locating and integrating behavioral health psychologists into four medical centers to work col-
40 laboratively with physicians to improve depression care. This article details the outcomes of the project's stated goals and describes the program in order that other psychologists considering clinical or research work in the primary care setting may benefit from the
45 lessons learned.

Pilot Project Goals

Goal 1: Improve Physician Diagnosis of Depression

Because of the underidentification of depression in primary care (U.S. Department of Health and Human Services, 1993), a goal was set to increase physicians' diagnoses of depression on encounter forms for pa-
50 tients prescribed antidepressant medication. It was expected that the percentage of all patients prescribed antidepressant medication by physicians at the four medical centers, with a corresponding depression diagnosis as captured through administrative data, would
55 increase by 50% as compared with a similar period of time prior to the pilot program.

Goal 2: Improve Patient Adherence to Antidepressant Medication

A goal was set to increase by at least 10% the proportion of patients with a new antidepressant medication prescription adherent for at least 3 months for the
60 entire population of patients who had been newly prescribed an antidepressant by a PCP in any of the four medical centers as compared with a similar time period prior to the program. Adherence was considered

120

achieved if pharmacy data indicated that the patient
65   fulfilled sufficient prescriptions to have continuous
daily medication for 3 months.

While a minimum of 6 months of antidepressant
medication adherence is recommended prior to medication termination (Lin, Von Korff, & Katon, 1995; Na-
70   tional Committee for Quality Assurance, 2003) because
of the very high rate of patients discontinuing within 3
months (Nemeroff, 2003; Unutzer, Katon, & Callahan,
2002; Wells, Sherbourne, & Schoenbaum, 2000), a
shorter 3-month period of adherence was chosen as an
75   outcome. Reporting 3-month adherence is also consistent with other studies in this area (Beck, 2001;
Dietrich et al., 2004).

*Goal 3: Improve Physician Comfort with Diagnosing
and Treating Depression*

Because of the low prevalence of depression diagnoses based on data from outpatient encounter forms, a
80   goal was set to demonstrate a statistically significant
improvement in physicians' self-reported comfort with
diagnosing and treating depression as measured by a
face valid, three-item physician comfort survey, following 6 months of working with a co-located, inte-
85   grated behavioral health psychologist.

Goal 4: Demonstrate Treatment Outcomes

To demonstrate high-quality depression care, a goal
was set that depressed patients receiving 3 months of
treatment in the four medical centers would demonstrate statistically significant improvements on meas-
90   ures of depression and health status. A 3-month time
period was selected for outcome measurement as initial
response to treatment is usually seen within 12 weeks
(MacArthur Initiative on Depression and Primary Care
at Dartmouth & Duke, 2003).

Goal 5: Physician Satisfaction with the Program

95   Critical to the success of any behavioral health program integrated into primary care is physician satisfaction. To demonstrate this, an eight-item, face valid survey assessing satisfaction with mental health services
was given to physicians working with a co-located be-
100   havioral health specialist in the medical centers. To
allow for comparisons, physicians in different medical
centers within the same medical group that were similar in size but utilized a specialty care, as opposed to an
integrated care model, were given the same survey. It
105   was expected that physicians working with a co-located
behavioral health psychologist would report greater
satisfaction than those using the specialty care model.

Time Line

All patients were referred to the psychologists during a 12-month period of time. Physician diagnosis of
110   depression and medication compliance results were
obtained for an 8-month period of time within the year
of the program.

Statistical Analysis

A pre-post analysis was used to assess changes in
percentage of patients diagnosed with depression by
115   PCPs, percentage of patients compliant with antidepressant medication, and physician comfort diagnosing
and treating depression. A Z test was utilized to evaluate differences between pre- and post-percentages.
Paired sample t tests were used to analyze change in
120   depression symptoms and health status from the beginning of treatment to 3 months following treatment. A t
test for independent samples was used to compare physician satisfaction with mental health at medical centers
with a co-located psychologist to medical centers with-
125   out one. Statistical significance for all tests was established at $p < .05$.

Integrating Behavioral Health into Primary Care Settings: A Pilot Project

Program Description

Each behavioral health psychologist was introduced
to the physicians of the medical centers during staff
meetings, and his or her new role as a collaborator for
130   the treatment of depression was described. The benefits
offered were clearly outlined: assisting in the diagnosis
of depression, monitoring/encouraging medication adherence, providing education, assessing treatment progress, providing therapy, and encouraging adherence
135   with medical regimens. While the physicians were specifically asked to refer depressed patients, all referrals
were evaluated and supported.

The pilot program specifically addressed variables
considered to be critical to the success of any inte-
140   grated program: location, availability, and collaboration (Blount, 1998; Farrar, Kates, Crustolo, & Nikolaou, 2001; Haley et al., 1998). The psychologists were
conveniently located in the same building as the primary care physicians, and great importance was placed
145   on maintaining availability to both patients and physicians. The psychologists maintained 30-min session
times, allowing for greater availability to patients. Specific time was also set aside for informal collaboration
with physicians.

150   The cornerstone of this pilot program was collaboration. While absolutely critical to success, collaboration can be difficult given the time constraints faced by
busy physicians. To overcome this challenge, collaboration was achieved formally and informally in a very
155   time efficient manner. Formal collaboration was conducted through the use of feedback forms. During the
first visit with the psychologist, the patient was asked
to sign a consent form allowing collaboration with the
PCP and to complete two depression questionnaires:
160   the Patient Health Questionnaire-9 (PHQ; Kroenke,
Spitzer, & Williams, 2001) and the Depression Screening Tool (DST; Strosahl & Quirk, 1998), a brief, valid,
and reliable measure of depression for use in primary
care settings. The Depression Screening Tool contains
165   5 items from the Outcome Questionnaire-45 (Lambert,

Lunnen, Umpress, Hansen, & Burlingame, 1994). These 5 items were selected because they were the most highly predictive of total depression scores on both the Beck Depression Inventory (Beck & Steer, 1993) and the structured interview (Williams, 1998) of the Hamilton Depression Scale (Hamilton, 1960). Patients also completed the 12-item SF-12 Health Survey (Ware, Kosinski, & Keller, 1996), a health survey containing eight different factors related to health and functional status. Following this visit, a feedback form indicating symptoms, diagnosis, and recommendations was sent to the PCP. The questionnaires were then repeated after 3 months of treatment. Updated feedback forms containing information on treatment progress, symptom severity, recommendations and so forth were also sent regularly. The PCPs reviewed the forms, initialed them, and placed them in the chart. Informal collaboration was achieved by the psychologists attending lunch with the physicians daily. During this time, the behavioral health psychologist and PCP would individually discuss the depression treatment of shared cases. The time spent together during lunch also served as a reminder of the psychologists' presence in the medical center and allowed for relationships to be developed while not impinging on the physicians' busy schedule.

Treatment for Depression

The psychologists, while each having different personal styles, maintained certain similarities. For patients on antidepressant medication, proper adherence was emphasized. This was done through education, which included several handouts on depression and medication treatment, and through an emphasis on alliance rather than on compliance. Over the course of therapy, the behavioral health specialist would work to develop a strong alliance with each patient, providing an environment to discuss concerns about the medication. As an alliance was formed, the psychologist and patient would work together to identify and overcome obstacles to medication adherence. It was felt that this work, critical to antidepressant medication treatment, is often difficult for PCPs because of time constraints. It should be noted that not all patients were on antidepressant medication; thus, for all patients adherence to treatment was also emphasized. In addition to the emphasis on adherence, the psychologists provided psychotherapy for depression that typically involved cognitive-behavioral interventions but did not utilize any manualized protocols for providing therapy. The therapists also worked with the patients to identify treatment goals that often centered on symptom reduction.

The behavioral health psychologists also placed emphasis on regular assessment of depressive symptoms. These assessments would then be used to help guide treatment and to provide feedback to both patients and physicians. For example, a change in symptom severity would often prompt discussions with pa-

tients and physicians about medication titration, adherence issues, or augmenting therapeutic services.

A team approach to depression treatment was also emphasized. Teaming with medical providers represented a shift from most specialty behavioral health work. In the primary care setting as opposed to specialty care, the psychologists found an increased need for engaging in consulting work, providing brief assessment, ruling out or diagnosing possible behavioral health conditions, and even conducting psychological evaluations for surgery.

Referrals to the Program

Patients were referred to the integrated behavioral health psychologists by PCPs. Ultimately, the physicians decided who they would refer to the behavioral health psychologist. Our experience was that referrals were slow at first but increased rapidly once the physicians got to know the psychologists better and began to receive positive feedback from the patients that they had referred. By the end of the pilot project, the psychologists typically had almost every available appointment booked daily.

Of the 47 PCPs in the four medical groups, 39 (83%) made referrals. They referred 358 adult patients to the behavioral health psychologists for treatment. Of those referred, 39.4% were men and 60.6% were women. The average age was 50.4 years, and 98.3% met the *Diagnostic and Statistical Manual of Mental Disorders* (American Psychiatric Association, 1994) criteria for a psychiatric diagnosis. Depression was the most common primary diagnosis, with 224 (62.6%) patients receiving this diagnosis. Diagnoses for all patients can be seen in Table 1.

Table 1

Primary Diagnosis of All Patients Referred to Behavioral Health for Treatment

Diagnosis	Frequency	%
MDD/Dysthymia	224	62.6
Adjustment disorder	58	16.2
Anxiety NOS	21	5.9
Panic disorder	16	4.5
Dementia	7	2.0
GAD	4	1.1
Bipolar disorder	4	1.1
PTSD	3	0.8
OCD	3	0.8
Developmental disorder	3	0.8
Psychotic disorder NOS	2	0.6
ODD	2	0.6
Bereavement	1	0.3
Eating disorder	1	0.3
Substance abuser	1	0.3
Depression NOS	1	0.3
Social phobia	1	0.3
No diagnosis	6	1.7
Total	358	100

Note. MDD = major depressive disorder; NOS = not otherwise specified; GAD = generalized anxiety disorder; PTSD = posttraumatic stress disorder; OCD = obsessive–compulsive disorder; ODD = oppositional defiant disorder.

Of those diagnosed with depression, only 98 were within the time window for this study and were able to complete 3 months of treatment within the centers participating in this study. A total of 76 of these patients (77.6%) completed the questionnaires and 3 months of treatment, while 22 patients dropped out of treatment in less than 3 months. A list of progress toward completion of 3 months of treatment is presented in Table 2.

Table 2
Progress Toward Completion of 3 Months of Treatment for Depressed Patients

Reason	Frequency	%
Completed 3 months of treatment	76	33.9
In active treatment but < 3 months	51	22.8
Referred out after consultation	50	22.3
Patient terminated treatment	22	9.8
Completed treatment in < 3 months	16	7.1
Referred out when clinician left	5	2.2
Patient refused treatment	1	0.5
Patient died	1	0.5
Insurance terminated	1	0.5
One-time-only appointment	1	0.5
Total	224	100

Type of Depression Treatment

The 224 depressed patients referred to the psychologists fell into one of three categories: medication plus therapy (74.1%), therapy only (25%), and medication only (0.9%). The type of treatment was determined by patient preference, as well as clinical indication, and was typically determined after discussion between the patient, physician, and psychologist. Of the 76 depressed patients completing 3 months of treatment, 15.8% received therapy only and 84.2% received both therapy and medication. These depressed patients were seen for an average of 6.24 visits. The higher rate of therapy plus medication may reflect the fact that all patients were seen at the medical center and were referred by a PCP as opposed to self-referred patients seen in specialty care who may be less likely to start with medication before seeing a therapist.

Of the 22 depressed patients who dropped out of treatment, 13 (59.1%) were receiving therapy only and 9 (40.9%) were receiving therapy and medication. Thus, the majority of depressed patients who completed 3 months of treatment were receiving combination treatment (therapy and medication), whereas the majority of the depressed patients who did not complete 3 months of treatment were receiving therapy only. While it is impossible to determine why those receiving medication would have a lower dropout rate, one reason may be that those receiving medication had higher initial depression scores and thus may be more motivated to stay in treatment. Similarly, committing to taking medication may be reflective of a commitment to overall treatment. However, future research is needed to replicate this finding and to determine factors contributing to adherence to therapeutic treatment.

Outcome 1: Improve Physician Diagnosis of Depression

No improvement was observed for physician diagnosis of depression on encounter forms when prescribing antidepressant medication. Prior to the program, the rate of diagnosis for the entire population of members prescribed antidepressant medication at the four medical centers was 8%, during the program it was 7%. Discussions with PCPs revealed that this finding may be partially an artifact of the current forms and procedures used by the PCPs and concerns about reimbursement. Frequency data on physician diagnosis of depression are presented in Table 3.

Outcome 2: Improve Patient Adherence with Antidepressant Medication

The 3-month antidepressant medication adherence rate for all patients placed on antidepressant medication by physicians in the four medical centers prior to the integrated program was 20%. During the integrated program this rate rose to 22%. Thus, there was a 10% increase in antidepressant medication compliance for the entire population of patients prescribed antidepressant medication in the four medical centers. Descriptive data on adherence are presented in Table 3.

Outcome 3: Improve Physician Comfort with Diagnosing and Treating Depression

Twenty-three physicians were handed and completed the Physician Comfort Survey just prior to the pilot program, during lunch meetings. The remaining 24 PCPs were not seen in person and thus did not complete the survey. In total, 49% of the PCPs completed the survey. An overwhelming majority of these physicians (91.3%) reported that they were "comfortable" or "very comfortable" evaluating depression, and 73.9% reported that they were "comfortable" or "very comfortable" treating depression. Although not all physicians responded, almost half did, and all who were available on the days the surveys were conducted did complete them. Frequency data regarding physician self-report comfort evaluating and treating depression are presented in Table 4.

The very high levels of self-reported comfort evaluating and treating depression were surprising given the 7% to 8% of depression diagnoses accompanying antidepressant medication prescriptions. However, because the reported comfort level was so high it was decided that a follow-up measurement would not be conducted as it was felt that little if any improvement in self-reported confidence level would be possible.

Outcome 4: Demonstrate Treatment Outcomes

All depressed patients completing 3 months of treatment with the behavioral health psychologists completed the Depression Screening Tool and the SF-12 prior to starting treatment and at 3 months. In addi-

Table 3

Physician Diagnosis of Depression and Medication Adherence for All Patients with a New Prescription for Antidepressant Medication: Pre- and Postprogram

Program	Prior to program		During program	
	Frequency	%	Frequency	%
Patients with a new prescription	2,213		2,233	
Patients with a corresponding diagnosis	181	8.2	165	7.4
Patients compliant for 3 months	453	20.4	501	22.4

Note. This includes all members prescribed antidepressant medication at the four medical centers.

Table 4

Physician Self-Reported Comfort Evaluating and Treating Depression

Comfort level	Evaluating depression		Treating depression	
	Frequency	%	Frequency	%
Very uncomfortable	0	0	1	4.3
Uncomfortable	2	8.7	5	21.7
Comfortable	14	60.9	10	43.5
Very comfortable	7	30.4	7	30.4

tion, 27 of these depressed patients also completed the Patient Health Questionnaire depression questionnaire that was added midway through the project, when starting treatment and at 3 months. Results indicated that 88% and 100% of these patients demonstrated at least a reduction on the DST and PHQ, respectively. The average DST score at the initial assessment was 11.08, after 3 months it was significantly reduced to 7.55, $t(75) = 9.54$, $p < .001$. The average PHQ score at the initial assessment was 15.33, falling into the moderately severe depression category. Following 3 months of treatment, it was significantly reduced to 8.93, which falls into the mild depression category representing a significant two-category reduction in depression severity, $t(26) = 9.09$, $p < .001$. Of those completing the PHQ, 40.7% demonstrated a reduction in depressive severity by two full depression categories, and 48.2% demonstrated a reduction in depressive severity by one depressive category. Approximately 1% of these patients demonstrated a reduction in depressive severity yet remained in the same category.

Also of note was the finding that of the 60 depressed patients completing an initial PHQ who received medication as part of the treatment, the average depression severity score was 15.40, which falls into the moderately severe depression category. As expected, the 19 depressed patients who completed an initial PHQ and who did not receive medication as part of treatment had a lower initial average depression score of 12.68, which falls into the moderately depressed category. This finding suggests that as appropriate, medication tended to be included in the more severe cases of depression.

The 49 depressed patients who completed the SF-12 health survey during the initial session and following 3 months of treatment demonstrated significant improvements in vitality, $t(48) = -2.07$, $p < .05$, social functioning, $t(48) = -3.89$, $p < .001$, emotional health,

$t(48) = -3.89$, $p < .001$, and mental health, $t(48) = -7.43$, $p < .001$.

Outcome 5: Physician Satisfaction with the Program

Twenty-three PCPs working with co-located psychologists and 13 PCPs working in selected centers without a co-located behavioral health specialist completed the satisfaction survey, with a response rate of 48.9% and 46.4%, respectively. Results indicated that on each of the eight items assessing satisfaction with mental health services, the physicians working with a co-located behavioral health specialist reported significantly greater satisfaction ($p < .05$). The PCPs working within the integrated program reported greater overall satisfaction, collaboration, convenience, and access for both physician and patient.

Implications

Our results demonstrate that by forging alliances between psychology and primary care, high-quality depression care can be provided in a setting in which it is truly needed. The findings of this pilot project have prompted an expanded integration of behavioral health into the primary care setting within our organization. These findings, taken together with other studies demonstrating the benefits of integrating care, should encourage other psychologists to initiate similar programs in primary care. Several lessons were learned during our project that may guide behavioral health specialists beginning work in the primary care setting.

Because the presence of an integrated psychologist is new to many physicians, behavioral health specialists should keep in mind the need to "sell" his or her role. To do this, a clear outline of the psychologist's role and potential benefits should be presented. Our experience taught us that using outcome measures and conducting regular assessment while providing feedback are very helpful in clearly establishing the benefit of utilizing an integrated team approach to treating depression.

Other important lessons learned were that the behavioral health specialist's relationship with the physicians is the key to a successful program. To facilitate this relationship, availability must be maintained to both patients and physicians, and a system for regular and continuous collaboration with physicians must be established in a manner that takes into account limits to the physician's time. Using feedback forms and regularly collaborating during lunch periods were highly effective in our program. Once this system was in place, the PCPs greatly appreciated having a specialist to work with who was able to provide information on depression, encourage and monitor adherence, and provide psychological interventions. Similarly, the behavioral health specialists found work in the medical centers to be very rewarding and the physicians extremely accommodating, as well as eager to help both the specialist and the patient.

For any integrated program to succeed, referrals are needed. Our experience taught us that once physicians developed a solid relationship with the behavioral health specialists, saw them on a regular basis, and started to receive positive feedback from referred patients, referrals increased quickly. Those who were referred also noted that it was very convenient to see a behavioral health specialist in the same building with their medical provider.

Behavioral health specialists working in primary care should also be aware that while physicians may report feeling comfortable diagnosing and working with depression, this may not actually be the case. In fact, many physicians may feel that they are not comfortable, have not had the necessary training, or that diagnosing depression may create additional work when they may already be overburdened. This further underscores the value of having an integrated behavioral health specialist to assist in making diagnoses. While physicians may be hesitant to make behavioral health diagnoses, the psychologists were able to document a diagnosis for every depressed patient referred to them.

While the results from our pilot study are encouraging, the study has important limitations, most notably the lack of a control group. There is a need for future research involving similar integrative programs utilizing randomized control groups (Gill & Dansky, 2003). Because this was not possible in our pilot program, it is impossible to compare the improvements seen in this study to the outcomes associated with nonintegrated care or to no care at all. Further research is also needed to better understand physician comfort level while diagnosing and treating depression as well as to identify factors associated with dropping out of treatment.

The time constraints of our pilot project represent another limitation of our study. Our measures of medication adherence and symptom severity were conducted following 3 months of treatment. Because of the chronic nature of depression, and the fact that complete symptom remission does not usually occur for most patients within 3 months (Lam & Kennedy, 2004), future research is needed to extend the outcome measures to 6 months and beyond.

Our project was unable to demonstrate an improvement in physician diagnosis of depression for patients placed on antidepressant medication. While physicians did not diagnose depression frequently, data indicated that antidepressant medication was prescribed appropriately and that excellent referrals were made to the behavioral health specialist. Improving physician diagnosis remains an important challenge for specialists working in the primary care setting, and future research should test other possible interventions. While our project focused on the diagnosis of patients who were prescribed medication, future research should also address physician diagnosis of depression for patients who were not prescribed antidepressant medication.

The integration of behavioral health specialists into the primary care setting represents an area of exciting opportunities for clinicians and researchers. This pilot program outlines a successfully integrated program, which will hopefully be replicated and expanded on. The lessons learned from this pilot should be helpful to psychologists looking to develop roles within the primary care setting where improved behavioral health care is greatly needed. It should be noted, however, that the value of collaborating with PCPs is not confined to psychologists working in the primary care setting. Increasing appropriate collaboration is a worthy aim for all psychologists, and strategies used in this pilot project may be applied to other settings.

To further advance the importance of collaborative care for depression, clinical and research work should include not only clinical outcomes but also physician satisfaction. While the primary care setting may represent a shift in the practice of many psychologists, such as shorter session times and an increased need for consultation, collaboration, and relationship building, the behavioral health specialists in our program found the work highly rewarding, greatly appreciated, and above all very much needed.

References

American Psychiatric Association (1994). *Diagnostic and statistical manual of mental disorders* (4th ed.). Washington, DC: Author.

Beck, A. (2001). Collaborative behavioral health in primary care. *Group Practice Journal, 50,* 22–26.

Beck, A. T., & Steer, R. A. (1993). *Manual for the Beck Depression Inventory.* San Antonio, TX: Psychological Corporation.

Blount, A. (Ed.) (1998). *Integrated primary care: The future of medical and mental health collaboration.* New York: Norton.

Coyne, J. C., Thompson, R., Klinkman, M., & Nease, D. (2002). Emotional disorders in primary care. *Journal of Consulting and Clinical Psychology, 70,* 789–809.

Dietrich, A., Oxman, T., Williams, J., Schulberg, H., Lee, M., Barry, P. et al. (2004). Re-engineering systems for the treatment of depression in primary care: Cluster randomized controlled trial. *British Medical Journal, 329,* 602.

Farrar, S., Kates, N., Crustolo, A., & Nikolaou, L. (2001). Integrated model for mental health care: Are health care providers satisfied with it? *Canadian Family Physician, 47,* 2483–2488.

Finley, P., Rens, H., & Pont, J. (2003). Impact of a collaborative care model on depression in a primary care setting: A randomized control trial. *Pharmacotherapy, 23*, 1175–1185.

Gill, J. M., & Dansky, B. S. (2003). Use of an electronic medical record to facilitate screening for depression in primary care. *Primary Care Companion Journal of Clinical Psychiatry, 5*, 125–128.

Haley, W., McDaniel, S., Bray, J., Frank, R., Heldring, M., Johnson, S. et al. (1998). Psychological practice in primary care settings: Practical tips for clinicians. *Professional Psychology: Research and Practice, 3*, 237–244.

Hamilton, M. (1960). Rating scale for depression. *Journal of Neurology, Neurosurgery, and Psychiatry, 23*, 56–61.

Kaintz, K. (2002). Barriers and enhancements to physician-psychologist collaboration. *Professional Psychology: Research and Practice, 33*, 169–175.

Kanapaux, W. (2004). The road to integrated care: Commitment is the key. *Behavioral Health Tomorrow, 13*, 10–16.

Katon, W., Russo, J., & Von Korff, M. (2002). Long-term effects of a collaborative care intervention in persistently depressed primary care patients. *Journal of General Internal Medicine, 17*, 741–748.

Katon, W., Von Korff, M., & Lin, E. (1995). Collaborative management to achieve treatment guidelines: Impact of depression in primary care. *Journal of the American Medical Association, 273*, 1026–1031.

Katon, W., Von Korff, M., & Lin, E. (1997). Collaborative management to achieve depression treatment guidelines. *Journal of Clinical Psychiatry, 58*, 20–23.

Kroenke, K., Spitzer, R., & Williams, J. (2001). The PHQ-9: Validity of a brief depression severity measure. *Journal of General Internal Medicine, 16*, 606–613.

Lam, R., & Kennedy, S. (2004). Evidence-based strategies for achieving and sustaining full remission in depression: Focus on meta-analysis. *Canadian Journal of Psychiatry, 49*, 17S–26S.

Lambert, M., Lunnen, K., Umpress, V., Hansen, N., & Burlingame, G. (1994). *Administration and scoring manual for the Outcome Questionnaire (OQ-45)*. Salt Lake City, UT: IHC Center for Behavioral Healthcare Efficiency.

Lin, E., Von Korff, M., & Katon, W. (1995). The role of primary care physicians in patients' adherence to antidepressant therapy. *Medical Care, 33*, 67–74.

MacArthur Initiative on Depression and Primary Care at Dartmouth & Duke (2003). *Depression management tool kit*. Retrieved September 2, 2004, from www.depression-primarycare.org

McDaniel, S., Belar, C., Schroeder, C., Hargrove, D., & Freeman, E. (2002). A training curriculum for professional psychologists in primary care. *Professional Psychology: Research and Practice, 33*, 65–72.

National Committee for Quality Assurance (2003). *HEDIS 2004 technical specifications* (Vol. 2). Washington, DC: National Committee for Quality Assurance.

Nemeroff, C. (2003). Improving antidepressant adherence. *Journal of Clinical Psychiatry, 64*, 25–30.

Pruitt, S., Klapow, J., Epping-Jordan, J., & Dresselhaus, T. (1998). Moving behavioral medicine to the "front line": A model for integration of behavioral and medical sciences in primary care. *Professional Psychology: Research and Practice, 29*, 230–236.

Strosahl, K., & Quirk, M. (1998). *Depression clinical roadmap toolkit*. Group Health Cooperative, Puget Sound, Washington. Unpublished manuscript.

Unutzer, J., Katon, W., & Callahan, C. (2002). Collaborative care management and late life depression in the primary care setting: A randomized controlled trial. *Journal of the American Medical Association, 288*, 2836–2845.

U.S. Department of Health and Human Services (1993). *Depression in primary care: Treatment of major depression* (Vol. 2; AHCPR Publication. No. 93-0551). Rockville, MD: Agency for Health Care Policy and Research.

Ware, J., Kosinski, M., & Keller, S. (1996). A 12-item short form health survey: Construction of scales and preliminary tests of reliability and validity. *Medical Care, 34*, 220–233.

Wells, K., Sherbourne, C., & Schoenbaum, M. (2000). Impact of disseminating quality improvement programs for depression in managed primary care: A randomized controlled trial. *Journal of the American Medical Association, 283*, 212–220.

Williams, J. (1998). A structured interview guide for the Hamilton Depression Rating Scale. *Archives of General Psychiatry, 45*, 742–747.

Acknowledgment: This project was funded with a grant from the New York State Department of Health.

About the authors: *Andrew Kolbasovsky* holds a PhD in clinical psychology from the University of Hartford. He is director of Clinical Development and Behavioral Medicine at the Health Insurance Plan of New York. His area of research interest includes behavioral medicine and integrating behavioral health and primary care services. *Leonard Reich* holds a PhD in counseling psychology from Arizona State University. He is vice president of Mental Health Services at the Health Insurance Plan of New York. His area of research interest includes quality improvement, behavioral health, depression care, and medication adherence. *Israel Romano* holds a PhD in clinical and school psychology from the Derner Institute of Adelphi University. He is director of Quality Management at the Health Insurance Plan of New York. His research interests include screening and treatment of depression, and the use of databases and Web technology for disease management and preventive health. *Beatriz Jaramillo* holds a PhD in public health-epidemiology from the School of Public Health, Columbia University. She is managing director of Health Services and Performance Analysis at the Health Insurance Plan of New York. Her area of research is psychiatric epidemiology-health services.

Address correspondence to: Andrew Kolbasovsky, 55 Water Street, 12th Floor, New York, NY 10041. E-mail: akolbasovsky@hipusa.com

Exercise for Article 26

Factual Questions

1. How was adherence to antidepressant medication defined?

2. Why did the psychologists maintain 30-minute session times?

3. How was "informal collaboration" between psychologists and physicians achieved?

4. Of the 224 patients with depression as a primary diagnosis, how many were within the time window for this study?

5. Antidepressant medication adherence was 20% prior to the program. During the program, it rose to what percentage?

6. Was the difference from the initial session to the follow-up on "mental health" section of the SF-12 health survey statistically significant? If yes, at what probability level?

7. The researchers explicitly mention two specific limitations of their evaluation of the program. What is the second limitation that they mention?

Questions for Discussion

8. In lines 97–98, the researchers refer to a "face valid survey." What is your understanding of the meaning of this term?

9. Is the program description in lines 127–191 described in sufficient detail that you have a good understanding of its components and operation? Explain.

10. In your opinion, how important is it to know how many clients dropped out? Is it important to know why they dropped out? Should dropouts be considered program "failures"? (See lines 278–294.)

11. The researchers administered the Physician Comfort Survey just prior to the program, but decided not to administer it as a follow-up at the end of the program. What is your opinion on the researchers' decision? (See lines 315–338.)

12. In your opinion, is material in lines 444–451 based largely on the data in this article? Is it speculation? Explain.

13. The researchers note that a limitation of this evaluation is the lack of a control group. In your opinion, how important is this limitation? (See lines 458–466.)

Quality Ratings

Directions: Indicate your level of agreement with each of the following statements by circling a number from 5 for strongly agree (SA) to 1 for strongly disagree (SD). If you believe an item is not applicable to this research article, leave it blank. Be prepared to explain your ratings. When responding to criteria A and B below, keep in mind that brief titles and abstracts are conventional in published research.

A. The title of the article is appropriate.

SA   5   4   3   2   1   SD

B. The abstract provides an effective overview of the research article.

SA   5   4   3   2   1   SD

C. The introduction establishes the importance of the study.

SA   5   4   3   2   1   SD

D. The literature review establishes the context for the study.

SA   5   4   3   2   1   SD

E. The research purpose, question, or hypothesis is clearly stated.

SA   5   4   3   2   1   SD

F. The method of sampling is sound.

SA   5   4   3   2   1   SD

G. Relevant demographics (for example, age, gender, and ethnicity) are described.

SA   5   4   3   2   1   SD

H. Measurement procedures are adequate.

SA   5   4   3   2   1   SD

I. All procedures have been described in sufficient detail to permit a replication of the study.

SA   5   4   3   2   1   SD

J. The participants have been adequately protected from potential harm.

SA   5   4   3   2   1   SD

K. The results are clearly described.

SA   5   4   3   2   1   SD

L. The discussion/conclusion is appropriate.

SA   5   4   3   2   1   SD

M. Despite any flaws, the report is worthy of publication.

SA   5   4   3   2   1   SD

127

Article 27

Technology-Mediated versus Face-to-Face Intergenerational Programming

MARCIA S. MARX
Research Institute on Aging of the
Hebrew Home of Greater Washington

JISKA COHEN-MANSFIELD
Research Institute on Aging of the
Hebrew Home of Greater Washington,
George Washington University
Medical Center

KARINE RENAUDAT
Research Institute on Aging of the
Hebrew Home of Greater Washington

ALEXANDER LIBIN
Research Institute on Aging of the
Hebrew Home of Greater Washington,
Georgetown University

KHIN THEIN
Research Institute on Aging of the
Hebrew Home of Greater Washington,
George Washington University Medical Center

ABSTRACT. Elderly computer novices received 1-on-1 e-mail training, which enabled them to communicate electronically with elementary school-aged pen-pals. A traditional intergenerational visiting program was conducted concurrently. Program evaluation revealed that the intergenerational visiting program was rated favorably by 88% of the participating seniors and the intergenerational e-mail program was rated favorably by 57% of the seniors. Yet only 6 (out of 23) seniors expressed interest in continuing to e-mail their pen-pals beyond the program period. While technology may never take the place of human contact for some seniors, increased computer support as well as arranging for e-mail pen-pals to meet in person might help boost the popularity of this form of intergenerational communication.

From *Journal of Intergenerational Relationships*, 3, 101–118. Copyright © 2005 by The Haworth Press, Inc. Reprinted with permission.

Introduction

Intergenerational communication between non-family members often takes the form of scheduled visits of school-aged children to a senior facility. This type of interaction is very popular, and the research
5 literature has many descriptions of benefits to both old and young such as positive change in one's perceptions of the other generation (Carstensen, Mason, & Caldwell, 1982; Newman, Faux, & Larimer, 1997; Aday, Rice, & Evans, 1991; Cummings, Williams, & Ellis,
10 2002), increased empathy toward seniors (Schwalbach & Kiernan, 2002), increased self-esteem in children (Bocian & Newman, 1989; Proller, 1989), increased prosocial behaviors in children (Lambert, Dellmann-Jenkins, & Fruit, 1990), feeling more in touch with
15 one's community (Carstensen et al., 1982), and supplying a positive experience for seniors (Kuehne, 1992). Yet many excellent intergenerational visiting programs

survive for only 1 or 2 years because the sponsoring agencies disband, a key individual leaves the program,
20 the initial grant or funding source expires, or the amount of time involved in coordinating and transporting the children to meet with the seniors becomes a burden (Hamilton et al., 1998).

Recognizing the value of intergenerational pro-
25 gramming as well as the need for an alternative mode of intergenerational communication between non-family members, we examined the usefulness of an intergenerational program in which both children and elderly persons interacted as e-mail "pen-pals" for a
30 period of 6 months. An e-mail program has the benefits of ongoing communication and connectedness without the time and monetary constraints that typically plague traditional face-to-face intergenerational programs. Prior to undertaking this project, we expected that
35 communicating through e-mail would be attractive to children who, in general, enjoy using computers and are proficient with e-mail, and we were hopeful that the seniors would also react positively to the program. Previous research on computers and healthy, active seniors
40 has shown that when older adults gain experience with computer tasks, their attitudes toward computer technology become more positive (Jay & Willis, 1992) and are comparable to those of younger or middle-aged persons (Czaja & Sharit, 1998). However, in a group of
45 frail seniors—77.5% of whom were considered "vulnerable" on the basis of health, poverty level status, and recent (within the previous 5 years) loss of mobility, significant other, and/or income, Billipp (2001) found mixed reactions to computer use. For instance, at
50 the conclusion of the 3-month period of personalized in-home computer training, 87% of the seniors said that they would not choose to have a computer in their houses (Billipp, 2001). While research has indicated that older persons, relative to their younger counter-

Table 1

Demographic, Health, Background, Psychosocial, and Computer Use Data for Seniors Participating in the Intergenerational E-mail Pen-pal and Visiting Programs, the Intergenerational E-mail Pen-pal Program Only, the Intergenerational Visiting Program Only, and the Control Group

	E-mail Pen-pal and Visiting Programs ($n = 27$)	E-mail Pen-pal Program only ($n = 11$)	Visiting Program only ($n = 4$)	Control group ($n = 27$)
Age (mean)	84 years	80 years	86 years	83 years
Gender	82% female	55% female	50% female	70% female
Marital status[a] (% married)	11% married	55% married	0% married	27% married
Education (% high school grad or above)	85%	90%	50%	85%
Country of origin (% born in U.S.)	70%	46%	50%	82%
Number of years in U.S.[b] (mean)	78 years*	52 years	65 years	79 years*
Self-reported health (% with good to excellent health)	70%	91%	75%	63%
Walking aids (% who use a walking aid)	26%	18%	50%	41%
MMSE (mean)	26.0	28.2	23.5	24.8
Time with grandchildren[c] (% who say it is not enough time)	44%	82%	33%	24%
Minutes of TV on a weekday[d] (mean)	113	96	75	176
Leave building (% who go out daily)	82%	73%	50%	67%
Loneliness (% sometimes or always lonely)	63%	27%	100%	56%
Depressed affect (% with depressed affect)	48%	27%	75%	48%
Connectedness to community (% who feel connected)	48%	43%	0%	44%
Computer experience (% with experience)	26%	46%	0%	22%
E-mail experience (% who use e-mail)	11%	27%	0%	11%

[a]Not married includes widowed, divorced, separated, and never married; $\chi^2_{(2)} = 7.95, p = .019$.
[b]$F_{(2,59)} = 6.82, p = .002$; *group is significantly different from e-mail pen-pal only group (Scheffe test, $p < .05$).
[c]Time spent includes both visits and telephone calls; $\chi^2_{(2)} = 10.48, p = .005$.
[d]$F_{(2,64)} = 3.77, p = 0.29$

Note. Data from the visiting program only group were not included in the statistical analyses due to small n.

55 parts, are at a disadvantage when using computers due to a variety of experiential, physiological, and cognitive factors (as summarized in Westerman & Davies, 2000), one should not conclude that elderly persons are not able to use computers. Indeed, researchers have
60 found that many frail elderly persons do master how to send e-mail independently when provided with intensive support from tutors as well as continuous practice (van Berlo & van Valen, 1998; Nahm & Resnick, 2001). In order to give every possible advantage to the
65 seniors in our intergenerational e-mail pen-pal program, we modeled our tutorials on the findings of previous research such that we offered ongoing individualized e-mail instruction and ample opportunity for the seniors to practice.
70   The present study was conducted in order to explore whether or not frail seniors with little or no computer experience are interested in participating in an intergenerational e-mail pen-pal program. In addition, as we were curious as to whether or not face-to-face
75 contact is a necessary component for effective intergenerational programming, we compared outcomes of our intergenerational e-mail program with those of a traditional intergenerational visiting program.

Methods

Participants

   A total of 69 seniors from a suburban federally sub-
105

80 sidized apartment building (occupancy = 278) were recruited for this study. We did not assign the seniors to groups, but rather let them choose according to their interests, as we felt we could not ethically deny program membership to any interested senior. Of the 69
85 seniors, 27 seniors enrolled in both the intergenerational e-mail pen-pal and visiting programs, 11 in the intergenerational e-mail pen-pal program only, 4 in the intergenerational visiting program only, and 27 seniors participated in neither program and served as a control
90 group. Since the visiting program only group consisted of only 4 seniors, this group was excluded from statistical analyses; however, we have presented mean and percentage data from those in the visiting program only group throughout this paper in order to allow for pre-
95 liminary comparisons with the other 3 groups.

Procedure

   All residents of the senior apartment building were invited to attend a group meeting in which we described the upcoming intergenerational e-mail and visiting programs, and interested persons were recruited at
100 that time. Seniors were also recruited by word-of-mouth (i.e., snowball referrals). Once a senior provided written informed consent for participation, we collected demographic, health, background data, and psychosocial data as well as information pertaining to computer use during an interview with the senior. Data pertaining

to program outcomes were obtained at the termination of the intergenerational programs.

Initial Assessments

Demographics. We recorded the senior's date of birth, gender, marital status, level of education, country of origin, and number of years living in the United States. The mean age for the group of 69 seniors was 83 years, with the mean age ranging from 80 to 86 years across the 4 groups (see Table 1). The majority of the seniors were female, although men made up about half of the participants in the e-mail pen-pal program only and in the visiting program only groups. Significant differences existed between the 4 groups with regard to marital status. Specifically, 55% of the seniors in the e-mail pen-pal program only group were married (or living as married), while only 27% of the control participants, 11% of those in both intergenerational programs, and none of the seniors in the visiting program only group were married ($\chi^2_{(2)} = 7.95$, $p = .019$). As is suggested by the data presented in Table 1, a significant relationship existed between gender and marital status for this sample in that 63% of the men were married in comparison to only 38% of the women being married ($\chi^2_{(1)} = 11.03$, $p = .001$). Significant differences did not emerge between groups with respect to level of education, with most participants having graduated high school (and some having received higher degrees) (see Table 1). While there were no significant differences between groups with respect to country of origin, seniors in the e-mail pen-pal program only group had lived in the United States for significantly fewer years (mean = 52 years) than had those who participated in only the visiting program (mean = 65 years), those in both the e-mail and visiting programs (mean = 78 years), and those in the control group (mean = 79 years) ($F_{(2,59)} = 6.82$, $p = .002$; Scheffe test < .05).

Health information. This category included measurements of self-reported health, use of walking aids, and cognitive status. Health was tapped using the global self-rated health item from the SF-36 (Samani, Willett, & Ware, 1988). Seniors supplied information as to whether or not they used walking aids (including a cane, walker, or motorized scooter) while in the apartment building. Cognitive status was assessed via the Mini-Mental State Examination (MMSE; Folstein, Folstein, & McHugh, 1975), which was administered by a research assistant trained in standardized administration and scoring procedures. Low scores on the MMSE are suggestive of cognitive impairment and scores above 24 indicate adequate cognitive functioning.

There were no differences between groups with regard to the 3 indicators of health (see Table 1). The majority of seniors in all 4 groups reported their health as "good" to "excellent." As to the use of walking aids while in the apartment building, this percentage ranged from 18% to 50% across the 4 groups. The mean score on the Mini-Mental State Examination (MMSE; Folstein et al., 1975) was 26 (out of 30) for the total group of 69 participants, and for the individual groups was 28.2 for those in the e-mail pen-pal program only group, 26.0 for those in both the e-mail pen-pal and visiting programs, 24.8 for the control subjects, and 23.5 for those in the visiting program only.

Background data. We asked participants how they felt about the amount of time they spent (either in person or by telephone) with their grandchildren (grandnieces or grandnephews and great-grandchildren were also included). We also recorded the number of minutes of television watched on an average weekday, and whether or not the seniors tended to go out of the apartment building on a daily basis.

As many as 82% of the seniors in the e-mail pen-pal program only group felt that they did not spend enough time with their grandchildren while this proportion was significantly lower for those in both the e-mail pen-pal and visiting programs (44%), the visiting program only (33%), and the control group (24%) ($\chi^2_{(2)} = 10.48$, $p = .005$) (see Table 1). A significant difference was seen between groups with respect to the number of minutes that seniors spent watching television on a typical weekday, with those in the control group watching the most television (mean = 176 minutes; $F_{(2,62)} = 3.77$, $p = .029$). Overall, more than half of the participants tended to go out from the apartment building on a daily basis.

Psychosocial data. This category included items pertaining to loneliness, depressed affect, and whether or not the participant felt connected to the community. Loneliness was tapped using an item from the UCLA Loneliness Scale (Russell, Peplau, & Cutrona, 1980), Are you lonely?, which was rated as 1 (never), 2 (sometimes), or 3 (always). The 4-item Geriatric Depression Scale (GDS4) (D'Ath, Katona, Mullan, Evans, & Katona, 1994) was administered by a research assistant. If a participant gave a response suggestive of depressed affect to any of the 4 items, this person was coded as positive for depressed affect. Finally, participants were asked how strongly they agreed or disagreed with this statement: I feel that I am connected to my community.

While statistical analysis did not reveal significant differences between groups with respect to our measurement of loneliness, the lowest percentage of loneliness was found in the e-mail pen-pal program only group (27%), and the highest, in the visiting program only group (100%) (see Table 1). As had been seen with the loneliness data, the same trend toward differences between groups emerged in the assessment of depressed affect in that the occurrence of depressed affect was least in those seniors in the e-mail program only group (27%) and greatest for those in the visiting program only group (75%). As to connectedness to one's community, none of those in the visiting program

220 only group agreed with the statement that they were connected to the community while little variability was seen across the other 3 groups (48% of those in the e-mail pen-pal and visiting programs, 43% of those in the e-mail pen-pal program, and 44% of the control par-

225 ticipants agreed or strongly agreed that they were connected to their community, see Table 1).

Computer use. Participants were asked how often they used a computer for any purpose and how often they used e-mail. Both items were rated on a 7-point

230 scale, ranging from 1 (never) to 7 (several times a day). For those seniors who were currently using e-mail, we asked them to name their relationships with the person(s) with whom they communicated.

Those in the e-mail pen-pal program only group

235 had comparatively more experience with computers as well as e-mail than did those in the other 3 groups, although differences between groups were not significant (see Table 1). Nine of the 69 seniors were currently using e-mail. Specifically, of those in the e-mail pen-

240 pal program only group, 2 seniors e-mailed their grandchildren and 1 senior e-mailed friends; of those in the e-mail pen-pal and visiting programs, 2 seniors e-mailed friends and family (excluding grandchildren) and 1 senior e-mailed relatives; and, of those in the

245 control group, 3 seniors e-mailed friends and family (including grandchildren).

Outcome Measures

Program evaluation. Following the completion of both intergenerational programs, participants rated the extent to which they had enjoyed each program [each

250 item rated as: 1 (no), 2 (some of the time), 3 (most of the time), 4 (all of the time)]. Participants were also asked these 3 open-ended questions about each program: What did you like best about the program? What did you dislike about the program? If you could, what

255 would you change about the program? For those who participated in both intergenerational programs, we also asked if they had a preference for one program over the other or if they had liked the programs equally.

260 The program evaluation phase was completed for 3 of the 4 seniors in the visiting program only group (75%), for 3 of the 11 persons in the e-mail pen-pal program only group (27%), for 20 of the 27 seniors who participated in both the visiting and e-mail pen-pal

265 programs (74%), and for 13 of the 27 control participants (48%). Reasons for not completing the program evaluation phase included failing health and death, unwillingness to complete the questionnaire, loss of interest in the intergenerational program, and for the e-

270 mail pen-pal program only group, a language barrier (i.e., four seniors in the e-mail pen-pal program only group spoke little English, and the Russian–English translators who had been available during the first 3 months of the project were no longer available at its

275 completion).

Interest in e-mail. At the termination of the e-mail pen-pal program, we asked participating seniors if they would like to continue e-mailing or to start e-mailing any person(s). Whenever we received an affirmative

280 response, we recorded the relationships of these persons to the seniors (e.g., pen-pal, relative, friend).

Description of intergenerational programs. Both intergenerational programs were conducted concurrently. These programs were scheduled to coincide

285 with the elementary school's 9-month calendar such that the visiting program began in October and ended in May and the e-mail pen-pal program ran from December through May. The e-mail pen-pal program had a later start date as it took time to set up the computer

290 center for the seniors.

Intergenerational E-Mail Pen-Pal Program

Each senior was assigned an elementary school-aged e-mail pen-pal (range: 2nd to 5th grade). Pen-pal dyads did not know each other prior to the e-mail communication. At no cost to the seniors, we set up a

295 computer center on the ground floor of their apartment building (complete with free tech support), and offered 1-on-1 e-mail tutorial sessions. A sign-up sheet was provided so that seniors could schedule a tutorial session at their convenience. We offered daytime as well

300 as evening hours and also a choice of 5 tutors—1 research assistant, 2 senior volunteers, and 2 high school student volunteers. Sessions typically lasted from 45 minutes to 1 hour. In addition, the computer center remained open 24 hours a day, allowing the seniors the

305 opportunity to practice whenever they wished.

The level of need for e-mail assistance varied among the seniors. While some seniors chose to sit at the computer and type their e-mails, others preferred to dictate their e-mail to a tutor and then to push the send

310 button upon completion. The seniors were provided with a large-print written protocol for sending e-mail which started with how to turn on the computer, how to get connected to the Internet, how to send an e-mail, and how to turn off the computer (as well as everything

315 in between). The seniors were also provided with a list of writing prompts that included items such as: Write about yourself (your name, where you were born, former occupation); write about what life was like without television, VCRs, and computers; and, write about cur-

320 rent events.

Intergenerational Visiting Program

Seniors participated in structured activities with a group of 20 elementary school children (from grades 2–5) who visited monthly for a total of 8 visits. Every month, we put a reminder flyer in each senior's mail-

325 box 2 days before a visit, and reminded each senior by phone on the day before a visit. Each visit lasted approximately 90 minutes. Activities included a talent show, playing board games (e.g., checkers), group sing-alongs, solving a crossword puzzle (the clues were

330 based on things that the seniors and children had done

131

on the previous visit), 1-on-1 interviews of the seniors by the children, and always juice and cookies (which were very well received). With the exception of introducing a senior and child who were both fluent in Spanish (the child spoke little English), we did not pair up specific seniors with children as we found it impossible to predict which senior–child dyads would hit it off and did not want to force friendships.

Data analysis. Data were entered separately onto a computer by 2 different persons, and then checked and corrected for data entry errors. Differences between the 4 groups were examined using chi-squares and analyses of variance. All analyses were performed via SPSS 11.0.

Results

Data analysis revealed that 88% of those who responded to our exit questionnaire had enjoyed the intergenerational visiting program most or all of the time, and 57% had enjoyed the intergenerational e-mail pen-pal program most or all of the time (see Table 2). As to there being a preference for one program over the other, we found that 2 seniors preferred the intergenerational e-mail pen-pal program to the visiting program, 6 seniors preferred the intergenerational visiting program to the e-mail pen-pal program, and 11 seniors liked the programs equally. Findings specific to the two programs are described below.

Table 2
Counts and Percentages of Seniors' Responses to: Did you enjoy participating in the Intergenerational E-mail Pen-pal Program? The Intergenerational Visiting Program?[a]

	E-mail Pen-pal Program ($n = 24$)	Visiting Program ($n = 21$)
No	3 (14%)	1[b] (4%)
Some of the time	6 (29%)	2 (8%)
Most of the time	1 (5%)	4 (17%)
All of the time	11 (52%)	17 (71%)

[a]Some seniors participated in both programs.
[b]The senior who said "no" to enjoying the visiting program attended 5 of the 8 visits.

Intergenerational E-Mail Pen-Pal Program

Over the course of the 6-month program, the seniors sent a total of 131 e-mails to their pen-pals and received 110 e-mails from the children. An example of e-mail correspondence between an intergenerational pen-pal dyad is provided in the Appendix [at the end of this article]. At the termination of the e-mail pen-pal program, thirteen seniors responded to the open-ended question, What did you like best about the e-mail pen-pal program? The response given most often ($n = 8$) was *communicating with/getting to know a child.* The seniors were very enthusiastic about how much they had enjoyed the questions and answers that were part of their e-mail correspondence with the children. Other responses to the open-ended questions included: *the challenge of learning something new, the convenience*

(the computers and tutors were all on the ground floor of the apartment building), and *"I just liked it."*

Fifteen participants responded to our open-ended question, What did you dislike about the intergenerational e-mail pen-pal program? Seven reported *no dislikes,* 3 reported *problems with learning to use a computer,* one senior had *"no need for it,"* one felt that the computer's response time was too slow, one was frustrated because she had *wanted to meet her pen-pal in person,* one senior referred to the program as a *"big, fat nothing,"* and one senior asked us, *"What should I write to a 10 year old?"*

When we asked the seniors what we could do to improve the e-mail pen-pal program, we received the following suggestions: *extend the program to include e-mailing grandchildren; let the pen-pals meet in person at least one time prior to initiating e-mail communication,* and *provide basic computer instruction.*

Special relationships were formed as a result of the intergenerational e-mail pen-pal program. In one instance, a 9-year-old girl and her senior e-mail pen-pal had exchanged several e-mails and were starting to build a relationship when the senior was suddenly hospitalized due to a fall and subsequent broken hip. When the senior was well enough to be transferred to a rehabilitative facility, the child insisted on going to visit her. Had it not been for the e-mail pen-pal program, it is doubtful that these two would ever have met face-to-face. In another case, one pair of pen-pals had so much fun corresponding through their e-mails that the child decided to join the visiting program so that the two could continue their relationship in person. Unfortunately, one week prior to the child's first visit with the group, the woman was injured in a fall and underwent arm surgery. She was in so much pain that she found it difficult to go out from her apartment. However, meeting her pen-pal was so important to this woman that she pulled herself together, attended the visit, and was thrilled to meet her pen-pal in person.

At the conclusion of the e-mail pen-pal program, we asked the seniors if they would like to continue the e-mail communication with their pen-pals. Of the 23 who responded to this question, 6 (26%) said that they would like to keep in touch with their pen-pals while 17 (74%) were not interested. It is noteworthy that the 6 seniors who wished to continue e-mailing their pen-pals had actually spent time with their pen-pals during the intergenerational visiting program. Yet spending time is clearly not the only factor that determines whether a senior will want to maintain an intergenerational e-mail relationship as there were 4 seniors who met their pen-pals during the intergenerational visiting program and were not interested in continuing to e-mail them at the end of the program.

In addition to the 6 seniors who were interested in continuing to e-mail their pen-pals beyond the termination of the e-mail pen-pal program, another 9 said that there was a person(s) (other than a pen-pal) to whom

430 they were interested in e-mailing, yielding a total of 15 seniors who were interested in continuing to send and receive e-mails. Three seniors named only one person, while the remaining 12 seniors named multiple persons. Specifically, 40% of these seniors (6/15) wished
435 to continue e-mailing their pen-pals, 67% (10/15) wanted to e-mail their grandchildren, 60% (9/15) wanted to e-mail their children, 67% (10/15) expressed interest in e-mailing other relatives (excluding children and grandchildren), and 33% (5/15) wanted to e-mail
440 friends. Clearly, these seniors had enjoyed e-mail as a mode of communication and had generalized its use beyond the intergenerational e-mail pen-pal program.

Intergenerational Visiting Program

While all those enrolled in the visiting program attended at least one visit, 2 seniors attended all 8 visits
445 and another 3 seniors attended 7 of the visits. An additional 21 seniors, who chose not to be enrolled in either program or as control participants, attended some of the visits. Of these, 15 attended 1 visit, three seniors attended 2 visits, and one senior attended 4 of the 8
450 visits.

At the exit interview, we asked this open-ended question, What did you like best about the intergenerational visiting program? We obtained responses from 21 seniors, all of whom gave answers that pertained to
455 the children rather than to features relating to programming (e.g., convenience of the meeting place). Nine seniors simply *enjoyed being with the children*, three *liked to observe the comfortable interaction between the children and seniors*, and another 2 seniors
460 noted *how smart the children are*. Other responses given were: *the age of the children, playing games with the children, when the children smiled, noticing differences from when the senior was a child, anticipating the children's visits*, and one senior *liked that she got to*
465 *see her e-mail pen-pal in person*.

When asked what they had disliked about the intergenerational visiting program, 15 seniors said that they had *liked everything* about the program, one reported *difficulties due to poor eyesight*, one *felt nervous*
470 *around the children and had trouble hearing*, and one senior felt there was *not enough time to speak with the children* (although the visits lasted 90 minutes).

As to changes for the visiting program, suggestions from the seniors were: *introduce phrases in languages*
475 *other than English* (since many of the seniors and children were originally from non-English speaking countries), *meet more often than once a month*, and *arrange for the e-mail pen-pals to come to the visits*.

The best part for us was watching as special senior-
480 child relationships developed over the months. For instance, there was a child who spoke little English at the onset of the intergenerational visiting program as her family had recently moved to the United States from South America. She was having difficulty at
485 school due to both the language barrier and cultural

differences. We approached a senior who is fluent in Spanish and had lived in South America for many years, and he agreed to come to the visits and to sit with this child. We are happy to report that the two
490 became close friends. In another case, a senior became so attached to a child that she met at the intergenerational visits that she requested him as an e-mail pen-pal, and we gladly complied. She frequently e-mailed this child in between the monthly visits.

Discussion

495 Both intergenerational programs were enjoyed by more than half of the seniors. A larger percentage of seniors enjoyed the intergenerational visiting program, presumably because they preferred meeting the children in person rather than as an unknown on the Inter-
500 net. However, this does not mean that the e-mail pen-pal program was a failure. We found that 57% of the seniors enjoyed the intergenerational e-mail pen-pal program most or all of the time. Moreover, 11 out of 19 seniors liked it equally well to the intergenerational
505 visiting program, and another 2 seniors preferred it to the visiting program. Taken together, these findings suggest that an e-mail pen-pal program is a viable form of intergenerational communication.

At the onset of this project, we found that a specific
510 group of seniors was interested in participating exclusively in our intergenerational e-mail pen-pal program. Specifically, these seniors were more likely to have had some experience with computers and e-mail, were comparatively healthier, more educated, and had lived
515 comparatively fewer years in the United States (4 of the 11 seniors could read and write simple English but were not able to speak the language fluently). Also, they felt that they had too little communication with their grandchildren. The salience of this subgroup is
520 supported by results of an earlier study that found that the seniors in an Internet training program who chose to use e-mail (in comparison to those who tended to limit their Internet experience to the World Wide Web) had previous computer experience, more education,
525 and self-reported health of good or excellent (White et al., 2002). Not only were we able to discern a profile to describe the type of senior who was drawn to our intergenerational e-mail pen-pal program, we also saw that a different profile emerged for those seniors who chose
530 to participate in only the visiting program. In this case, the seniors tended to be frailer, with respect to physical and emotional functioning (see Table 1).

We are aware that our allowing self-selection of seniors into programs rather than using randomized
535 group assignment introduced bias into the subject selection process. However, we felt that this was necessary as we wished to be sensitive to the preferences of the seniors. Had we not permitted seniors to select the programs in which they wished to participate, we
540 would have missed clues about the type of senior who is drawn to intergenerational programming that in-

cludes a technology piece but does not include a face-to-face component versus the type of person who seeks in-person contact. We propose that intergenerational researchers must sometimes move outside of the rigid guidelines for quantitative research design in order to really understand the underlying processes influencing their programming.

In order to improve our intergenerational e-mail pen-pal program, we asked the seniors for their suggestions. The two suggestions given most often by seniors were: provide basic computer instruction; and, let the pen-pals meet at least one time prior to starting their e-mail correspondence. As to the first suggestion, since we tailored each session to each senior's needs, basic computer training was included in the tutorial sessions whenever requested. However, this was not enough for some of the highly motivated seniors who we referred to a computer class at a nearby senior center. For the majority of seniors, however, we were hesitant to institute basic computer instruction as part of the tutorial sessions for they seemed challenged enough by just the task of e-mailing. Further discussion with seniors revealed that some had been frustrated with the amount of time spent connecting to the Internet (we used dial-up with Erol's) and with the number of pop-up advertisements that they needed to navigate through to get to their e-mail mailboxes (we used Yahoo for e-mailing). Long waits led them to think they had done something wrong or the computer was broken, and having a screen cluttered with advertisements made it difficult for the seniors, many of whom have decreasing visual functioning, to find the icon that they wanted to click on. While more expensive, the use of a cable Internet service as well as pop-up blocking software would make e-mailing much faster and less cluttered for the seniors involved in future intergenerational e-mail pen-pal programs.

The second suggestion by the seniors concerned meeting the pen-pals in person. This seems to be a good idea as previous studies of intergenerational pen-pals who communicated through the regular United States mail service reported positive outcomes when the pen-pals met in person. Bales, Eklund, and Siffin (2000) found that an 8-week period of intergenerational pen-pal letter writing followed by 4 hour-long face-to-face intergenerational meetings with structured activities served to promote positive attitudes about the seniors and to foster relationships between generations. In addition, Kiernan and Mosher-Ashley (2002) have reported about a letter exchange program that began as simple correspondence between generations and over the course of 8 years, has expanded to include face-to-face structured activities such as the children visiting the senior center, the seniors visiting the classroom, and an intergenerational holiday concert. An intriguing idea for future study would be a combination intergenerational visiting/e-mail pen-pal program in which seniors and children first develop a relationship in person

during scheduled visits, and then decide if they want to extend this relationship to include e-mail correspondence. While we found that the 6 seniors in our study who had wanted to continue e-mailing had all met their pen-pals in person, we also found that face-to-face contact alone is not sufficient as an additional 4 seniors who had met their pen-pals in person were not interested in continuing to e-mail. These findings lead us to suggest that meeting several times in person is not adequate for ensuring an enjoyable e-mail pen-pal experience, while meeting *and* developing a mutually satisfying relationship may be the necessary components. Clearly, this is a topic for future research.

The potential of intergenerational e-mailing extends beyond the pen-pal program presented here. Contact through e-mail could be used for a variety of intergenerational programming including outreach for seniors who are uncomfortable with face-to-face programs due to a language barrier, mentoring of at-risk children, and of course, helping seniors keep in touch with their grandchildren. A senior participant from the present study remarked that e-mailing was the best way for her to communicate with her grandchildren as they were always busy with homework and chores. Moreover, future intergenerational programs could move from e-mail pen-pal programs to supervised intergenerational chat rooms. Results from a study of Internet training for seniors living in sheltered housing in the Netherlands revealed that the seniors were not very interested in e-mail but were very eager to be involved in ongoing chat groups with people they did not know (van Berlo & van Valen, 1998).

In summary, while e-mail communication is clearly different from the traditional intergenerational programming, this type of intergenerational contact is enjoyable to elderly persons, filling a need for a distinct subset of seniors. Based on the suggestions of the seniors in the present study, we are now in a good position to develop intergenerational Internet programming that will appeal to a larger number of seniors.

APPENDIX

Example of E-mail Correspondence Between an Intergenerational Pen-Pal Dyad

Dear Amy (child):

I am your pen-pal. I moved from New York to Rockville 3 years ago. How long have you lived in Rockville and how long have you been going to your school?

Do you like your teacher? Do you like school? I only remember when I went to Kindergarten and my teacher lived in my apartment. So I was the teacher's pet. She taught me how to knit. Then we took a picture with our teacher.

When I was 16 my mother left me in Europe to go to America. Then she sent papers for me to come to

America with her. I went with my uncle on a boat. When I came off the boat I lost my shoe. I ran to my mother and lost my shoe because I was so excited to see her. I had not seen her for 4 or 5 years.

I look forward to hearing from you.

Good Luck,
Bessie (senior)

Dear Bessie,

I am 9 years old. I am in the third grade. I actually live in Chevy Chase. I love my school and my teacher. It was my birthday yesterday. I got a flute! To me it would be very exciting if I hadn't seen my mom in 4 or 5 years and then I finally saw her. I look forward to hearing from you again!

Love,
Amy

Dear Amy,

I am very glad for you that you got a flute. I have been here 3 years already. I am very happy because my son takes me places. He takes me to doctors. He took me from Queens to here because I was all alone after my husband died. I had 4 rooms. What did I need with 4 rooms? When they took me here, they lost some stuff from my place. But what can I do? My daughter lives in Seattle.

It took a long time for my mother to bring me to this country. I lived with my uncles and I gave up that she would ever bring me. But my mother didn't give up.

When my son went to college, he got an A on an essay he had written about a story I had told him. I have stories to tell. I'll keep them for the next time.

I hope to hear from you soon,
Bessie

Dear Bessie,

I think it's very good that your son does those things for you. He sounds like a good boy. Now I want to tell you something about my flute. Yesterday I would have had my 5th flute lesson but I got a big headache so I didn't go. But I am feeling much better now. My family is thinking about going to Paramus, New Jersey for Spring Break since my mom's family lives there. But we might not because my dad is very busy with work.

Love,
Amy

[Note: Some details have been changed to protect confidentiality.]

References

Aday, R. H., Rice, C., & Evans, E. (1991). Intergenerational partners project: A model linking elementary students with senior center volunteers. *The Gerontologist, 31,* 263–266.

Bales, S. S., Eklund, S. J., & Siffin, C. F. (2000). Children's perceptions of elders before and after a school-based intergenerational program. *Educational Gerontology, 26,* 677–689.

Billipp, S. H. (2001). The psychosocial impact of interactive computer use within a vulnerable elderly population: A report on a randomized prospective trial in a home health care setting. *Public Health Nursing, 18,* 138–145.

Bocian, K., & Newman, S. (1989). Evaluation of intergenerational programs: Why and how? *Journal of Children in Contemporary Society, 29,* 147–163.

Carstensen, L., Mason, S. E., & Caldwell, E. C. (1982). Children's attitudes toward the elderly: An intergenerational technique for change. *Educational Gerontology, 8,* 291–301.

Cummings, S. M., Williams, M. M., & Ellis, R. A. (2002). Impact of an intergenerational program on 4th graders' attitudes toward elders and school behaviors. *Journal of Human Behavior in the Social Environment, 6,* 91–107.

Czaja, S.J., & Sharit, J. (1998). Aged differences in attitudes toward computers. *Journal of Gerontology: Psychological Sciences, 538,* P329–P340.

D' Ath, P., Katona, P., Mullan, E., Evans, S., & Katona, C. (1994). Screening, detection and management of depression in elderly primary care attenders. I: The acceptability and performance of the 15 item Geriatric Depression Scale (GDS 15) and the development of short versions. *Family Practice, 11,* 260–266.

Folstein, M. F., Folstein, S. E., & McHugh, P. R. (1975). Mini-mental state: A practical method for grading the cognitive state of patients for the clinician. *Journal of Psychiatric Research, 12,* 189–198.

Hamilton, G., Brown, S., Alonzo, T., Glover, M., Mersereau, Y., & Wilson, P. (1998). Building community for the long term: An intergenerational commitment. *The Gerontologist, 39,* 235–238.

Jay, G. M., & Willis, S. L. (1992). Influence of direct computer experience on older adults' attitudes toward computers. *The Journals of Gerontology, 47,* P250–257.

Kiernan, H. W., & Mosher-Ashley, P. M. (2002). Strategies to expand a pen pal program from simple letters into a full intergenerational experience. *Educational Gerontology, 28,* 337–345.

Kuehne, V. S. (1992). Older adults in intergenerational programs: What are their experiences really like? *Activities, Adaptation & Aging, 16,* 49–67.

Lambert, D. J., Delimann-Jenkins, M., & Fruit, D. (1990). Planning for contact between the generations: An effective approach. *The Gerontologist, 30,* 553–556.

Nahm, E. S., & Resnick, B. (2001). Homebound older adults' experiences with the internet and e-mail. *Computers in Nursing, 19,* 257–263.

Newman, S., Faux, R., & Larimer, B. (1997). Children's views on aging: Their attitudes and values. *The Gerontologist, 37,* 412–417.

Proller, N. L. (1989). The effects of an adoptive grandparent program on youth and elderly participants. In S. Newman & S. Brummel (Eds.), *Intergenerational Programs: Programs, Imperatives, Strategies, Trends* (pp. 195–203). New York: Haworth Press.

Russell, D., Peplau, L. A., & Cutrona, C. E. (1980). The revised UCLA loneliness scale: Concurrent and discriminant validity evidence. *Journal of Personality and Social Psychology, 39,* 472–480.

Samani, E. F. Z., Willett, W. C., & Ware, J. H. (1988). Association of malnutrition and diarrhea in children aged under five years. *American Journal of Epidemiology, 128,* 93–105.

Schwalbach, E., & Kiernan, S. (2002). Effects of an intergenerational friendly visit program on the attitudes of fourth graders toward elders. *Educational Gerontology, 28,* 175–187.

van Berlo, A., & van Valen, C. (1998). First experiences with using e-mail and internet by elderly living in sheltered housing. *Studies in Health Technology Information, 48,* 150–153.

Westerman, S. J., & Davies, D. R. (2000). Acquisition and application of new technology skills: The influence of age. *Occupational Medicine, 50,* 478–482.

White, H., McConnell, E., Clipp, E., Branch, L.G., Sloane, R., Pieper, C., & Box, T. L. (2002). A randomized controlled trial of the psychosocial impact of providing internet training and access to older adults. *Aging & Mental Health, 6,* 213–221.

Acknowledgment: This study was supported by a Montgomery County Empowerment Grant.

About the authors: *Marcia S. Marx* is affiliated with the Research Institute on Aging of the Hebrew Home of Greater Washington. *Jiska Cohen-Mansfield* is affiliated with the Research Institute on Aging of the Hebrew Home of Greater Washington and the George Washington University Medical Center. *Karine Renaudat* is affiliated with the Research Institute on Aging of the Hebrew Home of Greater Washington. *Alexander Libin* is affiliated with the Research Institute on Aging of the Hebrew Home of Greater Washington and the Georgetown University Department of Psychology. *Khin Thein* is affiliated with the Research Institute on Aging of the Hebrew Home of Greater Washington and the George Washington University Medical Center.

Address correspondence to: Marcia S. Marx, 6121 Montrose Road, Rockville, MD 20852. E-mail: marx@hebrew-home.org

Exercise for Article 27

Factual Questions

1. The researchers indicate that they modeled the tutorials for the e-mail pen-pal program on the findings of previous research such that they offered what?

2. Was the background data collected with an "interview" *or* with a "questionnaire"?

3. Was there a significant difference among the groups in terms of the average number of minutes seniors watched television?

4. Were there significant differences among the groups in computer/e-mail experience compared to those among the groups on the initial assessment?

5. Were both programs conducted concurrently?

6. Did a majority of those in both programs report enjoying the programs (at least most or all of the time)?

Questions for Discussion

7. The researchers did not assign the seniors to groups. Rather, they let them choose the group(s) they wanted to join. In your opinion, is this a serious flaw of this program evaluation? Explain. (See lines 81–84 and 533–548.)

8. The group that had the visiting program only consisted of four seniors for the initial assessment and only three for the program evaluation phase. In your opinion, is this a sufficient number? Explain. (See lines 90–95 and 260–261.)

9. The researchers provide extensive information on the initial assessments of demographics, health data, background data, psychosocial data, and computer use data separately for each group. Are these data an important part of the study? Why? Why not? (See lines 108–246 and Table 1.)

10. Are the two programs described in sufficient detail to give you a good idea of how they operated? Explain. (See lines 291–338.)

11. In the results section, the researchers provide quotations from seniors (in italics) as well as statistical results. To what extent are the quotations useful in helping you understand the results of this study? Would the results section be as effective if the quotations were omitted? Explain. (See lines 345–478.)

12. In your opinion, is the Appendix at the end of the article an important part of this research report? Explain.

13. If you were a voting member of a funding agency, would this study convince you to vote for extensive additional funding to extend e-mail programs for seniors in additional locations? Explain.

Quality Ratings

Directions: Indicate your level of agreement with each of the following statements by circling a number from 5 for strongly agree (SA) to 1 for strongly disagree (SD). If you believe an item is not applicable to this research article, leave it blank. Be prepared to explain your ratings. When responding to criteria A and B below, keep in mind that brief titles and abstracts are conventional in published research.

A. The title of the article is appropriate.

    SA   5   4   3   2   1   SD

B. The abstract provides an effective overview of the research article.

    SA   5   4   3   2   1   SD

C. The introduction establishes the importance of the study.

    SA   5   4   3   2   1   SD

D. The literature review establishes the context for the study.

    SA   5   4   3   2   1   SD

E. The research purpose, question, or hypothesis is clearly stated.

    SA   5   4   3   2   1   SD

F. The method of sampling is sound.

    SA   5   4   3   2   1   SD

G. Relevant demographics (for example, age, gender, and ethnicity) are described.

    SA   5   4   3   2   1   SD

H. Measurement procedures are adequate.

    SA   5   4   3   2   1   SD

I.   All procedures have been described in sufficient detail to permit a replication of the study.

SA   5   4   3   2   1   SD

J.   The participants have been adequately protected from potential harm.

SA   5   4   3   2   1   SD

K.   The results are clearly described.

SA   5   4   3   2   1   SD

L.   The discussion/conclusion is appropriate.

SA   5   4   3   2   1   SD

M.   Despite any flaws, the report is worthy of publication.

SA   5   4   3   2   1   SD

Article 28

Family-Focused Smoking Cessation: Enhanced Efficacy by the Addition of Partner Support and Group Therapy

JANICE D. KEY
The Medical University of
South Carolina

LINDA D. MARSH
The Medical University of
South Carolina

CINDY L. CARTER
The Medical University of
South Carolina

ROBERT J. MALCOLM
The Medical University of South Carolina

DEBAJYOTI SINHA
The Medical University of South Carolina

ABSTRACT. While partner support has been found to be an important factor in smoking cessation, programs with partner training have not demonstrated improved efficacy. The goal of this project was to evaluate the effectiveness of a smoking cessation treatment program that included partner support in an innovative education/therapy model similar to alcohol and drug treatment programs. Subjects included 23 smokers, 71% with a support partner. The program consisted of a smoking cessation curriculum, combined with facilitated group therapy for participants and partners, and individualized medication evaluation. Smoking abstinence was 87% at program completion and 80% at one month follow up, 100% abstinence in participants with support and 50% in participants without support (p < 0.05). Smoking Stage of Change at enrollment was: contemplation 22%, preparation 70%, and action 8%, with 87% movement toward action stage. In the present study, partner support enhanced short-term abstinence from smoking.

From *Substance Abuse*, 25, 37–41. Copyright © 2004 by The Haworth Press, Inc. Reprinted with permission.

Introduction

Tobacco use remains the leading preventable cause of death in the United States, with 32% of adults smoking, resulting in more than 419,000 deaths each year at an annual cost of more than $50 billion.[1] Smoking ces-
5 sation programs are an essential component of reducing this burden of disease.[2] The majority of adult smokers want to quit and assistance with their tobacco dependence should be a part of standard medical care.[3] Smoking cessation programs have included pharmacotherapy
10 (nicotine replacement and antidepressant medication), counseling (cognitive behavioral approach used individually, by telephone, or in groups), and the combination of these two methods.[4] Smoking cessation treatment outcomes currently average only about 30% abstinence for the 6–12 month period following treat-
15 ment, with lower rates in patients who already have smoking related illnesses.[5] Research has focused largely on pharmacological rather than behavioral interventions. Additional research efforts to evaluate and
20 improve smoking cessation counseling programs will enhance treatment of tobacco addiction.

Over the last two decades there has been increased use of a family-centered approach in the treatment of alcohol and other drug addiction and mental health
25 disorders.[6] Professionals in these fields realize that providing services to individuals outside of the family context is less effective. Social support has also been found to be an important predictor of smoking abstinence. The success of a smoker in a treatment program
30 is associated with factors such as educational status (higher education), age (older age), health status (development of coronary artery disease but not cancer or obstructive pulmonary disease) and marital status (married).[7] Positive partner support is predictive of in-
35 creased rates of abstinence and decreased rates of relapse, especially when the supporting partner is an ex-smoker.[8–10] Despite evidence of the importance of partner support and the success of this model in treatment of other addictions, the inclusion of a family member
40 or supportive partner with a group therapy model has not been investigated in tobacco treatment programs. This preliminary study evaluates the effectiveness of a smoking cessation program that incorporates group therapy with partner support and a smoking cessation
45 curriculum.

Methods

This study was a prospective cohort study of an experimental intervention, combining a standard smoking cessation curriculum[11] with group therapy and individualized medication assessment. The institutional
50 review board reviewed and approved the study prior to enrollment. The intervention consisted of ten weekly 90-minute smoking cessation groups, each enrolling 12–16 participants and support partners, held in the

evenings, with facilitation of each session by a substance abuse counselor and clinical psychologist. Participants were individually evaluated by a primary care physician and a psychiatrist for medication including nicotine replacement and antidepressant medication.

Subjects

Participants were recruited through university medical center clinics (oncology, pulmonology, and cardiology) as well as advertisements in the local newspaper and throughout the medical center. Enrollment criteria were age over 18 years and current smoking. Exclusion criteria were cognitive impairment that precluded completion of the survey instruments. Participants were encouraged to include a support partner, either smoking or nonsmoking, who attended the entire program with the participant. Smoking support partners were not required to actively participate in smoking cessation for themselves. Enrollment occurred after an informational session about the program.

Measures

Tobacco use was measured using a self-reported smoking history. Nicotine dependence was measured using the Fagerström Test for Nicotine Dependence, with scores ranging from 0 to 11, 0 indicating minimum dependence to 11 indicating maximum dependence (mean score in smokers is usually 5–7).[12] Motivation to quit was measured using the Smoking Stage of Change.[13,14] These measurements were obtained at enrollment, completion of the group, and by telephone at one month following group completion. Smoking self-report was confirmed with exhaled carbon monoxide, with ≤ 6 ppm indicating nonsmoking, 7–11 ppm, light current smoking, and > 12 ppm, heavy current smoking.[15] Exhaled carbon monoxide was obtained at enrollment, at several group meetings, and at group completion.

The Family Adaptability Cohesion Evaluation Scale was used to measure family cohesion and adaptability, with an overall calculated score from 1–8 indicating family functioning, categorized as "extreme, mid-range, moderately balanced, or balanced."[16] Participants completed the self-report measurement based on the family in which they were currently living or functioning, either spouse or significant other and other household members. Individual distress was measured with the Beck Depression Inventory (BDI), with > 18 indicating severe depressive symptoms.[17] These measurements were obtained at enrollment and group completion. Demographic and descriptive individual variables were obtained by participant survey at enrollment. Group variables were attendance and curriculum topic (measured at each session), and self-reported participant satisfaction using a 5 item Likert scale ranging from 1 ("not at all satisfied") to 5 ("very satisfied") measured at the fourth session.

Data Analysis

Comparison of the subject groups included Fisher's exact test for categorical data and ANOVA method for continuous variables.

Results

Subjects included 23 smokers with the following demographic characteristics: 58% women, 83% Caucasian and 17% African-American, 17% low SES (< $20,000/year income), 61% married, and 22–75 years old (mean age 51 years). Twenty subjects had a support partner enroll with them in the program, including 10 spouses (5 smokers and 5 nonsmokers), 4 significant others (2 smokers and 2 nonsmokers), and 6 other family members (sibling, parent, or child) all of whom were smokers. Self-reported smoking history included: age at initiation of smoking 13–26 years old (mean age 18 years), 4–60 years of smoking (mean 33 years), and 0–100 previous quit attempts (mean 12). The Fagerström Test for Nicotine Dependence score ranged from 0–8 (mean 4.8, SD 2.8). Exhaled carbon monoxide at enrollment ranged from 0–20 ppm (mean 12 ppm) with 60% consistent with heavy current smoking, 20%, light current smoking, and 20%, no current smoking. Those 4 participants with exhaled carbon monoxide in the nonsmoking range and a Fagerström Test for Nicotine Dependence score of 0 had quit smoking only days before enrollment. Tobacco-related illnesses were present in 7, 2 of whom had a history of cancer, and 6 with coronary artery disease. Sixty-three percent of subjects (15/23) completed the program. Participants who completed the program did not differ from total enrolled subjects except for race as all the participants who completed the program were Caucasian. Sixty percent (9/15) of participants had a support partner in the program. Support partners consisted of non-smokers, smokers who also participated in the program, and a smoker who attended but did not want to participate in the smoking cessation program.

Measures of individual distress and of family cohesion and support were the BDI and FACES scores. The BDI score at enrollment ranged from 1–25 (mean 9.6), with only one participant's score indicating serious depressive symptoms (> 18). The BDI score at group completion ranged from 0–29 (mean 5.2), with improved scores in 86% of participants. The same participant with an elevated BDI at enrollment had an elevated BDI at completion. FACES scores ranged from 1.5–7.0 (mean 4.6, family type "moderately balanced"). All participants were offered individualized physician evaluation for medication, with 80% electing to use this service. Bupropion was prescribed for 75% ($n = 9$) and nicotine replacement for 42% ($n = 5$) of those who were medically evaluated. The attendance in group sessions was excellent, with a range of 70–100% of sessions attended (mean 93%). The majority of participants indicated they were "very satisfied" at the midprogram survey (mean score 4.6).

165 For the entire sample that completed the program, smoking abstinence was 87% (13/15) at program completion, measured by self-report and confirmed by exhaled carbon monoxide. At the one and three month telephone follow up, 80% (12/15) reported continued abstinence. The abstinence rate in participants with
170 partner support was 92% (12/13) at program completion and 85% (11/13) at one and three month follow-up. Utilizing an intent to treat analysis including all enrollees and assuming that participants that withdrew were all smoking at follow up, the abstinence rates
175 were 56% (13/23) at group completion and 52% (12/23) at one and three month follow up.

At enrollment the Smoking Stage of Change for all participants was: contemplation 22%, preparation 70%, and action 8%. By completion of the program, 87% of
180 the participants had moved their stage of change toward action stage, including the one smoking support partner who did not "actively" participate in cessation efforts.

Discussion

This study demonstrates an increased efficacy of
185 smoking cessation with the addition of group therapy and a support partner to a standard smoking cessation curriculum. The overall abstinence rate at completion of the group, 87%, and at one month after completion, 80%, was much higher than the smoking cessation
190 rate with cognitive behavioral interventions even with the addition of pharmacotherapy, where the reported abstinence rates are rarely greater than 30%. This increase in the abstinence rate was significantly greater and more likely to be sustained at least one
195 month when the participant had a support partner in the program than when they did not. However, this difference was lost when adjusted for dropping-out of the program. There was also a notable racial difference in program completion as the African-American
200 participants all withdrew.

Support through the difficulties of nicotine withdrawal is reported as an important factor by those smokers who have been able to quit. This program utilizes a new method of including support in a model
205 with group therapy/education. Although cognitive behavioral interventions are an important component of smoking cessation programs, the addition of group therapy/education and the presence of a supporting partner at each session addresses the stresses and is-
210 sues faced by smokers and their families as they battle nicotine addiction. This has been found to be essential in the treatment of alcohol and other drug addiction, where family and group therapy are common components of treatment programs.[6] Although nicotine ad-
215 diction is often viewed as less destructive to the family system than other addictions, the process of withdrawal can be just as difficult. Therefore, the addition of group therapy/education with partner support, as in

220 this program, taps the power of that support and greatly magnifies smoking cessation efficacy.

Surveys of smokers have reported the importance of partner support in smoking cessation.[8-10] In a community-wide smoking cessation "contest," those smok-
225 ers who listed a support person were more likely to report that they quit smoking than those who did not, 35% compared to 27%, and those who reported a higher level of positive support had up to 37% abstinence.[18] However, incorporation of partner support into treatment in an effective model has not been demon-
230 strated. An initial report of a partner support treatment program reported increased efficacy when partners encouraged self-mastery and autonomy of the smoker and were not negative toward the smoker.[19] However, further evaluation of this model in a randomized trial
235 using three interventions, nicotine gum alone, nicotine gum and psychological treatment, and nicotine gum and psychological treatment combined with partner support, found a fairly low abstinence rate in all three groups (overall about 18%) and no statistically signifi-
240 cant difference between the groups.[20] This program was designed as a cognitive behavioral intervention with a concurrent cognitive behavioral intervention for partner support strategy training. While the evaluation did find that perceived partner support increased during
245 the program, there was no improvement in abstinence with partner support. Although this study is similar to our program in that it includes "partner support," the approach is entirely different. Rather than relying on a cognitive behavioral approach to partner support train-
250 ing, our program incorporates support through group therapy. Of course, facts about nicotine addiction and strategies for quitting and supporting a smoker who is trying to quit must be addressed in an educational curriculum using a cognitive behavioral strategy. How-
255 ever, the incorporation of group therapy, with the partner present throughout every session of the program, allows each participant to explore and address their common and unique family and individual struggles as they become intensified during withdrawal.

260 There are a number of limitations in the present trial. This is a preliminary study limited by a small sample size, and therefore unable to evaluate the contribution of specific components of partner support. In addition, the sample is not demographically representa-
265 tive of many smokers in that it is entirely Caucasian and largely upper socioeconomic status with a relatively high educational level, and with most of the participants suffering a tobacco related illness. The differences in program completion, by race and also by part-
270 ner support, need to be explored further. Perhaps the quality of support offered by the smoker's partner is both essential to program continuation and to success in achieving abstinence. Likewise, culturally specific approaches that incorporate factors such as partner
275 support must be developed and tested. The qualities of partner support that assist a smoker may very well be

culturally distinct. To confirm these results, a larger randomized study is necessary.

280   Tobacco addiction research is a priority and should include behavioral interventions in addition to physiology and pharmacology research. The addition of partner support should be studied in larger trials. However, the method in which support is incorporated may be important in its effect, and therefore studies that in-
285 clude group therapy as well as standard cognitive behavioral intervention are areas of future research. This simple change in approach may have a profound effect and help smokers achieve their goal, to quit smoking.

References

1. Substance Abuse Resource Guide: Tobacco. Center for Substance Abuse Prevention, Substance Abuse and Mental Health Services Administration: U.S. Department of Health and Human Services; 1999.
2. The Surgeon General's 1990 Report on the health benefits of smoking cessation executive summary. MMWR Recommendations and Reports 1990; 39:6–7.
3. Treating Tobacco Use and Dependence: Quick Reference Guide for Clinicians. Rockville, MD: U.S. Department of Health and Human Services Public Health Service; 2000.
4. Rigotti, NA: Treatment of tobacco use and dependence. N Engl J Med 2002; 346(7):506–512.
5. Shiffman S: Smoking cessation treatment: Any progress? J Consult Clin Psychol 1993; 61(5):718–722.
6. Berenson D, Schrier EW: Current family treatment approaches. In: Graham AW, Schultz TK, eds. Principles of Addiction Medicine, 2nd ed. Chevy Chase, MD: American Society of Addiction Medicine; 1998; 4:1115–1125.
7. Freund KM, D'Agostino RB, Belanger AJ, Kannel WB, Stokes J: Predictors of smoking cessation: The Framingham study. Am J Epidemiol 1992; 135(9):957–964.
8. Roski J, Schmid LA, Lando HA: Long-term associations of helpful and harmful spousal behaviors with smoking cessation. Addict Behav 1996; 21(2):173–185.
9. Gulliver SB, Hughes JR, Solomon LJ, Dey AN: An investigation of self-efficacy, partner support and daily stresses as predictors of relapse to smoking in self-quitters. Addiction 1995; 90:767–772.
10. Murray RP, Johnston JJ, Dolce JJ, Lee WW, O'Hara P: Social support for smoking cessation and abstinence: The lung health study. Addict Behav 1995; 20(2):159–170.
11. Shipley RH: Quit Smart Leadership Manual. Durham, NC: Quitsmart Stop Smoking Resources; 1998.
12. Fagerström KO, Schneider NG: Measuring nicotine dependence: A review of the Fagerström tolerance questionnaire. J Behav Med 1989; 12:159–182.
13. DiClemente CC, Prochaska JO, Fairhurst S, Velicer WF, Rossi JS, Velasquez M: The process of smoking cessation: An analysis of precontemplation, contemplation and contemplation/action. J Consult Clin Psychol 1991; 59:295–304.
14. Velicer WF, Fava JL, Prochaska JO, Abrams DB, Emmons KM, Pierce J: Distribution of smokers by stage in three representative samples. Prev Med 1995; 24:401–411.
15. Vitalograph: Vitalograph Inc; 2000.
16. Olson DH: Commentary: Three Dimensional (3-D) Circumplex Model and revised scoring of FACES III. Fam Process 1991; 30:74–79.
17. Beck A, Ward C, Mendelson M, Mock J, Erbaugh J: An inventory for measuring depression. Arch Gen Psychiatry 1969; 4:53–63.
18. Pirie PL, Rooney BD, Pechacek TF, Lando HA, Schmid LA: Incorporating social support into a community-wide smoking-cessation contest. Addict Behav 1997; 22(1):131–137.
19. Ginsberg D, Hall SM, Rosinski M: Partner interaction and smoking cessation: A pilot study. Addict Behav 1991; 16:195–202.
20. Ginsberg D, Hall SM, Rosinski M: Partner support, psychological treatment, and nicotine guru in smoking treatment: An incremental study. Int J Addict 1992; 27(5):503–514.

Acknowledgments: This research was funded by a grant from the Department of Defense (project #82889), through the Hollings Cancer Center at the Medical University of South Carolina, Charleston, SC.

About the authors: Janice D. Key and Linda D. Marsh are affiliated with the Department of Pediatrics, Cindy L. Carter is affiliated with the Hollings Cancer Center, Robert J. Malcolm is affiliated with the Department of Psychiatry, and Debajyoti Sinha is affiliated with the Department of Biometry, The Medical University of South Carolina, Charleston, SC.

Address correspondence to: Janice D. Key, MD, Department of Pediatrics, The Medical University of South Carolina, 135 Rutledge Avenue, P.O. Box 250560, Charleston, SC 29425.

Exercise for Article 28

Factual Questions

1. Who facilitated each session?

2. How were participants recruited?

3. What instrument was used to measure "distress"?

4. Of the 23 original subjects, how many completed the program?

5. Did a majority of the participants report that they were "very satisfied" with the program?

6. At program completion, what percentage of the program participants were abstinent?

Questions for Discussion

7. Would you be interested in having more information on the Fagerström Test for Nicotine Dependence? Explain. (See lines 74–78.)

8. In your opinion, how important was it to confirm self-reported smoking with exhaled carbon monoxide tests? (See lines 83–88 and 164–167.)

9. Nine of the participants had a support partner in the program and six did not. In your opinion, how important would it be to use larger numbers of participants in future studies on this topic? (See lines 139–141 and 261–263.)

10. In your opinion, would it be worthwhile in a future study for researchers to assign some individuals to group therapy with partners, while assigning other individuals to group therapy without partners? Would random assignment be helpful? Explain.

11. In your opinion, does the use of prescription drugs complicate the interpretation of this study? Explain. (See lines 155–159.)

12. The researchers conducted follow ups at one and three months after the program. Is this an important strength of this study? Explain. (See lines 167–176.)

13. Keeping in mind that this is a pilot study with a small sample, are you convinced by this study that group therapy with partner support is a promising approach? Explain.

Quality Ratings

Directions: Indicate your level of agreement with each of the following statements by circling a number from 5 for strongly agree (SA) to 1 for strongly disagree (SD). If you believe an item is not applicable to this research article, leave it blank. Be prepared to explain your ratings. When responding to criteria A and B below, keep in mind that brief titles and abstracts are conventional in published research.

A. The title of the article is appropriate.

   SA   5   4   3   2   1   SD

B. The abstract provides an effective overview of the research article.

   SA   5   4   3   2   1   SD

C. The introduction establishes the importance of the study.

   SA   5   4   3   2   1   SD

D. The literature review establishes the context for the study.

   SA   5   4   3   2   1   SD

E. The research purpose, question, or hypothesis is clearly stated.

   SA   5   4   3   2   1   SD

F. The method of sampling is sound.

   SA   5   4   3   2   1   SD

G. Relevant demographics (for example, age, gender, and ethnicity) are described.

   SA   5   4   3   2   1   SD

H. Measurement procedures are adequate.

   SA   5   4   3   2   1   SD

I. All procedures have been described in sufficient detail to permit a replication of the study.

   SA   5   4   3   2   1   SD

J. The participants have been adequately protected from potential harm.

   SA   5   4   3   2   1   SD

K. The results are clearly described.

   SA   5   4   3   2   1   SD

L. The discussion/conclusion is appropriate.

   SA   5   4   3   2   1   SD

M. Despite any flaws, the report is worthy of publication.

   SA   5   4   3   2   1   SD

Article 29

Then and Now: A Follow-Up Study of Professionals' Perceptions of Parenting after Divorce Classes

RAYMOND J. TAYLOR
Colorado State University

ABSTRACT. Fifteen million children experienced a divorce in their families in the 1990s. The primary determinant of adverse outcome in children is ongoing parental hostility after the divorce. A study in 1996 of community professionals (ministers, pediatricians, attorneys, school counselors and divorce mediators) in a western Colorado county demonstrated the need for parenting after divorce classes. It has now been seven years since the beginning of those classes; the views and perceptions of those professionals are reexamined.

From *Journal of Divorce & Remarriage, 41*, 135–142. Copyright © 2004 by the Haworth Press, Inc. Reprinted with permission.

Introduction

During the 1990s almost 15 million children, most of them younger than eight years of age, experienced a divorce (Sammons 2001). Research indicates that the primary determinant of adverse outcome in children is
5 ongoing parental hostility after the divorce (Sammons 2001, Wallerstein, & Blakeslee, 1989). It is also found that children's emotional and economic stability are better maintained when both parents continue to play an active and positive role in their lives (Sammons
10 2001). Parenting after divorce counseling and education classes have been seen as a "doable" intervention and have been offered in various jurisdictions in the United States for going on three decades (Salem, 1995). The variety of these programs varies between
15 voluntary and mandatory, low and high intensity. Whether voluntary or mandatory, generally the first referral tends to come from the court when a divorce is filed; though it is reasonable to assume that professionals in the community may also start to make referrals to
20 their clientele in need. For this to happen, they must first be aware of the program, content and process.

Taylor (1999) demonstrated in a community in Western Colorado (Mesa County), which at that time did not have such a program, the differences of percep-
25 tions of community professionals (attorneys, divorce mediators, school counselors, pediatricians, ministers, judges, and divorced parents) regarding the need of children of divorce and the educational need of parents experiencing a divorce. The result of the 1996 study is
30 summarized on Table 1, demonstrating the distinct differences of professional populations within the community. All subgroups agreed that such a program was necessary for divorcing parents and children of divorce. The significant difference between subgroups
35 was that of the attorneys. Attorneys strongly and significantly disagreed with the other subgroups on the content of material offered within the divorce education sessions. On the other hand, it is the subgroups of the school counselors, ministers, and pediatricians who
40 work on the front line with children of divorce every day that strongly and significantly agreed (in disagreement with attorneys) that certain materials should be offered within the course context. The qualitative aspect of the study interviewed seven professionals from
45 each subgroup; all unanimously agreed that community training should occur, making professionals not only aware of the dynamics of divorce and the complication confronting the children, but also what interventions and programs were available within the community.
50 At the same time that this study was being conducted, the state of Colorado passed legislation, Colorado Senate Bill 96-141, enabling judges in each district to mandate such parenting after divorce classes. Approximately one year later, Mesa County started
55 offering such classes. The evaluation of the program has relied on "presenter/program" evaluation completed at the end of the same-day course. To date, there has not been an evaluation of the results and process.

Method

This study again takes place in Grand Junction,
60 Colorado, a semirural high-desert community in western Colorado with a population in the city of 65,000 and surrounding county of 150,000. The Mesa County parenting after divorce education program is now in its seventh year. This study completes the 1996 study of
65 perceptions of professionals regarding the need for parenting after divorce programs. The format of the study is the same as the 1996 study, where a total of 123 questionnaires were mailed nonrandomly to ministers of churches (30), school counselors (35), divorce

Table 1

List of Elements Felt to Be Important to the Divorced Parenting Program with Differences Between Populations as Signified by Chi-Square Analysis (1996 study results)

EXTREME NEGATIVE		PROGRAM ASPECTS	EXTREME POSITIVE	

1,4	*	Court-ordered program
		    Overview of divorce procedure
		    Definition of custody, parenting time and residential custodian issues
			+	3

1	*	Legal rights of parents	+	2,5

1	*	Parenting skills
		    Emotional responsibilities of parents
		    Responsibilities of noncustodian parents
		    Responsibilities of custodian parents (i.e., encouraging parenting time)
		    Post-divorce reactions of parents
			+	3,5

1	*
	*
	*
		Developing a parenting time schedule
		Post-divorce reactions of children
		Developmental needs of children
		    Benefits of parental cooperation vs. cost of parental fighting
		    Impact of brainwashing and parental alienation
		    Conflict management skills
			+	3

1	*	Calculation of child support using state guidelines Issues concerning domestic violence and child abuse	+	6

1	*
	
	*
		Emotional impact of post-divorce decisions
		    Issues of step-parents and blended families
		Techniques and importance of effective communication between parents
		    Divorce information workshop for children
			+	5,6

1	*	Information regarding divorce support and adjustment groups	+	2,3,5
1	*	Financial impact of divorce	+	2,3,5
		OTHER ASPECTS REGARDING CHILDREN OF DIVORCE IDENTIFIED NOT RELATED TO PARENTING PROGRAM		
		The need for a neutral location for transition of children during visitation		
1	*	Alternatives to divorce	+	2,4,5
1,3	*	Information regarding custody evaluations and litigation		

Code: 1 = attorneys, 2 = teachers, 3 = divorce mediators, 4 = physicians, 5 = ministers, 6 = parents
"*" = chi-square significant difference negatively from rest of sample
"+" = chi-square significant difference more positive than rest of sample

70 mediators (15), pediatricians (8), and divorce attorneys (35) in that area. Addresses were obtained from the local yellow pages. The community professionals were asked to participate anonymously; the only demographic that was asked was profession. All potential 75 participants were sent a cover letter explaining that this was a follow-up to the 1996 study, a questionnaire, and an addressed stamped envelope. The questionnaire consisted of four questions, the first being: Was that professional aware of the parenting after divorce edu- 80 cational program provided by the courts? (If participants answer "no," they were instructed not to proceed with the questions and return the questionnaire in the given envelope. If participants answered "yes" to being aware of the program in the area, they were to proceed 85 with the rest of the questionnaire.) The second question was: If they were aware of the program, did they believe that it was having a positive impact upon the community? The third question was: Did they believe that the program needed to be changed or remain the 90 same? The fourth question was an open-ended question

regarding any comments they may have regarding the parenting after divorce educational program.

Results

Of the 123 surveys distributed, 69 (56.09%) were returned. This was above the expected 20% return rate 95 for mail-based survey questionnaires (Braver et al., 1997). Of the 69 surveys returned, all were useful for quantitative and qualitative analysis. Return rates per sample populations are demonstrated in Table 2. Data were analyzed via chi-square analysis to determine 100 differences between sample populations. The data were also analyzed and reviewed regarding the whole sample as representative of the professional community.

Of the 69 returned questionnaires, 21 (30.43%) of the total sample were aware of the parenting after di- 105 vorce program in Mesa County, Colorado. Table 3 demonstrates the breakdown of professional groups and their responses to questions 1–3. Of the responding professionals, 0% of the pediatricians, 4.8% of the clergy, 44% of the divorce attorneys, 47% of the school

Table 2
Summary Response Rate from Different Sample Populations

Sample	# sent out	# received back	% received back
Pediatricians	8	5	62.5%
Clergy	30	21	70.0%
Divorce mediators	15	12	80.0%
Divorce attorneys	35	9	25.7%
School counselors	35	22	62.9%
Total	123	69	56.09%

Table 3
Summary Answers and Percentages from Questions 1–3 by Different Sample Populations

	1 aware of program		2 making a + impact upon community			3 keep program same or change		
Sample	Y	N	Y	N	??	same	changes	??
Pediatricians	0	8	*not applicable*			*not applicable*		
Clergy	1	20	1	0	0	0	0	1
Divorce mediators	9	3	8	1	0	4	3	2
Divorce attorneys	4	5	3	0	1	2	0	2
School counselors	7	15	6	1	0	1	2	4
Total	21	46	18	2	1	7	5	9
Percent	30.9%	69.1%	85.7%	9.5%	4.8%	33.3%	23.8%	42.9%

110 counselors, and 75% of the divorce mediators were aware of the program in the community. Those who were aware of the program within the community were made aware by legal orders, informed by their clients, friends, and coworkers, and "word of mouth but of no 115 substantive merit."

Thus, of the remaining 21 respondents who were aware of the program in the Mesa County, Colorado, area, 85.7% felt that the program was making a positive impact upon the community. One respondent from 120 each group of divorce mediators, divorce attorneys, and school counselors felt that no or questionable impact was being made. The majority of the qualitative comments suggested that any program attempting to help children in the community would have a positive influence: 33.3% felt that the program should be kept the 125 same as it is, 23.8% felt that changes were in order, and 42.9% weren't sure. Of the 42.9% that weren't sure if changes in the program should be made, the majority stated that they didn't know enough of the program to make those kinds of suggestions and called for an edu- 130 cation of the program, then leading to an evalutory program. Unlike the results of the 1996 study, there was no significant difference (chi-square) between sample populations on all questions.

None of the attorneys answered the open-ended 135 question regarding their perceptions of the parenting after divorce program. The one minister respondent had concerns that divorce continues to affect other areas in the children's lives including the spiritual, and 140 that one may see a decline in church or church school

attendance after a divorce. Of the three divorce mediators who commented on this question, all agreed that the program had value, and one thought it was interesting that he/she was never contacted for his/her opinion 145 or expertise. Of the six school counselors who commented, all believe that the program was important to children and would like the existing program to advise counselors of their services and referral process.

Discussion

Although only 30.9% of the returned surveys were 150 aware of the post-divorce education program, it shouldn't be assumed that the program is not functioning properly or contributing to the community. It is indicative only that those professionals have not had an opportunity to know about the program. It is important 155 for programs to share community services information with the community professionals who see children of divorce or divorcing parents in their field or line of work. It is only when one is aware of such programs that they may use them as referral sources when prob- 160 lems are observed or diagnosed in their clientele. Therefore, community professionals (not limited to school counselors, attorneys, ministers, pediatricians, and divorce mediators) should seek out information of services within the community related to children and 165 their parents. The professionals conducting such parenting after divorce classes should also network within the community to enlist and educate those community professionals. One such viable option would be to either have a class for professionals or to periodically

170 have professionals from the community invited (*gratis*) to observe and educate themselves and enhance a referral resource of a service available within the community.

The participants in the 1996 study unanimously 175 stated that annual in-services should occur educating community professionals about the dynamics and programs available. According to this year's result, this isn't happening. The participants have suggested in large numbers that they do not know enough of the 180 program to make suggestions for change if needed. This sample included professionals who see children of divorce and parents every day with expertise in education, childhood development, communication, and dispute resolution. One such solution is to form a community 185 task force of community volunteers to evaluate the process and ensure that professionals in the community are aware of the program. Once community professionals are educated as to the services, then they may be utilized regarding their varied professional expertise 190 and observations regarding the program and population-at-risk.

References

Arbuthnot, J., & Gordon, D. (January 1996). Does mandatory divorce education for parents work? A six-month outcome evaluation. *Family and Conciliation Courts Review, 34* (1).

Blaisure, K., & Geasler, M. (January 1996). Results of a survey of court-connected parent education programs in U.S. counties. *Family and Conciliation Court Review, 34*(1), 23–40.

Braver, S., Salem, P., Pearson, J., & DeLuse, S. (January 1996). The content of divorce education programs: results of a survey. *Family and Conciliation Court Review, 34* (1), 41–59.

Geasler, M.J., & Blaissure, K. R. (1999). Nationwide survey of court-connected divorce education programs. *Family Conciliation Court Review, 37,* 36–63.

Kline, M., Johnston, J., & Tschann, J. (1991). The long shadow of marital conflict: a model of children's post-divorce adjustment. *Journal of Marriage and Family, 53,* 297.

Sammons, W. & Lewis, J. (2001). Helping children survive divorce. *Contemporary Pediatrics, 43,* 103.

Taylor, R. (1999). Attitudes of professionals toward parenting programs after divorce. *Journal of Divorce & Remarriage, 32*(1/2), 159–165.

Wallerstein, J. & Blakeslee (1989). *Second chances: men, women, and children a decade after divorce.* New York: Ticker and Fields.

About the author: J Raymond J. Taylor, PhD, is assistant professor, Colorado State University at Pueblo.

Address correspondence to: Raymond J. Taylor, Colorado State University at Pueblo, 2200 South Bonforte Boulevard, Pueblo, CO 81001. E-mail: raymond.taylor@colostate-pueblo.edu

Exercise for Article 29

Factual Questions

1. How did the researcher obtain the addresses of the community professionals?

2. What were participants asked to do if they answered "no" in response to the question on whether they were aware of the program?

3. Sixty-nine of the questionnaires were returned. Of the participants who returned questionnaires, how many indicated being aware of the program?

4. Which professional group had the lowest return rate?

5. How many of the attorneys answered the open-ended question regarding their perceptions of the parenting after divorce program?

6. Of the 21 respondents, what percentage thought that the program was making a positive impact on the community?

Questions for Discussion

7. Speculate on why the researcher asked the participants to participate anonymously. (See lines 72–73.)

8. "Profession" was the only demographic information requested in this evaluation. If you had been conducting this study, would you have asked for additional demographics (e.g., age, race)? Explain. (See lines 73–74.)

9. What is your opinion on the return rate? Is it adequate? (See lines 93–96.)

10. The qualitative results are intermingled with some quantitative results in lines 122–148. In your opinion, how helpful are the qualitative results in learning how to improve the program?

11. This evaluation was not designed to evaluate the impact of the program from the point of view of the individuals who took the classes. In your opinion, would it be important to do so in a future evaluation? Explain.

12. The researcher suggests that a task force of community volunteers be used to make more community professionals aware of the program. In your opinion, how important is this suggestion for improving the program? (See lines 184–187.)

Quality Ratings

Directions: Indicate your level of agreement with each of the following statements by circling a number from 5 for strongly agree (SA) to 1 for strongly disagree (SD). If you believe an item is not applicable to this research article, leave it blank. Be prepared to explain your ratings. When responding to criteria A and B below, keep in mind that brief titles and abstracts are conventional in published research.

A.   The title of the article is appropriate.

SA   5   4   3   2   1   SD

B.   The abstract provides an effective overview of the research article.

SA   5   4   3   2   1   SD

C.   The introduction establishes the importance of the study.

SA   5   4   3   2   1   SD

D.   The literature review establishes the context for the study.

SA   5   4   3   2   1   SD

E.   The research purpose, question, or hypothesis is clearly stated.

SA   5   4   3   2   1   SD

F.   The method of sampling is sound.

SA   5   4   3   2   1   SD

G.   Relevant demographics (for example, age, gender, and ethnicity) are described.

SA   5   4   3   2   1   SD

H.   Measurement procedures are adequate.

SA   5   4   3   2   1   SD

I.   All procedures have been described in sufficient detail to permit a replication of the study.

SA   5   4   3   2   1   SD

J.   The participants have been adequately protected from potential harm.

SA   5   4   3   2   1   SD

K.   The results are clearly described.

SA   5   4   3   2   1   SD

L.   The discussion/conclusion is appropriate.

SA   5   4   3   2   1   SD

M.   Despite any flaws, the report is worthy of publication.

SA   5   4   3   2   1   SD

Article 30

Relationship Between Mental Toughness and Physical Endurance

LEE CRUST
York St. John College

PETER J. CLOUGH
Hull University

ABSTRACT. This study tested the criterion validity of the inventory, Mental Toughness 48, by assessing the correlation between mental toughness and physical endurance for 41 male undergraduate sports students. A significant correlation of .34 was found between scores for overall mental toughness and the time a relative weight could be held suspended. Results support the criterion-related validity of the Mental Toughness 48.

From *Perceptual and Motor Skills, 100,* 192–194. Copyright © 2005 by Perceptual and Motor Skills. Reprinted with permission.

Mental toughness has recently been conceptualised as a trait-like dimension of personality (1). These authors integrated studies of hardy personality and the stress-illness relationship from health psychology (4, 5)
5 into a model that represents the unique demands of sports and exercise. Clough, et al. (1) conceptualised mental toughness and hardiness as similar constructs, with the only notable difference being the addition of confidence into their model. The four components of
10 mental toughness, according to this model of mental toughness, are Control, Commitment, Challenge, and Confidence. Mentally tough individuals are considered to be competitive, resilient to errors or stress, and have high self-confidence and low anxiety.
15 The Mental Toughness 48 has 48 statements (1) to measure mental toughness and to reflect the new model. Responses are made on a 5-point Likert scale anchored by 1: strongly disagree and 5: strongly agree. Average completion time is approximately 10 min. The
20 MT48 has an overall test–retest coefficient of .90, with the internal consistency of the subscales (Control, Commitment, Challenge, and Confidence) of .73, .71, .71, and .80, respectively (1). In testing the MT48's construct validity, its authors identified significant cor-
25 relations with optimism of .48 (Life Orientation Test; 8), self-image .42 (Self-esteem Scale; 7), life satisfaction .56 (Satisfaction with Life Scale; 2), self-efficacy .68 (Self-efficacy Scale; 10), and trait anxiety .57 (State Trait Anxiety Inventory; 9). Clough, et al. (1)
30 cited their own work in supporting criterion validity by finding participants with high as opposed to low scores on mental toughness reported lower ratings of exertion during a 30-min. cycle ride at 70% VO_2 max. However,
35 further assessment of criterion validity for the MT48 is needed by using a measure of physical performance.
Applying the model, it was hypothesised that participants' endurance of a standardized physical endurance task would be significantly and positively related to scores on mental toughness.

Method

40 Participants were 41 male undergraduate students in sports and exercise science who volunteered. Their mean age was 21.0 yr. ($SD = 2.7$) and weight 79.6 kg ($SD = 5.0$). All participants gave informed consent prior to individual testing.
45 Each sat at a desk in a quiet room before being asked to lift a dumbbell constituting approximately 1.5% of the participant's body weight (*Note:* A low resistance was chosen to enable the afferent signals of pain to impinge on participant's sensations gradually.
50 A heavier weight would likely have been more physically rather than mentally demanding) using the dominant arm and an over-hand grip from its resting position on the desk to a holding position. Participants were instructed to hold the weight suspended with a straight
55 arm directly in front of the body and over the desk, with a 90° angle between arm and torso for as long as possible. A reward was offered for the best performance to limit differences in motivation. With a stopwatch time of the hold from lift of the weight into the
60 holding position and return to the resting position on the desktop was the measure of endurance. Following completion of the weight-holding task, participants completed the MT48 to obtain their self-ratings of mental toughness.

Results

65 To assess the relationship between Mental Toughness 48 scores ($M = 3.6$, $SD = 0.3$) and isometric endurance times ($M = 213.6$, $SD = 43.4$), Pearson correlations were calculated. These values were significant ($p < .05$) for overall Mental Toughness 48 with time ($r = $
70 .34), Control ($r = .37$), and Confidence ($r = .29$) but not for Challenge ($r = .22$) or Commitment ($r = .23$).
The results support the criterion validity of the MT48 given that weight-holding endurance was positively and significantly related to overall scores on

75 mental toughness. This finding is consistent with experimental work by Clough, et al. (1) and also with Maddi and Hess (6) who found the related concept of hardiness correlated with seven out of eight basketball performance indicators during a season-long investiga-
80 tion.

Previous findings on hardiness (5) may offer a theoretical explanation for the relationship between mental toughness and performance. It is possible that participants with greater mental toughness benefit from
85 a buffering effect (resistance resource), given differences in how demanding conditions are cognitively appraised or how situations are dealt with (i.e., exerting control by blocking out pain). Since changes in physiological measures (epinephrine, norepinephrine, and
90 cortisol) have correlated with a variety of performance measures and significantly with dimensions of personality (cf. 3), researchers might test for physiological correlates of the MT48 scores in mentally or physically demanding conditions to enable more clear understand-
95 ing.

References

1. Clough, P. J., Earle, K., & Sewell, D. (2002). Mental toughness: the concept and its measurement. In I. Cockerill (Ed.), *Solutions in sport psychology* (pp. 32–43). London: Thomson.
2. Diener, E., Emmons, R., Larsen, J., & Griffin, S. (1985). The Satisfaction with Life Scale. *Journal of Personality Assessment, 49*, 71–75.
3. Dienstbier, R. A. (1989). Arousal and physiological toughness: implications for mental and physical health. *Psychological Review, 96*, 84–100.
4. Kobasa, S. C. (1979). Stressful life events, personality and health: an enquiry into hardiness. *Journal of Personality and Social Psychology, 37*, 1–11.
5. Kobasa, S. C., Maddi, S. R., & Kahn, S. (1982). Hardiness and health: a prospective study. *Journal of Personality and Social Psychology, 42*, 168–177.
6. Maddi, S. R., & Hess, M. J. (1992). Personality, hardiness and success in basketball. *International Journal of Sport Psychology, 23*, 360–368.
7. Rosenberg, M. (1989). *Society and adolescent self-image.* Middletown, CT: Wesleyan Univer. Press.
8. Scheier, M. F., & Carver, C. S. (1985). Optimism, coping and health: assessment and implications of generalized outcome expectancies. *Health Psychology, 4*, 219–247.
9. Spielberger, C. D. (1968). *State Trait Anxiety Inventory.* San Diego, CA: Consulting Psychologists Press.
10. Wegner, M., Schwarzer, R., & Jerusalem, M. (1993). Generalized self-efficacy scale. In R. Schwarzer (Ed.), *Measurement of perceived self-efficacy: psychometric scales for cross-cultural research.* Berlin, Ger.: Berlini Freie Universitat.

Address correspondence to: Lee Crust, School of Sports Science and Psychology, York St. John College, Lord Mayor's Walk, York Y031 7EX, United Kingdom.

Exercise for Article 30

Factual Questions

1. What is the value of the test–retest reliability coefficient for the MT48?

2. Who were the participants in this study?

3. According to the literature review, what was the correlation of MT48 scores with optimism?

4. Why didn't the researchers use a heavier weight?

5. In the Results section of this study, how many statistically significant relationships were identified?

6. Why was a reward offered for the best performance?

7. What is the value of the correlation coefficient between time (time of the hold from lift of the weight to the resting position) and overall mental toughness?

Questions for Discussion

8. In your opinion, is the MT48 described in sufficient detail? Explain. (See lines 15–35.)

9. What is your understanding of the term "internal consistency" in line 21?

10. Would you be willing to generalize the results of this study to students who are not in sports and exercise science? Explain. (See lines 40–41.)

11. Would you describe any of the correlation coefficients reported in the Results section as representing very strong relationships? (See lines 68–71.)

12. Would you characterize the results of this study as offering very strong evidence of the validity of the MT48? Explain.

13. Even though this is a short research report, do you think that it provides information of value for individuals interested in the validity of the MT48? Explain.

Quality Ratings

Directions: Indicate your level of agreement with each of the following statements by circling a number from 5 for strongly agree (SA) to 1 for strongly disagree (SD). If you believe an item is not applicable to this research article, leave it blank. Be prepared to explain your ratings. When responding to criteria A and B below, keep in mind that brief titles and abstracts are conventional in published research.

A. The title of the article is appropriate.

    SA   5   4   3   2   1   SD

B. The abstract provides an effective overview of the research article.

    SA   5   4   3   2   1   SD

C.   The introduction establishes the importance of the study.

SA   5   4   3   2   1   SD

D.   The literature review establishes the context for the study.

SA   5   4   3   2   1   SD

E.   The research purpose, question, or hypothesis is clearly stated.

SA   5   4   3   2   1   SD

F.   The method of sampling is sound.

SA   5   4   3   2   1   SD

G.   Relevant demographics (for example, age, gender, and ethnicity) are described.

SA   5   4   3   2   1   SD

H.   Measurement procedures are adequate.

SA   5   4   3   2   1   SD

I.   All procedures have been described in sufficient detail to permit a replication of the study.

SA   5   4   3   2   1   SD

J.   The participants have been adequately protected from potential harm.

SA   5   4   3   2   1   SD

K.   The results are clearly described.

SA   5   4   3   2   1   SD

L.   The discussion/conclusion is appropriate.

SA   5   4   3   2   1   SD

M.   Despite any flaws, the report is worthy of publication.

SA   5   4   3   2   1   SD

Article 31

Temporal Stability of the Francis Scale of Attitude Toward Christianity Short-Form: Test–Retest Data over One Week

CHRISTOPHER ALAN LEWIS
University of Ulster at Magee College

SHARON MARY CRUISE
University of Ulster at Magee College

CONOR McGUCKIN
Dublin Business School of Arts

ABSTRACT. This study evaluated the test–retest reliability of the Francis Scale of Attitude toward Christianity short-form. Thirty-nine Northern Irish undergraduate students completed the measure on two occasions separated by one week. Stability across the two administrations was high, $r = .92$, and there was no significant change between Time 1 ($M = 25.2$, $SD = 5.4$) and Time 2 ($M = 25.7$, $SD = 6.2$). These data support the short-term test–retest reliability of the Francis Scale of Attitude toward Christianity short-form.

From *Psychological Reports, 96,* 266–268. Copyright © 2005 by Psychological Reports. Reprinted with permission.

Over the last 25 years, there have been more than 200 published studies examining the measurement, correlates, and consequences of variation in attitude toward Christianity among children, adolescents, and
5 adults (see Kay & Francis, 1996). At the centre of this work has been the 24-item Francis Scale of Attitude toward Christianity (Francis & Stubbs, 1987). Subsequently, Francis, Greer, and Gibson (1991) developed a 7-item short-form of the scale, intended to be a re-
10 placement for the full version when administration time is short. This short-form has demonstrated good psychometric properties (Francis, 1993), including high internal consistency (Lewis, 2001), a one-factor structure (Lewis, Shevlin, Lloyd, & Adamson, 1998), high
15 positive correlations with attitudinal and behavioural measures of religiosity (Maltby & Lewis, 1997), and is not affected by social desirability (Lewis, 1999, 2000).

To date no information on the test–retest reliability of this measure has been reported. Hill and Hood
20 (1999), in their review of measures in the psychology of religion, noted that "Test–retest reliabilities are not common in this area, despite their obvious value in identifying stable scores over time" (p. 7). Exceptions include data reported on the stability of the Duke Re-
25 ligion Index (Storch, Strawser, & Storch, 2004), the Religious Commitment Inventory–10 (Worthington, Wade, Hight, Ripley, McCullough, Berry, Schmitt, Berry, Bursley, & O'Connor, 2003), and the Systems of Belief Inventory (Holland, Kash, Passik, Gronert,
30 Sison, Lederberg, Russak, Baider, & Fox, 1998). The present aim was to evaluate the 1-wk. test–retest reliability of the Francis Scale of Attitude toward Christianity short-form among a sample of Northern Irish university students.

Method

Sample
35 Thirty-nine students (5 men and 34 women) whose mean age was 27.4 yr. ($SD = 10.0$), all in attendance at the University of Ulster at Magee College, Londonderry, Northern Ireland, and enrolled in a course in psychology, were employed as respondents.

Measure
40 The Francis Scale of Attitude toward Christianity short-form concerns attitude toward the Bible, prayer, church, God, and Jesus, a sample question being "I know that Jesus helps me" (Item 1). Items are scored on a 5-point scale with anchors of "agree strongly" (5)
45 through "uncertain'"(3) and "disagree strongly" (1). Scores range from 7 to 35, higher scores indicating a more positive attitude toward Christianity. A satisfactory estimate of internal consistency has been reported in Northern Ireland among undergraduate students (.90;
50 Maltby & Lewis, 1997).

Procedure
The short-form was completed during class time on two occasions separated by a period of 1 wk. as part of a practical class. Participants recorded their names and age but were assured of confidentiality, and participa-
55 tion was voluntary. None of the class declined to participate, and no credit was given for completing the questionnaires on either occasion. The participants were not informed that the measure would be readministered.

Results
60 Satisfactory estimates of internal reliability (Cronbach, 1951) were found for the Francis Scale of Attitude toward Christianity short-form at both Time 1 (Cronbach alpha = .91) and Time 2 (Cronbach alpha = .93). Scores on the scale for Time 1 and Time 2 were

65 highly correlated ($r = .92$). No significant difference was found in the mean scores ($t_{38} = -2.43$, ns) between Time 1 (M = 25.2, SD = 5.4, range 14–35) and Time 2 ($M = 25.7, SD = 6.2$, range 12–35).

Discussion

The present data provide evidence for the test–
70 retest reliability over a 1-wk. period for the Francis Scale of Attitude toward Christianity short-form among a sample of Northern Irish university students. Furthermore, satisfactory values of internal reliability were also found, in line with previous research (e.g., Lewis,
75 2001). Although the generalisability of these findings is limited given the small sample, the selectivity of the sample (i.e., university students, mainly female, and the small duration of the intervening period between tests), the short-form does appear temporally stable.
80 These findings provide additional psychometric evidence which attests to the stability of the measure (Lewis & Maltby, 2000). Further research is required to examine the stability of the Francis Scale of Attitude toward Christianity short-form among large and more
85 representative samples and over longer testing periods.

References

Cronbach, L. J. (1951). Coefficient alpha and the internal structure of tests. *Psychometrika, 16,* 297–334.

Francis, L. J. (1993). Reliability and validity of a short scale of attitude towards Christianity among adults. *Psychological Reports, 72,* 615–618.

Francis, L. J., Greer, J. E., & Gibson, H. M. (1991). Reliability and validity of a short measure of attitude toward Christianity among secondary school pupils in England, Scotland, and Northern Ireland. *Collected Original Resources in Education, 15,* Fiche 2, G09.

Francis, L. J., & Stubbs, M. T. (1987). Measuring attitudes towards Christianity: From childhood to adulthood. *Personality and Individual Differences, 8,* 741–743.

Hill, P C., & Hood, R. W. (1999). Measures of religiosity. Birmingham, AL: Religious Education Press.

Holland, J. C., Kash, K. M., Passik, S., Gronert, M. K., Sison, A., Lederberg, M., Russak, S. M., Baider, L., & Fox, B. (1998). A brief spiritual beliefs inventory for use in quality of life research in life-threatening illness. *Psycho-oncology, 7,* 460–469.

Kay, W. K., & Francis, L. J. (1996). *Drift from the churches: attitude toward Christianity during childhood and adolescence.* Cardiff, Wales: University. of Wales Press.

Lewis, C. A. (1999). Is the relationship between religiosity and personality 'contaminated' by social desirability as assessed by the Lie Scale? A methodological reply to Michael W. Eysenck (1998). *Mental Health, Religion and Culture, 2,* 105–114.

Lewis, C. A. (2000). The religiosity-psychoticism relationship and the two factors of social desirability: A response to Michael W. Eysenck (1999). *Mental Health, Religion and Culture, 3,* 39–45.

Lewis, C. A. (2001). Cultural stereotype of the effects of religion on mental health. *British Journal of Medical Psychology, 74,* 359–367.

Lewis, C. A., & Maltby, J. (2000). The Francis Scale of Attitude Toward Christianity (Adult Version: Short-Scale). In J. Maltby, C. A. Lewis, & A. Hill (Eds.), *Commissioned reviews of 250 psychological tests, 1,* (pp. 301–306). Cardiff, Wales, UK: Edwin Mellen Press.

Lewis, C. A., Shevlin, M. E., Lloyd, N. S. V., & Adamson, G. (1998). The Francis Scale of Attitude Toward Christianity (short-scale): exploratory and confirmatory factor analysis among English students. *Journal of Social Behavior and Personality, 13,* 167–175.

Maltby, J., & Lewis, C. A. (1997) The reliability and validity of a short scale of attitude towards Christianity among USA, English, Republic of Ireland, and Northern Ireland adults. *Personality and Individual Differences, 22,* 649–654.

Storch, E. A., Strawser, M. S., & Storch, J. B. (2004). Two-week test–retest reliability of the Duke Religion Index. *Psychological Reports, 94,* 993–994.

Worthington, E. L., Jr., Wade, N. G., Hight, T L., Ripley, J. S., McCullough, M. E., Berry, J. W., Schmitt, M. M., Berry, J. T., Bursley, K. H., & O'Connor, L. (2003). The Religious Commitment Inventory-10: development, refinement, and validation of a brief measure for research and counseling. *Journal of Counseling Psychology, 50,* 84–96.

Address correspondence to: Dr. Christopher Alan Lewis, School of Psychology, University of Ulster at Magee College, Londonderry, Northern Ireland, UK, BT48 7JL. E-mail: ca.lewis@ ulster.ac.uk

Exercise for Article 31

Factual Questions

1. The 7-item short-form of the scale is intended to be a replacement for what?

2. Do "higher scores" *or* "lower scores" indicate a more positive attitude toward Christianity?

3. What is the value of Cronbach alpha (a measure of internal reliability) at Time 2 (i.e., the second administration)?

4. What is the value of the test–retest reliability coefficient?

5. Did the mean scores differ significantly from the first week to the second week?

Questions for Discussion

6. The researchers cite research that suggests that the Francis Scale is not affected by "social desirability." What is your understanding of the meaning of this term?

7. The researchers provide a sample question from the Francis Scale. How helpful is this to you in understanding what the scale measures? Explain. (See lines 42–43.)

8. Although participants recorded their names and age on the scale, they were assured of confidentiality. Is this important? Explain. (See lines 53–54.)

9. In your opinion, do the results reported in this study indicate that the Francis Scale has adequate test–retest reliability? Explain. (See lines 64–65.)

10. What is your understanding of the difference between "internal reliability" and "test–retest reliability"?

11. To what extent do you agree with the researchers that the generalizability of their findings is limited? (See lines 75–79.)

12. The researchers suggest that in future research it would be desirable to examine the stability of the scale "over longer testing periods." (See lines 82–85.) If your textbook addresses this issue, what time period(s) does it suggest as being suitable?

Quality Ratings

Directions: Indicate your level of agreement with each of the following statements by circling a number from 5 for strongly agree (SA) to 1 for strongly disagree (SD). If you believe an item is not applicable to this research article, leave it blank. Be prepared to explain your ratings. When responding to criteria A and B below, keep in mind that brief titles and abstracts are conventional in published research.

A. The title of the article is appropriate.

SA   5   4   3   2   1   SD

B. The abstract provides an effective overview of the research article.

SA   5   4   3   2   1   SD

C. The introduction establishes the importance of the study.

SA   5   4   3   2   1   SD

D. The literature review establishes the context for the study.

SA   5   4   3   2   1   SD

E. The research purpose, question, or hypothesis is clearly stated.

SA   5   4   3   2   1   SD

F. The method of sampling is sound.

SA   5   4   3   2   1   SD

G. Relevant demographics (for example, age, gender, and ethnicity) are described.

SA   5   4   3   2   1   SD

H. Measurement procedures are adequate.

SA   5   4   3   2   1   SD

I. All procedures have been described in sufficient detail to permit a replication of the study.

SA   5   4   3   2   1   SD

J. The participants have been adequately protected from potential harm.

SA   5   4   3   2   1   SD

K. The results are clearly described.

SA   5   4   3   2   1   SD

L. The discussion/conclusion is appropriate.

SA   5   4   3   2   1   SD

M. Despite any flaws, the report is worthy of publication.

SA   5   4   3   2   1   SD

Article 32

Cross-Informant Agreement of the Behavioral and Emotional Rating Scale-2nd Edition (BERS-2) Parent and Youth Rating Scales

LORI L. SYNHORST
University of Nebraska-Lincoln

JACQUELYN A. BUCKLEY
Johns Hopkins Bloomberg School of
Public Health

ROBERT REID
University of Nebraska-Lincoln

MICHAEL H. EPSTEIN
University of Nebraska-Lincoln

GAIL RYSER
PRO-ED

ABSTRACT. Behavior rating scales are important tools in the process of assessing students' emotional and behavioral needs. Best practices in behavioral assessment dictate that the perspectives of multiple informants (e.g., teacher, parent, youth) should be considered. Overall, agreement between multiple informants is modest at best and is especially low between adult and youth respondents. Low cross-informant agreement has primarily been determined with behavior rating scales that are deficit-based; the scales almost exclusively measure behavior deficits and pathologies. Recently developed strength-based instruments examine the students' behavioral and emotional strengths and competencies. Cross-informant agreement, however, has not been examined with most strength-based scales. The purpose of this study is to evaluate the cross-informant agreement between parents and youth on the Behavioral and Emotional Rating Scale-2 (BERS-2), a standardized instrument that assesses children's emotional and behavioral strengths. The results of this study suggest that the BERS-2 possesses moderate to high cross-informant agreement with coefficients ranging from .50 to .63.
From *Child & Family Behavior Therapy*, 27, 1–11. Copyright © 2005 by The Haworth Press, Inc. Reprinted with permission.

School professionals are faced with the challenge of effectively assessing and serving students with mental health needs, including students with emotional and behavioral disorders (EBD). Best practices in behav-
5   ioral assessment dictate that professionals use psychometrically sound instruments that will allow for multiple perspectives on a child's behavior. Information gathered from multiple contexts and environments is important; it provides a more holistic picture of the
10 youth because informants may interact differently with the youth, observe the youth in different contexts, and contribute unique and divergent perspectives on children's behavior (Phares, Compas, & Howell, 1989; Achenbach et al., 1987). Furthermore, multiple per-
15 spectives of children's behavior provide valuable in-

formation necessary to identify problems and plan interventions (Grills & Ollendick, 2003).

Behavioral rating scales are one of the most popular methods for gathering information from multiple in-
20 formants (e.g., teacher, parent, child) (Merrell, 2000). Agreement among multiple informants, referred to as cross-informant reliability, is frequently discussed in the mental health and educational literature. Cross-informant reliability refers to the extent to which rat-
25 ings from raters in different roles (e.g., parents, youth, teachers) agree. This is important because many behavior rating scales are designed to collect assessment information from multiple informants who may differ in their roles or the environments in which they interact
30 with students (e.g., home or school) (Myers & Winters, 2002). Evaluators attempt to collect and summarize information from a variety of informants across a variety of settings, and then consolidate that information to gain a more complete understanding of a child's behav-
35 ior. This can be problematic because unfortunately, rating scale results from multiple informants rarely agree.

Research has shown that agreement between different person's ratings of the child's behavior is modest at
40 best (McConaughy, Stanger, & Achenbach, 1992). Studies have suggested that multiple informant agreement is higher for externalizing versus internalizing behaviors (Costello & Edelbrock, 1985; Silverman & Eisen, 1992). Furthermore, agreement among infor-
45 mants with similar roles (e.g., teacher to teacher) is higher than agreement among informants with dissimilar roles (e.g., parent to teacher). For example, one of the most influential reports about cross-informant agreement came from a meta-analysis of 269 samples
50 in 119 studies conducted by Achenbach, McConaughy, and Howell (1987) that reported the correlations between ratings by parents, teachers, mental health workers, observers, peers, and self-reports. The average cross-informant reliability coefficients reported for

55 informants who played similar roles with respect to the children (e.g., two parents, two teachers) was .60 in contrast to .28 for different informants in different situations (e.g., parent and teachers).

60 When cross-informant agreement is further examined, higher levels of agreement are usually reached when comparing any adult dyads (e.g., parent and teacher) rather than youth-adult dyads. The lowest cross-informant agreement appears to be between youth self-report and adult reports (e.g., teachers, parents) of the student's behavior (Achenbach et al., 65 1987). The average reported cross-informant correlation (weighted *r)* was .28, with a range of .24 (parent and mental health worker) to .42 (teacher and observer). Youth self-report agreement with other informants was particularly low; correlations ranged from 70 .20 (self-report and teacher) to .27 (self-report and mental health worker). All correlations were significant, meaning that the correlations did not occur by chance, but the authors concluded that low correlations between youth self-reports and adult reports indicated 75 that youth self-reports are not providing the same data as adult informants, and therefore both perspectives are important.

Additional research on the standardization data for 80 the Achenbach scales indicated a similar pattern of low correlations between youth self-report and adult reports. When examining the total-problems items on Achenbach scales, average agreement between teacher and youth was .17, and .29 for caregiver and youth 85 pairs (Arnold & Jacobowitz, 1993). Research with adolescents further verified low agreement between youth and adults' agreement about levels of problems, with average correlations ranging from .07 to .24 (Younstrom, Loeber, & Stouthamer-Loeber, 2000). Further-90 more, researchers using the CBCL and YSR to examine race/ethnicity differences in inter-informant agreement in adolescents also found agreement between parents and student ranged from approximately .14 to .29 (Lau et al., in press).

95 Most of what is known about youth and adult cross-informant agreement comes from research on scales such as the CBCL, which is primarily deficit-based. In other words, the majority of information obtained is about a child's behavioral deficits, with minimal con-100 sideration of assessing strengths and competencies. Much less is known about cross-informant agreement on behavioral rating scales that are strength-based, whose primary purpose is to assess behavioral and emotional strengths and competencies. The last decade 105 has seen an increase in mental health and educational initiatives advocating the importance of documenting the strengths and resources of youth and families in treatment planning and outcomes measures (Epstein, Cullinan, Ryser, & Pearson, 2002). From a strength-110 based perspective, even children with the most challenging behaviors have strengths that can be identified and used to develop intervention or treatment plans that

build upon these strengths (Epstein, 1999; Provence, Erikson, Vater, & Palmeri, 1995). School personnel 115 need to be able to utilize strength-based assessments for screening, planning, and educational interventions around the positive behaviors and characteristics that are stable over time and witnessed across different observers (Epstein, Hertzog, & Reid, 2001).

120 The *Behavioral and Emotional Rating Scale* (BERS; Epstein & Sharma, 1998) was originally developed in response to the need for psychometrically sound strength-based measurement tools. Although the advancement of strength-based assessment tools is still 125 in developmental stages, the *Behavioral and Emotional Rating Scale* (BERS; Epstein & Sharma, 1998) emerged as a widely used standardized instrument designed specifically to assess children's emotional and behavioral strengths. The BERS was renormed in 130 2001–2002 to become more comprehensive by creating separate teacher and parent scales as well as a new youth self-report scale. It is unknown if higher agreement would occur between parents and youth on ratings of positive behaviors and competencies of students 135 rather than negative behaviors or deficits. Therefore, the purpose of this study was to determine the cross-informant agreement between youth self-report and parent report with the Behavioral and Emotional Rating Scale-2 (BERS-2).

Method

Participants

140 Participants were drawn from the BERS-2 normative sample. The BERS-2 Parent Rating Scale was normed on a sample of 927 persons in 34 states and Washington, DC; the Youth Rating Scale was normed on a sample of 1,301 youth in 30 states and Washing-145 ton, DC. The participants completed the BERS-2 between the fall of 2001 and the spring of 2002. To select a nationally representative sample, the following variables were considered during the recruitment process: geographic region (Northeast, Midwest, 150 South, West); Hispanic (Hispanic, non-Hispanic), and race (White, Black, Other). In order to obtain a distribution of BERS-2 data that was more proportional to the U.S. school-age population, the samples for the Parent and Youth Rating Scales were weighted based 155 on three sampling variables: race, Hispanic origin, and geographic region during normative development and data analyses. According to Salvia and Ysseldyke (2001), this procedure is an acceptable method to use to ensure that normative samples conform to popula-160 tion characteristics. These procedures resulted in nationally representative samples.

From the normative group, 296 matched sets of youth and parents' data were selected. All students were in general education programming, not receiving 165 any special education services. The youth ranged in age from 11–18, and the majority were female (50.3%). The ethnicity of the youth was as follows:

Caucasian (80.1%), African American (15.9%), and other (4.0%).

Instruments

170   The original BERS scale contains 52 items. These 52 items were included in the BERS-2 Parent Rating Scale. Parents rated the items on a 4-point Likert scale that ranges from 0 (not at all like my child) to 3 (very much like my child). Parents also answered 8
175 open-ended questions designed to target the child's academic, social, athletic, family, and community strengths. Parents can complete the BERS-2 in approximately 10 minutes. The scale provides an overall Strength Index, which is a single summary score of
180 strengths, and five subscales: Interpersonal strength (e.g., accepts criticism), Family involvement (e.g., complies with rules at home), Intrapersonal strength (e.g., is self-confident), School functioning (e.g., pays attention in class), and Affective strength (e.g., ac-
185 cepts a hug). The five subscales have a mean standard score of 10 and a standard deviation of 3. The sum of the five subscale standard scores is transformed into the Strength Index. The Strength Index has a mean of 100 and standard deviation of 15.

190   The BERS-2 Youth Rating Scale for ages 11–18 is a replica design of the parent scale instrument; however, the youth self-report includes minor wording changes to reflect the youth's perspective. For example, "Uses anger management skills" was changed to
195 "I use anger management skills." The 52 items on the Youth Rating Scale can also be completed in approximately 10 minutes. The scale has a reading level of approximately 5th grade.

Data Analysis

    Pearson product moment correlations for each
200 BERS-2 subscale and for the overall Strength Index were computed to assess the BERS-2 cross-informant reliability. To control for possible Type I error due to computing multiple correlations, an adjusted alpha level (two-tailed) was computed by dividing .05 by the
205 number of correlations computed resulting in an adjusted alpha level of .007. To determine whether there were differences between the scaled scores for the subscales and total Strength Index, we conducted paired samples t tests. Paired samples t tests were used be-
210 cause the participants were the youth who completed the youth self-report and the caregivers of those youth.

Results

    Standard score means and standard deviations for the parents' and youths' rating scales across the six subscales and the Strength Index are reported in Table
215 1. Parent and youth reported strengths fell within the average range on the BERS-2 Strength Index as well as all of the subscales. Correlations ranged from a low of .50 for the Intrapersonal Strength subscale to a high of .63 for the Interpersonal Strength subscale, with a cor-
220 relation of .54 for the Strength Index. All correlations

were significant. Consistent with the observed correlations, no significant difference between means was found for any of the subscales or the Total Strength Index across parent and youth informants.

Table 1
Means, Standard Deviations, and Agreement Correlations for the Parent and Youth BERS-2 Ratings Scales

BERS-2 subscale	Parent report		Youth self-report		
	M	*SD*	*M*	*SD*	*r*
Strength Index	97	18	99	16	.54
Interpersonal strength	10	3	10	3	.63
Family involvement	9	3	10	3	.59
Intrapersonal strength	10	3	10	3	.50
School functioning	10	3	10	3	.53
Affective strength	9	3	10	3	.50

Note. All correlations significant at $p < .007$.

Discussion

225   The purpose of this study is to evaluate the cross-informant agreement of parent and youth ratings of behavioral strengths with the Behavioral and Emotional Rating Scale-2. The results of this study suggest that the BERS-2 possesses good cross-informant
230 agreement between parents and youth, with agreement coefficients ranging from .50 to .63. These findings provide insight into the extent to which observers in different roles (i.e., parents and youth) agree in their perception of youth's positive behaviors; parents and
235 youth are providing fairly consistent reports of youth strengths and competencies.

    This study shows that agreement between parents and youth is higher than typically found with deficit-based measures. The majority of previous research on
240 scales such as the CBCL indicates that the typical range for parent and youth agreement is low (e.g., .17–.25). To further compound the disagreement, more depressed or stressed parents reported higher levels of behavior problems than did their children
245 (Younstrom, Loeber & Stouthamer-Loeber, 2000). The higher agreement between youth and parents on the BERS-2 scales may be due to the nature of the scale. For example, the BERS-2 scales ask informants to rate positive behaviors such as "smiles often" and
250 "enjoys a hobby" compared to the primarily deficit-based scales that ask informants to rate problems and pathologies. Informants may be more apt to agree about the presence or absence of positive rather than negative behaviors, or are at least more likely to en-
255 dorse the existence of positive behaviors.

    In addition, behavioral and emotional strengths may not necessarily be situationally specific. Strengths assessed with the BERS-2 may be more likely to be identified across different informants
260 across different settings. In contrast, negative externalizing and internalizing behaviors may be more situational specific and therefore would not be as easily identified across multiple informants.

Furthermore, youth may be less likely or less able to identify their individual problems and deficits, yet those deficits are identified by parents resulting in low parent-youth agreement about deficits. Youth may be more likely to identify their strengths and therefore agreement between parents and youth is higher.

Limitations and Future Research

There are general limitations to this study. First, the population included in the sample has limitations. The ratings obtained were primarily based on students in general education. The profile of strengths and competencies may differ for students in special education and therefore cross-informant agreement may be different. Also, the number of participants limited our ability to analyze the results based on demographic characteristics. For example, the sample was not ethnically diverse, and results may not generalize to students from other ethnicities. Using larger samples in future research would allow for such analyses.

Second, additional cross-informant agreement analyses need to be conducted. Although the results of this study indicate that cross-informant agreement between parents and youth with a strength-based scale is higher than with a deficit-based scale, it would be important to compare the parent-youth agreement on the BERS-2 with other parent and youth measures of behavioral and emotional strengths.

Agreement between additional informants should also be examined with the BERS-2. For example, agreement between teacher perceptions and youth perceptions should also be explored, as well as teacher and parent agreement with the BERS-2. Although youth-parent agreement on the BERS-2 was higher than youth-parent agreement with other deficit measures, it would be interesting to know if other BERS-2 cross-informant agreement results between teacher to youth and teacher to parent would be higher as well.

Furthermore, cross-informant agreement should be measured with both deficit and strength-based measures to determine the differences in agreement, using the same sample, on deficit-based and strength-based measures. When using the same sample, more direct comparisons can be made between the agreement on strength-based and deficit-based measures.

Implications for Clinical Services

The overall findings indicate that youth and parents are more likely to agree on a strength-based rather than deficit-based measure. Despite these promising results, assessment of the behavioral and emotional needs of youth continues to be a complex task of integrating multiple informants' reports. It should not be assumed that one informant's information is more valuable than another informant's, and therefore the collection of information from multiple informants across multiple settings is still highly encouraged. Rating scale results must always be complimented with additional informa-

tion such as interviews and observations that allow evaluators to obtain the most comprehensive picture of the behavioral and emotional strengths and needs of youth.

However, incorporating information from the BERS-2 offers an approach to behavioral assessment that empowers students and families by focusing on strengths. As with any instrument, the BERS-2 should not be the sole determining factor of whether a child qualifies for special services. However, the identification of strengths is an important part of the process. The BERS-2 can be used as an instrument to help identify children who may qualify for special support services. Furthermore, knowledge of a child's strengths will aid in service planning and delivery, development of Individual Education Plans (IEP), planning and evaluating interventions. The high cross-informant agreement strengthens the confidence with which practitioners can identify strengths for planning. Strength-based assessment has the potential to focus attention on the ways practitioners can support and foster students' strengths.

References

Achenbach, T. M., McConaughy, S.H., & Howell, C.T. (1987). Child/adolescent behavioral and emotional problems: Implications of cross-informant correlations for situational specificity. *Psychological Bulletin, 101,* 213–232.

Arnold, J., & Jacobowitz, D. (1993). The cross-informant program for the CBCL/4-18, YSR, and TRF (version 4.1) [DOS]. Burlington, VT: University Associates in Psychiatry.

Cohen, J. (1977). *Statistical power analysis for the behavioral sciences* (rev. ed.) New York: Academic Press.

Costello, E. J., & Edelbrock, C. S. (1985). Detection of psychiatric disorders in pediatric primary care: A preliminary report. *Journal of the American Academy of Child Psychiatry, 24,* 771–774.

Epstein, M. H. (1999). The development and validation of a scale to assess the emotional and behavioral strengths of children and adolescents. *Remedial and Special Education, 20,* 258–262.

Epstein, M. H., Cullinan, D., Ryser, G., & Pearson, N. (2002). Development of a scale to assess emotional disturbance. *Behavioral Disorders, 28,* 5–22.

Epstein, M. H., Hertzog, M. A., & Reid, R. (2001). The behavioral and emotional rating scale: Long term test–retest reliability. *Behavioral Disorders, 26,* 314–320.

Epstein, M. H., & Sharma, J. (1998). Behavioral and Emotional Rating Scale: A strengths-based approach to assessment. Austin, TX: PRO-ED.

Grills, A. E., & Ollendick, T. H. (2003). Multiple informant agreement and the anxiety disorders interview schedule for parents and children. *Journal of the American Academy of Child & Adolescent Psychiatry, 42,* 30–40.

Lau, A. S., Garland, A. F., Yeh, M., McCabe, K. M., Wood, P. A., & Hough, R. L. (in press). Race/Ethnicity and Inter-informant agreement in assessing adolescent psychopathology. *Journal of Emotional & Behavioral Disorders.*

McConaughy, S. H., Stanger, C., & Achenbach, T. M. (1992). Three-year course of behavioral/emotional problems in a national sample of 4- to 16-year-olds: I. Agreement among informants. *Journal of the American Academy of Child & Adolescent Psychiatry, 31,* 932–940.

Merrill, K. (2000). Informant reports: Theory and research in using child behavior rating sales in school settings. In E. Shapiro and T. Kratochwill (Eds.), *Behavioral assessment in schools (2nd ed.)* (pp. 233–256). New York: The Guilford Press.

Myers, K., & Winters, N. (2002). Ten-year review of rating scales: I. Overview of scale functioning, psychometric properties, and selection. (Research Update Review.) *Journal of the American Academy of Child & Adolescent Psychiatry, 41,* 114–122.

Phares, V., Compas, B., & Howell, D. (1989). Perspectives on child behavior problems: Comparisons of children's self-reports with parent and teacher reports. *Psychological Assessment: A Journal of Consulting and Clinical Psychology, 1,* 68–71.

Provence, S., Erikson, J., Vater, S., & Palmeri, S. (1995). *Infant-Toddler Development Assessment.* IDA. Chicago: Riverside Publishing.

Salvia, J., & Ysseldyke, J. (1998). Assessment (7th ed.). Boston: Houghton Mifflin.

Silverman, W. K., & Eisen, A. R. (1992). Age differences in the reliability of parent and child reports of child anxious symptomatology using a structured

Article 32   Cross-Informant Agreement of the Behavioral and Emotional Rating Scale-2nd Edition (BERS-2) Parent
and Youth Rating Scales

interview. *Journal of the American Academy of Child & Adolescent Psychiatry, 31,* 117–124.

Younstrom, E., Loeber, R., & Stouthamer-Loeber, M. (2000). Patterns and correlates of agreement between parent, teacher, and male adolescent ratings of externalizing and internalizing problems. *Journal of Consulting & Clinical Psychology, 68,* 1038–1050.

Acknowledgments: This research was supported in part by grants from the Center for Mental Health Services and U.S. Department of Education, Office of Special Education Programs. Opinions expressed do not necessarily reflect the position of the funding agencies and no endorsement should be inferred.

About the authors: *Lori L. Synhorst*, PhD, is assistant professor, Department of Special Education and Communication Disorders, University of Nebraska-Lincoln, Lincoln, NE. *Jacquelyn A. Buckley*, PhD, is postdoctoral research fellow, Prevention Research Center, Johns Hopkins Bloomberg School of Public Health, Baltimore, MD. *Robert Reid*, PhD, is professor, Department of Special Education and Communication Disorders, University of Nebraska-Lincoln, Lincoln, NE. *Michael H. Epstein*, PhD, is professor and co-director, Center for At-Risk Children's Services, University of Nebraska-Lincoln, Lincoln, NE. *Gail Ryser*, PhD, is assistant director of research, PRO-ED, Austin, TX.

Address correspondence to: Lori L. Synhorst, University of Nebraska-Lincoln, 247H Barkley Memorial Center, Lincoln, NE 68583. E-mail: lsynhorst2@unl.edu

Exercise for Article 32

Factual Questions

1. "Cross-informant" reliability refers to the extent to which what is true?

2. In the literature review, the researchers cite a meta-analysis which indicates which of the following?
   A. Cross-informant reliability tends to be higher for those with similar roles.
   B. Cross-informant reliability tends to be higher for those with different roles.

3. According to the literature review, is the BERS designed to assess children's "strengths" *or* "weaknesses"?

4. Were all correlations in the results section of this research report significant?

5. What is the value of the correlation coefficient for the agreement of parents and youth on the family involvement subscale?

6. Were any of the differences between the means for the parents and the means for youth in Table 1 significant?

Questions for Discussion

7. The normative sample from which the sample for this study was drawn is geographically diverse. In your opinion, is this an important strength of this study? Explain. (See lines 141–145.)

8. How informative is it to know that the scale has a reading level of approximately 5th grade? (See lines 197–198.)

9. The researchers mention "Type I error" in line 202. Do you know the meaning of this term? If so, define it.

10. In your opinion, do any of the correlation coefficients in Table 1 represent very strong relationships? Explain.

11. Do you agree with the researchers' statement that the BERS-2 possesses good cross-informant agreement between parents and youth? (See lines 228–231.)

12. If you had been planning this study, would you have expected to find nearly perfect agreement between parents and youth on the BERS-2? Explain.

Quality Ratings

Directions: Indicate your level of agreement with each of the following statements by circling a number from 5 for strongly agree (SA) to 1 for strongly disagree (SD). If you believe an item is not applicable to this research article, leave it blank. Be prepared to explain your ratings. When responding to criteria A and B below, keep in mind that brief titles and abstracts are conventional in published research.

A. The title of the article is appropriate.
SA   5   4   3   2   1   SD

B. The abstract provides an effective overview of the research article.
SA   5   4   3   2   1   SD

C. The introduction establishes the importance of the study.
SA   5   4   3   2   1   SD

D. The literature review establishes the context for the study.
SA   5   4   3   2   1   SD

E. The research purpose, question, or hypothesis is clearly stated.
SA   5   4   3   2   1   SD

158

F. The method of sampling is sound.

        SA   5   4   3   2   1   SD

G. Relevant demographics (for example, age, gender, and ethnicity) are described.

        SA   5   4   3   2   1   SD

H. Measurement procedures are adequate.

        SA   5   4   3   2   1   SD

I. All procedures have been described in sufficient detail to permit a replication of the study.

        SA   5   4   3   2   1   SD

J. The participants have been adequately protected from potential harm.

        SA   5   4   3   2   1   SD

K. The results are clearly described.

        SA   5   4   3   2   1   SD

L. The discussion/conclusion is appropriate.

        SA   5   4   3   2   1   SD

M. Despite any flaws, the report is worthy of publication.

        SA   5   4   3   2   1   SD

Article 33

Reliability and Validity of the Wender Utah Rating Scale for College Students

MICHAEL WIERZBICKI

Marquette University

SUMMARY. The Wender Utah Rating Scale was developed to assess adults' retrospective account of the childhood occurrence of symptoms associated with attention-deficit/hyperactivity disorder (ADHD). As little work has focused on psychometric properties of the scale for college students, it was administered to 111 college students. Because college students with ADHD experience more symptoms of depression than other students, three measures of mood-related symptoms were also administered. One month later, the Wender scale and the Beck Depression Inventory were readministered to 67 participants. On both occasions, the Wender scale had high internal consistency ($r \geq .87$) and was modestly but significantly correlated with measures of mood disorder symptoms (rs ranging from .33 to .47). The scale had high test–retest reliability ($r = .68$). These results support its use as a component of assessment of ADHD in college students.

From *Psychological Reports*, 96, 833–839. Copyright © 2005 by Psychological Reports. Reprinted with permission.

Psychological research has shown that children with attention-deficit/hyperactivity disorder (ADHD) often continue to experience problems associated with impulsivity and inattentiveness in adulthood.[19,20] This

5 has led to an increased interest in the assessment and treatment of ADHD of adults.[13] The assessment of ADHD in adults, however, is complicated by the fact that diagnostic criteria for ADHD require that symptoms be present and cause problems in adaptive func-

10 tioning by age seven years.[1] If school records or psychological evaluations from the client's childhood are not available, then clinicians must rely on retrospective accounts of childhood problems.

Wender and his colleagues[18] developed the Wender

15 Utah Rating Scale (WURS) as an aid in the retrospective assessment of the childhood occurrence of ADHD symptoms. Wender and others have reported the scale has good internal consistency and test–retest reliability.[17,18] In addition, several studies have shown that the

20 scale is valid in that it successfully distinguishes between ADHD adults and both patient and nonpatient groups.[16,18,21]

Although attention to adults with ADHD has increased, there remains a need for research on ADHD in

25 young adults, including college students.[20] Although individuals with ADHD continue to experience academic difficulties throughout adolescence and adulthood,[19] at least some of them are successful to the extent that they attend and complete college. Several re-

30 cent studies have examined ADHD in college students. Self-reported symptoms distinguished between college students with and without prior diagnoses of ADHD.[14] Psychometric properties of self- and parent-report scales of ADHD-related behaviors of college students

35 have been discussed in detail.[7] Also, both sex and national differences in ADHD symptoms in college students have been studied.[5] This research with college students is important for several reasons. Some college students who are experiencing academic difficulty may

40 have as-of-yet undiagnosed cases of ADHD.[23] In addition, college students who have ADHD and other types of learning disabilities report higher severity of depressive symptoms than other college students.[12]

It is unclear whether the norms reported for the

45 general adult population apply to college students. Only a small number of studies to date have examined the Wender scale in college students. Internal consistency and 1-mo. test–retest reliability in a sample of 83 college students are adequate.[15] Italian and Spanish

50 versions of the test have good reliability and at least moderate validity.[6,10] In the largest study to date using the scale with college students, internal consistency and 2-wk. test–retest reliabilities plus moderate validity in terms of its correlation with self-reported ADHD

55 symptoms in adulthood have been reported.[22] Still, there remains a need for continuing research on the Wender scale with college students, both to document its psychometric characteristics and to evaluate its usefulness as an aid to the assessment of ADHD.

60 This study evaluated the reliability and validity of the Wender scale in a sample of college students. Students were administered the test and three measures of depressive symptoms. One month later, a subsample was readministered the scale and one measure of de-

65 pressive symptoms. The internal consistency, test–retest reliability, and validity in terms of correlations to measures of depressive symptoms were examined.

Method

Participants were 111 students enrolled in introductory psychology courses at a private university in a midwestern city. They volunteered to participate in research as one means of obtaining additional course credit. Participants included 24 men and 86 women (and one participant who did not respond to the question regarding sex) and ranged in age from 18 to 24 years (M = 19.4, SD = 1.3). The greater number of female participants was likely due to their greater representation (about 60%) on the class rosters.

Participants completed a questionnaire battery in groups of about 25 people. The questionnaire battery included the Wender scale, the Beck Depression Inventory,[2] the mood-related events of the Unpleasant Events Schedule,[11] and the Automatic Thoughts Questionnaire.[9] Completion of these measures required about 45 minutes. Four weeks later, participants were invited to attend a second 20-min. session. At this session, participants completed the Wender scale and the Beck Depression Inventory in groups of 15 to 20 people. Sixty-seven of the original 111 participants responded to this invitation and completed the second set of measures.

The Wender scale assesses childhood symptoms associated with ADHD (e.g., concentration problems, being easily distracted). It consists of 61 items that are rated on a 5-point scale with anchors of 1 = "Not at all or very slightly" and 5 = "Very much." The scale has good reliability for adults.[18] In addition, Ward, et al.[18] described a 25-item form, which includes these items, which most strongly discriminated between adults with and without the diagnosis of ADHD. Throughout the rest of this paper, the original version of the scale is referred to as the WURS-61, and the 25-item version of the test is termed the WURS-25.

Stein, et al.[17] used factor analysis to identify five factors of the WURS-61 for men: Conduct Problems (10 items), Learning Problems (7 items), Stress Intolerance (9 items), Attention Problems (7 items), and Poor Social Skills (9 items). Stein, et al. also used factor analysis to derive five factors of the WURS-61 for women: Dysphoria (10 items), Impulsive (10 items), Learning Problems (7 items), Attention Problems (8 items), and Unpopular (4 items). Stein, et al. stated that, in a population of adults referred to a specialty clinic for evaluation of ADHD, these 10 subscales have adequate internal consistency (rs > .69) and test–retest reliability over a 1-mo. interval (rs > .70).

Three measures of depressive symptoms were administered because college students with ADHD and other learning problems report more severe depressive symptoms than other students[12] and because dysphoria has been an important factor in ADHD symptoms.[17] These measures are commonly used by psychologists to assess depressive symptomatology.

The Beck Depression Inventory has 21 items, each concerning a symptom of depression that is rated for severity. Estimates for this measure have indicated it is reliable and valid for mild and moderate depression with non-patient and outpatient groups.[3]

The mood-related items of the Unpleasant Events Schedule are 36 unpleasant activities that Lewinsohn and Amenson[11] found most strongly associated with depressed mood. Participants rate each activity on a 3-point scale for Frequency and Unpleasantness; the cross-product of the frequency and unpleasantness ratings forms a Total Unpleasantness score. Lewinsohn and Amenson reported that this measure is reliable, even over a 2-yr. period, and is sensitive to changes in mood. Here, only the Total Unpleasantness score is reported.

The Automatic Thoughts Questionnaire has 30 items, each consisting of a negative thought that commonly occurs during depression and is rated for its frequency during the previous week (e.g., "I feel like I'm up against the world."). The scale has substantial reliability and validity in terms of its association with symptoms of depression.[4,8]

Results

Preliminary analyses were conducted to assess sex differences on the Wender scale. Univariate analyses of variance showed that, at Time 1, men and women did not differ on either the WURS-61 ($F_{1,108}$ = 3.10, ns) or the WURS-25 ($F_{1,108}$ = 1.33, ns). For this reason, data for men and women were combined throughout the remaining analyses. Means and standard deviations for men and women on both forms at Time 1 are in Table 1. A second analysis was conducted to compare participants who did and did not attend the second session, to assess whether they were comparable. Analyses of variance showed that the two groups did not differ significantly on the demographic variables of age, sex (coded as 1 = male, 2 = female), and year in school. This indicated that the two groups were comparable in demographic characteristics.

Table 1
Means and Standard Deviations of Men and Women on Two Forms of the Wender Utah Rating Scale

Form	Men (n = 24)		Women (n = 86)	
	M	SD	M	SD
WURS-61	67.8	21.8	59.2	21.2
WURS-25	28.0	13.2	24.7	12.2

Reliability of the Wender scale was examined in two ways. First, internal consistency was calculated for both forms of the test at Times 1 and 2. At Times 1 (n = 110) and 2 (n = 67), the coefficient alpha for the WURS-61 was .87 and .89, respectively; for the WURS-25, the coefficient alpha was .89 and .91, respectively. To estimate 1-mo. test–retest reliability, Pearson product-moment correlation coefficients were calculated between Times 1 and 2 for the total scores of the two forms and for the five WURS-61 subscales for the men and five subscales for the women of the

Table 2

One-Month Test–Retest Reliability Coefficients for Wender Utah Rating Scale: Total Score and Subscale Scores

Test	r	Subscale			
		For Men ($n = 15$)		For Women ($n = 51$)	
WURS-25 Total Score	.62[†]	Conduct Problems	.77[†]	Dysphoria	.53[†]
WURS-61 Total Score	.68[†]	Learning Problems	.64[†]	Impulsive	.47[†]
		Stress Intolerance	.84[†]	Learning Problems	.72[†]
		Attention Problems	.86[†]	Attention Problems	.67[†]
		Poor Social Skills	.53[*]	Unpopular	.56[†]

*$p < .05$. [†]$p < .01$.

Table 3

Pearson Correlations between Wender Utah Rating Scale and Measures of Depression

Measure	Time 1			Time 2		
	WURS-25 ($n = 111$)	WURS-61 ($n = 111$)	Dysphoria ($n = 86$)	WURS-25 ($n = 67$)	WURS-61 ($n = 67$)	Dysphoria ($n = 51$)
Beck Depression Inventory	.38[†]	.33[†]	.42[*]	.45[†]	.42[†]	.35[†]
Automatic Thoughts Questionnaire	.43[†]	.43[†]	.55[*]			
Unpleasant Events Schedule[a]	.44[†]	.47[†]	.49[*]			

[a]Total Unpleasantness score. *$p < .05$. [†]$p < .01$.

WURS-61. These test–retest correlation coefficients are presented in Table 2. Test-retest reliability coefficients for the WURS-61 ($r = .68$) and WURS-25 ($r = .62$) were significantly different from zero. In addition, test–retest reliability coefficients for the five subscales for the men and the five subscales for the women were also significant ($rs > .47$).

The construct validity of the Wender Utah Rating Scale was estimated by calculating the correlations between the two forms of the scale and the measures of depressive symptoms at Times 1 and 2. These correlations are presented in Table 3. The Wender scale was moderately but statistically significantly correlated with depressive symptoms (rs ranging from .33 to .47, $p < .01$). The correlations between scores on the Dysphoria subscale and on the measures of depressive symptoms at Times 1 and 2 were also calculated. These correlations, which ranged from .35 to .55 and appear in Table 3, were significant.

Discussion

This study investigated the Wender Utah Rating Scale for a college student population. It found that the scale has high internal consistency and test–retest reliability over a 1-mo. interval. This was true both for the total scores of its two forms, as well as for the five subscales for male subjects and five subscales for female subjects as developed by Stein, et al.[17] These findings are consistent with those of Wender and others, who have reported that the Wender scale has good reliability within the general adult population.[17,18] In addition, these findings are also consistent with the results of several studies that have shown that it has adequate reliability in college student populations.[6,10,15,22] Thus, research to date has supported its reliability in populations of both general adults and college students.

This study also showed that the scale has at least moderate construct validity, in that it is related to depressive symptoms commonly experienced by adults with ADHD. It is important to recognize that this study examined the relationship between scores on the Wender scale and three measures of depressive symptoms. Because ADHD and depressive symptoms represent distinct constructs, this study does not directly support the criterion-related validity of the Wender scale. However, because college students with ADHD report more depressive symptoms than other students[12] and because dysphoric mood represents a factor in the symptoms of ADHD for women,[17] it should be expected that high scores on the Wender scale would be correlated with higher reports of depressive symptoms. In this way, this study can be viewed as supporting the construct validity of attentional problems as assessed by the scale.

Researchers should continue to explore methods for evaluating ADHD in college students. Because the diagnosis of ADHD requires evidence that the client experienced problems in functioning due to attentional difficulties prior to age seven years, clinicians must seek information concerning the client's childhood functioning. When school and psychological records from the client's childhood are not available or do not clearly address the issue of attentional symptoms, then the clinician must rely on retrospective accounts of the client or others, such as the client's parents. Still, such retrospective accounts may be inaccurate, both due to memory gaps[20] and to possible bias given that the client and the parents are aware of the client's adult functioning. Despite the limitations of retrospective accounts, the Wender Utah Rating Scale appears to be a useful method of assessing childhood attentional symptoms in adults, including college students.

240

References

1. American Psychiatric Association. (2000). *Diagnostic and statistical manual of mental disorders.* (4th ed., Text Rev.) Washington, DC: American Psychiatric Association.
2. Beck, A. T., Rush, A. J., Shaw, B. F., & Emery, G. (1979). *Cognitive therapy of depression.* New York: Guilford.
3. Beck, A. T., Steer, R. A., & Garbin, M. G. (1988). Psychometric properties of the Beck Depression Inventory: Twenty-five years of evaluation. *Clinical Psychology Review, 8,* 77–100.
4. Dobson, K. S., & Breiter, H. J. (1983). Cognitive assessment of depression: Reliability and validity of three measures. *Journal of Abnormal Psychology, 92,* 108–109.
5. DuPaul, G. J., Shaughency, E. A., Weyandt, L. L., Tripp, G., Kiesner, J., Ota, K., & Stanish, H. (2001). Self-report of ADHD symptoms in university students: Cross-gender and cross-national prevalence. *Journal of Learning Disabilities, 34,* 370–379.
6. Fossati, A., Di Ceglie, A., Acquarini, E., Donati, D., Donini, M., Novella, L., & Maffei, C. (2001). The retrospective assessment of childhood attention deficit hyperactivity disorder in adults: Reliability and validity of the Italian version of the Wender Utah Rating Scale. *Comprehensive Psychiatry, 42,* 326–336.
7. Glutting, J. J., Monaghan, M. C., Adams, W., & Sheslow, D. (2002). Some psychometric properties of a system to measure ADHD among college students: Factor pattern, reliability, and one-year predictive validity. *Measurement and Evaluation in Counseling and Development, 34,* 194–209.
8. Harrell, H. H., & Ryon, N. B. (1983). Cognitive-behavioral assessment of depression: Clinical validation of the Automatic Thoughts Questionnaire. *Journal of Consulting and Clinical Psychology, 51,* 721–725.
9. Hollon, S. D., & Kendall, P. C. (1980). Cognitive self-statements in depression: Development of an automatic thoughts questionnaire. *Cognitive Therapy and Research, 4,* 383–395.
10. Lara-Munoz, C., Herrera-Garcia, S., Romero-Ogawa, T., Torija, L., & Garcia, M. L. (1998). Caracteristicas psicometricas de la escala de evaluacion retrospectiva del trastorno por deficit de atencion e hiperactividad Wender-Utah en espanol. *Actas Luso-espanolas de Neurologia, Psiquiatria y Ciencia Alines, 26,* 165–171.
11. Lewinsohn, P. M., & Amenson, L. S. (1978). Some relations between pleasant and unpleasant mood-related events and depression. *Journal of Abnormal Psychology, 87,* 644–654.
12. Mattek, W, & Wierzbicki, M. (1998). Cognitive and behavioral correlates of depression in learning disabled and nonlearning disabled adult students. *Journal of Clinical Psychology, 54,* 831–837.
13. Nadeau, K. G. (Ed.) (1995). *A comprehensive guide to attention deficit disorder in adults: research, diagnosis, and treatment.* New York: Brunner/Mazel.
14. O'Donnell, J. P., McCann, K. K., & Pluth, S. (2001). Assessing adult ADHD using a self-report symptom checklist. *Psychological Reports, 88,* 871–881.
15. Rossini, E. D., & O'Connor, M. A. (1995). Retrospective self-reported symptoms of attention-deficit hyperactivity disorder: reliability of the Wender Utah Rating Scale. *Psychological Reports, 77,* 751–754.
16. Stein, M. A., Fischer, M., & Szumowski, E. (1999). Evaluation of adults for ADHD. *Journal of the American Academy of Child and Adolescent Psychiatry, 38,* 940–941.
17. Stein, M. A., Sandoval, R., Szumowski, E., Roizen, N., Reinecke, M. A., Blondis, T. A., & Klein, Z. (1995). Psychometric characteristics of the Wender Utah Rating Scale (WURS): Reliability and factor structure for men and women. *Psychopharmacology Bulletin, 31,* 425–433.
18. Ward, M. F., Wender, P. H., & Reimherr, F. W. (1993). The Wender Utah Rating Scale: An aid in the retrospective diagnosis of childhood attention deficit hyperactivity disorder. *American Journal of Psychiatry, 150,* 885–890.
19. Weiss, G., & Hechtman, L. T. (1986). *Hyperactive children grown up: empirical findings and theoretical considerations.* New York: Guilford.
20. Wender, P. H. (1995). *Attention-deficit hyperactivity disorder in adults.* New York: Oxford Univer. Press.
21. Wender, P. H., Ward, M. F., Reimherr, F. W., & Marchant, B. K. (2000). ADHD in adults. *Journal of the American Academy of Child and Adolescent Psychiatry, 39,* 543.
22. Weyandt, L. L., Linterman, I., & Rice, J. A. (1995). Reported prevalence of attentional difficulties in a general sample of college students. *Journal of Psychopathology and Behavioral Assessment, 17,* 293–304.
23. Wierzbicki, M. (2002). The occurrence of LD and ADHD in college students referred for evaluation of academic problems. Poster session presented at the annual meeting of the Midwestern Psychological Association, Chicago, IL, May.

Acknowledgment: The author thanks Scott Langenecker for his assistance in collecting the data reported in this paper.

Address correspondence to: Michael Wierzbicki, Department of Psychology, Marquette University, Milwaukee, WI 53201-1881. E-mail: michael.wierzbicki@marquette.edu

Exercise for Article 33

Factual Questions

1. The students in this study volunteered to participate in order to obtain what?

2. After the first session, how many weeks later were the participants invited to attend a second session?

3. The WURS-25 contains 25 items from the WURS-61, which contains 61 items. On what basis were the 25 items selected?

4. On the WURS-61, did men or women have a higher mean score? Is the difference between the means for men and women statistically significant?

5. For women, which WURS subscale has the highest test–retest reliability coefficient?

Questions for Discussion

6. Many of the participants who attended Time 1 failed to attend Time 2. In your opinion, how important is it to know that those who did and those who did not attend at Time 2 were similar in their demographics? Explain. (See lines 154–161.)

7. Values of coefficient alpha are reported in lines 164–168. What is your understanding of what these coefficients indicate?

8. In lines 174–176 and in Table 2, the values of the test–retest reliability coefficients for total scores are reported (i.e., .62 and .68). Based on your knowledge of reliability, do these coefficients indicate satisfactory test–retest reliability? Explain.

9. Examine the correlation coefficients in Table 3, all of which are statistically significant. In your opinion, do they all represent very strong relationships? Explain.

10. The researcher uses the term "construct validity" in lines 180, 208, and 223. What is your understanding of the meaning of this term?

11. To what extent has this study convinced you that the WURS has adequate reliability and validity for use with college students?

Quality Ratings

Directions: Indicate your level of agreement with each of the following statements by circling a number from 5 for strongly agree (SA) to 1 for strongly disagree (SD). If you believe an item is not applicable to this research article, leave it blank. Be prepared to explain your ratings. When responding to criteria A and B below, keep in mind that brief titles and abstracts are conventional in published research.

A. The title of the article is appropriate.

SA 5 4 3 2 1 SD

B. The abstract provides an effective overview of the research article.

SA 5 4 3 2 1 SD

C. The introduction establishes the importance of the study.

SA 5 4 3 2 1 SD

D. The literature review establishes the context for the study.

SA 5 4 3 2 1 SD

E. The research purpose, question, or hypothesis is clearly stated.

SA 5 4 3 2 1 SD

F. The method of sampling is sound.

SA 5 4 3 2 1 SD

G. Relevant demographics (for example, age, gender, and ethnicity) are described.

SA 5 4 3 2 1 SD

H. Measurement procedures are adequate.

SA 5 4 3 2 1 SD

I. All procedures have been described in sufficient detail to permit a replication of the study.

SA 5 4 3 2 1 SD

J. The participants have been adequately protected from potential harm.

SA 5 4 3 2 1 SD

K. The results are clearly described.

SA 5 4 3 2 1 SD

L. The discussion/conclusion is appropriate.

SA 5 4 3 2 1 SD

M. Despite any flaws, the report is worthy of publication.

SA 5 4 3 2 1 SD

Article 34

Sex Differences in Portuguese Lonely Hearts Advertisements

Universidade do Porto, Portugal

ABSTRACT. Advertisements from "Lonely Hearts" columns in the major daily Portuguese newspaper (*Jornal de Notícias*) were used to test hypotheses about the mate preferences of men and women. A total of 484 advertisements were coded for demographic descriptors and offers of and appeals for attractiveness, financial security, sincerity, expressiveness, and instrumentality (e.g., intelligence and ambition). Some results supported social exchange and evolutionary predictions: men sought younger women and offered security; women sought older men with status and resources. However, other results challenged such predictions: attractiveness and expressiveness did not differ by sex.

From *Perceptual and Motor Skills, 101*, 393–400. Copyright © 2005 by Perceptual and Motor Skills. Reprinted with permission.

Research on mate preferences has typically relied on one of two sources of data, self-report of preferences (Buss, 1989; Sprecher, Sullivan, & Hatfield, 1994) or the attributes requested in personal advertisements (Harrison & Saeed, 1977; Deaux & Hanna, 1984). Lynn and Bolig (1985) have suggested that personal advertisements can be an excellent source of data for social science research. They noted that personal advertisements have at least three positive features to recommend them: (1) subjects are not aware that they are being studied; (2) the consequences of placing personal advertisements are more representative of naturalistic settings than are the consequences of the typical interpersonal behavior in laboratory settings; (3) personal advertisers better represent the population at large on many dimensions than do college subjects used in typical laboratory experiments. However, advertisers probably also differ from the general population (Goodwin, 1990). Probably advertisers lack social support networks which are usually used to find mates, with the result that advertisers must use impersonal means.

Personal advertisements contain information about the supposedly attractive traits of the advertiser (offered traits) and also about traits that the advertiser is looking for in a potential partner (sought traits). The likelihood that particular attributes such as physical attractiveness, resources, commitment, or social skills will be mentioned depends strongly on the sex of the advertisers (Kenrick, Groth, Trost, & Sadalla, 1993; Waynforth & Dunbar, 1995). This research has been expanded over the years to compare the advertisements of heterosexuals and homosexuals (Gonzales & Meyers, 1993), with the general finding that sex seems to predict the characteristics of these advertisements better than sexual orientation does.

Most research about sex differences in personal advertisements has addressed hypotheses based on social exchange theory (e.g., Deaux & Hanna, 1984; Hirschman, 1987) and evolutionary theory (e.g., Kenrick, et al., 1993; Waynforth & Dunbar, 1995). For Rajecki, Bledsoe, and Rasmussen (1991), the essential contrast between these two theoretical orientations is the emphasis they place on proximal (social) or distal (evolutionary) factors. However, it is thought that the orientations are not necessarily incompatible (Kenrick, et al., 1993).

Social exchange models suggest that individuals seek the "best value" they can achieve in a mate. Each individual is assumed to carry an approximate "market value," depending on the extent to which the person possesses valued traits such as beauty, intelligence, wealth, and social status. It is assumed that, if every individual seeks the best value in a mate, individuals of approximately equal value will tend to pair up (Murstein, 1986). Cameron, Oskamp, and Sparks (1977) described advertisements by single persons as depicting a "heterosexual stock market" and noted that "the ads in this paper read a little bit like the ask-bid columns of the New York Stock Exchange. Potential partners seek to strike bargains which maximize their rewards in the exchange of assets" (Cameron, et al., 1977, p. 28). Harrison and Saeed (1977) found evidence of exchange across certain characteristics: men were more likely to offer financial security and seek attractiveness and a younger partner, whereas women were more likely to offer attractiveness and seek financial security and an older partner. Deaux and Hanna (1984) reported that men seek physical attractiveness and offer financial security, whereas women offer physical attractiveness and seek financial security. Also, Koestner and Wheeler (1988) found men offered expressive traits (traditionally feminine traits; e.g., caring and affection) and sought instrumental traits (traditionally masculine traits; e.g., intelligence and ambition), whereas women's advertisements showed the reverse pattern. Why are advertisers portraying themselves counter to traditional sex-role stereotypes? Koestner and Wheeler suggested two explanations. First, they speculated that their sample of advertisements was biased toward nontraditional individuals. Second, they suggested that this occurred due to the advertisers' awareness of what to do to attract a partner. In other words, men assumed that women would be attracted to them if they had expressive traits, and women assumed that men would be attracted to them if they had instrumental traits.

Social evolutionary models focus on a different level of historical analysis (Kenrick et al., 1993). However, they share several basic assumptions with the social exchange models, such as resource exchange as a basis for courtship, and envision a more or less selfish individual acting in ways designed to maximize personal gain from a relationship. Social evolutionary models, instead of focusing on the exchange of socially defined rewards, view individuals as acting on evolved mechanisms that were selected because they helped maximize our ancestors' genetic fitness.

Because women have a shorter reproductive life span than men, men are therefore attracted to women primarily by visual cues such as youth and physical attractiveness that signal the capacity to reproduce, and women seek nonappearance-related factors such as financial strength and group occupation that maximize the survival prospects of their children (Feingold, 1992). As predicted by the evolutionary hypothesis, women report physical attractiveness to be less important to them than do men, and they value socioeconomic status more than men. Because the character (sincerity, honesty) of men has import for the survival of their mate's offspring, women should seek these characteristics more than do men.

Thus, the contents of personal advertisements have been extensively examined for sex differences, mainly in the United States. The present study is in line with the observations of Cicerello and Sheehan (1995, p. 756) that "future research should investigate whether evidence of exchange across attractiveness, financial security, and age desired in a partner may be limited to American culture."

The present study may be seen as a replication of earlier research, using a Portuguese setting and thus contributes to the cross-cultural scope of such analyses. During the 1970s and 1980s, Portugal, like most developed countries, experienced substantial increases in the proportion of women in the workplace. In 2000, the female employment rate was 44.9% (Instituto Nacional de Estatística, 2001). In the context of the European Union, Portugal is one of the countries with the highest female employment rate. The Government increased legislation to prohibit sex discrimination and appointed Comissão para a Igualdade e Direitos da Mulher (CIDM) whose office constitutes the governmental mechanism to supervise equality of opportunities and of rights. Surveys of family roles indicate some shifts in the patterns of division of household labor. In 1997/98, women constituted 56% of the students enrolled in college education. In sum, in recent decades, Portugal, a small Catholic European nation, has experienced ideological, political, and economic pressures concerning sex roles similar to those of other Western nations (Neto & Pinto, 1998). Our specific hypotheses, which are based on a consideration of social exchange theory, evolutionary theory, and previous research on the differences about the mate preferences of men and women, were (H_1) Women will be more likely to offer attractiveness, and men will be more likely to seek attractiveness. (H_2) Women will be more likely to seek financial security, while men will be more likely to offer financial security. (H_3) Women will be more likely to seek sincerity, while men will be more likely to offer sincerity. (H_4) Women will be more likely to seek expressive traits, while men will be more likely to offer expressive traits. (H_5) Women will be more likely to offer instrumental traits, while men will be more likely to seek instrumental traits. (H_6) Men will be more likely to seek younger women, whereas women will be more likely to seek older men.

Method

Advertisements

Personal advertisements were drawn from the major national newspaper, *Jornal de Notícias*. Several decision rules were established in the selection of the advertisements for the sample. The advertisement had to specify both the sex of the advertiser and the sex of the person sought. Advertisements in which the advertisers specified they were looking for a same-sex dating partner were excluded from the sample. Advertisements placed by foreigners seeking a Portuguese mate were excluded from our analysis. This was partly because we wanted to focus only on the Portuguese mate-seekers and partly because of the small number of such advertisements. Advertisements were closely examined to ensure that these were not reruns, although it was impossible to control for the possibility of rewrites.

All advertisements placed by women throughout the year 2000 in the *Jornal de Notícias* personal sections from Saturday and Sunday were selected for study. Women placed a total of 242 advertisements. The same number of advertisements placed by men was selected, using a random number table. Thus, a total 484 advertisements were coded. The attempt to sample through the calendar year was made, in an effort to avoid any unspecified seasonal effect.

Procedure

Offers and requests were analyzed in terms of the following coding categories, selected on the basis of

Table 1

Number and Percentage of Advertisers Who Offered and Solicited Characteristics in Each of the Content Categories (n = 242)

Advertisement content	Men		Women		χ^2	df
	n	%	n	%		
Attractiveness offer	59	24.4	54	22.3	0.29	1
Attractiveness appeal	36	14.9	26	10.7	1.8	1
Security offer	88	36.4	49	20.2	15.5†	1
Security appeal	6	2.5	55	22.7	45.0†	1
Sincerity offer	135	55.8	127	52.5	0.53	1
Sincerity appeal	46	19.0	81	33.5	13.1†	1
Expressiveness offer	69	33.5	64	26.4	0.26	1
Expressiveness appeal	53	21.9	41	16.9	1.9	1
Instrumental offer	51	21.1	73	30.2	5.4	1
Instrumental appeal	35	14.5	76	31.4	19.7†	1
Age						
Older sought	7	6.3	73	80.2	135.4†	2
Same age	23	20.7	18	19.9		2
Younger sought	81	73.0	0	0.0		2

†$p < .001$.

185 previous research (Harrison & Saeed, 1977; Deaux & Hanna, 1984; Koestner & Wheeler, 1988): attractiveness (good-looking, cute), financial security (independent, professional), sincerity (honest, loyal), expressiveness (caring, loving), and instrumentality (active, competent). 190 Criteria for inclusion were strict. A master list of all words subsumed by any given category was compiled, and advertisement contents were compared with the master list. This list was initially based on classifications used in previous research. However, the 195 list was also in part empirically derived. During the rater's training period, some words not in the original master list were added to yield a final list of words encompassed by any given category. When mentioned, the following demographic characteristics pertaining to 200 each advertiser were also recorded: age, sex, marital status, race, and religion.

The same rater coded all advertisements. The rater was trained in the use of coding criteria and was required to meet high standards of reliability prior to 205 coding. In addition, 10% of the coded advertisements were randomly selected and coded independently by a second rater, with resultant kappas varying between .91 and 1.00.

Results

The age distributions of male and female advertisers 210 were similar ($\chi_4^2 = 2.1$, *ns*) for the five age groups: 20 to 29, 30 to 39, 40 to 49, 50 to 59, and 60 yr. and above. These age groups included 10.1%, 23.7%, 25.4%, 25.4%, and 15.4% of the male advertisers, respectively, and 10.5%, 21.7%, 32.2%, 23.0%, and 215 12.5% of the female advertisers. One hundred and sixty-three cases (33.7%) counted as missing data in that the age was not specified or was vague. Forty-seven percent indicated their marital status, single advertisers being 27.8%, married 3.1%, divorced 39.2%, 220 widowed 24.7%, and separated 5.3%. None of the advertisers described themselves as being nonwhite. A small number (1.4%) stated their religion as Christian. No other religion was mentioned.

Table 1 shows the number and percentage of male 225 and female advertisers who made an offer or request for at least one characteristic in each of the content categories. The chi-square analyses indicate that men more often than women offered their financial security. Women, on the other hand, were more likely to seek 230 financial security, sincerity, and instrumental characteristics. Also, women were more likely to offer instrumental characteristics, those traits generally characteristic of men. The results indicated that the attractiveness and the expressiveness categories were not sig- 235 nificantly associated with sex. Men were more likely to seek younger women, whereas women were more likely to seek older men.

Discussion

In personal advertisements, advertisers describe themselves as potential partners in a relationship and 240 frequently describe their "ideal" man or woman. The contents of these advertisements are not randomly generated: men and women use systematic strategies to manage an impression and attract desirable others. Although it cannot be claimed that people who advertise 245 in the personal section of a selected newspaper are representative of the population at large, they do provide one perspective on the issues of sex in this society. Although this study and previous research provide support for exchange and evolutionary theories, this pic- 250 ture is more complicated than is first apparent. In fact, in this study men and women indicated that not always do women in general differ from men in terms of the advertisements they write.

From the perspective of social theories of mate 255 preferences, some expectations are that women, who as a class are more likely to be excluded from social power, would seek mates with access to such resources and would offer their physical characteristics in return. For men, the quality of the exchange object would be at premium, so they would seek physical beauty in return for their power resources.

However, evolutionary theories of mate selection predict that women, whose own parental investment in producing offspring is large, would seek mates with characteristics that could ensure the survival of progeny. These male characteristics would be some form of material advantage. For their part, men would seek mates with the potential to reproduce and would seek characteristics in mates that correlate with reproductive success, such as beauty and youth.

The results of the content analyses of the 484 personal advertisements supported two social exchange and evolutionary predictions about mate choice in this Portuguese sample. First, women were relatively more likely to seek financial security, while men were more likely to offer financial security. Second, men and women in our sample did show differences in age preferences in mates or partners. The results showed that, as groups, women tend to stipulate older men, and men tend to stipulate younger women. Such findings agree with a variety of studies into the context of personal advertisements (e.g., Cameron, et al., 1977; Harrison & Saeed, 1977; Rajecki, et al., 1991) as well as cross-cultural research (Buss, 1989) and data from national probability samples (Sprecher, et al., 1994). They support also the claim of the universality of this sex difference in age preferences.

The findings regarding sex differences in advertisers' descriptions of themselves and potential dating partners in terms of attractiveness and of expressiveness did not support the hypotheses, and the sex differences in sincerity and in self-presentation of instrumental personality traits were only partially supported. In contrast with previous studies based on exchange theory (Cicerello & Sheehan, 1995) or on evolutionary theory (e.g., Waynforth & Dunbar, 1995), women were not relatively more likely to offer physical attractiveness, and men were not relatively more likely to seek attractiveness. Thus, the attractiveness exchange and evolutionary hypothesis were not supported. Men and women sought and offered similarly physical attractiveness. Although this null finding contradicts some previous findings in the domain of personal advertisements, Gonzales and Meyers (1993) pointed out that other research in social psychology suggests that attractiveness has an important role for both men and women. Kenrick, et al. (1993) noted that the subjects of both sexes placed high value on attractiveness. As Regan (1998) pointed out, in modern, industrialized societies the physical and social environments are such that both men and women have considerable powers of selection, and this may explain the sexes' similar emphasis on physical appearance. The sociocultural changes occurring in the Portuguese society in the last

decades, particularly the increased number of women earning higher degrees and entering the workplace, probably contribute to explain the similar search for physical attractiveness by women.

Women were more likely to seek sincerity in agreement with evolutionary theory (Feingold, 1992), while men were not more likely to offer sincerity. Also, women were relatively more likely to offer instrumental or "male-valued" traits in their advertisements, while men did not seek instrumental traits. Our findings did not show sex differences in expressive traits. These findings on the role of personality, as expressed in personal advertisements, were somewhat mixed, in agreement with some previous research. For example, results of American studies concerning instrumentality did not differ by sex, contrary to the prediction of social exchange theory (Cicerello & Sheehan, 1995).

In summary, in this study, we have found that the Portuguese people writing these advertisements behaved in ways that exchange and evolutionary theories would predict, at least as far as mate-searching is concerned, in terms of the descriptors of age and financial security. These results provide independent cross-cultural support for similar findings from other United States (Thiessen, Young, & Burroughs, 1993) and the United Kingdom (Greenlees & McGrew, 1994) "Lonely Hearts" data sets.

More important, perhaps, our data also suggest that descriptors such as physical attractiveness and expressive traits may not be used universally among humans. In this respect, our results support the argument from Smuts (1991) and Waynforth and Dunbar (1995) for context-dependency of people's behavioural strategies against those who have argued that such characteristics are evolved adaptations that occur universally among humans, regardless of cultural and ecological context. In the same vein, implicit in social exchange models is the assumption that the value of a particular quality varies with culture.

In closing, it should be noted that there are other considerations in using personal advertisement data to test general hypotheses from theories. Do personal advertisements really lead to courtship, marriage, and reproduction for older singles? These are questions about external validation essential for future research.

References

Buss, D. M. (1989). Sex differences in human mate preferences: Evolutionary hypotheses tested in 37 cultures. *Behavioral and Brain Sciences, 12,* 1–49.

Cameron, C. Oskamp, S., & Sparks, W. (1977) Courtship American style: Newspaper ads. *The Family Coordinator, 26,* 27–30.

Cicerello, A., & Sheehan, E. (1995) Personal advertisements: A content analysis. *Journal of Social Behavior and Personality, 10,* 751–756.

Deaux, K., & Hanna, R. (1984) Courtship in the personal column: The influence of gender and sexual orientation. *Sex Roles, 11,* 363–375.

Feingold, A. (1992) Gender differences in mate selection preferences: A test of parental investment model. *Psychological Bulletin, 11,* 125–139.

Gonzales, M. H., & Meyers, S. A. (1993) "Your mother would like me": Self-presentation in the personal ads of heterosexual and homosexual men and women. *Personality and Social Psychology Bulletin, 19,* 131–142.

Goodwin, R. (1990) Dating agency members: Are they different? *Journal of Social and Personal Relationships, 7,* 423–430.

Greenlees, T. A., & McGrew, W C. (1994) Sex and age differences in preferences and tactics of mate attraction: Analysis of published advertisements. *Ethology and Sociobiology*, *15*, 59–72.

Harrison, A. A., & Saeed, L. (1977) Let's make a deal: An analysis of revelations and stipulations in lonely hearts advertisements. *Journal of Personality and Social Psychology*, *35*, 257–264.

Hirschman, E. C. (1987) People as products: Analysis of a complex marketing exchange. *Journal of Marketing*, *51*, 98–108.

Instituto Nacional de Estatística. (2001) *Anuário estatístico de Portugal*. Lisboa: I. N. E.

Kenrick, D., Groth, G., Trost, M., & Sadalla, E, K. (1993) Integrating evolutionary and social exchange perspectives on relationships: Effects of gender, self-appraisal, and involvement level on mate selection criteria. *Journal of Personality and Social Psychology*, *64*, 951–969.

Koestner, R., & Wheeler, L. (1988) Self-presentation in the personal advertisements: The influence of implicit notions of attraction and role expectations. *Journal of Social and Personal Relationships*, *5*, 149–160.

Lynn, W. M., & Bolig, R. (1985) Personal advertisements: Sources of data about relationships. *Journal of Social and Personal Relationships*, *2*, 377–383.

Murstein, B. I. (1986) *Paths to marriage*. Beverly Hills, CA: Sage.

Neto, F., & Pinto, I. (1998) Gender stereotypes in Portuguese television advertisements. *Sex Roles*, *39*, 153–164.

Rajecki, D. W., Bledsoe, S. B., & Rasmussen, J. L. (1991) Successful personal ads: Gender differences and similarities in offers, stipulations, and outcomes. *Basic and Applied Social Psychology*, *12*, 457–469.

Regan, P. (1998) What if you can't get what you want? Willingness to compromise ideal mate selection standards as a function of sex, mate value, and relationship context. *Personality and Social Psychology Bulletin*, *24*, 1294–1303.

Smuts, R. (1991) The present also explains the past. *Ethology and Sociobiology*, *12*, 409–410.

Sprecher, S., Sullivan, Q., & Hatfield, E. (1994) Mate selection preferences: Gender differences examined in a national sample. *Journal of Personality and Social Psychology*, *66*, 1074–1080.

Thiessen, D., Young, R. K., & Burroughs, R. C. (1993) Lonely hearts advertisements reflect sexuality dimorphic mating strategies. *Ethology and Sociobiology*, *14*, 209–229.

Waynforth, D., & Dunbar, R. I. M, (1995) Conditional mate choice strategies in humans: Evidence from " 'Lonely hearts' advertisements." *Behaviour*, *132*, 755–779.

Acknowledgment: I am grateful to anonymous reviewers for their thoughtful comments on an earlier draft of this paper.

Address correspondence to: Félix Neto, Faculdade de Psicologia e de Ciências da Educação, Universidade do Porto, Rua do Campo Alegre, 1055, P-4150 Porto, Portugal. E-mail: fneto@psi.up.pt

Exercise for Article 34

Factual Questions

1. In the literature review, two possible explanations are offered for why men and women sometimes portray themselves counter to traditional sex-role stereotypes. What is the first explanation?

2. What is the first specific hypothesis stated by the researcher?

3. Did the researcher try to eliminate advertisements placed more than once (i.e., reruns)?

4. All advertisements placed by women during the time period were analyzed in this study. Only a sample of the ones placed by men during the time period was used. How was the sample selected?

5. Was the difference between men and women in "security offer" (i.e., offering their financial security) statistically significant? If yes, at what probability level?

6. In Table 1, how many of the differences were statistically significant?

Questions for Discussion

7. In lines 37–112 and in the Discussion section of the research report, the researcher discusses two theories, which are also referred to as "models." In your opinion, is this discussion a strength of this article? Would the article be as interesting without this discussion? Would the article be as informative without it? Explain.

8. What is your opinion on the researcher's decision to exclude advertisements in which the advertisers specified they were looking for same-sex partners? Explain. (See lines 164–166.)

9. In lines 190–198, the researcher describes a master list of words used to categorize the advertisements. In your opinion, is the master list described in sufficient detail?

10. In your opinion, is the coding of a sample of the advertisements by a second rater an important strength of this study? Explain. (See lines 205–208.)

11. Is it important to know that the age distributions of male and female advertisers were similar? Explain. (See lines 209–215.)

12. Do you agree with the researcher that it cannot be claimed that people who advertise in the personal section of a selected newspaper are representative of the population at large? Explain. (See lines 243–247.)

Quality Ratings

Directions: Indicate your level of agreement with each of the following statements by circling a number from 5 for strongly agree (SA) to 1 for strongly disagree (SD). If you believe an item is not applicable to this research article, leave it blank. Be prepared to explain your ratings. When responding to criteria A and B below, keep in mind that brief titles and abstracts are conventional in published research.

A. The title of the article is appropriate.

SA   5   4   3   2   1   SD

B. The abstract provides an effective overview of the research article.

SA   5   4   3   2   1   SD

C. The introduction establishes the importance of the study.

SA   5   4   3   2   1   SD

D. The literature review establishes the context for the study.

SA   5   4   3   2   1   SD

E. The research purpose, question, or hypothesis is clearly stated.

SA   5   4   3   2   1   SD

F. The method of sampling is sound.

SA   5   4   3   2   1   SD

G. Relevant demographics (for example, age, gender, and ethnicity) are described.

SA   5   4   3   2   1   SD

H. Measurement procedures are adequate.

SA   5   4   3   2   1   SD

I. All procedures have been described in sufficient detail to permit a replication of the study.

SA   5   4   3   2   1   SD

J. The participants have been adequately protected from potential harm.

SA   5   4   3   2   1   SD

K. The results are clearly described.

SA   5   4   3   2   1   SD

L. The discussion/conclusion is appropriate.

SA   5   4   3   2   1   SD

M. Despite any flaws, the report is worthy of publication.

SA   5   4   3   2   1   SD

Article 35

The Reporting of Therapist Sample Data in the *Journal of Counseling Psychology*

JAMES P. GUINEE

University of Central Arkansas

ABSTRACT. Adequate reporting of sample characteristics is necessary in conducting, reviewing, and replicating research studies. In this study, the author reviewed *Journal of Counseling Psychology* studies from 1988 to 1997 that used therapists in their research samples and examined the type and consistency of therapist sample reporting. Researchers report as many as 9 different therapist variables, and overall there is a lack of consistency in how often each variable is reported and how it is measured. The implications for the lack of uniformity in reporting are discussed.

From *Journal of Counseling Psychology*, 47, 266–270. Copyright © 2000 by the Educational Publishing Foundation. Reprinted with permission.

Appropriate identification of research participants is critical to the science of psychology (American Psychological Association, 1994; Smith & Glass, 1987). Moreover, in the psychotherapy literature, adequate
5 information about research samples is necessary in order to determine to which clinical and therapist populations the results can be generalized (Hill, Nutt, & Jackson, 1994); furthermore, replications and extensions of studies, vital to counseling research (Hill,
10 1993), require comprehensive descriptions of research participants in previous studies. Finally, without consistent reporting of data in the use of aggregate studies (e.g., meta-analysis), little can be concluded about what variables matter (Smith & Glass, 1987).
15 Given the importance of consistent reporting of sample information, has an adequate description of information about research samples been consistently provided in the *Journal of Counseling Psychology* (*JCP*)? Although I could find no articles that specifi-
20 cally addressed this question, two reviews of reporting trends in *JCP* studies imply that the answer is no. Meier and Davis (1990) found that quantitative reports of scale reliability and validity estimates in *JCP* studies are often incomplete. More recently, Hill et al. (1994)
25 examined trends in psychotherapy process research from 1978 to 1992. They found that although the majority of *JCP* studies report therapist and client gender, minimal information is typically reported about thera-

pist and client race. They did not examine the reporting
30 of other therapist or client variables.

To examine the reporting of sample information in *JCP*, I examined the type of therapist sample data and how consistently it is reported. According to Beutler, Crago, and Arizmendi (1986), virtually every psycho-
35 therapy study directly or indirectly examines the role of therapist characteristics in affecting therapeutic change; therefore, an adequate knowledge about the therapist influences generalizability and replication of the results. Furthermore, given the therapist's importance to
40 the psychotherapy process and outcome (e.g., Gelso & Carter, 1994; Whiston & Sexton, 1993), researchers that fail to report therapist variables perpetuate the uniformity myth that all therapists are the same, regardless of age, theoretical orientation, setting, and combina-
45 tions thereof (Ellis & Chartrand, 1999).

Therefore, I investigated all studies published in *JCP* during the past 10 years that used therapists as part or all of their research samples. I was specifically interested in the following questions: (a) What data do
50 researchers solicit and report regarding therapist–participants? (b) What percentage of studies report each therapist characteristic? and (c) How consistently are these characteristics measured?

Method

I searched the Method section of every *JCP* article
55 published from 1988 to 1997 as well as other sections of the article if the authors indicated that participant data could be found elsewhere.

Total Number of Studies with Therapists As Participants

All studies that included therapists in their research samples were then counted for each issue. In line with
60 Hill et al. (1994), I defined *therapist* as one who has been specifically trained as a professional therapist (e.g., counseling or clinical psychologists, psychiatrists, counselors, or social workers) or as a therapist in training (e.g., prepracticum student, practicum student,
65 and intern). Furthermore, because I was interested in the proportion of samples composed of professional therapists and therapists in training, I eliminated all psychotherapy studies specifically focusing on supervi-

sion and training, as these studies would inflate the percentage of trainees in the general therapist research samples.

Therapist Data

For each study that included therapists in the research sample, I recorded all reported therapist data. In a given study, therefore, researchers report as many as nine different criteria regarding therapists: (a) number (i.e., the number of therapists in the sample); (b) age; (c) gender; (d) race/ethnicity; (e) professional status—whether the therapist is primarily a professional therapist or a therapist in training; (f) setting (e.g., counseling center, private practice, or academic department); (g) academic training (e.g., counseling psychology, clinical psychology); (h) level of experience (e.g., years of experience, number of clients); and (i) theoretical orientation (e.g., psychodynamic, cognitive–behavioral, or humanistic).

I then recorded how many of the therapist variables were reported for each article and how many different methods were used to measure a given characteristic (e.g., reporting therapist experience by degree status vs. years of clinical experience). Finally, for the sake of accuracy, I double-checked every article for each type of therapist data it included.

Results

Percentage of Studies with Therapist–Participants

There was a total of 560 studies published in *JCP* from 1988 to 1997, of which 123 (22%) included therapists in their research samples. Discarding the data on training and supervision studies resulted in a total of 100 articles. The percentage of *JCP* studies with therapists in the research sample ranged from 10% (1988) to 36% (1994), with a 10-year percentage of 18%.

Therapist Number

One hundred percent of the studies reported the number of therapists in the research sample. The mean number of reported therapists was 30.4, with a standard deviation of 49.23, and a range from 1 to 320. The median number of therapists was 12, and in approximately two-thirds of the studies the therapist sample size ranged from 1 to 15.

Therapist Age, Gender, and Race/Ethnicity

For 44% of the studies that reported therapist age, the mean age of therapist samples was 36.2, with a standard deviation of 7.5, and aggregate means ranged from 22.5 to 51.5. The median age of samples was 34.0, and in approximately one-half of the studies the mean age of the therapist sample ranged from 22.5 to 32.0. For 80% of the studies that reported therapist gender, the percentage of female therapists in research samples was 59%, compared with 42% for male therapists. Finally, for 47% of the studies that report therapist race/ethnicity, European American therapists dominated the research samples, accounting for an average of 86% of the sample, whereas other racial/ethnic groups composed a considerably smaller percentage of the sample (14%).

Therapist Professional Status and Setting

For 89% of the studies that reported professional status, graduate students composed 52% of the sample, compared with 48% for professional therapists. Furthermore, the results show that for 50% of the studies that reported therapist setting, the most frequent site was a university/college counseling center (25%), followed by a combination of different (i.e., counseling center and hospital clinic) settings (9%), academic departments (8%), and mental health centers (4%).

Therapist Academic Training

For 34% of the studies that reported academic training, the more common method involved the breakdown of clinical psychologists, counseling psychologists, and so forth (23%). The other method (11%) made a general reference to participants' background but did not specify the number of therapists from each type of degree program. For example, Worthington et al. (1995) described their participants in the following manner: "…6 had their master's degrees in clinical or counseling psychology…" (p. 467).

Therapist Level of Experience

Most studies (i.e., 93%) reported level of experience. Researchers most commonly (44% of studies) reported experience by means of the therapist's degree (e.g., master's vs. doctorate), followed closely (42%) by reporting the therapist's years of experience. Common labels included *postdegree, postdoctorate,* or even *postlicensure* (Turner, Valtierra, Talken, Miller, & DeAnda, 1996) *years of experience,* although experience is sometimes simply described as *years of counseling experience* (e.g., Gati, Garty, & Fassa, 1996), without indicating whether all or part of that experience is postdegree or postdoctorate.

Studies that tended to use graduate students as the therapist research sample varied widely in their assessment of experience level. The most common method (23%) for describing a trainee's level of experience is reporting the student's current status in his or her academic program (i.e., master's or doctoral student), followed by dividing trainees into different experimental groups (16%) on the basis of the number of practica (e.g., Porter, Wagner, Johnson, & Cox, 1996). Other methods include a graduate student's number of years in school, number of hours of supervised therapy experience, and Stein and Lambert's categorization (1984)—*novice* (i.e., less than two completed semesters of supervised practicum experience), and *advanced* (i.e., two or more completed semesters of supervised practicum experience), and *experienced* (i.e., postdoctoral psychologist).

Theoretical Orientation

Theoretical orientation was the least frequently reported (i.e., 33%) of all therapist variables and was assessed in three different ways. The most common method is a numerical breakdown of how many therapists adhere to each therapeutic approach listed. This categorization is typically based on therapist self-reports, such as "...six preferred emotionally focused couples' therapy; 5 preferred cognitive-behavioral...." (Worthington et al., 1997). The second method for reporting involves a simple reference to theoretical orientation, using descriptive phrases such as "...collectively adhered to person-centered, gestalt, transactional analytic...orientations..." (Rennie, 1994) and "all of the counselors an eclectic blend of cognitive–behavioral, person-centered, and experiential approaches..." (Cummings, Hallberg, & Slemon, 1994).

The third, and least used method, involves therapists rating their relative adherence to different major theoretical approaches. Gelso, Kivlighan, Wine, Jones, and Friedman (1997) had therapists rate their theoretical orientation on a 7-point Likert-type scale (1 = *not at all*, 7 = *greatly*) for *behavioral and/or cognitive therapy, existential–humanistic therapy,* and *psychoanalytic and/or dynamic therapy.* Other studies (e.g., Hill, Diemer, & Heaton, 1997; Hill, Thompson, Cogar, & Denman, 1993; Hill, Helms, Spiegel, & Tichenor, 1988) involve a similar method but use the labels *psychoanalytic, humanistic,* and *cognitive–behavioral* for the theoretical orientations.

Discussion

What therapist variables are reported in psychotherapy studies? On the basis of a perusal of all *JCP* studies from 1988 to 1997 that included therapists as participants, a given study may report as many as nine different variables when describing the therapist research sample: number, age, gender, race/ethnicity, professional status, setting, academic training, level of experience, and theoretical orientation. Interestingly, the Beutler et al. (1986) taxonomy of therapist variables that affect therapeutic effectiveness show some overlap with the variables reported in *JCP* studies; however, other salient variables (e.g., socioeconomic status) do not.

How consistently are these therapist variables reported? The concept of consistency can be construed in two different ways: How often is the characteristic reported, and is the characteristic measured in the same manner in each study? In general, the majority of *JCP* articles from 1988 to 1997 with therapists as participants were inconsistent by either definition.

The only therapist characteristic that was reported in all *JCP* studies was the number of therapists in the sample. This should not be surprising, given that reporting of the sample size is expected in scientific research (American Psychological Association, 1994). However, it is interesting to note that in approximately two-thirds of the studies the size of the research sample ranged from 1 to 15 therapists. Although the size of a sample is not necessarily indicative of the quality of a study (Tracey, 1983), obtaining adequate samples of therapists has been a major problem in psychotherapy research (e.g., Gelso, 1979; Vachon et al., 1995). A related finding in this study was that therapists in training accounted for approximately 52% of participants in the research sample, suggesting that psychotherapy studies continue to rely unduly on using graduate students (Gelso, 1979; Hill & Corbett, 1993).

JCP articles examined frequently omitted relatively obtainable therapist information—that is, *externally observed characteristics* (Beutler et al., 1986)—therapist gender (80%), therapist setting (50%), therapist race/ethnicity (47%), therapist age (44%), and therapist academic training (34%). Although there are occasions where sample characteristics are not reported due to confidentiality purposes (American Psychological Association, 1994), the lack of uniformity in reporting these characteristics leads one to question whether the methodology of psychotherapy research is indeed imprecise (Kazdin, 1980), or perhaps there is a lack of agreement on which therapist variables should be routinely reported.

Therapist experience level is one variable that shows high agreement among researchers with respect to reporting (i.e., 93% of studies); however, there is much variation on how it is measured. Kivlighan, Patton, and Foote (1998) noted that an agreed-on definition of therapist experience does not exist. They also stated that many researchers confuse experience level with type of training (e.g., paraprofessional vs. professional), and furthermore, "...experience level has often been used as a convenient proxy for the counselor's level of knowledge development..." (p. 274). Beutler et al. (1986) reaffirmed this position, suggesting that defining a therapist's level of experience should minimally include the amount (e.g., number of years) and type (e.g., professional discipline) of training.

The problem with defining level of experience is even more problematic with therapists in training. I found five different methods for defining a therapist-in-training's level of experience, and the most common one was whether the trainee–participant was a master's or doctoral level student. However, because it is possible for a first-year student to be in a doctoral program, this categorization is not an accurate measure of experience. Traccy, Hays, Malone, and Herman (1988) suggested that Stein and Lambert's (1984) definition of experience—novice, advanced, and professional—may be the most efficient method for defining level of experience because it categorizes therapists on the basis of concrete experiences more than on the type of degree or years in school. Furthermore, this categorization has been found to differentiate therapeutic interventions and effectiveness of trainees (e.g., Guinee & Tracey, 1994; Robyak, 1981; Robyak, Goodyear, Prange, & Donham, 1986).

Theoretical orientation was the least frequently reported therapist characteristic in this study. Assessing a therapist's theoretical orientation is clearly a difficult endeavor, possibly because of the approximately 250 different theoretical schools now in existence (Corsini, 1984). Gelso (1995) implied that another reason for underreporting theoretical orientation is the famous dodo bird hypothesis: Widely differing theoretical approaches to therapy appear to produce generally equivocal results (Luborsky, Singer, & Luborksy, 1975), and therefore if all theories are equally effective, then theoretical orientation becomes much less appealing.

For the studies that did report therapist theoretical orientation, it was typically reported by means of therapists simply endorsing a major therapeutic philosophy (e.g., psychodynamic, cognitive–behavioral) that presumably is closest to their therapeutic style. Gelso (1995) argued that this method of assessing theoretical orientation is simplistic and vague. Furthermore, he suggested that when practitioners are asked what their theoretical orientations are, they typically talk about the extent to which they adhere to the tenets of multiple theories (vs. just one). Gelso recommended that studies follow Hill and O'Grady's (1985) lead by having therapists rate degree of adherence to various theories. Therefore, therapists can get a score on preference for and adherence to whatever theory or theories are being examined. Yet, the results of this study indicate that Gelso's recommendations have not been followed.

A limitation of the present investigation is that I only examined studies in *JCP* that used therapists in their research samples, therefore I cannot generalize the findings to any other journal or to reporting practices of other types of research samples (e.g., clients). Nevertheless, I believe that, similar to Meier and Davis (1990) and Hill et al. (1994), the reporting practices of researchers suggest an unacceptable degree of incomplete and inconsistent reporting of important information. Clearly the field of counseling psychology research cannot progress if it stumbles over even the smallest of obstacles (Strong, 1991); therefore, it is hoped that the results of this study would serve as a reminder for researchers to present adequate sample information.

It is also hoped that researchers would use this study to establish a basic template of information in reporting information about therapist samples. The therapist is a vital participant in the therapeutic endeavor, yet many *JCP* studies that use therapists present an unclear picture of the therapist population studied and present significant obstacles to generalizing or replicating the results. By consistently reporting a minimum set of characteristics, a clearer picture of therapist research samples will emerge: How many therapists participated? How many professionals versus graduate students participated? How many men and women participated? What was their age range? What was the racial/ethnic composition? Where were they primarily employed or trained? What kind of academic training did they have? How many years of experience and what type of training did they have? and, to what degree did they subscribe to different theoretical orientations?

References

American Psychological Association (1994). *Publication Manual of the American Psychological Association.* Washington, DC: Author.

Beutler, L. E., Crago, M., & Arizmendi, T. G. (1986). Therapist variables in psychotherapy process and outcome. In S. L. Garfield & A. E. Bergin (Eds.), *Handbook of psychotherapy and behavior change* (3rd ed., pp. 257–310), Hillside, NJ: Wiley.

Corsini, R. J. (1984). *Current psychotherapies.* Itasca, IL: F. E. Peacock.

Cummings, A. L., Hallberg, E. T., & Slemon, A. G. (1994). Templates of client change in short-term counseling. *Journal of Counseling Psychology, 41,* 464–472.

Ellis, M. V., & Chartrand, J. M. (1999). Advanced quantitative methods in counseling psychology: Synthesis. *The Counseling Psychologist, 27,* 579–588.

Gati, I., Garty, Y., & Fassa, N. (1996). Using career-related aspects to assess person–environment fit. *Journal of Counseling Psychology, 43,* 196–206.

Gelso, C. J. (1979). Research in counseling: Methodological and professional issues. *The Counseling Psychologist, 8,* 7–35.

Gelso, C. J. (1995). Theories, theoretical orientation, and theoretical dimensions: Comment on Poznanski and McLennan (1995). *Journal of Counseling Psychology, 42,* 426–427.

Gelso, C. J., & Carter, J. A. (1994). Components of the psychotherapy relationship: Their interaction and unfolding during treatment. *Journal of Counseling Psychology, 41,* 296–306.

Gelso, C. J., Kivlighan, D. M., Jr., Wine, B., Jones, A., & Friedman, S. C. (1997). Transference, insight, and the course of time-limited therapy. *Journal of Counseling Psychology, 44,* 209–217.

Guinee, J. P., & Tracey, T. J. (1994). Counselor interpersonal power base preference: An examination of counselor and client variables. *Counselor Education and Supervision, 34,* 92–101.

Hill, C. E. (1993). Editorial. *Journal of Counseling Psychology, 40,* 252–256.

Hill, C. E., & Corbett, M. M. (1993). A perspective on the history of outcome research in counseling psychology. *Journal of Counseling Psychology, 40,* 3–24.

Hill, C. E., Diemer, R. A., & Heaton, K. J. (1997). Dream interpretation sessions: Who volunteers, who benefits, and what volunteer clients view as most and least helpful. *Journal of Counseling Psychology, 44,* 53–62.

Hill, C. E., Helms, J. E., Spiegel, S. B., & Tichenor, V. (1988). Development of a system for categorizing client reactions to therapist interventions. *Journal of Counseling Psychology, 35,* 27–36.

Hill, C. E., Nutt, E. A., & Jackson, S. (1994). Trends in psychotherapy process research: Samples, measures, researchers, and classic publications. *Journal of Counseling Psychology, 41,* 364–377.

Hill, C. E., & O'Grady, K. E. (1985). List of therapist intentions illustrated in a case study and with therapists of varying theoretical orientations. *Journal of Counseling Psychology, 32,* 3–22.

Hill, C. E., Thompson, B. J., Cogar, M. C., & Denman, D. W. (1993). Beneath the surface of long-term therapy: Therapist and client report of their own and each other's covert processes. *Journal of Counseling Psychology, 40,* 278–287.

Kazdin, A. E. (1980). *Research design in clinical psychology.* New York: Harper & Row.

Kivlighan, D. M., Jr., Patton, M. J., & Foote, D. (1998). Moderating effects of client attachment on the counselor experience–working alliance relationship. *Journal of Counseling Psychology, 45,* 274–278.

Luborsky, L., Singer, B., & Luborsky, L. (1975). Comparative studies of psychotherapy. *Archives of General Psychiatry, 32,* 995–1008.

Meier, S. T., & Davis, S. R. (1990). Trends in reporting psychometric properties of scales used in counseling psychology research. *Journal of Counseling Psychology, 37,* 113–115.

Porter, R. L., Wagner, W. G., Johnson, J. T., & Cox, L. M. (1996). Sexually abused girls' verbalizations in counseling: An application of the client behavior system. *Journal of Counseling Psychology, 43,* 383–388.

Rennie, D. L. (1994). Clients' deference in psychotherapy. *Journal of Counseling Psychology, 41,* 427–437.

Robyak, J. E. (1981). Effects of gender on the counselor's preference for methods of influence. *Journal of Counseling Psychology, 28,* 7–12.

Robyak, J. E., Goodyear, R. K., Prange, M. E., & Donham, G. (1986). Effects of gender, supervision, and presenting problems on practicum students' preference for interpersonal power bases. *Journal of Counseling Psychology, 33,* 159–163.

Smith, M. L., & Glass, G. V. (1987). *Research and evaluation in education and the social sciences.* Englewood Cliffs, NJ: Prentice Hall.

Stein, D. M., & Lambert, M. J. (1984). On the relationship between therapist experience and therapy outcome. *Clinical Psychology Review, 4*, 127–142.

Strong, S. R. (1991). Theory-driven science and naive empiricism in counseling psychology. *Journal of Counseling Psychology, 38*, 204–210.

Tracey, T. J. (1983). Single case research: An added tool for the counselor and supervisor. *Counselor Education and Supervision, 22*, 197–206.

Tracey, T. J., Hays, K. A., Malone, J., & Herman, B. (1988). Changes in counselor response as a function of experience. *Journal of Counseling Psychology, 35*, 119–126.

Turner, P. R., Valtierra, M., Talken, T. R., Miller, V. I., & DeAnda, J. R. (1996). Effect of session length on treatment outcome for college students in brief therapy. *Journal of Counseling Psychology, 43*, 228–232.

Vachon, D. O., Susman, M., Wynne, M. E., Birringer, J., Olshefsky, L., & Cox, K. (1995). Reasons therapists give for refusing to participate in psychotherapy research. *Journal of Counseling Psychology, 42*, 380–382.

Whiston, S. C., & Sexton, T. L. (1993). An overview of psychotherapy outcome research: Implications for practice. *Professional Psychology: Research and Practice, 24*, 43–51.

Worthington, E. L., Jr., Hight, T. L., Ripley, J. S., Perrone, K. M., Kurusu, T. A., & Jones, D. R. (1997). Strategic hope-focused relationship-enrichment counseling with individual couples. *Journal of Counseling Psychology, 44*, 381–389.

Worthington, E. L., Jr., McCullough, M. E., Shortz, J. L., Mindes, E. L., Sandage, S. J., & Chartrand, J. M. (1995). Can couples assessment and feedback improve relationships? Assessment as a brief relationship enrichment procedure. *Journal of Counseling Psychology, 42*, 466–475.

Acknowledgment: I thank Ernie Ness for his feedback on an earlier version of this article.

Address correspondence to: James P. Guinee, Counseling Center, University of Central Arkansas, 313 Bernard Hall, 201 Donaghey Avenue, Conway, AK 72035. E-mail: jamesg@mail.uca.edu

Exercise for Article 35

Factual Questions

1. According to the literature review, what is the "uniformity myth"?

2. Did the researcher include psychotherapy studies focusing on supervision and training?

3. For the studies that reported therapist gender, what percentage of the therapists was female?

4. Which racial/ethnic group dominated the research samples?

5. According to the researcher, the concept of consistency in how therapist variables are reported can be construed in two different ways. What are they?

6. According to the researcher, what is a "limitation" of his study?

Questions for Discussion

7. The researcher double-checked every article for each type of therapist data it included. In your opinion, would it have been better to have another person do the double-checking? Explain. (See lines 90–92.)

8. The researcher states that the mean number of reported therapists in the research samples was 30.4, while the median number was 12. Speculate on why these two averages are different. (See lines 101–106.)

9. Does it surprise you that a majority of the therapists were graduate students? Explain. (See lines 122–124.)

10. The researcher states that theoretical orientation was the least frequently reported of all therapist variables. In your opinion, is this an important omission in studies of therapy? Explain. (See lines 170–171 and 289–296.)

11. Do you believe that it would be helpful in future studies to examine reporting practices of other types of research samples, such as clients? Explain. (See lines 317–319.)

12. Do you believe that, overall, the results of this study indicate an "unacceptable degree of incomplete and inconsistent reporting of important information"? Explain. (See lines 320–324.)

Quality Ratings

Directions: Indicate your level of agreement with each of the following statements by circling a number from 5 for strongly agree (SA) to 1 for strongly disagree (SD). If you believe an item is not applicable to this research article, leave it blank. Be prepared to explain your ratings. When responding to criteria A and B below, keep in mind that brief titles and abstracts are conventional in published research.

A. The title of the article is appropriate.
SA   5   4   3   2   1   SD

B. The abstract provides an effective overview of the research article.
SA   5   4   3   2   1   SD

C. The introduction establishes the importance of the study.
SA   5   4   3   2   1   SD

D. The literature review establishes the context for the study.
SA   5   4   3   2   1   SD

E. The research purpose, question, or hypothesis is clearly stated.
SA   5   4   3   2   1   SD

F. The method of sampling is sound.
SA   5   4   3   2   1   SD

G. Relevant demographics (for example, age, gender, and ethnicity) are described.

       SA   5   4   3   2   1   SD

H. Measurement procedures are adequate.

       SA   5   4   3   2   1   SD

I. All procedures have been described in sufficient detail to permit a replication of the study.

       SA   5   4   3   2   1   SD

J. The participants have been adequately protected from potential harm.

       SA   5   4   3   2   1   SD

K. The results are clearly described.

       SA   5   4   3   2   1   SD

L. The discussion/conclusion is appropriate.

       SA   5   4   3   2   1   SD

M. Despite any flaws, the report is worthy of publication.

       SA   5   4   3   2   1   SD

Article 36

Project D.A.R.E. Outcome
Effectiveness Revisited

STEVEN L. WEST
Virginia Commonwealth University

KERI K. O'NEAL
University of North Carolina, Chapel Hill

OBJECTIVES. We provide an updated meta-analysis on the effectiveness of Project D.A.R.E. in preventing alcohol, tobacco, and illicit drug use among school-aged youths.
METHODS. We used meta-analytic techniques to create an overall effect size for D.A.R.E. outcome evaluations reported in scientific journals.
RESULTS. The overall weighted effect size for the included D.A.R.E. studies was extremely small (correlation coefficient = 0.011; Cohen's d = 0.023; 95% confidence interval = –0.04, 0.08) and nonsignificant (z = 0.73, NS).
CONCLUSIONS. Our study supports previous findings indicating that D.A.R.E. is ineffective.

From *American Journal of Public Health*, 94, 1027–1029. Copyright © 2004 by American Journal of Public Health. Reprinted with permission.

In the United States, Project D.A.R.E. (Drug Abuse Resistance Education) is one of the most widely used substance abuse prevention programs targeted at school-aged youths. In recent years, D.A.R.E. has been the country's largest single school-based prevention program in terms of federal expenditures, with an average of three-quarters of a billion dollars spent on its provision annually.[1] Although its effectiveness in preventing substance use has been called into question, its application in our nation's schools remains very extensive.[2–6]

Given the recent increases in alcohol and other drug use among high school and college students,[7] the continued use of D.A.R.E. and similar programs seems likely. In a meta-analysis examining the effectiveness of D.A.R.E., Ennett et al.[3] noted negligible yet positive effect sizes (ranging from 0.00 to 0.11) when outcomes occurring immediately after program completion were considered. However, this analysis involved 2 major limitations. First, Ennett et al. included research from nonpeer-reviewed sources, including annual reports produced for agencies associated with the provision of D.A.R.E. services. While such an inclusion does not necessarily represent a serious methodological flaw, use of such sources has been called into question.[8]

Second, Ennett and colleagues included only studies in which postintervention assessment was conducted immediately at program termination. As noted by Lynam et al.,[6] the developmental trajectories of drug experimentation and use vary over time. Thus, if individuals are assessed during periods in which rates of experimentation and use are naturally high, any positive effects that could be found at times of lower experimentation will be deflated. Likewise, assessments made during periods in which experimentation and use are slight will exaggerate the overall effect of the intervention.

Ideally, problems such as those just described could be solved by the use of large-scale longitudinal studies involving extensive follow-up over a period of years. There have been several longer-term follow-ups, but the cost of such efforts may limit the number of longitudinal studies that can be conducted. In the present analysis, we attempted to overcome this difficulty by including a wider range of follow-up reports, from immediate posttests to 10-year postintervention assessments, in an updated meta-analysis of all currently available research articles reporting an outcome evaluation of Project D.A.R.E.

Methods

We conducted computer searches of the *ERIC*, *MEDLINE*, and *PsycINFO* databases in late fall 2002 to obtain articles for the present study. In addition, we reviewed the reference lists of the acquired articles for other potential sources. We initially reviewed roughly 40 articles from these efforts; 11 studies appearing in the literature from 1991 to 2002 met our 3 inclusion criteria, which were as follows:

1. The research was reported in a peer-reviewed journal; reports from dissertations/theses, books, and unpublished manuscripts were not included. We selected this criterion in an attempt to ensure inclusion of only those studies with rigorous methodologies. As noted, a previous meta-analysis of Project D.A.R.E. included research from nonreviewed sources, a fact that critics have suggested may have added error to the reported findings.[8]

2. The research included a control or comparison group (i.e., the research must have involved an experimental or quasi-experimental design).

Table 1
Primary Articles Included in the Meta-Analysis

Study (year)	Sample	r	d	95% confidence interval
Ringwalt et al. (1991)[18]	5th and 6th graders (*n* = 1270; 52% female/48% male; 50% African American/40% Anglo/10% other), posttested immediately	0.025	0.056	−0.06, 0.16
Becker et al. (1992)[19]	5th graders (*n* = 2878), posttested immediately	−0.058	−0.117	−0.19, −0.04
Harmon (1993)[20]	5th graders (*n* = 708), posttested immediately	0.015	0.030	−0.12, 0.18
Ennett et al. (1994)[21]	7th and 8th graders (*n* = 1334; 54% Anglo/22% African American/9% Hispanic/15% other), 2 years post-D.A.R.E.	0.000	0.000[a]	−0.11, 0.11
Rosenbaum et al. (1994)[22]	6th and 7th graders (*n* = 1584; 49.7% female/50.3% male; 49.9% Anglo/24.7% African American/8.9% Hispanic/16.5% other), 1 year post-D.A.R.E.	0.000	0.000[a]	−0.10, 0.10
Wysong et al. (1994)[23]	12th graders (*n* = 619), 5 years post-D.A.R.E.	0.000	0.000[a]	−0.16, 0.16
Dukes et al. (1996)[24]	9th graders (*n* = 849), 3 years post-D.A.R.E.	0.035	0.072	−0.06, 0.21
Zagumny & Thompson (1997)[25]	6th graders (*n* = 395; 48% female/52% male), 4–5 years post-D.A.R.E.	0.184	0.376	0.07, 0.68
Lynam et al. (1999)[6]	6th graders (*n* = 1002; 57% female/43% male; 75.1% Anglo/20.4% African American/0.5% other), 10 years post-D.A.R.E.	0.000	0.000[a]	−0.15, 0.15
Thombs (2000)[26]	5th through 10th graders (*n* = 630; 90.4% Anglo/5.5% African American/4.1% other), posttested at least 1 to 6 years post-D.A.R.E.	0.025	0.038	−0.15, 0.23
Ahmed et al. (2002)[14]	5th and 6th graders (*n* = 236; 50% female/50% male/69% Anglo/24% African American/7% other), posttested immediately	0.198	0.405	0.01, 0.80

Note. r = correlation coefficient; *d* = difference in the means of the treatment and control conditions divided by the pooled standard deviation. Negative signs for *r* and *d* indicate greater effectiveness of control/comparison group.
[a]Assumed effect size.

3. The research included both preintervention and postintervention assessments of at least 1 of 3 key variables: alcohol use, illicit drug use, and tobacco use. We chose to include only those effect sizes that concerned actual substance use behaviors, since the true test of a substance use prevention effort is its impact on actual rates of use.

Using these criteria, we refined the original list of studies to 11 studies (Table 1). We calculated effect sizes using the procedures outlined by Rosenthal.[9] Meta-analysis results are commonly presented in the form of either a correlation coefficient (*r*) or the difference in the means of the treatment and control conditions divided by the pooled standard deviation (Cohen's *d*).[10] Since both are ratings of effect size, they can readily be converted to one another, and, if not provided in the original analyses, they can be calculated via F, *t*, and χ^2 statistics as well as means and standard deviations.[9]

We calculated both estimations for the individual included studies and for the overall analysis. As discussed by Amato and Keith,[11] tests of significance used in meta-analyses require that effect sizes be independent; therefore, if 2 or more effect sizes were generated within the same outcome category, we used the mean effect size. We also used the procedure for weighting effect sizes suggested by Shadish and Haddock[12] to ensure that all effect sizes were in the form of a common metric. In addition, we calculated 95% confidence intervals (CIs) for each study and for the overall analysis.

Results

The average weighted effect size (*r*) for all studies was 0.011 (*d* = 0.023; 95% CI = −0.04, 0.08), indicating marginally better outcomes for individuals participating in D.A.R.E. relative to participants in control conditions. The fact that the associated CI included a negative value indicates that the average effect size was not significantly greater than zero at $p < .05$. According to the guidelines developed by Cohen,[13] both of the effect sizes obtained were below the level normally considered small. Four of the included studies noted no effect of D.A.R.E. relative to control conditions, and 1 study noted that D.A.R.E. was less effective than the control condition.

Furthermore, the 6 reports indicating that D.A.R.E. had more positive effects were for the most part small (Figure 1). The largest effect size was found in a report in which the only outcome examined was smoking. Finally, we conducted a test of cumulative significance to determine whether differences existed between D.A.R.E. participants and non-D.A.R.E. participants. This test produced nonsignificant results (*z* = 0.73, NS).

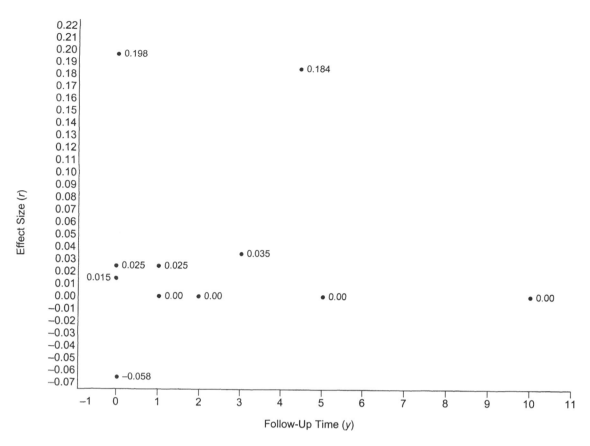

Figure 1. Plot of effect sizes, by follow-up time.

Discussion

Our results confirm the findings of a previous meta-analysis[3] indicating that Project D.A.R.E. is ineffective.
125 This is not surprising, given the substantial information developed over the past decade to that effect. Critics of the present analysis might argue that, despite the magnitude of our findings, the direction of the effect of D.A.R.E. was generally positive. While this is the case,
130 it should be emphasized that the effects we found did not differ significantly from the variation one would expect by chance. According to Cohen's guidelines,[13] the effect size we obtained would have needed to be 20 times larger to be considered even small. Given the
135 tremendous expenditures in time and money involved with D.A.R.E., it would appear that continued efforts should focus on other techniques and programs that might produce more substantial effects.

Our findings also indicate that D.A.R.E. was mini-
140 mally effective during the follow-up periods that would place its participants in the very age groups targeted. Indeed, no noticeable effects could be discerned in nearly half of the reports, including the study involving the longest follow-up period. This is an important con-
145 sideration for those involved in program planning and development.

As noted earlier, progression in regard to experimentation and use varies over time. Use of alcohol and other drugs reaches a peak during adolescence or
150 young adulthood and decreases steadily thereafter.[7,15] Such a developmental path would be expected of all individuals, regardless of their exposure to a prevention effort. Ideally, individuals enrolled in a program such as D.A.R.E. would report limited or no use during their
155 adolescent and young adult years. The fact that half of the included studies reported no beneficial effect of D.A.R.E. beyond what would be expected by chance casts serious doubt on its utility.

One shortcoming of our analysis should be noted.
160 In many of the studies we included, individual students were the unit of analysis in calculating effects. As noted by Rosenbaum and Hanson,[16] this practice tends to lead to overestimates of program effectiveness, since the true unit of analysis is the schools in which the stu-
165 dents are "nested." Because our meta-analysis was limited to the types of data and related information available from the original articles, the potential for such inflation of program effectiveness exists. However, the overall effect sizes calculated here were small and non-
170 significant, and thus it is unlikely that inclusion of studies making this error had a significant impact on the current findings.

An additional caveat is that all of the studies included in this analysis represent evaluations of what is
175 commonly referred to as the "old D.A.R.E.": programs generally based on the original formulations of the D.A.R.E. model. In response to the many critiques of

the program, the D.A.R.E. prevention model was substantially revamped in 2001, thanks in part to a \$13.6
180 million grant provided by the Robert Wood Johnson
Foundation.[17] The revisions to the model have since
given rise to programs working under the "new
D.A.R.E." paradigm. However, at the time of the writing of this article we were unable to find any major
185 evaluation of the new D.A.R.E. model in the research
literature, and the effectiveness of such efforts has yet
to be determined.

References

1. McNeal RB, Hanson WB. An examination of strategies for gaining convergent validity in natural experiments: D.A.R.E. as an illustrative case
study. *Eval Rev.* 1995;19:141–158.
2. Donnermeyer J, Wurschmidt T. Educators' perceptions of the D.A.R.E.
program. *J Drug Educ.* 1997;27:259–276.
3. Ennett ST, Tobler NS, Ringwalt CL, Flewelling RL. How effective is
Drug Abuse Resistance Education? A meta-analysis of Project D.A.R.E.
outcome evaluations. *Am J Public Health.* 1994;84:1394–1401.
4. Hanson WB. Pilot test results comparing the All Stars Program with
seventh-grade D.A.R.E.: Program integrity and mediating variable
analysis. *Subst Use Misuse.* 1996;31:1359–1377.
5. Hanson WB, McNeal RB. How D.A.R.E. works: An examination of
program effects on mediating variables. *Health Educ Behav.*
1997;24:165–176.
6. Lynam DR, Milich R, Zimmerman R, et al. Project D.A.R.E: No effects
at 10-year follow-up. *J Consult Clin Psychol.* 1999;67:590–593.
7. Johnston LD, O'Malley PM, Bachman JG. *National Survey Results on
Drug Use From the Monitoring the Future Study, 1975–1998. Volume 1:
Secondary School Students.* Rockville, Md: National Institute on Drug
Abuse; 1999. NIH publication 99–4660.
8. Gorman DM. The effectiveness of D.A.R.E. and other drug use prevention programs. *Am J Public Health.* 1995;85:873.
9. Rosenthal R. *Meta-Analytic Procedures for Social Research.* 2nd ed.
Thousand Oaks, Calif: Sage Publications; 1991.
10. DasEiden R, Reifman A. Effects of Brazelton demonstrations on later
parenting: A meta-analysis. *J Pediatr Psychol.* 1996;21:857–868.
11. Amato PH, Keith B. Parental divorce and well-being of children: A
meta-analysis. *Psychol Bull.* 1991;110:26–46.
12. Shadish WR, Haddock CK. Combining estimates of effect size. In: Cooper H, Hedges LV, eds. *The Handbook of Research Synthesis.* New
York. NY: Russell Sage Foundation; 1994:261–281.
13. Cohen J. *Statistical Power Analysis for the Behavioral Sciences.* 2nd ed.
Hillsdale, NJ: Lawrence Erlbaum Associates; 1998.
14. Ahmed NU, Ahmed NS, Bennett CR, Hinds JE. Impact of a drug abuse
resistance education (D.A.R.E.) program in preventing the initiation of
cigarette smoking in fifth- and sixth-grade students. *J Natl Med Assoc.*
2002;94:249–256.
15. Shedler J, Block J. Adolescent drug use and psychological health: A
longitudinal inquiry. *Am Psychol.* 1990;45:612–630.
16. Rosenbaum DP, Hanson GS. Assessing the effects of a school-based
drug education: A six-year multilevel analysis of Project D.A.R.E. *J Res
Crime Delinquency.* 1998;35:381–412.
17. Improving and evaluating the D.A.R.E. school-based substance abuse
prevention curriculum. Available at: http://www.rwjf.org/programs/
grantDetail.jsp?id=040371. Accessed January 8, 2003.
18. Ringwalt C, Ennett ST, Holt KD. An outcome evaluation of Project
D.A.R.E. (Drug Abuse Resistance Education). *Health Educ Res.*
1991;6:327–337.
19. Becker HK, Agopian MW, Yeh S. Impact evaluation of drug abuse resistance education (D.A.R.E.). *J Drug Educ.* 1992;22:283–291.
20. Harmon MA. Reducing the risk of drug involvement among early adolescents: An evaluation of drug abuse resistance education (D.A.R.E.).
Eval Rev. 1993;17:221–239.
21. Ennett ST, Rosenbaum DP, Flewelling RL, Bieler GS, Ringwalt CL,
Bailey SL. Long-term evaluation of drug abuse resistance education.
Addict Behav. 1994;19:113–125.
22. Rosenbaum DP, Flewelling RL, Bailey SL, Ringwalt CL, Wilkinson DL.
Cops in the classroom: A longitudinal evaluation of drug abuse resistance education (D.A.R.E.). *J Res Crime Delinquency.* 1994;31:3–31.
23. Wysong E, Aniskiewicz R, Wright D. Truth and D.A.R.E.: Tracking
drug education to graduation and as symbolic politics. *Soc Probl.*
1994;41:448–472.
24. Dukes RL, Ulllman JB, Stein JA. Three-year follow-up of drug abuse
resistance education (D.A.R.E.). *Eval Rev.* 1996;20:49–66.
25. Zagumny MJ, Thompson MK. Does D.A.R.E. work? An evaluation in
rural Tennessee. *J Alcohol Drug Educ.* 1997;42:32–41.
26. Thombs DL. A retrospective study of D.A.R.E.: Substantive effects not
detected in undergraduates. *J Alcohol Drug Educ.* 2000;46:27–40.

Acknowledgments: Portions of this research were presented at the
Eighth Annual Meeting of the Society for Prevention Research,
Montreal, Quebec, Canada, June 2000.

About the authors: *Steven L. West* is with the Department of Rehabilitation Counseling, Virginia Commonwealth University, Richmond. *Keri K. O'Neal* is with the Center for Developmental Science,
University of North Carolina, Chapel Hill. Drs. West and O'Neal
contributed equally to all aspects of study design, data analysis, and
the writing of this article. No protocol approval was needed for this
study.

Address correspondence to: Steven L. West, Ph.D., Virginia Commonwealth University, Department of Rehabilitation Counseling,
1112 East Clay St., Box 980330, Richmond, VA 23298-0330.
E-mail: slwest2@vcu.edu

Exercise for Article 36

Factual Questions

1. To identify the articles for this meta-analysis, the
researchers conducted computer searches of which
three databases?

2. Which study had the largest effect size (r)? (Identify it by the name of the author and year of publication.) What was the value of r in this study?

3. What was the average weighted effect size (r) for
all studies included in this meta-analysis?

4. The study with the largest effect size examined
only one outcome. What was the outcome?

5. According to Figure 1, the study with the longest
follow-up time had what effect size?

6. Were the researchers able to find any major
evaluations of the *new* D.A.R.E. paradigm?

Questions for Discussion

7. The researchers do not describe the D.A.R.E. program components. In your opinion, would it have
been desirable for them to do so? Explain.

8. What is your opinion of the researchers' decision
to include only research reported in peer-reviewed
journals? (See lines 58–66.)

9. What is your opinion of the researchers' decision
to include only evaluations that included a control
or comparison group? (See lines 67–69.)

10. Does it surprise you that the study by Becker et al. in Table 1 has negative effect sizes? Explain.

11. In Table 1, 95% confidence intervals are reported. What is your understanding of the meaning of these intervals?

12. What is your opinion on the researchers' suggestion in lines 134–138? Is your opinion based on the data in this meta-analysis? Explain.

Quality Ratings

Directions: Indicate your level of agreement with each of the following statements by circling a number from 5 for strongly agree (SA) to 1 for strongly disagree (SD). If you believe an item is not applicable to this research article, leave it blank. Be prepared to explain your ratings. When responding to criteria A and B below, keep in mind that brief titles and abstracts are conventional in published research.

A. The title of the article is appropriate.

SA   5   4   3   2   1   SD

B. The abstract provides an effective overview of the research article.

SA   5   4   3   2   1   SD

C. The introduction establishes the importance of the study.

SA   5   4   3   2   1   SD

D. The literature review establishes the context for the study.

SA   5   4   3   2   1   SD

E. The research purpose, question, or hypothesis is clearly stated.

SA   5   4   3   2   1   SD

F. The method of sampling is sound.

SA   5   4   3   2   1   SD

G. Relevant demographics (for example, age, gender, and ethnicity) are described.

SA   5   4   3   2   1   SD

H. Measurement procedures are adequate.

SA   5   4   3   2   1   SD

I. All procedures have been described in sufficient detail to permit a replication of the study.

SA   5   4   3   2   1   SD

J. The participants have been adequately protected from potential harm.

SA   5   4   3   2   1   SD

K. The results are clearly described.

SA   5   4   3   2   1   SD

L. The discussion/conclusion is appropriate.

SA   5   4   3   2   1   SD

M. Despite any flaws, the report is worthy of publication.

SA   5   4   3   2   1   SD

Article 37

Risk Taking As Developmentally Appropriate Experimentation for College Students

JODI DWORKIN
University of Minnesota

ABSTRACT. Researchers have suggested that experimentation may be a necessary, constructive component of identity formation. However, these researchers have also noted the paradox of risk taking; an individual may experience both positive and negative precursors and consequences of risk taking. The present investigation used qualitative methods to explore the personal meaning of experimentation behaviors and of this paradox to college students. A stratified sample of 12 community college students (6 female) and 20 university students (10 female) was interviewed. Data were analyzed using grounded theory methods. Students described a deliberate and functional process of experimenting with a variety of risk behaviors. This included articulating the ways in which the college culture promotes participation in risk behaviors as developmentally appropriate experimentation.

From *Journal of Adolescent Research, 20,* 219–241. Copyright © 2005 by Sage Publications. Reprinted with permission.

The concept of risks as opportunities for adolescents can be traced back to the work of G. Stanley Hall (1904). Hall argued that parents and educators should exert limited control over adolescents, thereby enabling their experimentation. However, this perspective has not received serious attention until recently (Lightfoot, 1997). From this perspective, it has been suggested that risk behaviors are deliberate and goal directed, the product of subjectively rational decisions. In fact, scholars have posited that adolescents actively choose and shape their environment and actively seek out risks because of the potential for challenge and excitement (Chassin, 1997; Lightfoot, 1997). It has further been argued that experimentation serves developmentally appropriate functions (Baumrind, 1985; Jessor & Jessor, 1977; Maggs, Almeida, & Galambos, 1995; Silbereisen, Noack, & Reitzle, 1987), such as facilitating peer interactions, teaching youth to negotiate behaviors that become legal post-adolescence, and facilitating identity achievement. This perspective challenges the traditional assumption that adolescents are merely victims of antisocial peer influences (Chassin, 1997) and presents risk behaviors as experimentation behaviors that afford youth positive developmental opportunities.

However, researchers have also noted the paradox of risk taking; an individual may experience both positive and negative precursors and consequences of risk taking (Maggs et al., 1995; Maggs & Hurrelmann, 1998). The present investigation used qualitative methods to explore the personal meaning of experimentation behaviors and of this paradox to emerging adults in college. Emerging adults are in a transitional period between adolescence and young adulthood, actively experimenting to figure out who they are (Arnett, 2000). College students are often immersed in an anti-academic culture of athletics, campus parties, drinking, fraternities and sororities, and dating (Sperber, 2000). Thus, emerging adults in college are an ideal population to ask about their experiences.

Literature Review

During college, the majority of individuals participate in at least one behavior that adults would consider dangerous and health compromising. Specifically, rates of participation with most substance use, alcohol use, and unprotected sexual activity have been found to peak during emerging adulthood (Johnston, O'Malley, & Bachman, 2003). In addition, college students are more likely to be binge drinkers than their same-age noncollege counterparts. However, in high school, college-bound seniors are less likely to report heavy drinking than noncollege-bound youth. This suggests that emerging adults in college "catch up to and pass" their noncollege peers (Johnston et al., 2003, p. 21). This is not surprising given that college students are in a life stage characterized by risk and testing their limits to find out who they are, living in a relatively unregulated environment surrounded by same-age peers (Arnett, 2000). Fortunately, the majority of these emerging adults are not subject to drastic consequences (Arnett, 1991). Still, there is tremendous concern among parents and educators regarding how to protect emerging adults from these outcomes. Parents and educators strive to help emerging adults make responsible decisions about potentially risky behaviors and to reduce the number of tragedies resulting from poor decisions.

In a study of college students, Parsons, Siegel, and Cousins (1997) found that the perceived benefits of an outcome were more predictive of participation in risky

182

behaviors than students' assessment of the perceived risks. Emerging adults seeking out these benefits might
70 be described as sensation seeking (Zuckerman, 1990). Individuals high on the sensation-seeking personality trait desire sensory stimulation. College students high in sensation seeking, immersed in the college culture, are likely to be seduced by the excitement and intensity
75 of risk behaviors (Horvath & Zuckerman, 1993). And the college culture abounds with opportunities for risk. Unfortunately, the line at which experimentation behaviors become dangerous is often blurred. It is a challenge to determine the point at which developmentally
80 beneficial behaviors become dangerous (Irwin, 1993).

Experimentation behaviors are not inherently dangerous or problematic; rather, negative outcomes occur under certain conditions. It is unlikely that a behavior will be either entirely problematic or conventional. It is
85 possible to engage in both groups of behaviors simultaneously. College students may participate to a greater or lesser degree in a problem behavior and may do so independently of, or in addition to, engaging in more conventional behavior (Jessor & Jessor, 1977). For
90 example, all alcohol use is not the same. There is a difference between having a few sips of beer and getting drunk four times a week. There is a difference between having alcohol during a holiday dinner with family and drinking with friends. There is a difference
95 between drinking and drinking that is followed by driving. Behavior is the product of the interaction between a person and his or her environment. Therefore, to fully understand college student behavior, the influence of both these factors must be examined simultaneously
100 (Jessor, 1987).

To begin to explore this, Shedler and Block (1990) categorized a sample of young people into three groups based on their level of substance use. They defined frequent users as youth who used marijuana frequently
105 and had tried at least one other drug. Abstainers were defined as youth who had never tried drugs. Experimenters were defined as youth who used marijuana no more than once a month and who had tried no more than one other drug. Their data revealed that beginning
110 in childhood, experimenters demonstrated the most positive outcomes. Frequent users were described as undercontrolled, and these youth reported being more alienated, distressed, and having less impulse control than experimenters. Abstainers were described as over-
115 controlled and unnecessarily delaying gratification. These youth reported feeling more anxious, emotionally constricted, and having poorer social skills than experimenters.

Maggs and colleagues (e.g., Maggs et al., 1995;
120 Maggs & Hurrelmann, 1998; Schulenberg, Maggs, & Hurrelmann, 1997) have consistently found that young people who experiment, in a controlled way, with risk behaviors, show the most positive developmental outcomes. For instance, substance use has been found to
125 facilitate peer relationships for adolescents. Research has concluded that adolescents who experiment with substances show higher levels of peer acceptance and involvement, compared with young people participating in more delinquent, antisocial behavior who have
130 fewer and less satisfying peer relationships (Maggs et al., 1995; Maggs & Hurrelmann, 1998).

The finding that participation in risk behaviors often accompanies positive developmental outcomes, in combination with high rates of participation in certain
135 risk-taking behaviors, such as alcohol use, supports the contention that a certain level of risk taking is normative for young people (Baumrind, 1985; Schulenberg et al., 1997; Shedler & Block, 1990). Consequently, to fully understand risk during emerging adulthood, we
140 must recognize and consider both risks and opportunities. The present study builds on this perspective by exploring emerging adults' perspectives of risk behaviors.

Present Investigation

145 College creates an experience that encourages a period of experimentation that is longer than experienced by previous generations and perhaps longer than experienced by emerging adults who do not attend college full-time immediately following high school. As a
150 result, college students are at risk for crossing the unclear boundary between healthy experimentation and dangerous risk taking by participating in behaviors such as binge drinking and unprotected sexual activity. Sperber (2000) even argues that colleges advertise an
155 uninhibited collegiate subculture centered around leisure to attract students, and this culture "demands beer" (p. 192).

The present study is designed to explore the process of experimentation from the viewpoint of the ex-
160 perimenters and to work toward a better understanding of experimentation behaviors. The following questions are addressed:

1. In what ways do emerging adults view risk behavior as a form of developmentally appropriate ex-
165 perimentation?
2. How does the college culture promote risk as experimentation?
3. How does experimentation reflect what is going on developmentally during emerging adulthood?
170 4. What are the implications of these findings for research and for outreach?

The present investigation used in-depth interviews. In-depth interviewing provides access to a clearer understanding of why people act as they do by working
175 toward an appreciation of the meaning they give to their behaviors (Jones, 1985). Interviews address an individual's subjective experience of a preanalyzed situation in an attempt to draw out his or her definitions of the situation. Allowing emerging adults to describe
180 their experiences, in-depth, using their own words, provides the best understanding of their construction of

their experiences with experimentation (Jones, 1985). Interviews help formulate new hypotheses that will support the systematic examination of experimentation behaviors in the future (Merton, Fiske, & Kendall, 1990).

Method

To obtain a more holistic view of experimentation, I used a dual interpretive methodology. First, a phenomenological perspective guided data collection and analysis (van Manen, 1984) to provide access to the meanings that individuals assign to the process of experimentation (Morse, 1994). Second, grounded theory (Glaser & Strauss, 1967) provided a method for building a theory of experimentation usable by scholars (Morse, 1994), without being limited by preconceived notions of risk taking (Glaser, 1978).

Participants

A stratified sample of 32 college students was interviewed for this research (see Table 1). The sample was stratified across institution, gender, age, and ethnic group. Twenty students were recruited from a large midwestern university, and 12 students were recruited from a midwestern community college. Incorporating student experiences at different types of institutions allows for a sample and an experience more representative of college students. At the time of the study, all participants were full-time students. To assist with stratification, students were recruited through student organizations on each campus, including cultural, ethnic, arts, academic, and athletic organizations.

Table 1
Participants

Demographics	Community College (*n* = 20)	University (*n* = 20)
Age		
18 years	2	1
19 years	4	5
20 years	3	4
21 years	2	7
22 years	1	3
Gender		
Female	6	10
Male	6	10
Ethnicity		
Latino	0	6
African American	3	6
White	8	8
Asian (not U.S. born)	1	0
Hometown		
Urban	2	8
Suburban	4	7
Rural	6	5
Family Structure		
Two-parent family	7	14
Single-parent family	4	5
Grandparents	1	1

Note. Cells = *n*

To recruit university students, an electronic mail message was forwarded to at least 1,500 students who were involved in registered student organizations. Students who had already participated recruited a few students through word of mouth. Interested participants were asked to contact me directly to learn more about the study and arrange a time for an interview. Because of the large number of university students who volunteered to participate, I was able to select the students I chose to interview. Interested students were sent an electronic mail message requesting their gender, age, academic year, ethnicity, and when they would be available for an interview. University students were then selected for interviews based on gender, academic year, and ethnicity. Every student I contacted to participate in an interview participated. The lower response rate at the community college did not allow me to be as selective.

To recruit students at the community college, I contacted the director of student life who provided me with a list of student organizations. Because of the limited number of organizations, an electronic mail message describing the study was sent to the 15 faculty advisors who were responsible for active student organizations. Six advisors responded to my initial electronic mail. Phone calls were then made to the advisors who did not respond. As a result of this effort, three advisors agreed to forward an electronic mail message to group members. The electronic mail message described the study and requested that interested students contact me directly to learn more about the study and arrange a time for an interview. Two advisors agreed to allow me to speak to their groups. In the groups, I handed out fliers and had interested students provide contact information. The sixth advisor was responsible for an inactive organization. She agreed to mention the study to students with whom she still had contact. Approximately 100 students were contacted either via electronic mail or in person about the study. Again, a few participants were recruited through word of mouth, by students who had already participated, and by the director of student life. With the exception of one, all students whom I contacted to participate in an interview, participated.

There was much diversity among the community college students whom I interviewed, which reflects the diversity of community college students. The majority of students whom I spoke with were planning on transferring to a 4-year college. One student attended a state university and only attended classes at the community college in the summer. Three students were attending the community college because they had academic trouble at a 4-year university and decided they wanted to remain in college. One of these students was planning on returning to the university to graduate.

Data Collection

Students were interviewed individually, face to face. Interviews were in-depth and semistructured.

Questions were developed from a thorough review of the literature to explore the meaning of risk taking and experimentation to college students (see the Appendix at the end of this article for the core interview ques-
270 tions relevant to the present analyses). Interviews lasted between 50 and 90 minutes and were audiotaped. They were held at a time that was convenient for the student, either on the university campus or on the community college campus. Following the interview,
275 participants completed a brief background questionnaire and a checklist assessing how frequently they participated in a variety of experimentation behaviors. Students received $10 for their participation.

The first five interviews were conducted to pilot the
280 interview protocol and are included in the data analysis. This allowed me to generate additional questions, eliminate questions, and adjust the order of the questions as needed. However, it should be noted that adaptations were made throughout the process of data col-
285 lection to continuously adapt the interview and obtain the most complete data. This modification process is consistent with grounded theory methods (Strauss & Corbin, 1990).

Throughout data collection, I maintained a journal.
290 Immediately following each interview, I recorded nonverbal expressions, emerging themes, interpretations, details of the interview, and conversations that were not recorded (Taylor & Bogdan, 1998). This information was treated as data and analyzed accordingly.

Data Analysis

295 The present investigation relied on the constant comparative method of interpretive analysis. This method of analysis encourages systematic generation of theory through inductive coding and analysis (Glaser & Strauss, 1967).

300 These data were analyzed under the assumption that the data provided by participants corresponds to their actual experiences and to the meanings they apply to these experiences. In addition, interpretation of the data included distinguishing between solicited and unsolic-
305 ited statements and considering how my background affected the direction of the interview and influenced the data (Taylor & Bogdan, 1998).

Consistent with the constant comparative method of interpretive analysis, data analysis consisted of seven
310 steps, using three levels of coding. First, I transcribed the interviews verbatim, noting salient features such as long pauses and laughter (Riessman, 1993). To preserve participant confidentiality, the interviews were transcribed using pseudonyms and eliminating any
315 identifying information. To ensure accuracy, I then carefully checked the transcripts against the tapes. The second step was to read the transcripts many times, looking for themes, patterns, and concepts. Each interview was summarized. Third, the interview data were
320 sorted by the eliciting empirical interview question (see the Appendix for the interview questions). Fourth, to

categorize and sort the interview data, the data were coded into conceptual categories within empirical questions. This was the first level of coding (Charmaz,
325 1988; Taylor & Bogdan, 1998). Every event and idea of a given phenomenon was named. Data were then grouped around phenomena, or categorized, thereby reducing the number of units of analysis (Strauss & Corbin, 1990). For example, in one set of analyses,
330 data were grouped around the type of activity the student described.

Fifth, I performed axial coding, the second level of coding. Axial coding is a more intense form of coding centered on a specific phenomenon or category. It is
335 used to identify the properties of the already identified categories, thereby providing more specificity. I labeled specific events and experiences within each phenomenon, thereby generating subcategories (Strauss, 1987). Analyses were conducted both within and be-
340 tween categories and within and between subcategories. For instance, grouping data by activity allowed for analyses both within and between social activities that did and did not involve substance use. I was then able to identify shared experiences between individuals and
345 those experiences that were unique (Patton, 1990; Taylor & Bogdan, 1998).

Sixth, I performed selective coding, the third level of coding. To gain even more specificity, I coded those subcategories that were significantly tied to the core
350 category and that facilitated an understanding of this category (Strauss, 1987). Finally, I identified the cases that did not fit the model as a way to either discount part of the model or for suggesting additional relationships (Strauss & Corbin, 1990; Taylor & Bogdan,
355 1998).

Following grounded theory procedures, after the data were coded, I diagrammed the relationships between constructs (Strauss & Corbin, 1990). Diagrams allowed me to visually depict the relationships between
360 concepts and move from coding to defining the emerging concepts. After data analysis was complete, I went back to the literature to improve my understanding of the findings, not to support, discount, or provide additional data but to help explain the findings, and put
365 them in a context (Strauss & Corbin, 1990).

The relationships that emerged from students' descriptions of their experiences and that were diagrammed are described in the following sections. These relationships are exemplified by direct quotes
370 from students (Ryan & Bernard, 2000). Consistent with this process, the results and discussion are presented as one section.

Results and Discussion

Although risk taking has been explored extensively (Bell & Bell, 1993; Jessor & Jessor, 1977), researchers
375 have yet to give as much attention to experimentation and include the emerging adult perspective in this definition. First, the relationship between experimentation

and risk taking from the perspective of emerging adults will be explored. Next, I will consider the ways in
380 which the college culture promotes emerging adult experimentation. Third, the ways in which experimentation is developmentally appropriate for college students will be considered. Finally, there will be a discussion of the implications of these findings for re-
385 search and outreach.

Relationship Between Experimentation and Risk Taking

Experimentation. Students described experimentation as an active process of figuring out who they are and what they are capable of through making intentional and deliberate decisions. For instance, Alexis
390 said, "you have to experiment to find out who you are, and what you like. It's like as little as trying new foods to whether or not you want to sleep around." These emerging adults described a process of experimentation consistent with the process of decision making about
395 risky behavior described by Furby and Beyth-Marom (1992). They described being motivated to experiment by a desire to test their limits, both their personal limits and the limits of the behavior.

Emerging adults described experimenting with a
400 variety of different behaviors. Many students described starting to question the religious beliefs their parents raised them with and having the opportunity in college to experiment with other religions through coursework. Next, students described meeting new people, more
405 specifically meeting people different from them. For instance, a few students mentioned that dating someone of a different race was a form of experimentation. Through experimentation, they could learn about others and have their stereotypes debunked, not only stereo-
410 types based on race or ethnicity but also on sexual orientation, or stereotypes based on whether someone grew up in a city or on a farm. Students also talked about experimenting with taking different classes and with extracurricular activities, such as joining a new
415 club or trying a new sport.

In addition, the overwhelming majority of students mentioned substance use, alcohol use, or sexual activity. Ben described experimenting with alcohol: "I think it's important for people to test alcohol out. You know
420 part of that is you're gonna get sick sometimes but hopefully that's in the beginning stages and you learn from that."

Risk taking. Students defined risk taking as intentional and functional behavior. They described a delib-
425 erate process of trial and error, taking a chance, or a risk, to see what would happen. Many of these emerging adults were unclear about whether the risk was the behavior, and, as such, certain behaviors were inherently risky, or whether the risk was the outcome, and a
430 behavior could not be defined as risk taking until after experiencing the outcome. Nearly every student described risk taking based on the outcome. For instance,

Gabriel, a substance user, believed drugs were not inherently risky and noted that whether an individual
435 views them as risky is dependent on the outcome.

> If people value their body as a temple, then taking drugs is a risk because you're harming your body. If you see your body as just a vessel that you're in then it's not really risky, then it's just experimentation, how much can
440 you do to this vessel before it collapses.

Consequently, whether emerging adults choose to take a risk is based on their understanding of the potential outcomes, their assessment of the probability of the outcomes, the personal value of the outcomes, and
445 whether they see themselves as vulnerable to experiencing the outcomes, regardless of the probability that each will actually occur. This is consistent with past research (Beyth-Marom & Fischhoff, 1997; Fischhoff, Lichtenstein, Slovic, Derby, & Keeney, 1981; Furby &
450 Beyth-Marom, 1992). Individuals are willing to risk different things and see themselves as more or less vulnerable to actually experiencing those outcomes. As Jacob said, "the risk is defined by what you view as acceptable."
455 Consistent with this, when asked to identify behaviors they viewed as risk taking, there was a huge range in students' responses. The most frequently mentioned behaviors were applying for a job, drinking to excess, drunk driving, drag racing, unprotected sexual activity,
460 stealing, and certain drugs, with only three to six out of 32 emerging adults mentioning each.

Risk taking as a form of experimentation. After considering experimentation and risk taking independently, students were asked to discuss the relationship
465 between the two. Students offered three possible relationships: experimentation and risk taking are the same, experimentation and risk taking are opposite ends of one continuum, and experimentation and risk taking are two separate constructs. When describing
470 the first scenario, which was only endorsed by four students, students discussed that there are many similarities between experimentation and risk taking. Perhaps most important, both are functional and intentional behaviors. For instance, emerging adults de-
475 scribed a similar process for assessing the outcome of experimentation and risk-taking behaviors. Dalila described her impressions of the similarities between experimentation and risk taking.

> With experimenting you're trying to see if it's gonna
480 work or not, and that's what you're doing with risk taking. And they both do have side effects....I think they go hand in hand because when you take a risk or when you experiment, you're gonna find out a solution that's good or bad.
485 In the second scenario, in which experimentation and risk taking are opposite ends of one continuum, which again was only supported by four students, the intensity of the behavior determines whether a behavior is experimentation or risk taking. Although unable to

490 identify the point at which behaviors become dangerous, students were clear that an acceptable risk reaches
a threshold at which point it becomes dangerous. For
instance, Amanda said,

495 I think there's a point to where you're experimenting,
like...if it's your first time drinking...I think that that's
when you're experimenting, but after awhile it just becomes risk taking...you know whether you like it....I think
there is a point to where it kind of switches over...you're
just plain taking a risk.

500 In this example, casual drinking might be experimentation, whereas habitual drinking would be risk taking.

The final relationship, that experimentation and risk
taking are unique constructs, earned the most endorsement from students. This relationship suggests that a
505 behavior could be experimentation, it could be risk
taking, or it could be both. Therefore, although they are
two unique constructs, they are not mutually exclusive
categories. Gabriel explained this well when he said,

You can experiment with something and it can also be a
510 risk, just as you can take a risk which might be an experiment. But you can also do an experiment that has no
risk to it, and you can also take risks that aren't experiments. So I mean, I think they're sort of interrelated, but
they don't have to be.

515 When discussing experimentation and risk taking as
two separate constructs, emerging adults distinguished
between them in two ways. They described a public
distinction and a personal distinction. The public distinction lies in other's perceptions, particularly the per-
520 ceptions of parents and other adult authority figures, of
what emerging adults do and the connotation of the
language used by the general public to describe emerging adult behavior. From this perspective, risk-taking
behaviors are most often functionally irrelevant. The
525 personal distinction, or how emerging adults understand their experimentation, will be highlighted here.

The primary distinction between experimentation
and risk taking articulated by emerging adults was in
the process. Experimentation was described as a learn-
530 ing process, a process designed to achieve a goal. Risk
taking was more likely to be spontaneous and motivated by a desire to be challenged. Participants described risk taking as inherently more dangerous.

Students also described the personal distinction as
535 being influenced by their knowledge and preparation
before participating in a given behavior, including
whether they were aware of the potential consequences
and whether they took precautions to avoid a negative
outcome. With experimentation, emerging adults de-
540 scribed being more prepared and taking precautions to
avoid undesirable outcomes. They described risk taking
as less likely to be planned. And some emerging adults
explained that whether a behavior was experimentation
or risk taking was determined simply by their personal
545 values and how they felt about the behavior.

In these descriptions, students explained that there
is something about college that is conducive to and
encourages, or perhaps even facilitates, experimentation in a way that other contexts do not. To gain a bet-
550 ter understanding of this, students were asked to describe "what is it about college that encourages experimentation." In their explanations, students sponta-
neously produced the phrase *college culture*. They
were then asked to describe the college culture.

College Culture

555 Students' descriptions of the college culture were
consistent with the image of college portrayed in the
media and described by Sperber (2000): students struggling academically, all night parties that include drinking alcohol, promiscuous sex, and drug use. For exam-
560 ple, Paul said, "I hear college student, I think, alright
this guy drinks every weekend, keeps a 2.5 maybe."
And many emerging adults described entering college
with the expectation that their experiences were going
to be consistent with this image. Stacey, a community
565 college student, described her expectations: "You're
supposed to drink, and you're supposed to listen to
Dave Mathews Band....It's just the rule when you're in
college." Students described the college culture as providing them with the free time and opportunity to ex-
570 periment with what it meant to be independent from
their parents, including questioning the things their
parents had always told them. Alexis described this
experience:

You have adolescents, and they're all trying to figure out
575 who they are, and they're all saying, well my parents said
this was wrong, well really is it? Everything comes into
question. Is it really wrong to smoke pot? Is it really
wrong to sleep around? Is it really wrong to swear?

Community college students who were still living
580 at home described maintaining much more contact with
their families and, therefore, being more influenced by
their parents' beliefs or at least feeling obligated to
respect their parents' beliefs while they were still living
with them.

585 Both university and community college students
explained that many things contribute to college students' high rates of participation in risk behaviors, such
as drinking alcohol, using substances, and sexual activity. Emerging adults said that participation in risk be-
590 haviors and the development of a college culture was
most influenced by independence and living away from
their parents, or at least spending significantly more
time away from their parents. Most students reported
having few real world responsibilities. For example,
595 most said they were not financially independent from
their parents, thus, they did not have to worry about
budgeting their money between leisure activities, such
as buying alcohol and paying their bills. Emerging
adults described college as an environment in which
600 they were responsible for making their own decisions,
relatively unburdened by real world responsibilities,

surrounded by other young people making the same decisions. For example, Jacob, a university student said,

There's a carefree attitude experiencing college...my friends and I refer to as the safety bubble of school, you can do whatever you want. You can get up at 8 in the morning and drink for a football game, you're not an alcoholic, you're a party animal. But if you do that in the real world, then you'll go to treatment.

Most students expressed this same sentiment, that there were few or no consequences to their behaviors. This is consistent with past research, which has found that the majority of young people do not experience negative consequences as a result of participating in risky behaviors (Arnett, 1991).

Another important contributor to the development of the college culture described by these young people was the college environment. They defined the college environment to include the opportunities for experimentation that were available and the array of new experiences, people, and ideas to which students were exposed. Alexis, a community college student, described how she felt the college environment contributed to the college culture.

You stick 36,000 students who are basically between the ages of 18 and 25 together, without parents...they're on their own for the first time, they're all going to school...when you shove all of these people in a small area, I think it's gonna develop a culture of its own, and I think that would be the weekend ritual of getting dressed up and going out and getting blitzed [drunk] or going dancing or finding a guy to sleep with. Not everybody does it, but a lot of people do. It's kind of more acceptable.

As highlighted by Alexis, college students are surrounded by opportunity, with plenty of free time to act on those opportunities. This represents one extreme of how students described their experiences.

At the other extreme, students described adamantly opposing the stereotypical college culture and working hard to not behave in ways consistent with that image. The group of emerging adults in the middle described behaving with moderation, refusing to accept the college culture without experiencing it for themselves. They described a process of negotiating the image of the college student and figuring out how that fit into their developing sense of self. For example, Jacob, a university student, said,

The first thing I saw was a frat house, with girls in bikinis and guys throwing beer cans at cars, and I was like, this place is gonna be awesome. That was my idea of school then....All these beautiful girls who are just willing to have sex on a drop of a dime....I opted to change that rather quickly. I didn't find it to be as rewarding as most people think....It kind of lured me away from the stereotypical idea of fun, kinda made hanging out and relaxing with a smaller group of people who you really value as your friends...much more important.

Negotiating where they fit into the college culture might be seen as one part of the larger process of finding their niche in society. For instance, Amina said, "I think the whole time in college it's just about learning about yourself and then learning about things that are interesting to you, just exploring the different parts of your identity or interests."

Moratorium and the college culture. Emerging adults' descriptions of the college culture suggest that although they believed that they would be actively experimenting throughout their lives to constantly refine who they are, rates of experimentation are particularly high throughout college. For instance, Stacey said,

Right now, you're just kinda in between. You're about to be on your own, where you have to decide everything for yourself. I think before I make those decisions without anything to back me up, I think right now is a good time to kind of figure all that stuff out before I get more into a job and a family and things like that.

This period of active exploration described by students is consistent with Erikson's (1959, 1965, 1968) description of the period of moratorium, a period characterized by change and transition during which individuals search for their niche in society. Moratorium is characterized by experimentation and learning about oneself to move closer to a stable identity. In moratorium, young people experiment with many different things that facilitate learning about self, including learning their limits; learning how things affect them; learning about others; learning about society and social norms; learning facts, skills, and information; and gaining experiences to use for future reference (Erikson, 1959; Grotevant, 1992).

Emerging adulthood, characterized as a period of moratorium for many young people, may be the most intense time of life. Young people have survived the dependence associated with adolescence, but having not yet earned all of the responsibilities of adulthood (Arnett, 2000). During this transition, young people approach the adult world and work toward accepting an introductory adult identity, making commitments to interpersonal relationships and occupational undertakings, and identifying a value system that is consistent with both self and society (Hauser & Greene, 1991).

When asked whether they felt they were "in a period of active exploration to figure out who you are," overwhelmingly, students reported they were. In the interview, 25 students said they were definitely in a period of active exploration, four students said "sort of," two students said they were not exploring but their responses suggested otherwise, and one student was not asked because he had to end the interview early to keep a prior commitment. In the interview, all students described extremely high rates of trying new things, evidence they were actively involved in this process of exploration. In the questionnaire, 77% of all emerging adults reported having changed peer groups, 91%

joined or quit an activity, 75% began or ended an intimate relationship, and 81% changed fashion, at least once in the past year, indications of being in moratorium.

This group of emerging adults attributed their high rates of experimentation to two primary transitions: the transition out of high school and into college and the transition to greater independence. What they described as most meaningful about the transition from high school to college was that it was a transition to a new environment. Data revealed that the intensity of this experience varied by whether they moved away from home, how far they moved, and how different the new location was. These emerging adults explained that a new environment provided access to many new opportunities, experiences, behaviors, ideas, options, and people who provided access to many of these opportunities. Because the majority of the community college students were still living at home or in their hometown, they described having access to different experiences than university students. They had access to fewer extracurricular activities, but to a student body that was more diverse in terms of age and life stage. This group of community college students described being more committed to their education than the university students and was more certain about their career goals.

The second major transition described was increased independence. The development of independence was greatly affected by the factors just described. Regardless of whether students continued to live at home or moved away, they described spending significantly more time away from their parents and, thus, felt they had more responsibility for making their own decisions.

Emerging adults' descriptions of being in moratorium and actively working to figure out who they are serves as further support for the contention that experimentation is intentional and functional behavior, which is developmentally appropriate for college students.

Implications

This study focused on the ways emerging adults in college view risk behavior as a form of developmentally appropriate experimentation, providing many implications for research and for outreach.

Implications for Research

These data provide a foundation for future research in numerous ways. First, these students did not identify themselves as risk takers. They identified themselves as experimenters. This suggests that it may be more effective to talk with emerging adults about experimentation rather than a continued focus on risk taking. However, the use of the word experimentation may have confounded the process of data collection. The word experimentation connotes a systematic scientific process. Consequently, some students may have been defining the word *experimentation* rather than describing how they viewed their experiences with experimentation.

Second, students made a distinction between behavioral extremes, suggesting that consistent with the findings of other researchers, emerging adults do not view their activities as inherently risky (Graber & Brooks-Gunn, 1995; Jessor, 1987).

Third, college students' descriptions suggest that research needs to study a variety of behaviors to identify healthy experimentation behaviors that are functionally equivalent to dangerous risk taking behaviors and would therefore help emerging adults avoid negative consequences from risk behaviors (Silbereisen et al., 1987; Silbereisen & Reitzle, 1991). Research needs to work toward identifying the point in the process of experimentation at which participation in these behaviors becomes dangerous, the point at which the potential for negative outcomes greatly increases, and the point at which participation in dangerous behaviors becomes habitual.

Implications for Outreach

The challenge of outreach becomes evident very quickly when talking with college students about experimentation and risk taking. These students defined behaviors as dangerous based on the outcome. If a behavior cannot be identified as dangerous until after a negative outcome has been experienced, how can prevention efforts aimed at identifying and avoiding dangerous risk taking be successful? Although there is still a tremendous amount of research to be conducted, these data are critical for a new approach to outreach.

Outreach efforts that have focused on prevention and intervention typically target the minority of youth who are inexperienced risk takers or experimenters and the minority of youth experiencing real crisis. However, there is a large, often neglected number of youth in a middle group, a group described as experimenters (Shedler & Block, 1990) who experiment with a variety of behaviors and often demonstrate optimal outcomes but could experience crisis. Identifying the process of experimentation and the functions that experimentation behaviors serve, outreach efforts can begin to target experimenters and work to redirect youth behaviors, provide youth with alternatives to dangerous behavior, encourage youth to take precautions when participating in potentially dangerous behaviors, and prevent youth from experiencing real crisis.

Preventing participation in dangerous risk taking might also be achieved by promoting positive behaviors. Rather than trying to directly prevent youth substance use, an alternative approach would be to promote social activities that do not involve substances but fulfill the same needs of young people and thereby eliminate the need for substances, what others have referred to as functionally equivalent behaviors (Silbereisen & Reitzle, 1991). Jason, a heavy drug user, said,

> I think they're [drugs] important because it has added beneficial aspect, but if I had to do without and was said, okay you just have to party without drugs and without alcohol, that wouldn't be a big deal because...it's not really a focus, it's just something we do.

Thus, outreach efforts might be directed toward strengthening and promoting healthy experimentation and risk taking and responsible decision making rather than only working to prevent youth participation in dangerous risk taking. Students supported this. Josh, who had been a heavy substance and alcohol user, described changing his activities:

> I still take risks. I just changed it. I do more [rock] climbing and stuff like that....I always like that sense of danger a little bit, that risk to take, but I just do it in other ways.

Limitations and Future Directions

Although the present investigation begins to elucidate the process of experimentation for emerging adults in college, this study is limited. First, these students represent volunteers from one large public university and one community college, both in the same midwestern town. It is also cautioned that these results not be generalized to the experiences of emerging adults who do not attend college, the "forgotten half" ("The Forgotten Half," 1988), or to younger youth. Second, although the sample was relatively diverse in terms of gender and race and ethnicity, the small sample size does not allow for analyses within or between groups. Future research should explore experimentation from the perspective of different populations and should explore gender, racial and ethnic, and socioeconomic differences in young people's experiences with both healthy experimentation and dangerous risk taking. Quantitative measures are needed to survey much larger samples of young people to better understand their experiences with experimentation and risk taking. Third, although most students were describing behaviors that they were still participating in, hindsight self-report may have distorted their understanding of their experiences. Future research might work to capture young people's experiences, when they are in the moment, so to speak.

Conclusion

The concept of experimentation as distinct from risk taking was salient for nearly every student interviewed. Although researchers (e.g., Baumrind, 1985; Jessor & Jessor, 1977; Maggs et al., 1995) have suggested a definition of experimentation as functional and intentional, the present results contribute the emerging adult perspective to this definition. Students were able to articulate the relationship between experimentation and risk taking and distinguish between functional experimentation and dangerous risk taking. They situated experimentation in the college culture, an environment

resulting from increased independence and spending less time with their parents.

Overwhelmingly, this group of emerging adults described their experiments as successful, even the decisions that might have had an undesirable outcome. The majority agreed that "I wouldn't change anything ...because it's a learning experience." With each behavior providing emerging adults with opportunities for learning and growth, perhaps emerging adults need to experiment with a variety of behaviors to gain the full array of skills necessary for adult life. Mark said, "I think if you want to learn a really good lesson, the best way to learn it is by experiencing it and knowing first hand that I can't do that or else such and such will happen." Students' ability to articulate their process of experimentation is extremely valuable, and their words have many implications for research and for outreach.

Appendix–Partial Interview Guide

Today, I would like to hear about your experiences of trying things as you work to figure out who you are. This might include clothes, activities, alcohol, drugs, driving, art, poetry, friendships, intimate relationships, sexuality and anything else, whether it is legal or illegal. I want this to be a casual conversation, and I want to hear your opinions and your stories. My goal is to develop a more realistic definition and understanding of young adults' experiences.

1. What new behaviors have you tried since starting college?
2. How do you think you have changed since starting college?
3. How would you describe yourself?
4. What sorts of things do you do to help you figure out who you are?

A. I would like to start off by talking specifically about your experiences with these behaviors. (I will go through the following questions for one or two of the behaviors identified above. In the first few interviews, I will ask which behavior they would like to talk about. As I conduct more interviews, I may choose which behaviors we discuss to ensure a diversity of behaviors.)

1. What are the different reasons that you do [the behavior]?
2. What, if anything, is dangerous or risky about this?
3. What, if anything, is safe or positive about this?
4. How likely are these outcomes?
5. How important are the risks to you?
6. How important are the positive things to you?
7. What do you learn about yourself from this experience?
8. What do you learn about others from this experience?
9. How does it help you grow as a person?
10. How does it help you develop your sense of self?
11. How do you feel about yourself when you do it?

12. How do you feel about yourself afterwards?

13. Would you make the same decision again? Why or why not?

14. Would you recommend this behavior to someone else? Why or why not?

15. What do you tell people about it?

16. What would your parents or guardians think about it?

17. How does being X (gender, race or ethnicity, social class, religion) influence what you do or how you feel about it?

B. Application

1. How do you decide if a behavior is too dangerous or too risky?

2. How do your friends or peers make this distinction?

C. I'm interested in how you define experimentation and risk taking.

1. How do you define experimentation?

2. What things do people do that count as experimenting?

3. How do you define risk taking?

4. What things do people do that count as risk taking?

5. Do the reasons you would experiment differ from the reasons you might take risks?

6. Can you give some specific examples?

7. Talk about the similarities and differences between risk taking and experimentation.

8. How does being X (gender, race or ethnicity, social class, religion) influence how you think about experimentation or risk taking?

Moratorium

1. Some people believe that college students are in a period of active experimentation as they work to figure out who they are. Tell me about how this does or does not describe you right now.

2. What is it about college that allows you to do that?

References

Arnett, J. (1991). Still crazy after all these years: Reckless behavior among young adults aged 23–27. *Personality and Individual Differences, 12,* 1305–1313.

Arnett, J. J. (2000). Emerging adulthood: A theory of development from the late teens through the twenties. *American Psychologist, 55,* 469–480.

Baumrind, D. (1985). Familial antecedents of adolescent drug use: A developmental perspective. *National Institute on Drug Abuse: Research Monograph Series, 56,* 13–44.

Bell, N. J., & Bell, R. W. (1993). *Adolescent risk taking.* Newbury Park, CA: Sage.

Beyth-Marom, R., & Fischhoff, B. (1997). Adolescents' decisions about risks: A cognitive perspective. In J. Schulenberg, J. L. Maggs, & K. Hurrelmann (Eds.), *Health risks and developmental transitions during adolescence* (pp. 110–135). Cambridge, UK: Cambridge University Press.

Charmaz, K. (1988). The grounded theory method: An explication and interpretation. In R. M. Emerson (Ed.), *Contemporary field research: A collection of readings* (pp. 109–126). Prospect Heights, IL: Waveland.

Chassin, L. (1997). Foreword. In J. Schulenberg, J. L. Maggs, & K. Hurrelmann (Eds.), *Health risks and developmental transitions during adolescence* (pp. xiii–xvi). Cambridge, UK: Cambridge University Press.

Erikson, E. H. (1959). Identity and the life cycle. *Psychological Issues, 1*(1, Monograph 1).

Erikson, E. H. (1965). Youth: Fidelity and diversity. In E. H. Erikson (Ed.), *The challenge of youth* (pp. 1–28). Garden City, NY: Anchor.

Erikson, E. H. (1968). *Identity: Youth and crisis.* New York: Norton.

Fischhoff, B., Lichtenstein, S., Slovic, P., Derby, S. L., & Keeney, R. L. (1981). *Acceptable risk.* New York: Cambridge University Press.

The forgotten half: Pathways to success for American's youth and young families. (1988). Washington, DC: Youth and America's Future.

Furby, L., & Beyth-Marom, R. (1992). Risk taking in adolescence: A decision-making perspective. *Developmental Review, 12,* 1–44.

Glaser, B. G. (1978). *Theoretical sensitivity: Advances in the methodology of grounded theory.* Mill Valley, CA: Sociology Press.

Glaser, B. G., & Strauss, A. L. (1967). *The discovery of grounded theory: Strategies for qualitative research.* Chicago: Aldine.

Graber, J. A., & Brooks-Gunn, J. (1995). Models of development: Understanding risk in adolescence. *Suicide and Life-Threatening Behavior, 25,* 18–25.

Grotevant, H. D. (1992). Assigned and chosen identity components: A process perspective on their integration. In G. R. Adams, T. P. Gullotta, & R. Montemayor (Eds.), *Adolescent identity formation* (pp. 73–90). Newbury Park, CA: Sage.

Hall, G. S. (1904). *Adolescence: Its psychology and its relations to physiology, anthropology, sociology, sex, crime, religion, and education.* New York: Appleton-Century-Crofts.

Hauser, S. T., & Greene, W. M. (1991). Passages from late adolescence to early adulthood. In S. I. Greenspan, & G. H. Pollock (Eds.), *The course of life: Vol. 4. Adolescence* (pp. 377–405). Madison, CT: International Universities Press.

Horvath, P., & Zuckerman, M. (1993). Sensation seeking, risk appraisal, and risky behavior. *Personality & Individual Differences, 14,* 41–52.

Irwin, C. (1993). Adolescence and risk taking: How are they related? In N. J. Bell & R.W. Bell (Eds.), *Adolescent risk taking* (pp. 7–28). Newbury Park, CA: Sage.

Jessor, R. (1987). Problem-behavior theory, psychosocial development, and adolescent problem drinking. *British Journal of Addiction, 82,* 331–342.

Jessor, R., & Jessor, S. L. (1977). *Problem behavior and psychosocial development: A longitudinal study of youth.* New York: Academic Press.

Johnston, L. D., O'Malley, P. M., & Bachman, J. G. (2003). *Monitoring the Future: National survey results on drug use, 1975–2002. Volume II: College students and adults ages 19–40* (NIH Publication No. 03-5376). Bethesda, MD: National Institute on Drug Abuse.

Jones, S. (1985). Depth interviewing. In R. Walker (Ed.), *Applied qualitative research* (pp. 45–55). Aldershot, UK: Gower.

Lightfoot, C. (1997). *The culture of adolescent risk-taking.* New York: Guilford.

Maggs, J. L., Almeida, D. M., & Galambos, N. L. (1995). Risky business: The paradoxical meaning of problem behavior for young adolescents. *Journal of Early Adolescence, 15,* 344–362.

Maggs, J. L., & Hurrelmann, K. (1998). Do substance use and delinquency have differential associations with adolescents' peer relations? *International Journal of Behavioral Development, 22,* 367–388.

Merton, R. K., Fiske, M., & Kendall, P. L. (1990). *The focused interview: A manual of problems and procedures* (2nd ed.). New York: Free Press.

Morse, J. M. (1994). Designing funded qualitative research. In N. K. Denzin & Y. S. Lincoln (Eds.), *Handbook of qualitative research* (pp. 220–235). Thousand Oaks, CA: Sage.

Parsons, J. T., Siegel, A.W., & Cousins, J. H. (1997). Late adolescent risk-taking: Effects of perceived benefits and perceived risks on behavioral intentions and behavioral change. *Journal of Adolescence, 20,* 381–392.

Patton, M. Q. (1990). *Qualitative evaluation and research methods* (2nd ed.). Newbury Park, CA: Sage.

Riessman, C. K. (1993). *Narrative analysis* (Vol. 30). Newbury Park, CA: Sage.

Ryan, G.W., & Bernard, H. R. (2000). Data management and analysis methods. In N. K. Denzin & Y. S. Lincoln (Eds.), *Handbook of qualitative research* (2nd ed., pp. 769–802). Thousand Oaks, CA: Sage.

Schulenberg, J., Maggs, J. L., & Hurrelmann, K. (Eds.). (1997). *Health risks and developmental transitions during adolescence.* Cambridge, UK: Cambridge University Press.

Shedler, J., & Block, J. (1990). Adolescent drug use and psychological health: A longitudinal inquiry. *American Psychologist, 45,* 612–630.

Silbereisen, R. K., Noack, P., & Reitzle, M. (1987). Developmental perspectives on problem behavior and prevention in adolescence. In K. Hurrelmann, F. Kaufmann, & F. Losel (Eds.), *Social intervention: Potential and constraints* (pp. 205–218). New York: de Gruyter.

Silbereisen, R. K., & Reitzle, M. (1991). On the constructive role of problem behavior in adolescence: Further evidence on alcohol use. In L. P. Lipsitt & L. L. Mitnick (Eds.), *Self-regulatory behavior and risk taking: Causes and consequences* (pp. 199–217). Norwood, NJ: Ablex.

Sperber, M. (2000). *Beer and circus: How big-time college sports is crippling undergraduate education.* New York: Henry Holt.

Strauss, A. L. (1987). *Qualitative analysis for social scientists.* New York: Cambridge University Press.

Strauss, A. L., & Corbin, J. (1990). *Basics of qualitative research: Grounded theory procedures and techniques.* Newbury Park, CA: Sage.

Taylor, S. J., & Bogdan, R. (1998). *Introduction to qualitative research methods: A guidebook and resources* (3rd ed.). New York: John Wiley.

van Manen, M. (1984). Practicing phenomenological writing. *Phenomenology and Pedagogy, 2*, 36–69.

Zuckerman, M. (1990). The psychophysiology of sensation seeking. *Journal of Personality, 58*, 313–345.

About the author: Jodi Dworkin earned her Ph.D. in 2002 in human development and family studies from the University of Illinois, Urbana-Champaign. She is currently an assistant professor and extension specialist at the University of Minnesota in the Department of Family Social Science. Her research interests include promoting positive family development, normative adolescent development, adolescent and emerging-adult risk behavior, and parenting.

Address correspondence to: Jodi Dworkin, Department of Family Social Science, 1985 Buford Ave., 290 McNeal Hall, University of Minnesota, St. Paul, MN 55108. E-mail: jdworkin@che.umn.edu

Exercise for Article 37

Factual Questions

1. How many students participated in this study?

2. How many of the students in this study were Latino?

3. To recruit university students, an electronic mail message was forwarded to at least 1,500 students who were involved in what?

4. Did all the community college students the researcher contacted agree to participate? If not, how many did not?

5. In this study, a checklist was used to assess what?

6. According to the researcher, what word might have confounded the process of data collection because it connotes a systematic scientific process?

Questions for Discussion

7. In your opinion, has the researcher provided a convincing argument for the use of in-depth interviews for this study? (See lines 172–186.)

8. In your opinion, to what extent is the use of both community college students and university students a strength of this study? Explain. (See lines 202–205.)

9. In your opinion, are there advantages to audiotaping interviews? Are there disadvantages? Explain. (See lines 270–271 and 310–316.)

10. Before reading this article, how familiar were you with the constant comparative method of qualitative data analysis? To what extent did the description of the data analysis in lines 308–372 in this article improve your understanding of this type of data analysis? Explain.

11. In the results section of qualitative research articles, it is common to provide quotations in the word of the participants. To what extent do the quotations in the results section of this article help you understand the results? In your opinion, would the report of results in this article be as effective without the quotations? Explain. (See lines 373–756.)

12. It is common for the results sections of research reports on qualitative research to be longer than the results sections in reports on quantitative research. In your opinion, could the results section of this article have been shortened without losing important information? Explain. (See lines 373–756.)

13. The researcher describes three limitations of her research in lines 844–869. Do you think that all three are equally important? Is one more important than the others? Explain.

Quality Ratings

Directions: Indicate your level of agreement with each of the following statements by circling a number from 5 for strongly agree (SA) to 1 for strongly disagree (SD). If you believe an item is not applicable to this research article, leave it blank. Be prepared to explain your ratings. When responding to criteria A and B below, keep in mind that brief titles and abstracts are conventional in published research.

A. The title of the article is appropriate.

SA   5   4   3   2   1   SD

B. The abstract provides an effective overview of the research article.

SA   5   4   3   2   1   SD

C. The introduction establishes the importance of the study.

SA   5   4   3   2   1   SD

D. The literature review establishes the context for the study.

SA   5   4   3   2   1   SD

E. The research purpose, question, or hypothesis is clearly stated.

SA   5   4   3   2   1   SD

F. The method of sampling is sound.

SA   5   4   3   2   1   SD

G. Relevant demographics (for example, age, gender, and ethnicity) are described.

SA   5   4   3   2   1   SD

H. Measurement procedures are adequate.

SA   5   4   3   2   1   SD

I. All procedures have been described in sufficient detail to permit a replication of the study.

SA   5   4   3   2   1   SD

J. The participants have been adequately protected from potential harm.

SA   5   4   3   2   1   SD

K. The results are clearly described.

SA   5   4   3   2   1   SD

L. The discussion/conclusion is appropriate.

SA   5   4   3   2   1   SD

M. Despite any flaws, the report is worthy of publication.

SA   5   4   3   2   1   SD

Article 38

Conceptions of Work: The View from Urban Youth

ANNA P. CHAVES
Boston College

MATTHEW A. DIEMER
Boston College

DAVID L. BLUSTEIN
Boston College

LAURA A. GALLAGHER
Boston College

JULIA E. DeVOY
Boston College

MARIA T. CASARES
Boston College

JUSTIN C. PERRY
Boston College

ABSTRACT. This study sought to examine how poor and working-class urban adolescents conceive of work as well as the work-related messages they receive from their families. Data were collected to understand how 9th-grade urban students perceive work using an exploratory and qualitative research methodology. Although the data suggested that urban youths' conceptions of work were complex and varied, the conceptual array of urban youths' perceptions of work suggested that work does not generally represent a means of self-concept expression or the expression of one's interest in the world of work. Specifically, urban youth tended to define work in terms of external outcomes (e.g., money), which was also a common theme among the messages they received about work from their families.

From *Journal of Counseling Psychology, 51*, 275–286. Copyright © 2004 by the American Psychological Association. Reprinted with permission.

Many urban youth in the United States are at a considerable risk for experiencing unsuccessful school-to-work transitions (Blustein, Juntunen, & Worthington, 2000; Wilson, 1996), which increase their chances of
5 engaging in unsatisfying and low-income work (Glover & Marshall, 1993), and facing chronic joblessness and underemployment (Hotchkiss & Borow, 1996). (In this study, the term *urban youth* is used to denote young people who live in urban areas whose families, some of
10 whom are recent immigrants, are financially impoverished or struggling to make ends meet. Naturally, we are aware that not all urban youth are poor or working class.) Significant external challenges hinder the vocational development of urban youth, including racism
15 and discrimination, poverty, and access to fewer resources such as adequate job training and quality schooling (Constantine, Erikson, Banks, & Timberlake, 1998; Newman, 1996; Wilson, 1996). In short, urban youth, particularly racial-ethnic minority youth, often
20 experience considerable difficulty in obtaining access to employment that is stable and meaningful (Carter & Cook, 1992; Wilson, 1996).

In an attempt to address many of these inequities and provide a more equitable playing field, recent
25 school-to-work interventions have been developed as a means to promote optimal transitions for urban youth (Blustein et al., 2000). Similarly, educational reform efforts, many of which are based on school-to-work initiatives and other vocationally oriented themes, have
30 sought to improve access to occupational opportunities for adolescents by providing them with the necessary skills to become successful participants in the world of work (Stone & Mortimer, 1998). For the most part, existing school-to-work initiatives have been designed
35 without an explicit awareness of how the recipients of these efforts conceive of the relationships between themselves and their vocational worlds. Without a clear sense of how urban youth understand the experience of work, present educational and psychological interven-
40 tions may not be sufficiently relevant to the inner lives of the urban students. This study was designed, therefore, to begin mapping the internal landscape of concepts, beliefs, and values that urban youth, who have been at the margins of our scholarship, hold about
45 work. The inclusion of knowledge derived from the inner lives of the recipients of our educational and psychological reform efforts has the clear potential to improve the efficacy of initiatives such as school-to-work interventions and related counseling and psychoeduca-
50 tional efforts.

Many of the organized school-to-work interventions begin when students transition into high school, which generally occurs in the ninth grade. As such, we have targeted a group of 9th-grade urban students to
55 explore how they conceive of work. Middle adolescence has been identified as a critical period for the development and crystallization of educational and vocational foundations and perceptions (Super, Savickas, & Super, 1996; Vondracek, Lerner, &
60 Schulenberg, 1986) as well as a sensitive time for the

formation of long-lasting attitudes and beliefs (Alwin & Krosnick, 1991; Kelloway & Harvey, 1999). As such, the decision to involve 9th-grade students as participants represents a concerted effort to explore conceptions of work at a key stage of their development, thereby informing knowledge about how such conceptions may impact major decisions about school and postsecondary plans.

One of the most compelling critiques of present career development discourse is that many of the ideas that have guided theory and practice have been derived from the experiences of the middle class within affluent and market-based societies (Blustein, 2001; Richardson, 1993; Savickas, 1993). Underlying the view of work within middle-class and relatively well-educated populations in Western cultures is the notion that people have choice or volition in their work lives and that work offers an outlet for one's interests, abilities, and values (Blustein, 2001). Existing theoretical traditions, however, have been criticized for failing to adequately address the lack of volition that many poor and working-class populations as well as individuals of color face in their work lives (Blustein, 2001; Carter & Cook, 1992; Leong & Brown, 1995). Indeed, scholars have increasingly recognized that vocational development occurs within multiple contexts that include the influence of social, political, and economic factors (Vondracek et al., 1986). For example, the labor market in most Western cultures functions in a manner in which individuals who have greater access to economic and familial resources have more choices or volition in their work lives (e.g., Bynner, Ferri, & Shepherd, 1997; Ellwood et al., 2000). Conversely, residents of inner-city communities, and poor racial-ethnic minority youth in particular, face several external obstacles that make it difficult for them to become successful participants in the world of work (Constantine et al., 1998; Wilson, 1996). Barriers such as racial-ethnic and gender discrimination, the higher incidence of violence in many urban communities, poverty, and lack of accessible jobs complicate the transition of poor and working-class youth into the workforce (Wilson, 1996) and constrain the choices they may exercise in transitioning to the world of work (Helms & Cook, 1999). Furthermore, recent technological developments have had a significant impact on the availability of jobs for youth (Rifkin, 1995). With the rise of technological advancement, the labor market is increasingly requiring employees to possess specialized training and skills to function successfully in the workforce (R. Marshall & Tucker, 1992). The barriers that are often present in the lives of many inner-city youth make it difficult for them to attain the education and training necessary to compete in the new global economy (Wilson, 1996). For instance, inequities in school funding make it less likely that urban schools possess the technological resources and educational and vocational programs that more affluent schools may provide for their students

(Kozol, 1991). The concept of career choice on the basis of the expression of interests or values, therefore, may be less relevant for social groups (e.g., the poor and working class, recent immigrants, students of color) that are not afforded the same resources as other social groups (e.g., the middle and upper classes).

The theoretical premises of traditional career development theory, which are slanted toward the experience of middle-class individuals, in turn, have influenced the construction of career-focused and school-to-work interventions. The interventions that have been designed under the rubric of the school-to-work movement have generally been based on assumptions about work that are rooted in a culture that has relatively affirming views about the role of work in education and in overall human development (Blustein et al., 2000). Indeed, a core assumption of school-to-work interventions is that students will become more connected to their education by embedding many academic tasks in a work-based context (Blustein et al., 2000). For example, the use of work-based learning in school-to-work programs assumes that youth would find such experiences meaningful and relevant. However, a cursory review of the lives of poor and working-class individuals in the United States and other Western countries suggests that the experiences of work may not be inherently interesting (Helms & Cook, 1999; Riverin-Simard, 1991; Smith, 1983; Wilson, 1996). The fact that work may not provide intrinsic rewards is inadequately represented in many present career development theories. For example, one of the major assumptions of many traditional career choice theories (e.g., Holland, 1997; Super et al., 1996) is that people strive for a congruent fit between their vocational activities and their interests. The fact that many poor and working-class youth do not have access to educational opportunities and labor markets that will allow for self-concept expression or a congruent person-environment fit raises serious questions about the relevance and effectiveness of existing school-to-work interventions. Indeed, in critique of the relevance of traditional theories to the school-to-work transition for working-class and poor youth, Blustein (1999) argued,

...depending exclusively on an existing array of theoretical ideas may result in a loss of information...and may inadvertently result in scholars and practitioners missing an opportunity to build ideas from the voices of work-bound youth and working class adults, whose input into policy and educational reform efforts to date has been minimal. (p. 350)

In reality, this struggle to find meaning in work is a challenge for all youth who must navigate the transition from high school to work (Schneider & Stevenson, 1999). However, we argue that the developmental task of finding work that offers meaning and advancement is even more of a pronounced dilemma for poor and working-class youth. If the work opportunities available in work-based learning programs and other transition interventions are not meaningful and relevant, then it is unlikely that these experiences would effectively facilitate participants' engagement with the world of work and, consequently, may not function to enhance student commitment to learning.

The existing literature in psychology and related social sciences that has explicitly focused on individuals' conceptions of work is modest, yet informative to this investigation. A number of important explorations of conceptions of work have been advanced within sociological and anthropological perspectives (e.g., Bowe, Bowe, & Streeter, 2000; Donkin, 2001; Gini, 2000; Wilson, 1996). A collection of vignettes prepared by Bowe et al. (2000) provided a powerful and popular account of the diversity of working experiences of North American workers. The views of work that are found in the Bowe et al. volume also range across a wide array of feelings and positions. When considering the narrative entries of the Bowe et al. participants collectively, a picture emerges of individuals seeking to make meaning of their working experiences, often by placing their observations into a context defined by their family history, cultural background, or individual dreams. In another relevant project, Schneider and Stevenson (1999) conducted a comprehensive study of high school students' goals and ambitions after high school. Although not overtly focusing on the students' conceptions of work, this investigation explored the nature of high school students' aspirations about their careers, thereby offering some informative insights into the construction of adolescents' beliefs about the connections between work and education. Schneider and Stevenson defined students' ambitions by the extent to which they are aligned (i.e., the students' goals being consistent with their educational aspirations) using a global index of the degree to which students' knowledge about the educational requirements of their goals were consistent with their stated aspirations. They concluded that students had relatively high aspirations, but that they were typically not consistent with their actual educational plans. In exploring the lack of aligned ambitions in many of their respondents, Schneider and Stevenson suggested that such contextual factors as the family, community, and the labor market played a strong role in shaping the degree of fit between students' ambition and their educational/career plan.

Two extensive interdisciplinary studies (i.e., Csikszlentmihalyi & Schneider, 2000; Wilson, 1996) have perhaps the most relevance to the present discussion. Csikszlentmihalyi and Schneider used the experience sampling method (ESM) to explore the types of activities that students considered to be work, play, or neither work nor play. The ESM is a method that assesses the respondents' specific activities and their cognitive and affective states at random times throughout the day. Csikszlentmihalyi and Schneider used a national sample of 33 schools and concluded that,

...(y)oung people in general are developing rather negative images of work. Even though everyone agrees that work is important to one's future, it is still, by and large, felt to be depressing and dull. Contrary to received wisdom it is not the more affluent white, middle-class children who support the work ethic. Work appears to be a more integral part of the self-concept of minority children. Hispanics and African Americans from families of lower socioeconomic status experience work as more intrinsically rewarding. Of course, this initial attraction to work by the underprivileged may later change into bitterness when underemployment and unemployment take their toll. (p. 93)

A somewhat different view is offered in Wilson's (1996) study of the impact of loss of employment among urban youth and adults. Wilson cited the important role of work in organizing people's lives, particularly work that offers a connection to mainstream economic and social activities within society. Wilson's analysis provides some basic insights into the inner lives of urban youth who are now confronting a world where sustainable and meaningful work is not readily available in their communities. One of Wilson's more provocative points is that the decline of work within urban communities is a leading cause of the growing sense of despair, alienation, and disengagement that pervades the lives of many poor inner-city residents of color. The participants in Wilson's study reported considerable pessimism about their futures, a view that was clearly embedded within their life experiences. One of the reasons for the distinction between the Wilson findings and the results reported by Csikszlentmihalyi and Schneider (2000) is that Wilson's sample included primarily young adults and older adults. It may be that the Csikszlentmihalyi and Schneider prognosis regarding the potential cynicism of adults of color who confront a world that offers disappointing job options after having such high hopes in adolescence is manifested in Wilson's sample of urban men and women who have not fared well in the present labor market.

A number of potentially important observations have emerged in recent qualitative explorations of work among working-class and poor individuals (e.g., Blustein et al., 2002; Phillips, Blustein, Jobin-Davis, & White, 2002). One of the most important findings from this line of work is found in the Blustein et al. study of working-class young adults. The Blustein et al. team divided participants' narratives by socioeconomic status and found that young adults from higher socioeconomic backgrounds tended to view work as having greater meaning and potential for self-expression. In contrast, a similar cohort of young adults from lower socioeconomic backgrounds viewed work primarily as a means of earning a living. The Phillips et al. study, which explored the views of the school-to-work transition from the perspective of high school juniors, captured a complex sense of work that also seemed to be related to the participants' overall experiences of school and future career planning. Some of the participants were anxious about the need to consider work as a major life activity; indeed, Phillips and her colleagues found that this anxiety actually seemed to mobilize some of the students to engage more in school and in active career planning. Although the aforementioned literature and research point to some potentially informative directions in the study of conceptions of work, far more research is needed to explore how urban youth, particularly racial and ethnic minority urban youth, conceive of work in light of sociopolitical effects and economic changes that have diminished opportunities within urban communities (Wilson, 1996).

In addition to the sociopolitical and economic levels of influence, the family plays a critical role in the work orientations of youth (Blustein et al., 2002; Kelloway & Harvey, 1999; Loughlin & Barling, 2001; Vondracek et al., 1986). Conceptions and belief systems about work are constructed in large measure on the basis of an individual's proximal and distal contexts (Vondracek et al., 1986). Researchers have documented that by the age of 7, children have already begun to understand the relationship between monetary gain and employment, and by the ages 10–14, children have developed an understanding of the relationships that exist among employers, employees, and consumers (Berti & Bombi, 1988). Galambos and Sears (1998) suggested that the family serves as one level of context that influences youths' views about the purpose, values, and attitudes about work. Because the family is typically the primary socialization agent for youth, children begin to make meaning of the world of work as they observe their family members in the workforce and listen to them discuss their work experiences (Barling, Dupre, & Hepburn, 1998). The observations they make of their family members' experiences very likely have an impact on their own beliefs and attitudes about the labor force. Thus, inner-city youth, particularly urban racial-ethnic minority youth, who have learned of discrimination and racial and economic inequities through observations and conversations with family members, may expect that they will not be successful in their work lives and anticipate job failure well before entering the workforce (Barling et al., 1998). When considered collectively, the theoretical and research literature point to the family as a key factor in the occupational socialization process, which would entail the internalization of many attitudes, values, and beliefs about work. Naturally, other social and psychological contexts also are relevant in the development of conceptions of working. Thus, to understand how youth make meaning of the world of work, we have also elected to examine the work-related messages they have received from their families.

In summary, exploring conceptions of work is critical because the perceptions that inner-city adolescents have of work may impact their decisions about postsecondary plans concerning education and work, thereby influencing their motivation to engage in academic and vocational tasks (Lent, Brown, & Hackett, 1994; Loughlin & Barling, 2001). For example, if students do not view education as relevant to their future work, they are more likely to become academically and socially disengaged from school (Worthington & Juntunen, 1997). Similarly, conceptions of work will likely affect the way in which career interventions will be understood by youth. An intervention will likely be hindered if counselors use a perspective of work that differs radically from the ideas and beliefs of the recipients of the intervention. Given that the family serves as a primary socialization agent (Barling et al., 1998), it is also important for counselors to consider the influence of messages that urban adolescents receive from their parents and other family members about the purpose of work. In addition, interventions need to address the sociopolitical realities that participants face to effectively meet their needs.

We initiated this study, therefore, to fill a considerable gap in the literature in both counseling psychology and in the broader educational and public policy communities. Given the unfavorable educational and vocational outcomes faced by many urban youth (U. S. Department of Education, 1996), we have elected to turn our scholarly attention to the thoughts and beliefs about work of inner-city adolescents. Furthermore, we have chosen to use a qualitative design as a way to give voice to urban youths' thoughts and ideas about work. Qualitative methodologies are particularly useful for exploratory investigations, or when no clear a priori theoretical model currently exists (C. Marshall & Rossman, 1989). Qualitative research typically focuses on the meanings participants assign to themselves and their worlds (Patton, 1990). Given that school-to-work interventions and educational reform efforts have been traditionally void of input from the recipients of these initiatives (McIntyre, 2000), this study seeks to solicit the conceptions of work that are prevalent among urban youth as well as the messages they have learned about the world of work from their families. We intend to provide the sort of knowledge that will help to bring our field closer toward a more truly inclusive psychology of working, which seeks to give voice to all people who work, not just those who have traditional careers based on volitional choices (Blustein, 2001; Richardson, 1993).

Method

This study was conducted in two parts using a discovery-oriented qualitative methodology. Informed by existing qualitative methods, such as grounded theory (Strauss & Corbin, 1998) and consensual qualitative research (CQR; Hill, Thompson, & Williams, 1997), we developed a rigorous, integrative qualitative approach that was specifically designed to respond to the questions that we raised in this study. The overall approach to the narrative data was based on our intention to develop overarching categories that emerged from the participants' responses. Once we developed categories to organize the analyses, we explored the frequency of responses to ascertain the prevalence of specific beliefs and conceptions among our participants. Initially, a pilot study was completed to develop a coding scheme from qualitative data regarding urban adolescents' views of work as well as the work-related messages they have received from their families. Subsequently, the main study attempted to confirm and modify the initial coding system as a means to further elucidate urban youths' conceptions of work.

Participants

Pilot study. The pilot study consisted of 80 randomly selected 9th-grade students from two urban high schools in the northeastern United States who were participating in a vocational and psychological intervention designed to link school and work. At one of the high schools, which consisted of approximately 1,078 students, the whole student body racially identified as 50% Black, 36% Hispanic, 8% Asian, and 8% White. At the second high school, which consisted of approximately 1,335 students, the whole student body racially identified as 66% Black, 22% Hispanic, 11% White, and 2% Asian. According to federal guidelines, 65% of the students from the whole school district qualified for free lunch, whereas 9% qualified for reduced lunch. The pilot sample, which consisted of 38 boys and 40 girls, was predominantly African American/Black Caribbean (n = 42), with 20 Hispanic, 8 White, 6 Asian, and 2 Native American participants and 2 participants who did not report any identifying information.

Main study. Following revisions to the data collection protocol and the development of an initial coding scheme, an additional 80 9th-grade students were randomly selected from the same two urban public high schools to participate in the main study. The participants were enrolled in the same vocational and psychosocial program during the following academic year. The main study sample consisted of 48 boys and 32 girls, with 37 African American/Black Caribbean, 25 Hispanic, 12 White, and 6 Asian participants.

Instruments

Demographic information. Demographic information related to race-ethnicity and gender was extrapolated from the high schools' student database with the students' assent.

Data collection worksheet. A worksheet of questions was generated to understand how urban youth conceive of work. Specifically, the interest was in the youths' meaning and definition of work and the messages they have received about work from their family. A pilot test of this preliminary worksheet was conducted to ascertain the usefulness, readability, and applicability of the questions posed for participants. The preliminary worksheet also was used to develop an initial coding scheme. A set of three questions was asked during the pilot investigation: (a) What is your personal definition of work? (b) Would you work if you could do something else that would give you money? Please tell us your thinking about this. (c) What have you been told in your family about working?

Revisions were made to improve the clarity and readability of the worksheet following the pilot data collection and preliminary analysis of both the data and the data collection worksheet. The research team felt that a number of the participants appeared to misunderstand the intent of the questions asked and gave responses that reflected this misunderstanding. With the intent of more clearly exploring conceptions of work, the worksheet was revised and composed of the following questions: (a) What is your definition of work? (b) If you had all the money you could ever want, would you work? Why/Why not? (c) What have you learned from your family about work? Our experiences administering the worksheets to participants, and the participants' responses, suggested that the revisions improved the data collection worksheet.

Procedure

Data collection. The pilot and main study data were collected by means of a worksheet that was distributed and completed by all 9th-grade students who were participating in the aforementioned vocational and psychosocial intervention linking school to work. At one of the high schools, all 9th-grade students received this intervention, whereas at the second high school, all 9th-grade students enrolled in the media arts career pathway received this intervention. The worksheets were incorporated into the intervention curriculum as a means to begin discussing work-based issues with the students. Facilitators of the intervention project, which included four of the investigators as well as several additional graduate students in counseling psychology, distributed the worksheets. Facilitators and classroom teachers were available to answer questions posed by the students regarding the content and meaning of the worksheet questions. Parental consent for participation in this study was obtained at the inception of the intervention project. Similarly, students were notified of their right to confidentiality and to withdraw from any aspects of the intervention, including the data collection worksheet. After completing the data collection efforts, the pilot and main study participants were randomly selected from the stack of worksheets completed by the entire sample of 9th-grade students involved in the intervention.

Research team. The research team for this study consisted of four judges, two auditors, and a research consultant. All four of the judges and the two auditors were doctoral students in either counseling or developmental psychology and consisted of two European American female doctoral students, a Latina female doctoral student, a European American/Native American female doctoral student, a European American male doctoral student, and an Asian American male doctoral student. The research consultant was a European American male counseling psychology faculty member. Each member of the research team maintained professional interests in culture, social class, and career development. Given the importance of addressing researcher bias throughout the data collection and data analyses (Hill et al., 1997; Lincoln & Guba, 1985; Miles & Huberman, 1994), the research team members discussed their beliefs, values, and expectations during each of the research meetings. The research consultant assisted in raising the team's awareness of bias and in preventing the bias from influencing the data collection and analysis process.

Development of coding scheme. To develop the coding scheme, 40 of the worksheets from the pilot data were randomly selected from the pool of available data and distributed to the judges during the first year of the intervention. Following the CQR approach (Hill et al., 1997), the judges each independently coded (i.e., identified concepts) the written responses to the first (i.e., "What is your personal definition of work?") and third (i.e., "What have you been told in your family about working?") questions of the worksheet. A decision was made not to analyze the data to the second question (i.e., "Would you work if you could do something else that would give you money? Please tell us your thinking about this.") in this initial pilot phase of coding because it appeared that several of the students misunderstood the intent of the question. This second question was later revised to ensure understanding of the purpose of the question. In an effort to develop the coding scheme, each of the judges began reviewing the data by engaging in a line-by-line analysis (Strauss & Corbin, 1998). Codes, which were used to cluster similar information, were then developed as a way to capture the concept or essence of the data (Strauss & Corbin, 1998). Individual responses were commonly assigned multiple codes, as responses often contained multiple concepts. Each judge then met with another judge, forming a dyad to compare, contrast, and refine the codes. Then, both dyads of judges met with the research consultant to generate an initial coding system, which consisted of a list of all codes that emerged from the pilot data. The judges discussed the codes and arrived at consensual agreement about the most appropriate codes that captured the essence of the data. The coding scheme served as a conceptual framework to organize the data (Miles & Huberman, 1994).

Moreover, to devise a coding scheme for the revised Question 2 (i.e., "If you had all the money you could ever want, would you work? Why/Why not?"), 40 cases were randomly selected from the pool of data available the following academic year, after revisions had been made to the data collection worksheet. These 40 cases were separate from the data used in the main

study. The data analysis for Question 2 proceeded in the same aforementioned manner, yielding a coding system applicable for all three questions during the main phase of the investigation. The two auditors reviewed the initial coding scheme and confirmed both the process and content of the judges' coding (cf. Hill et al., 1997). That is, they confirmed the methodological procedures the judges used. Although the auditors were in agreement with the initial coding system, they offered minor revisions to improve the clarification of the codes in the coding scheme.

Main study data analysis. After the coding scheme was developed, analysis of the data derived in the main study was initiated. Following the same data analytic procedure as in the pilot study, each judge was given an additional 80 randomly selected worksheets from the pool of available data during the second year of the intervention. These 80 worksheets were separate from the worksheets used in the pilot investigation. Again, each judge coded the worksheets individually, assigning multiple codes to individual responses, and then met with the other judge in their dyad to reach consensus about the coding. Judges coded the data using the existing coding scheme while also expanding the coding scheme to incorporate the additional voices of the participants from the main study. All four judges met with the research consultant to discuss and reach consensus about the coding.

The judges then sought to collapse, revise, or discard their codes into overarching categories using the constant comparative method (Strauss & Corbin, 1998) and a consensual decision-making process (Hill et al., 1997). The categories represented superordinate themes that cut across the codes developed. These findings were then presented to the auditors. The auditors noted inconsistencies (e.g., the same response being assigned different codes) and aspects of the coding system that lacked clarity (e.g., meaning of a particular code). The four judges then began another iteration of refining the categories, making consensual decisions in response to the auditor's feedback, and making revisions to the codes assigned and coding scheme. The auditors served as valuable means of triangulating the data analytic procedure of the four judges throughout the research process (Hill et al., 1997; Patton, 1990) and were used to increase the trustworthiness of the study results (Lincoln & Guba, 1985). The auditors also assisted in reaching consensus with the judges that data saturation had been achieved (cf. Bogdan & Biklen, 1992; Morrow & Smith, 2000; Patton, 1990) after the 80 cases had been analyzed. Through the process of developing the categories, the research team was able to ensure that no new themes emerged from the data and that the categories were representative of the experiences of all the youth in this study. In summary, the discovery-oriented data analysis approach yielded a final conceptual network of urban youths' perceptions

199

635 of work as well as the messages they have received from their families about work.

Results

The findings of our study were organized according to the responses provided to each individual question. For each question, we established categories that were generated from the data. Within each category, sub-
640 categories also were developed as a way to elucidate urban youths' conceptions of work. The categories within each question are described below according to their prevalence. Given that individual responses were periodically double-coded among categories, the total
645 frequencies subsequently provided for each subcategory may exceed the total number of participants who responded within each specific category. Additionally, we provided vignettes to illustrate the themes that emerged from the data and to vivify the voice and per-
650 spective of our participants.

Definitions of Work

The participants in the study described their definitions of work in a number of ways that varied in their degree of complexity and sophistication. The categories of participants' definitions of work included the
655 following four headings: *Outcomes of work*, *Dimensions of work*, *Attitudes of work*, and *Personal development* (see Table 1).

Table 1
Students' Definitions of Work

Category	Subcategory	Frequency
Outcomes of work		60
	Money	55
	Goal accomplishment	6
Dimensions of work		33
	Physical/mental action	12
	Self-occupied	9
	Subordination	7
	Helping others/community	7
	Schoolwork	5
Attitudes of work		32
	Positive	14
	Multidimensional	7
	Requires effort/energy	7
	Negative	5
Personal development		13
	Self-concept implementation	5
	Responsibility/maturity	4
	School and work connection	3
	Work-based learning	2

Outcomes of work. The most common definition of work provided by 60 different participants was related
660 to external outcomes of working; that is, participants prominently conceptualized work as a means for obtaining money or income and accomplishing tangible goals. Among the external outcomes coded, money was described as a salient aspect of work among a total of
665 55 participants. Participant 3, for instance, defined work as, "A place where you go and you get paid for

what you do." Similarly, Participant 114 wrote, "Something you go to 5 days a week and get paid for what you do. Lots of money." Although these vignettes
670 clearly evidence the notion that the participants viewed money in general terms, the following responses demonstrated that participants also more specifically conceived of work as a means for obtaining money for basic necessities, to support themselves, and/or to sup-
675 port their families. To illustrate these more differentiated conceptualizations of external outcomes, Participant 34 indicated, "Work is a necessity. A person must work to provide for themselves and their family." In a similar vein, Participant 44 defined work as, "A job
680 that supports you or your family. It provides food and shelter."

Furthermore, the notion of goal accomplishment was articulated by only 6 participants. Participant 7 suggested that work "Is to try hard to achieve some-
685 thing you want or want to do," and Participant 93 indicated, "My definition of work is doing something to achieve a goal or standard."

Dimensions of work. As a second category, a modest number ($n = 33$) of the participants defined work in
690 terms of a range of behavioral and psychological dimensions. For example, 12 students defined work in terms of a physical or mental action. To illustrate this, Participant 42 indicated, "Work is a form of manual labor whether physical or mental," and Participant 82
695 wrote, "Doing some kind of labor or service for someone."

Another subcategory under this category revealed that 9 students conceived of work as a way to keep oneself occupied. Participant 5 indicated that work is
700 "Something that makes you occupied." Additionally, Participant 54 defined work as, "A way to get money…. Work is also to pass time and not stay home all day."

Participants reporting dimensions of work also revealed subordinate aspects of work; that is, 7 partici-
705 pants reflected a belief that work is something done under someone else. Participant 24, for instance, wrote, "I think work is labor that you do for people that pay you." Similarly, Participant 94 suggested, "My definition of work is doing something for another person and
710 struggling."

Seven participants also viewed work in terms of helping others and the community. Using this more interpersonal conceptualization, Participant 16 defined
715 work as, "Getting up early in the morning. Getting in on time and staying in all day. Working hard and helping the customers or patients." Participant 20 also conceptualized work in a similar manner, suggesting that work is done "to earn money by helping out your
720 community."

Last, 5 participants associated to their schoolwork when they were asked to define work. Participant 26 viewed work as, "Something that you do for a purpose. Like it could be a job or work in school." Participant

725 69 also articulated this subcategory by stating, "Work could either be having a job or doing work in school."

Attitudes of work. A third type of definition that was identified in a modest proportion (n = 32) of the participants' responses pertained to a category related to general attitudes about work. For example, in 14 cases, work was perceived in a positive light, as illustrated by Participant 123: "My definition of work is something you love doing. Something that you wake up every morning for and can't wait to do." Participant 735 44 indicated, "I would like to have a job that I enjoy, and have fun doing it."

Alternatively, 5 participants perceived work in a negative manner. For example, Participant 147 described work as, "A boring stupid thing to do for the 740 rest of your life." Participant 78 suggested that work is "doing tasks or hard labor for money." Yet, our findings revealed that a more positive view of work was more common than a negatively valenced view.

Although these responses suggested that students 745 wrote about work in relatively one-sided or simplistic terms, 7 students reflected a multidimensional understanding about work that integrated both positive and negative aspects. For example, the definition of work by Participant 77 was, "Punishment and stress and 750 sometimes depending on what you do, work can be fun." Following this more flexible view of work, Participant 115 wrote, "Whether you like your job or not is up to you and the position you are in."

Additionally, 7 participants described work as an 755 activity that requires a lot of effort and energy. Participant 73, for example, suggested that work is "A strong force of learning to do something in which you put a lot of effort to it." Participant 81 echoed similar sentiments: "Something that you use your time and do put 760 an effort into it."

Personal development. A fourth and final category that was coded among participants' responses related to work as a sense of personal development. In contrast to the aforementioned categories, this conceptual category 765 was coded for only a few students (n = 13) in the sample. Five participants described work as a means of implementing one's self-concept. For example, Participant 109 stated, "To me work is something … that tells about your personality. What you do should reflect a 770 bit on who you are," and Participant 87 suggested, "My definition of work is experience, something that you are good at it."

Similarly, 4 participants perceived work as a way to develop responsibility and maturity. Participant 36 775 stated, "A job is a part of maturity and responsibility." Participant 140 echoed similar sentiments: "Work means to me is be mature and ready for responsibility."

Participants in this category also discussed the relationship between training and work. For instance, 3 780 participants acknowledged a link between education and future work opportunities. Participant 113 suggested, "The less education you have, the more likely

you are to have a worse job." Two participants also thought of work as a place to acquire skills and experi-785 ence. Participant 87 defined work as "Experience. Something that you are good at it. You get money from it. You also get to learn from it."

Purpose of Work

We designed the second question of the data collection instrument to assess the salience of money in par-790 ticipants' reasons for working. Our decision to ask participants if they would continue to work even if all of their economic needs were met was designed to assess the reasons and motivations participants would offer for either working or not working. The categories that 795 emerged were as follows: *Reasons for working* and *Reasons for not working* (see Table 2).

Table 2
Purpose of Work

Category	Subcategory	Frequency
Reasons for working		54
	Economic insecurity	25
	Intrinsic meaning	17
	Self-occupied	11
	Extra wealth/luxury	9
Reasons for not working		23

Reasons for working. The majority of the participants (n = 54) suggested that they would continue to work in some capacity, even if they "had all the money 800 they could ever want." Of the participants who did indicate that they would continue working, a reason for doing so among 25 participants was related to economic insecurity. These participants perceived "all the money they could ever want" as still not being enough 805 money to feel financially secure. For example, Participant 50 indicated, " 'Cause people that have a lot of money tend to lose it. So I would work even though I had all the money." Similarly, Participant 127 stated that he would continue working, "because your money 810 would run out, then I would work to keep it coming;" and Participant 149 indicated, "I would still work because eventually you'll run out of money. I'll just keep the money coming." In summary, despite the promise of having unlimited finances, these participants indi-815 cated that they would continue working out of a fear of being unable to meet basic needs.

In contrast, 17 participants endorsed intrinsic reasons for their continuing to work. These participants expressed a sense of satisfaction or meaning they 820 would derive from working and, for this reason, indicated they would continue working. For example, when answering Question 2, Participant 20 responded, "Yes, because I would want to affect my community in a positive way and still make money." Similarly, Partici-825 pant 30 indicated, "Because I would want to help benefit others even though I already have enough money to benefit myself." Participant 90 wrote, "Because that way you could feel like you are earning your money."

Finally, Participant 34 explained, "If I had all the money I could ever want, I must have gotten it from working. And I would keep working because it would be something I enjoy doing."

Eleven participants within this category also appeared to conceptualize work as an activity that kept them occupied and reported that they would continue to work to avoid being bored. For example, Participant 109 indicated, "I can't sit at home every day and do nothing. I'd feel useless to the world." Similarly, Participant 38 stated, "Because I feel that it is boring sitting at home all the time. Work is not always a bad thing, it is fun."

Finally, despite the promise of "all the money you could ever want," 9 participants also indicated that they would continue working to accumulate more money and to be able to acquire more material things. For example, Participant 13 reported,

> Yes, if I had all the money I could ever want I would still want to work. Because I love to spend money and it will be gone in a minute, so I have to work so I can still have more money.

Similarly, referring to money, Participant 18 stated, "Yes, because I can never get enough of it;" and Participant 147 indicated a desire to continue working "Because I want more and more." It is important to note that these participants would continue to work not out of fear of being unable to meet basic needs, as mentioned previously, but out of a desire to acquire more wealth and luxuries.

Reasons for not working. A minority of the participants (*n* = 23) indicated that they would not continue working if they had unlimited finances. There was less divergence in the reasons participants provided for why they would not work. That is, participants' responses centered on the notion that the only reason for working would be for financial reasons. In essence, once these participants' motivation for working was satisfied, they offered no other reasons for working. For example, Participant 113 wrote,

> No, the point of work is to make money. There are also other ways to make money. It is what people base their life on. If someone handed it to me, without work, why would I waste my time for money I don't need?

Similarly, Participant 16 indicated, "I wouldn't work because if I had all the money, why work? To me working is to get money to pay bills, taxes, etc. So I wouldn't work if I could pay everything." Participant 78 stated, "No because I have all the money to get anything I want, so what is the point? When you work, you work for money. I have all the money, so why still do it?" In other words, individuals who suggested they would not continue working if they had unlimited funds perceived work solely as a means to obtain money to support themselves and their families.

Lessons Learned from Family About Work

When participants were asked what they had learned from their families about work, five categories emerged. These categories included *Attributes of adaptive workers*, *Outcomes of work*, *Familial experience of work*, *Positive aspirations*, and *Nothing* (see Table 3).

Table 3
Lessons Learned from Family About Work

Category	Subcategory	Frequency
Attributes of adaptive workers		35
	Work ethics/attitudes	24
	School and work connection	6
	General work skills/habits	6
Outcomes of work		32
	Money	25
	Goal accomplishment	6
	Better life/success	5
Familial experience of work		27
	Negative	15
	Multidimensional	8
	Positive	6
Positive aspirations		8
Nothing		6

Attributes of adaptive workers. A modest number of participants (*n* = 35) suggested that their families have provided them with a sense of those attributes that are necessary and beneficial for successful participation in the world of work. Twenty-four of the participants reported attributes related to work ethics and attitudes possessed by their families. The participants, for example, noted that their families work hard to receive some type of reward or payoff. Participant 20 remarked, "I have learned that work can sometimes be hard or difficult, but it pays off in the end, and you're helping people in need." Similarly, participants in this category also highlighted a sense of perseverance by their families, a theme that is evident in the response given by Participant 101: "Work must be completed whatever the cost." Participants have also learned that work requires responsibility and maturity on the part of the worker. For instance, Participant 115 indicated, "From my family I have learned that…work is a commitment that should be taken seriously."

Another attribute noted by 6 participants in this category was related to the connection between school and work. For example, participants discussed the messages they received concerning the role that completing high school, college, or postsecondary training would play in their work lives. Participant 2 wrote, "I learned that the only way you can feel good about working is by going to college and studying your goal." Additionally, Participant 161 stressed that, "If you do not have a good education, you have to work really hard and…you will end up in the street."

Finally, 6 participants provided a variety of responses reflecting general work skills and habits learned from their families, which dealt with themes from being on time to being efficient. As a case in point, Participant 109 wrote, "I've learned you have to go as much as possible, do a lot there, be on time, work hard and efficiently…" Similarly, Participant 16 noted, "I learned that you have to get up early, take everything serious, and you have to be on time."

Outcomes of work. When participants were asked what they had learned from their families about work, a modest proportion of the participants ($n = 32$) noted lessons related to the external outcomes of working. For example, 25 participants have learned that work provides a means to obtain money to support oneself, one's family, and to obtain basic necessities for living and survival. The following narratives illustrated these themes aptly. Participant 135 stated, "You need a job because when you get older, you are going to need money so you can pay your bills and support yourself." Participant 32 wrote, "Working is a very important step that you take…to support members of your family." Similarly, Participant 155 noted, "Work is important because it's what gives you money to eat and the other important things."

Under this category, 6 participants learned that working provides a means to accomplish one's goals. For instance, Participant 11 noted, "I learned … that in order to get what I want, I need to work hard and that way I will achieve my goals." Correspondingly, Participant 74 wrote, "I have learned that if you don't work in life you probably can't accomplish anything…"

Five participants also received messages from their families regarding the role work plays in building a better life, promoting success, or both for themselves and for their families. To illustrate, Participant 22 described her home life and her mother's guidance in the following way: "I live with my mother and my two sisters. My mother is a lawyer for legal aid. In my eyes, she is working to take care of her responsibilities…. She always tells me to be better than her." Likewise, Participant 110 learned, "Even though they don't want to go to work, they still go—no matter what—because they want their kids and family to have the best life that they can have."

Familial experience of work. A modest number of participants ($n = 27$) also discussed the personal work experiences of their families. Under this category, the data generally conveyed a negative parental experience of work, as evidenced by the comments of 15 participants. For example, Participant 56 explained, "It's very hard, but you need it to live." Similarly, Participant 40 wrote, "Work is hard and difficult, that is what I learned from my family." In contrast, the four responses of solely positive experiences included replies such as "Jobs can be fun…" from Participant 8 and "That working is good" from Participant 60.

Eight participants expressed their family's multidimensional experiences of work. For instance, Participant 131 stated, "I learned that it takes a great deal of time and can be frustrating and tiring or easy and fun…" Participant 89 wrote, "It is sometimes stressful and hard…but work can also be a great learning experience." Interestingly, in this combined subcategory, participants indicated they learned that work experience was positive for their male family members and negative for female family members. In other words, the participants tended to perceive that their male family members had more positive work lives compared with their female family members. For example, female Participant 50 suggested, "My family all works for [a major telephone company]. I don't really wanna work there. My mother does not like the people who she works with. My dad, he likes the people. My sister doesn't like her job…." Similarly, female Participant 110 revealed, "…the men in my family seem to love working, but the women hate it."

Positive aspirations. A minority of the participants ($n = 8$) suggested that their families convey positive future aspirations for their children. For example, familial aspirations for their children were related to being content at work and being proud of their work. Participant 38 wrote, "My mom has taught me that if you don't enjoy working in a particular place then it is not worthwhile;" and Participant 109 indicated, "I've learned that if you don't like it, quit. Do what makes you happy." Participant 28 also suggested receiving messages related to "Being honest and proud of your work."

Nothing. Finally, 6 participants indicated that they learned nothing from their families regarding work. Participants 127, 143, 147, and 156 simply stated, "Nothing," whereas Participant 145 wrote, "Nothing, they never talk about it."

Discussion

In this investigation, we have reported the major thematic findings that emerged in a qualitative analysis of written text about the meaning of work within a sample of 9th-grade urban high school students. The results of this study underscore a reality that is increasingly apparent in counseling and vocational psychology research and practice: Access to opportunities is not distributed equally (Blustein, 2001; Richardson, 1993). Indeed, this study gives powerful evidence that considerable diversity exists in how young people understand the meaning of work in their lives. In this discussion, we examine each set of findings in light of previous research, followed by an analysis of the overall impact of this study for research and practice in counseling psychology.

The first major area that we explored in this study encompassed the participants' personal definitions of work. The most common category that we identified within this domain is the notion that work is primarily understood as a means to specific outcomes. More specifically, the participants tended to cite external outcomes as the primary way of defining the experience of work (i.e., money, goal attainment). This finding is similar to the results reported in the Blustein et al. (2002) study, which used a somewhat older sample of working-class young adults. In the Blustein et al. study, the participants, who were from lower socioeconomic backgrounds, viewed work primarily as a means to obtain money and to earn a living. Consistent with the observations of Wilson (1996) and Smith (1983), our findings suggest that inner-city youth tend to adopt a very practical view of work, which may be a reflection of a reality of constrained opportunities, inadequate schools, and limited access to diverse occupational role models. However, the present findings contrast with the results reported by Csikszlentmihalyi and Schneider (2000), who found that students of color (most of whom were poor or working class in their sample) have positive views about work in relation to European American youth. One plausible explanation for the discrepancy between our findings and the results reported by Csikszlentmihalyi and Schneider may be in the mode of assessing attitudes or conceptions about work. Moreover, Csikszlentmihalyi and Schneider noted that the students of color in their sample did not report satisfying play activities and were more likely to report states of disengagement than their European American counterparts. Thus, another explanation of the differences between the conceptions of work found in our findings and the results of the Csikszlentmihalyi and Schneider project may be inferred by seeking out a broader view of the lives of the urban youth. A full picture of the lives of the urban youth in the Csikszlentmihalyi and Schneider study suggests that their lives were characterized by a relative absence of other engaging activities, which may have enhanced their experience of work-related activities.

Another category within the first area, which was endorsed by a modest number of participants, described various dimensions of work, ranging from different types of work to specific psychological and behavioral attributes of working. In this category, the participants sought to describe the various modalities in which people work within contemporary society. For example, some of the participants defined work by identifying the various tasks that characterize specific job responsibilities (e.g., manual labor, service to others). Another attribute within the first domain was the discussion of the participants' attitudes or feelings about work. Some of the participants saw work in a positive light, whereas others viewed work in a more negative manner. In addition, a number of other participants were able to maintain the positive and negative views in tandem. Although occurring among only a few of the participants, we did observe that some of the participants mentioned work as a source of personal development (e.g., self-expression, a means of obtaining maturity, and greater work-based skills). Taken together, the contributions within the first domain suggest that the majority of urban youth tend to view work

primarily as a means to an end. This view contrasts sharply with many of the views of work that have been detailed in major career development and choice theories (e.g., Holland, 1997; Super et al., 1996) in which work is presented as a means of expressing one's interests or implementing one's self-concept. Although these observations are not consistent with the results of the Csikszlentmihalyi and Schneider (2000) study, a number of other studies seem to confirm these findings (e.g., Blustein et al., 2002; Wilson, 1996). For example, the young adults in the Blustein et al. (2002) study who were from lower socioeconomic backgrounds tended to work primarily to ensure survival and not primarily as a means of attaining internal satisfaction, whereas the participants from more affluent backgrounds were more likely to report that working fulfilled their interests.

In the second question, we sought to explore the conceptions of work without the influence of any financial considerations. Consistent with the purpose of this question, the observations reported by the participants provided insights into the diverse spectrum of motivational factors that play a role in conceptions of working. In the first category of responses, the participants noted that they would continue to work, even if they were wealthy. However, nearly half these participants indicated that they would continue working because they believed they would still feel concerned about financial security even if they had all of the money they wanted. This finding suggests that the sense of economic insecurity presently may be so pervasive that it would be difficult to consider life without worries about money. A minority of these participants, however, reported intrinsic reasons for continuing to work in this hypothetical scenario. The participants who reported that they would not work if they had access to unlimited funds primarily indicated that the primary goal of work is to earn money, and that without that incentive, they would likely not want to engage in working. When considered collectively, this set of findings suggests that working among inner-city adolescents is primarily viewed as a means to an end. Yet, the diverse responses here, especially from the minority of students who referred to some intrinsic work motivations, conveys a reality that the views of working among inner-city youth may in fact be more pluralistic than is evident in the modest literature in this area. The adolescents who seem to value work for its own sake may be similar to the youth who are described in Newman's (1999) ethnographic study of urban youth who work in fast-food restaurants. In Newman's account of youth working in hamburger restaurants in an urban inner-city community, she described how some of the workers become very attached to their work and begin to feel more connected to others and to their communities via the working process. Although it is premature to infer this sort of causal scenario in the comments of the participants who seemed to consider

some intrinsic reasons for working, future research on the motivational factors inherent in working would be
1155   very informative. In effect, the data reported here suggest that a small, but sizable proportion of students seem to have more intrinsically motivated views of working, thereby suggesting that different pathways may exist in the development of conceptions of work-
1160   ing. In effect, the diversity of findings reported here are consistent with the inconclusive results that characterize the literature on conceptions of work (e.g., Blustein et al., 2002; Csikszlentmihalyi & Schneider, 2000). The diversity of responses observed in our study sug-
1165   gests that multiple pathways exist in the development and expression of conceptions of working.

The third question revealed important insights about the lessons the participants learned from their families about work. One of the most prominent cate-
1170   gories included a focus on the function of work in obtaining money to support oneself and one's family. This finding parallels the qualitative studies by both Newman (1999) and Wilson (1996) that have identified the important role of supporting one's family in their
1175   participants' views of their working lives. In addition, some of the participants described how their families constructed work as a means to accomplish goals and to enhance one's overall life. Indeed, the fact that a sizable proportion of participants indicated that they
1180   learned about some of the adaptive features of working from their families conveys the complexity of the conceptions of working that were identified in this study. The participants also learned about the attributes of successful workers from their families (e.g., the impor-
1185   tance of working hard, the need for perseverance). Another category that emerged in this domain was descriptions of family experiences at work, many of which conveyed a negative view of work. These findings suggest that the family socialization process has
1190   the potential to convey highly disparate views of working, depending perhaps on the experiences of the adults in the family and other contextual factors. The results observed in this study also support the position advocated by Loughlin and Barling (2001), who argued that
1195   young workers' values, beliefs, and attitudes are strongly influenced by their families.

Taken together, the results from this study suggest that for many (but clearly not all) urban high school students, work is viewed as a necessity and not as a
1200   means of self-expression. This view is consistent with the broader visions of vocational psychology that have been advocated by Blustein (2001) and Richardson (1993), who have argued that most people in the world do not have access to work lives that offer them much
1205   volition in terms of the types of occupations they can obtain. The responses that have been conveyed by the participants underscore that the experience of a lack of volition in working is not the exclusive phenomenon of poor, Third World countries but exists in the United
1210   States at the core of many of our urban centers. The

results from this study also underscore the importance of incorporating context into theoretical formulations. The fact that the conceptions of working were gener-
1215   ally different from the views espoused in major career choice and development theories (e.g., Holland, 1997; Lent et al., 1994; Super et al., 1996) merits careful attention. In our view, many of the prevalent theories in vocational psychology have long incorporated context,
1220   although often these contextual influences are not well integrated into theoretical formulations. The findings from this study suggest that these contextual factors need to be given more attention in research, practice, and policy recommendations. The theoretical formula-
1225   tions of the developmental perspectives (e.g., Super et al., 1996; Vondracek et al., 1986) and social cognitive career theory (Lent et al., 1994) offer particularly compelling explications of context that may be helpful in understanding the development and expression of con-
1230   ceptions of working. Although these theoretical positions have included contextual factors, the present findings, when considered in light of some previous research (e.g., Blustein et al., 2002; Wilson, 1996), suggest that the notion of work offering intrinsic rewards
1235   and serving as an outlet for one's interests needs to be questioned more overtly in theory construction, research, and counseling practice. More precisely, the theoretical assumptions of the Super et al. and Vondracek et al. studies assume that people have some de-
1240   gree of volition in their work lives and that they have an opportunity to express their interests in their careers. The Lent, Brown, and Hackett (2002) social cognitive career theory relies on an assumption that "… people (are) active agents in, or shapers of, their career devel-
1245   opment" (p. 255). Similarly, the person-environment fit view of Holland (1997) assumes that "…(p)eople search for environments [in this case, work] that will let them exercise their skills and abilities, express their attitudes and values, and take on agreeable problems
1250   and roles" (p. 4). Although some of the participants in this study did seem to express hope that they could influence the course of their working lives, many others conveyed less optimistic views of their career options. These views did not generally reflect the agentic
1255   and self-determined behavior that underlies much of the existing career choice and development theory.

In our view, the parallel results that we found in the first and third questions lead us to speculate that there may be a deep connection between how work is viewed
1260   in one's family and by the adolescents themselves. The findings that we have reported are consistent with family socialization literature that has highlighted the important crucible that families provide in the development and acquisition of beliefs, attitudes, and behaviors
1265   in adolescence (e.g., Loughlin & Barling, 2001; Vondracek et al., 1986). Although this observation may be obvious to many readers, it suggests that schools and agencies may need to work hard on expanding visions of work. Without taking into account the cultural and

familial attributes that frame how people experience working, interventions and policy initiatives that are developed may be too distant from the internal belief systems of students and client groups to be maximally effective.

One of the most interesting findings in this study is the modest multidimensionality of the students' responses. Whereas most of the participants conveyed rather bleak views of working, some students tended to have more positive views of work. These responses were the most similar to the views of working that have been prevalent in the traditional career development literature, in which people are thought to have opportunities to express their interests in the occupational world. The fact that these responses were in the minority underscores the reality that the traditional career narrative (Super et al., 1996) in which people have choices that reflect their interests and values is not a common belief system in the inner-city world of adolescents. However, one very compelling direction for future research would be to identify the factors in the lives of urban youth that function to create such diverse narratives about working. In addition, it would be useful to explore the cultural, historical, and economic factors that provide the broader framework for the development of conceptions of work.

Given that the study of conceptions of working is relatively new to vocational and counseling psychology, we believe that our findings may be most useful in suggesting future directions for research. In addition to the study of the outliers in our sample, which we noted previously, we also recommend studies that would examine the impact of developmental differences in conceptions of work. For example, would variations in cognitive development account for some of the differences in conceptions of working that arose in this study? Another critically needed study is the exploration of how social class influences conceptions of working. In addition, studies examining sources of positive intrinsic and extrinsic motivation in conceptions of work would be useful. Another important area that merits attention is a systematic exploration of the relationship between cultural beliefs and conceptions of work. We also need to understand how conceptions of work are related to other aspects of human development in related domains of human functioning (e.g., school engagement, vocational development). In addition, we believe that it may be timely to develop quantitative measures of conceptions of working that can be tailored for specific populations and different developmental stages. Measures of this nature would allow investigators to understand some of the complex linkages between conceptions of working and various outcomes in educational and vocational functioning. With a coherent and flexible measure of conceptions of working, investigators may be able to combine quantitative and qualitative methods to explore the meaning and implications of one's values, beliefs, and attitudes about working.

The data revealed that the majority of urban youth and their families view work as a means to an end and not necessarily as an activity for personal growth and development. The parallel results that we found among our participants' and their family's messages lead us to speculate that there is a connection between how work is viewed in one's family and by adolescents themselves. Interventions that assist urban teenagers in career exploration and planning should be created with an awareness of the relevant work narratives that are shared and transmitted through familial generations (cf. Loughlin & Barling, 2001; Young & Friesen, 1992). For example, counselors may find it useful to include some discussion of students' conceptions of work and their family work messages in individual, preventive, and group-level interventions. It would be important to include this focus early in the course of counseling and psychoeducational interventions.

Our results have the potential to enlighten the fundamental assumption of many secondary school reform efforts that are predicated on the notion that enhancing work-based learning will enhance the motivation of students (e.g., Blustein et al., 2000; Worthington & Juntunen, 1997). Given the finding that urban high school youth conceive of work primarily as a means to external outcomes, positioning schoolwork within a work-based rubric may not lead to the desired effects of improving student engagement. The difficulty in framing education as a means toward the attainment of a stable working life is that working does not necessarily represent a particularly exciting or intrinsically interesting endeavor. Therefore, although students may be motivated to work to maximize their earning potential, the actual experience of working itself may not be sufficiently motivating to engage students in their academic tasks. More precisely, the combination of these two extrinsically valued tasks may not result in the sort of intrinsic motivation that may actually yield gains in student engagement and performance. In our view, the question of how to use work-based experiences as a means of engaging students in their school tasks needs careful research attention, ideally using the latest theoretical innovations from motivational psychology (Ryan & Deci, 2000). More important, we recommend that educational analysts and counseling professionals develop interventions and reform efforts that are constructed in the baseline conceptions of working that urban youth hold (Blustein et al., 2000). If we learn in subsequent research that positive and hopeful views of working are associated with academic success and resilience in the face of obstacles, we may find it useful to develop interventions that will result in the expansion of conceptions of working. For example, it may be that multiple views of working that include the option of moving into satisfying work would be most productive for urban youth.

Our study has attempted to make sense of how urban youth experience work. Although our sample was circumscribed, we feel it is justified, as we are focusing on a population that clearly needs a great deal of attention. Our analysis provides initial information regarding urban youths' conceptions of work; however, the findings from this study are not generalizable to other groups of urban youth. Although more in-depth interviews would have been useful to further inquire about the conceptions of work of these students and their families, having participants write short responses to three questions gave students a degree of anonymity to voice private concerns and gave us the ability to collect and analyze a large amount of qualitative data. Furthermore, although attempts were made to minimize the impact of researcher bias by articulating and becoming aware of bias throughout the study, it is important to note that there is always a risk for researcher bias to influence the research process. As such, the perspectives of the research team may have influenced the findings that emerged from this study. Finally, it is difficult to clearly understand all the factors that may have contributed to our findings; however, the results reported in this investigation provide future investigators with some viable ideas about the factors that may be playing a role in the development and expression of conceptions of work within an inner-city population.

References

Alwin, D. F., & Krosnick, J. A. (1991). Aging, cohorts, and the stability of sociopolitical orientations over the life span. *American Journal of Sociology, 97,* 169–195.

Barling, J., Dupre, K. E., & Hepburn, C. G. (1998). Effects of parents' job insecurity on children's work beliefs and attitudes. *Journal of Applied Psychology, 83,* 112–118.

Berti, A. E., & Bombi, A. S. (1988). *The child's construction of economics.* Cambridge, England: Cambridge University Press.

Blustein, D. L. (1999). A match made in heaven? Career development theories and the school-to-work transition. *Career Development Quarterly, 47,* 348–352.

Blustein, D. L. (2001). Extending the reach of vocational psychology: Toward an inclusive and integrative psychology of working. *Journal of Vocational Behavior, 59,* 171–182.

Blustein, D. L., Chaves, A. P., Diemer, M. A., Gallagher, L. A., Marshall, K. G., Sirin, S., & Bhati, K. S. (2002). Voices of the forgotten half: The role of social class in the school-to-work transition. *Journal of Counseling Psychology, 49,* 311–323.

Blustein, D. L., Juntunen, C. L., & Worthington, R. L. (2000). The school-to-work transition: Adjustment challenges of the forgotten half. In S. D. Brown & R. W. Lent (Eds.), *Handbook of counseling psychology* (3rd ed., pp. 435–470). New York: Wiley.

Bogdan, R. C., & Biklen, S. K. (1992). *Qualitative research for education: An introduction to theory and methods.* Needham Heights, MA: Allyn & Bacon.

Bowe, J., Bowe, M., & Streeter, S. (2000). *Gig: Americans talk about their jobs.* New York: Three Rivers Press.

Bynner, J., Ferri, E., & Shepherd, P. (Eds.) (1997). *Twenty-something in the 1990s: Getting on, getting by, getting nowhere.* Brookfield, VT: Ashgate Publishing.

Carter, R. T., & Cook, D. A. (1992). A culturally relevant perspective for understanding the career paths of visible racial/ethnic group people. In H. D. Lea & Z. B. Leibowitz (Eds.), *Adult career development: Concepts, issues, and practice* (pp. 192–217). Alexandria, VA: National Career Development Association.

Constantine, M. G., Erikson, C. D., Banks, R. W., & Timberlake, T. L. (1998). Challenges to the career development of urban racial and ethnic minority youth: Implications for vocational intervention. *Journal of Multicultural Counseling and Development, 26,* 83–95.

Csikszentmihalyi, M., & Schneider, B. (2000). *Becoming adult: How teenagers prepare for the world of work.* New York: Basic Books.

Donkin, R. (2001). *Blood, sweat, & tears: The evolution of work.* New York: Texere.

Ellwood, D. T., Blank, R. M., Blasi, J., Kruse, D., Niskanen, W. A., & Lynn-Dyson, K. (2000). *A working nation: Workers, work, and government in the new economy.* New York: Russell Sage Foundation.

Galambos, N. L., & Sears, H. A. (1998). Adolescents' perceptions of parents' work and adolescents' work values in two-earner families. *Journal of Early Adolescence, 18,* 397–420.

Gini, A. (2000). *My job, my self: Work and the creation of the modern individual.* New York: Routledge.

Glover, R. W., & Marshall, R. (1993). Improving the school-to-work transition of American adolescents. *Teachers College Record, 94,* 588–610.

Helms, J. E., & Cook, D. A. (1999). *Using race and culture in counseling and psychotherapy: Theory and process.* Boston: Allyn & Bacon.

Hill, C. E., Thompson, B. J., & Williams, E. N. (1997). A guide to conducting consensual qualitative research. *The Counseling Psychologist, 25,* 517–572.

Holland, J. L. (1997). *Making vocational choices: A theory of vocational personalities and work environments* (3rd ed.). Odessa, FL: Psychological Assessment Resources.

Hotchkiss, L., & Borow, H. (1996). Sociological perspective on work and career development. In D. Brown & L. Brooks (Eds.), *Career choice and development* (3rd ed., pp. 281–336). San Francisco: Jossey-Bass.

Kelloway, E. K., & Harvey, S. (1999). Learning to work: The development of work beliefs. In J. Barling & E. K. Kelloway (Eds.), *Young workers: Varieties of experience* (pp. 37–57). Washington, DC: American Psychological Association.

Kozol, J. (1991). *Savage inequalities: Children in America's schools.* New York: HarperCollins.

Lent, R. W., Brown, S. D., & Hackett, G. (1994). Toward a unifying social cognitive theory of career and academic interest, choice, and performance. *Journal of Vocational Behavior, 45,* 79–122.

Lent, R. W., Brown, S. D., & Hackett, G. (2002). Social cognitive career theory. In D. Brown (Ed.), *Career choice and development* (4th ed., pp. 255–311). San Francisco: Jossey-Bass.

Leong, F. T. L., & Brown, M. T. (1995). Theoretical issues in cross-cultural career development: Cultural validity and cultural specificity. In W. B. Walsh & S. H. Osipow (Eds.), *Handbook of vocational psychology: Theory, research, and practice* (2nd ed., pp. 143–180). Mahwah, NJ: Erlbaum.

Lincoln, Y. S., & Guba, E. G. (1985). *Naturalistic inquiry.* Newbury Park, CA: Sage.

Loughlin, C., & Barling, J. (2001). Young workers' work values, attitudes, and behaviours. *Journal of Occupational and Organizational Psychology, 74,* 543–558.

Marshall, C., & Rossman, G. (1989). *Designing qualitative research.* Newbury Park, CA: Sage.

Marshall, R., & Tucker, M. (1992). *Thinking for a living: Education and the wealth of nations.* New York: Basic Books.

McIntyre, A. (2000). Constructing meaning about violence, school, and community: Participatory action research with urban youth. *The Urban Review, 32,* 123–154.

Miles, M. B., & Huberman, A. M. (1994). *Qualitative data analysis* (2nd ed.). Thousand Oaks, CA: Sage.

Morrow, S. L., & Smith, M. L. (2000). Qualitative research for counseling psychology. In S. D. Brown & R. W. Lent (Eds.), *Handbook of counseling psychology* (3rd ed., pp. 199–230). New York: Wiley.

Newman, K. S. (1996). Working poor: Low-wage employment in the lives of Harlem youth. In J. A. Grager & J. Brooks-Gunn (Eds.), *Transitions through adolescence: Interpersonal domains and context* (pp. 323–343). Hillsdale, NJ: Erlbaum.

Newman, K. S. (1999). *No shame in my game.* New York: Vintage.

Patton, M. G. (1990). *Qualitative evaluation and research methods.* Newbury Park, CA: Sage.

Phillips, S. D., Blustein, D. L., Jobin-Davis, K., & White, S. F. (2002). Preparation for the school-to-work transition: The view from high school. *Journal of Vocational Behavior, 61,* 202–216.

Richardson, M. S. (1993). Work in people's lives: A location for counseling psychologists. *Journal of Counseling Psychology, 40,* 425–433.

Rifkin, J. (1995). *The end of work: The decline of the global labor market force and the dawn of the post-market era.* New York: Tarcher.

Riverin-Simard, D. (1991). *Careers and social classes.* Montreal, Canada: Meriden Press.

Ryan, R. M., & Deci, E. L. (2000). Self-determination theory and the facilitation of intrinsic motivation, social development, and well-being. *American Psychologist, 55,* 68–78.

Savickas, M. L. (1993). Career counseling in the postmodern era. *Journal of Cognitive Psychotherapy, 7,* 205–215.

Schneider, B., & Stevenson, D. (1999). *The ambitious generation: America's teenagers—Motivated but directionless.* New Haven, CT: Yale University Press.

Smith, E. J. (1983). Issues in racial minorities' career behavior. In W. B. Walsh & S. H. Osipow (Eds.), *Handbook of vocational psychology: Vol. 1, Foundations* (pp. 161–222). Hillsdale, NJ: Erlbaum.

Stone, J. R., & Mortimer, J. T. (1998). The effect of adolescent employment on vocational development: Public and educational policy implications. *Journal of Vocational Behavior, 53,* 184–214.

Strauss, A., & Corbin, J. (1998). *Basics of qualitative research* (2nd ed.). Newbury Park, CA: Sage.

Super, D. E., Savickas, M. L., & Super, C. M. (1996). The life-span, life-space approach to careers. In D. Brown & L. Brooks (Eds.), *Career choice and development* (3rd ed., pp. 121–178). San Francisco: Jossey-Bass.

U.S. Department of Education (1996). *Urban schools: The challenge of location and poverty* (NCES Publication No. 96–184r). Washington, DC: U.S. Government Printing Office.

Vondracek, F. W., Lerner, R. M., & Schulenberg, J. E. (1986). *Career development: A life-span, developmental approach.* Hillsdale, NJ: Erlbaum.

Wilson, W. J. (1996). *When work disappears: The world of the new urban poor.* New York: Random House.

Worthington, R. L., & Juntunen, C. L. (1997). The vocational development of non-college-bound youth: Counseling psychology and the school-to-work transition movement. *The Counseling Psychologist, 25,* 323–363.

Young, R. A., & Friesen, J. D. (1992). The intentions of parents in influencing the career development of their children. *Career Development Quarterly, 40,* 198–207.

Acknowledgments: This research was supported in part by Boston Public Schools, the Boston College Lynch School of Education Collaborative Fellows program, Massachusetts Department of Education, and the American Honda Foundation grants awarded to David L. Blustein.

Address correspondence to: David L. Blustein, Department of Counseling, Developmental, and Educational Psychology, Boston College, Campion Hall 315, Chestnut Hill, MA 02467. E-mail: blusteid@bc.edu

Exercise for Article 38

Factual Questions

1. How many students participated in the pilot study?

2. How were the students for the main study selected?

3. Were the three questions revised on the basis of the pilot study?

4. Was parental consent obtained?

5. How many students referred to money in their definitions of work?

6. Did a majority of the participants suggest that they would continue to work in some capacity, even if they "had all the money they could ever want"?

Questions for Discussion

7. The introduction (including the literature review) in lines 1–398 is longer than the ones in most articles in this book. In your opinion, is the long introduction a strength of this study? Explain.

8. The researchers studied only urban youth. In your opinion, would it be desirable to include middle-class youth (in order to compare the two groups) in future studies on this topic? Why? Why not?

9. Students were notified of their right to confidentiality. Is this important? Explain. (See lines 505–508.)

10. The researchers mention the possibility of "researcher bias" at several points. In your opinion, is researcher bias a more important consideration in qualitative studies than it is in quantitative studies? Explain. (See lines 526–534 and 1395–1402.)

11. The role of auditors is mentioned at various points such as in lines 610–627. To what extent does the use of auditors increase your confidence in the results of this study?

12. The researchers mention "data saturation" in line 625. Speculate on the meaning of this term.

13. The results and discussion sections in lines 636–1410 are longer than most others in this book. In your opinion, could this material be abbreviated without affecting the usefulness of this report? Explain.

14. The participants filled out worksheets (i.e., brief questionnaires). Would you recommend using interviews in follow-up studies on this topic? Explain. (See lines 1391–1397.)

Quality Ratings

Directions: Indicate your level of agreement with each of the following statements by circling a number from 5 for strongly agree (SA) to 1 for strongly disagree (SD). If you believe an item is not applicable to this research article, leave it blank. Be prepared to explain your ratings. When responding to criteria A and B below, keep in mind that brief titles and abstracts are conventional in published research.

A. The title of the article is appropriate.

SA   5   4   3   2   1   SD

B. The abstract provides an effective overview of the research article.

SA   5   4   3   2   1   SD

C. The introduction establishes the importance of the study.

SA   5   4   3   2   1   SD

D. The literature review establishes the context for the study.

SA   5   4   3   2   1   SD

E. The research purpose, question, or hypothesis is clearly stated.

SA   5   4   3   2   1   SD

F. The method of sampling is sound.

SA   5   4   3   2   1   SD

G. Relevant demographics (for example, age, gender, and ethnicity) are described.

SA   5   4   3   2   1   SD

H. Measurement procedures are adequate.

SA   5   4   3   2   1   SD

I. All procedures have been described in sufficient detail to permit a replication of the study.

SA   5   4   3   2   1   SD

J. The participants have been adequately protected from potential harm.

SA   5   4   3   2   1   SD

K. The results are clearly described.

SA   5   4   3   2   1   SD

L. The discussion/conclusion is appropriate.

SA   5   4   3   2   1   SD

M. Despite any flaws, the report is worthy of publication.

SA   5   4   3   2   1   SD

Article 39

Interdependent Self: Self-Perceptions of Vietnamese-American Youths

TAN PHAN
San Diego State University

ABSTRACT. This study examined how Vietnamese-American adolescents perceive themselves in relation to their families. Qualitative, criterion-based sampling and "snowball" or "chain sampling" strategies were used as well as in-depth interviews with 10 Vietnamese-American adolescents. The research focused on parental interactions, family climate, and parental control. The study also looked at peer relationships, parental input, and adolescents' academic achievement orientation. The adolescents described grow closer to, and more emotionally dependent upon, their parents over time. The parents see their children's education as an effective instrument of empowerment and liberation for the entire family, and as providing hope for the future.

From *Adolescence*, 40, 425–441. Copyright © 2005 by Libra Publishers, Inc. Reprinted with permission.

Introduction

Theories of Self

Western psychology presumes that individuals carry within themselves, as an essential self, an autonomous "self" which exists independently of the social order. At the core of each self-contained individual resides an identity, a persistent self that transcends particular contexts and comprises the essence of the person (e.g., Cushman, 1990, 1995; Gergen, 1991, 1994, 1999; Sampson, 1989, 1993; Shotter, 1993; Wilkinson, 1997). Postmodernist thinkers have deconstructed this notion, arguing that there is no core, or essential self, that persists across situations. Instead, the self is described as perpetually in flux and inextricably linked to social exchange. The self is constituted in ever-changing social contexts, especially in the discourses that are the vehicle of social exchange; different selves emerge in differing circumstances of relationships. It is not just simply that an individual or an identity acts as an agent manifesting different aspects of his/her autonomous, continuous core self in varying circumstances but rather that the self exists only through integration with the process of relationship in the context of the communal. The self does not exist within the individual but in the space between and among people, in conversational exchange (e.g., Cushman, 1990, 1995; Geertz, 1997; Gergen, 1991, 1994, 1999, 2001; Gergen & Gergen, 1988; Harre, 1984; Sampson, 1977, 1985, 1989, 1993; Shotter, 1993).

Psychosocial Development

Like postmodernist thinkers, some feminists have reappraised femininity. Such feminists have adapted sociological and psychological theories to explain the nature and the origin of gender.

In the realm of socialization, it has been argued that gender is rooted so early and so profoundly within the personality that prior to its acquisition there is no self at all. Femininity is seen not as an impoverished identity but is praised for its social rather than individualistic qualities. This view emphasizes the social aspects of the self since it focuses on the development of selves through their relations (of separation and intimacy) with others (their "objects"). This object relations theory associates maturity with separation and autonomy, but feminists detected in this a specifically masculine bias and urged a focus on the differential evolution of feminine selves.

While Miller (1976) associates gender difference with masculine activity versus feminine passivity, object-relations theory equates it with separation versus attachment. Chodorow (1977) explains that the distinct different masculine and feminine personalities are not a result of internalizing different values, but a function of the asymmetrical family: mothers elicit contrasting responses from daughters and sons. Looking at parenting patterns where the mothers carry out the primary care-taking activities, girls develop their identity through connection with their mother. Identity comes to be defined by connection. Girls remain longer in the primary relational mode. In contrast, boys are pushed to separate from their mothers earlier. They develop a self in opposition to the feminine with more rigid ego boundaries but a weak, defensive gender identity. Boys must separate from their mothers in order to develop their masculine identity. Thus, identity becomes grounded in separation and independence. In effect, boys are drawn to a value system and subject-orientation centered on autonomy and detachment. Girls' feminine selves are constituted through relatedness, connectedness, and intimacy. Female selves have a stronger tendency to experience the needs and feelings of others as their own; they feel more continuous with nature and more embedded in social contexts.

Similar distinctions have been drawn by Lykes (1985) in her study of autonomous individualism and social individuality. Lykes (1985, 1989) examined conceptions of self among Guatemalan women who were exiled and at that time living in Mexico. Her analysis demonstrates the critical roles that power status and material conditions exert on one's sense of self in social and individual distinctions. In equating an ethic of care with powerlessness, Puka (1989) relates Gilligan's ethic to women's subordinate positions and describes care as a defensive response to sexism. These researchers view status, not gender, as the basis for the development of a moral self.

Gilligan claims that the experiences of inequality and subordination that circumscribe the lives of women also give rise to a moral self grounded in human connections and characterized by concerns with relationships (Gilligan & Attanucci, 1988). Emphasizing the differences between men and women and boys and girls, Gilligan and others (Chodorow, 1978; Miller & Prentice, 1994; Miller, 1976, 1984; Noddings, 1984) celebrate the essential "feminine" self and the feminine values associated with what they characterized as "the feminine voice." The "feminine voice emerges with great clarity, defining the self and proclaiming its worth on the basis of the ability to care for and protect others" (Gilligan, 1982, p. 79). In contrast, is the masculine voice. "Instead of attachment, individual achievement rivals the male imagination and great ideas or distinctive activity defines the standard of self-assessment and success" (Gilligan, 1982, p. 79).

The Eastern Concept of Self

The self-in-relation theory of female development parallels the argument of Markus and Kitayama (1991), which suggests that many Asian cultures insist on the fundamental relatedness of individuals to each other. The emphasis is on attending to others, fitting in, and harmonious interdependence. These authors make a distinction between independent self and interdependent self. People in different cultures have different concepts of self, of others, and of the interdependence of the two. The interdependent view is comparable to the feminist's self-in-relation theory. The independent self is the prototypical Western cultural view of the self, a view most characteristic of white, middle-class men with a Western European ethnic background (Markus & Kitayama, 1991).

Markus and Kitayama (1991) suggest that the view of the self-in-relation to specific others emphasizes the individual not separated from the social context, but as more connected and less differentiated from others. Individuals are motivated to find a way to fit, to fulfill and create obligation, and to become part of various interpersonal relationships. The focus of the interdependent self is the relationship of the individual to other actors in the social context. To know and understand their social surroundings, it is important for persons to be sensitive to and knowledgeable about the others who are the co-participants in various relationships and about the social situations that enable these relationships. When individuals are in direct interaction with others, and when they perceive themselves as interdependent parts of larger social wholes, these individuals require a complete understanding of others to maintain relationships and to ensure a harmonious social interaction. By knowing how others are feeling and thinking, they are likely to understand the contexts of their relationship to them. Consequently, these interdependent selves may develop a dense and richly elaborated store of information about others and of the self-in-relation.

Chu's (1985) definition of self considers some of the salient aspects in many Asian societies. The self is defined as a configuration of roles expressed in self-other expectations and observable in self-other interactions. Chu explains that it is not so much how individuals "see" themselves; rather, it is the fundamental behavioral expectations that individuals have of themselves when interacting with others. Chu suggests the self develops out of interactions with three broad entities in one's environment: (a) significant others, (b) objects and ideas, and (c) beliefs and values. A conceptual configuration emerges from these interactions with regard to one's self. This has implications, and guides one's further interactions with significant others, materials, objects, and ideas. According to Chu, of all these entities, it is the significant others who are crucially important to the formation of an individual's self. Significant others included in one's environment are the products of the cultural milieu in which the significant others and the self live and function. Individuals learn from these interactions and internalize the ideological content of their society. They learn to manage and manipulate their material environment for their survival. Thus, the self is seen as a configuration of role relations with significant others. The direction is oriented primarily toward significant others in a manner defined by predominant cultural values. The self seeks to accommodate others and, in return, to receive enduring support. The self of this nature is not very assertive. For example, assertion in Japanese culture is viewed as being immature and the individual is regarded as lacking self-control. The Japanese notion of control is inwardly directed. The individual adjusts to various interpersonal contingencies by controlling inner attributes such as desires, personal goals, and private emotion, which can disturb the harmonious equilibrium of interpersonal transactions (DeVos, 1985). Yielding, in Asian culture, is not a sign of weakness; rather it reflects tolerance, self-control, reflexibility, and maturity (Chu, 1985).

Purpose of the Study

This study examined how adolescent male and female Vietnamese-American youths perceive "self" in relation to their family. It focused on parental interactions, family climate, and parental control as variables relevant to these perceptions. It also looked at peer relationships, parental input, and adolescents' academic achievement orientation.

Method

Sampling Strategies

Data for this paper were drawn from a larger ongoing longitudinal qualitative research project focusing on the academic resiliency of 40 Vietnamese-American youths (ages 17 and 18), who had received academic scholarships to attend a university. I used purposeful, criterion-based sampling strategies (Glaser & Strauss, 1967; Patton, 1990; Strauss & Corbin, 1990, 1998; Taylor & Bogdan, 1998) to recruit Vietnamese-American students who were graduating from high school with an above 4.00 grade point average (GPA). In order to recruit the students, I started sampling by attending Vietnamese cultural festivities, religious institutions, and Vietnamese language schools in Southern California in order to introduce my research to these organizations, announce the project, distribute the research description, and ask for volunteers. I also employed "snowball" or "chain sampling" (Patton, 1990). That is, before or at the end of each interview, I asked the participants if they would identify others that fit the study's selection criteria. I telephoned those who expressed interest, standardizing contacts by using the same research description.

Participants

This paper presents data that were collected from five boys and five girls, to whom I have assigned fictitious names. For purposes of this study, the boys' names are Khoa, Binh, Quan, Don, and Trung, and the girls' names are Ngoc, Kim, Giang, Lien, and Phoung. Of the ten students, one was going to attend Yale, one Harvard, one Stanford, and seven the University of California (UC) at San Diego, Los Angeles, or Berkeley. Of those seven at UC schools, three were high school valedictorians. All of them had received scholarships and each of their GPAs was above 4.00. These students were also actively involved in extracurricular activities and did volunteer work in their community. Those who chose to go to UC schools did so because they did not want to be too far away from their families. All of them came from poor, working-class families and lived in low-income neighborhoods of Southern California.

Procedure

In-depth personal interviews were conducted with each participant soon after they had received awards for academic achievements. The interviews involved semi-structured, open-ended questionnaires. They were conducted in their homes, were recorded on tape, and later transcribed verbatim by the researcher of this study. The participants were interviewed individually at the end of high school. Most of the interviews lasted between two to three hours. There were five parts to the questionnaires. The first, third, and fourth parts examined the youths' (a) parental interaction, (b) family climate, and (c) parental control and peer relationships, and parental input and academic achievement orientation. The second and fifth parts of the interview questionnaires explored the youths' relationship with siblings, family rules, personal concerns, decision-making, and plans for the future. Throughout this paper, participants' voices are included to give texture to the analytic conclusions and to provide samples of the kind of evidence upon which those conclusions are based. Furthermore, as is common in qualitative studies, rich detail about the participants, the process, and the analysis also invites readers to determine transferability of results (Creswell, 2002; Mertens, 1998; Patton, 1990; Taylor & Bogdan, 1998).

Data Analysis

Although no method is completely neutral, some methods may result in an analysis that is closer to reality. Therefore, in this study I proposed no formal hypothesis for testing (Strauss & Corbin, 1990, 1998). During the interviews, I let the concepts, explanations, and interpretations of those participating in the study become the data I analyzed (Strauss & Corbin, 1990). Data were analyzed throughout the study, rather than after the data collection. This served two purposes: (a) it enabled me to make decisions in data collection, and (b) to identify emerging topics and recurring patterns. The data were analyzed through a process of analytic induction (Glaser & Strauss, 1967; Miles & Huberman, 1994; Strauss & Corbin, 1990, 1998) in which field notes and interview transcripts were compared in order to identify an initial set of coding categories based on emerging patterns in the data. Field notes included descriptions and my reflections on observations and conversations before, during, and after each interview. The interview transcriptions and documents were read and reread to determine relevant themes.

I then generated topics from the data. According to McMillan and Shumacher (1989), "a topic is the descriptive name for the subject matter of the segment. The topic identifies the meaning of the segment" (p. 488). I noted duplication of topics and overlapping meanings. Each data segment was given a code—or abbreviation for the topic. Thus, some segments might have two or three codes at this point. The topics were then grouped into categories and subcategories. According to McMillan and Schumacher (1989), "A category is an abstract name that represents the meaning of similar topics" (p. 492). I looked for patterns or relationships among categories in order to determine the connections between various aspects of people's situa-

tions, mental processes, beliefs, and actions. This qualitative analysis depended on salient "grounded categories of meanings" held by the participants in the situation (McMillan & Schumacher, 1989, p. 495).

Through extensive in-depth interviews, I sought to
explore views of self from these Vietnamese-American
youths' relationships to their parents, siblings, extended families, and communities. In this article, the
discussion is based on a portion of the data that focused
on the psychosocial development of the participants.

Results

Family Ties

The youths' values reflect a sense of moral self
which is communal and is connected to others. They
are demonstrating what Lykes (1985) would call a notion of "social individuality." The portrait of Vietnamese youths I am painting here is one that emphasizes
their strengths. These strengths are tied to their connection to others and their view of self as a moral agent
responsible for the well-being of others. Their values
and sense of self are attributable to the family and cultural values; alternatively, these values may be attributable to their socialization within a culture that emphasizes the well-being of the group over the individual.
Bruner (1995) suggests the self is as much a product of
our culturally mediated ways for determining meaning
as it is a presupposition. As a psychologist, Bruner
explores relations between the concepts of meaning,
culture, and the self. He suggests that no single theory
of meaning can be adequate; his focus is on how meaning is developed in human beings' interactions with
each other and in their world, a world that is as much a
product of their modes of interpretation as it is an antecedent influence upon them. This examination raises
questions about the universality of the psychological
models that posit an individualistic, separate self as the
end point of development. Phuong described her family
involvement: "I visit my aunts, uncles, and my grandparents. I take my grandparents to the Buddhist temple
when I have time on Sunday. I try to make time for my
grandparents." Don offered the analysis of his feelings
and relationships with his family: "We have a close
relationship; my dad and I are really close."

Khoa stated:

Our family environment is good. Family is really important. I stay home in the summer. My oldest brother is
studying medicine in Boston. We are very close. I feel
bad because I live on campus. I should live at home so I
can look after my sister. When I lived at home, I kind of
looked out for her. She is 12 years old. She is going
through the adolescence stage, but I am not very worried
because she is really mature for her age. I guess my
brother taught her that. I talk to her once or twice a week.
I talk to my brother frequently. He calls my sister and me
a few times a week. My sister talks to my brother more
often than she talks to me. My brother always checks on
me and provides me with support and guidance. He
knows how our uncles were. If I didn't know, then he'd

think I was a bad boy. He thinks I should relate well to
our family and relatives.

Quan expressed a similar theme: "My parents are
very important to me. I appreciate their guidance and
their disciplines. I really appreciate their advice. I love
both of them equally. I feel obligated to do well for
them and for our honor, as well as for myself. My family is the main motivator along with our Vietnamese
history. I like to learn Vietnamese history." And Giang
commented: "I discuss schoolwork with my parents. I
don't hide anything from them. I can't stand hiding or
being secretive to my parents. If I have concerns, I will
tell my parents. I need my parents' input. I value their
advice." Likewise Binh commented: "Family is important. My family provides me emotional and moral support. I appreciate the values they have taught me."

Establishing Relational Bonds: Mothers and Children

The youths spoke about their mothers with great
love, respect, and sympathy. The specificity of girls'
socialization lies in their special closeness to the primary caregiver; the distinctness of the feminine personality lies in this capacity for empathetic connectedness. The girls showed respect and admiration for their
mothers and fathers. Their parents showed confidence
in their daughters' abilities. The mothers believed their
daughters were smart and through their guidance would
make intelligent decisions. The material reality of
one's economic, social, power status, as well as one's
cultural history affects one's sense of self. This gives
rise to a womanist ethic of liberation, as Eugene (1989)
found among Black women. Phoung reported her relationship with her mother was important because "I can
talk to her about anything. I ask her for advice. My
mother is my mentor and my role model." Phoung said
her mother taught her to grow up to be a kind and responsible person.

The fathers and mothers protect their daughters
and, at the same time, give them freedom. I found the
girls in my study wanted to protect their mothers, as
much as they felt protected by them. Giang described
the differential treatment of women and her feelings of
wanting to protect her mother:

My mother is my role model. I admire her. I love her
dearly. She has only a grade 5 education. She is the
sweetest woman on this earth. I feel sorry for my mother
and love her. My father's family does not treat her very
well. She can't speak English, only Vietnamese. My
dad's family does not accept her because she came from
a poor family and now we are still poor.

The girls and the boys in the study spoke with passion about the importance of their parents.

Khoa stated:

I admire my parents. They live in a new country. It is difficult for them, yet they still support and sacrifice for us.
My parents would be happier if they were in Vietnam
where they feel they belong since they can speak the language and grew up there. Here, they are very lonely. I

213

feel sorry for them. I can see their sadness and nostalgia for family in Vietnam, but they try to hide this. The only thing that helps make them happy is that we are good citizens, and we study hard for a higher education. My dad talked about how someday we have to leave home. I'm sad about it.

The girls spoke with passion about their mothers. To the girls, their mothers are their role models and their mentors. Ngoc, for example, said: "When I am unsure of anything, I'll just ask my mother and she'll give me advice. She is always right. I value her wisdom, her perception, and her observations."

Lien reported:

I love my house and my room. As you see, my room has only the necessities. There is nothing extravagant but I love it. When I come home late, my mother looks out the living room window watching for me. Every day, when I get home from school, I love to hang out in the kitchen helping my mother cook because she always tells us stories. Her voice is so sweet. She is so pretty, so gentle and naive. She is a good storyteller. My mother recalls her childhood, her village, Vietnamese folklore, and the history against the Chinese. She also tells us the famous story of two women who fought the Chinese and brought independence to Vietnam.

Both the boys and girls spoke about their mothers. They were referred to as women who were nurturing, supportive, and caring. They also said their mothers showed them they could thrive in this world. Their mothers gave them strength and courage, as they watched their mothers sacrifice and suffer. While some of the adolescents spoke about the significance of both parents, most believed their relationships with their mothers were very important. The mother's stories of influence were apparent throughout their lives.

Separation / Connection

The young Vietnamese-American males I interviewed have a concept of self that, contrary to Gilligan's (1982) predictions about males, seems to be more communal and relational than that of the American youths. For example, Quan said: "Definitely, I'll look after my mother. I owe her everything." Binh: "Five years from now, hopefully, I will still be in California because my family is here. With a computer science degree, I could get a job anywhere but I want to stay here." Don stated: "I talked to my father about everything, just like a friend. He jokes around a lot. They listen to me. They maintain their old ways, although I try to get them to be more open. Just like being at home (Vietnam), they expect us to be respectful to the elders. When we go to my grandparents' house, we have to be very respectful. I have ten aunts and uncles."

Trung's parents were divorced, and he had lived only with his father for most of his childhood and adolescence. He felt strongly about his father because of the care and support he received from him. Trung continually referred to his father and the important role he plays in his life. He attributed his success almost exclu-

sively to his father. Of all the relationships with friends, Trung said his relationship with his father was the most important: "I would give up my girlfriend or wife if I had to choose between them and my father." He wanted to get a Ph.D. in computer science. Trung said for now he just wanted to complete his bachelor's degree in computer science and get a job. That way, he could support his father. Trung wanted his father to retire and he wanted to buy a house for him. He said he knew his father wanted to visit his homeland, his village, his family, and his friends in Vietnam but he put Trung's needs before his own. He burst into tears when he talked about his father. His most important goal was to look after his father, "I owe him so much." In the future, Trung planned to take care of his father. He anticipated that his father would live with him and his wife, because he wanted to make sure his father would be cared for by him.

I admire my father even though he does not have a high status job. He can't speak English well but I admire him the most. He sacrificed everything for me. My father is the one I admire and worship. I put him first; he is the most important person in my life. I pledge that I will have a good job so my father will have a good life. He does everything for me. I owe him for everything I have. My education is extremely important to me because I owe it to my father. My father wants me to continue studying as high as I can go. In fact, he wants me to get my Ph.D. He says the higher, the better. I think I will get my computer degree and work for a big company so that I can provide my father a better life. I want to buy a house for my father, let him travel, and enjoy himself. After that, I will pursue graduate work. I'm anxious to help my father even though he would be happy to support me as long as I want to study. He has sacrificed all of his life for me. When I get married or have a girlfriend, I will still put my father first. I would let my wife go if she does not approve of my father. I could never let him be alone. No one is more important to me than my father. My father does not worry about me anymore because I always do what he wants.

The boys and girls viewed their family members as the most important people in their lives. They were motivated by their parents' hard work and the fact that they had little material wealth. Giang: "Most of my friends' houses are rich and nice but they like my house because it's warm and full of love. Their parents work most of the time so my friends feel neglected. They feel lonely, and here I am always happy, so they envy me. Even if we lived in public housing, I would have lots of love from my parents. My parents are always there for us. They always support us in any way."

Don, Quan, Binh, Khoa, Kim, Phoung, Ngoc, Lien, and Giang reported that their mothers' endurance motivated them. They took their parents' experience as proof that they, too, must survive and excel. They described growing closer to and feeling more dependent on their parents as they grew older. Don, for example, stated:

My parents don't want me to be without money. When I need money, my dad deposits thousands of dollars into my bank account. They pay for my brother's tuition also. I am worried about my father; he works very hard to make money. I feel guilty about asking him, but he told me he is happy to help me. We all remind him to look after himself. I worry about him getting sick. My family and relatives are in San Diego so I don't want to move anywhere else. I want to stay here so I can be close to them.

When Ngoc was asked if there was any particular adult she looked up to, without hesitance she responded, "My mother; she went through a lot." To explain why her mother is the most important person in her life, Ngoc said:

She left everything behind. She risked her life to escape so we would have a better future in a new country. We would learn a different language and culture. She did not want us to live in poverty. I know she misses her family, but she never says it to us. I can see the sadness in her eyes when she talks about her family. She takes care of us. She sacrifices everything for our father and us in order to give us a happy life.

Watching their parents experience arduous times had a profound effect on these youths. As Trung and others pointed out, they too could be resilient. As Binh said, seeing their parents "struggle but stay happy and optimistic through difficult times" provided them with a model to which they could aspire.

The youths' attitudes and behaviors challenged mainstream developmental beliefs about adolescents. Khoa: "My brother is more attentive to my sister. He takes her shopping, and to movies. I play basketball with her." They are aware of societal expectations concerning the need for adolescents to separate from their parents, but unapologetically explained as they grew older they were becoming closer to their parents.

Phoung: "My family is most important to me. We are very close. School is very important too but my family is the most important to me. I love everyone dearly." Lien: "I would never miss our family's dinner. I like to see my grandparents at least once a week. I see my parents every night before I go to bed. When I get home late I still like to see my parents and kiss them goodnight even now that I am in university." As they spoke about their parents, they commonly told stories about being cared for, supported by, and being inspired by them. Also they said they were becoming increasingly dependent on and growing closer to their parents over time. The youths saw their parents as a source of strength and of motivation. Their parents were also viewed as their role models, and as the most important relationship in their lives. They idealized their parents but also learned practical survival skills from them.

Cultural and Religious Values

Traditional Vietnamese culture is influenced by both Confucianism and Buddhism. Confucianism has long been deeply rooted in Vietnamese society and its family system. The family is the chief source of social identity for the elderly and the young. The family provides the strongest motivation, much stronger than religion or nationality. Confucianism prescribes communal salvation and emphasizes ancestor worship, respect for authority, the belief in consensus, and a willingness to put society's or the family's interests before individual interests. The family generally consists of father, as head of the household, grandparents, the mother and the children, the sons- and daughters-in-law, other relatives, and also all the spirits of the dead ancestors. In every house I visited, there was an altar with a picture or statute of Buddha along with the family's ancestors' photographs.

Cultural traditions and meanings are ingrained in the children's relationships with their parents. Quan explained: "My mom takes us to Buddhist temple. My mom teaches us Buddhist philosophy." Listen to Ngoc: "I like to listen to Vietnamese music because it always conveys meaningful moral values. It praises Vietnamese mothers. It also teaches us to be good daughters and sons. The music teaches us to learn to appreciate and love life, and care for others. Western music is too individualistic, too empty, and promotes violence."

Trung commented: "In Vietnam, people are closer to each other. Here people are very individualistic." And Don: "I don't have close Vietnamese friends but I participated in the community events. Now, I am too busy so I don't participate as much. I should be more involved. My brother was very active in the community." Binh, a young man, said: "My brother, my sister, and my parents are most important to me; also my other relatives. I visit my relatives when I have time. I visit them in the summer. They gossip a lot. My brother visits my relatives regularly. My parents are Buddhist. My grandparents go to Buddhist temple regularly. I went with them when I was little."

Gilligan's (1988) work, describing the ethic of care, has made a contribution to moral development theory. She argues that the masculine voice is concerned with abstract rules of justice. According to Gilligan (1982), the male's "I" (self) is defined by separation. She asserts that women and girls are more relational and thus more likely to invoke a care ethic than do men and boys. Gilligan raised the possibility of a different moral self. However, cross-cultural researchers suggest that the self is better described as collective or communal rather than individualistic.

From Kim:

I try to keep good Vietnamese traditions and adapt the good traditions. I'm very proud to be a Vietnamese girl. I feel that Vietnamese girls are more responsible. I have a lot more responsibility to my younger siblings, my parents, and to my relatives. I'm not just caring for myself, unlike Western girls of my age; they have only themselves to worry about. I treasure these responsibilities. My parents have always taught us that we should be caring and responsible for each other, not just for one's self.

635   We can't live alone on this earth. We need each other so we should support each other. If you don't have a family, then you should care for your community, your country, and the people around you. My parents don't tell me to do household chores. I do [them] because I'm the only daughter. I feel obligated to. As a Vietnamese daughter I want to keep this tradition. My mother makes dinner and after dinner I wash the dishes. I have worked extremely

640   hard since I was 14 years old. I worked whenever I could to earn money for my parents. After school, I went straight to work.

Kim added: "I learned lots from my father as well as my mother. I am close to my mother too. My mother

645   wants me to maintain the Vietnamese traditions. I keep the good traditions and adapt the good American values too." I see Chu (1985) as taking a similar position in the theory of the individual's self as distinguished by the continuity having two characteristics. They are the

650   relations which are oriented toward significant others rather than toward the self, and the basis of self-other relations as defined by cultural ideas and materials (Chu, 1985; Wei-Ming, 1985).

Thus, self-in-relation highlights the intrinsically in-

655   terdependent, interrelated quality of the self. This challenges psychology's long-standing allegiance to the notion of the self-contained individual as the unit of discourse. Gender is not a trait of individuals but a form of discourse; self is not the essential core of indi-

660   vidual identity, but a phenomenon emerging within social exchange.

Discussion

The values that play a key role in these students' lives are respect for the family; commitment to honor the family and community; respect for learning and for

665   teachers, elders, mentors, and scholars; and a strong sense of belonging to a family, a community, and a nation. Their close relationships with their mothers, fathers, and siblings may have been a critical factor in their academic resiliency. It is important to recognize

670   that these youths were academically successful and socially integrated. They were actively involved in extracurricular activities and volunteered in their communities.

Different students play different roles in their fami-

675   lies depending on their particular place among siblings. Most students expressed in vivid terms their love for family members. When the boys talked about their relationships with their parents, no one seemed preoccupied with or focused on issues of separation. The self

680   is transformed and guided by others: "The self-knowledge that guides behavior is of the self-in-relation to specific others in particular contexts. The fundamental units of the self system, the core conceptions, or self-schemata are thus predicated on signifi-

685   cant interpersonal relationships" (Markus & Kitayama, 1991, p. 227). Their struggles, concerns, and questions were about connections and how to maintain them. These concerns only grew stronger over time. Both the

690   boys and girls told stories about growing closer and more emotionally dependent on their parents over time, particularly to their mothers.

The mothers in this study were portrayed as deeply caring, supportive, and inspirational. Khoa, Binh, Quan, Don, Ngoc, Kim, Giang, Lien, and Phoung cred-

695   ited their mothers with much of their own success. They spoke of admiration for their mothers' competence, strength, and independence. For the girls, their relationship with their mothers seemed to provide the trusting companionship for which they yearned. They

700   were uninhibited and proud to let their mothers be part of their world, and they actively resisted separating from them. The boys felt close to their mothers and took great care to emphasize the relationship. This challenges the widely held notion that male children

705   require male role models. The boys believed, articulated, and demonstrated through their words and their achievements that their mothers and fathers had raised them to be mature, sensitive, and caring people. The pride in Vietnam's long rich history and ethnic identity

710   and the sense of obligation and responsibility to family, community, and nation gives motivation, energy, and inspiration to these students to work hard in school in order to repay the obligations of love and sacrifice. These youths have a strong sense of their own identity.

715   In other words, these Vietnamese students assumed their individual responsibility for their academic successes within the collective spirit of the previous and current generations. Their identities are shaped through relations to others—especially, family, community,

720   nation—as well as history, culture, and traditions. Similarly, their actions do not occur in isolation: virtually all accomplishments occur through the efforts and spirits of many. Each day there are vivid reminders of the generational contrasts that shape the ways these

725   narrators construct their lives. This reflects Chu's (1985) explanation, with regard to an individual's sense of self-worth or even purpose in life, that the way the person can cope and survive is a measure of the strength of self. The most essential source of strength

730   derives from significant others. Another source of strength is cultural ideas, including moral values and religious beliefs. The last source, perhaps a fragile one, is material assets, another source of strength for self (Chu, 1985).

735   The results of interviews, examining their learning environments and analyzing their narratives, led to the realization that education is seen by parents as an effective instrument of empowerment and liberation for the entire family, providing hope for the future. Values of

740   friendship and connection, of relationship and context, of cycles and growth, of cultures and beauty, of ritual and respect for the new land, of learning and achievement, so common in the youths' ways of knowing, are central to the Vietnamese culture. It is not the details of

745   the Vietnamese culture alone that are important to us here, but the notion that out of the youths' experiences

216

and consciousness, values and knowledge, a workable ordering of the interdependence between the two cultures is possible.

References

Brown, L. M., & Gilligan, C. (1992). *Meeting at the crossroads: Women's psychology and girls' development.* Cambridge, MA: Harvard University Press.

Bruner, J. S. (1995). Meaning and self in cultural perspective. In D. Bakhurst & C. Sypnowich (Eds.), *The social self* (18–29). Thousand Oaks, CA: Sage.

Chodorow, N. (1977). *The reproduction of mothering: Psychoanalysis and the sociology of gender.* Berkeley, CA: University of California Press.

Chu, G. (1985). The changing concept of self in contemporary China. In A. Marsella, G, DeVos, & F. L. Hsu (Eds.), *Culture and self.* London: Tavistock.

Coole, D. (1995). The gendered self. In D. Bakhurst & C. Sypnowich (Eds.), *The social self* (123–139). Thousand Oaks, CA: Sage.

Creswell, J. (2002). *Educational research: Planning, conducting, and evaluating quantitative and qualitative research.* New Jersey: Prentice-Hall.

Cushman, P. (1990). Why the self is empty. *American Psychologist, 45,* 599–611.

Cushman, P. (1995). *Constructing the self, constructing America: A cultural history of psychotherapy.* New York: Addison-Wesley.

DeVos, G. A. (1985). Dimensions of the self in Japanese culture. In A. Marsella, G. DeVos, & F. L. K. Hsu (Eds.), *Culture and self* (149–184). London: Tavistock.

Eugene, T. (1989). Sometimes I feel like a motherless child: The call and response for a liberational ethic of care by Black feminists. In M. Brabeck (Ed.), *Who cares? Theory research and educational implications of the ethic of care* (45–63). New York: Praeger.

Geertz, C. (1979). From the native's point of view: On the nature of anthropological understanding. In P. Rabinow & W. M. Sullivan (Eds.), *Interpretive social science.* Berkeley: University of California Press.

Gergen, K. (1991). *The saturated self. Dilemmas of identity in contemporary life.* New York: Harper Collins.

Gergen, K. (1994). *Realities and relationships: Soundings in social construction.* Cambridge, MA: Harvard University Press.

Gergen, K. (1999). *An invitation to social construction.* London: Sage.

Gergen, K. (2001). *Social construction in context.* London: Sage.

Gergen, K., & Gergen, M. (1988). Narrative and the self as relationship. *Advances in Experimental Social Psychology, 21,* 17–56.

Gilligan, C. (1982). *In a different voice: Psychological theory and women's development.* Cambridge, MA: Harvard University Press.

Gilligan, C., & Attanucci, J. (1988). The origins of morality in early childhood relationships. In C. Gilligan, J. V. Ward, & J. M. Taylor (Eds.), *Mapping the moral domain* (111–138). Cambridge, MA: Harvard University Press.

Glaser, B. G., & Strauss, A. L. (1967). *The discovery of grounded theory: Strategies for qualitative research.* Chicago: Aldine.

Harre, R. (1984). *Personal being: A theory for individual psychology.* Cambridge, MA: Harvard University Press.

Lykes, M. B. (1985). Gender and individualistic vs. collectivist bases for notions about the self. *Journal of Personality, 53,* 356–383.

Lykes, M. B. (1989). The caring self: Social experiences of power and powerlessness. In M. Brabeck (Ed.), *Who cares: Theory research and educational implications of the ethic of care* (164–180). New York: Praeger.

Markus, H. R., & Kitayama, S. (1991). Culture and the self: Implications for cognition, emotion and motivation. *Psychological Review, 98,* 224–253.

McMillan, J. H., & Schumacher, S. (1989). *Research in education: A conceptual introduction* (2nd ed.). Glenview, IL: Scott, Foresman.

Mertens, D. (1998). *Research methods in education and psychology: Integrating diversity with quantitative and qualitative approaches.* Thousand Oaks, CA: Sage.

Miles, M., & Huberman, A. (1994). *Qualitative data analysis. An expanded sourcebook* (2nd ed.). Newbury Park: Sage.

Miller, D. T., & Prentice, D. A. (1994). The self and the collective. *Personality and Social Psychology Bulletin, 20,* 451–453.

Miller, J. (1976). *Toward a new psychology of women.* Boston, MA: Beacon Press.

Miller, J. (1984). Culture and the development of everyday social explanation. *Journal of Personality and Social Psychology, 46,* 961–978.

Noddings, N. (1984). *Caring: A feminine approach to ethics and moral education.* Berkeley, CA: University of California Press.

Patton, M. (1990). *Qualitative evaluation and research methods* (2nd ed.). Newbury Park: Sage.

Puka, B. (1989). The liberation of caring: A different voice for Gilligan's "different voice." In M. Brabeck (Ed.), *Who cares? Theory research and educational implications of the ethic of care* (19–44). New York: Praeger.

Sampson, E. (1977). Psychology and the American ideal. *Journal of Personality and Social Psychology, 35,* 767–782.

Sampson, E. (1985). The decentralization of group identity: Toward a revised concept of personal and social order. *American Psychologist, 44,* 914–921.

Sampson, E. (1989). The challenge of social change for psychology: Globalization and psychology's theory of the person. *American Psychologist, 44,* 914–921.

Sampson, E. (1993). *Celebrating the other: A dialogic account of human nature.* Boulder, CO: Westview.

Shotter, J. (1993). *Conversational realities.* London: Sage.

Strauss, A., & Corbin, J. (1990). *Basics of qualitative research: Grounded theory procedures and techniques.* Newbury Park, CA: Sage.

Strauss, A., & Corbin, J. (1998). *Basics of qualitative research: Technique and procedures for developing grounded theory* (2nd ed.). Newbury Park, CA: Sage.

Taylor, S., & Bogdan, R. (1998). *Introduction to qualitative research methods: A guidebook and resource* (3rd ed.). New York: Springer.

Wei-Ming, T. (1985). Selfhood and otherness in Confucian thought. In A. Marsella, G. DeVos, & F. L. Hsu (Eds.), *Culture and self.* London: Tavistock.

Wilkinson, S. (1997). Feminist psychologist. In D. Fox & I. Prilleltensky (Eds.), *Critical psychology: An introduction* (247–264). London: Sage.

Acknowledgments: The author gratefully acknowledges Rena Lewis and anonymous reviewers for their helpful comments and suggestions. The research for this article was supported by the San Diego State University's Research Scholarship and Creative Activity Grant.

Address correspondence to: Tan Phan, College of Education, School of Teacher Education, San Diego State University, 5500 Campanile Drive, San Diego, California 92181. E-mail: tphan@mail.sdsu.edu

Exercise for Article 39

Factual Questions

1. According to the literature review, postmodernist thinkers argue that the self is "inextricably linked" to what?

2. According to the literature review, how did Chu (1985) define "self"?

3. How did the researcher implement "snowball" sampling?

4. Did the participants come from upper-class families?

5. What is the sample size for this study?

6. Were the interviews based on fully structured questionnaires?

7. Did the researcher propose a hypothesis for this study?

Questions for Discussion

8. What is your opinion on the selection of only students with GPAs above 4.00? (See lines 193–198.)

9. What is your opinion on the researcher's decision to analyze data throughout the study rather than only after the data collection? (See lines 261–264.)

10. The researcher describes the coding for the analysis in lines 265–292. In your opinion, is this description clear? Is it sufficiently detailed? Explain.

11. The researcher states that participants' voices (i.e., quotations of the participants' actual words) are included in order "to give texture to the analytic conclusions and to provide samples of the kind of evidence upon which those conclusions are based." (See lines 245–249.) Consider the quotations relating to "family ties" in lines 299–360. In your opinion, do these quotations provide "texture"? Do they provide adequate "evidence"? Explain.

12. For the research topic of this study, do you think that a quantitative study (with statistical results) would also be informative? Explain.

Quality Ratings

Directions: Indicate your level of agreement with each of the following statements by circling a number from 5 for strongly agree (SA) to 1 for strongly disagree (SD). If you believe an item is not applicable to this research article, leave it blank. Be prepared to explain your ratings. When responding to criteria A and B below, keep in mind that brief titles and abstracts are conventional in published research.

A. The title of the article is appropriate.

SA 5 4 3 2 1 SD

B. The abstract provides an effective overview of the research article.

SA 5 4 3 2 1 SD

C. The introduction establishes the importance of the study.

SA 5 4 3 2 1 SD

D. The literature review establishes the context for the study.

SA 5 4 3 2 1 SD

E. The research purpose, question, or hypothesis is clearly stated.

SA 5 4 3 2 1 SD

F. The method of sampling is sound.

SA 5 4 3 2 1 SD

G. Relevant demographics (for example, age, gender, and ethnicity) are described.

SA 5 4 3 2 1 SD

H. Measurement procedures are adequate.

SA 5 4 3 2 1 SD

I. All procedures have been described in sufficient detail to permit a replication of the study.

SA 5 4 3 2 1 SD

J. The participants have been adequately protected from potential harm.

SA 5 4 3 2 1 SD

K. The results are clearly described.

SA 5 4 3 2 1 SD

L. The discussion/conclusion is appropriate.

SA 5 4 3 2 1 SD

M. Despite any flaws, the report is worthy of publication.

SA 5 4 3 2 1 SD

Article 40

Contributions to Family and Household Activities by the Husbands of Midlife Professional Women

JUDITH R. GORDON
Boston College

KAREN S. WHELAN-BERRY
Utah Valley State College

ABSTRACT. This article presents an exploratory study that furthers our understanding of the functioning of two-career couples at midlife and, in particular, our understanding of the husband's contributions to family and household activities. More specifically, it addresses the following questions regarding dual-career couples: (a) Whose career has precedence? (b) What is the nature of the husband's contributions to the family and household? and (c) What types of support result? This study is part of a larger research project that focuses on the professional and personal lives of a group of midlife professional women who were married, had children, and had enduring careers. The results presented here describe the women's perceptions of support (or lack of support) provided by their spouses in their family and household. It discusses the implications of such support for family functioning and for the ability of midlife women to pursue full-time careers.

From *Journal of Family Issues*, 26, 899–923. Copyright © 2005 by Sage Publications. Reprinted with permission.

Recent research has suggested that between one-third and one-half of women in top executive and professional positions at midlife do not have children. They remain childless as a result of a "creeping 'non-
5   choice' " because they cannot successfully combine employment and family responsibilities and still rise to high-level positions (Hewlett, 2002). Although organizations have instituted family-friendly programs as one way of supporting women employees, most of these
10 programs address concerns of women early in their careers. Husbands are another potential source of support for midlife professional women; in fact, such support has been shown to result in greater well-being for the women (Cutrona & Russell, 1990; Greenglass,
15 1993). Although research has recognized the contributions of men in two-career families, their involvement has been studied primarily for families with young children (Barnett & Rivers, 1996; Deutsch, 1999; Deutsch, Lussier, & Servis, 1993; Ehrensraft, 1987;
20 Gilbert, 1993). Are these contributions the same for the families of midlife professional women? As more

women have moved into higher positions at midlife, have the contributions of their spouses changed?

The study reported here examines the contributions
25 of husbands of midlife women in helping them balance employment and family demands. More specifically, it addresses the following questions: (a) Whose career has precedence? (b) What is the nature of the husband's contributions to the family and household? and
30 (c) What types of support result?

A great deal has been written about women who work outside the home and the special challenges women with children face in balancing employment and family. During the past 20 years most of this work
35 has focused on women in early career stages, although some of the more recent research has examined women at midlife (e.g., Apter, 1995; Borysenko, 1996; Gordon & Whelan, 1998; James & Liewkowicz, 1997; Levinson, 1996; J. Marshall, 1994). We have been particu-
40 larly interested in studying professional women at midlife who are married, have children, but also have had enduring careers because they have likely experienced the potential conflict between employment and family. Because they have had enduring careers, they most
45 likely have established a workable division of responsibilities with their husbands and have found ways to either overcome or minimize this conflict.

Women who reached midlife in the mid-1980s to early 1990s were among the first who attempted to
50 work full-time throughout their adult life while still marrying and having children without significant time away from the workforce as a result of childbearing. As pioneers, they faced special challenges in dealing with employment and home in ways that professional
55 men had never considered. Some of these professional women achieved a degree of success previously unknown for women who were married and had children. This particular group of women, one that has been able to meld the responsibilities of employment and family,
60 provides insight into the broader array of challenges women who work outside the home face and the ways their partners help or hinder their balancing act.

This article describes a group of midlife professional women with enduring careers and their percep-
65 tions of the role their husbands played in sustaining and supporting their careers. As an exploratory study, it attempts to delineate the participation by the husbands of professional midlife women in the family and household arena. Although these contributions repre-
70 sent only part of the potential support that husbands can provide (e.g., they can also offer emotional or financial support), they represent areas that appear to be important for balancing employment and family. Subsequent research examines other areas of support.

75 We first present some background about the functioning of two-career families. Next we describe the research method, including data collection, analysis procedures, and an overview of the sample. Then we consider the results of the analysis, looking specifically
80 at the midlife women's perceptions of their husband's involvement and support in employment and family domains. Finally, we discuss the implications of the results, as well as limitations to the study and directions for future research.

Background

85 As the baby boomers reach midlife and beyond, they have swelled the ranks of workers between the ages of 40 and 50 years. For example, the percentage of the labor force between the ages of 35 and 54 years increased from 42% in 1990 to 47% in 2004 (U.S. Bu-
90 reau of Labor Statistics, 2004). The number of women between the ages of 35 and 44 years was 16.6 million in 2004, as compared to 11.7 million in 1985 (U.S. Bureau of Labor Statistics, 2004). Understanding the issues faced by these workers at midlife and beyond
95 can facilitate the development of appropriate policies and practices.

Although some research has addressed the issues of midlife workers (A. Kruger, 1994; Levinson, 1978; O'Connor & Wolfe, 1991) and now midlife women
100 (Apter, 1995; Gordon & Whelan, 1998; Grambs, 1989; Jacobson, 1995; Levinson, 1996; J. Marshall, 1995), little of this work has looked at women with enduring careers at midlife and similarly at the roles their spouses play in their lives. Women at midlife typically
105 have established their careers and home and family life (Gordon & Whelan, 1998; Reid & Willis, 1999; White, 1995). They often have school-age or young-adult children although can still have preschool children at home. Other published data from this study of married
110 midlife women with enduring professional careers and families (Gordon & Whelan, 1998) indicated that these women had needs for renewed work-family balance, more personal time, and continued achievement, accomplishment, and perceived value to the organization.
115 They also perceived a need for assistance in preparing for the next decade's challenges, which included good mothering, especially of adolescents; building their career path and continuing to advance in their organi-

zation; maintaining balance in their lives; developing
120 career competencies; and dealing with their aging parents. Most of these women developed personal coping strategies as ways of meeting these needs. Yet Gordon and Whelan's (1998) study did not address the role that husbands played in the midlife of these professional
125 women. As the number of dual-career couples continues to increase and the workforce continues to age, a significant number of dual-career couples at midlife and beyond will continue to face the challenge of balancing employment and family responsibilities.

Support Provided by Wives and Husbands in Two-Career Families

130 Prior research indicates that many women significantly support their husband's careers. Women provide support by taking primary responsibility for family and household (Beck, 1998; Bonney, Kelley, & Levant, 1999; P. Kruger, 1998; Manke, Seery, Crouter, &
135 McHale, 1994; Shelton & John, 1993). Historically, employed women have done a greater share of family work than their husbands (Biernat & Wortman, 1991; Coverman, 1989). Even when women jointly own family companies with their husbands, they have assumed
140 more family and household responsibilities (Marshack, 1994). Wives have also been viewed as partners in their husband's careers. Recruitment for executive positions, for example, has often included the husband and wife in interviews and on-site visits, even investi-
145 gating the wife's character, personality, and marital relations (Murray, 1986). Women with careers may relinquish them or reduce their career advancement as a result of their spouse's career moves, thus becoming the trailing spouse.

150 Women have rarely experienced the same type of support from their spouse, even if they have equal or primary careers, although husbands contributed more to household labor in a younger cohort of spouses (Pleck, 1997; Robinson & Godbey, 1997; Rogers &
155 Amato, 2000). A study, for example, indicated that husbands' participation in childcare increases as mothers have extended work hours (Bonney et al., 1999). Traditionally, however, men have worked outside the home and women worked inside the home. Employed
160 women merely added job-related responsibilities to their home responsibilities (Potuchek, 1997). In large part, this lack of support results from the competing career obligations that the husbands have because their participation in dual-career families has personal and
165 professional consequences (Rosin, 1990). The amount and sharing of household, childcare, and family work evolves, increasing and decreasing, as children and parents age or are ill. At midlife, women and men may find themselves sandwiched between generational re-
170 sponsibilities, placing additional burdens on them.

Outcomes in Two-Career Couples

Satisfaction with the division of household labor influences marital happiness (Suitor, 1991). A larger percentage of wives than husbands restructured their work for family reasons (Karambayya & Reilly, 1992). Even though the men were equally involved with their families, they did not restructure their employment as much as the women to meet family obligations, instead making so-called special arrangements instead of more consistent adjustments. Some men felt stuck in what has been called the "daddy trap" (Hammonds & Palmer, 1998), where they face significant work demands that conflict with their (and their wife's) desire for them to be equal participants in dealing with family and household responsibilities (Hertz, 1999). Women were more satisfied when their husbands shared the chores they had traditionally performed rather than spent more time performing household chores in general (Benin & Agostinelli, 1988). Clearly, the intertwining of their careers and lives can create problems for the advancement of one member of the couple if relocation is required (Cohen, 1994; Taylor & Lounsbury, 1988). Yet their relationship and support for each other can overcome some of these negative outcomes (Gilbert, 1985, 1993). Special cases exist when husband and wife work in the same business, altering and increasing the requirements for support (Marshack, 1994). Decision making and responsibilities in these careers are not equal, with women primarily responsible for the home arena and husbands for the work arena (Marshack, 1994; Ponthieu & Caudill, 1993; Wicker & Burley, 1991).

In addition to the impact of the actual attitudes and behaviors on the wives' outcomes, the wives' perceptions can also influence their attitudes and behaviors. Wives' perceptions of their husbands' attitudes toward the wives working influenced the wives' attitudes about their own work (Spitze & Waite, 1981). The impact of perceptions is further illustrated in a study where perceptions of unfairness in household chores and spending money were significantly related to husbands' and wives' assessment of marital quality (Blair, 1993). Perceptions of equity play a key role in marital satisfaction and quality (Gager, 1998; Gilbert, 1993).

Summary and Unanswered Questions

As more women have entered the workforce, their husbands have contributed to the family by helping with household and child care tasks. Most of the research so far has focused on men and women at early career stages with young children. Husbands' contributions to two-career families have been chronicled in numerous studies, although most have not specifically considered the nature of participation in couples at midlife (Aldous, Mulligan, & Bjarnasin, 1998; Barnett & Baruch, 1987; Barnett & Rivers, 1996; Deutsch, 1999; Gilbert, 1993). This stage of career and life offers new complexities and poses special challenges that make understanding the role of husbands important. Does one person's career take precedence, or does true equality exist in the careers of husbands and wives at

midlife? What happens at midcareer to career precedence and sharing of home and family responsibilities, for example, when both partners are highly successful in their careers? Furthermore, what do these pioneering women have to say about their husbands' contributions to family life? To what extent do the husbands share in the work of the family? What happens when the husband and wife have career aspirations that call for spending significant time on job-related activities and also have children who require attention?

The current exploratory study attempted to take a first step in addressing these unanswered questions by looking at the husbands' involvement in employment and family in midlife dual-career couples. We focus on three questions: (a) Whose career has precedence? (b) What is the nature of the husband's contributions to the family and household? and (c) What types of support result? In the current study, we report the results in the women's voice as a way of better identifying, describing, and understanding the subtleties, complexities, and common issues of the families of midlife professional women.

Method

We used a qualitative methodology in the current exploratory study because it provides a richness of data that helps identify key themes that can form the basis of subsequent quantitative studies (Denzin & Lincoln, 1998; C. Marshall & Rossman, 1999; Strauss & Corbin, 1990). We interviewed 36 professional women between the ages of 36 and 50 years. These women were part of a pioneering group who combined marriage and parenting with enduring and relatively uninterrupted full-time work throughout their adult lives. They are an unusual group because of the degree of their career accomplishments—each woman had attained significant professional stature; the sample included top business executives, well-regarded physicians, partners in major legal firms, and successful self-employed consultants and businesswomen. Their husbands were equally accomplished, holding high-level business, not-for-profit, legal, and medical positions. Most of the women and men in the sample were at the pinnacle of demanding careers that required large amounts of time and energy and gave no indication of diminishing in importance during the next 10 years.

Data Collection and Analysis

Although the current study was part of a larger one that involved an extensive interview protocol, the results of the current study were based primarily on the women's responses to the following questions, which allowed us to delineate the contributions made by the husbands of the midlife professional women: "What role has your husband played in helping you manage family and career?" "How do you interface with your husband's career and vice versa?" We also coded comments about the woman's spouse in other parts of the interview, which included questions about the nature of their employment and family responsibilities, the way they manage these responsibilities now and in the past, their key challenges, the major issues they faced at various times in their lives, the nature of the transition between life stages, the impact and contributions of their organization in handling their employment and family responsibilities, and their satisfaction with their job, career, and life.

We used a nonrandom sample of Boston-area professionals; securing a random sample or a complete sample of the population would have been desirable but was unrealistic because of difficulty in locating married, professional women with children and enduring careers. The first author contacted a small group of women who could help identify women in professional-level jobs who had worked full-time throughout their adult lives, were married, and had at least one child. The women identified in this way were contacted by telephone and asked to participate in the current study. All but two of the women contacted agreed to be interviewed; these two women declined to participate, not because of lack of interest, but because of significant time demands on their lives at that time. The women who participated were then asked to suggest additional women. This snowball technique resulted in a convenience sample, which is appropriate for an exploratory study. The interviews lasted between 1 and 3 hours and were audiotaped. The first author conducted all interviews to ensure relative consistency in their content.

Each interview was transcribed. We analyzed the transcripts using the qualitative analysis approach suggested by Miles and Huberman (1994) as follows: We created a data set with the responses to questions that related directly to the husband, household and family management, and career interfaces between the husband's and wife's career. We then searched the full interview transcript and included any interviewee comments that related to the spouses of the women interviewed. We first coded the responses according to the broad, thematic areas of the interview questions related to spouse, for example, the role the husband played in helping manage family and career, and the nature of the two careers. During this coding, we focused on and identified the themes that related to the involvement of the spouses in helping the women handle career and family responsibilities, although the larger research project addressed multiple themes and issues. Next, we reviewed each transcript to identify any additional thematic areas not yet specified and to ensure that all relevant themes were identified. For this article, we focused on career precedence and the husband's contribution to family and household. A second coder then coded the nature of career precedence and the husband's contribution to family and household based on comments about the husband previously extracted from the interviews. The interrater agreement (Miles & Huberman, 1994) between the two coders

initially was 83% for career precedence and 69% for husband's contributions. When the second coder read the entire transcript of the interviews of the women where coding differences existed, and after discussing discrepancies between the two sets of codes and trying to reconcile them, the agreement rose to 97% and 81%, respectively. In cases where no agreement could be reached, the codings by the first coder are reported in this article.

Sample

The women in the sample were all White, and the majority were between the ages of 40 and 45 years, although younger and older women were included in the sample to capture the breadth of experiences at midlife. The length of their marriage varied from fewer than 5 years to more than 20 years, with most of the women having marriages of 15 to 20 years, followed in frequency by 11 to 15 and 6 to 10 years, respectively. Some women had been divorced previously; however, all were married at the time of the interview. More than one-half of the sample had two children, and one-third had only one child; having three or more children was less common. These children ranged in age from preschool to adult. Table 1 provides more specific information about the sample.

Table 1
Age, Marital Status, and Children of the Women in the Sample (N =36)

	Number of women
Age of the women (M)	(41)
36 to 39 years	8
40 to 45 years	26
46 to 50 years	2
Length of marriage (M)	(15)
0 to 5 years	1
6 to 10 years	8
11 to 15 years	10
15 to 20 years	12
More than 20 years	5
Number of children (M)	(2)
1	12
2	20
3 or more	4
Age of youngest child	
Preschool	9
Elementary school	20
Secondary school	6
College or older	1
Age of oldest child	
Preschool	4
Elementary school	19
Secondary school	5
College or older	8

The women in our sample were quite successful and worked in an array of professions, as shown in the left-hand column of Table 2. Many held high-level positions in major Boston-area organizations; they

Table 2
Occupations of the Women and Their Husbands (N = 36)

Woman's occupation	Number of women with this occupation	Woman's description of husband's occupation				
Account manager	1	Self-employed				
Attorney	3	Attorney (2)	Bank executive			
Bank executive	4	Consultant	Development officer	Higher education executive	High technology manager	
Chief financial officer	1	Psychologist				
Consultant	3	Administrative judge	Consultant	Medical researcher		
Development officer[a]	1	N/A				
Film producer	2	Media executive	Television reporter			
Financial manager	1	Attorney				
Human resources manager[a]	5	Development director	Executive chef	Human resources manager	Psychoanalyst	N/A
Information systems manager	2	Attorney	Professor			
Investment banker	1	Consultant				
Physician	4	Physician (4)				
Professor	1	Hotel administrator				
Psychologist	1	Hospital administrator				
Real estate developer	1	Real estate developer				
Senior administrator	2	Attorney	Politician			
Social worker	1	Physician				
Systems engineer	1	Architect				
Systems planning manager	1	Physician				

[a]The data from the interviews of one of the women with this occupation did not include the husband's occupation, shown in the table as N/A.

370 were partners in law firms, well-regarded physicians, top human resources executives, senior vice presidents in financial services organizations, and top managers in the nonprofit sector. The husbands of these women also held professional-level positions, as shown in Table 2; 375 the right-hand column lists the professions of the husband of each woman with the specified occupation. One-fourth held the same type of job as their wives; for example, the sample included couples who were attorneys, physicians, media-related professionals, or human 380 resources managers. This sample was unusual because in most of the couples the husband and wife had achieved a high, relatively equal level of success in their careers.

Results

We present the results as they answer our three re-385 search questions. First, we analyze whose career has precedence. Next, we present the data regarding the husband's contribution to the family and household. Finally, we combine these data into a typology of four types of husbands to describe the overall type of sup-390 port they offer.

Career Precedence

Career precedence was reflected either in whose career was the primary focus of career decisions or in who assumed the burden of balancing employment and family. The women in the current study described 395 whose career took precedence in one of three ways: their husband's, their own, or equal.

Husband's career had precedence. The husband's career took precedence for 22% of the couples. The

women explained this precedence as occurring for four 400 reasons. First, the salaries associated with the two careers may have resulted in the husband's career having precedence. A social worker reported, for example, that her husband's career took precedence because he made a higher salary: "I still did most of the daytime stuff, I 405 mean, that was an economic reality." Second, decisions about job location, such as whether the wife trailed the husband in job relocations, reflected the type of career precedence. A husband's career took precedence, for example, because job mobility for the wife was easier. 410 Third, the husband may have had ego needs, such as providing security for his family or having status or power, that were met by his having the dominant career. The wife in a physician couple noted this motivation:

415 His career is skyrocketing and all that, and I've come to realize that that's important to him. Because of his needs and deprivations and so on as a child [his career] is something he just had to keep working at until he feels comfortable.

420 Finally, this traditional attitude toward career precedence may be a function of many men's socialization to expect to be the family's breadwinner.

One attorney noted this influence when she described her husband's career having precedence:

425 Oh, definitely if there has to be any give it seems to be mine.... Men have a fascinating way of forgetting that they had to be home at six.... I think they just naturally assume they're primo. I think women are by nature more accommodating.

223

430   *Wife's career had precedence.* For a slightly
smaller percentage of couples, 19%, the wife's career
had precedence. For these couples, only two of the
factors—salary and job mobility—seemed to play a
major role in the decision. For a human resources man-
435   ager, for example, her higher salary resulted in her career having precedence. She believed that her husband
also felt comfortable limiting his career achievement:

It just sort of happened gradually because of my advancement. It wasn't a choice, do you take this promotion
440   or not? And the fact that he also was someone who has a
lot of interests around the home, is very interested in the
computer, and is project oriented. [He] didn't feel like he
had to prove himself professionally. And we just felt for
the total family, this was the best thing to do.

445   A physician described the lesser mobility of her career because of job vacancies or the special nature of
her work: "In many ways, he has a more common and
saleable job…. So when we've talked about moving,
it's always been with an eye to what academic jobs are
450   out there for me that he could find a job around."

The careers had equal precedence. The largest
group of the women interviewed, 58%, either stated or
implied that the two careers held equal precedence, as
captured in one attorney's comment about her husband,
455   also an attorney: "Every time I go to give up mine, he
says he'll retire too." Yet the equality is not without
some tension and trade-offs. As one physician noted,
"We're even. If anything, I got to be an associate professor a year ahead…[however,] I would have left sev-
460   eral times for good job offers, but [my husband] does
not want to leave Boston." A human resources manager
commented,

We both sacrifice somewhat in our career. My husband is
an executive chef, and in that business if you're really go-
465   ing to get ahead, you have to be willing to put in the 60,
70, 80 hours per week. You have to be willing to relocate
with some of the bigger chains or work in Boston and
make the long commute, put in the hours. He has sacrificed that to help maintain the family life at home. So in
470   that respect he sacrificed, and I have sacrificed also.

Another woman described the trade-offs in her family:

Now I'm reaching another sort of crossroads where I'm
feeling maybe the business isn't really going to bring in
475   enough money in the next few years to pay all those bills
easily. The other dilemma is that my husband has been
working at his job for so many years…and he's got a
great job but he's also in midlife crisis. I mean, he
doesn't want to do that forever. And I'm feeling a bit
480   more pressure to pull a little more weight so he can slack
off a little and try something new in a couple of years. So
there's always a dilemma, there's always a trade-off. You
know, things change.

Trade-offs have a lot to do with managing the logis-
485   tics of the two careers. They also relate to personal
issues about growing older, accomplishing desired
goals, and an equal commitment to ensuring that family

needs are met. It is a dynamic process, with adjustments occurring continuously.

Contributions to Family and Household
490   No midlife woman did all of the family and child
care herself. Most husbands made some contributions
to the family and household activities, although some
contributions were extremely limited. The husbands'
contributions ranged from doing a small part, to shar-
495   ing relatively equally, to the husband's having primary
responsibility. Our thematic analysis indicated that
many of the husbands played specific supportive roles,
as well as offered general support. This support helped
the wife handle the challenges created by the require-
500   ments of a professional career and a demanding family.
For example, an information systems manager noted
that "I think having a supportive husband and a supportive daughter have always been important." A business
executive noted,

505   I think that [my husband] has always been real supportive
around my career and very supportive around the intel-
lectual challenges that I find associated with my work.
Not that it doesn't create stress, when there's not enough
clean underwear, but I think that's [support's] the key.

510   Without this basic type of support, managing employment and family likely would be even more stressful for the midlife women.

Although most families purchased extensive child
care and household services (depending, of course, on
515   the ages of their children), significant responsibilities
for managing and implementing family-related activities remained. Of the wives, 42% explicitly characterized their husband's involvement using the language of
"managing" and "doing." In the remainder of the cases,
520   this distinction was based on women's description of
the tasks and responsibilities performed by themselves
and their husbands. *Managing* refers to the planning,
coordinating, and initiating of all household and family-related activities. The person or persons who man-
525   age to carry the emotional burden or psychological
responsibility for making sure that the household runs
smoothly and that children receive appropriate care.
The manager often initiates and delegates various family and household activities to other family members or
530   paid caregivers or household service providers. One
woman, for example, described herself as the "domestic coordinator" of her family. Another noted about her
husband, "On a day-to-day basis, he does more of the
planning part of it."

535   *Doing* refers to the carrying out, performing, or implementing of a sequence of household activities.
Typically, these activities occur in response to initiatives or requests by the person who manages the
household and family-related activities. The same per-
540   son can manage and do, or one person can manage
while the other person does the family and household
work. Often, the women describe their husbands as
helping in the household. As one woman noted, "He

Table 3
Types of Support Provided by Husbands (N = 36)

		Managing	
		Low	High
Doing	Low	Uninvolved (*n* = 5) The au pair does it.... Oh, he couldn't plan [household responsibilities] if his life depended on it.... We have to send somebody to do the grocery shopping.... The major need is for carpooling, baseball. I mean [the nanny] doesn't really take care of the kids.	Coordinator (*n* = 3) [Husband] probably [makes greater contributions]. It's changing. Right now, it's about 60–40, but until recently, it's probably been 90–10.... [My husband] always has the higher percentage. He would do drop off and pick up. He would do teacher conferences. He would do whatever.
	High	Helpmate (*n* = 18) [He's] a great husband. He'll do anything I ask him to do. He doesn't necessarily think of things on his own. And there were a number of years when that bothered me, but then I realized that...I ought to be thankful that he does these things, and all I have to do is say, "Would you do this?" and he says, "Sure, fine."	Egalitarian (*n* = 10) But he was always very good about [my traveling on short notice]. He certainly did more than half, pitching in, running errands, and taking kids to the doctor and making sure that there was food in the house and that kind of thing.... It's always been shared. I think I did more of some things than he did all along, even when my career was maybe even busier than his.

couldn't plan it if his life depended on it." Another woman described doing as follows: "Sometimes you just have to ask him. He knows the basics. He cooks, he cleans, he grocery shops, he does errands. It's just part of the routine. He's there to help out."

Categories of Support

Based on the wives' perceptions as expressed during our interviews, we identified the extent to which husbands manage or do most activities regarding family and household as high or low. We characterized (not counted) the content of the wives' comments to determine the level of each type of support by their husbands. We categorized a husband as high on managing if the wife reported that he consistently and of his own initiative performed numerous tasks related to the planning, coordinating, and initiating of activities; we categorized a husband as low on managing if the wife described him as rarely performing such activities. Similarly, we categorized a husband as high on doing if his wife described him as implementing household-related activities, typically after she specified that they needed to be done; we categorized a husband as low on doing if he rarely performed any household-related activities.

This results in four possible combinations. Table 3 illustrates the combinations and offers an example of a woman's comments about husbands who fall into each category. We have chosen descriptive names—uninvolved, helpmate, egalitarian, and coordinator—to reflect the underlying approach of these husbands to the sharing of household and family responsibilities. The labels are intended solely to differentiate about possibilities rather than definitively characterize each husband.

Uninvolved husbands. Of the husbands, 14% were low on managing and doing household and family activities and so were perceived as making very limited contributions in these areas. Some men lack the time because of extensive career commitments. As one physician commented, "If I ever had any question about where my focus would be, knowing that he's so busy means that somebody has to be home running the show."

Other men remain uninvolved because they believe that they can completely enjoy their family in less time than their wives need. Still, others have retained a view, often based on early socialization, that women should assume primary responsibilities for their family and household. These husbands can serve as a source of security by providing the financial backing that allows their wife the freedom to work at any career, regardless of its compensation: "His doing all of the things he's doing gives us a lot of security." The husband can also give his wife the opportunity to opt out of working because the family does not need her salary to maintain its standard of living: "My husband refers to it as 'women have this net.' They can always say 'I'll just stop working.'"

Helpmate husbands. One-half of the husbands are low on managing and high on doing. They help with family and household either by doing the chores men typically do or by willingly doing whatever their wives ask them to do. One woman described her husband's contribution as follows:

I went and I did laundry, and I had a laundry basket, and I carried it and put it at the foot of the stairs. And all the clothes were folded and the laundry basket sat there for a day. And so the next day I put a second laundry basket

225

next to it. And the next day I had like three laundry baskets sitting at the bottom of the stairs. Everybody stepped over them. The kids took out what they needed. After the third or fourth day, I said to [my husband], "Could you take these upstairs?" "Oh, sure dear. No problem."…. I probably do more than he does…but I probably could get him to do more by asking him to do more.

Helpmate husbands can also serve as a personal lifeline. In this role, the husband acts as a stabilizing force by being a calm center or reminding his wife about the importance of her personal health and well-being:

My husband, who has just been the most consistent center of my life, [is] a very calm, tranquil being that I've kind of run around for 20 years. I think that to the extent that that has been a center of my life, it's been a quiet center, and it's been an extremely important one in that we've always kind of figured out how to get things done together.

In some families, the wives preferred to retain responsibility for, control of, and psychological oversight of the family and child care. Perhaps because many of the women care more about the details of home life, they spend more energy than their husbands in this regard. As one senior executive noted,

I probably have always done more of that [managing the household]. I think that's pretty classic, too. And that's by choice…I can't stand a messy house. So if nobody else in the house is going to do it, I'm going to do it. And I feel guilty if my kids don't have sort of a square meal at the end of the day…. But I clearly impose on myself a level of responsibility that's ridiculous.

Even if husbands share child care, the couple may take a more traditional approach to household management, resulting in the husbands acting as helpmates rather than truly egalitarian:

I'd say [we divide up] the child care responsibilities 50-50. With the running of the house and making decisions for the house and all that kind of thing, 90/10, with me taking 90% and him taking 10%. Because no matter what I do, no matter how many agreements we make, no matter how we sit down and write it down on paper, after 3 weeks it just goes back to me taking responsibility for it. It doesn't get done. He says that, although he thinks that he is very liberated and that he thinks I have every much a right to a career as he does, when it comes right down to it, he thinks he has old-fashioned values about who is going to be in charge of the house and he just won't help with it.

Helpmate husbands can also act as team players, playing the role of facilitator or partner. One woman noted, "He's a facilitator because when he's home he's a 50-50 participant." Another commented,

He's been very, very much a partner. He really encouraged me to take advantage of the work opportunities [to be self-employed] and convinced me that whatever support I needed at home to make that work out would be, we'd make it.

Egalitarian husbands. Of the husbands, 28% shared responsibilities for managing and doing family and household responsibilities relatively equally. As one woman commented, "Absolutely [he still does half]. More if I can get him to." Such sharing results in more positive balance between employment and family responsibilities, although the negotiations involved in allocating responsibilities and ensuring that either the husband or wife has the so-called big picture can sometimes be associated with more stress and reduced life satisfaction in the short run.

Our strategy has been that I do mornings and my husband does the evenings and afternoon type thing. So whatever I do workwise, I am always going to be late for work [in comparison to other employees] in the morning…. We use chores actually as trade-offs because I hate to clean the bathroom; he hates to iron. So this Sunday I ironed 10 shirts so he's cleaned the bathroom; I had to sort of learn to not want the housework done as I would do it, but just, you know, done.

Although a number of the women say that their husbands share the responsibilities relatively equally, the men do not assume quite as much responsibility for organizing or managing as their wives. If they straddle the helpmate and egalitarian categories, they likely spend more time in doing than managing family and household activities than the typical helpmate. Yet a number of the wives justify this less-than-equal contribution by acknowledging that their husbands do more than most husbands do. This seems particularly the case in household work as opposed to childcare.

Coordinator husbands. Of the husbands, 8% were perceived to have the primary responsibility for managing the family and household responsibilities and rely on their wives' help in doing the related activities. This type of activity by the husband as manager and wife as doer is analogous to the helpmate type; however, the roles are reversed. The coordinator husbands may make it possible for some women to work at all and for others to have high-level, high-profile, extremely demanding careers. As one woman noted,

But over the years…because of what was happening in my career in terms of advancement and because he had flexibility…we decided that we didn't need more money. We needed more time, and we needed to have some semblance of sanity in our life. He has continued to cut back…. Realistically, I could never have done this if my husband had a career that required him to be gone from 7:00 in the morning till 7:00 at night or traveling.

One woman described her husband's attitude in assuming the coordinator role that she should "do what you need to do." Another husband felt that he was missing important times with his children, so changed his priorities and schedule to take responsibility for them.

Coordinator husbands can serve as the family manager, such as by organizing family activities. One woman described her husband's role: "[My husband]

organizes field trips for us all the time, which we joke about, [calling him] Mr. Field Trip." It is also possible for the husband to take charge of all household and family activities. The wife of one husband who had this role estimated that she had only 10% of the responsibility in the household or family.

Discussion

Families with both spouses employed are the major pattern in the United States (Elloy & Flynn, 1998); however, most of the research attention has been paid to young couples early in their careers. By midlife, such couples have likely established workable patterns of sharing responsibilities. The current study was a first step in documenting the nature of this pattern and, more specifically, the husband's contribution to the family and household in which the wife held a high-level professional job. This article presented preliminary results regarding the career precedence of spouses in the families of midlife professional women, the contributions to family and household by husbands in those families, and the pattern of overall support offered by the husbands to the midlife women. In this section, we discuss the results in each of these areas.

Career Precedence

Our results suggest that equal career precedence is more common than either the husband's or the wife's career having precedence. Yet even when the wives report equal career precedence, creating truly equal careers often requires trade-offs and sacrifices from one or both partners that may be extremely difficult, often testing their commitment to their careers and sometimes to their families. In almost all cases, precedence is economically driven; however, equal economic contributions do not necessarily translate into equal precedence because other factors, such as logistics, early socialization, or personal ego needs may moderate the impact of the economic contributions. At the same time, organizations need to better appreciate the movement toward greater equality in career precedence. For example, managers are more likely to assume that female employees who are mothers would handle any household or family emergencies that occur (Hammonds & Palmer, 1998). Such assumptions may be inaccurate and negatively affect the wife's career advancement, increase stress for male employees who have assumed such responsibilities, or undermine the arrangements made by spouses for handling the challenges posed by the interaction of employment and family.

We captured these couples at one time in their careers. Over time, shifts in career precedence to ensure a sense of fairness in the marriage occurred for many couples, as either the husband or wife wished to change his or her level of involvement with family or as job opportunities opened or closed. This dynamic, somewhat free-form texture reflects the value partners placed on ensuring their husband's or wife's happiness and fulfillment. The couples continually renegotiated priorities as a way of making the family situation work and the partners feel happy and successful.

Contributions to Family and Household

Not unexpectedly, the contributions by husbands of midlife women vary significantly. When we categorized the contributions as managing and doing, we noted that some midlife professional women characterized their husbands as contributing in neither, one, or both ways. Regardless of their relative contributions, men still spend more time doing than managing in the household. This pattern of contribution continues to put the psychological burden on women, causing them to face the necessity of either acting as so-called superwoman or finding other ways of handling the overload at work or home. Because of their relatively high income, many of the professional women we interviewed bought household services as a way of handling this potential conflict, a solution available only to those women or families with sufficient discretionary income. Still, the nature of the husband's contribution likely has a psychological impact and hence consequences for the life satisfaction, career commitment, and job satisfaction of the midlife professional women (and their husbands).

Some husbands may complement or substitute for their performance of household or family responsibilities by providing support in other ways. For example, some act as career advisors to their working wives. As sounding boards, the husbands may offer advice about career-related issues that range from decisions about returning to work after a maternity leave to how to handle specific personnel problems. In this role, they might also serve as mentors or role models in which they demonstrate desirable professional behavior.

A number of the women described their relationships with their husbands as ones of "independence and dependence." The analysis we presented about husband's contributions highlights this tension. By midlife, however, the couples have developed the mechanisms, such as hiring household staff, alternating whose job requirements receive priority, or developing responsive scheduling patterns, for resolving conflicting demands.

Support Provided by the Husbands

We presented the beginnings of a four-cell typology of support provided by the husbands of midlife professional women. Such a typology highlights the critical role that husbands play in supporting the individual work–life balance of professional midlife women. The typology provides a way for husbands and wives to consider all the tasks necessary to support effective, functional home and family life. Such intentional consideration may provide a more satisfactory division of these responsibilities and related work than a division based on family-of-origin patterns or traditional gender roles and responsibilities.

840 Where the husband falls in the typology could provide insight into the amount and type of support needed from the husband's and the wife's employer. For example, the woman with a helpmate may need less flexibility and more referral services; the woman with a coordinator husband may need the reverse. This high-
845 lights the need for use of benefits to be equally accepted for men and women. Until recently, it was more acceptable for women than men to take advantage of various benefits, such as leave following the birth of a child or flextime to attend children's activities.

Just as career precedence and contributions to household and family may change during an individ-
850 ual's life span, so may a husband's place in the typology. Although a husband may act as a helpmate early in his and his wife's career, later he may shift to a co-ordinator as the demands of his work lessen and his wife's increase. Organizations, too, must be flexible in
855 responding to such changes. They must offer an array of benefits so that professional women and their spouses can tailor their choices to their specific needs.

Limitations and Future Research

Although the current study has taken a first step in trying to understand the contributions and support that
860 the husbands of midlife professional women provide, future research should involve a larger study that would verify our results. The work on career precedence could be extended, such as by measuring career precedence on a 100% scale, where husbands and
865 wives are asked to divide the percentage according to the contribution of each spouse. How career precedence changes during the course of the marriage would also provide interesting insights into husbands' support in dual-career families. Future research might also in-
870 volve obtaining data about career precedence and family and household contributions from the husbands and comparing the two sets of perceptions. In addition, the typology proposed here should be tested and expanded to describe the wife's role as perceived by the husband
875 and the relationship as perceived by the husband and wife.

Future research should also test specific hypotheses about the impact of perceived or actual behaviors and attitudes on both spouses' job, family, life satisfaction,
880 employment and family balance, and stress. Additional research should compare perceptions to actual attitudes and behavior to determine which has the greater impact on these outcomes. Replicating this research with younger and older workers will also provide insight
885 into whether this support is a unique midlife phenomenon or a general set of behaviors and attitudes in dual-career couples. This research should also be extended to different racial and ethnic groups, occupational categories, and geographical locations. In addition, the role
890 of children in performing household chores and supporting their parents' careers should be considered.

Conclusion

Personal, relationship, and societal factors affect the way partners combine occupational and family roles (Gilbert, 1988, 1993). The extent of the husbands'
895 contributions depended on factors such as the husband's ego, the relative salaries of the spouses, their job mobility, the flexibility of their work situations, and the early socialization of husband and wife regarding the appropriate roles for each spouse. The current
900 study suggested that wives' perceptions of their husbands' attitudes and behaviors about employment and family are important. It represents a next step in understanding the complex dynamics of dual-career families at midlife. The midlife professional women whom we
905 interviewed were almost uniformly enthusiastic about the support they received from their husbands. This support facilitated their management of employment and family obligations. Although the nature of support varied, knowing that their husbands valued them and
910 their careers helped them deal with the challenges of balancing the many facets of their lives.

References

Aldous, J., Mulligan, G. M., & Bjarnasin, R. (1998). Fathering over time: What makes the difference? *Journal of Marriage and the Family, 60*, 809–820.

Apter, T. (1995). *Secret paths: Women in the new midlife.* New York: Norton.

Barnett, R. C., & Baruch, G. K. (1987). Determinants of fathers' participation in the family work. *Journal of Marriage and the Family, 49*, 29–40.

Barnett, R. C., & Rivers, C. (1996). *She works/he works: How two-income families are happier, healthier, and better-off.* San Francisco: Harper San Francisco.

Beck, B. (1998). Women and work: At the double. *Economist, 348*(8077), S12–S16.

Benin, M. H., & Agostinelli, J. (1988). Husbands' and wives' satisfaction with the division of labor. *Journal of Marriage and the Family, 50*, 349–361.

Biernat, M., & Wortman, C. (1991). Sharing of home responsibilities between professionally employed women and their husbands. *Journal of Personality and Social Psychology, 60*, 844–860.

Blair, S. L. (1993). Employment, family, and perceptions of marital quality among husbands and wives. *Journal of Family Issues, 14*, 189–212.

Bonney, J. F., Kelley, M. L., & Levant, R. F. (1999). A model of fathers' behavioral involvement in child care in dual-earner families. *Journal of Family Psychology, 13*, 401–415.

Borysenko, J. (1996). *A woman's book of life: The biology, psychology, and spirituality of the feminine life cycle.* New York: Riverhead Books.

Cohen, C. E. (1994). The trailing-spouse dilemma. *Working Woman, 19*, 69–70.

Coverman, S. (1989). Women's work is never done: The division of domestic labor. In J. Freeman (Ed.), *Women: A feminist perspective* (pp. 356–368). Palo Alto, CA: Mayfield.

Cutrona, C., & Russell, D. (1990). Type of social support and specific stress: Toward a theory of optimal matching. In B. Sarason, I. Sarason, & G. Pierce (Eds.), *Social support: An Interactional View* (pp. 319–366). New York: John Wiley.

Denzin, N. K., & Lincoln, Y. S. (1998). Introduction: Entering the field of qualitative research. In N. K. Denzin & Y. S. Lincoln (Eds.), *Strategies of qualitative inquiry* (pp. 1–17). Thousand Oaks, CA: Sage.

Deutsch, F. M. (1999). *Halving it all: How equally shared parenting works.* Cambridge, MA: Harvard University Press.

Deutsch, F. M., Lussier, J. B., & Servis, L. J. (1993). Husbands at home: Predictors of paternal participation in childcare and housework. *Journal of Personality and Social Psychology, 65*, 1154–1166.

Ehrensraft, D. (1987). *Parenting together: Men and women sharing the care of children.* New York: Free Press.

Elloy, D. F., & Flynn, W. R. (1998). Job involvement and organization commitment among dual-income and single-income families: A multiple-site study. *Journal of Social Psychology, 138*, 93–101.

Gager, C. T. (1998). The role of valued outcomes, justifications, and comparison referents in perceptions of fairness among dual-earner couples. *Journal of Family Issues, 19*, 622–648.

Gilbert, L. A. (1985). *Men in dual-career families: Current realities and future prospects.* Hillsdale, NJ: Lawrence Erlbaum.

Gilbert, L. A. (1988). *Sharing it all: The rewards and struggles of two-career families*. New York: Plenum.

Gilbert, L. A. (1993). *Two careers/one family: The promise of gender equality*. Newbury Park, CA: Sage.

Gordon, J. R., & Whelan, K. S. (1998). Successful professional women in midlife: How organizations can more effectively understand and respond to the challenges. *Academy of Management Executive, 12*, 8–24.

Grambs, J. D. (1989). *Women over forty: Visions and realities*. New York: Springer.

Greenglass, E. R. (1993). Social support and coping of employed women. In B. C. Long & S. E. Kahn (Eds.), *Women, work, and copying: A multidisciplinary approach to workplace stress* (pp. 215–239). Montreal, Canada: McGill-Queen's University Press.

Hammonds, K. H., & Palmer, A. T. (1998, September 21). The daddy trap. *Business Week, 3596*, 56–60.

Hertz, R. (1999). Working to place family at the center of life: Dual-earner and single-parent strategies. *Annals of the American Academy of Political and Social Science, 562*, 16–31.

Hewlett, S. A. (2002). Executive women and the myth of having it all. *Harvard Business Review, 80*, 66–72.

Jacobson, J. M. (1995). *Midlife women: Contemporary issues*. Boston: Jones and Bartlett.

James, J. B., & Liewkowicz, C. (1997). Themes of power and affiliation across time. In M. E. Lachman & J. B. James (Eds.), *Multiple paths of mid life development* (pp. 109–144). Chicago: University of Chicago Press.

Karambayya, R., & Reilly, A. H. (1992). Dual earner couples: Attitudes and actions in restructuring work for family. *Journal of Organizational Behavior, 13*, 585–601.

Kruger, A. (1994). The midlife transition: Crisis or chimera? *Psychological Reports, 75*, 1299–1305.

Kruger, P. (1998). The good news about working couples. *Parenting, 12*, 69.

Levinson, D. J. (1978). *The seasons of a man's life*. New York: Knopf.

Levinson, D. J. (1996). *The seasons of a woman's life*. New York: Knopf.

Manke, B., Seery, B. L., Crouter, A. C., & McHale, S. M. (1994). The three corners of domestic labor: Mothers, fathers, and children's weekday and weekend housework. *Journal of Marriage and the Family, 56*, 657–668.

Marshack, K. J. (1994). Copreneurs and dual-career couples: Are they different? *Entrepreneurship Theory and Practice, 19*, 49–69.

Marshall, C., & Rossman, G. B. (1999). *Designing qualitative research* (3rd ed.). Thousand Oaks, CA: Sage.

Marshall, J. (1994). Why women leave senior management jobs. In M. Tanton (Ed.), *Women in management: A developing presence* (pp. 185–201). London: Routledge.

Marshall, J. (1995). Working at senior management and board levels: Some of the issues for women. *Women in Management Review, 10*, 21–25.

Miles, M. B., & Huberman, A. M. (1994). *Qualitative data analysis*. Thousand Oaks, CA: Sage.

Murray, T. J. (1986). Checking out the new corporate wife. *Dun's Business Month, 128*, 50–51.

O'Connor, D., & Wolfe, D. M. (1991). From crisis to growth at midlife: Changes in personal paradigm. *Journal of Organizational Behavior, 12*, 323–340.

Pleck, J. (1997). Paternal involvement: Levels, sources, and consequences. In M. E. Lamb (Ed.), *The role of the father in child development* (3rd ed., pp. 66–103). New York: John Wiley.

Ponthieu, L., & Caudill, H. (1993). Who's the boss? Responsibility and decision making in copreneurial ventures. *Family Business Review, 6*, 3–17.

Potuchek, J. L. (1997). *Who supports the family? Gender and breadwinning in dual-earner marriages*. Stanford, CA: Stanford University Press.

Reid, J. D., & Willis, S. L. (1999). Middle age: New thoughts, new directions. In S. L. Willis & J. D. Reid (Eds.), *Life in the middle: Psychological and social development in middle age* (pp. 276–280). San Diego, CA: Academic Press.

Robinson, J. P., & Godbey, G. (1997). *Time for life: The surprising ways Americans use their time*. State College: Pennsylvania State University Press.

Rogers, S. J., & Amato, P. R. (2000). Have changes in gender relations affected marital quality? *Social Forces, 79*, 731–754.

Rosin, H. M. (1990). Consequences for men of dual career marriages: Implications for organizations. *Journal of Managerial Psychology, 5*, 3–8.

Shelton, B. A., & John, D. (1993). Does marital status make a difference? Housework among married and cohabiting men and women. *Journal of Family Issues, 14*, 401–423.

Spitze, G. D., & Waite, L. J. (1981). Wives' employment: The role of husbands' perceived attitudes. *Journal of Marriage and the Family, 45*, 117–124.

Strauss, A., & Corbin, J. (1990). *Basics of qualitative research: Grounded theory procedures and techniques*. Newbury Park, CA: Sage.

Suitor, J. J. (1991). Marital quality and satisfaction with the division of household labor across the family life cycle. *Journal of Marriage and the Family, 53*, 221–230.

Taylor, A. S., & Lounsbury, J. W. (1988). Dual-career couples and geographic transfer: Executives' reactions to commuter marriage and attitude toward the move. *Human Relations, 41*, 407–424.

U.S. Bureau of Labor Statistics. (2004). *Employment status of the population by sex and age*. Available at www.bls.gov/cps/home.htm

White, B. (1995). The career development of successful women. *Women in Management Review, 10*, 4–15.

Wicker, A., & Burley, K. (1991). Close coupling in work–family relationships: Making and implementing decisions in a new family business and at home. *Human Relations, 44*, 77–92.

Acknowledgment: We thank Mary Dunn and Peter Rivard for their assistance with the data analysis for this article.

Exercise for Article 40

Factual Questions

1. The researchers state that they are "particularly interested in studying professional women at midlife who are married, have children, but also have had enduring careers." What reason do they give for this interest?

2. The results of this study are based primarily on the women's responses to two questions. What is the first question?

3. The researchers indicate that securing a random sample would have been desirable but was unrealistic for what reason?

4. Why were all interviews conducted by only one of the authors (i.e., researchers)?

5. According to the researchers, why were younger and older women included in the sample?

6. What was the mean (average) age of the women in the sample?

7. In their conclusion, do the researchers conclude that the women were enthusiastic about the support they received from their husbands?

Questions for Discussion

8. The researchers provide "Background" for this study in lines 85–250. How helpful is this background in establishing the context for this study? Would the report of the study be as effective without the background material? Explain.

9. The researchers indicate that this study is an "exploratory study." Do you agree with this characterization? If yes, what could be done in future studies on this topic to make them more definitive? (See lines 66, 239, 252, and 309–310.)

10. In your opinion, is the process of coding the participants' responses described in sufficient detail? (See lines 314–350.)

11. The researchers describe interrater reliability in lines 336–350. In your opinion, how important is this information? Would it be a weakness of the report if this information were not given? Explain.

12. The women in this study had diverse occupations. Is this a strength of this study? Explain. (See Table 2.)

13. How helpful are the direct quotations of the words of the women in this study in helping you understand the results? Are there a sufficient number of quotations? Are there too many? Explain. (See lines 384–732.)

14. The researchers make suggestions for future research in lines 858–891. Do some of these seem more important than others? Explain.

Quality Ratings

Directions: Indicate your level of agreement with each of the following statements by circling a number from 5 for strongly agree (SA) to 1 for strongly disagree (SD). If you believe an item is not applicable to this research article, leave it blank. Be prepared to explain your ratings. When responding to criteria A and B below, keep in mind that brief titles and abstracts are conventional in published research.

A. The title of the article is appropriate.

    SA   5   4   3   2   1   SD

B. The abstract provides an effective overview of the research article.

    SA   5   4   3   2   1   SD

C. The introduction establishes the importance of the study.

    SA   5   4   3   2   1   SD

D. The literature review establishes the context for the study.

    SA   5   4   3   2   1   SD

E. The research purpose, question, or hypothesis is clearly stated.

    SA   5   4   3   2   1   SD

F. The method of sampling is sound.

    SA   5   4   3   2   1   SD

G. Relevant demographics (for example, age, gender, and ethnicity) are described.

    SA   5   4   3   2   1   SD

H. Measurement procedures are adequate.

    SA   5   4   3   2   1   SD

I. All procedures have been described in sufficient detail to permit a replication of the study.

    SA   5   4   3   2   1   SD

J. The participants have been adequately protected from potential harm.

    SA   5   4   3   2   1   SD

K. The results are clearly described.

    SA   5   4   3   2   1   SD

L. The discussion/conclusion is appropriate.

    SA   5   4   3   2   1   SD

M. Despite any flaws, the report is worthy of publication.

    SA   5   4   3   2   1   SD

Article 41

Adult Helping Qualities Preferred by Adolescents

JUNE MARTIN
Fielding Graduate University

MICHAEL ROMAS
Fielding Graduate University

MARSHA MEDFORD
Fielding Graduate University

NANCY LEFFERT
Fielding Graduate University

SHERRY L. HATCHER
Fielding Graduate University

ABSTRACT. Most studies of therapeutic alliance have focused on adult populations and been written from the therapist's perspective. Thus, there is a clear need for studies of therapeutic alliance that focus on adolescent populations from the perspective of the adolescents. The current study is an exploratory process investigation using a focus group methodology with a nonclinical sample of adolescents to determine which traits in adults might foster alliance, with the assumption that the same traits would apply to therapeutic settings. A content analytic approach was used, and 12 adult qualities found to be preferred by adolescents from most to least cited were: respect, time shared, openness, role characteristics, recognition, guidance, identification, trust, freedom, like/dislike, responsibility, and familiarity.

Client expectations are a predominant indicator of treatment outcome and client satisfaction (Horvath, 2001). Adult and adolescent therapeutic treatments have increasingly focused on the alliance between cli-
5   ent and therapist. However, adolescents pose unique challenges for therapists (Blos, 1962; Kazdin & Wassell, 1999; Masterson, 1968). Historically, clinicians and researchers have maintained that adolescents are in a crucial and formative stage of development whereby
10   they may have a "second chance" to resolve earlier conflicts from childhood, prior to consolidating their adult identities (Blos, 1962). Masterson's (1968) classic research suggests that psychological problems appearing in adolescence are unlikely to be "outgrown,"
15   and immediate therapeutic intervention may prevent the development of future, if not greater, psychopathology.

A lack of measures of adolescents' preferred adult qualities in helping relationships with adults led to our
20   attempt to derive indicators of therapeutic alliance for use with adolescent clients. Available scales that are currently reported in the literature primarily focus on the therapeutic relationship from the perspective of the therapist. Consequently, knowledge of adolescents'
25   perspectives on the helping relationship is unknown. The focus group study reported here was undertaken to determine helping qualities in adults that may be sought by pre-therapy adolescents.

Literature Review

A comprehensive search of the literature failed to
30   reveal more than a few articles related to qualities sought by adolescents in people from whom they might seek help. Although there have been studies of therapist–client alliance measures for use with adolescents, these have been only from the perspective of the thera-
35   pist (Barber, Connolly, Crits-Christoph, Gladis, & Siqueland, 2000; Hatcher, 1999; Hatcher & Barends, 1996; Joyce, Ogrodniczuk, Piper, & McCallum, 2003). Numerous studies have measured the impact of the therapeutic alliance on treatment outcomes, but these
40   have primarily evaluated adult populations (e.g., Farber, 2003; Horvath, 2001; Martin, Garske, & Davis, 2000).

Roberts, Lazicki-Puddy, Puddy, and Johnson (2003) reviewed past studies of adolescent therapy
45   outcomes within specific diagnostic categories. Hatcher, Barends, Hansell, and Gutfreund (1995) compared patient and therapist views of the alliance, but again utilizing an adult population. In other words, the therapeutic alliance-process outcome literature has his-
50   torically been written from the therapist's perspective, not the client's (Bachelor, 1995). However valid this may be, attempts to generalize these findings to adolescent populations present problems (Cobb, 1992; Everall & Paulson, 2002; Foreman, Gibbins, Grienenberger,
55   & Berry, 2000; Liddle & Schwartz, 2002; Oetzel & Scherer, 2003; Paulson, Truscott, & Stuart, 1999; Robbins, Turner, & Alexander, 2003; Weisz & Hawley, 2002).

For example, Oetzel and Scherer (2003) suggest
60   that adolescent development is a key component in engaging adolescents in psychotherapy. Adolescents manifest psychopathology differently from adults, and they differ in their ability to cognitively understand their problems or deal with change strategies. Accord-
65   ing to Scales and Leffert (1999), youth typically experience a significant decrease in support during middle school and high school and "about three out of every four adolescents say they do not have positive

family communication or a caring school" (p. 41).
Numerous researchers have noted that the challenges
presented by cognitive developmental change and emotional processing during adolescence require separate
empirical investigation into adolescent alliance process-outcome studies (Everall & Paulson, 2002; Kazdin,
1991; Kazdin & Weisz, 1998).

Everall and Paulson (2002) identified three themes
that are unique to the development of adolescent alliance: "therapeutic environment, uniqueness of the
therapeutic relationship, and therapist characteristics"
(p. 81). Additionally, several researchers who have
studied therapeutic process have identified issues of
building trust, being helpful, and listening as important
to developing therapeutic alliance with adolescents
(e.g., Diamond, Liddle, Hogue, & Dakof, 1999; Lambert, Whipple, & Hawkins, 2003). Other researchers
have emphasized the importance of offering adolescents therapeutic support, not advice, in recognition of
the importance of developing autonomy among adolescents (Church, 1994; DiGiuseppe, Linscott, & Jilton,
1996). Oetzel and Scherer (2003), in pointing out how
little is known about adolescent treatment issues, suggested that studies be conducted to determine how adolescents view the process of engagement in therapy and
to find methods for overcoming barriers to effective
engagement.

Timlin-Scalera, Ponterotto, Blumberg, and Jackson
(2003) noted specific barriers to formal help-seeking
by Caucasian adolescent males in an affluent community. These barriers included concerns about confidentiality, unfamiliarity with mental health professionals,
reluctance to burden others, and the belief that males
are weak if they seek help. However, it may not be just
male adolescents who tend to feel weak in seeking
therapy. Adolescents in therapy differ from adults in
therapy in that the adolescent's therapist needs to be
more active than the typical adult therapist (Balser,
1957; Weiner, 1992). Additionally, adolescents tend to
be receptive to a therapist's honesty and directness, yet
they are likely to forgive a therapist's evasiveness
(Weiner, 1992).

Therapists use various methods to address such
concerns (Oetzel & Scherer, 2003; Weersing, Weisz, &
Donenberg, 2002). These strategies include providing
empathy, genuineness, trust, nonjudgmental stance,
respect for adolescent perspectives, and choice in decision-making (Liddle & Schwartz, 2002; Oetzel &
Scherer, 2003). Other researchers have emphasized the
importance of establishing and demonstrating the relevance of the treatment to adolescents' emotional and
interpersonal needs (Kazdin, 1991; Kazdin & Wassell,
1999).

In their meta-analysis of child and adolescent (ages
4 to 18) psychotherapy research, Kazdin, Bass, Ayers,
and Rogers (1990) focused on those between the ages
of 6 and 11. This age group focus limits the authors'
ability to generalize their meta-analytic findings about

empirically supported psychotherapy outcome studies
to an adolescent population—those between the ages of
12 and 18. In sum, researchers have noted the lack of
knowledge of empirically supported therapeutic process variables among adolescents (Diamond et al., 1999;
Shirk & Karver, 2003; Shirk & Saiz, 1992).

Current studies in the therapeutic alliance literature
primarily focus on the perspective of adolescent alliance during rather than before clinical treatment
(Foreman et al., 2000; Joyce et al., 2003). These studies typically adhere to a retrospective methodology and
use clinical populations. Although investigations of
therapist characteristics have begun to appear in the
literature (e.g., Everall & Paulson, 2002), nonclinical
adolescent perceptions of adult qualities that could
facilitate a counseling alliance have yet to be fully examined. The traits of adolescents that could encourage
them to engage in help-seeking behavior from an adult
are predominantly lacking in the literature. The goal of
the present study was to explore the perceptions of a
sample of nonclinical adolescents that might prompt
them to confide their conflicts and concerns to an adult.
As such, this would have implications for clinicians
who seek to form a counseling alliance with adolescent
clients.

We suggest that adolescents will perceive qualities
of adults in nontherapeutic helping relationships that
are generalizable to their alliance with therapists. Furthermore, this correlation can be objectively demonstrated.

Method

Research Design

This study used a focus group methodology with a
nonclinical sample of adolescents. Qualitative and
quantitative methods devised by Morgan (1998) and
Roberts and Robinson (2004) were used to analyze the
categories of helpful adult qualities perceived by this
sample.

Participants

A convenience sample of adolescent research participants was recruited, and an electronic message was
sent via Internet postings on the psychology student
and/or faculty sites forums at a geographically diverse
doctoral program in psychology. The message asked
readers to invite adolescents to participate in a focus
group study. Age (12 to 17 years) was the only exclusionary criterion. In addition, the participants were not
selected from a population of present or potential psychotherapy patients, and they were not asked to disclose whether or not they were or had been in a counseling or psychotherapy relationship.

Participants were given a written description of the
research topic, which noted that the purpose of the
study was to ultimately develop an interpersonal counseling alliance scale for adolescents. All participants
and at least one parent signed an informed consent letter, which was then collected by the primary investiga-

Table 1
Focus Group Questions

1.   What do you like/dislike about school?
2.   Tell us about your favorite/least favorite teacher?
3.   Who do you go to when you have a problem?
4.   Imagine that you had a secret/problem; what would the adult have to be like to share that secret?
5.   What adult do you admire most in the world?
5a. Why?
6.   What kind of adult do you want to be?
7.   How necessary do you think it would be for an adult to appreciate or like you, if you wanted to confide in that adult?
8.   What would make you feel appreciated in a relationship with an adult?
9.   What would make you feel accepted in a relationship with an adult?
10. What makes you feel respected in a relationship with an adult?
11. What is it that would make you feel understood when you are talking with an adult?
12. What do you hate when you are talking to a grownup?
12a. What do you hate that they do?
13. When can you feel like a teammate with an adult?
13a. What makes you feel that you are part of the team with an adult?
14. What makes you see an adult as a helpful person?
15. Is there anything in our talking that we have not covered that you think is important?

tor prior to participation in the study. In addition, written permission was obtained from the participants and their parents for the 2-hour focus group to be audiotaped.

Ultimately, there were 7 participants: six females and one male. The mean age was 14.6 years (range = 12 to 17 years), 71% of the participants were Caucasian (*n* = 5 females), and 29% were Hispanic (*n* = 2, one male and one female).

Measures

Following the study of Hatcher (1995), the researchers reviewed facilitative techniques used in peer counseling to develop the questions asked of the participants. In addition, statements from the Combined Alliance Scale (CAS) (Hatcher & Barends, 1996), an established measure of therapeutic alliance previously used exclusively with adults, were selectively adapted for the open-ended format used in the focus group. For example, the CAS statement, "I believe my therapist appreciates and likes me" became "How necessary do you think it would be for an adult to appreciate or like you if you wanted to confide in that adult?"

Procedures

The participants were asked 15 semistructured questions (see Table 1) as posed by one primary facilitator, followed by further questions from four other researchers in attendance. The participants were first told that the focus group was entirely confidential and they were asked to speak as often and as freely as they felt comfortable.

The questions centered on the types of characteristics that adolescents might seek in adults to whom they might turn for assistance with their concerns. Two questions had follow-up probes to clarify intent, and one probed the content of responses (see Table 1). The researchers sought to extrapolate indicators applicable in a noncounseling setting from the adolescents' statements of characteristics fostering interpersonal alliance with adults.

Participants were offered refreshments and at the end of their participation each was awarded a $15 bookstore gift certificate as a token of appreciation.

Data Analysis

The adolescents' verbal responses to semistructured questions about perceived qualities of helpful adults were transcribed from an audiotape recording and then coded using a version of Krippendorff's (2004) and other researchers' content analytic approaches (e.g., Hogenraad, McKenzie, & Peladeau, 2003; Neuendorf, 2002; Roberts & Robinson, 2004). The researchers initially identified 47 categories of helpful adult qualities. After removing overlapping themes, they ultimately reduced the categories to 12: trust, familiarity, identification, respect, recognition, openness, time shared, freedom, responsibility, guidance, role characteristics, and like/dislike. Each word, sentence, or thematic paragraph was coded by two of the researchers (Coder 1 and Coder 2) as a unit measure of the 12 thematic categories.

First, the coders independently rated the adolescents' responses in the transcript. When the results were compared, some discrepancies were found in the way some of the data had been coded. For example, Coder 1 categorized a passage as an example of recognition, whereas Coder 2 categorized it as an example of respect. In order to come to agreements, definitions in the 1996, 1998 version of *Webster's Revised Unabridged Dictionary* were used and a second round of coding was then done.

Results

The participants named one or more of the 12 categories a total of 250 times. The frequency with which

Table 2
Highest to Lowest Adult Helping Quality Categories for Two Rounds of Coding

Category	First round of coding			Second round of coding		
	Rank	Frequency	%	Rank	Frequency	%
Respect	1	39	15.6	1	41	16.4
Time shared	2	36	14.4	2	36	14.4
Openness	3	34	13.6	3	35	14.0
Role characteristics	4	28	11.2	4	27	10.8
Recognition	5	24	9.6	5	23	9.2
Guidance	6	23	9.2	6	22	8.8
Identification	7	21	8.4	7	21	8.4
Trust	8	14	5.6	8	14	5.6
Freedom	9	8	3.2	10	8	3.2
Like/dislike	10	8	3.2	9	12	4.8
Responsibility	11	6	2.4	11	6	2.4
Familiarity	12	4	1.6	12	5	2.0

each category was named allowed the coders to rank the categories from 1 to 12. In the first round, there were 5 occasions (2%) in which one coder did not code a category while the other coder did. Occasionally, a speaker mentioned two or more different qualities in his or her paragraph response, which may have led to one of the two coders missing or overcoding a helping quality. The strength of each category was rated from highest to lowest based on the number of times each category was coded by the two independent raters over two different time periods (see Table 2).

On the category qualities, interrater agreement between the coders ranged from perfect agreement for trust (kappa = 1.0) to kappa = .57 for like/dislike. The highest rate of kappa agreement between the two coders was for trust, identification, time shared, guidance, role characteristics, freedom, and responsibility, which ranged from kappa = 1.0 to .91. The second group of helping qualities included recognition, respect, and openness, with the range of interrater agreement being kappa = .88 to .85. The least agreement between the two raters occurred in the familiarity and like/dislike categories (kappa = .66 to .57). The mean kappa agreement (Cohen, 1960, 1968) between the coders on all variables for this first round of coding was .88, with a confidence interval set at .80. The second round of coding resulted in an improved interrater coding agreement (kappa = 1.00).[1]

Adult demonstrations of respecting adolescents include inviting an adolescent into a conversation. Another participant reported being respected when an adult treated her as an equal. The second most fre-

quently cited category, time shared, included the notion that adults like to spend time with adolescents. The third most frequently cited category, being open, was defined here as the adult's ability to listen nonjudgmentally, without lecturing and by being available to receive new ideas from the adolescent. See Table 3 for representative quotes.

Discussion and Conclusion

For both the first and second rounds of coding, the top three adult qualities preferred by the adolescents were respect, time shared, and openness. This finding differs from other studies. For example, Diamond et al. (1999) found that the top three issues in working therapeutically with adolescents were building trust, being helpful, and listening. Additionally, Everall and Paulson (2002) found three alliance themes: therapeutic environment, uniqueness of the therapeutic relationship, and therapist characteristics.

Because of the exploratory nature of this study and the small sample, inferential or nonparametric statistics were not used. However, frequencies and interrater reliability were calculated. In terms of internal validity, the measures matched the conceptual definitions of the 12 categories. The generalizability of findings in this exploratory study may be limited to a nonclinical adolescent population. In addition, the participants were predominantly Caucasian females.

This study found that adolescents like adults to demonstrate specific role characteristics that are useful and relevant, and they also like adults to view them as mature, capable, and aware. The finding in this study that adolescents identified adult qualities of role characteristics, togetherness time, and being open to an adolescent's ideas is consistent with the emphasis by Kazdin (1991) and Kazdin and Wassell (1999) on attending to the relevance of the "help" in relation to an adolescent's emotional and interpersonal needs. However, this study also found that adolescents like adults to empathetically support them yet guide them—a

---

[1] Using Neuendorf's (2002) "utterance coding system," an a priori coding scheme was established in which all measures were described. For coding the responses, a code book was developed in which all variables were defined by a standard dictionary definition, and a standardized coding rating was applied to each variable. For the categorical terms, frequency lists of key words and phrases were generated from the transcript.

Table 3

Qualitative Illustrations from the Adolescent Focus Group Transcript

Category	Example statements from adolescent transcript
1. Respect	If you don't have respect for somebody, then you obviously wouldn't want to start a friendship with them…. But if you respect somebody and they respect you back, then it's a really healthy relationship, and you guys can ask each other questions and it's not a lopsided relationship.
2. Time shared	I think it's really important to spend a lot of time with people that if you're trying to connect or if you're trying to get close to someone you knew, that's not really going to happen unless you spend time with them. And the more time you spend with someone, the more comfortable you become with them. That's really important.
3. Openness	If you're telling them something that's majorly serious, and you're feeling really bad about it, and then they change the subject to something lighthearted or something. They're like, "Oh, let's do that," and "Oh, let's talk about school or something." And, like, you know that they didn't get the end at that point, that it was really, like, something bothering you, but if they really, like, give it the amount of attention, you know, like the severity that you think it deserves, it means something.
4. Role characteristics	Because they could tell you in, you know, a million different ways to solve this problem, but you're not going to feel like you've been helped unless you feel confident like it's going to work.
5. Recognition	He, like, talks to us, like, at his level and no other teachers do that. They talk to us like we're stupid or something.
6. Guidance	I just feel like someone or that I've been helped by an adult if after I'm done talking with them or consulting with them, I feel, I feel more confident and ready to address certain things.
7. Identification	Like, you know, they react the same way I would, you know, or you know I could expect them, you know.
8. Trust	Like, someone that hangs around with you, that you hang around with a lot that you know, and I don't know, just someone that you trust a lot, someone that won't tell. Kind of maybe someone that, like, looks, that you think is looking out for your best interests rather than their own.
9. Freedom	The pressure that people put on you, like, not even just your own peers, but your teachers…and, like, counselors as far as, like, colleges and stuff like that. They think that you need to be going to the greatest schools around and just trying to get you to go to school.
10. Like/Dislike	As if you, if you don't like them, you're not linking with them. Why would you tell them?
11. Responsibility	I admire my English teacher, my favorite teacher, because he's the only person that really kind of forces you to deal with yourself that makes sense, but he holds you to, like, he holds you responsible for everything that you should be accountable for, but, I don't know how to say it. He makes you deal with your weaknesses and not only in writing, but in life. I really admire that about him, because you know, it takes a lot of, like, courage and strength to, like, tell someone this is what you need to do and you're doing this really badly, you know, but he said that you can do this well, and, like, I appreciate that. I appreciate his honesty and his bluntness.
12. Familiarity	It makes me feel like I'm human, like a friend of his and it's just learning something from a friend other than, you know, learning something from this teacher who's on a higher level than you so that it makes it easier to learn.

320 point noted in other studies (e.g., Church, 1994; DiGiuseppe et al., 1996).

Empirically supported therapeutic process variables are lacking for adolescents. Suggestions for future research include developing measures of adolescent therapeutic alliance scales that include the 12 categories found in this study. Empirically supported therapeutic process investigations that use such alliance measures are needed. Additionally, there is a need for cluster analyses of the 12 variables to examine factors that influence the rank order of importance and the association they have with the therapeutic alliance.

Often, psychotherapists have preconceived notions of what may be important to their clients, especially adolescents. Determining types of interventions that may be viewed more positively by adolescent clients and may therefore further a therapeutic alliance repre-

sents a critical first step toward optimal treatment of adolescents. Therapists must allow adolescents a voice that will inform our knowledge of what is important to them when they are seeking help. As they do so, therapists may wish to emphasize the characteristics identified in this exploratory focus group study, especially the top three: respect, time-sharing, and openness.

References

Bachelor, A. (1995). Clients' perception of the therapeutic alliance: A qualitative analysis. *Journal of Counseling Psychology, 42*, 323–337.

Balser, B. H. (Ed.). (1957). *Psychotherapy of the adolescent.* New York: International.

Barber, J. P., Connolly, M. B., Crits-Christoph, P., Gladis, L., & Siqueland, L. (2000). Alliance predicts patients' outcome beyond in-treatment change in symptoms. *Journal of Consulting and Clinical Psychology, 68*, 1027–1032.

Blos, P. (1962). *On adolescence.* Oxford, England: Free Press of Glencoe.

Church, E. (1994). The role of autonomy in adolescent psychotherapy. *Psychotherapy: Theory, Research, Practice, Training, 31*, 101–108.

Cobb, N. (1992). *Adolescence: Continuity, change, and diversity.* Mountain View, CA: Mayfield.

Cohen, J. (1960). A coefficient of agreement for nominal scales. *Education and Psychological Measurement, 20*, 37–48.

Cohen, J. (1968). Weighted kappa: Nominal scale agreement with provision for scaled disagreement or partial credit. *Psychological Bulletin, 70*, 213–220.

Diamond, G. M., Liddle, H. A., Hogue, A., & Dakof, G. A. (1999). Alliance-building interventions with adolescents in family therapy: A process study. *Psychotherapy: Theory, Research, Practice, Training, 36*, 355–368.

DiGiuseppe, R., Linscott, J., & Jilton R. (1996). Developing the therapeutic alliance in child–adolescent psychotherapy. *Applied and Preventive Psychology, 5*, 85–100.

Everall, R., & Paulson, B. (2002). The therapeutic alliance: Adolescent perspectives. *Counseling and Psychotherapy Research, 2*, 78–87.

Farber, B. A. (2003). Patient self-disclosure: A review of the research. *Journal of Clinical Psychology/In Session, 59*, 589–600.

Foreman, S. A., Gibbins, J., Grienenberger, J., & Berry, J. W. (2000). Developing methods to study child psychotherapy using new scales of therapeutic alliance and progressiveness. *Psychotherapy Research, 10*, 450–461.

Hatcher, R. L. (1999). Therapists' views of treatment alliance and collaboration in therapy. *Psychotherapy Research, 9*, 405–423.

Hatcher, R. L., & Barends, A. W. (1996). Patients' view of the alliance in psychotherapy: Exploratory factor analysis of three alliance measures. *Journal of Consulting and Clinical Psychology, 64*, 1326–1336.

Hatcher, R. L., Barends, A. W., Hansell, J., & Gutfreund, M. J. (1995). Patients' and therapists' shared and unique views of the therapeutic alliance: An investigation using confirmatory factor analysis in a nested design. *Journal of Consulting and Clinical Psychology, 63*, 636–643.

Hatcher, S. (Ed.). (1995). *Peer programs on the college campus: Theory, training, and "voice of the peers."* San Jose, CA: Resource.

Hogenraad, R., McKenzie, D. P., & Peladeau, N. (2003). Force and influence in content analysis: The production of new social knowledge. *Quality and Quantity, 37*, 221–238.

Horvath, A. O. (2001). The therapeutic alliance: Concepts, research and training. *Australian Psychologist, 36*, 170–176.

Joyce, A. S., Ogrodniczuk, J. S., Piper, W. E., & McCallum, M. (2003). The alliance as mediator of expectancy effects in short-term individual therapy. *Journal of Consulting and Clinical Psychology, 71*, 672–679.

Kazdin, A. E. (1991). Effectiveness of psychotherapy with children and adolescents. *Journal of Consulting and Clinical Psychology, 59*, 785–798.

Kazdin, A. E., Bass, D., Ayers, W. A., & Rogers, J. (1990). Empirical and clinical focus of child and adolescent psychotherapy research. *Journal of Consulting and Clinical Psychology, 58*, 729–740.

Kazdin, A. E., & Wassell, G. (1999). Barriers to treatment participation and therapeutic change among children referred for conduct disorder. *Journal of Clinical Child Psychology, 28*, 160–172.

Kazdin, A. E., & Weisz, J. R. (1998). Identifying and developing empirically supported child and adolescent treatments. *Journal of Consulting and Clinical Psychology, 66*, 19–36.

Krippendorff, K. (2004a). *Content analysis: An introduction to its methodology* (2nd ed.). Thousand Oaks, CA: Sage.

Krippendorff, K. (2004b). Reliability in content analysis: Some common misconceptions and recommendations. *Human Communication Research, 30*, 411–433.

Lambert, M. J., Whipple, J. L., & Hawkins, E. J. (2003). Is it time for clinicians to routinely track patient outcome? A meta-analysis. *Clinical Psychology: Science and Practice, 10*, 288–301.

Liddle, H. A., & Schwartz, S. J. (2002). Attachment and family therapy: Clinical utility of adolescent–family research. *Family Process, 41*, 455–476.

Martin, D. J., Garske, J. P., & Davis, M. K. (2002). Relation of the therapeutic alliance with outcome and other variables: A meta-analytic review. *Journal of Consulting and Clinical Psychology, 68*, 438–450.

Masterson, J. F. (1968). The psychiatric significance of adolescent turmoil. *American Journal of Psychiatry, 124*, 1549–1554.

Merriam-Webster's Collegiate Dictionary (11th ed.). (2003). Springfield, MA: Merriam-Webster.

Morgan, D. L. (1998). Practical strategies for combining qualitative and quantitative methods: Applications to health research. *Qualitative Health Research, 8*, 363–377.

Neuendorf, K. A. (2002). *The content analysis guidebook.* Thousand Oaks, CA: Sage.

Oetzel, K. B., & Scherer, D. G. (2003). Therapeutic engagement with adolescents in psychotherapy. *Psychotherapy: Theory, Research, Practice, Training, 40*, 215–225.

Paulson, B. L., Truscott, D., & Stuart, J. (1999). Clients' perceptions of helpful experiences in counseling. *Journal of Counseling Psychology, 46*, 317.

Robbins, M. S., Turner, C. W., & Alexander, J. F. (2003). Alliance and dropout in family therapy for adolescents with behavior problems: Individual and systemic effects. *Journal of Family Psychology, 17*, 534–544.

Roberts, F., & Robinson, J. D. (2004). Interobserver agreement on first-stage conversation analytic transcription. *Human Communication Research, 30*, 376–410.

Roberts, M. C., Lazicki-Puddy, T. A., Puddy, R. W., & Johnson, R. J. (2003). The outcomes of psychotherapy with adolescents: A practitioner-friendly research review. *Journal of Clinical Psychology, 59*, 1177–1191.

Scales, P., & Leffert, N. (1999). *Developmental assets: A synthesis of the scientific research on adolescent development.* Minneapolis, MN: Search Institute.

Shirk, S. R., & Karver, M. (2003). Prediction of treatment outcome from relationship variables in child and adolescent therapy: A meta-analytic review. *Journal of Consulting and Clinical Psychology, 71*, 452–464.

Shirk, S. R., & Saiz, C. C. (1992). Clinical, empirical, and developmental perspectives on the therapeutic relationship in child psychotherapy. *Development and Psychopathology, 4*, 713–728.

Timlin-Scalera, R. M., Ponterotto, J. G., Blumberg, F. C., & Jackson, M. A. (2003). A grounded theory study of help-seeking behaviors among white male high school students. *Journal of Counseling Psychology, 50*, 339–350.

Webster's Revised Unabridged Dictionary. (1996, 1998). Plainfield, NJ: MICRA.

Weersing, V. R., Weisz, J. R., & Donenberg, G. R. (2002). Development of the therapy procedures checklist: A therapist-report measure of technique use in child and adolescent treatment. *Journal of Clinical Child and Adolescent Psychology, 31*, 168–180.

Weiner, I. (1992). *Psychological disturbance in adolescence* (2nd ed.). Oxford, England: Wiley.

Weisz, J. R., & Hawley, K. M. (2002). Developmental factors in the treatment of adolescents. *Journal of Consulting and Clinical Psychology, 70*, 21–43.

Acknowledgments: The authors wish to acknowledge the assistance of the adolescents who participated in this study. We thank the following Fielding Graduate University graduate students: Missi Trzeciak-Kerr, Stephanie Morris, and Razia Siddiqui for their research assistance. We also thank Katherine Randazzo, Ph.D., for her statistical assistance.

Address correspondence to: Nancy Leffert, Ph.D., Fielding Graduate University, 2112 Santa Barbara Street, Santa Barbara, CA 93105. E-mail: nleffert@fielding.edu

Exercise for Article 41

Factual Questions

1. What was the only exclusionary criterion for the selection of participants in this study?

2. How many of the participants were male?

3. When analyzing the results, the researchers initially identified how many categories of helpful adult qualities?

4. The strength of each of the 12 categories was rated from highest to lowest based on what?

5. Was the interrater agreement for "trust" high? Explain.

6. How was "being open" defined by the researchers?

Questions for Discussion

7. The researchers use the term "convenience sample" in line 163. What is your understanding of the meaning of this term?

8. If you had conducted this study, would you have asked the participants whether they were or had been in a counseling or psychotherapy relationships? Why? Why not? (See lines 170–174.)

9. In lines 178–184, the researchers indicate that informed consent was obtained. In your opinion, is it important to mention this in a research report?

10. In your opinion, is the focus group procedure described in sufficient detail? Explain. (See lines 202–220.)

11. Was the fact that the researchers "independently rated" the responses important? Explain. (See lines 237–238.)

12. To what extent do the quotations in Table 3 help you understand the meaning of the 12 categories? Are the meanings of all 12 clear to you? Explain.

13. If you had conducted this study, would you have used focus groups (i.e., asking the questions to groups of participants) or individual interviews? Explain.

14. In your opinion, how important is this study for helping therapists understand how to work with adolescents? Explain.

Quality Ratings

Directions: Indicate your level of agreement with each of the following statements by circling a number from 5 for strongly agree (SA) to 1 for strongly disagree (SD). If you believe an item is not applicable to this research article, leave it blank. Be prepared to explain your ratings. When responding to criteria A and B below, keep in mind that brief titles and abstracts are conventional in published research.

A. The title of the article is appropriate.
   SA 5 4 3 2 1 SD

B. The abstract provides an effective overview of the research article.
   SA 5 4 3 2 1 SD

C. The introduction establishes the importance of the study.
   SA 5 4 3 2 1 SD

D. The literature review establishes the context for the study.
   SA 5 4 3 2 1 SD

E. The research purpose, question, or hypothesis is clearly stated.
   SA 5 4 3 2 1 SD

F. The method of sampling is sound.
   SA 5 4 3 2 1 SD

G. Relevant demographics (for example, age, gender, and ethnicity) are described.
   SA 5 4 3 2 1 SD

H. Measurement procedures are adequate.
   SA 5 4 3 2 1 SD

I. All procedures have been described in sufficient detail to permit a replication of the study.
   SA 5 4 3 2 1 SD

J. The participants have been adequately protected from potential harm.
   SA 5 4 3 2 1 SD

K. The results are clearly described.
   SA 5 4 3 2 1 SD

L. The discussion/conclusion is appropriate.
   SA 5 4 3 2 1 SD

M. Despite any flaws, the report is worthy of publication.
   SA 5 4 3 2 1 SD

Appendix A

A Reader's, Writer's, and Reviewer's Guide to Assessing Research Reports in Clinical Psychology

BRENDAN A. MAHER
Harvard University

Adapted from Maher, B. A. (1978). A Reader's, Writer's, and Reviewer's Guide to Assessing Research Reports in Clinical Psychology. *Journal of Consulting and Clinical Psychology, 46,* 835–838. Published by the American Psychological Association. This material may be reproduced in whole or in part without permission, provided that acknowledgment is made to Brendan A. Maher and the American Psychological Association. Copyright 1978 by the American Psychological Association, Inc. 0022-006X/78/4604-0835$00.75.

Many detailed responses to a first draft were reviewed. Particular acknowledgment is due Thomas Achenbach, George Chartier, Andrew Comrey, Jesse Harris, Mary B. Harris, Alan Kazdin, Richard Lanyon, Eric Mash, Martha Mednick, Peter Nathan, K. Daniel O'Leary, N. D. Reppucci, Robert Rosenthal, Richard Suinn, and Norman Watt.

Requests for reprints should be sent to Brendan A. Maher, Department of Psychology and Social Relations, Harvard University, Cambridge, MA 02138.

The editors of the *Journal of Consulting and Clinical Psychology* who served between 1974 and 1978 have seen some 3,500 manuscripts in the area of consulting and clinical psychology. Working with this number of manuscripts has made it possible to formulate a set of general guidelines that may be helpful in the assessment of research reports. Originally developed by and for journal reviewers, the guidelines are necessarily skeletal and summary and omit many methodological concerns. They do, however, address the methodological concerns that have proved to be significant in a number of cases. In response to a number of requests, the guidelines are being made available here.

Topic Content

1. Is the article appropriate to this journal? Does it fall within the boundaries mandated in the masthead description?

Style

1. Does the manuscript conform to APA style in its major aspects?

Introduction

1. Is the introduction as brief as possible given the topic of the article?
2. Are all of the citations correct and necessary, or is there padding? Are important citations missing? Has the author been careful to cite prior reports contrary to the current hypothesis?
3. Is there an explicit hypothesis?
4. Has the *origin* of the hypothesis been made explicit?
5. Was the hypothesis *correctly* derived from the theory that has been cited? Are other, contrary hypotheses compatible with the same theory?
6. Is there an explicit rationale for the selection of measures, and was it derived logically from the hypothesis?

Method

1. Is the method so described that replication is possible without further information?
2. *Subjects*: Were they sampled randomly from the population to which the results will be generalized?
3. Under what circumstances was informed consent obtained?
4. Are there probable biases in sampling (e.g. volunteers, high refusal rates, institution population atypical for the country at large, etc.)?
5. What was the "set" given to subjects? Was there deception? Was there control for experimenter influence and expectancy effects?
6. How were subjects debriefed?
7. Were subjects (patients) led to believe that they were receiving "treatment"?
8. Were there special variables affecting the subjects, such as medication, fatigue, and threats that were not part of the experimental manipulation? In

clinical samples, was "organicity" measured and/or eliminated?

9. *Controls*: Were there appropriate control groups? What was being controlled for?

10. When more than one measure was used, was the order counterbalanced? If so, were order effects actually analyzed statistically?

11. Was there a control task(s) to confirm specificity of results?

12. *Measures*: For both dependent and independent variable measures—was validity and reliability established and reported? When a measure is tailor-made for a study, this is very important. When validities and reliabilities are already available in the literature, it is less important.

13. Is there adequate description of tasks, materials, apparatus, and so forth?

14. Is there discriminant validity of the measures?

15. Are distributions of scores on measures typical of scores that have been reported for similar samples in previous literature?

16. Are measures free from biases such as
    a. Social desirability?
    b. Yeasaying and naysaying?
    c. Correlations with general responsivity?
    d. Verbal ability, intelligence?

17. If measures are scored by observers using categories or codes, what is the interrater reliability?

18. Was administration and scoring of the measures done blind?

19. If short versions, foreign-language translations, and so forth, of common measures are used, has the validity and reliability of these been established?

20. In correlational designs, do the two measures have theoretical and/or methodologies independence?

Representative Design

1. When the stimulus is human (e.g., in clinical judgments of clients of differing race, sex, etc.), is there a *sample* of stimuli (e.g., more than one client of each race or each sex)?

2. When only one stimulus or a few human stimuli were used, was an adequate explanation of the failure to sample given?

Statistics

1. Were the statistics used with appropriate assumptions fulfilled by the data (e.g., normalcy of distributions for parametric techniques)? Where neces-

sary, have scores been transformed appropriately?

2. Were tests of significance properly used and reported? For example, did the author use the *p* value of a correlation to justify conclusions when the actual size of the correlation suggests little common variance between two measures?

3. Have statistical significance levels been accompanied by an analysis of practical significance levels?

4. Has the author considered the effects of a limited range of scores, and so forth, in using correlations?

5. Is the basic statistical strategy that of a "fishing expedition"; that is, if many comparisons are made, were the obtained significance levels predicted in advance? Consider the number of significance levels as a function of the total number of comparisons made.

Figures and Tables

1. Are the figures and tables (a) necessary and (b) self-explanatory? Large tables of nonsignificant differences, for example, should be eliminated if the few obtained significances can be reported in a sentence or two in the text. Could several tables be combined into a smaller number?

2. Are the axes of figures identified clearly?

3. Do graphs correspond logically to the textual argument of the article? (E.g., if the text states that a certain technique leads to an *increment* of mental health and the accompanying graph shows a *decline* in symptoms, the point is not as clear to the reader as it would be if the text or the graph were amended to achieve visual and verbal congruence.)

Discussion and Conclusion

1. Is the discussion properly confined to the findings or is it digressive, including new post hoc speculations?

2. Has the author explicitly considered and discussed viable alternative explanations of the findings?

3. Have nonsignificant trends in the data been promoted to "findings"?

4. Are the limits of the generalizations possible from the data made clear? Has the author identified his/her own methodological difficulties in the study?

5. Has the author "accepted" the null hypothesis?

6. Has the author considered the possible methodological bases for discrepancies between the results reported and other findings in the literature?

Appendix B

Quality Control in Qualitative Research

MILDRED L. PATTEN

From Patten, M. L. (2005). *Understanding research methods: An overview of the essentials* (5th ed.). Los Angeles: Pyrczak Publishing. Reprinted with permission.

This topic describes some of the specific techniques that qualitative researchers use to establish the dependability and trustworthiness of their data.[1]

One technique is to use multiple sources for obtaining data on the research topic. The technical name for this is **data triangulation**. For instance, for a qualitative study of discrimination in an employment setting, a researcher might interview employees, their supervisors, and the responsible personnel officers. To the extent that the various sources provide similar information, the data can be said to be corroborated.

The methods used to collect data can also be triangulated. For instance, a researcher might conduct individual interviews with parents regarding their child-rearing practices and then have the same participants provide data via focus groups. This would be an example of **methods triangulation**.

Note that in *data triangulation*, typically two or more types of participants (such as employees and supervisors) are used to collect data on a research topic. In contrast, in *methods triangulation*, only one type of participant (such as parents) is used to provide data but two or more methods are used to collect the data.

An important technique to assure the quality of qualitative research is to form a *research team*, with each member of the team participating in the collection and analysis of data. This can be thought of as **researcher triangulation**, which reduces the possibility that the results of qualitative research represent only the idiosyncratic views of one individual researcher.

Sometimes, it is helpful to form a **team of researchers with diverse backgrounds**. For instance, for a study on the success of minority students in medical school, a team of researchers that consists of both medical school instructors and medical school students might strengthen the study by providing more than one perspective when collecting and analyzing the data.

The issue of having diversity in a research team is addressed in Example 1, which is from a qualitative research report on gender issues. The researchers point out that gender diversity in their research team helps to provide a "comprehensive view."

Example 1:

Diversity in a research team: Gender and sexuality issues were analyzed by all three researchers. That our research team included one man and two women probably helped us have a comprehensive view of the different meanings of gender issues.[2]

Oral interviews and focus groups are typically audiotaped and then transcribed. Sometimes, transcription is difficult because some participants might not speak distinctly. In addition, transcribers sometimes make errors. Therefore, checking the accuracy of a transcription helps to ensure the quality of the data. In Example 2, a sample of segments was checked.

Example 2:

Checking the accuracy of transcriptions: Each audiotaped session was transcribed verbatim. Segments of the transcriptions were checked randomly against the audiotapes for accuracy.[3]

In the analysis of data, each member of a research team should initially work independently (without consulting each other) and then compare the results of their analyses. To the extent that they agree, the results are said to be dependable. This technique examines what is called **interobserver agreement**.[4] When there are disagreements, often they can be resolved by having the researchers discuss their differences until they reach a consensus.

The use of an outside expert can also help to ensure the quality of the research. A researcher's peer (such as another experienced qualitative researcher) can examine the process used to collect data, the resulting data

---

[1] The terms "dependability" and "trustworthiness" in qualitative research loosely correspond to the terms "reliability" and "validity" in quantitative research.

[2] Rasera, E. F., Vieira, E. M., & Japur, M. (2004). Influence of gender and sexuality on the construction of being HIV positive as experienced in a support group in Brazil. *Families, Systems, & Health, 22*, 340–351.

[3] Lukens, E. P., Thorning, H., & Lohrer, S. (2004). Sibling perspectives on severe mental illness: Reflections on self and family. *American Journal of Orthopsychiatry, 74*, 489–501.

[4] In qualitative research, this is sometimes called *intercoder agreement*. In quantitative research, this concept is called *interobserver reliability*.

and the conclusions, and then provide feedback to the researcher. This process is called **peer review**. Under certain circumstances, the peer who provides the review is called an **auditor**.

The dependability of the results can also be enhanced by a process called **member checking**. This term is based on the idea that the participants are "members" of the research team. By having the participants/members review the results of the analysis, researchers can determine whether their results "ring true" to the participants. If not, adjustments can be made in the description of the results.

Notes:

Notes:

Notes:

Notes:

Notes:

ANSWERS

A Cross Section of Psychological Research

Journal Articles for Discussion and Evaluation

SECOND EDITION

Andrea K. Milinki

Editor

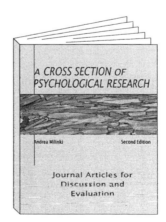

Pyrczak Publishing
P.O. Box 250430
Glendale, CA 91225

"Pyrczak Publishing" is an imprint of Fred Pyrczak, Publisher, A California Corporation.

Visit us at **www.Pyrczak.com** to learn more about our titles and to request examination copies.

Answers to Factual Questions

Article 1: Factors That Influence Fee Setting by Male and Female Psychologists

1. 39. (See lines 88–89.)   **2.** Self-pay clients seen in self-employed private practice. (See lines 97–99.)
3. Yes. (See line 150.)   **4.** No. (See lines 152–156.)   **5.** No. (See lines 188–192.)   **6.** The difference
regarding local competition. (See lines 269–274 and 285–288.)

Article 2:   Involvement of Fathers in Therapy: A Survey of Clinicians

1. 135. (See lines 180–182.)   **2.** 27.0%. (See lines 197–198.)   **3.** 62.00. (See Table 2.)   **4.** 39.46. (See
Table 2; note that this is rounded to 39.5% in line 307.)   **5.** Yes, at the $p < .01$ level. (See Table 2 and the
footnote to the table.)   **6.** Yes, the r for this relationship is .32, which is significant at the .01 level. (See
lines 393–395.)

Article 3: Screening for Domestic Violence: Recommendations Based on a Practice Survey

1. 12%. (See lines 53–57.)   **2.** Yes. (See lines 161–165.)   **3.** They were randomly selected. (See lines
183–184.)   **4.** 2% to 80%. (See lines 203–207.)   **5.** Females. (Scc Table 2.)   **6.** No. (See lines 240–
245.)

Article 4: Students' Ratings of Teaching Effectiveness: A Laughing Matter?

1. 1 for Strongly Disagree and 5 for Strongly Agree. (See lines 28–32.)   **2.** 453. (See Abstract and lines
32–33.)   **3.** 21. (See Abstract and line 35.)   **4.** .49 (See lines 41–45.)   **5.** "The lecturer helped me to
develop an interest in the subject matter," with $r = .60$. (See lines 40–48.)   **6.** Yes. (See lines 40–48.)

Article 5: Psychological Correlates of Optimism in College Students

1. That students who rated optimism high would also score more positively on adjustment, higher on self-
esteem, and lower on loneliness. (See lines 18–21.)   **2.** Yes. (See lines 22–24.)   **3.** Life Orientation Test.
(See lines 24–26.)   **4.** Yes. (See lines 28–37.)   **5.** $r = .51$ for Total adjustment score ratings and scores
on the Rosenberg scale. (See lines 54–56.)   **6.** One. (See lines 51–58.)

**Article 6: Relationships of Assertiveness, Depression, and Social Support Among Older Nursing
        Home Residents**

1. No. (See lines 57–58 and 174–182.)   **2.** No, because the mean score was 9.0, while the highest
possible score is 30. (See lines 67–71 and 83–84.)   **3.** $r = -.33$. (See lines 85–86.)   **4.** No. (See lines 88–
91.)   **5.** No. (See lines 88–89.)   **6.** Inverse. (See lines 98–101.)

Article 7: Correlations Between Humor Styles and Loneliness

1. Loneliness and self-defeating humor. (See lines 37–39.)   **2.** 23.5. (See lines 65–66.)   **3.** Choice A.
(See lines 110–112.)   **4.** The $r = -.47$ for the relationship between Loneliness and Affiliative Humor.
(See lines 111–112.)   **5.** Yes, at the $p < .001$ level. (See lines 111–113.)   **6.** No. (See lines 115–117.)

Article 8: Effects of Laughing, Smiling, and Howling on Mood

1. To control for the first issue raised by Provine in 2000, which was that no previous study separated the effects of laughter from those of humor. (See lines 10–14 and 27–28.) **2.** 22. (See line 34.) **3.** Faces from one with a broad smile to one with a broad frown. (See lines 40–45.) **4.** 27. (See lines 50–51.) **5.** No. (See lines 52–56.) **6.** Yes, at the *p* < .01 level. (See lines 56–58.)

Article 9: Alcohol, Tobacco and Other Drugs: College Student Satisfaction with an Interactive Educational Software Program

1. 16. (See lines 50–51.) **2.** 20 to 30 minutes. (See lines 102–103.) **3.** Course credit. (See lines 110–111.) **4.** No. (See lines 112–113.) **5.** Agree and Strongly Agree. (See lines 116–118.) **6.** Revealed a personal limitation. (See Table 1.)

Article 10: Multimodal Behavioral Treatment of Nonrepetitive, Treatment-Resistant Nightmares: A Case Report

1. This case did not have recurrent dreams (i.e., the nightmares did not share common content). (See lines 74–80.) **2.** "I must remember when I'm dreaming to remind myself that I'm dreaming." (See lines 121–124.) **3.** Yes. (See lines 93–96.) **4.** No. (See lines 198–203.) **5.** Yes. (See lines 223–229.) **6.** Of successful treatment of nonrepetitive, chronic nightmares with combined direct treatment. (See lines 241–245.)

Article 11: Continuous White Noise to Reduce Resistance Going to Sleep and Night Wakings In Toddlers

1. The entire range of human hearing from 20–20,000 Hertz. (See lines 30–32.) **2.** No. (See lines 115–121.) **3.** To collect data and promote compliance. (See lines 180–181.) **4.** Turning the sound down approximately 5 to 10 dB every night until the machine was off. (See lines 183–186.) **5.** 0.3. (See lines 219–223.) **6.** Rose. (See lines 246–253.)

Article 12: Multiple Uses of a Word Study Technique

1. Two. (See lines 93–95 and the top section of Figure 1.) **2.** Yes. (See lines 106–108.) **3.** 90% of the words read correctly on the probes during two consecutive instructional probes. (See lines 111–113.) **4.** Yes. (See lines 163–165.) **5.** Gradual. (See lines 187–192 and Figure 2.) **6.** No. (See lines 216–218.)

Article 13: Use of an Antecedent Procedure to Decrease Night Awakening in an Infant: A Replication

1. Yes. (See line 56.) **2.** 90%. (See lines 99–100.) **3.** Four. (See lines 102–103.) **4.** 1.3. (See lines 104–105.) **5.** The parents. (See lines 75–81 and 106–110.)

Article 14: Brief Functional Analysis and Intervention Evaluation for Treatment of Saliva-Play

1. In a designated location in the classroom. (See lines 45–47.) **2.** As anytime Matt's hand crossed the plane of his lips, or if he expectorated saliva onto his chin and "sucked" it back into his mouth. (See lines

55–59.) **3.** 10. (See lines 70–72.) **4.** The demand condition. (See lines 96–98 and Figure 1.) **5.** 45.3. (See lines 150–151.) **6.** No. (See lines 152–154 and Figure 2.)

Article 15: Sex Differences on a Measure of Conformity in Automated Teller Machine Lines

1. Conformity was operationally defined by number of times a participant stood in line behind the confederates for at least 5 sec. instead of using the vacant ATM. (See lines 46–49.) **2.** Two women behind another woman. (See lines 70–73.) **3.** 91% of the women and 66% of the men. (See lines 99–101.) **4.** Yes, at the $p < .01$ level. (See lines 102–103.) **5.** 81%. (See lines 103–105.) **6.** The experiment was conducted in a small coastal town in California. It is unclear whether the results would remain consistent in a different setting. (See lines 130–134.)

Article 16: Effects of Participants' Sex and Targets' Perceived Need on Supermarket Helping Behavior

1. Yes. (See lines 13–20.) **2.** As a shopper with a cart. (See lines 60–61.) **3.** The participant's response of help or no help. (See lines 74–75.) **4.** No. (See lines 88–91.) **5.** Yes. (See lines 100–105.) **6.** 45. (See Table 1.)

Article 17: Failure of a Traffic Control "Fatality" Sign to Affect Pedestrians' and Motorists' Behavior

1. 80. (See lines 21–24 and 81–83.) **2.** Looking both ways. (See lines 57–58.) **3.** 6. (See lines 67–68.) **4.** 29.5%. (See lines 99–105.) **5.** 4.6 with the sign present; 4.5 at the control intersection. (See lines 111–113 and Table 1.) **6.** No. (See lines 119–126.)

Article 18: Project Trust: Breaking Down Barriers Between Middle School Children

1. A list of 24 groups, active within the school, emerged from them. (See lines 71–73.) **2.** Choose to eat lunch with. (See line 157.) **3.** The greatest degree. (See lines 153–156.) **4.** "Dirties." (See lines 198–200.) **5.** "Whites." (See Table 1 where $p = .255$ for "Whites." Also, see lines 193–195.) **6.** Yes, at the $p < .01$ level. (See lines 214–219.)

Article 19: Psychotherapy Using Distance Technology: A Comparison of Face-to-Face, Video, and Audio Treatment

1. From radio and print ads. (See lines 46–47.) **2.** 19 to 75. (See lines 71–72.) **3.** Yes. (See lines 113–117.) **4.** Less. (See lines 267–269 and Table 1.) **5.** Because randomization equalized pretreatment conditions across groups, making unnecessary any further operations to adjust for pretest scores. (See lines 312–316.) **6.** .15. (See lines 300–305.)

Article 20: Differences in Readers' Response Toward Advertising versus Publicity

1. A higher proportion of the readers will recall the publicity message than a comparable advertisement. (See lines 45–47.) **2.** Random assignment. (See lines 92–94.) **3.** 77%. (See lines 143–146.) **4.** The publicity group. (See lines 161–165 and Table 1.) **5.** All twelve. (See the values of p in Table 1.) **6.** t test. (See Table 1.)

Article 21: Online Instruction: Are the Outcomes the Same?

1. 52. (See line 68.) **2.** Randomly. (See lines 71–72.) **3.** The instructor's overall effectiveness. (See lines 102–111.) **4.** No. (See lines 112–119.) **5.** Yes, because the highest possible score was 7. The face-to-face group earned an average of 6.00, and the online group earned an average of 6.25. (See lines 114–119.) **6.** Yes, because the face-to-face group had an average of 6.7, and the online group had an average of 6.8. (See lines 135–138.)

Article 22: Effect of Petting a Dog on Immune System Function

1. That petting the dog would have a positive effect on IgA. (See lines 45–47.) **2.** They were randomly assigned. (See lines 51–53.) **3.** Tactile stimulation. (See lines 58–61.) **4.** The *t* test. (See lines 120–122.) **5.** .62. (See lines 122–130.) **6.** 705.8 on the pretest and 910.3 on the posttest. (See Table 1.)

Article 23: The Profession of Psychology Scale: Sophisticated and Naïve Students' Responses

1. Yes. (See lines 7–9.) **2.** The more psychology courses students completed, the more knowledgeable they would be of the profession. (See lines 24–26.) **3.** 20.1 for the Naïve group, and 23.2 for the Sophisticated group. (See lines 37–45.) **4.** Yes. (See lines 59–60.) **5.** No. (See lines 77–83.) **6.** "What percentage of psychologists can write prescriptions?" (See lines 114–116.)

Article 24: Untreated Recovery from Eating Disorders

1. Yes. (See line 33.) **2.** Yes. (See line 48.) **3.** On bulletin boards throughout the campus. (See lines 56–57.) **4.** 18. (See lines 79–80.) **5.** 1.94 years. (See lines 102–104.)

Article 25: Does Therapist Experience Influence Interruptions of Women Clients?

1. A negative relationship. (See lines 61–64.) **2.** To dominate conversation and keep women in a subordinate position. (See lines 124–130.) **3.** Five minutes. (See lines 203–207.) **4.** As an overlap of speech that is disruptive or intrusive. (See lines 235–237.) **5.** Yes, at the $p < .05$ level. (See lines 275–277 and the footnote in Table 2.) **6.** No. (See lines 315–319 and Table 2.)

Article 26: Integrating Behavioral Health into Primary Care Settings: A Pilot Project

1. If pharmacy data indicated that the patient fulfilled sufficient prescriptions to have continuous daily medication for three months. (See lines 63–66.) **2.** To allow for greater availability to patients. (See lines 146–147.) **3.** By the psychologists attending lunch with the physicians daily. (See lines 182–184.) **4.** 98. (See lines 254–255.) **5.** 22%. (See lines 306–310 and Table 3, where the result without rounding is 22.4%.) **6.** Yes, at the $p < .001$. (See lines 376–382.) **7.** The time constraints; three months instead of a more desirable six months. (See lines 470–478.)

Article 27: Technology-Mediated versus Face-to-Face Intergenerational Programming

1. Ongoing individualized e-mail instruction and ample opportunity for the seniors to practice. (See lines 64–69.) **2.** Interview. (See lines 101–105.) **3.** Yes. (See lines 184–189 and Table 1.) **4.** No. (See lines 234–238.) **5.** Yes. (See lines 282–290.) **6.** Yes. (See lines 345–349 and Table 2.)

Article 28: Family-Focused Smoking Cessation: Enhanced Efficacy by the Addition of Partner Support and Group Therapy

1. A substance abuse counselor and clinical psychologist. (See lines 54–55.) **2.** Through university medical clinics (oncology, pulmonology, and cardiology) as well as advertisements in the local newspaper and throughout the medical center. (See lines 59–62.) **3.** The Beck Depression Inventory. (See lines 97–100.) **4.** 15. (See lines 135–136.) **5.** Yes. (See lines 161–163.) **6.** 87%. (See lines 164–167 and lines 187–188.)

Article 29: Then and Now: A Follow-Up Study of Professionals' Perceptions of Parenting after Divorce Classes

1. From the local yellow pages. (See lines 71–72.) **2.** Not to proceed with the questions and return the questionnaire in the given envelope. (See lines 80–83.) **3.** 21. (See lines 103–105.) **4.** Divorce attorneys. (See Table 2.) **5.** None. (See lines 135–137.) **6.** 85.7%. (See lines 116–119 and the last row in Table 3.)

Article 30: Relationship Between Mental Toughness and Physical Endurance

1. .90. (See line 20.) **2.** Forty-one male undergraduate students in sports and exercise science. (See lines 40–41.) **3.** .48. (See lines 23–25.) **4.** It would likely have been more physically rather than mentally demanding. (See lines 50–51.) **5.** Three. (See lines 68–71.) **6.** To limit differences in motivation. (See lines 57–58.) **7.** .34. (See lines 58–61 and 68–71.)

Article 31: Temporal Stability of the Francis Scale of Attitude Toward Christianity Short-Form: Test–Retest Data over One Week

1. The full version when administration time is short. (See lines 9–11.) **2.** Higher scores. (See lines 46–47.) **3.** .93. (See lines 63–64.) **4.** $r = .92$. (See lines 64–65.) **5.** No. (See lines 65–68.)

Article 32: Cross-Informant Agreement of the Behavioral and Emotional Rating Scale-2nd Edition (BERS-2) Parent and Youth Rating Scales

1. To the extent to which ratings from raters in different roles (e.g., parents, youth, teachers) agree. (See lines 23–26.) **2.** Choice A. (See lines 47–58.) **3.** Strengths. (See lines 125–129.) **4.** Yes. (See lines 220–221.) **5.** .59. (See Table 1.) 6. No. (See lines 221–224.)

Article 33: Reliability and Validity of the Wender Utah Rating Scale for College Students

1. Additional course credit. (See lines 70–72.) **2.** Four weeks. (See lines 84–85.) **3.** They were the 25 items that most strongly discriminated between adults with and without the diagnosis of ADHD. (See lines 91–102.) **4.** Men had a higher mean. The difference is not significant. (See lines 146–152 and Table 1.) **5.** Learning problems. (See Table 2.)

Article 34: Sex Differences in Portuguese Lonely Hearts Advertisements

1. That their sample of advertisements was biased toward nontraditional individuals. (See lines 80–81.)
2. Women will be more likely to offer attractiveness, and men will be more likely to seek attractiveness.

(See lines 142–148.) **3.** Yes. (See lines 171–173.) **4.** Using a random number table. (See lines 174–179.) **5.** Yes, at the $p < .001$ level. (See lines 227–228 and Table 1.) **6.** Five. (See the footnote to Table 1.)

Article 35: The Reporting of Therapist Sample Data in the *Journal of Counseling Psychology*

1. That all therapists are the same, regardless of age, theoretical orientation, setting, and combinations thereof. (See lines 39–45.) **2.** No. (See lines 67–71.) **3.** 59%. (See lines 113–116.) **4.** European American. (See lines 116–121.) **5.** How often is the characteristic reported, and is the characteristic measured in the same manner in each study? (See lines 213–216.) **6.** He only examined studies in *JCP* that used therapists in their research samples; therefore, he cannot generalize the findings to any other journal or to reporting practices of other types of research samples (e.g., clients). (See lines 315–319.)

Article 36: Project D.A.R.E. Outcome Effectiveness Revisited

1. *ERIC*, *MEDLINE*, and *PsycINFO*. (See lines 50–51.) **2.** Ahmed et al. (2002). $r = 0.198$. (See the last reference in Table 1.) **3.** 0.011. (See lines 101–102.) **4.** Smoking. (See lines 116–117.)
5. 0.00. (See the effect size farthest to the right in Figure 1.) **6.** No. (See lines 183–187.)

Article 37: Risk Taking As Developmentally Appropriate Experimentation for College Students

1. 32. (See lines 197–198.) **2.** 6. (See Table 1.) **3.** Registered student organizations. (See lines 210–212.) **4.** No, one did not participate. (See lines 251–252.) **5.** How frequently students participated in a variety of experimentation behaviors. (See lines 274–277.) **6.** Experimentation. (See lines 767–773.)

Article 38: Conceptions of Work: The View from Urban Youth

1. 80. (See lines 420–421.) **2.** Randomly. (See lines 440–444.) **3.** Yes. (See lines 463–485.) **4.** Yes. (See lines 503–505.) **5.** 55. (See Table 1 and lines 663–665.) **6.** Yes. (See lines 797–800).

Article 39: Interdependent Self: Self-Perceptions of Vietnamese-American Youths

1. Social exchange. (See lines 9–13.) **2.** As a configuration of roles expressed in self-other expectations and observable in self-other interactions. (See lines 143–146.) **3.** Before or at the end of each interview, the researcher asked the participants if they would identify others that fit the study's selection criteria. (See lines 206–208.) **4.** No. (See lines 226–228.) **5.** 10. (While the researcher mentions that there were 40 in a larger ongoing study in lines 189–193, the sample size for this study is given in lines 211–212.)
6. No. (See lines 231–232.) **7.** No. (See lines 256–257.)

Article 40: Contributions to Family and Household Activities by the Husbands of Midlife Professional Women

1. Because they have likely experienced the potential conflict between employment and family. (See lines 39–43.) **2.** What role has your husband played in helping you manage family and career? (See lines 274–280.) **3.** Because of the difficulty in locating married, professional women with children and enduring careers. (See lines 292–297.) **4.** To ensure relative consistency in their content. (See lines 311–313.) **5.** To capture the breadth of experiences at midlife. (See lines 351–355.) **6.** 41. (See Table 1, where the mean age is given in parentheses.) **7.** Yes. (See lines 904–906.)

Article 41: Adult Helping Qualities Preferred by Adolescents

1. Age; ages 12 to 17 years. (See lines 169–170.)   **2.** One. (See lines 185–186.)   **3.** 47. (See lines 227–229.)   **4.** The number of times each category was coded. (See lines 256–259.)   **5.** Yes, it was perfect with a kappa of 1.0. (See lines 260–262.)   **6.** The adult's ability to listen nonjudgmentally, without lecturing and by being available to receive new ideas from the adolescent. (See lines 282–287.)

Notes:

Notes: